THE PAPERS OF
BENJAMIN FRANKLIN

SPONSORED BY

The American Philosophical Society

and Yale University

The Pennsylvania State House or Independence Hall

THE PAPERS OF

Benjamin Franklin

VOLUME 22 *March 23, 1775, through October 27, 1776*

WILLIAM B. WILLCOX, *Editor*

Douglas M. Arnold, Dorothy W. Bridgwater, Jonathan R. Dull, Claude A. Lopez, and Catherine M. Prelinger, Assistant Editors

New Haven and London: YALE UNIVERSITY PRESS, 1982

Funds for editing this volume of The Papers of Benjamin Franklin *have been provided by three sources, for all of which the editors are most grateful: the Andrew W. Mellon Foundation, the American Philosophical Society, and the National Historical Publications and Records Commission under the chairmanship of the Archivist of the United States.*

Published with assistance from the National Endowment for the Humanities.

Library of Congress catalog card number: 59–12697
International standard book number: 0–300–02618–8

Printed in the U.S.A.

10 9 8 7 6 5 4 3 2 1

Contents

CONTENTS

xi

CONTENTS

CONTENTS

CONTENTS

CONTENTS

CONTENTS

CONTENTS

CONTENTS

CONTENTS

CONTENTS

List of Illustrations

LIST OF ILLUSTRATIONS

Contributors to Volume 22

The ownership of each manuscript, or the location of the particular copy used by the editors of each rare contemporary pamphlet or similar printed work, is indicated where the document appears in the text. The sponsors and editors are deeply grateful to the following institutions and individuals for permission to print or otherwise use in the present volume manuscripts or other materials which they own.

INSTITUTIONS

Algemeen Rijksarchief, The Hague
American Philosophical Society
Amherst College Library
Archives du Ministère des affaires étrangères, Paris
Bristol, R. I., Historical Society
British Museum
John Carter Brown Library
Central Library, Sheffield
Château de Ramezay Museum, Montreal
Chicago Historical Society
Clements Library, University of Michigan
Connecticut Historical Society
Connecticut State Library
Dartmouth College Library
Department of Records, Recorder of Deeds, City of Philadelphia
Duke University Library
Folger Shakespeare Library
Harvard University Library
Haverford College Library
Historical Society of Pennsylvania
Henry E. Huntington Library
Kunstsammlungen der Veste Coburg
Robert E. Lee Memorial Foundation, Stratford Hall, Va.
Library Company of Philadelphia
Library of Congress
Maine Historical Society

Marietta College Library
Maryland Historical Society
Massachusetts Archives
Massachusetts Historical Society
Moravian Archives, Bethlehem, Pa.
Morristown National Historical Park
National Archives
New-York Historical Society
New York Public Library
New York State Library
Oesterreichische Nationalbibliothek, Vienna
Pennsylvania State Library
Pierpont Morgan Library
Princeton University Library
Public Record Office
Ringwood Manor Museum, Ringwood State Park, N.J.
Rosenbach Foundation
South Carolina Historical Society
Staffordshire County Record Office
University of Indiana Library
University of North Carolina Library
University of Pennsylvania Library
University of Virginia Library
Warren, R.I., Baptist Church Benevolent Society
Williams College Library
Yale University Library

CONTRIBUTORS TO VOLUME 22

INDIVIDUALS

Morris Duane, Philadelphia

Dr. Joseph E. Fields, Joliet, Ill.

Robert B. Gillespie, Lake Forest, Ill.

Bruce Gimelson, Chalfont, Pa.

D. A. F. H. H. Hartley Russell, Reading, Berks.

Ben Hibbs, Philadelphia

Mrs. Arthur Loeb, Philadelphia

Miss Helen Newman, Washington, D.C.

Mrs. Norman H. Pearson, Hamden, Conn.

Mrs. Henry M. Sage, Albany, N.Y.

Theodore Sheldon, Chicago

Joseph G. Turner, Los Angeles

Method of Textual Reproduction

An extended statement of the principles of selection, arrangement, form of presentation, and method of textual reproduction observed in this edition appears in the Introduction to the first volume, pp. xxiv-xlvii. What follows is a condensation and revision of part of it.

Printed Material:

Those of Franklin's writings that were printed under his direction presumably appeared as he wanted them to, and should therefore be reproduced with no changes except what modern typography requires. In some cases, however, printers carelessly or willfully altered his text without his consent; or the journeymen who set it had different notions from his—and from each other's—of capitalization, spelling, and punctuation. Such of his letters as survive only in nineteenth-century printings, furthermore, have often been vigorously edited by William Temple Franklin, Duane, or Sparks. In all these cases the original has suffered some degree of distortion, which the modern editor may guess at but, in the absence of the manuscript, cannot remedy. We therefore follow the printed texts as we find them, and note only obvious misreadings.

We observe the following rules in reproducing printed materials:

1. The place and date of composition of letters are set at the top, regardless of their location in the original printing; the complimentary close is set continuously with the text.

2. Proper nouns, including personal names, which were often printed in italics, are set in roman except when the original was italicized for emphasis.

3. Prefaces and other long passages, though italicized in the original, are set in roman. Long italicized quotations are set in roman within quotation marks.

4. Words in full capitals are set in small capitals, with initial letters in full capitals if required by Franklin's normal usage.

5. All signatures are set in capitals and small capitals.

6. We silently correct obvious typographical errors, such as the omission of a single parenthesis or quotation mark.

7. We close a sentence by supplying, when needed, a period or question mark.

Manuscript Material:

a. *Letters* are presented in the following form:

1. The place and date of composition are set at the top, regardless of their location in the original; the complimentary close is set continuously with the text.

2. Addresses, endorsements, and notations are so labelled and printed at the end of the letter. An endorsement is to the best of our belief by the recipient, a notation by someone else, whereas in a document that is not a letter an endorsement is by the writer.

b. *Spelling* of the original we retain. When it is so abnormal as to obscure the meaning, we supply the correct form in brackets or a footnote, as "yf [wife]."

c. *Capitalization* we retain as written, except that every sentence is made to begin with a capital. When we cannot decide whether a letter is a capital, we follow modern usage.

d. Words underlined once in the manuscripts are printed in italics; words underlined twice or written in large letters or full capitals are printed in small capitals.

e. *Punctuation* has been retained as in the original, except:

1. We close a sentence by supplying, when needed, a period or question mark. When it is unclear where the sentence ends, we retain the original punctuation or lack of it.

2. Dashes used in place of commas, semicolons, colons, or periods are replaced by the appropriate marks; when a sentence ends with both a dash and a period, the dash is omitted.

3. Commas scattered meaninglessly through a manuscript are eliminated.

4. When a mark of punctuation is not clear or can be read as one of two marks, we follow modern usage.[1]

5. Some documents, especially legal ones, have no punctuation; others have so little as to obscure the meaning. In such cases we silently supply the minimum needed for clarity.

f. *Contractions and abbreviations* in general are retained. The ampersand is rendered as "and," except in the names of business firms, in the form "&c.," and in a few other cases. Letters represented by the thorn or tilde are printed. The tailed "p" is spelled out as per, pre, or pro. Symbols of weights, measures, and monetary values follow modern usage, as: £34. Superscript letters are lowered.

g. *Omitted or illegible words or letters* are treated as follows:

1. If not more than four letters are missing, we supply them silently when we have no doubt what they should be.

2. If more than four letters are missing, we supply them in brackets, with or without a question mark depending on our confidence in the insertion.

3. Other omissions are shown as follows: [*illegible*], [*torn*], [*remainder missing*], or the like.

4. Missing or illegible digits are indicated by suspension points in brackets, the number of points corresponding to the estimated number of missing figures.

5. When the writer has omitted a word required for clarity, we insert it in brackets and italics.

h. *Author's additions and corrections:*

1. Interlineations and brief marginal notes are normally incorporated in the text without comment, and longer notes with the notation [*in the margin*] unless they were clearly intended as footnotes, in which case they are printed with our notes and with a bracketed indication of the source.

2. Canceled words and phrases are in general omitted without notice; if significant, they are printed in footnotes.

1. The typescripts from which these papers are printed have been made from photocopies of the manuscripts; marks of punctuation are sometimes blurred or lost in photography, and it has often been impossible to consult the original.

3. When alternative words and phrases have been inserted in a manuscript but the original remains uncanceled, the alternatives are given in brackets, preceded by explanatory words in italics, as: "it is [*written above:* may be] true."

4. Variant readings of several versions are noted if important.

Abbreviations and Short Titles

Acts Privy Coun., Col.	W. L. Grant and James Munro, eds., *Acts of the Privy Council of England, Colonial Series, 1613–1783* (6 vols., London, 1908–12).
AD	Autograph document.[1]
ADS	Autograph document signed.
AL	Autograph letter.
ALS	Autograph letter signed.
Amer.	American.
Ammerman, *Common Cause*	David Ammerman, *In the Common Cause: American Response to the Coercive Acts of 1774* (Charlottesville, Va., [1974]).
APS	American Philosophical Society.
Archaeol.	Archaeological.
Assn.	Association.
Autobiog.	Leonard W. Labaree, Ralph L. Ketcham, Helen C. Boatfield, and Helene H. Fineman, eds., *The Autobiography of Benjamin Franklin* (New Haven, 1964).
Bargar, *Dartmouth*	Bradley D. Bargar, *Lord Dartmouth and the American Revolution* (Columbia, S.C., 1965).
BF	Benjamin Franklin.
Bigelow, *Works*	John Bigelow, ed., *The Works of Benjamin Franklin* . . . (12 vols., New York and London, 1904).
Board of Trade Jour.	*Journal of the Commissioners for Trade and Plantations* . . . *April 1704 to* . . . *May 1782* (14 vols., London, 1920–38).
Boyd, *Jefferson Papers*	Julian P. Boyd *et al.*, eds., *The Papers of Thomas Jefferson* (19 vols. to date, Princeton, 1950 —).
Burke's Peerage	Sir Bernard Burke, *Burke's Genealogical and Heraldic History of the Peerage Baronetage and Knightage with War Gazette and Corrigenda* (98th ed., London, 1940). References in exceptional cases to other editions are so indicated.
Burnett, *Continental Congress*	Edmund C. Burnett, *The Continental Congress* (New York, 1941).
Burnett, *Letters*	Edmund C. Burnett, ed., *Letters of Members of the Continental Congress* (8 vols., Washington, 1921–36).

---

1. For definitions of types of manuscripts see above, 1, xliv-xlvii.

Butterfield, *Adams Correspondence*	Lyman H. Butterfield *et al.*, eds., *Adams Family Correspondence* (4 vols. to date, Cambridge, Mass., 1963 –).
Butterfield, *John Adams Diary*	Lyman H. Butterfield *et al.*, eds., *Diary and Autobiography of John Adams* (4 vols., Cambridge, Mass., 1961).
Candler, *Ga. Col. Recs.*	Allen D. Candler, ed., *The Colonial Records of the State of Georgia . . .* (26 vols., Atlanta, 1904–16).
Carroll, *Journal*	Brantz Mayer, ed., *Journal of Charles Carroll of Carrollton, during His Visit to Canada in 1776, as One of the Commissioners from Congress . . .* (Baltimore, Md., 1845).
Carter, *Gage Correspondence*	Clarence E. Carter, ed., *The Correspondence of General Thomas Gage . . .* (2 vols., New Haven and London, 1931–33).
Chron.	*Chronicle.*
Clark, *Wickes*	William Bell Clark, *Lambert Wickes, Sea Raider and Diplomat: the Story of a Naval Captain of the Revolution* (New Haven and London, 1932).
Cobbett, *Parliamentary History*	William Cobbett and Thomas C. Hansard, eds., *The Parliamentary History of England from the Earliest Period to 1803* (36 vols., London, 1806–20).
Col.	Column.
Coll.	*Collections.*
Commons Jours.	*Journals of the House of Commons* (233 vols. to date, [London,] 1803–); vols. I–LI are reprints.
Crout, "Diplomacy of Trade"	Robert R. Crout, "The Diplomacy of Trade: the Influence of Commercial Considerations on French Involvement in the Anglo-American War of Independence, 1775–78" (Ph.D. dissertation, University of Georgia, 1977).
Cushing, *Writings of Samuel Adams*	Harry Alonzo Cushing, ed., *The Writings of Samuel Adams . . .* (4 vols., New York, 1904–08).
D	Document unsigned.
DAB	*Dictionary of American Biography.*
Dartmouth MSS	Historical Manuscripts Commission, *The Manuscripts of the Earl of Dartmouth . . .: Eleventh Report*, appendix, part 5; *Fourteenth Report*, appendix, part 10; *Fifteenth Report*, appendix, part 1 (3.vols., London, 1887–96).

Deane Papers	*The Deane Papers*, 1774–90 (5 vols.; New-York Historical Society *Collections*, XIX–XXIII; New York, 1887–91).
DF	Deborah Franklin.
Dictionnaire de biographie	*Dictionnaire de biographie française* . . . (14 vols. to date, Paris, 1933–).
DNB	*Dictionary of National Biography.*
Doniol, *Histoire*	Henri Doniol, *Histoire de la participation de la France à l'établissement des États-Unis d'Amérique. Correspondance diplomatique et documents* (5 vols., Paris, 1886–89).
Donoughue, *British Politics*	Bernard Donoughue, *British Politics and the American Revolution: the Path to War, 1773–75* (London and New York, 1964).
DS	Document signed.
Duane, *Works*	William Duane, ed., *The Works of Dr. Benjamin Franklin* . . . (6 vols., Philadelphia, 1808–18). Title varies in the several volumes.
Dubourg, *Œuvres*	Jacques Barbeu-Dubourg, ed., *Œuvres de M. Franklin* . . . (2 vols., Paris, 1773).
Dull, *French Navy*	Jonathan R. Dull, *The French Navy and American Independence: a Study of Arms and Diplomacy, 1774–1787* (Princeton, 1975).
Ed.	Edition or editor.
Exper. and Obser.	*Experiments and Observations on Electricity, made at Philadelphia in America, by Mr. Benjamin Franklin* . . . (London, 1751). Revised and enlarged editions were published in 1754, 1760, 1769, and 1774 with slightly varying titles. In each case the edition cited will be indicated, e.g., *Exper. and Obser.* (1751).
Ferguson, *Power of the Purse*	Elmer James Ferguson, *The Power of the Purse: a History of American Public Finance* . . . (Chapel Hill, N.C., [1961]).
Fitzpatrick, *Writings of Washington*	John C. Fitzpatrick, ed., *The Writings of George Washington* . . . (39 vols., Washington, D.C., [1931–44]).
Force, *Amer. Arch.*	Peter Force, ed., *American Archives: Consisting of a Collection of Authentic Records, State Papers, Debates, and Letters and Other Notices of Publick Affairs* . . ., fourth series, March 7, 1774 to July 4, 1776 (6 vols., [Washington, 1837–46]); fifth series, July 4, 1776 to September 3, 1783 (3 vols., [Washington, 1848–53]).

Freeman, *Washington*   Douglas S. Freeman (completed by John A. Carroll and Mary W. Ashworth), *George Washington: a Biography* (7 vols., New York, [1948–57]).

Gaz.   *Gazette.*

Geneal.   *Genealogical.*

Gent. Mag.   *The Gentleman's Magazine, and Historical Chronicle.*

Gipson, *British Empire*   Lawrence H. Gipson, *The British Empire before the American Revolution* (15 vols., New York, 1939–70; I–III, revised ed., N.Y., 1958–60).

Gruber, *Howe Brothers*   Ira D. Gruber, *The Howe Brothers and the American Revolution* (New York, 1972).

Heitman, *Register of Officers*   Francis B. Heitman, *Historical Register of Officers in the War of the Revolution* . . . (Washington, D.C., 1893).

Hinshaw, *Amer. Quaker Genealogy*   William W. Hinshaw, *Encyclopedia of American Quaker Genealogy* (6 vols. Ann Arbor, Mich., 1936–50).

Hist.   *Historical.*

Hutchinson, *Diary*   Peter O. Hutchinson, ed., *The Diary and Letters of His Excellency Thomas Hutchinson, Esq.* . . . (2 vols., London, 1883–86).

Hutchinson, *History*   Thomas Hutchinson, *The History of the Colony and Province of Massachusetts-Bay* . . . (Lawrence S. Mayo, ed.; 3 vols., Cambridge, Mass., 1936).

JCC   Worthington C. Ford *et al.*, eds., *Journals of the Continental Congress, 1774–1789* (34 vols., Washington, 1904–37).

Jensen, *Founding of a Nation*   Merrill Jensen, *The Founding of a Nation: a History of the American Revolution, 1763–1776* (New York, etc., 1968).

Jour.   *Journal.* The citation "Jour." is of Franklin's MS account book described above, xi, 518–20.

JW   Jonathan Williams, Jr.

Kammen, *Rope of Sand*   Michael G. Kammen, *A Rope of Sand: the Colonial Agents, British Politics, and the American Revolution* (Ithaca, N.Y., [1968]).

Larousse, *Dictionnaire universel*   Pierre Larousse, *Grand dictionnaire universel du XIXe siècle* . . . (17 vols., Paris, [n.d.]).

Lasseray, *Les Français*   André Lasseray, *Les Français sous les treize étoiles, 1775–1783* (2 vols., Paris, 1935).

Ledger   The Franklin MS described above, XI, 518–20.

Lee Family Papers   Paul P. Hoffman, ed., *The Lee Family Papers,*

	1742–1795 (University of Virginia Library *Microfilm Publication* No. 1; 8 reels, Charlottesville, Va., 1966).
Lee Papers	*The Lee Papers*, 1754–1811 (4 vols.; New-York Historical Society *Collections*, IV–VII; New York, 1872–75).
Lewis, *Indiana Co.*	George E. Lewis, *The Indiana Company, 1763–1798: a Study in Eighteenth Century Frontier Land Speculation and Business Venture* (Glendale, Cal., 1941).
LS	Letter signed.
Mackesy, *War for America*	Piers Mackesy, *The War for America, 1775–1783* (Cambridge, Mass., 1965).
Mag.	*Magazine.*
Mass. Acts and Resolves	Abner C. Goodell *et al.*, eds., *The Acts and Resolves, Public and Private, of the Province of Massachusetts Bay* . . . (21 vols., Boston, 1869–1922).
Mass. Arch.	Massachusetts Archives, State House, Boston.
MS, MSS	Manuscript, manuscripts.
Namier and Brooke, *House of Commons*	Sir Lewis Namier and John Brooke, *The History of Parliament. The House of Commons 1754–1790* (3 vols., London and N.Y., 1964).
Naval Docs.	William B. Clark, William J. Morgan, *et al.*, eds., *Naval Documents of the American Revolution* (8 vols. to date, Washington, D.C., 1964 —).
N.J. Arch.	William A. Whitehead *et al.*, eds., *Archives of the State of New Jersey* (2 series, Newark and elsewhere, 1880—). Editors, subtitles, and places of publication vary.
N.Y. Col. Docs.	E. B. O'Callaghan, ed., *Documents Relative to the Colonial History of the State of New York* (15 vols., Albany, 1853–87).
Pa. Arch.	Samuel Hazard *et al.*, eds., *Pennsylvania Archives* (9 series, Philadelphia and Harrisburg, 1852–1935).
Pa. Col. Recs.	*Minutes of the Provincial Council of Pennsylvania* . . . (16 vols., Harrisburg, 1851–53). Volumes I–III are reprints published in Philadelphia, 1852. Title changes with Volume XI to *Supreme Executive Council.*
Phil. Trans.	The Royal Society, *Philosophical Transactions.*
PMHB	*Pennsylvania Magazine of History and Biography.*

Price, *France and the Chesapeake*

Jacob M. Price, *France and the Chesapeake: a History of the French Tobacco Monopoly, 1674–1791, and of Its Relationship to the British and American Tobacco Trade* (2 vols., Ann Arbor, Mich., [1973]).

Proc.

Proceedings.

Pub.

Publications.

Quincy, *Memoir*

Josiah Quincy, *Memoir of the Life of Josiah Quincy Jun. of Massachusetts* (Boston, 1825).

RB

Richard Bache.

Rev.

Review.

Ryerson, *Revolution Is Now Begun*

Richard A. Ryerson, *"The Revolution Is Now Begun": the Radical Committees of Philadelphia, 1765–1776* ([Philadelphia,] 1978).

Sabine, *Loyalists*

Lorenzo Sabine, *Biographical Sketches of Loyalists of the American Revolution . . .* (2 vols., Boston, 1864).

Sibley's Harvard Graduates

John L. Sibley, *Biographical Sketches of Graduates of Harvard University* (Cambridge, Mass., 1873—). Continued from Volume IV by Clifford K. Shipton.

Smith, *Letters*

Paul H. Smith et al., eds., *Letters of Delegates to Congress* (5 vols. to date, Washington, D.C., 1976 —).

Smyth, *Writings*

Albert H. Smyth, ed., *The Writings of Benjamin Franklin . . .* (10 vols., N.Y., 1905–07).

Soc.

Society.

Sparks, *Works*

Jared Sparks, ed., *The Works of Benjamin Franklin . . .* (10 vols., Boston, 1836–40).

Stevens, *Facsimiles*

Benjamin F. Stevens, ed., *Facsimiles of Manuscripts in European Archives Relating to America, 1773–1783* (25 vols., London, 1889–98).

Taylor, *Adams Papers*

Robert J. Taylor et al., eds., *Papers of John Adams* (4 vols. to date, Cambridge, Mass., 1977 —).

Trans.

Translator.

Trans.

Transactions.

Van Doren, *Franklin*

Carl Van Doren, *Benjamin Franklin* (N.Y., 1938).

Van Doren, *Franklin—Mecom*

Carl Van Doren, ed., *The Letters of Benjamin Franklin & Jane Mecom* (American Philosophical Society *Memoirs*, XXVII, Princeton; 1950).

Votes, N.J.

Votes and Proceedings of the General Assembly of the Province of New Jersey . . . (New York,

Woodbridge, etc., 1711—). A separate volume was published for each session and is so designated, e.g., *Votes, N.J.* (Oct.–Dec., 1771).

W&MQ *William and Mary Quarterly*, first or third series as indicated.

WF William Franklin.

Wharton, *Diplomatic Correspondence* Francis Wharton, ed., *The Revolutionary Diplomatic Correspondence of the United States* (6 vols., Washington, D.C., 1889).

Wroth, *Province in Rebellion* L. Kinvin Wroth, *et al.*, eds., *Province in Rebellion: a Documentary History of the Founding of the Commonwealth of Massachusetts, 1774–1775* (Cambridge, Mass., and London, 1972). I: introduction, catalogue, and indices; II: microfiche supplement.

WTF William Temple Franklin.

WTF, *Memoirs* William Temple Franklin, ed., *Memoirs of the Life and Writings of Benjamin Franklin, LL.D., F.R.S., &c. . . .* (3 vols., 4to, London, 1817–18).

Introduction

The months of Franklin's stay in America, sandwiched between his years in England and in France, were probably the most strenuous period of his life; on the average, he said later, he devoted twelve hours a day to public affairs.[1] When he turned seventy in January, 1776, neither he nor any one else seems to have noticed the occasion, doubtless because the rush of business overshadowed it. Rush was inherent in the situation that faced the colonies. The war into which they had been precipitated forced them to create a government capable of waging it, and to do so quickly before the British mobilized their strength and brought it to bear. For almost a year after Lexington the King's small army was mewed up in Boston, and the King's ships were too few to be more than a nuisance; not until the Howe brothers arrived at Staten Island in the summer of 1776 did the war begin in earnest. By then the activities of Congress, with Franklin in the midst of them, had produced in the nick of time the wherewithal to fight.

The way in which this was done, Franklin said a year and a half later, he could not have understood if he had not lived through it. A people without laws or government, warships or soldiers or military supplies, was faced by invasion from abroad and by hostility at home from "all those whom contrariety of opinion, tory principles, personal animosities, fear of so dreadful and dubious an undertaking, joined with the artful promises and threats of the enemy rendered open or concealed opposers, or timid neutrals, or lukewarm friends to the proposed revolution." Yet energetic leadership worked its wonders: governments and codes of law were created, warships built and armies raised; the enemy was halted, and "the greatest revolution the world ever saw, is likely to be effected in a few years."[2]

On May 6, the day after Franklin landed, he was elected a delegate from Pennsylvania to the Congress that was about to convene, and when it met he was plunged into the problems that

1. From Arthur Lee's journal, Oct. 25, 1777: Richard Henry Lee, *Life of Arthur Lee* . . . (2 vols., Boston, 1829), I, 345.
2. *Ibid.*, pp. 343–5.

confronted it. They were awesome. Dissenters had to be contained, but not at the cost of mob rule; and conscientious objectors, as Franklin slowly discovered, could neither be dragooned into service nor allowed to escape it scot free. An army had to be created, clothed and fed and armed and kept in being; the difficulties involved were more than Washington and his staff could handle, and were brought to Congress through delegates, Franklin among them, who visited headquarters at Cambridge. The army still lacked munitions and engineers, but by the end of 1775 hope was dawning that both could be obtained from France; here again Franklin was in the thick of the negotiations. When the invasion of Canada was on the verge of collapse, Congress sent him and others to Montreal to try, without chance of success, to redeem the disaster. A few months later he renewed by letter his old acquaintance with Lord Howe, after the Admiral and his brother arrived with their commission to negotiate peace, and then as one of three Congressional representatives listened to the terms they brought. Almost every major problem before the delegates, in short, was one in which Franklin had a hand.

His chief contribution was as a committeeman. Major issues, along with a great number of trivial ones, were decided on the floor of Congress; but the main work was done in committee. Matters of transient importance were delegated to ad hoc committees, of which Franklin had his full share. On most of them, such as that to consider Lord North's conciliatory resolution, or to find lead and saltpetre, he seems to have played a negligible part if any; on one, to establish a postal system, he was the expert and must have been influential, but the records have disappeared.[3] Although his three missions as a representative of Congress, to Washington's camp, to Canada, and to Howe, are well documented, his role can rarely be distinguished from that of his fellow representatives. The same is true of his work on the two standing committees of Congress, which became in effect its executive arms. The secret committee, charged with obtaining military

3. See the editorial note on the Post Office, July 26, 1775. We have included in the chronology all BF's Congressional committees and other assignments, as recorded in the *JCC*, together with his election to local Pa. bodies. He was appointed to so many committees, John Adams claimed later, because of his reputation; in their meetings, as in Congress, he kept silent when not asleep in his chair. 5 Mass. Hist. Soc. *Coll.*, IV (1878), 431.

supplies from abroad, gave him training in the business of logistics that later stood him in good stead.[4] The committee of secret correspondence, established to make contact with friends of America overseas, did not confine itself to that function but was soon directing agents in the West Indies, the Netherlands, and France; and for a time before Franklin's departure for Europe he and his close colleague, Robert Morris, were the committee.[5]

Twice during his stay in America Franklin was as deeply involved in the affairs of Pennsylvania as in those of Congress. The first time was the summer and fall of 1775: at the end of June of that year the Assembly created a committee of safety to organize defense, and Franklin at once became its president and attended faithfully until the year's end; defense proved to be such a broad rubric that the committee, as the crisis pushed the Governor into the background, became the de facto executive of the province. The second time was the summer of 1776: the internal revolution swept away the Assembly and replaced it with a convention, of which Franklin again was president; and that body acted as a legislature while framing a constitution.[6] No one in those two periods was more visible in local politics.

Visibility was assured by Franklin's name and by his responsibilities in the province and in Congress, but his personal influence through his many positions is impossible to evaluate. The reason is obvious. Members of a group in day-to-day contact leave at most a record of their joint decisions, and whatever we know about who said what comes only by accident. Franklin's role in Philadelphia, far more than his role in London, was played orally. The only evidence that survives is in other men's letters, diaries, and later memoirs, which give nothing more than glimpses, often unreliable and sometimes contradictory, of what that role was. As a consequence, although his political activities in this period were more important than ever before, we know less about them.

Neither does the evidence throw much light on the two personal crises in which he was involved after he landed, his alien-

---

4. See the editorial note on the committee, Sept. 18, 1775.

5. See the headnotes on the committee to Lee, Nov. 30, and on BF's notes on committee business, under Jan. 25.

6. See the editorial notes on the committee of safety, June 30, 1775, and on the convention, July 15, 1776.

ation from Joseph Galloway and from William Franklin. He was eager to see both men as soon as he arrived, and in the next few weeks did see them, separately and then together. These interviews seem to have brought on the breach with Galloway, whose recollections of them years later, and at second hand, are all we know of what occurred.[7] The breach between father and son was more gradual. In the summer Franklin twice visited the Governor in New Jersey; whatever passed between them did not bring a complete rupture, for the senior Franklin and Jane Mecom, coming from Cambridge in November, stopped at Perth Amboy and dined, if they did not spend the night, with William and his wife. Elizabeth Franklin urged them to stay for a while, but they would not; "Pappa," she wrote, "was anxious to get Home."[8] This was apparently the last time he saw her, or his son except for a brief encounter in England after the war. He wrote Elizabeth in 1776 after her husband's arrest, and she replied;[9] but no letter between father and son survives, if any was written, between September of 1775 and the summer of 1784, when William, a refugee in London, tried tentatively and unsuccessfully to renew their relationship.[1] The break seems to have come before the end of 1775, and what it cost Franklin we do not know. Within less than a year he lost in turn, by death and then by politics, his wife and one of his oldest friends and his son; and he kept his own counsels about the loss.

The old man, as he was by the standards of his time, gave few signs of aging. He was as robust physically, except for one brief period, as he was mentally. The exception was his mission to Canada, which he began in the belief that he might not survive it[2] and from which he returned, before the other commissioners, complaining of many ailments. His ill health, according to one of his companions, combined with his sense of a hopeless mission to shorten his stay;[3] and he reached Philadelphia sick and exhausted.

7. See the headnote on BF to Galloway, May 8, 1775.
8. To WTF, Nov. 9, 1775: APS.
9. See her letter of Aug. 6, 1776.
1. WF's letter of July 22 to Aug. 6, 1784, is in the APS, and BF's reply in Smyth, *Writings*, IX, 252–4.
2. To Quincy, April 15, 1776.
3. See the note on John Carroll to BF, May 11, 1776.

During the next crucial weeks, when Congress was deciding the issue of independence, he was laid low by gout.[4]

He consequently played no part in the debates that culminated in the Declaration, but he had done his part in preparing the way for it. Before his departure from England he had concluded that the ministry's choice was between retreat and war; and he must have suspected that war would lead, much as he might regret it, to separation. A few weeks after his return he was saying, according to Galloway, that independence was inevitable.[5] By summer he was ready for the substance of it: he proposed to abolish the Navigation Acts and to establish a confederation with the powers of a sovereign state, proposals that at the time were far too radical for the majority in Congress. Yet he was still too much attached to "that fine and noble china vase the British Empire"[6] to smash it except as a last resort. His proposals were conditional: they were to lapse if Whitehall reversed its policy within a given time, and in that case he suggested that Congress offer Britain, in lieu of taxation, an annual subsidy for a hundred years.[7] He expected independence, nevertheless, long before it was declared, and a month after Bunker Hill was ready for an overt breach although not for a final one. In the months that followed came news from England of the Prohibitory Act, the King's proclamation of rebellion, and military preparations for the campaign of 1776; and these developments must have killed his last hope of reconciliation.[8] His mission to Canada and his subsequent illness detached him from the crucial debates, but he was more fully prepared than most for independence when it came.

After that issue was settled, and Franklin journeyed to Staten Island to learn that Lord Howe's peace negotiations were meaningless, he returned to find himself at the center of quite different negotiations. The previous March, in response to hints that the French government might be well disposed, Silas Deane had been sent to Paris; before he arrived Versailles had decided to make a

---

4. See the note on Mecom to Greene, June 16, and BF to Washington, June 21, 1776.

5. See the headnote on BF to Galloway, May 8, 1775.

6. To Lord Howe, July 20, 1776.

7. These three proposals are all below under July 21, 1775.

8. Compare his letter to Don Gabriel of Dec. 12, 1775, with that to Quincy of April 15, 1776.

surreptitious loan, and Madrid followed suit. Congress read into these decisions more than was there; it created a commission to negotiate a commercial treaty with France and, if all went well, to secure by purchase or on loan eight ships of the line.[9] Deane, Franklin, and Jefferson were named as commissioners, but Jefferson declined to serve; Arthur Lee, then in London, was chosen to replace him. On October 26, after only seventeen and a half months in America, Franklin sailed to join Deane and Lee in Paris.

The material of those months raises editorial problems that are new in this series, and it remains to explain their nature and our handling of them. The first problem is what to do with the correspondence of Franklin's major committees (the minor ones left almost no records) and with documents relating to the Pennsylvania convention. The most influential committee was that of secret correspondence, which a Frenchman called the "privy council."[1] We print the significant letters from it when Franklin was concerned with them, and as examples of its work a few routine ones that he signed; the rest we summarize or notice in our annotation. The important letters to the committee were those from its agents abroad, which were commonly sent by circuitous routes and took months to reach Philadelphia; the question here is which Franklin saw and which came after his departure. We print or summarize only those that we believe he could have seen, and explain why we think the others, even if written long before he sailed, arrived too late.[2]

Two of his standing committees, and the convention, produced records that are too arid or too voluminous, or both, to be reproduced or even summarized. The secret committee of Congress, in the six months of his attendance, wrote a few letters and numerous contracts, and all that are extant are readily available in print; we confine ourselves to summarizing only those that Franklin happened to sign, which are a fair sample of the committee's work. The correspondence of the Pennsylvania committee of safety, even in the short period when Franklin presided over it, is too bulky

9. See the commissioners' instructions of Oct. 22, printed below under Sept. 24, 1776.

1. Bonvouloir to de Guines, Dec. 28, 1775.

2. See the note on Deane to Morris, June 23, 1776.

for individual mention, as is the material addressed to or emanating from the Pennsylvania convention. Again a sampling is necessary, and our sample is documents on which Franklin's name appears; these we do not summarize if they are routine (individual commissions, for example), but we take some notice of all that we have found.

A second problem is how to describe the genesis and functioning of an institution without adding an unnecessary document in order to append a headnote. The ordinance of the Pennsylvania Assembly that created the committee of safety, for instance, is not within our rubric; neither are the Congressional resolutions that established the Post Office, or the action of the Pennsylvania conference that led to the convention of 1776. In such cases we insert an editorial note, under the date when the institution was authorized or began its work; the purpose is to provide a background for later documents and to explain from contemporary sources, when possible, Franklin's relationship to that institution. In a few other cases, for reasons that will be apparent, we introduce similar notes.

A third problem will grow larger as the series progresses: how to treat material that has already been published in one of the other modern editions of the Founding Fathers. The major example in this volume is documents that have appeared in *The Papers of Thomas Jefferson*. We cannot omit them without leaving a serious gap; but to summarize, let alone recapitulate, the monumental annotation of Julian Boyd and his fellow editors would be presumptuous and preposterous. We therefore refer the reader to that edition and add to it, if at all, only such supplementary annotation as our different focus requires.

This volume differs in kind from its predecessors. A revolution crowds events tightly together and they jostle each other; Franklin is often involved with many at once. He hobnobs with men now famous, and with hundreds of others who appear, like crowds in a spectacular film, and never reappear. He and they seem to be constantly in action. Some of what they did is unknown because no record survives, and some of what is known was aridly recorded. The documents, nevertheless, tell their story. It is one of confusion, divided counsels, and sometimes disaster; but it also reveals, as Franklin said, a singular energy. He and his younger colleagues improvised a government and army. Their spirits survived the Canadian debacle and the retreat from Manhattan, and were increasingly nourished by hope of French assistance. Just when the military prospects grew black, in the autumn of 1776, that hope began to burgeon; and the story of the volume ends with the septuagenarian embarking on the greatest political gamble of his life.

\

Chronology

March 23, 1775, through October 27, 1776

1775
April 19: The Battles of Lexington and Concord.

May 5: BF lands in Philadelphia.

May 6: The Pennsylvania Assembly adds BF and others to its Congressional delegation.

May 9: The Pennsylvania Assembly instructs its Congressional delegation.

May 10: Congress convenes.

May 29: Congress appoints BF to a committee to consider means of establishing a postal service.

Late May or early June: BF meets with WF and Galloway.

June 3: Congress appoints BF to a committee to draw up a petition to the King.

June 10: Congress appoints BF to a committee to consider means of introducing the domestic manufacture of saltpetre.

June 17: The Battle of Bunker Hill.

June 23: Congress appoints BF to two committees, one to draft Washington's declaration of the causes of taking up arms, the other to supervise the issuance of paper currency.

June 30: The Pennsylvania Assembly creates a committee of safety and appoints BF to it; he is chosen president on July 3.

July 6: Congress approves the declaration of the causes of taking up arms.

July 8: Congress signs the Olive Branch Petition.

July 12: Congress appoints BF to a committee to consider the protection of American trade.

July 13: Congress appoints BF to a committee to supervise Indian affairs in the middle department.

July 14: BF reports out of committee the resolutions on trade, which are adopted on July 15.

July 22: Congress appoints BF to a committee to consider Lord North's conciliatory resolution; its report, rejecting the resolution, is adopted on July 31.

July 26: Congress adopts the report of the post office committee and appoints BF postmaster general.

July 31: Congress appoints BF to a committee to encourage the domestic manufacture of lead.

August 1: Congress adjourns.

August 16: BF is elected to the Philadelphia committee of inspection and observation.

August 23: The King proclaims the colonies in rebellion.

August 29: BF goes to Perth Amboy to visit WF.

September 13: Congress reconvenes.

September 18: Congress creates a standing secret committee to supervise the importation of arms and ammunition, and appoints BF to it on September 19.

September 22: Congress appoints BF to a committee to consider the state of American trade.

September 30: Congress appoints BF to a committee to confer with General Washington at headquarters.

October 2: BF is elected from Philadelphia to the Pennsylvania Assembly.

October 4: BF leaves for Cambridge.

October 15–29: BF in Cambridge.

October 19: The Pennsylvania Assembly reappoints BF to the committee of safety.

October 29–November 9: BF returns from Cambridge via Warwick and Perth Amboy, bringing Jane Mecom.

November 4: The Pennsylvania Assembly reappoints BF as a delegate to Congress.

November 9: The Pennsylvania Assembly instructs its Congressional delegation.

November 11: Congress appoints BF to a committee to consider a treaty negotiated with the Indians.

November 16: Congress appoints BF to a committee on the use of packet ships.

November 17: Congress appoints BF to a committee to consider a letter from Washington.

November 23: Congress appoints BF to a committee to consider the treatment of those who refuse to honor the paper currency issued by the Pennsylvania Assembly and by Congress.

November 29: Congress creates the standing committee of secret correspondence and appoints BF to it.

December 2: Congress appoints BF to a committee to establish express riders for carrying intelligence.

December 13: Congress appoints BF to a committee to instruct the committee that sits during the Congressional recess.

December 22: Congress appoints BF to a committee to record unfinished Congressional business.

Late December: The committee of secret correspondence meets with Bonvouloir.

December 31: The assault on Quebec and the death of General Montgomery.

1776

January 5: WF is deprived of his official functions.

January 9: The publication of *Common Sense*.

January 22: Congress appoints BF to a committee to prepare a tribute to General Montgomery.

January 24: Congress appoints BF to a committee to consider the establishment of a war office.

January 25: Congress instructs BF to obtain from France a memorial to General Montgomery.

February 1: Congress instructs BF to inquire from local postmasters about establishing express riders.

February 14: The committee of secret correspondence reports its discussion of the Canadian situation with La Jeunesse.

February 15: Congress appoints BF as a commissioner to Canada.

February 16: BF is elected to the new Philadelphia committee of inspection and observation.

February 26: BF resigns from the Pennsylvania Assembly and committee of safety.

March 1: Congress appoints BF to a committee to consider a New Hampshire petition.

March 2: The committee of secret correspondence appoints Silas Deane as its agent in France.

March 15: Congress appoints BF to a committee to direct General Lee to assume the southern command.

March 17: The British evacuate Boston.

March 20: Congress appoints BF to a committee to examine the qualifications of a would-be officer, and adopts the commission and instructions for the commissioners to Canada.

March 26: BF leaves Philadelphia with the other commissioners to Canada.

March 26–April 29: The commissioners travel to Montreal via New York, Fort Constitution, Albany, Saratoga, and St. Johns.

April 29–May 11: BF in Montreal.

May 2: Louis XVI authorizes the funding of military supplies for America.

May 3: Admiral and General Howe are appointed commissioners to negotiate peace.

May 6: The Americans begin their retreat from Quebec.

May 11–30: BF returns from Montreal to Philadelphia via New York.

May 16: American defeat at the Cedars.

June 5: Congress appoints BF to a committee to establish express riders between army posts.

June 7: Richard Henry Lee introduces his resolutions providing for confederation, independence, and foreign alliances.

June 8: American defeat at Trois Rivières.

June 11: Congress appoints BF to a committee to draft a declaration of independence.

June 12: Congress appoints BF to a committee to draft a plan of treaties with foreign powers.

June 24: Congress orders WF removed to Connecticut.

July 2: Congress declares the colonies independent.

July 4: Congress adopts the Declaration of Independence. The Congress appoints BF to a committee to obtain the attendance of commissioners for Indian affairs at a forthcoming conference, and to another to design a seal for the United States.

July 8: BF is elected from Philadelphia as a delegate to the Pennsylvania convention.

July 16: BF is chosen president of the Pennsylvania convention.

July 20: The Pennsylvania convention names BF as a Congressional delegate. Congress authorizes BF to answer a letter from Lord Howe.

July 26: The Pennsylvania convention instructs its Congressional delegation.

July 30–August 1: Congress debates the Articles of Confederation; BF speaks on representation and taxation.

August 14: Congress appoints BF to a committee to encourage desertions among foreign troops in British service.

August 20: Congress appoints BF to a committee to consider a letter from Washington, and to another to investigate the capture of American vessels by their mutinous crews.

August 26: Congress appoints BF to a committee to consider a letter from Col. James Wilson about encouraging Hessian officers to desert.

August 27: The Battle of Long Island.

September 6: Congress appoints BF to a committee to meet with Lord Howe.

September 11: The committee meets with Lord Howe on Staten Island.

C. September 15: Congress learns of French willingness to furnish financial assistance.

September 15: The British capture New York.

September 17: Congress approves the plan of a treaty to be proposed to France.

September 24: Congress adopts the first set of instructions for its agent or agents in France.

September 26: Congress elects BF, Deane, and Jefferson as commissioners to France.

September 28: The Pennsylvania convention adopts a constitution. Congress approves a letter of credence and financial arrangements for the commissioners to France.

October 1: Thomas Story reports from Arthur Lee to the committee of secret correspondence.

October 16: Congress adopts additional instructions to the commissioners to France.

October 22: Congress elects Arthur Lee to replace Jefferson as a commissioner to France, and adopts the final instructions.

October 26: BF leaves Philadelphia.

October 27: BF sails for France on the *Reprisal*.

THE PAPERS OF
BENJAMIN FRANKLIN

VOLUME 22

March 23, 1775, through October 27, 1776

From Josiah Quincy, Sr.[1]

ALS: Massachusetts Historical Society

Honoured Sir,   Braintree March 25th: 1775.

My dear Son has repeatedly acknowledged your friendly Reception and Patronage of him, since his Arrival in London:[2] Be pleased, therefore, to accept of my gratefull Sense of your Goodness to him; with my ardent Wishes, that your united Endeavors to preserve your native Country from impending Ruin may be attended with Success.

You would hardly be perswaded to believe, did not melancholly Experience evince the Truth of it, that such a Number of infamous WRETCHES could be found upon the Continent, as are now group'd together in Boston under Pretence of flying thither from the Rage of popular Fury; when every Body knows, and their own Consciences cannot but dictate to them, that all they aim at, is, to recommend themselves to the first Offices of Trust and Power, in Case the Plan of subverting the present Constitution, and establishing a despotic Government in its Stead, can be successfully carried into Execution: Some of them are already gratified with lucrative Posts and Pensions, as a Reward for prostituting their venal Pens in Defence of the arbitrary and violent Measures of an abandoned A[dministratio]n; which, doubtless, stimulates the rest to exert their little Abilities to effect the Ruin of their Country; in Hopes they also may have an Opportunity to riot in the Spoils of it: May that all perfect BEING, who governs the Universe, turn their Councils into *Foolishness*; and cause them to repent of their complicated Crimes, or to experience the fatal Consequences of their wicked Apostacy!

The News Papers will discover to you the shamefull Artifices they have been practicing to flatter the Hopes and alarm the Fears of their fellow Citizens; and thereby not only to disunite and divide, but discourage them from pursuing those Measures which the Wisdom of the Continent has devised and recommended, as most salutary and effectual for our Preservation and Security: But, happily for our dear native Country, Providence has been gra-

1. BF's old friend: above, VI, 3–4, and subsequent volumes. This letter, the first to BF that is extant, shows an addiction to commas; we have deleted those that obscure the meaning.
2. For young Quincy's mission to England, and his opinion of BF, see above, XXI, 513. He was homeward bound when this letter was written, and died at sea a month later.

3

ciously pleased to raise up such powerfull Advocates, in Defence of our Claim to be exempted from parliamentary Legislation, by Arguments drawn from those fundamental Principles of natural and civil Law, which form the *Basis* of the english Consitution, as must be sufficient to inform the most ignorant, and convince the most obstinate, of the justness of our Claim; and therefore cannot be invalidated by the futile Productions of those mercenary Scriblers that have appeared in Opposition to it.

May I be permitted, upon this Occasion, without Offence, to present to your View the following Queries; as containing my Sentiments upon the present gloomy Aspect of our publick Affairs: What gave Rise to them was a number of Queries which were published in Drapers Paper of the 14th: of last November:[3] but my Diffidence prevented mine from being published.

Is not human Happiness the End of every good Government?

Can the Happiness of a People be secure and permanent, where the Government is despotic?

Is it not, therefore, absolutely necessary that the supreme Magistrate should be restrained by Law from doing evil or becoming despotic; whilst his Power to Good should be as extensive as his Capacity?

Is not the british Constitution guarded against Despotism, by making the Minister answerable for his Sovereign's mal Administration?

If an abandoned Ministry, by Bribery and Corruption, had procured a Law to be made whereby the Constitution was subverted, and the Sovereigns Power rendered absolute, would the People be obliged to submit to it?

Suppose a Law enacted, to render the King's Power absolute in

---

3. American Loyalists, including many prominent royal appointees, had moved to Boston for protection and were making their voices heard in the press. Perhaps the best known of their "shamefull Artifices" were the letters of Daniel Leonard, one of the newly appointed councillors, under the pseudonym "Massachusettensis," which appeared in the winter and spring of 1774–75 in the *Mass. Gaz. and the Boston Post-Boy and Advertiser*. Among the "powerfull Advocates" of the colonial position Quincy must have had particularly in mind John Adams, who answered Leonard in the *Boston Gaz.*, from January on, in the famous "Novanglus" letters; they defended the American position in the way described. The published queries, thirty in number, were in the *Mass. Gaz.; and the Boston Weekly News-Letter* of Nov. 24, 1774. They harped on the benefits of the British constitution, the duty of obedience, and the sin of precipitating a civil war.

Part of his Dominions; would it not be repugnant to the fundamental Principles of the Constitution and therefore void?

Would not every Member of Parliament who voted for such a
Law incur the Guilt of high Treason against the State?

Would not the Minister, who advised his Sovereign to give his
Consent to it, be equally guilty?

Would not the People throughout his Dominions be justified
were they to rise up, as one Man, and oppose the Execution of
such a Law?

Is not the Kings Power in Canada, by a late Law of the british
Parliament rendered as absolute, as that of an asiatic DESPOT?[4]

Are not ALL concerned in Government there, whether in the
legislative or executive Departments, appointed by the Crown;
paid by the Crown and removeable at Pleasure?

If Despotism is established in Canada, why may it not by another Law be established in all the Colonies upon this Continent?

The Idea is horrible! and it is with inexpressible Anguish I
proceed to ask:

If the Acts of Parliament relative to these Colonies, especially
for these ten Years past, are not almost all of them calculated to
subjugate the Inhabitants to a legislative Power in which they
have no Share?

Can Property be secure, or the People free, who are subjected
to a legislative Power in which they have no Share, and over which
they have no Controul? Is not this a compleat Definition of a
despotic Government?

Are not *Americans* equally intituled with *Britons* to be governed
by those Laws only, to which they have given their Consent, either
personally, or by Representation?

Is it not a *natural Right* given by God to Man with Life, and
therefore as unalienable as Life it Self?

Is it not a *civil Right* stipulated and secured to the Subject, not
only by magna Charta, but by all those Statutes, Compacts, Cove-
nants and Agreements, by and between the Sovereign and Subject, upon which the Constitution is founded; and therefore as
indefeazable as the Rights of the Crown?

Does it not, therefore, necessarily follow, that as Allegiance and
Protection are reciprocal, so Legislation and Representation are
inseperable?

4. For the Quebec Act see above, XXI, 228 n.

Has not the rapid Increase of the Colonies in Numbers and Property been owing as much, at least, to the Peoples equal Share in their respective Legislatures, as to the natural Advantages of their Soil and Climate?

Had they not from the begining enjoyed this inestimable Privilege, would not this extensive Continent have remained a Desart still or been possessed by the Subjects of some other european Power?

Were they by Force or Fraud to be deprived of it, would not the Country soon become again a howling Wilderness?

Has not the Increase and Prosperity of the Colonies greatly contributed to the Wealth and Grandeur of the Nation, and the distinguished Rank she sustains among the Powers of the World?

Have the Colonies either unitedly or seperately renounced their Allegiance to their Sovereign; or by any Misconduct forfieted their Claim to his Protection, and lost those Rights and Privileges, which are granted and secured to them by their respective Charters?

If they have not, why are their repeated humble Petitions to the Throne disregarded, and the Prayer of them ungranted?

Before their Patience was worn out, by repeated Provocations, and unparalelled Injuries: Did the Colonies ever discover any want of Attachment to the Parent State?

As a dutifull Son, settled at a Distance from his Father's House considers it as his *Home*: Have not the Colonies, in like manner considered England as their *Home*; and behaved towards the Parent State with most cordial and filial Affection?

Have they not ever rejoiced in her Prosperity sympathized with Her in Adversity, and occasionally afforded her Aid, even beyond their Abilities? and has she not been so sensible of this, as more than once to remunerate them for their extraordinary Services?

Has not the Protection of the Colonies, *exaggerated as it is*, been more than compensated by the Profits of an exclusive Commerce?

Is not the Claim, therefore, of the british House of Commons to *give* and *grant* the Property of their american fellow Subjects, *without their Consent*, repugnant to every Idea of natural Equity and Justice?

Are we Bastards, and not Children, that a Prince, who is celebrated as the best of Kings, has given his Consent to so many and such unprecedented and oppressive Acts of Parliament, as if carried into Execution must eventually render the Condition of his *american Subjects* no better than that of *Slaves* to his *british Subjects?*

Are they not so disgracefully humiliating, as no Society of Men would submit to, who had any Sense of Freedom: the least Spark of Virtue, or any Power of Resistance?

Is not the enforcing the Execution of them, with Fleets and Armies, as inhumane as it is unjust?

Who are answerable for all the horrid Consequences of a long and bloody civil War? They who from Motives of Avarice and Ambition attack; or They who from a Principle of Selfpreservation defend?

If the Seat of Goverment was transferred from Britain to America; and an american House of Commons were to give and grant the Property of their british fellow Subjects, without their Consent, would they not loudly as well as justly complain of such Treatment as arbitrary and oppressive?

Can They do that, justly, which upon a supposed Change of Situation and Circumstances They would with reason complain of, as in the highest Degree unjust?

Will not the Subversion of the american Constitutions of Government, and subjugating the People to an arbitrary Jurisdiction produce, sooner or later, the same Effects in every other Part of the King's Dominions?

When the Sovereign's Power over his american Dominions becomes absolute, will not Americans from a Spirit of just Resentment endeavor to extend it over the whole Empire?

Will not an immense american Revenue, at the Disposal of a corrupt and corrupting Administration, easily effect such a Plan of universal Despotism?

Can Britons, therefore, who have for Ages been the sucessful Defenders of civil and religious Liberty, remain any longer silent Spectators of the hostile Measures that are pursuing in America; or unconcerned about the Event of them?

If they are, may we not venture to foretel, without the Spirit of Prophecy, that it will not be much longer they will remain a FREE PEOPLE?

If you should find it as difficult to excuse me, as I find it to apologize for the Errors and Imperfections of so long a Letter, I shall be heartily sorry I have wrote it: But, if it meets with so favorable a Reception, as in Return you will please to gratifie me with your own Sentiments respecting the present Controversy between the Parent State and these Colonies, I shall not only be greatly obliged, but promise you that no Extracts from them shall be communicated to the Publick; nor to any, but such of your Friends as you shall be pleased to point out: Indeed, there is no Injunction you can lay upon me, that I would not chearfully comply with, rather than be deprived of an entertaining and instructive Epistle from You, as often as you can spare Time to bestow such an inestimable Favor upon Your most obliged and obedient Servant   JOSA: QUINCY

P:S: I have desired my Son communicate to you any Part of my Letter to him which he thinks worthy your Notice.

Doctor Franklin

Addressed: To / Doctor Franklin / in Craven Street / London / per Favr: of Fran: Dana Esqr.[5] / Q D C

Notation: From *Josiah Quincy* March 25. 1775.

From James Kinsey[6]   ALS: American Philosophical Society

Sir   Burlington March 26 1775.
      By the favor of Mr. Wister I transmitt the Votes and Laws of the last Session of Assembly, Which I hope will be delivered safely to you together with this inclosing a Duplicate of the petition to the King.[7]

5. Francis Dana (1743–1811), later famous as a diplomat and jurist, was on a mission to England to present the American case there and sound out opinion; he returned almost a year later, convinced that reconciliation was impossible. *DAB.* He left from Rhode Island in late April (*Newport Mercury*, April 24, 1775), and carried not only this letter but those to BF below from Winthrop, Cooper, and Warren (March 28, April 1, 3); when he could not deliver them he must have kept them, for they came by way of his descendants to the Mass. Hist. Soc. See its *Proc.*, VII (1863), 117–25, and Elizabeth E. Dana, *The Dana Family in America* (Cambridge, Mass., 1956), pp. 485, 500, 502.
6. The Burlington lawyer identified above, XXI, 112 n. He was writing as a member of the N.J. Assembly's committee of correspondence.
7. Bartholomew Wistar (1754–96), the grandson of Caspar Wistar (above, III, 114), left for London in late March or early April with a certificate from a Friends' meeting, and apparently stayed for three years. Hinshaw, *Quaker Genealogy*, II, 438, 691; Negly K. Teeters, *They Were in Prison . . .* (Philadelphia, [1937]), p. 119. He carried with him *Votes, N.J.* (Jan.–Feb., 1775), and a

In my last I Stated Mr. Wilmotts Affair fully, hope he will see by it that the Colony has not been to blame and that he will speedily receive his Money.[8]

It Woud give us pleasure to hear of the Approbation of the Crown to the Law for instituting a suit against the late Eastern Treasurer: If there shoud be any Opposition made pray do the Committee of Correspondence the favor to Acquaint them therewith.[9] With great Respect I am Your Most humble Servant

J KINSEY

Addressed: To / Dr Benjamin Franklin / Craven Street / London

Notation by Jonathan Williams, Jr.: J Kinsey New Jersey Mar. 26. 1775 recd July 7 1775 Answd 12th & 19th July 1775

From John Winthrop   ALS: Massachusetts Historical Society

Dear Sir   Cambridge New England 28 March 1775

I did my self the honor to write you, 13 Septr last, by Mr. Quincy, acknowleging the receit of several curious Pamphlets, for which am much obliged to you, and beg the favor of you to present my respectful Compliments to Sir John Pringle, and Mr. Henley, for the particular honor they have done me, in sending me their curious Productions. Since that, I have received the last Vol. of the Philosophical Transactions,[1] for which I return you my

---

petition to the King, approved by the Assembly on Feb. 13, which listed colonial grievances and was in part drawn verbatim from the petition sent by the Continental Congress: *Minutes of the Provincial Congress and the Council of Safety of the State of New Jersey* (Trenton, 1879), pp. 88–92. Wistar, when he found that BF had returned home, delivered the duplicate to JW, who endorsed this letter. The original petition reached London soon after BF's departure. Arthur Lee, who was acting informally as N.J. agent, received and presented it to Dartmouth, but it was returned to him on the ground that he was not authorized to act for the colony. *Dartmouth MSS,* II, 288; Lee to Kinsey, April 17, 1775, 4 Force, *Amer. Arch.,* II, 339. JW, unaware of this development, tried in turn to present the petition; see his letter to BF below, July 19.

8. See above XXI, 404.

9. *Ibid.,* p. 260 n. No opposition had been recorded when the law, with others from New Jersey, had come before the Board of Trade the previous December: *Board of Trade Jour.,* 1768–75, pp. 403–5.

1. Part 2, we assume, of *Phil. Trans.,* LXIV (1774). The disappearance of Winthrop's earlier letter makes the pamphlets impossible to identify, but in all

thanks. I must confess, I was not a little mortified, when I opened the package, in not finding a line from my ever honored Friend, whose correspondence always gives me the greatest pleasure. Whether it were occasioned by the multiplicity of most important affairs, in which I know you are involved; or, whether any Letter of yours has been intercepted, I am not able to say. My suspicion of the last has been strengthned by the circumstances, in which the last Vol. of Transactions came to my hand. It was only tied up loosely in a brown paper cover, without any seal.

However the case may be, I cannot neglect so good an opportunity as now offers, of paying my respects to You. My neighbour, Francis Dana Esq, is embarking for London. He was a Gentleman of the Law in this town, while there was any Law; a modest, sensible, intelligent person, and a true Friend to Liberty. He had the firmness to oppose the address to Mr. H. when it was in agitation among the Lawyers.[2] I need say nothing of the situation of our public affairs, as Mr. Dana will be able to give you full information. I cannot, however, forbear observing, to the honor of the people of this Province, that ever since the resignation of the Mandamus Councillors,[3] they have been as quiet and peaceable as any Colony on the Continent, tho' under a total suspension of government, and an accumulation of grievances. We are now in a state of the most anxious suspense, but preparing for the worst. God send better times!

I have desired Mr. Dana to deliver you 52 *s.* sterl. for another annual payment to the Royal Society. With sentiments of the

---

likelihood two of them were Pringle's *Discourse on the Different Kinds of Air* . . . (above, XXI, 148) and a paper by William Henly read before the Royal Society and reprinted separately, in which the author referred to Winthrop's observations on lightning: *Phil. Trans.*, LXIV, 146–7.

2. For Dana's mission see the note on Quincy's letter above, March 25. The address to Hutchinson from a number of lawyers on the eve of the Governor's departure, May 29, 1774, may be found in Force, 4 *Amer. Arch.*, I, 363.

3. Those appointed by the crown under the Massachusetts Government Act. By the previous September twenty out of thirty-six had either initially refused the oath or later resigned: *Boston Gaz.*, Sept. 5, 1774. Some new appointments were made in London, but by December the Council existed only in name. "The taking any Step by their Advice," the Governor reported to Dartmouth, "would add no weight to the Authority of Government, but rather be an Argument for Disobedience." Carter, *Gage Correspondence*, I, 387; see also pp. 364–5, 370, 372–3.

highest respect and esteem I am Sir Your most obliged humble
Servant   JOHN WINTHROP

Dr Franklin.

Addressed: Benjamin Franklin Esq / London / Favord by Fras
Dana Esq

Notation: John Winthrop to Dr Franklin 1775.

From Samuel Cooper

ALS: Massachusetts Historical Society; draft: British Museum[4]

Dear Sir,   Boston N.E. 1 Apr. 1775.
I wrote you in Septr and Aug: last, and it is a great While
indeed since I have had the Pleasure of a Line from you.[5] The
Anxiety and Distress bro't upon us by the Port Bill and other
Acts, and the Troops and Ships of War station'd here have been
great; and much Art and Pains have been employ'd to dismay us,
or provoke us to some rash Action, but hitherto the People have
behav'd with an astonishing Calmness and Resolution. The Union
and Firmness of this and the other Colonies have rather grown
than diminished; and they seem prepar'd for all Events. Had I not
learn'd in these Days to wonder at Nothing I should have been
surpriz'd at the Inconsistency of the Manner in which the Petition
from the Congress was receiv'd, and Lord Dartmouth's circular
Letter to the Governor, on that Subject.[6] It will however have no
Effect, or one directly contrary to the Views of Administration.
The Colonies highly approve the Proceedings of the Congress and
have voted Delegates for the new one in May. The Assembly at N.
York forbore an express approbation; but have resolv'd almost all

4. We publish as usual the ALS, from which the draft differs only in inconsequential details.
5. Cooper's letters are above, XXI, 273–6, 297–302; the latest extant letter
from BF was of Feb. 25, 1774.
6. On March 27 the *Boston Gaz.* had published the circular letter from the
agents to the colonial speakers (XXI, 399), announcing that the King had
graciously received the petition and recognized its importance. Alongside that
text appeared Dartmouth's circular letter to the governors of Jan. 4, 1775
(Carter, *Gage Correspondence*, II, 179), in which he made disparaging comments
on the first Congress and instructed the recipients to do all in their power to
prevent the choice of delegates to the second.

the Acts complain'd of by the Congress to be Grievances, and County Assemblies in that Province will probably by a large Majority appoint Delegates for the approaching Congress. One would have imagin'd that Ministerial Influence and Bribes would have had a much greater Effect upon that Province than has hitherto appear'd.[7]

We have heard that the Merchants and Manufacturers in Britain are petitioning on our, or rather their own Behalf, that no more Troops are to be sent; and the Acts likely to be repeal'd:[8] Other Accounts from your Side the Water say, that the same or similar Measures will still be pursued. The Determination here seems to be, not to abate our Vigilance, and to act as tho we expected no Favor till adequate Relief is granted. I send this by a safe hand, Mr. Dana, a Gentleman of the Law, much esteemd here, and tho a Nephew of Judg Trowbridg, a firm Friend to the Liberties of his Country.[9] He carries with him Papers containing particular Accounts of our Affairs, and I think you may rely on his Representations: He can inform you minutely of Things that have taken place since Mr. Quincy left us,[1] and of our present State. I hope it will not be long before my Country will find itself in a Situation to give some Testimony of it's Sense of your great Services to it, and Sufferings, in it's Cause. With the most respectful and warm Attachment I am Sir, Your obedient humble Servant

SAML COOPER.

Dr Franklin.

Addressed: To / Benjn. Franklin Esqr. / L L D. F R S / London

Notation: From Samuel Cooper.   April 1. 1775.

---

7. The N.Y. Assembly had refused, by a narrow margin, to consider the proceedings of the first Continental Congress or to elect delegates to the second. But it had passed resolutions, published in the *Boston Evening Post* of March 27, denouncing a large number of British statutes as infringements on American liberty. The calling of an extralegal provincial convention had been announced on March 7, and Cooper proved right in guessing that it would choose Congressional delegates. Jensen, *Founding of a Nation*, pp. 532–3.

8. The Boston press in March had reported the merchants' petitions, which BF and Barclay had been abetting since the previous December; see Vol. XXI.

9. Edmund Trowbridge (1709–93), Dana's uncle under whom he had studied, was a Loyalist by temperament but held aloof from the struggle. *DAB*.

1. In other words since the end of September: above, XXI, 346 n.

From William Lee[2]

ALS: American Philosophical Society

Dear Sir.   London 3 Apl. 1775.

I wrote you the other day about an hundred pounds which the Constitutional Society here had orderd to be given for releif of the poor sufferers in Boston and now inclose you Mr. Olivers letter respecting that business.[3] I presume you are fully informed from other hands of all the public transactions here since you left us. Therefore shall only beg you to believe me to be sincerely and with the highest esteem Dear Sir Your most Obliged and Obedient Humble Servant   WILLIAM LEE

Addressed: To / Doctor Benjamin Franklin Esqr. / L.L.D. / Philadelphia / via Maryland

Endorsed: W Lee Esqr April 3. 75

From Joseph Warren[4]

ALS (facsimile):[5] Massachusetts Historical Society

Sir,   Boston April 3rd 1775.

Altho' I have not the pleasure either of a personal or epistolary acquaintance with you, I have taken the liberty of sending you by

2. The brother of Arthur and Richard Henry Lee, who made a name for himself in London politics: above, xx, 308 n.

3. Lee's earlier letter, and the enclosure in this one, have disappeared. Alderman Richard Oliver, M.P. (1735–84), was a former supporter of Wilkes, but broke with him in 1771 and became a founder of the Constitutional Society: *DNB*; Namier and Brooke, *House of Commons*, III, 224. In February the Society had voted £100 for the Bostonians; Oliver had presented the money to BF, who had returned his thanks. *London Chron.*, Feb. 9–11; *London Evening Post*, Feb. 21–3, 1775. Lee is here alluding to a second donation of the same amount, voted on March 21: *Public Advertiser*, March 23, 1775. BF sent the first gift, as a draft on London, by Josiah Quincy, Jr., in mid-March, and transmitted what we presume was the second by another draft, which he gave to John and Samuel Adams in Philadelphia but which they did not forward to London; he subsequently paid the money in Mass. Memorandum Book (above, VII, 167–8), entries of Aug. 2 and Nov. 20, 1775.

4. Warren (1741–75), the well known physician-turned-soldier, author of the Suffolk resolves (above, XXI, 342–3) and a leader among the Boston Whigs, was killed at Bunker Hill. *DAB*.

5. The original, when it came to the Society, was printed in its *Proc.*, VII (1863), 125, and has been missing for many years. The facsimile, of unknown provenance, is not of that printed text, but differs from it in minor details and

Mr. Dana a pamphlet which I wish was more deserving of your notice.[6] The ability and firmness with which you have defended the Rights of Mankind and the Liberties of this Country in particular have rendered you dear to all America. May you soon see your enemies deprived of the power of injuring you and your friends in a situation to discover the grateful sense they have of your exertions in the cause of freedom. I am, Sir, with the greatest esteem and respect, your most obedient humble servant

JOSEPH WARREN

Doctor Franklin.

From John Foxcroft

ALS: American Philosophical Society

My Dear Friend New York April 4th 1775
Your very agreable favour of the 4th. of Janry. I rec'd by the last Packet informing of your having drawn on me for the Ballance of our Acct. as it Stands in your Books[7] a Copy of which I rec'd by a Ship Via Philada. Mr. Bache will inform you that at his desire the Bill was paid in Philadelphia when due. The Acct. as you say may be easly rectify'd when we meet.

My sincere thanks are due to you, for your goodness in assuring Mr. Todd that you would chearfully become my Security whenever call'd upon for that purpose. I had a very Polite Letter from Mr. Boldero on the Occasion Signifying how Sorry he was that the Articles of their partnership prevented his complying with my request;[8] I have wrote to Mr. Todd by this packet, which I hope will settle the matter. I think the Post Office escapes the Political

---

adds a superscription: "Doctor Benjamin Franklin, London. / Pr. favr. Mr. Dana."

6. *An Oration: Delivered March Sixth,* 1775 . . . *to Commemorate the Bloody Tragedy of the Fifth of March,* 1770. *By Dr. Joseph Warren.* (Boston, 1775). For Dana's mission see the note on the first document.

7. BF's letter is lost, but the bill was undoubtedly that to which Foxcroft had referred in his of Feb. 1: above, XXI, 464.

8. This is our only evidence that BF gave surety for his friend when Foxcroft was reappointed, and Hugh Finlay appointed, deputy postmasters general in North America. Mr. Boldero was either Henry or John, two brothers who were London bankers and who died in 1789: *Kent's Directory* . . . (London, 1775); *The European Mag. and London Rev.* . . . , XV (1789), 352, 504: Joseph J. Muskett, *Suffolk Manorial Families* . . . (3 vols., Exeter, 1900–14), I, 188.

14

Storm which now Rages, thus far none of our Riders have met with the least Interuption, and have the pleasure to inform you that in consequence of some New Regulations we made last Winter the Posts are very Regular once a Week as far as St. Augustine and twice a Week between this City and Quebec.[9]

Pray what is become of the Ohio Scheme? I have heard nothing from your side the Water concerning it for this Six Months past.[1] The Virginians are setling that Country very fast since the Peace which Ld. Dunmore concluded with the Indians renders it impossible for the Latter ever again disturbing them in the peaceable possession of that Montpelier of America.[2]

My two Charming Sweet little Girls together with Mrs. Foxcroft are pure[3] well thank God. She joins me in sincere Regards and best wishes for the health and happiness of you and the good Family in Craven Street. I am and ever shall remain with the greatest Esteem and Regard your obliged Friend and very humble Servant   JOHN FOXCROFT

I expect Mr. Finlay from Quebec by the 20th. of May.[4]

Endorsed: Mr Foxcroft 1775

9. The new regulations were doubtless an outgrowth of Hugh Finlay's tour of inspection in 1773–74, which he recorded in [Frank H. Norton, ed.,] *Journal Kept by Hugh Finlay* . . . (Brooklyn, N.Y., 1867). But the days of the royal post were numbered. A month after Foxcroft made this optimistic statement he was compelled to discharge the postriders between New York and Boston because they were being stopped and their mail opened; official correspondence had to be sent by sea. The overland route from Quebec was cut at the same time, and Finlay had to open communication with Halifax and thence by water to New York. Force, 4 *Amer. Arch.*, II, 480–1: Ruth L. Butler, *Doctor Franklin, Postmaster General* (New York, 1928), pp. 160–2.

1. The Vandalia grant was still buried in the glacial proceedings of Whitehall, and was never confirmed: above, XXI, 288n.

2. Presumably a reference to Montpellier, the old capital of Languedoc, noted for the beauty of its surroundings. Lord Dunmore's incursion down the Ohio in 1774, in the small war that bears his name, produced in the autumn a preliminary settlement with the Indians by which they surrendered to the whites their claim to all land south of the Ohio. Reuben G. Thwaites and Louise P. Kellogg, eds., *Documentary History of Dunmore's War* . . . (Madison, Wis., 1905), especially pp. 385–6.

3. In the now obsolete sense of "very."

4. Finlay had delivered dispatches to Gage in Boston and then gone to Quebec to cope with the postal problems there. Butler, *op. cit.*, p. 162. We have found no evidence that he returned to New York.

15

Speculation on the Speed of Ships   MS: Library of Congress

During his homeward voyage Franklin took time off from writing his journal of the peace negotiations in London to return to a question that had intrigued him for years: why do westbound ships have a longer crossing of the Atlantic than eastbound? Almost three decades earlier he had advanced a tentative answer in terms of the earth's rotation;[5] he now sketched a new one that was essentially a recapitulation of the old, and apparently prevailed on his grandson to write it out.[6] It remained with him for another decade until August, 1785, when he was again homeward bound after his years in France; he then embodied this paragraph of speculation in a long set of maritime observations. By January, 1786, however, he convinced himself that the earth's rotation was irrelevant,[7] and appended a note to that effect when his observations were published.[8]

On board the Pennsylvania Packet, Capt. Osborn at Sea,

April 5. 1775.

Suppose a Ship to make a Voyage Eastward from a Place in Lat: 40. North, to a Place in Lat 50. North, Distance in Longitude 75 Degrees.

In sailing from 40 to 50 she goes from a Place where a Degree of Longitude is about 8 miles greater than in the Place she is going to. A Degree is equal to 4 Minutes of Time. Consequently the Ship in the Harbour she leaves partaking of the Diurnal Motion of the Earth, moves two miles in a minute faster, than when in the Port she is going to; which is 120 miles in an Hour.

This motion in a Ship and Cargo is of great force; and if she could be lifted up suddenly from the Harbour in which she lay quiet, and set down instantly in the Latitude of the Port she was bound to, tho' in a Calm, that Force contained in her would make her run a great Way at a Prodigious Rate. This Force must be lost gradually in her Voyage, by gradual Impulse against the water, and probably thence shorten the Voyage. In returning just the contrary must happen and her Voyage be retarded and lengthned.

BF.

Endorsed: Voyages from & to America why not of equal Length

5. Above, III, 67–8.
6. The heading and date, and the endorsement at the end, are in BF's hand; the body of the text appears to be in WTF's.
7. BF to Jonathan Williams, Jr., Jan. 19, 1786, APS.
8. In the form of a letter to Julien-David (misnamed Alphonsus) LeRoy,

Observations at Sea on Temperatures of Air and Water

Printed in *Transactions of the American Philosophical Society* . . . , II (1786), 325.

On his voyage to America Franklin was wondering about the sea around him. Soon after setting down his speculation on the speed of ships (the preceding document) he, or perhaps his grandson under his direction, began to record the temperature of the water. For the first four days it varied little, and perhaps for that reason the readings were abandoned for the next eleven days. They were resumed on the 26th, and from the 28th were made at various times of day and evening, accompanied by other observations, until the ship was at or near the mouth of the Delaware. From these data the following table was compiled. The manuscript has been lost, and the table did not appear in print until more than a decade later.[9] Hence we do not know when the data collected on shipboard were cast in their present form, but the form has no bearing on their significance. For years Franklin had been interested in the Gulf Stream.[1] Now for the first time he had the evidence to detect it. "Besides the gulph weed with which it is interspersed," he wrote years later in the light of this and subsequent evidence, "I find that it is always warmer than the sea on each side of it, and that it does not sparkle in the night."[2]

[April 10 to May 3, 1775]

Observations of the warmth of the sea-water, &c. by Fahrenheit's thermometer, in crossing the Gulph stream; with other remarks made on board the Pennsylvania packet, Capt. Osborne, bound from London to Philadelphia, in April and May 1775.

Jean-Baptiste's brother, which the editor or editors entitled "Maritime Observations": APS *Trans.*, II (1786), 294–324; BF's note is on p. 317.

9. Incorporated as an appendix to BF's "Maritime Observations," for which see the preceding document.

1. See above, X, 94; XV, 246–8.

2. APS *Trans.*, II, 315–16.

Date.	Hour.	Temp. of Air.	Temp. of Wat.	Wind.	Course.	Distance.	Latitude N.	Longitude W.	Remarks.
April 10			62						
11			61						
12			64						
13			65						
14			65						
26		60	70				37 39	60 38	Much gulph weed; saw a whale.
27		60	70				37 13	62 29	Colour of water changed.
28		70	64				37 48	64 35	No gulph weed.
—	8 A.M.	67	60	S S E	W b S	34			Sounded, no bottom.
—	6 P.M.	63	71	S W	W N W	44			Much light in the water last night.
29	8 A.M.	65	72	N	W	57 }	37 26	66 0 }	Water again of the usual deep sea colour, little or no light in it at night.
—	5 P.M.	66	66	N E	W b S	69			
—	11 dit.	64	70	N WbN	W b N	24			
30	8 A.M.	62	70	N E	E b S	43	37 20	68 53 }	Frequent gulph weed, water continues of sea colour, little light.
—	12	64	72	E S E	W b N	25			
—	6 P.M.	65	65	S	W N W	60			Much light.
—	10 dit.	68	63			44			Much light all last night.
May 1	7 A.M.	65	56	S S W	W b N	21	38 13	72 23	Colour of water changed.
—	12	64	56		W N W	31			
—	4 P.M.	64	57	S W	N W	18			Much light.
—	10 dit.	62	53		W S W	18			Much light. Thunder-gust.
2	8 A.M.	60	53	W S W	W b N	15	38 43	74 3	
—	12	64	55	N W		10			
—	6 P.M.	65	55	N b W		30			
3	7 A.M.	62	54				38 30	75 0	

Franklin, Thomas Walpole, Samuel Wharton, and John Sargent: Power of Attorney to William Trent

DS: Historical Society of Pennsylvania

The promoters of the Walpole grant in London were becoming more and more unsure of obtaining it. Franklin's ostensible withdrawal from their group in January, 1774,[3] had had no perceptible effect in forwarding their cause, and their chance of success diminished as war drew nearer. They waited for over a year. Then in the spring of 1775 they apparently concluded that the immediate prospect in Whitehall was so unpromising that they would be well advised to turn their attention to America, to find out whether there might not be a market there for at least some of their vast tract. At the same time, no doubt with an eye on the need for influence in Philadelphia, they reinstated Franklin in absentia as one of their principals. At a meeting on April 11 they empowered Major William Trent, who was returning home after his years as a lobbyist in London, to be their agent in disposing of what the crown, they still purported to believe, was about to convey to them.[4] Trent arrived in Philadelphia on June 7[5] and soon thereafter, presumably, secured Franklin's signature to complete those already on his power of attorney.

The instrument on the face of it authorized him to deal in any land within the Walpole grant. A now missing letter from Thomas Walpole and John Sargent to Franklin, written in late spring or early summer, referred to "their Plan of Possessing and Leasing the Lands contracted for with Government," which could scarcely be anything but the entire twenty million acres.[6] The promoters were sending Trent to explore an unknown market, in a political situation that could not be foreseen, and perhaps expected him to dispose of any lands he could in any way he could. Those to which the Walpole Company had the most plausible claim were only a small part of the whole, and Samuel Wharton, at least, was particularly concerned with that part. The time had come, he wrote Franklin in a letter that Trent delivered, "to establish Titles for Lands, fairly obtained from the native Proprietors."[7] Those proprietors were the Indians who, at Fort Stanwix in 1768, had ceded to the "suffering traders" a tract that had subsequently been incorporated in the Walpole grant.[8]

---

3. Above, XXI, 31–4.
4. Lewis, *Indiana Co.*, p. 150. Trent appears often in vols. XVI, XVIII–XX.
5. Philip Skene, his shipmate, arrived on that date: Wharton to BF below, April 17, 1775; *JCC*, II, 82.
6. As paraphrased by WF in his letter below, Aug. 14, 1775.
7. Wharton to BF below, April 17, 1775.
8. The remainder of the grant requested was land that had been purchased at

Trent brought with him two legal opinions, which Wharton had secured in London, that title obtained from the Indians needed no validation by the crown.[9] Wharton and Franklin had long held this view.[1] It justified the Company in disposing without royal consent of what it had acquired without royal intervention, in other words the traders' grant; and the sale of that land was in fact proposed the following August.[2] This scheme, whether or not it was what the promoters had had in mind in their power of attorney, had some color of legality; and they hoped that Congress would deepen the color by declaring that the Indians had an unconditional right to alienate. Such a declaration might be procured, Wharton suggested before the summer was out, by offering a few key delegates half-shares in the Company.[3] The will-o'-the-wisp that the promoters had chased for six years in Whitehall now moved to Philadelphia.

⟨April 11, 1775: Walpole and his associates petitioned the King to be allowed to acquire, at a price and subject to conditions that might be thought reasonable, part of a tract of land on the Ohio purchased by the crown at a congress with the Six Nations at Fort Stanwix on November 5, 1768. After a number of orders from the Treasury, the Board of Trade, and the Committee of Council for Plantation Affairs, a report by the Board of Trade on May 6, 1773, proposed the terms of the grant and a plan for establishing a government. An order in council of May 19 referred this report to the Committee of Council, which on July 3 ordered the law officers of the crown to draft an instrument, embodying the conditions set forth in the report, to be issued under the great seal.[4] On the 16th the law officers made their report; on October 28, 1773, the Committee of Council instructed them to prepare the instrument,[5] and transmitted to the petitioners a map of the lands in question. Those lands and others purchased at the aforesaid congress were ordered to be erected into a colony under the name of Vandalia.

Fort Stanwix for the king, whose proprietary rights the Company had acknowledged in offering to pay quitrents. Above, XV, 265, 275–9; XVI, 163; XVII, 8–9.

9. See the headnote below, July 12, 1775.

1. Above, XX, 300–4.

2. See the letter from WF cited above.

3. Lewis, *Indiana Co.*, pp. 160–1. See also Bancroft to BF below, Aug. 7, 1775.

4. Above, XX, 298–9n.

5. *Ibid.*, pp. 327–8 n.

Various persons and their families have taken unauthorized possession of parts of the grant to be made to the petitioners, who wish that these settlers may hold on the same terms that are to be set for the rest of the land. William Trent, one of the aforesaid associates, is about to leave for America. The signers, on behalf of themselves, their heirs, assigns, and associates, constitute him their attorney to manage their interests in the tract and to lease, at such rents and other terms as he considers most for their benefit, such parts of it as have been or may in future be settled; to make agreements with the lessees for the preemption [*torn*] of their leases on the same terms on which the signers, their heirs, assigns, and associates, shall sell unsettled neighboring land of the same quality and situation; and in general to act as the signers might if present in person. They ratify in advance whatever legal steps Trent may take.⟩

Sealed and Delivered by the above named Thomas Walpole and John Sargent (being first duly stamp't) in Presence of
    JNO DAGGE
    WILL ROSS
Sealed and delivered by the above named Samuel Wharton in the Presence of
    WILL ROSS
    JOHN LILLEY[7]

Sealed and delivered by the above named Benjamin Franklin in the presence of us[6]
(4) RICHD. BACHE
    JAMES BRYSON

(2) THOMAS
    WALPOLE
SAML. WHARTON
(3) B FRANKLIN
    J. SARGENT

6. In BF's hand.
7. We have no explanation of the numbers, and cannot identify Lilley. For John Dagge see above, XVI, 167 n, where we should have added (if we had known) that Henry was his brother: Sir John Maclean, *The Parochial and Family History of Trig Minor* . . . (3 vols., London, 1873), I, 295, 297. Ross was probably William Ross, a lawyer in Boswell Court, St. Clement's Danes: *The Records of the Honorable Society of Lincoln's Inn . . . Admissions* . . . (2 vols., [London,] 1896), I, 531. Bryson was later postmaster of Philadelphia, a surveyor general of the Post Office, and in 1782–86 a tenant of BF. *JCC*, IX, 816, 860; John C. Fitzpatrick, "The Post Office of the Revolutionary War," *Daughters of the Amer. Revolution Mag.*, LVI (1922), 582; J. Thomas Scharf and Thompson

From Alexander Dalrymple[8]

ALS: American Philosophical Society

My Dear Sir   Soho Square 17th April 1775

The Bearer Mr. William Whitchurch finding his Health much impaired by his assiduous application to his Business has been induced to make a Voyage to America; I believe you are not unacquainted with his Works as a Writing Engraver and if he finds the Climate agrees with him and that he can find suitable occupation he may remain at Philadelphia and I hope may be the means of improving this Branch of art in the Western World.[9] You will very much oblige me by giving him your advice and Countenance. I shall leave England in a very few days having been lately appointed by the East India Company in my Standing in the Council of Fort St. George[1] where I shall be happy to hear from You and glad of every opportunity to testify how sincerely I am My Dear sir Your most Obliged humble servant

A DALRYMPLE

Addressed: To / Benjamin Franklin LLD / Philadelphia

Endorsed: Dalrimple 17. Ap. 1775.

Westcott, *History of Philadelphia* . . . (3 vols., Philadelphia, 1884), III, 1812; Penrose B. Hoopes, "Cash Dr to Benjamin Franklin," *PMHB,* LXXX (1956), 61–9 *passim.*

8. For the explorer and hydrographer see above, XVIII, 214–15 n.

9. Whitchurch was later described as an "engenious Mapengraver" and "the ablest artist in that branch." Rudolph Raspe to BF, Aug. 14, 1777 (APS); Georg Foster, *A Voyage round the World in His Britannic Majesty's Sloop, Resolution* . . . (2 vols., London, 1779), I, xiv. The engraver apparently did not go to Philadelphia, and certainly did not stay there; for in 1777 Dalrymple gave him a second letter of the same tenor, in response to which BF promised to write friends in America: Whitchurch to BF, March 2, 1778, APS. A second and undated Whitchurch letter in the APS suggests that he never did emigrate.

1. He was leaving for a short and stormy sojourn in India, where he had previously spent more than a decade in the Company's service when his patron, George Pigot (1719–77), had been governor of Madras. He was now returning with Pigot, who had been raised to the peerage and reappointed governor. They arrived at the end of the year, and Pigot promptly quarreled with a majority of the council; his opponents deposed and arrested him, and he died in confinement in May, 1777. Dalrymple was then recalled. *DNB* under Dalrymple and Pigot; Henry D. Love, *Vestiges of Old Madras* . . . (4 vols., London, 1913), III, 84, 103–6.

From Samuel Wharton ALS: American Philosophical Society

Dear Sir   Portsmouth April 17th. 1775.

As Major Trent is the Bearer of this Letter,[2] it is the less Necessary for Me *now* to be very particular in my Communications. I presented, as you desired, your Respects to Lord Camden, and his Lordship requested Me to tell You, that He should have been much pleased to have seen you, before you embarked; That the Chancellor's Decission in your Case is entirely *political*, And that, if during the Administration of the present Men, An Appeal should be made from the Court of Chancery to the House of Lords, you would certainly meet with the same Fate there, as you had below.[3] In a few Days after the Hollidays, His Lordship moves for the total Repeal of the Quebeck Act; And if Lord Chatham's Health will admit of it, He will certainly second the Motion; And in the House of Commons, Sir George Saville moves to *amend* this shameful Act. There have been several Conferences between Lord Camden And Sir George Upon the Subject; But although the latter Wishes the total Repeal, Yet some of the Rockingham's think it is too much to attempt, and therefore, in a friendly Way, it is settled between them, To move in the different Houses, in the different Ways I have mentioned. The Fate of these Motions, there can be no doubt about;[4] But yet, it is thought Right to lay a proper Ground for Repeal, In Case our Countrymen shall act so unitedly and decisively, in their Plans of *Non* Exportation &c., as to compel the Court to abandon the present Set of Ministers. I am realy grieved at the Publication of Mr. Galloway's extraordinary Pamphlet. Our great Friends in both Houses are extremely angry at it, and express themselves in most resentful Terms against the Author; While the Courtiers rejoice at that Part of the Pamphlet,

2. For Trent's return to America and the reasons for it see the headnote above, April 11. He reached Philadelphia, as mentioned there, on June 7.

3. Camden was presumably saying that the Chancellor's decision would be political. As far as we know none had yet been rendered; see the account of the proceedings above, XXI, 200–1. The appeal to the Lords was presumably the one that BF had been considering but ordered dropped two days before Trent landed; see BF to Life below, June 5, 1775.

4. The plan went through, with the result predicted, but Chatham did not participate. Camden introduced into the Lords on May 17, and Savile into the Commons the next day, a bill to repeal the Quebec Act; both houses rejected it by large majorities. Cobbett, *Parliamentary History*, XVIII (1774–77), 655–84.

23

which represents our Divisions and Controversys as to Boundaries and Modes of Religion, our Incompetency to resist the Power of this Country, And the undecided State of the Congress, for several Weeks, As to what realy were the *Rights* of America; Yet the Courtiers at the same Time treat with ineffable Contempt the Plan of Union proposed, and which they say, by *not* being adopted, offended the Authors Pride, and has been the happy Means of their being satisfactorily *confirmed* in their Ideas of the Weakness and Division of the Colonies; and that by Perseverance, They shall unquestionably obtain a perfect Submission.[5] Mr. Pope, you remember, has wisely said "How shall We reason but from what We know",[6] On which, I shall only make this short Observation, that if our Friend Mr. Galloway had *properly known* The real Plans of this arbitrary Administration, He would never, I am persuaded, have committed Himself, in the very indiscreet Manner, that He had done. Major Trent carrys out with Him the restraining Act for Pennsylvania, New-Jersey &c.; And least any News, unfavorable to the Designs of Government, might arrive from Governor Colden, Administration used great Industry in accelerating it through the House of Lords, In Order that New York might *Not*, if possible, be inserted in it; they placing much Confidence in the *Fidelity* and *Loyalty* of the Delancey's and their Friends, to dissolve the Union of America.[7] The Generals, Burgoyne, Howe and Clinton are now here, waiting only for a favorable Wind, To sail for Boston. There, it is to be determined, How two of them are to be disposed of; One of them, with two or three Regiments, it being *here* decided, shall be stationed at New York, to support the King's Friends, so called, in that Colony.[8] Several Persons, as Spies, are sent to each of the Provinces, to collect Intelligence, And observe,

5. Joseph Galloway, *A Candid Examination of the Mutual Claims of Great Britain and the Colonies* . . . (New York, 1775), contained the author's rejected plan of union described above, XXI, 469–70 n, and arraigned the proceedings of the Continental Congress.

6. "What can we reason," etc.: *Essay on Man*, I, 18.

7. For the extension of the New England Restraining Act to other colonies, and the government's hope that New York would remain loyal, see above, XXI, 521–2 n. The hope was not borne out, despite the best efforts of the De Lancey faction; see the note on BF to Hartley below, May 6, 1775.

8. The "triumvirate of reputation," as Burgoyne called them, sailed on April 20 and reached Boston on May 25: William B. Willcox, *Portrait of a General: Sir Henry Clinton in the War of Independence* . . . (New York, 1964), pp. 36, 43–5. Whitehall had not decided to send troops to New York.

and report, the Conduct of People in general, and *some* in particular. Major Skeene returns for that, or some other, such servile and dishonorable Purpose. He is in the same Ship with Major Trent.[9] It would surely be presumption in *Me*, to offer any Intimations to You, as to what Part America ought immediately to take; But it is Mr. Levy's and Mr. Steady's sincere Opinions, that if the next Congress will firmly insist on, and see inviolably maintained, throughout America, The NON-EXPORTATION and Non *Importation* Plans, And at the same Time will effectualy Arm, in Case of the Worst, that the Magnitude of these Measures will infallibly force its own Way; and American Freedom will be soon fixed, on an immoveable Basis. Whenever any Thing material occurs, you may depend upon having it immediately communicated to You; And in the mean Time, give Me leave to inform you, that I have obtained a very full, and satisfactory Opinion from Serjeant Glynn (The *best* Lawyer, Lord Camden assures Me, in England) Upon the Title to our Indian Lands, (Which Mr. Trent will shew You) And permit Me to ask the Favor of You, To assist this Gentleman, in obtaining *concurrant* Opinions from Mr. Galloway, Mr. Dickinson, and the Lawyers from Virginia &c., Who may be at the Congress;[1] As *this* is certainly the favorable Crisis, to establish Titles for Lands, fairly obtained from the native Proprietors. I am Dear Sir with the sincerest Esteem Your most obedient and faithful Servant

S WHARTON

Dr Franklin

Endorsed: S. Wharton April 17. 1775.

From Dorothea Blunt

ALS: American Philosophical Society

Dear Sir   Craven Street April the 19 1775

I have not been fortunate enough to be in Craven Street when letters have been forwarding to you and now have reason to fear that it will not be without some difficulty that mine will be of the happy number that will get to you, at least it seems so to me from

9. This reference to Skene was presumably a reason why Congress investigated and eventually confined him; see the letter from the Pa. delegates below, July 3, 1775.

1. For Glynn see above, XXI, 89 n. His and Henry Dagge's opinions and their endorsement by one Va. lawyer, Patrick Henry, are discussed in the headnote below, July 12, 1775.

a note that I have just now read of Sir Huttons.[2] However neither my small hopes, nor my great fears, shall prevent my writing this day, for if you have any feelings for me, that are but in the smallest degree in unison with mine for you, the shortest letter and the least will be farr from indifferent to you if it comes to hand; and if it should not, I shall have a self pleasing assurance of having done what you had reason to expect, and what I shall hope you will believe I had done tho you should not receive this. I have visited our valuable friend Mrs. Stevenson several times since you left us who tho she appears little different from what she did when you were here, yet gives frequent p[roof?] of weak spirits, which I am sure will be still [weak]er if your letter whenever it comes does not contain the strongest assurances of your return for I am firmly persuaded that without the animating hope of spending the remainder of Life with you, she wou'd be very wretched indeed, for tho many of your friends are also her friends, yet all of us are less to her than you. I hope you will bestow some kind epithet upon me for having said so much of another when I cou'd have said full as much of myself; but I will be just, and I will also acknowledge that Mrs. Stevenson has a prior claim to your regard and attention. Mrs. Hewson and Children I have just come from, Will recovering of the Measles, and the other two not vissibly affected.[3] I am going for a Month to Bath with Mrs. Scott,[4] shall return to Kensington tho not to continue long for the situation is by no means adapted to me. I am not happy nor do I think I ever shou'd be so in it. I may not be more so in another but it is natural to wish to make the trial.

My Brother and Lady Blunt are here for a few hours.[5] I have no

2. In "The Cravenstreet Gazette" BF had raised James Hutton to the peerage: above, XVII, 223.

3. They all had measles but with no bad results; see their mother's letter below, June 10, 1775.

4. Possibly Sarah Scott (1723–95), known in her day as a novelist and historian. She had married George Lewis Scott, through whom BF first met Tom Paine, but had been separated from him for some years. Her sister was Mrs. Elizabeth Montagu, one of the most famous hostesses in London; both women were habituées of Bath, and Mrs. Scott was there in the summer of 1775. John Doran, *Lady of the Last Century (Mrs. Elizabeth Montagu)* . . . (London, 1873), pp. 195, 202. For both sisters see also the *DNB*.

5. Sir Charles and his wife, we presume, had come to town from their home in Odiham. For the two see above, XIV, 93 n; XIX, 151 n; XXI, 613.

leisure nor shall I have before this must be sent so Adieu My Dear friend. May you who so well deserve peace and happiness not only enjoy it yourself but be the means of restoring it to others, which no one more sincerely prays for than your affectionate and oblig'd friend   D: BLUNT

Addressed: Dr Franklin

Endorsed: Miss Dolly Blunt 75

From Margaret Stevenson   ALS: American Philosophical Society

Dear Sir   April th[e] 24 1775
I have only time till [*to* tell] you I hope your wellcom, to Philada: welcom i am shuer you ar but I mean in good health, and safe arrived, and my Daer Temple, pray tell him too writ to Mrs. Wolford.[6] I hope you ar ashurd I take every opportunity to send your papers, by this Shipe. I am oblig'd to Mr. Baliy for Inquiring at the Coffehous. The Bishop sent to me to Let him know how to convey a letter to you: yesterday Mr. Alxander tuck me in his Coch to kins in town. I beg him to goe Jermen Street way: he dide. I cald at the Bishop was not at home. I left word withe the servant, but have not hearde, from his Lordship.[7] Sir John is well and exeeding polit he expects to hear from you inclousd he says to me.[8] Jonathan is not come I have not hard from him, I am told he is gon to Holland, Mr. Sthran is going to Bath much out of

6. Mrs. Woolford was a friend of Mrs. Stevenson about whom we have scanty information, derived from her letters to WTF after he left England: July 29, 1775; June 29, Oct. 15, 1781; and Feb. 29, 1784 (APS). She was an acquaintance of Dr. Alexander Small. She was close to Martha Harris Johnson, Grace Williams' sister and BF's niece, who was living in London, and followed with interest the careers of the Johnson children. She and her sister had known WF during his sojourn in England, and she had apparently been a surrogate mother to WTF since his boyhood. See also Hewson to BF below, Sept. 2, 1776.

7. Mr. Bailey, if that is how he spelled his name, we have never heard of; the Bishop was Jonathan Shipley, and Mrs. Stevenson was undoubtedly driven to his house by William Alexander, the banker who was then on the verge of bankruptcy: above, XIX, 316 n.

8. In a letter enclosed, Sir John Pringle presumably meant, in BF's next to Mrs. Stevenson.

heath.[9] All your friends ar well, excepct my selfe, and i am out of Sprits, but i hop my Dearst and Dear friend will whin he writs will rais them by saying he shall soon return. Oh my Dear Sir, I shall rejoys at that hapey day. I hop you recived your papers and letters by Magor Trent i wish him safe arrived, I wish to chat a grate dele with you if i cold drict [direct] my penn for you to read i should by [be] hapey [to] Enteartan you.

Well Sir wilst I was writing came Mr. Blowers off Boston his Wife a Daughter of Bengn. Kent, of the same place, he disered to Lodge hear for a month or too, as he is i Sad American; I wold make op Dr. Fs bead for him and he is a friend of Jona. Wiloms [Williams] so he and wife Sleeps hear to Mor: night, and Nany and I shall be full of Bissnes.[1] I most make up your Packit, and to the Coffee Hous with it my self that I see this Capt. Price, and beg his Specialle Care, I have inclosd all your lettrs,[2] and my Love to Mr. and Mrs. Bach Dear Temple &ct: &ct: My Prayrs and Besst wishes atand you in all place[s]. God Allmity Bless and keep you in health and give you all you wish or wante, which is the constant prayer, Dear Sir, Your Sincer freind and oblig'd Servant

MARGT STEVENSON

Mr. Gorman is come and tells me he has drawn on Mr. Tood for the six pip of Burgandy[3] he will write to you by the next opportuny. He has sent too hamprs of Shamppane for the Gentleman to tast. If Shold like he says he can sueply them.

Addressed: Dr. Franklin

Endorsed: Mrs. Stevenson

9. JW was in Holland at the time, and left for England on May 3; see his MS journal, Yale University Library. The invalid at Bath was William Strahan.

1. Sampson S. Blowers (1742–1842) had been one of the defense counsel in the trials following the Boston Massacre, and had incurred the enmity of the local Whigs. In 1774 he married Sarah Kent, the daughter of another Loyalist, and went with her to England. *DAB.* "Nany," alias Ann Hardy, was Mrs. Stevenson's old servant: above, XVII, 167.

2. William Price had been master of the *Aurora* two years before, and was perhaps the same captain with whom BF had been on bad terms a decade earlier: *PMHB*, XXVIII, 477; above, XII, 100–1. Price left at the beginning of May and reached Philadelphia six weeks later: *Public Advertiser*, May 4; *Pa. Gaz.*, June 21, 1775. BF's acknowledgment of this letter is below, July 17, 1775.

3. Thomas O'Gorman was tireless in publicizing his wine business; see above, XIX, 86–7. "Mr. Tood" must have been Anthony Todd, secretary of the Post Office (above, X, 217 n), but the six pipes of Burgundy elude us.

From the Massachusetts Provincial Congress

LS: Massachusetts Historical Society; draft: Massachusetts Archives; copies: National Archives and Connecticut State Library[4]

The second Massachusetts provincial congress, elected by the towns as the first had been, held two sessions between February 1 and April 15, 1775. It then recessed until May 10, but as a result of Lexington and Concord reconvened on April 22. By that time John Hancock had left for the second Continental Congress, and Joseph Warren succeeded him as president pro tempore. One of the first acts of the new session was to prepare an account of the events of April 19 and hurry it across the Atlantic for presentation to the British public.[5] A narrative printed in a local paper, accompanied by supporting depositions and an address to the people of Great Britain, was sent on April 28 to Franklin as the provincial agent; the covering letter below was drafted by a committee of which Warren was a member, and was signed by him for the congress. This material arrived in London in late May, almost two weeks before Gage's account, and Arthur Lee saw to it that the American side of the story received maximum publicity.[6]

4. The draft, in Warren's hand, has no significant differences from the LS that we print. Three other versions, the present whereabouts of which we do not know, have come to light in the past. They were advertised as follows: an LS, with interlineations by Elbridge Gerry, in Libbie's sale catalogue, March 17–21, 1891, p. 224; an ALS (in fact a copy) in the same firm's catalogue, May 8–10, 1894, p. 164; and an LS in Parke Bernet's catalogue, April 10, 1962, pp. 81–2.

5. See Wroth, *Province in Rebellion*, I, 109–10, 117.

6. The narrative was that in the *Essex Gaz.*, April 18–25, 1775. To carry the dispatches the congress employed Richard Derby's small, fast schooner, the *Quero*, commanded by the owner's son John. She left Salem on the night of April 28–29, and Derby reached London on May 28. William Lincoln, ed., *The Journals of Each Provincial Congress of Massachusetts . . .* (Boston, 1838), pp. 153–4, 159; Hutchinson, *Diary*, I, 455; James D. Phillips, *The Life and Times of Richard Derby . . .* (Cambridge, Mass., 1929), pp. 41–4; John H. Cary, *Joseph Warren . . .* (Urbana, Ill., 1961), p. 191; Robert S. Rantoul, "The Cruise of the 'Quero,'" Essex Institute *Hist. Coll.*, XXXVI (1900), 1–30. The account in the *Essex Gaz.* was published in London as an extra: *London Evening-Post Extraordinary*, May 29, 1775, reprinted in the issue of May 29–30. On the 30th it appeared in the *Public Advertiser* along with the address to the British people, and the next day the same paper carried a number of the supporting depositions, and Arthur Lee's invitation to the public to examine the originals deposited with the Lord Mayor. The British side of the story was not known until more than a week later. Gage's report, accompanied by letters from two officers on the expedition, went by the brigantine *Sukey* from Marblehead, and did not reach Lord Dartmouth until June 10; the government immediately

Sir,   In Provincial Congress. Watertown April 26th. 1775

From the entire confidence we repose in your faithfulness and abilities, we consider it the happiness of this Colony that the important trust of Agency for it, in this day of unequalled distress, is devolved on your hands: We doubt not your attachment to the cause of the Liberties of Mankind will make every possible exertion in *our* behalf a pleasure to you; although our circumstances will compell us often to interrupt your repose by matters that will surely give you pain. A singular Instance hereof is the occasion of the present Letter. The contents of this packet will be our apology for troubling you with it: from these you will see how and by whom we are at last plunged into the horrors of a most unnatural War: Our Enemies, we are told, have dispatch'd to Great Britain a fallacious Account of the Tragedy they have begun: to prevent the operation of which, to the public Injury, we have engaged the Vessel that conveys this to you, as a Packet in the Service of this Colony. And we request your assistance in supplying Capt. Derby, who commands her, with such necessaries as he shall want, on the credit of your Constituents in Massachusetts Bay. But we most ardently wish that the several Papers herewith inclosed may be immediately printed and dispersed thro' every Town in England, and especially communicated to the Lord Mayor, Aldermen, and Common Council of the City of London, that they may take such order thereon as they may think proper; and we are confident your fidelity will make such improvement of them as shall convince all who are not determin'd to be in everlasting blindness, that it is the united efforts of both Englands that must save either. But that whatever price our brethren in the *one* may be pleas'd to put on their constitutional Liberties we are authorized to assure you that the Inhabitants of the *other*, with the greatest unanimity, are inflexibly resolved to sell *theirs* only at the price of their Lives. Signed by order of Congress

JOS WARREN Presdt pro tem

To Benjamin Franklin Esqr Agent for the Colony of the Massachusetts-Bay now in London

Notation: Genl. Warren to Dr Franklin Watertown Congress

---

published an account based on this material. Anne R. Cunningham, ed., *Letters and Diary of John Rowe . . .* (Boston, 1903), p. 294; Carter, *Gage Correspondence*, I, 396–7; *London Gaz.*, June 10, 1775.

Extract of a Letter
From Philadelphia,

To a Gentleman in this City, dated the 6th inst.

YESTERDAY evening Dr. FRANKLIN arrived here from London in six weeks, which he left the 20th of March, which has given great joy to this town, he says we have no favours to expect from the Ministry, nothing but submission will satisfy them, they expect little or no opposition will be made to their troops, those that are now coming are for *New-York*, where it is expected they will be received with cordiality. As near as we can learn there are about four thousand troops coming in this fleet, the men of war and transports are in a great measure loaded with dry goods, to supply *New-York*, and the country round it, agents are coming over with them. Dr. *Franklin* is highly pleased to find us arming and preparing for the worst events, he thinks nothing else can save us from the most abject slavery and destruction, at the same time encourages us to believe a spirited opposition, will be the means of our salvation. The Ministry are alarmed at every opposition, and lifted up again at every thing which appears the least in their favour, every letter and every paper from hence, are read by them.

N E W - Y O R K:
Printed by JOHN ANDERSON, at Beekman's-Slip.

Broadside Announcing Franklin's Return from England

To David Hartley

ALS: Darmouth College Library

What as far as we know was the first letter Franklin wrote after landing was not to his son or sister or some close friend, as might be expected, but to an Englishman who three months earlier seems to have been no more than a casual acquaintance. In late February, when Hartley asked for information, Franklin furnished it in a formal, third-person note,[7] and a few weeks later left for home. In those weeks the relationship must have developed to the point where the two agreed to exchange news, the American under his own name and the Englishman, who as a member of Parliament had to be circumspect, under the initials "G. B." In this note and its sequel, two days later, Franklin began to fulfil the agreement.

His notes in juxtaposition are puzzling. Why did he take time from the rush of business to write two so close together? Why does he omit here his most momentous news, that war was begun? Why does the second, below, not mention the first and yet repeat what it says about New York? Perhaps because of the rush of business. This note is in obvious haste, and two days later he may have forgotten what, or even that, he had written before.

Hartley began to fulfil his side of the agreement in several letters early in the summer, carried by the same captain who brought him this one,[8] and the correspondence so initiated continued for years. The Englishman wrote at length (he was no more given to a short letter than to a short speech), while the American answered more succinctly. Both expressed themselves almost as if for publication, and Hartley did read one of his friend's letters to the House of Commons.[9] The two kept in touch in this way until the climax of their relationship in 1783, when they met to negotiate the final treaty of peace.

Dear Sir,   Philada May 6. 1775.

I arrived here last Night, and have the Pleasure to learn that there is the most perfect Unanimity throughout the Colonies; and that even N York, on whose Defection the Ministry so confidently rely'd, is as hearty and zealous as any of the rest.[1] I have not yet had time to collect particulars of Information for you; and there-

---

7. See above, XXI, 511–12.

8. The letters have disappeared, but see BF's note to him below, Sept. 12, 1775.

9. That below of Oct. 3, 1775.

1. For the ministry's optimism see above, XXI, 521–2 n. After the N.Y. Assembly refused to elect delegates to the second Congress, a provincial convention did so; see the note on Cooper to BF above, April 1. News of this action, which was doubtless behind BF's remark, was printed in the *Pa. Gaz.*, April 26, 1775.

fore the chief Intention of this Line is to introduce to you the Bearer Capt. Falconer, who is perfectly acquainted with the State of things here, and on whose Accounts you may depend.[2] With great Esteem I am, Sir, Your most obedient humble Servant

B FRANKLIN

D. Hartley Esqr

To Joseph Galloway ALS: Mrs. Arthur Loeb, Philadelphia (1955)

This short letter is tantalizingly uninformative. It touches on the two personal relationships that were in crisis when Franklin returned to America, with his son and with his oldest political ally; but it throws little light on either. Its contents make clear that it was in answer to a letter now missing, in which Galloway congratulated Franklin on his election to the Congress, announced his own intention of retiring from politics, and offered to send his carriage from his country estate, Trevose, to bring his friend to their first meeting in more than a decade. In this reply Franklin neither accepts nor declines, partly because he is unsure when and where he will see his son, whom in fact he was unable to meet until some weeks later.[3]

He apparently did go to Trevose and spend the night. In their conversation, as Galloway remembered it years afterward, the host was forthright in urging reconciliation with Britain; but the guest was guarded, and after the visit kept so much to himself that Samuel Adams suspected him of sinister designs. At a second meeting with Galloway, Franklin tried to demonstrate how stiffnecked the ministry was by reading him the journal of his peace negotiations in London; but the reading was

2. Nathaniel Falconer scarcely had enough time in Pennsylvania to become "perfectly acquainted with the State of things": his arrival and his entry outward bound were noted simultaneously in the *Pa.Gaz.*, May 3, and his clearance in the *Pa. Jour.*, May 10, 1775. He was at Deal on June 21 (*Public Advertiser*, June 23, 1775), and presumably delivered this note a few days later.

3. On May 7 WF heard to his surprise of his father's arrival: to Strahan, May 7, 1775, Pierpont Morgan Library. Partly because of that development, WF wrote Cadwallader Colden the next day, he could not come to New York, and would expect to hear from Colden at Perth Amboy: *The Letters and Papers of Cadwallader Colden* (N.-Y. Hist. Soc. *Coll.* for 1917–23, 1934–35), LVI (1923), 294. He could not in any case have hurried to Philadelphia, for he had called the Assembly to meet on the 15th and was preparing a lengthy address. He delivered it on the 16th, and met daily with the Council until the short session ended on the 20th: 1 *N.J. Arch.*, XVIII, 534–64. He therefore did not visit Philadelphia until after that date.

interrupted.[4] Some time in late May or early June William Franklin came to Philadelphia, met his father and the son whom he had not seen since babyhood, and took the boy back with him to New Jersey.[5] The Governor, presumably during that visit and again according to Galloway's recollection, spent a bibulous evening with the other two men; at the end of it the elder Franklin inveighed against British corruption and dissipation, assured them that the colonies would prevail, "and declared in favour of measures for attaining to Independence."[6] This seems to have been the moment of his open break with his friend, but precisely how and when that moment was reached remains unclear.

My dear Friend   Monday May 8. 75

I am much oblig'd by your kind Congratulations. I am concern'd at your Resolution of quitting public Life at a time when your Abilities are so much wanted. I hope you will change that Resolution.[7] I hear my Son is to be at Burlington this day Week to meet his Assembly. I had purposed (if he could not conveniently come hither) to meet him there, and in my Return to visit you at Trevose. I shall know in a Day or two, how that will be. But being impatient to see you, I believe I shall accept the kind Offer of your Carriage, and come to you directly. If I conclude upon that, I shall let you know. At present I am so taken up with People coming in contineually, that I cannot stir, and can scarce think what is proper

4. These were Galloway's recollections as imparted to Hutchinson in January, 1779. BF also told him, he added, that he left England a fortnight earlier than he had given out he would, in order not to be stopped. Hutchinson, *Diary*, II, 237–8. In fact BF broadcast to friends and acquaintances when he was sailing; see for example XXI, 523, 525–6. This discrepancy may call into question how accurately Galloway remembered, but the comment about BF's being distrusted has corroboration. During his early weeks in Congress he kept so silent that Richard Henry Lee, and apparently others, suspected he was a British spy; not until mid-July was the suspicion dissipated. William T. Hutchinson *et al.*, eds., *The Papers of James Madison* (12 vols., to date; [Chicago,] 1962 —), I, 149, 158. By that time a rumor was abroad in London that BF, disgusted by the delegates' refusal to consider any plan of reconciliation, was on his way back to England. *London Packet or, New Lloyd's Evening Post*, July 19, 1775.

5. See BF to Jane Mecom below, June 17, 1775. WF and WTF returned to New Jersey well before June 13, when BF acknowledged WTF's letter from Perth Amboy.

6. Hutchinson, *Diary, loc.cit.*

7. For Galloway's growing disillusionment, culminating in his resignation from the Congress on May 12, see Benjamin H. Newcomb, *Franklin and Galloway: a Political Partnership* (New Haven and London, 1972), pp. 271–8.

or practicable. I am ever, with unalterable Esteem and Affection, my Dear Friend, Yours most affectionately   B FRANKLIN

Addressed: To / Joseph Galloway Esq / Trevose / Bucks.

Endorsed: May 8. 1775 Dr. Franklin on his Arrival in Philadelphia

To David Hartley[8]   ALS: Harvard University Library

Dear Sir,   Philada. May 8. 1775. Monday

I arrived here on Friday Evening, and the next morning was unanimously chosen by the General Assembly a Delegate for the ensuing Congress, which is to meet on Wednesday.[9]

You will have heard before this reaches you of the Commencement of a Civil War; the End of it perhaps neither myself, nor you, who are much younger, may live to see. I find here all Ranks of People in Arms, disciplining themselves Morning and Evening,[1] and am informed that the firmest Union prevails throughout North America; New York as hearty as any of the rest. I purpose to communicate to you from time to time the most authentic Intelligence I can collect here, and hope to hear frequently from you in the same Way. I am with great Esteem, Dear Sir, Your most obedient humble Servant   B FRANKLIN

David Hartley Esqr

Endorsed: D F May 8 1775

8. For puzzling aspects of this and BF's earlier note to Hartley see the headnote above, May 6.

9. The Assembly unanimously elected BF a delegate on Saturday, May 6, and the Congress convened four days later. 8 *Pa. Arch.*, VIII, 7231; *JCC*, II, 11–12.

1. News of Lexington and Concord reached Philadelphia on April 24, and the next day a mass meeting resolved to co-operate for mutual defense; so originated the city associators. On the 29th another meeting decided that each ward should provide one or more companies, and on May 1 the officers were elected. John F. Roche, *Joseph Reed: a Moderate in the American Revolution* (New York, 1957), pp. 58–60. On the 5th drums were beating and flags flying as the militia paraded the streets; "the whole country appears determined to assume a military character, and this city, throwing off her pacific aspect, is forming military companies, a plan being laid for thirty-three . . . ." Even a faction of Quakers was raising two. George A. Ward, ed., *Journal and Letters of the Late Samuel Curwen* . . . (London, 1842), p. 26.

The Pennsylvania Assembly: Instructions to Its Delegates in Congress

Printed in *Votes and Proceedings of the Province of Pennsylvania* . . . (6 vols., Philadelphia, 1752–76), VI, 587.

Franklin had no more than set foot in Philadelphia before he was plunged into local as well as Congressional politics. The day after he arrived the Assembly chose him unanimously as a delegate to Congress. On June 30 he was appointed to the Pennsylvania committee of safety and three days later became its president.[2] On August 16 he was elected, at the head of all three tickets, to the Philadelphia committee of inspection and observation, and was re-elected on February 16, 1776; in August and February he was also appointed to a district committee.[3] On October 2, 1775, he was chosen as an Assemblyman from Philadelphia, and on the 19th reappointed to the committee of safety and on November 4 to Congress.[4] In June, 1776, the committee of inspection named him as a delegate to the provincial conference, a predecessor of the constitutional convention; on July 8 he was elected from Philadelphia to the convention itself, on the 16th became its president, and on the 20th was reappointed as one of its delegates to Congress.[5]

Although these many offices attest his popularity, no man could have filled them all; and Franklin did not try. He never took his seat in the Assembly. He worked hard on the committee of safety during its early months, but his attendance became sporadic as time wore on; and in February, 1776, he resigned from both the committee and the Assembly.[6] The focus of his activities was Congress, and there he worked within the framework of the Assembly's instructions to its delegates.

Those instructions had been under consideration for months before Franklin's return from England. The previous December the Assembly

2. See the editorial note on the committee below, June 30, 1775.

3. These committees, established to enforce the Continental Association, took on a variety of functions as the crisis deepened, and became a base for those who were pressing for an enlarged militia and for independence. Ryerson, *Revolution Is Now Begun*, pp. 128–31, 156–7, 272–4; see also the broadside *List of the Sub-Committees, appointed by the Committee for the City and Liberties of Philadelphia* . . . ([Philadelphia,] 1776). BF, to the best of our knowledge, took no part in these committees and was a member only on paper.

4. Ryerson, pp. 135–8; 8 *Pa. Arch.*, VIII, 7310, 7347.

5. James E. Gibson, "The Pennsylvania Provincial Conference of 1776," *PMHB*, LVIII (1934), 330; *Pa. Gaz.*, July 10, 1776; *The Proceedings . . . Relative to Calling the Conventions of 1776 and 1790* . . . (Harrisburg, Pa., 1825), p. 46.

6. See the note on the committee of safety, already cited, and the headnote on BF to the speaker of the Assembly below, Feb. 26.

had approved the proceedings of the first Continental Congress, selected seven delegates to the second, and appointed a committee to draft their instructions. The draft was repeatedly considered and repeatedly deferred.[7] On March 9 the Assembly repudiated the program of Joseph Galloway and his supporters, who opposed joint action through the coming Congress and urged that Pennsylvania petition on its own for redress of grievances. On May 9 the legislature, just after it had added Franklin and two others to its delegation and had had news of Lexington, adopted the instructions below. They were little different from those to the delegates to the first Congress.[8] The Assembly, once it had repudiated the proposal for separate action, did not commit its delegates to anything more than colonial unity and resistance.[9]

GENTLEMEN,   May 9, 1775.

The Trust reposed in you, is of such a Nature, and the Modes of executing it, may be so diversified in the Course of your Deliberations, that it is scarcely possible to give you particular Instructions respecting it.

We shall therefore, in general, direct that you meet in Congress the Delegates of the several British Colonies, to be held on the Tenth Instant, to consult together on the present critical and alarming Situation and State of the Colonies, and that you exert your utmost Endeavours to agree upon, and recommend, such further Measures, as shall afford the best Prospect of obtaining Redress of American Grievances, and restoring that Union and Harmony between Great-Britain and the Colonies so essential to the Welfare and Happiness of both Countries.

You are directed to make Report of your Proceedings to this House at their next Sessions after the Meeting of the Congress. Signed by Order of the House,   JOHN MORTON, Speaker.[1]

7. 8 *Pa. Arch.*, VIII, 7162, 7167–8, 7180, 7185.

8. For the earlier instructions see *ibid.*, p. 7100. The changes in the later ones were the omission of two clauses, one about ascertaining American rights and the other about avoiding disrespect to the mother country.

9. Even this commitment was too much for Galloway. On May 12 he resigned as a delegate to Congress. He also ceased attending the Assembly, which soon afterward voted funds for defense, organized the militia, rejected North's conciliatory plan, and established the committee of safety. See Ryerson, pp. 96–8, 100–12, 117–24; Benjamin M. Newcomb, *Franklin and Galloway: a Political Partnership* (New Haven and London, 1972), pp. 276–8; 8 *Pa. Arch.*, VIII, 7185–6, 7211–13, 7228–30, 7234, 7245–9.

1. Morton (*c.* 1724–77) was one of the delegates to Congress elected the previous December. He had been a member of the Assembly since 1756, with one brief intermission, and speaker since the previous March. *DAB*.

From Catharine Greene[2]

ALS: Yale University Library

My Dear Dear Friend   [May 14, 1775]

Welcom a Hundred times Welcom to our once happy Land. Are you in Health and allow me to ask you the old question over again if you are the Same good old Soul you used to be? Your arrival gives New Spring to all have heard mention it. When Shall We See you here? Do let it be as Soon as the Congress is adjournd or dont know but your good Sister and Self Shall mount our old Naggs and Come and See you. Mr. Greene would Send Plenty of love if at home. We are all well hope you found all that is Dear to you So. We Receivd your favors by Mr. Marchant[3] many thanks to you for them. This is but the forerunner of a longer letter from your affectionate Real Friend   CATY GREENE

From Jane Mecom

ALS: Yale University Library

Warrick 14 May 1775

My Ever Dear and much Honoured Brother

God be Praised for bring you Saif back to America and soporting you throw such fatuges as I know you have sufered while the minestry have been distresing Poor New England in such a Cruil maner. Your last by Poor Quensey[4] Advises me to keep up my Cuiridg and that foul wither does not last allways in any country. But I beleve you did not then Imagin the storm would have Arisen so high as for the General to have sent out a party to creep out in the night and slauter our Dear Brethern for Endevering to defend our own Property, but God Apear'd for us and drove them back with much Grater Lose than they are willing to own. There Countenances as well as confeshon of many of them shew they were much mistaken in the people they had to Deal with, but the

---

2. For BF's old friend, and her husband William, see the long biographical note above, V, 502 n. We have published BF's many letters to Catharine in 1772; this is the first but far from the last extant letter from her. It was written as a postscript to the one from Jane Mecom that follows.

3. Doubtless the Parmesan cheese, the recipe, and BF's covering letter, which we believe was written in January, 1772. Although Marchant did not sail until the following July, he was a natural person to carry the packet, because he was not only a Rhode Islander but also a distant relative of the Greenes. Above, X, 316 n; XIX, 25–6, 377 n.

4. For the death of young Josiah Quincy see above, XXI, 513.

distress it has ocationed is Past my discription. The Horror the Town was in when the Batle Aproch'd within Hearing Expecting they would Proceed quite in to town, the Comotion the Town was in after the batle ceas'd by the Parties coming in bringing in there wounded men caus'd such an Agetation of minde I beleve none had much sleep, since which we could have no quiet, as we understood our Bretheren without were determined to Disposes the Town of the Regelors, and the Generol shuting up the town not Leting any Pass out but throw such Grate Dificulties as were allmost insoportable. But throw the Goodnes of God I am at last Got saif Hear and kindly Recved by Mr. Green and His wife (who to my grate comfort when I had got Pac't up what I expected to have liberty to carey out intending to seek my fourtune with hundred others not knowing whither) sent me an Invitation in a leter to Mrs. Patridg of which I gladly acepted. On the day I arived at Provedence had the unspeakable Pleasure of hearing my Dear Brother was saif arived at His own home, Blessed be God for all His mercys to me an unworthy Creature. These People seemed formed for Hospetality Apear to be Pleas'd with the vast Adition to there famely which consists of old Mr. Gough and wife, there sons wife and negro boy, Mr. Thomas Leverett's wife 2 Children and a made, my self an Grand Daughter who I could not leve. If I had it would have been her Death, and they Expect this Day 3 more of Mr. Leveretts Chill'n young Mr. Gouge, Suckey and Mrs. Pateridg and Daughter and seem as tho there harts were open to all the world. They sent for old Mrs. Downs but dont know if she designs to come as it is so Extreemly dificult to git a line to pass to Each other. Mrs. Leveritt is trying to git a house to keep house by her self. My poor litle Delicat Nabour Mrs. Royall and Famely came out with me not knowing where she should find a Place.[5] I

5. The swarm of guests whom the Greenes had taken in was composed largely of Hubbarts, relatives through the marriage of Catharine Greene's sister, Judith Ray. Mrs. Partridge, who had with her her stepdaughter Rebecca, was Tuthill Hubbart's sister; another sister was "Sukey" Bean, and Mrs. Downes (the name was variously spelled) was the mother-in-law of one of the Hubbart brothers. "Mr. Gough and wife" were Capt. James and Elizabeth Craister Gooch; he was half-brother of Elizabeth Franklin, Tuthill's mother, and his son William had married a Hubbart. Thomas Leverett was a distant relative of the Hubbarts and Greenes. Jane's granddaughter was Jane Flagg, who soon afterward married a Greene. "My Poor litle Delicat Nabour," who ended in Worcester, was Abigail Tailer Royall, widow of Jacob Royall. See Van Doren, *Franklin—Mecom*, pp. 152–3.

left them at Cambridg in a most shocking Disagreable Place but since hear she is gone to wooster. My own Daughter had been at Board at Roxbury almost a year before but she with the famely were obliged to fly into the woods and tho they Returnd again they think themselves very unsaif[6] and she was in grate concern what cours to take when the day before I left her she Rec'd a leter from her husband that He was saif Arived at Bedford in Dartmouth[7] not Dareing to venture in to salem from whence they sail'd. This also was a grat Ease to my mind as she might now soon Expect her husband to take the care of her.

I am still under grate concern for Cousen williams. He was out of Town at the time of the batle and was Advised to keep out and His Poor wife slaved her self almost to Death to Pack up and secure what she could and sent away her two Daughters Intending to go to Him and behold in comes he in to town the day before I came out Imagining (as I was told for I did not see him) that was the saifest Place. I can hear nothing of Him since.[8]

You will have seen the Gener'l leter to Conettacut and be able to Judge of the truth of His Insineuations by his fidelity to us poor bostonions.[9]

I have wrot a grat number of leters to you the winter and spring Past but cannot Prercive by your self or Cousen Jonathan that you have recved any of them. I sent won about a month ago but as you are Return'd it is no mater if you never git it. Present my love to my Cousens Beaches and the Dear Children and Exept the same from your Ever Affectionat sister   JANE MECOM

Is Jona'n come with you? If he is remember my love to Him.

Dear Brother I am tould you will be joyn'd to the Congress and

6. For Jenny Collas' flight from Boston see above, XXI, 348.
7. New Bedford was then part of the town of Dartmouth.
8. For his vicissitudes see his letter below, June 19, 1775.
9. The Conn. Assembly asked Gage, through Gov. Trumbull, to explain what had happened. He responded by justifying the recent operation, in which the troops had committed no outrages but had shown tenderness to young and old, as a necessity forced upon him. When an illegal body was preparing for hostilities by stocking magazines, his duty was to destroy them in order to prevent the calamities of a civil war. His military operations had been and would remain defensive, but would not stop while Boston was beleaguered. The letter, along with news of BF's arrival, appeared on May 13 in the *Providence Gaz.; and Country Jour.* Jane's satiric reference to Gage's fidelity was to his breach, as many Bostonians saw it, of the agreement that those who would might leave the town; see Williams' letter just cited.

that they will Remove to Conetecut. Will you Premit me to come and see you there? Mrs. Green says she will go with me.[1]

Addressed: To / Doctr. Franklin / of / Philadelphia
Forwarded by / Yr. most obedt. hum Servt. / Eben Hazard[2] / New York / May 29th. 1775
Endorsed: Sister Mecom May 14. 1775

To Edmund Burke

ALS: Central Library, Sheffield

The background of this letter was conversations between the two men during Franklin's last months in London. Burke's record of their final meeting, even though not committed to paper until years later, is revealing enough to be worth extensive quotation. "As far as a man, so locked up as Dr. Franklin, could be expected to communicate his ideas, I believe he opened them to Mr. Burke. It was, I think, the very day before he set out for America,[3] that a very long conversation passed between them, and with a greater air of openness on the Doctor's side, than Mr. Burke had observed in him before. In this discourse Dr. Franklin lamented, and with apparent sincerity, the separation which he feared was inevitable between Great Britain and her colonies. He certainly spoke of it as an event which gave him the greatest concern. America, he said, would never again see such happy days as she had passed under the protection of England. He observed, that ours was the only instance of a great empire, in which the most distant parts and members had been as well governed as the metropolis and its vicinage:[4] But that the Americans were going to lose the means which secured to them this rare and precious advantage. The question with them was not whether they were to remain as they had been before the troubles, for better, he allowed they could not hope to be; but whether they were to give up so happy a situation without a struggle? Mr. Burke had several other conversations with him about that time, in none of which, soured and exasperated as his mind certainly was, did he discover any other

1. She wrote these sentences at the head of Catharine Greene's postscript, the preceding document.
2. For Ebenezer Hazard see the note on BF's letter to him below, Aug. 3, 1775.
3. Probably March 18. BF had given out that he was leaving the next day, but actually spent it with Priestley and set out for Portsmouth on the 20th; see above, XXI, 526 n.
4. An idea that BF had long held and had recently expounded to Chatham: above, XVII, 322; XXI, 548.

wish in favour of America than for a security to its *ancient* condition."[5]

Burke apparently did not answer this letter. The war obliged him to break off the correspondence, to his great regret, and he did not renew it until what he regarded as an emergency gave him reason to in 1781.[6]

Dear Sir, Philada. May 15. 75

You will see by the Papers that Gen. Gage call'd his Assembly to propose Lord North's pacific Plan,[7] but before they could meet drew the Sword, and began the War. His Troops made a most vigorous Retreat, 20 Miles in 3 Hours, scarce to be parallell'd in History: the feeble Americans, who pelted them all the Way, could scarce keep up with them.

All People here feel themselves much oblig'd by your Endeavours to serve them. I hear your propos'd Resolves were negativ'd by a great Majority;[8] which was denying the most notorious Truths; and a kind of national Lying, of which they may be convicted by their own Records.

The Congress is met here, pretty full. I had not been here a Day before I was return'd a Member. We din'd together on Saturday, when your Health was among the foremost. With the sincerest Esteem, I am ever Dear Sir, Your most obedient humble Servant

B FRANKLIN

Edm. Burke Esqr.

Addressed: To / Edmund Burke Esqr / [*illegible*] Street / London / Beaconsfiel / Bucks[9]

Endorsed: Franklin Philada. May 15 1775

5. [Edmund Burke,] *An Appeal from the New to the Old Whigs . . .* (London, 1791), pp. 37–8.
6. When Congress threatened to recall Burgoyne to captivity, and Burke asked for BF's good offices in preventing the move: Thomas W. Copeland *et al.*, eds., *The Correspondence of Edmund Burke* (9 vols., Chicago and Cambridge, 1958–70), IV, 362.
7. Whatever Gage's intention when he called the General Court, he soon afterward received instructions not to lay before it North's conciliatory resolution (above, XXI, 592); in fact the Court never met, for the provincial congress quashed the elections. Carter, *Gage Correspondence*, II, 187; Wroth, *Province in Rebellion*, I, 122.
8. The resolutions with which Burke concluded his famous speech on conciliation, March 22, 1775, were all rejected, the first by a margin of 270 to 78. Cobbett, *Parliamentary History*, XVIII (1774–77), 478–538, 540; see also Donoughue, *British Politics*, pp. 256–64.
9. BF's address has been deleted; the forwarding address to Beaconsfield is in another hand.

To Jonathan Shipley

ALS: Yale University Library

My dear Lord,   Philada. May 15, 1775

I arrived here well the 5th. after a pleasant Passage of 6 Weeks. I met with a most cordial Reception, I should say from all Parties, but that all Parties are now extinguish'd here. Britain has found means to unite us. I had not been here a Day before I was unanimously elected by our Assembly a Delegate to the Congress, which met the 10th and is now sitting. All the Governors have been instructed by the Ministry to call their Assemblies and propose to them Lord N's pacific Plan; Gen. Gage, call'd his;[1] but before they could meet, drew the Sword; and a War is commenc'd, which the youngest of us may not see the End of. My Endeavours will be if possible to quench it; as I know yours will be: but the Satisfaction of endeavouring to do good, is perhaps all we can obtain or effect. Being much hurried, I can only add my best Wishes of Happiness to you and all the dear Family, with Thanks for your many Kindnesses. I am, ever, with the highest Esteem and Respect, My Lord, Your Lordship's most obliged and obedient humble Servant   B FRANKLIN

Lord Bp. St. Asaph

Addressed: To / The right reverend the Bishop of St. Asaph / Jermyn Street / London

To [William?] Bradford[2]

ALS: Historical Society of Pennsylvania; draft: American Philosophical Society

Dear Sir,   Wednesday PM. May 16. [1775]

I have just now been urged to apply to you in behalf of a Stranger who is suppos'd to have spoken some disrespectful Words

1. See the note on the preceding document.

2. The well known Philadelphia printer, who has appeared frequently in earlier volumes (see for example above, II, 315 n), was a captain in the second battalion of Philadelphia associators: *Pa. Col. Recs.*, X, 302. At some time during the year his son Thomas also seems to have become a captain, but we have been unable to discover when; see the *Decennial Register of the Pennsylvania Society of Sons of the Revolution* (Philadelphia, 1898), p. 258. The younger man had just passed his thirtieth birthday (see the *DAB*), and BF could have been

of you, and who is apprehensive of the Resentment of your Company, as he is told they are exceedingly exasperated against him. He declares that the Words ascrib'd to him, are much misrepresented, and that if he had an Opportunity of giving you a true Account of them, you would be satisfy'd they were merely jocular, without the least Intention of offending you or any of your Corps. I do not presume to have any Influence with you, intitling me to mediate in any Affair that concerns you.[3] I only beg leave to mention, that as he is a Clergyman of the Church of England, and some pains has lately been taken in England to represent the Colonies as inimical to that Church, I hope you and the Company will on Enquiry find that the Offence is not so great as to require such Marks of Resentment as may be misconstrued there, and deemed the Effects of[4] Enmity to the Clergy; because at this Juncture it might create us some powerful Enemies, increase their number, and diminish that of our Friends.[5] Be so good as to excuse my giving you this Trouble, and believe me to be with sincere Esteem, Dear Sir, Your most obedient humble Servant

B FRANKLIN

Capt. Bradford

Endorsed: Benj Franklin May 16

---

writing to him. But we do not know that he was yet commissioned, and do know that his father was; hence our guess that the latter was the recipient.

3. Ever since the Stamp Act William Bradford and BF had been on bad terms; see above, XVI, 35.

4. The draft here inserts "a Spirit of Intolerance and."

5. We cannot confidently identify the worried cleric. All the known Anglican clergymen in Pennsylvania in 1775 had been there too long to qualify as strangers; see Edgar L. Pennington, "The Anglican Clergy of Pennsylvania in the American Revolution," *PMHB*, LXIII (1939), 414. The most likely candidate is a missionary whom the Society for the Propagation of the Gospel had sent to a nearby parish in Delaware. This was Sydenham Thorne (1748?–93), who had arrived and been ordained a few months before, and was soon in hot water because of his Loyalist leanings; see Nelson W. Rightmyer, *The Anglican Church in Delaware* (Philadelphia, [1947]), pp. 66–7, 169.

To [Joseph Priestley[6]]

Printed in Benjamin Vaughan, ed., *Political, Miscellaneous, and Philosophical Pieces . . . Written by Benj. Franklin . . .* (London, 1779), pp. 550–1.

Dear Friend,   Philadelphia, May 16, 1775.

You will have heard before this reaches you, of a march stolen by the regulars into the country by night, and of their *expedition* back again. They retreated 20 miles in [6][7] hours.

The Governor had called the Assembly to propose Lord North's pacific plan;[8] but before the time of their meeting, began cutting of throats; You know it was said he carried the sword in one hand, and the olive branch in the other; and it seems he chose to give them a taste of the sword first.

He is doubling his fortifications at Boston, and hopes to secure his troops till succour arrives.[9] The place indeed is naturally so defensible, that I think them in no danger.

All America is exasperated by his conduct, and more firmly united than ever. The breach between the two countries is grown wider, and in danger of becoming irreparable.

I had a passage of six weeks; the weather constantly so moderate that a London wherry might have accompanied us all the way. I got home in the evening, and the next morning was unanimously chosen by the Assembly a delegate to the Congress, now sitting.

In coming over I made a valuable philosophical discovery,[1] which I shall communicate to you, when I can get a little time. At present am extremely hurried. Yours most affectionately,

B. F.

6. WTF identified the recipient, in a note on one of the proof sheets of Vaughan's work (Library of Congress) that he used in preparing the *Memoirs*.

7. Brackets in the printed text. If the figure is BF's, he had come much closer to the actual time involved than in his letter to Burke the day before.

8. See the note on the letter just cited.

9. On the day after Concord a Bostonian noted in his diary that his fellow townsmen were alarmed, and "the entrenchments on Boston Neck double Guarded." Anne R. Cunningham, ed., *Letters and Diary of John Rowe* . . . (Boston, 1903), p. 292.

1. On the proof sheet mentioned above WTF here appended the following MS note: "Suppos'd to be relative to the different temperature of the Seas, in different Latitudes, and Currents." BF's discovery is discussed below in our headnote on what we believe to be his later, unfinished letter to Priestley at the end of the month.

From Noble Wimberly Jones

ALS: Duke University Library

Dear Sir   Savannah 16. May 1775

The frequent accounts of your Intentions of leaving England, also unwilling to intrude on time taken up with Matters of Consiquence prevented my Writing as often as I otherwise should have done, however constrained by a real Esteem for a Gentleman so great a friend [of] Mankind in general and of American in particular will I trust plead my Excuse for thus troubling you concern'd at the loss this Pro[vince] sustain'd thro I am pretty confident thro' the Ill conduct of our Assembly's Nominating another Person and I am positive your feelings for America must be great.[2] The present Sittuation is truely Alarming, by late Accounts from Boston there has been some Lives lost both on the side of the Soldiers and Americans but as you will have a more perfect Account before this can reach you I forbear mentioning our acct. Tis said the Americans had the best of it but bad is the best in Wars between Fathers, Sons Bretheren &c. as both lose let which will conquer, therefore the Vile advisers of such a Plan a[s h]as been adopted have the more to Answer for. God only know where such Matters may end especially in which our Lives Liberties and all that is dear to us depends, tho' our Province has not appeared outwardly forward in the Ma[tter,] thro' Influence of some Tools of Administration, yet am of oppinion a large Majority do heartily Join in sentiment with the other Colonies perhaps 9, out of ten or more.[3] God send that our Sovereign may [*dismiss?*] those base Men that advise such Measures that may prove destructive to his whole Dominion, and consider his Subjects in America with the same affection as those nearer to him and that they naturally must be entitled to the like Rights and Priveledges in one part of his

2. The syntax and also, apparently, an unintended repetition obscure Jones' meaning. His sentence, as we interpret it, should read: "[I am] concerned at the loss this Province sustain'd thro, I am pretty confident, the Ill conduct," etc. The reference is to the choice of Grey Elliott to succeed BF as agent: above, XXI, 142–4.

3. The day after news of Lexington and Concord reached Georgia on May 10, Jones and others raided the public powder magazine. Thereafter the "Tools of Administration"—Gov. Wright and his supporters—were forced onto the defensive, and by the 25th Wright admitted that he was faced by general rebellion. William W. Abbot, *The Royal Governors of Georgia* . . . (Chapel Hill, [1959]), pp. 171–2.

45

kindom as in the other, And then am [in m]y own mind Confident all disputes would subside. I conclude with best Respects that you may enjoy Life and Health to see these troubles all at an happy end And am Dear Sir Your Most Sincere and Obedient Humble Servant

N W JONES

Mr. Banks the Gentleman I trust you will receive this by[4] [has] been in this Province some year's (and probably with some [other bus]iness) goes to see his Father and other relations in England of Ch[oice?] I chose to send it by a Private Hand at this time he has promised if [he] can conveniently to deliver it himself.

Addressed: Benjamin Franklin Esqr / Georgia Coffe House / London / per favour of Mr Bankes

From Charles-Guillaume-Frédéric Dumas

ALS (draft):[5] Library of Congress

Monsieur,   La Haie 17e. May 1775

En attendant que j'aie l'avantage de répondre plus au long à la Lettre dont vous m'avez honoré de Londres par Mr. Rey en date du 24 fevr. 1774,[6] Celle-ci vous sera présentée par Messieurs Giraud et Planier et leurs Epouses, quatre braves et honnêtes gens, qui pour l'amour du plus précieux de tous les biens de l'homme, pour l'amour de la liberté, ont quitté leur patrie la France, et sont venus se réfugier ici, où ils se croyoient en sûreté; mais la tyrannie et le despotisme menacent de les faire réclamer, et en ce cas ils

4. Sutton Bankes sailed from Tybee on May 19 for London: *Ga. Gaz.*, May 24, 1775. We know nothing more about him except that he had been on a committee the summer before to draft resolutions against the Boston Port Act: *ibid.*, Aug. 3, 1774; Hugh M'Call, *The History of Georgia . . .* (2 vols., Savannah, 1811–16), II, 19.

5. The draft is in two parts: the bulk of it, down to where the date reappears, is on three consecutive sheets; and the concluding paragraph and signature are on the verso of the last sheet. These parts might conceivably have been separate letters, but we do not think so because one is unsigned and the other lacks a salutation. If they were a single letter, was it sent? BF acknowledged one of May 18 (below, Dec. 9), which would seem to be this one. But Dumas, writing on June 30, 1775, from outside the Hague, spoke of beginning a letter there and forgetting to bring it with him, and went on to repeat much of what is in the draft. Perhaps he forgot that he had finished and sent it?

6. BF's missing letter was undoubtedly in answer to Dumas' above, XXI, 34–7.

seroient livrés et sans doute perdus.[7] Dans cette inquiettante situation ils me paroissent disposés à aller chercher, dans le sein de l'heureuse Province dont vous êtes l'honneur et l'ornement, la douceur que l'Europe marâtre paroît leur refuser. Ils emportent avec eux quelque chose, mais peu. Les fraix du voyage payés, je ne crois pas qu'il leur restera plus de 150 Liv. Sterling en argent comptant. Il s'agira donc de pourvoir à leur subsistance par l'emploi sage et solide de cette petite somme, soit en achetant quelque fond modique dans l'intérieur de votre Province ou de celle de Jersey, soit en s'appliquant à quelque branche de Commerce en détail dans l'une de vos villes, où ils pourroient aussi gagner quelque chose en donnant leçon à la jeunesse; car ces Messieurs sont gens de Lettres. Quoiqu'ils entreprennent, votre protection, Monsieur, vos bons avis et votre sage direction feront le plus grand bien à ces étrangers, en les empêchant d'êtres dupés et frustrés de leur ressource pécuniaire dans l'emploi qu'ils en feront pour se procurer un petit établissement où leur industrie puisse les rendre heureux. Souffrez donc, Monsieur, que je recommande à votre humanité et soins paternels ces quatre personnes, que le hazard m'a fait connoître il y a deux mois. Témoin journalier depuis ce temps, de leurs manieres et sentimens honnêtes, et de leur agréable conversation, le seul regret que m'a occasionné leur connoissance, a été de ne pouvoir leur faire un sort heureux. *Homo sum, nilque humani a me alienum puto;*[8] et j'ai une si haute idée de vos nobles sentimens à cet égard, que quand même vous ne m'auriez pas obligeamment permis dans l'honneur de votre derniere de vous adresser quelque ami, j'aurois également pris cette liberté pour ceux-ci, vu leur situation critique.

Du reste, Monsieur, j'ai eu soin de les prévenir, qu'ils vont dans un pays où la vertu, la sagesse et l'humanité les accuilleront et les dirigeront, mais où leur industrie, leur travail et conduite constamment sage devront faire le reste.

7. We can find nothing about either of these couples. Dumas referred to them again, but not by name, in the June letter just cited; he then believed that they had already sailed with a note of introduction from him. Four months later two Frenchmen with quite different names, also *gens de lettres*, also with an introduction from him, and carrying his letters of May 18 and June 30, turned up in Philadelphia: BF to Dumas below, Dec. 9. Either last-minute substitutes replaced Giraud and Planier, or the latter renamed themselves.

8. *Homo sum; humani nil a me alienum puto*: "I am a man; I consider nothing human as alien to me." Terence, *Heauton Timoroumenos*, line 77.

Je vous rends bien des graces, Monsieur, de votre bel Ouvrage dont vous m'avez fait présent.[9] Je le conserverai précieusement, et y converserai souvent avec vous.

J'ai donné depuis peu une nouvelle Edition du Droit des Gens de Vatel in 4° avec des notes de ma façon, et une Lettre aussi de moi à la tête, où je parle de vos Provinces avec un intérêt qui part du fond du coeur.[1] J'en ai deux Exemplaires en réserve pour vous et pour la Bibliotheque de Philadelphie; j'y ajouterai quelques autres petites nouveautés que je croirai pouvoir vous faire plaisir, et ferai partir le paquet par le premier Vaisseau qui fera voile de Rotterdam pour Philadelphie.

17e May 1775 Minute de ma Lettre à Mr. B. Franklin
Je fais les voeux les plus sinceres, Monsieur, pour votre santé et conservation, pour celle de toute votre digne et honorée famille, pour la prospérité de votre Province et de toutes celles à qui leur liberté est plus précieuse que tous les autres biens du monde. Le plus ardent de mes voeux est que l'orage odieux qui gronde sur elles se dissipe, et que leurs libertés en sortent plus radieuses et mieux affermies que jamais: ou, si ce noir nuage doit crever sur des tetes humaines, que ce ne soit que sur les têtes coupables des monstres qui l'ont excité. Le voeu de tout ce qu'il y a encore de coeurs honnêtes en Europe est pour vous, Hommes vertueux! Votre sort interesse, inquiette tout ce qui n'est pas des âmes de boue. Le cri général est que votre cause est celle de la nature, celle du genre humain. On admire la conduite tout à la fois ferme et moderee que vous avez tenue jusqu'ici vis à vis de vos ennemis. Tous les yeux sont tournés sur celle que vous aller tenir, si l'on veut, comme il paroît, pousser à bout tant de braves gens. Dieu ben[isse] votre Congrès, que je suppose assemblé, y maintienne l'union fraternelle, couronne du plus heureux succès ses résolutions, et confonde vos ennemis, vos lâches et vos traîtres: car cette exécrable engeance se fourre partout. J'ai l'honneur d'être avec la

9. Undoubtedly the fifth ed. of *Exper. and Obser.*

1. Emmerichs de Vattel, *Le Droit des gens; ou, Principes de la loi naturelle, appliqués à la conduite et aux affaires des nations et des souverains* . . . (Amsterdam, 1775). The work first appeared in 1758; Dumas' edition was described as enlarged, revised, and corrected. He discusses it, and other gifts that he added, in the June letter already mentioned.

plus haute considération, et la plus respectueuse estime, Monsieur
votre très humble et très obéissant serviteur   C G F Dumas

From Jonathan Williams, Jr.

ALS: American Philosophical Society

Dear and honoured Sir   London May 20. 1775
   Since my last I have recvd from La Duchesse de Villroy the Plan
of your Armonica improved, which you will receive by this Ship.[2]
The Newspapers will give you all in the political Way. I have been
several Days shut up in your Room, so have not been able to
gather any thing more than the Public Prints contain. You will
see by the Fate of the N York and Quebec Petitions, that it is not
because what came from the Congress was illegal, that their Applications did not succeed, since both have been treated alike: I
think this must cure the N York Dissention if there remains any.[3]
   I have been down to Virginia Street and am in a good Way to

2. In April, during his visit to Paris, JW had met the duchesse de Villeroi
and learned of her improvement on BF's armonica. "Instead of playing with the
Fingers on the Glass she had contrived to fix Keys so that one Plays the same as
with the Harpsichord. Her Grace has engaged to give me a Plan and Description
of it." JW's MS journal, Yale University Library, entry of April 4, 1775. The
plan that he forwarded has since disappeared; but it could not have turned the
armonica into an effective keyboard instrument because all attempts to do so
failed: above, X, 124. For the Duchess (1731–1816) see Larousse, *Dictionnaire
universel*, under Villeroi, Gabriel-Louis de Neufville, duc de.
3. The N.Y. Assembly, after the actions to which Cooper referred in his letter
above of April 1, had sent petitions to the King, Lords, and Commons, denouncing British actions and requesting that Parliament restore to the colony
the rights it had enjoyed before the end of the previous war. An unofficial body
of British Protestants in Canada had petitioned for the recovery of their rights
as British subjects through repeal or amendment of the Quebec Act. The Commons refused to receive either petition. Force, 4 *Amer. Arch.*, I, 1318–22,
1834–8; *Commons Jours.*, XXXV (1774–76), 376, 384–5; Gipson, *British Empire*, XII, 307–10. The petition to the King from the first Continental Congress
had been received and buried: above, XXI, 476 n. JW is saying that of these
three petitions the only legal one, that from New York, suffered the same fate
as the others, which were from extralegal bodies; hence the colony must learn
that it cannot secure redress by itself.

get good Information relative to Mrs. Davys Affair.[4] I will write again when I have obtained it.

I recvd for you a large Packet from Carolina it was so Bulky that I thot best to examine it before I sent it, and as I find nothing but Newspapers in it shall keep it here.[5]

The Queen of Denmark is Dead 'tis whispered that she was poisoned but without much appearance of Truth.[6]

The inclosed is written by the Gentlemen and Ladies that did us the honor of their Company to day at Dinner.[7] I have stolen a few minutes from them to write the above, so hope you will excuse the hurry with which it is written. I am with unfeigned affection Your dutifull Kinsman   J WILLIAMS JUNR

Addressed: Doctor Franklin / Philadelphia

Endorsed: Jona Williams 75

To Humphry Marshall

Reprinted from William Darlington, *Memorials of John Bartram and Humphry Marshall* . . . (Philadelphia, 1849), p. 521.

Dear Sir: Philadelphia, May 23d. 1775.

I received your favour of the 13th inst. I think, with you, that the non-importation and non-exportation, well adhered to, will end the controversy in our favour. But, as Britain has begun to use

4. The affair, which BF presumably mentioned in a missing letter, remains in mystery. It may have had to do with the sea, for Virginia Street was near the docks; and it may have concerned the widow of BF's and Galloway's old friend Hugh Davy (above, IX, 17). She died in Philadelphia in 1782: Edward L. Clark, *A Record of the Inscriptions . . . in the Burial-Grounds of Christ Church* . . . (Philadelphia, 1864), p. 452.

5. Doubtless the consignment that BF had requested from Peter Timothy the previous September: above, XXI, 292.

6. The Queen, King George's youngest sister, had been imprisoned after the overthrow of Struensee: above, XIX, 73. She was then exiled to Celle in Hanover, where a group of Danes plotted to restore her to power. Before the plot matured she died of a disease, perhaps typhus, that was epidemic in Celle at the time; and in the circumstances poisoning was naturally suspected. Hester W. Chapman, *Caroline Matilda, Queen of Denmark, 1751–75* (London, [1971]), part iii.

7. The enclosure, now missing, was no doubt the product of the parlor game of *bouts-rimés*, which had long been popular in Craven Street: above, XVIII, 272.

force, it seems absolutely necessary that we should be prepared to repel force by force, which I think, united, we are well able to do.

It is a true old saying, that *make yourselves sheep and the wolves will eat you*: to which I may add another, *God helps them that help themselves*.[8] With much esteem, I am, sir, Your most obedient humble servant.[9]

To Jane Mecom

ALS: Marietta College Library; copy: Harvard University Library

Dear Sister   Philada. May 26. 1775.

I have just now heard by Mr. Adams, that you are come out of Boston, and are at Warwick in Rhodeisland Government: I suppose it must be at good Mr. and Mrs. Green's, to whom present my affectionate Respects.[1] I write this Line just to let you know I am return'd well from England; that I found my Family well; but have not found the Repose I wish'd for, being the next Morning after my Arrival delegated to the Congress by our Assembly. I wish to hear from you, and to know how you have left your Affairs [in] Boston; and whether it will be inconvenient for you to come hither, or you wish rather that I should come to see you, if the Business I am engag'd in will permit. Let me know if you want any Assistance; and what is become of Cousin Williams and Family, and other Friends. Jonathan was at Paris when I left England, but to return in a Week or two.[2] I am ever, my dear Sister Your very loving Brother   B FRANKLIN

Send me what News you can that is true.

Sally presents her Duty to you and Love to Mr & Mrs Green.

8. The first was an Italian proverb, and the second was adapted from Aesop in *Poor Richard*: above, XX, 10; II, 140.

9. We conjectured that BF left his previous letter to Marshall unsigned for the sake of security: above, XXI, 520 n. Why he handled this one the same way defies conjecture.

1. BF had obviously not yet received his sister's letter of May 14 with its news of the Greenes' household. We have no way of knowing whether he learned of her whereabouts from John or Samuel Adams, both of whom arrived in Philadelphia on May 10.

2. The father had fled with his family to Worcester; see his letter below, June 19, 1775. The son did not return to London until May 3; see the note on Mrs. Stevenson's letter above, April 24.

MAY 26, 1775

Notation: This Letter has been three Weeks in Newport office Forwarded to Mrs. Macom by her Hble Servt A. Maxwell Wedny 10 O'Clk ante M.[3]

From Richard Oliver[4]   ALS: American Philosophical Society

Dear Sir   London 31st May 1775
   Some time since Mr. Wm Lee forwarded my letter to you advising the payment of £100 from the Constitutional Society into the hands of your Bankers Messrs. Brown Collinson & Co. towards relieving the distress'd Inhabitants of Boston.
   On the 23d Inst. they voted £100 more for their relief which is also paid into the hands of the same Gentlemen on your Account and both sums wait your demand and application.[5]
   Recent accounts from America give information of an unprovoked attack by a detachment from the regular troops at Boston against the Provincials which as far as we yet know reflects as little honour on the Brittish Military as our Politicks do on the Brittish Legislature.[6]
   I entertain the best hopes that America directed by wisdom similar to your own will act with sufficient firmness to maintain the rights of free 'tho loyal subjects.
   All reasonable men with whom I converse still continue fixed in opinion against the right of taxing America not represented in

3. Missing from the ALS and supplied from the copy. Adam Maxwell, a friend of Ezra Stiles, was a Scottish-born schoolmaster in Newport, who soon afterward was instrumental in uncovering the treachery of Dr. Benjamin Church. See Richard K. Showman *et al.*, eds., *The Papers of General Nathanael Greene* (2 vols. to date, Chapel Hill, 1976–), p. 14 n.
   4. The London alderman and M.P.; see Lee to BF above, April 3.
   5. For the two earlier gifts from the Society, and BF's handling of them, see the letter just cited. We have found no record in BF's accounts of this third donation; a fourth, in early June, made a greater stir: the Society voted that a contribution of £100 be sent to BF for the relatives of "our BELOVED American Fellow Subjects, who, FAITHFUL to the Character of Englishmen, preferring Death to Slavery, were, for that Reason only, inhumanly murdered by the King's Troops at or near Lexington and Concord." *Public Advertiser*, June 9, 1775. The following October BF presented £100 from the Society to the Mass. General Court: Council minutes (Mass. Arch.), Oct. 25, 1775.
   6. The account had been published in London two days before; see the head-note on the Mass. provincial congress to BF above, April 26.

Parliament. I am with much respect and great Esteem Dear Sir Your very Obedient Humble Servant   RICHD OLIVER

Addressed: To / Dr Benjamn Franklyn / Philadelphia

Endorsed: Aldn Oliver

Proposed Resolutions of Thanks

AD: American Philosophical Society

The first Continental Congress had sent to London, along with its petition to the King and address to the British people, a resolution of thanks to all those in Britain who had attempted to defend the American cause.[7] The second Congress sent the Olive Branch Petition and another address, but no resolution of thanks to any of its British friends except the City of London.[8] At some point Franklin decided that such thanks were in order, and drafted the three resolves that follow. If he ever introduced them, no record seems to have survived; and there is neither internal nor external evidence of when he wrote them. In our opinion the most plausible bracket of time is between May, when his English friends and what they had tried to do were still fresh in memory, and July 8, when the Olive Branch Petition and address were adopted; and our practice is to assign a document to its earliest likely date.

Resolved   [May, June, or early July, 1775]
     That the Thanks of this Congress, of all America, and in our Opinion, of Britain likewise, are due to the Right Honourable the Earl of Chatham, for his benevolent Endeavours to accommodate the present unhappy Differences, and particularly for the wise and excellent Plan he offer'd in the House of Lords for that purpose, which was rejected by their Lordships without Consideration, and which if it had been received and attended to, might have been the Basis of a Reconciliation and lasting Agreement.[9]

Resolved,
     That the Thanks of the Congress be presented likewise to Edmund Burke Esqr. and to David Hartley, Esq. for their generous

7. Above, XXI, 337.
8. See the note on the petition below, July 8, 1775, and *JCC,* II, 158–71.
9. Chatham's first endeavor was his motion in January to withdraw the troops from Boston, and his second was the plan introduced on Feb. 1: above, XXI, 454, 459–61, 463–4, 576–83.

53

Endeavours in the same common Service to the whole British Empire.[1]

Resolved,

That the Thanks of this Congress be also presented to the Right Reverend the Bishop of St. Asaph, for his most excellent Sermon and Speech on American Affairs.[2] And to all the noble Lords and Commoners in both Houses of Parliament who have been pleased to espouse the Cause of our much injured and oppressed Country.

Endorsed: Resolutions of Thanks[3]

To [Joseph Priestley?]   Unfinished draft: Library of Congress

During his voyage to Philadelphia Franklin made the observations on the sea that appear above under April 10. On May 16 he promised in a letter to Priestley to communicate to him "a valuable philosophical discovery" that he had made on the voyage; years later William Temple Franklin conjectured, in a note on that letter, that the discovery was related to variations in the temperature of sea water. This draft justifies a further conjecture, that Franklin started to redeem his promise but broke off after a short introduction; and outside evidence suggests that what he was about to explain was how to recognize the presence of the Gulf Stream. Part of the evidence is in his April observations: at two periods on the crossing, close together, considerable seaweed appeared, phosphorescence vanished, and the temperature of the water rose. The rest of the evidence is what followed this fragment when he embodied it in his "Maritime Observations," completed in 1785: he described the

1. Burke's speech and motions on conciliation, March 22 (see BF to Burke above, May 15), and Hartley's on March 27 (above, XXI, 511).
2. The sermon in 1773 and the intended speech on the Mass. Government Bill the following year: above, XX, 140 n; XXI, 321–2.
3. On the verso of one sheet BF wrote "Portugal," and on the other an arithmetical jotting and beside it a column of figures relating to the emission of bills of credit. He was on a committee to supervise the printing of $2,000,000 in such bills in specified amounts and denominations (*JCC*, II, 103, 105–6), and was apparently satisfying himself that the totals accorded with the limits set. Although this is the only contemporary evidence we have that he was involved in the issue of paper money, he later said that during his Congressional term he had taken a more active part: he had made a number of proposals, which he thought would have been effectual but which were rejected, for preventing depreciation of the currency. These he listed in a letter to Samuel Cooper, April 22, 1779, Smyth, *Writings*, VII, 293.

same three changes in the sea as indications of the Gulf Stream.[4] By the time he disembarked from the *Pennsylvania Packet*, it seems reasonable to conclude, he had a method for identifying the great current; and soon afterward he set out to impart his discovery to Priestley. Then he stopped. Perhaps he was unwilling to commit himself without further tests, which he made years later; perhaps he was distracted by the press of business. In any case a decade passed before he resumed his inquiry into the Gulf Stream.

Sir   Philada. May 1775.

About 5 or 6 Years since, there was an Application made by the Board of Customs at Boston, to the Lords of the Treasury, complaining that the Packets between Falmouth and New York were generally a Fortnight longer in their Passages, than Merchant Ships from London to Rhodeisland, and proposing that for the future they should be ordered to Rhodeisland instead of New York.

Being then concern'd in the Management of the American Post-Office, I happened to be consulted on the Occasion: And it appearing strange to me, that there should be such a Difference between two Places scarce a Days Run asunder, especially when the Merchant Ships are generally deeper laden and more weakly mann'd than the Packets, and had from London the whole Length of the River and Channel farther to run before they left the Land of England, I could not but think the Fact misunderstood or misrepresented.[5]

From Nathaniel Seidel[6]

Two copies:[7] Moravian Archives, Bethlehem, Pennsylvania

Dear and honourd Sir   May 1775.

Your safe return from England into this Province, at so very

4. Smyth, *Writings*, IX, 394–7. For the "Maritime Observations" see the note on BF's speculation above, April 5.

5. See above, XV, 246–8.

6. Seidel (1718–82), born in Silesia of a Bohemian Protestant family, emigrated to America as a young man to work as a Moravian missionary. He was consecrated bishop in 1758, and four years later succeeded Bishop Spangenberg as head of the provincial board of the church in America. Edmund De Schweinitz, "Some of the Fathers of the American Moravian Church," Moravian Hist. Soc. *Trans.*, II (1877–86), 219–27.

7. By the same copyist, and of two distinct drafts. One, undated and with

critical a Time, has given me and my Brethren much Joy, we viewd and honor'd the Hand of God in it, hoping that your deep Knowledge and long Experience in the House of Assembly will once more be well apply'd for the good of this Country. I can therefore assure you that we thankd God for your safe Arrival and I most heartily wellcome you with this in Pensilvania.

Yet Dear Sir I have still another Reason to trouble you with these Lines and I hope you'll excuse my Freedom. Time and Circumstances have with a deep Regard for your Person implanted into us also a particular Confidence, which makes me address you in our present Situation.

I need not inform you of the present Ferment thru' the whole Province, which has brought us into a perplexed and distressed State here in this County and other Places. Our good Neighbours with whom we lived in the most cordial neighbourly Union and Love, seem to be quite out of Humour with the Br[ethre]n and others who can not join them in taking up Arms and do as they do.

Some good inoffensive Persons have been already ill treated on account of their religious Principles and some others are treadned with taring and feathering, ruining their Farms and burning their Houses and Barns. We know to excuse this vehement Heat, but are sore afraid of the bad consequences and the evil Effect such Excesses may have upon the Country in general.

I would therefore in the Name of the Brethren and others who conscientiously scruple to bear Arms in this and the other Provinces beg the Favour of you to be their Advocat in the present Congress and to use your undoubted influence with the Honorable Members: to give no occasion in their Resolves to the several Committees or others to attack their Neighbours and Fellow Subjects in the most tender and dearest Parts, their religious Liberties and Conscience, but that they rather recomend it to the good People of these Provinces, to keep the Peace and to let ev'ry reli-

---

interlineations and a clause in the margin, was published with occasional small misreadings in *PMHB*, xxix (1905), 245–6. The other, which we print, is a cleaner text and is dated and signed after a fashion. It contains a passage of some interest that Seidel deleted, and in places, as may be seen by comparing it with the *PMHB* version, differs substantially in wording.

gious Society enjoy their Priviledges fully and undisturbed, as long as they do not act against this Country.

I think none can or will withdraw themselves from the common Burden and Expence of the Province wherein they live.[8]

We know to value the good old English Liberty, which we have enjoyd thro' Gods Mercy so many years in this Country, we should think ourselves extream unhappy if the Strugle for Liberty should cost us our Liberty of Conscience for which we are come into America and which our Br[ethre]n now enjoy under Russia, Prussia and other Governments.

That the God of Peace may direct the Councils of the Americans and the Councils in England so, that both may meet one another in the Way of Peace is surely the Prayer of thousands. It is the constant Prayer of Honorable Sir your Humble Servant   N.S.

To Benj. Franklin Esqr.

To Nathaniel Seidel

ALS: Moravian Archives, Bethlehem, Pennsylvania

Philada June 2. 1775

Reverend and dear Sir, Nathanael Seidel.

I am much oblig'd by your kind Congratulations on my Return; and I rejoice to hear that the Brethren are well and prosper.[9] I am persuaded that the Congress will give no Encouragement to any to molest your People on Account of their Religious Principles;

---

8. Here follows the deleted passage: "but it would be Tyrany in extream to attempt to force from us a high valued Priviledge: the Exemption from bearing of Arms, which has been granted unto the Br[ethre]n even in Russian Prussia Danemark and where ever they settled and which has brought the Brethren at first into Pensilvania.

"We seek nothing but the Good of the Country where we live and that we ourselves may be able to lead a quiet and peaceable Life in all Godliness and Honesty."

On May 6, when companies of troops were being raised in every township, a Moravian conference urged the brethren to share in the expense as far as their means permitted, but to do nothing that might jeopardize the exemption from bearing arms that had been given them by statute (22 Geo. II, c. 30). See Kenneth G. Hamilton, "John Ettwein and the Moravian Church during the Revolutionary Period," Moravian Hist. Soc. *Trans.*, XII (1940), 234–6.

9. See the preceding document.

and tho' much is not in my Power, I shall on every Occasion exert my self to discountenance and prevent such infamous Practices. Permit me however to give a little Hint in point of Prudence. I remember that you put yourselves into a good Posture of Defence at the Beginning of the last War when I was at Bethlehem; and I then understood from my much respected Friend Bp. Spangenberg, that there were among the Brethren many who did not hold it unlawful to arm in a defensive War.[1] If there still [are] any such among your young Men, perhaps it would not be amiss to permit them to learn the military Discipline among their Neighbours, as this might conciliate those who at present express some Resentment, and having Arms in Readiness for all who may be able and willing to use them, will be a general Means of Protection against Enemies of all kinds. But a Declaration of your Society, that tho' they cannot in conscience compell their young Men to learn the Use of Arms, yet they do not restrain such as are so disposed, will operate in the Minds of People very greatly in your Favour. Excuse my Presumption in offering Advice,[2] which indeed may be of little Value, but proceeds from a Heart fill'd with Affection and Respect for a Society I have long highly esteem'd, and among whom I have many valuable Friends. I am with great Regard and Veneration, Revd. Sir, Your most obedient humble Servant

B FRANKLIN

Written in great Haste.

From John Jacob Friis[3]   ALS: American Philosophical Society

Honoured Sir,   Philada Jun. 2d. 177[5]
    Here inclosed I return the Letter, which You were so complaisant and kind to let me have the Reading of. Your Answer, which

1. During BF's long visit to the frontier in 1755–56 he stayed four times at Bethlehem and became acquainted with Seidel's predecessor, Bishop Spangenberg. See above, VI, 308, 362 n, and for the Bishop's statement *Autobiog.*, pp. 231–2. For Moravian views of military service see Peter Brock, *Pacifism in the United States from the Colonial Era to the First World War* (Princeton, 1968), pp. 285–321.

2. For more light on BF's ideas about the treatment of conscientious objectors see his proposals below, under Sept. 29, 1775.

3. Friis (1708–93) was a Dane, who taught in the Moravian seminary in Saxony before emigrating to America in 1753. He was an assistant to the

You were pleased to give to it I have forwarded already.[4] That our dear Lord may bless You and the whole Congress in all Your Deliberations and Councels is the most sincere and cordial Wish of Your devoted and most humble Servant J. FRIIS

Addressed: To / Doctor Benjn. Franklin / these

Endorsed: Moravians

To Thomas Life

> Extract: Papers of the Earl of Dartmouth deposited in the Staffordshire County Record Office

Philadelphia June 5. 1775.

I have just received your Favor of April 5. giving me an Account of the Progress of my Suit.[5] I called at your House just before I came away to settle Matters with You, and it was no small Disappointment to me that I did not meet with You. I did then propose returning in October, but I find Things here in such a Situation, that I now think it not likely I shall ever again see England, Hostilities being commenced by General Gage against America, and a Civil War begun, which I have no Chance of living to see the End of, being 70. Years of Age: So it seems not worth while to proceed in the Appeal to the House of Lords; especially as from the Troubles in New England, I am not likely to receive any Reimbursement of the Expence.[6] I have already written to You,

---

Philadelphia congregation until he became too ardent in the American cause and was recalled to Bethlehem, where he taught for the rest of his life. See Augustus Schultze, "The Old Moravian Cemetery of Bethlehem, Pa.," *Moravian Hist. Soc. Trans.*, V (1897–98), 99, 108–9; Kenneth G. Hamilton, "John Ettwein and the Moravian Church during the Revolutionary Period," *ibid.*, XII (1940), 264 n.

4. The letter and answer were undoubtedly the preceding documents.

5. For developments in William Whately's Chancery suit against BF see the headnote above, XXI, 200–1. Life's letter, now missing, is summarized in his accounts; it reported an order from the Lord Chancellor on the argument over the exceptions that BF's counsel had made to the report of the Master in Chancery. The matter came before the court on March 27, and the final argument was held on June 14: Mass. Hist. Soc. *Proc.*, LVI (1922–23), 111; Chancery Decrees and Orders, C 33/444/380, Public Record Office.

6. BF by this time could not have returned to England without facing arrest,

JUNE 5, 1775

that upon Sight of Your Bill I shall punctually discharge it; And I desire You to withdraw the Petition.   B. FRANKLIN.

Extract. To Thomas Life Esqr.

Docketed: Philadelphia, June 5. 1775 Extract of a Letter from Dr. Benjamin Franklin to Thomas Life Esqr.

From William Strahan

Extract:[7] Papers of the Earl of Dartmouth deposited in the Staffordshire County Record Office

William Strahan was one of the few British political correspondents whom Franklin retained after leaving England. The Scot had bought himself a seat in Parliament in 1774, and consistently supported the government's American policy. The outbreak of war, much as he regretted it, did not shake his faith in the British position; and in his letters he tried the impossible task of converting his old friend to his views.[8] The effect was to strain the friendship, which Franklin was at one point ready, until he had second thoughts, to break off,[9] but which in the end proved stronger than their political disagreement; for years to come they kept in touch by letter.

---

and an appeal to the House of Lords would have temporarily precluded that danger; see the headnote just cited. BF's pessimism about being repaid turned out to be unwarranted; see the action of the Mass. House and Council below, Oct. 23, 1775.

7. Strahan had promised to write BF by every packet, and did write monthly from April until packets were discontinued in October. On Aug. 2 and Sept. 6 he speaks of his other letters from April through July, and that of October is below. Of these seven, five are extant in whole or in part: June 7, July 5, Aug. 2, Sept. 6, and Oct. 4. All were intercepted, copied or extracted for Lord Dartmouth, and then sent on. The ALS of Sept. 6 is among BF's papers; the originals of the others have since been lost. Two letters, of April 8 and May 5, have vanished along with BF's reply to them of July 7, which Strahan mentioned on Sept. 6. The only extant letter that BF wrote and sent is below, Oct. 3, where he speaks of receiving four from Strahan, the latest dated Aug. 2. That was in fact the fifth; so one, written between May and August, must have gone astray. BF also received the September letter; five, therefore, are known to have arrived, and most if not all went by way of Whitehall.

8. See Namier and Brooke, *House of Commons*, III, 490–1; above, XIX, 91, 407; and the extant letters from Strahan just cited.

9. See below, the note that BF did not send of July 5 and the letter that he did of Oct. 3, 1775.

60

London, June 7. 1775.
We begin to expect to hear of the Proceedings of the Congress soon. I hope it is composed not of headstrong violent and unreasonable Men, but of plain, honest, cool, dispassionate, and impartial Representatives of the People; more ready to heal than to spread Misunderstandings, and perfectly disposed to promote a Reconciliation with the Mother Country by every Means in their Power, consistent with the Happiness and Liberty of their Constituents. If this should luckily happen to be the Case, I expect to see You quickly return to us with the Olive Branch in Your Hand, invested with full Powers to terminate all Differences upon reasonable and solid Terms.[1] Believe me, I think so well of this Office that I hope it is actually reserved for You, and that the successful Conclusion of so important a Treaty will crown the Operations of a Life spent in the Investigation of every useful Branch of Knowledge, and in the Service of his Country in particular. This is truly worthy of your highest Ambition, and I still hope to see it gratified in this Respect, however Appearances seem at present to be against it. WILL. STRAHAN.

Extract. To Dr. Franklin.

Notation: London. June 7, 1775. Extract of a Letter from William Strahan Esqr. to Dr. Franklin.

From Jonathan Williams, Jr.

ALS: Yale University Library

Dear and honoured Sir   London June 7. 1775
Agreeable to a Message from Lord Shelburn, I waited on the Prince de Masserano spanish ambassador, for a Book which his Lordship informed me was for You.[2] After my Name was sent up, his Secretary came and asked if I spoke French, and answering in

1. BF responded (*ibid.*) that he could not return to England without being imprisoned because of the Chancery suit.
2. Almost a decade earlier Shelburne, as secretary of state, had had considerable official contact with the Spanish Ambassador: Edmond G. Petty-Fitzmaurice, Baron Fitzmaurice, *Life of William Earl of Shelburne* . . . (2 vols., London, 1912), I, 287, 290–1, 324–5. Victor-Amé-Philippe Ferrero de Fiesque, Prince of Masserano (1713–77), was a popular figure at the British court, but for some time had been under treatment in Paris for a serious illness; he did not return to his post until late May: Doniol, *Histoire*, I, 56–7.

the affirmative I was immediately admitted into the Princes Chamber, where he was dressing. He then told me that the Infanta of Spain, desires his best regards to you, and requests you will accept a Volume of his Works, as a token of his affectionate Esteem.[3] The Prince at the same Time expressed his concern at not having the honor of presenting it to you in Person, and likewise desires his Compliments. I am Your dutifull and affectionate Kinsman

JONA WILLIAMS JUNR

I should have mentioned, that His Royal Highness has got the Armonica in thorough Repair, and is exceedingly pleased with it.[4] I send the Book and some Newspapers by Capt. Miller.

Doctor Franklin

From Mary Hewson

ALS: American Philosophical Society

My dear Sir   Craven Street June 10. 1775

My mother promis'd Lord Drummond to send a letter to you by him,[5] she deputed Mr. Williams to write it for her, but as he

3. Don Gabriel Antonio (1752–88), the fourth and favorite son of King Charles III, was a talented classicist as well as a trained musician; see John D. Bergamini, *The Spanish Bourbons: the History of a Tenacious Dynasty* (New York, [1974]), p. 100. The Infante was sending BF his translation of Sallust, *La Conjuracion de Catilina y la guerra de Jugurta* ([Madrid, 1772]). BF's receipt of the present, "beautifully and magnificently printed," was reported in the *Pa. Gaz.*, Aug. 30, 1775, and in the *Pa. Evening Post* the next day; yet his acknowledgment below, Dec. 12, indicates that the volume had just arrived. It is now in the Yale University Library, with a note in BF's hand: "A Present from Don Gabriel Infant of Spain, the Translator. to B. Franklin. Delivered to Mr. Williams for him by Prince Maserano, Ambassador from that Court, in England. 1775." Years later BF commented that the Sallust was still considered to be typographically superior to the best printing in Paris: Smyth, *Writings*, VIII, 336.

4. We have no other evidence for what seems to be suggested here, that BF had already been in touch with the Infante.

5. This is the first appearance on BF's horizon, as far as we know, of a man who was already attracting attention in Philadelphia and, by his own account, in Whitehall as well. Thomas Drummond (1742–80), a Scot who laid claim to a Jacobite title and styled himself Lord Drummond, first went to America in 1768 to look after a kinsman's estate, and remained until late in 1774. He conferred with some delegates to the first Continental Congress, and carried to the ministry their terms for a settlement. Lord North supposedly approved, and

has already written by this Vessel he desir'd me to do it. I pleaded being very sleepy and stupid, they said writing would rouse and enliven me, I do not find they said true, however, I will write on.

I have the pleasure to tell you that my dear little folks are all well, they have all had the measles. My mother was urging me to day to wean my little girl, I cannot tell why, for I never was in better health; I pleaded for her by saying that as she is to be your grand daughter you would be very angry if I did not let her suck a year, my mother then was silent, for absent as well as present your opinion is her Law.

The next Letter I write to you I hope to be able to tell you I have settled with Mr. Mure, for we are now ready to make our aplication to him. Mr. Alexander has very obligingly offer'd me his Assistance as a negociator.[6]

I ask'd my mother if she had any thing to say. Only her Love, and that her patience is almost exhausted, it will not hold out above ten days longer if she does not hear from you.

Dolly is with her sister at Bromley who has been extremely ill but is now better.[7] I do not attempt to give you any but domestic news, all the political you have from abler hands. I am as much as ever an American at heart and Dear Sir Your faithful and affection-ate   MARY HEWSON

Drummond was now on his way back to America to sound out members of the second Congress. He landed in Boston in August, stopped in New York, and eventually reached Philadelphia. His negotiations in America reached their climax in February, 1776, and then abruptly collapsed. Sir James B. Paul, *The Scots Peerage* . . . (9 vols., Edinburgh, 1904–14), VII, 58; Herbert A. Meistrich, "Lord Drummond and Reconciliation," N.J. Hist. Soc. *Proc.*, LXXXI (1963), 256–77; William M. MacBean, *Biographical Register of St. Andrews Society* . . . (2 vols., N.Y., 1922), I, 124; George A. Morrison, *History of St. Andrew's Society* (N.Y., 1906), pp. 73–6. Polly writes as though Drummond were too familiar to need introduction. He had been dealing with Whitehall at just the time that BF had been involved, through Barclay and Fothergill, in his own dealings; and it is tempting to believe, without a shred of evidence, that these parallel negotiations had brought the two men together.

6. Polly's letter below of Dec. 12 has a much fuller account of this settlement, which had to do with the legacy from her aunt; we discuss it there, along with Mr. Mure. The negotiator was doubtless BF's banker friend, William Alexander.

7. Catherine Blunt relapsed: by December she was in a "deep decline," and she died before the year was out; see Polly's letter just cited and above, IX, 327 n.

Remember me to Mr. and Mrs. Bache my Son and his Brother.[8]

[*In Mrs. Stevenson's hand:* My Love to Dear Temple I Long to hear.]

I hope he will forgive my neglect, I often think of him tho' I confess I at this time forgot he was with you.

Addressed: Dr Franklin

Endorsed: Polly Hewson

To William Temple Franklin

ALS: American Philosophical Society

My dear Billy,   Philada. June 13. 1775

I wonder'd it was so long before I heard from you. The Packet it seems was brought down to Philadelphia, and carry'd back to Burlington before it came hither. I am glad to learn by your Letters that you are happy in your new Situation, and that tho' you ride out sometimes, you do not neglect your Studies.[9] You are now in that time of Life which is the properest to store your Mind with such Knowledge as is hereafter to be ornamental and useful to you. I confide that you have too much Sense to let the Season slip. The Antients painted *Opportunity* as an old Man with Wings to his Feet and Shoulders, a great Lock of Hair on the fore part of his Head, but bald behind; whence comes our old Saying, *Take Time by the Forelock*; as much as to say, when it is past, there is no means of pulling it back again; as there is no Lock behind to take hold of for that purpose.

I am sorry your Things have suffer'd so much Damage in their

8. Her "Son," Benny Bache, and his brother William. For the family joke that Elizabeth Hewson was going to marry Benny see BF's letter to Polly below, July 8, 1775.

9. WTF's letters are missing. BF had reason to be concerned about his grandson's "new Situation," for WTF had never before been with his father and stepmother. The young man's studies were in preparation for entering the College of Philadelphia in the autumn. A few months earlier his father had intended him for King's College (above, XXI, 404), and may or may not have been consulted about the change in plan. If BF was not responsible for it, he had good reason to be: he was a founder of the Philadelphia institution, and the faculty of King's was suspect as a nest of Loyalists. Wallace Brown, *The King's Friends* (Providence, R.I., 1965), p. 99.

Way to you; and I fear if I send the Glass you write for, it may likewise be hurt in the Carriage, as I have no Convenience at present of packing it safely, and the Boatmen and Waggoners are very careless People. If you want to use a Glass, your Father has a better, which he will lend you. But a Perspective Glass is not so good as the Eye for Prospects, because it takes in too small a Field. It is only useful to discern better some particular Objects.[1] So, as I expect you here after the Vacation, to go to the College, I think it best to keep the Glass for you till you come, when you will find it in your Desk and Book Case with your little Beginning of a Library; and I hope about the same time your Books and Things from London will be arrived.

I have received a long Letter from Mrs. Stevenson. It is a kind of Journal for a Month after our Departure, written on different Days, and of different Dates, acquainting me who has call'd, and what is done, with all the small News. In four or five Places, she sends her Love to her dear Boy, hopes he was not very sick at Sea, &c. &c. Mrs. Hewson and the Children were well. She was afraid, she says, to see some of your Friends, not knowing how to excuse your not taking leave of them.

Your Shirts will go by to-morrow's Stage. They are in a little Trunk, and I hope will get safe to hand.

Mr. and Mrs. Bache send their Love to you. The young Gentlemen are well and pleas'd with your remembering them. Will has got a little Gun, marches with it, and whistles at the same time by way of Fife.[2] I am ever, Your affectionate Grandfather

B FRANKLIN

Addressed: Mr W. T. Franklin / at Govr Franklin's / Amboy

Endorsed: Answered July 13th. 1775

Notation: B. Franklin Esqr to his grandson June 13th. 1775

1. Perspective glasses or delineators were a device, as the name implies, to help in drawing accurate perspective. Apparently WF, as well as his son, was interested in sketching landscapes.

2. WTF's cousin William had just turned two: above, XX, 317.

To [Catharine Greene³]   Copy: American Philosophical Society

My Dear Friend   Philada June 17th 1775.

I received your kind congratulations with infinite pleasure, as I learn by them that you and yours are well. I long much to see once more my native Country, and my friends there, and none more than my dear Caty and her family. Mr. Green I hope will allow an old man of 70 to say he loves his wife, it is an innocent affection. I have great Obligations to him and you, for your hospitality to my sister. It is much too long a journey for her who is no good Horsewoman, and perhaps for you, though you used to ride admirably; Otherwise I should be pleased with the flattering idea you throw out to me, of mounting your nags to make me a visit. If I possibly can find time, I purpose to be in New England this summer, and you may be assured the *honest* old soul as you call him, will not pass your Door, without indulging himself with the pleasure of calling to see his friends. My love to Mr. Green and the Children, and believe me ever, my dear dear Friend Yours most affectionately.   B FRANKLIN.

Notation: Franklins letters   William Greene Esq

To Jane Mecom   ALS: American Philosophical Society

My dear Sister,   Philada. June 17. 1775.

I wrote to you some time since, having heard from one of the Delegates that you were at Warwick, and I supposed it must be with that good Family, so I directed my Letter to you there; I hope you receiv'd it.⁴ I have since received your kind Letter of May 14. with one from dear Mrs. Green. I sympathise most sincerely with you and the People of my native Town and Country. Your Account of the Distresses attending their Removal affects me greatly. I desired you to let me know if you wanted any thing, but have not since heard from you. I think so many People must be a great Burthen to that hospitable House; and I wish you to be other wise provided for as soon as possible, and I wish for the Pleasure of your Company, but I know not how long we may be allowed to con-

---

3. In answer to her note contained in Jane Mecom's letter above, May 14.
4. The letter above, May 26.

tinue in Quiet here if I stay here, nor how soon I may be ordered
from hence; nor how convenient or inconvenient it may be for you
to come hither, leaving your Goods as I suppose you have in
Boston. My Son tells me he has invited you to Amboy.[5] Perhaps
that may be a Retreat less liable to Disturbance than this: God
only knows, but you must judge. Let me know however if I can
render you any Service; and in what way. You know it will give
me Pleasure. I hear the Cousin Williams is at last got out with his
Family: I shall be glad to hear from them, and would write if I
knew where they were. I receiv'd the other Day here, a Letter I
wrote to you from London the 20th of February.[6] It has been to
New England, and I suppose your being not found there, occasion'd its being forwarded to me. I am, Thanks to God, very
hearty and well, as is this whole Family. The youngest Boy is the
strongest and stoutest Child of his Age that I have seen: He seems
an Infant Hercules.[7] I brought over a Grandson with me, a fine
Lad of about 15.[8] His Father has taken him to Amboy. You will

5. WF had been in Philadelphia in late May or early June; see the headnote on
BF to Galloway above, May 8. The Governor may have learned of Jane's straits
through her letter to BF of May 14, and sent his invitation to her in consequence.
6. Probably the brief note of Feb. 17 above, XXI, 103.
7. William Bache, marching and whistling at the age of two; see BF to WTF
above, June 13.
8. The date of WTF's birth has never been established. It was Feb. 22, 1762,
according to his tombstone in Paris; and we know that his birthday was celebrated on Feb. 22: Beatrix C. Davenport, ed., *Diary of the French Revolution by
Gouverneur Morris* (2 vols., Boston, 1939), II, 370. Our predecessors concluded
that the year was probably erroneous, and among other evidence they cited this
remark by BF and an earlier one to WF above, XXI, 266, both of which point to
1760: XIII, 443 n. We have since come on three other statements of the same
purport, one by BF in March, 1777, that his grandson was "about 17" and
another in 1781 that he was "now of age," and WTF's remark in 1790 that he
had "arrived to the senatorial age," in other words thirty. BF to Ingenhousz
below, Feb. 12–March 6, 1777, and to Samuel Huntington, March 12, 1781,
National Archives; WTF to George Washington, Jan. 9, 1790, Washington
Papers, Library of Congress. The only conflicting evidence that has come to
light, aside from the tombstone, is WTF's application for a French residence
permit in 1822, the year before his death; he is there described as the son of WF
and Elizabeth Franklin, born in 1762. (Minutier des notaires, Paris, Dec., 11,
1822, Notaire Philippe Fouché, XIII, 608, no. 20,717.) Because part of this
statement is false, the rest is suspect. WTF's remark on Jan. 9, 1790, that he
was then thirty raises a slight question about the day and month of his birth,
but it was probably on Feb. 22 and almost certainly in 1760.

be pleas'd with him when you see him. Jonathan Williams was in France when I left London. Since I have been here I receiv'd a Letter he sent me there: I enclose it for your Amusement; and to show to his Father and Mother, as it may be some Satisfaction to them, if they have not lately heard from him.[9] I am ever, my dear Sister Your affectionate Brother   B FRANKLIN

Addressed: To / Mrs Jane Mecom / at / Mr Green's / Warwick / Rhodeisland

From Jonathan Williams, Sr.   ALS: Yale University Library

Honoured sir   Worcester June 19the. 1775

Hearing that you was arrv'd in America and I being much Concrned for our belov'd Son, this is to desire you to Give us Some account of his Situation and Curcomstances. Poor fellow I feare he is now undon as a Merchant. We relying on the faith of General Gage packed up all his Goods in Order to remove them out of Boston, but was forbid by him out of whose Mouth proceds blessing and cursing.[1] They there remain with all my Estate Which

---

Before the young man's return to America only a few of those close to him, whether by blood or propinquity, seem to have been aware who he was. At Craven St. Mrs. Stevenson and her daughter guessed, but kept the guess to themselves; they saw a strong resemblance between grandfather and grandson, Polly Hewson wrote BF years later, "when we did not think ourselves at liberty to say we did, as we pretended to be as ignorant as you supposed we were, or chose we should be." Oct. 25, 1784, APS; see also her letter below, Sept. 5, 1776. JW seems to have been in the same position of knowing but not saying. A letter from WTF after returning to America made JW "happy in the Appelation of Kinsman which he gives me," apparently for the first time. To BF below, Nov. 23. What WF confided to his wife is their secret; all we know is that she adapted quickly to her "son" after his return. As for the others, the evidence suggests that DF lived and died in ignorance, and that Jane Mecom learned the truth for the first time from this letter. The only previous discussion of WTF as a scion of the family had been in correspondence between BF and WF.

9. Probably a letter now lost; JW's above of May 20 could scarcely have arrived by this time.

1. From the passage about good and evil in man's tongue: James 3:10. After Lexington thousands of Bostonians left town. Gage was anxious to be rid of them, and negotiated with the selectmen and town meeting the terms of evacuation. The agreement was that those who wished might, upon depositing their firearms with the selectmen, receive passes to leave with their families and

was indeed Sofficient for me and all my famley though a few days before I left that once happy Town which is now become a den of theaves and robers, to Compleat ruin my Stores With all my papers and Some of my Books Were Consumed by fire. I was Oblig'd to Leave all except a few trunk of Clouths and house linnen my Sons Goods nine houses one of Which I valued at £15.000 Sterling and all its valueable furnurture, but blessed be God I have now Colected my Scater'd famley Who are all hear in this Town,[2] in Comfortable Curcomstances at present, and rather then they Should want I will go to day Labour, though Old I have good helth (56 this day). My Greatest Concrn is to pay my debts though I have got my plate but that must if we tarrey Long in this State go to the Support of my famley. My debts that are due to me dose not follow me and was I to follow them I doobt whither I Should catch them, nor Could I as the Old Saying is make one hand Wash the other tho' the former is five times more then the Latter. However I doobt not we Shall git through the Wilderness and on those Accounts prehaps Sooner Arive too the promis'd Land.

Our Aunt Meccom Accept'd an Invitation from Mr: Green and is well there a few days ago and happy for every one is so that thinks themselves so. My wife and Children Joines in dutyfull

effects. The provincial congress arranged for their settlement, and for the passage of Loyalists into town. Difficulties arose at once, however, and the crux of them was the interpretation of "effects". Gage feared that Boston, once all the rebels' movable property was out of it, might be set afire. He interpreted effects to exclude first merchandise, then provisions and medical supplies, both of which were in short supply within his lines. The provincial congress thereupon limited what the Loyalists might carry in: clothing and household furniture. Resentment escalated, and Gage's conduct became a grievance that Congress included in its declaration of reasons for taking up arms. *Mass. Spy, or, American Oracle of Liberty*, May 3, and *Boston Gaz.*, June 5, 1775; Carter, *Gage Correspondence*, I, 397–8; Wroth, *Province in Rebellion*, I, 123; II, 1684, 2076; *JCC*, II, 151. See also Gerard B. Warden, *Boston, 1689–1776* (Boston and Toronto, [1970]), p. 319; Richard Frothingham, *History of the Siege of Boston . . .* (4th ed., Boston, 1873), pp. 93–6; John R. Alden, *General Gage in America . . .* (Baton Rouge, 1948), pp. 255–6.

2. They obviously included his wife, Grace Harris Williams, and no doubt some of their sons and daughters. The first eight in order of birth appear in *Report of the Record Commissioners of the City of Boston*, XXIV (1894), pp. 265, 275, 280, 285, 290, 293, 298, 300, and the other two in *The Manifesto Church: Records of the Church in Brattle Square Boston* (Boston, 1902), pp. 181, 183.

respects With Your Nephew and Humble Servant   J WILLIAMS

Please to direct to Worcester Which Lays in the post Rhode. Your being in the Congress will give you a better knoledge of our public State than I Can Write.

Addressed: To / The Honble. Benjamin Franklin Esqr / In / Philadelphia

From Samuel Vaughan[3]   ALS: American Philosophical Society

My dear Sir,   Montego Bay Jamaica 24 June 1775

I most sincerely congratulate you and your country, upon your safe arrival in America. After many years watchful attention to its interest and when you could render it no further service at home, You are at length arrived to the only Asylum and at the most critical juncture to take your place and to display your distinguished abilities among a sett of Worthies (whose fame will be immortal) struling for the preservation of the small remains of British Liberty, now banished from its once happy Isle, to America, the last place of its resort. God grant you success, equal to the justice and importance of your Cause, and that it may flourish there until the end of time.

I should have fulfilled my intention of making the tour of North America with my Son, had not the sword been drawn; had I went, I could not (with my quick sensibility) have refrained taking an active part, tho' without power to render adequate service, being unknown there, without acquaintance or natural interest to give me influence, and the certain consequence would have been, sequestration of all my property in this Island. I therefore thought it more prudent to continue here until the spring, in hopes by that time to have a more favourable prospect, for laying a plan for throwing my small mite with advantage into the public weal.

I have not had the favour of an answer from Messrs. Welleng's, or from Mr. Yates, whose character and conduct I truly revere;[4]

3. For Vaughan and his projected American tour, mentioned in the second paragraph, see above, XXI, 441–2.

4. "Welling's" was undoubtedly Thomas Willing, of Willing, Morris & Co., for whom see the *DAB* and Thomas W. Balch, "Thomas Willing of Philadelphia (1731–1821)," *PMHB*, XLVI (1922), 1–14. Yates may well have been Richard

their Virtue will be transmitted with its native lustre to Posterity. Should the times permit a few moments thought from more public concerns, may I hope you will bear in mind and procure if in Your power, proper settlements for my Sons John and Charles, for whom I will pledge my self, that they will not disgrace *even your* recommandation. My Son is at present in Hanover, or he would not have failed to have done himself the pleasure of writing You by this conveyance,[5] as I am sure he is equally with my self, Dear Sir Your affectionate and most obedient humble Servant

SAML VAUGHAN

Doctor Benjn Franklin

Addressed: To / Doct[or] Benjn. Franklin / Philadel[phia]

Endorsed: S. Vaughan

To Browns & Collinson[6]

ALS (draft): American Philosophical Society

Gentlemen,   London, June 27. 75.
 Pay the Ballance of my Account to John Sargent Esqr.[7] whose Receipt shall be your Discharge. I am, Gentlemen Your old Friend and humble Servant   BF.

Messrs Browns & Collinson

Yates, a New York merchant who had Philadelphia connections and traded with the West Indies: John A. Stevens, Jr., *Colonial New York: Sketches Biographical and Historical* . . . (New York, 1867), p. 172.

5. Vaughan had eleven children, most of whom grew to maturity and many of whom were remarkable for longevity; see John H. Sheppard, "Reminiscences and Genealogy of the Vaughan Family," *New England Hist. and Geneal. Register*, XIX (1865), 355. John (1756–1841) and Charles (1759–1839) were young enough so that neither of them was likely to have been on his own in Hanover. That son was doubtless either Benjamin (1751–1835) or William (1752–1850), and we suspect the former because of his connection with BF. The family went to America after the war, and four of the children settled there: Sarah P. Stetson, "The Philadelphia Sojourn of Samuel Vaughan," *PMHB*, LXXIII (1949), 459–74.

6. Why BF wrote as of London the reader must guess. No record of this transaction appears in his Jour. or Ledger, and all we know about it is contained in the note itself and in the following document.

7. The banker, one of BF's oldest English friends.

To John Sargent

ALS (draft): American Philosophical Society

Dear Sir, Philada. June 27. 1775.

I have written to Messrs. Browns and Collinson to pay the Ballance of my Acct to you;[8] and I beg you to take the Trouble of receiving and keeping it for me, or my Children. It may possibly soon be all I shall have left: as my American Property consists chiefly of Houses in our Seaport Towns, which your Ministry have begun to burn, and I suppose are wicked enough to burn them all.[9] It now requires great Wisdom on your Side the Water to prevent a total Separation; I hope it will be found among you. We shall give you one Opportunity more of recovering our Affections and retaining the Connection; and that I fear will be the last.[1] My Love to Mrs. Sargent and your Sons.[2] My best Wishes attend you all; being ever, with sincere Esteem, and the most grateful Sense of your long continu'd Friendship, Dear Sir, Your affectionate humble Servant   B FRANKLIN

Mr Sargent

Editorial Note on the Pennsylvania Committee of Safety

On June 30, 1775, in response to a recommendation from the Philadelphia committee of inspection and observation, the Pennsylvania Assembly created a committee of safety.[3] Twenty-five members were named, Franklin among them.[4] The committee's function was military: to call into service as many associators as it thought necessary, to pay them, and

---

8. The preceding document.

9. BF had expected this to happen when war began (above, XXI, 584), and perhaps for that reason jumped to the conclusion that it was happening. The first circumstantial account of the Battle of Bunker Hill reached Philadelphia on the 24th and was read to the Congress on the 26th; the burning of Charlestown during the battle was quickly seized upon as an example of wanton destruction. Burnett, *Continental Congress*, p. 83; *JCC*, II, 152, 165, 216.

1. The Olive Branch Petition (see the note on it below, July 8, 1775) had been before the Congress since June 19.

2. George, Arnold, and John: above, X, 365 n.

3. For the recommendation and the creation of the committee see 8 *Pa. Arch.* VIII, 7239–40, 7247.

4. Attendance shrank at times to three or four, and the committee continued to do business. See its minutes in *Pa. Col. Recs.*, X, 282–453.

to supply their necessities; to encourage the manufacture of saltpetre; and, a broad rubric, to provide for defending the province against insurrection and invasion. For these purposes the committee was to draw upon the provincial treasury. At the first committee meeting, on July 3, Franklin was unanimously chosen president. For the next seven weeks he attended assiduously; out of forty-six meetings he missed only three. From late August until he left for Cambridge in early October he was present roughly half the time. The new assembly reappointed him on October 19, when some members were dropped and others added, and the next day the committee re-elected him president.[5] But after he returned in November he attended only on rare occasions.

The various activities of the committee, as recorded in its minutes and in the fragments of its correspondence that survive, were as broad as its authorization implied. It sought out gunpowder, saltpetre, lead, and other military supplies; it organized a naval force and arranged, probably at Franklin's instigation, for the placement of chevaux-de-frise to block the Delaware;[6] it established regulations for the militia and recommended defensive measures to the Assembly; it interrogated suspects and disposed of prisoners of war; it negotiated with local committees and Congress about commissions in the armed forces of the province.[7] When at the end of 1775 Congress authorized four new battalions for continental service, the selection of their officers at the committee's meetings in early January brought out virtually all the members who had never before attended. Franklin was present on three of these occasions, and again on January 10. Thereafter he was absent, and in late February he resigned.[8]

5. *Ibid.*, pp. 373–4 and *passim*; Ryerson, *Revolution Is Now Begun*, p. 140.
6. These obstacles were commonly credited to BF: John W. Jackson, *The Pennsylvania Navy, 1775–1781: the Defense of the Delaware* (New Brunswick, N.J., [1974]), pp. 154, 156. Later evidence—his own—suggests that BF had the original idea, or at least came to believe so. "Il imagine les Chevaux de frise," Le Veillard reported his saying years later, "pour empêcher l'approche des Vaisseaux de guerre, c'est une nouvelle invention qui peut servir a fermer les Ports, elle a un très grande [*sic*] Effet . . . . " Boyd, *Jefferson Papers*, IX, 497.
7. In addition to the minutes just cited see Agnes Hunt, *The Provincial Committees of Safety in the American Revolution* (n. p., 1904), pp. 84–97. For the most recent interpretation of the committee's role see Ryerson, *op. cit.*, pp. 122–4, 126–8, 132–4, 140, 146, 150, 157, 164, 200–1, 225, 227, 235, 238–41.
8. BF to the Speaker of the Assembly below, Feb. 26. Robert Morris was elected vice president on Oct. 20 (*Pa. Col. Recs.*, X, 374); he attended regularly until November, and acted as chairman in BF's absence. Thereafter, when the minutes tell who was in the chair, a succession of members presided with no apparent pattern. On only two occasions was BF present and not chairing: on

During his term of service the committee carried on an extensive correspondence, much of which is included in its minutes. These letters and orders may be considered to fall within our original rubric, but are so numerous that to take notice of each would clutter the volume with routine business in which Franklin could have played at most an extremely minor part.[9] We have therefore confined ourselves to those documents that were addressed to or signed by him, and have summarized such of them as relate to relatively trivial matters. The result is a sample, wide-ranging if arbitrary, of the committee's work.

From Charles-Guillaume-Frédéric Dumas[1]

ALS: American Philosophical Society

Monsieur,   La Haie 30e Juin 1775

En réponse à la Lettre toute obligeante dont vous m'avez favorisé en date du 24 Fevrier 1774, puisque j'ai eu le bonheur de rencontrer votre goût dans le choix des nouvautés que vous avez bien voulu recevoir de moi, cela m'enhardit à continuer de vous payer le tribut de mes petits travaux. Je sens combien il est chétif; mais le desir *extrême* et constant que j'ai de faire exister les seuls témoignages en mon pouvoir de ma grande estime pour votre personne et pour tous les braves Américains, suppléera, j'espere, à ce qui lui manque de mérite intrinseque.

On a fini d'imprimer l'hiver passé une nouvelle édition du Droit des gens de Vattel. Je n'ai pu refuser aux sollicitations de certaines gens d'en être l'Editeur. Ce qu'il y a de curieux, c'est qu'à la réserve de mes idées touchant les peines, que ces gens connoissent et approuvent, toutes les autres theses que je soutiens, tant dans mes notes que dans une Lettre que j'ai mise à la tête de l'édition, sont justement l'opposé de ce qu'on vouloit de moi; et mon histoire à cet égard ressemble fort au conte de Balaam: on s'attendoit que je maudirois des tyrans beaucoup moins odieux que ceux que

---

Oct. 4, the day when he left for Cambridge, and on Jan. 10, his final meeting. *Ibid.*, pp. 354, 452.

9. The original rubric is open to interpretation, but seems to commit us to take notice of each document written to or by the committee: above, I, xxxiv–vi. To do so, when most of this material is in print in *Pa. Col. Recs.*, and *Pa. Arch.*, would be an unjustifiable waste of time, effort, and space.

1. Much of this letter repeats and expands on Dumas' earlier one above, May 17, part of which he summarizes in his postscript.

l'on bénit; et j'ai fait le rebours: je doute qu'on me le pardonne; et je m'en console.[2]

Voici donc, Monsieur, trois exemplaires de ce Vattel: un pour votre Bibliotheque, un autre pour celle de Philadelphie, et un troisieme pour telle autre Bibliotheque et Province que vous voudrez. Vous trouverez sur un feuillet blanc, à la tête de chacun, mon idée sur le Gouvernement et la Royauté. Je la crois neuve et pourtant la plus simple de toutes, et la seule juste et saine. Impraticable, et par conséquent inutile et dangereuse à discuter en Europe, j'ai cru que, semée en Amérique, elle y pourra prendre racine, germer et fructifier un jour.

J'ajoute au paquet une couple d'exemplaires d'une traduction hâtée que j'ai faite de l'Extrait des Actes de votre Congrès général dans le temps où ces pieces parurent chez nous dans leur primeur en Anglois.[3] Il me seroit difficile de vous dire, Monsieur, combien les Pieces qu'il contient ont été goûtées et admirées généralement, et l'horreur avec laquelle on voit Saturne dévorer ses enfans.

Vous trouverez encore, Monsieur, un petit Livre dans ce paquet, les Droits de Dieu de la Nature et des gens tirés de la Défense de la nation Britannique etc. par Abbadie, avec le Discours du Jurisconsulte Noodt sur les Droits des Souverains. On a réimprimé cela chez nous; on m'a fait présent d'un Exemplaire, et j'ai cru ne pouvoir mieux en disposer, que pour la Bibliotheque de Philadelphie, où je le crois à sa place, sur-tout dans les circonstances présentes.[4]

J'eusse voulu vous envoyer deux autres Pieces: mais elles ne sont

2. For the edition see the note on *ibid*; in his introductory letter Dumas hailed the voice of true liberty in the colonies. We do not follow his reference to tyrants, but the central point is clear. "Balak said unto Balaam, what hast thou done unto me? I took thee to curse mine enemies, and, behold, thou hast blessed them altogether." Numbers 23:11.

3. For the *Extracts* see above, XXI, 390–1. Dumas' translation may well have been, if the imprint is fictitious, *Lettres du congres general de Philadelphie aux habitans des colonies americaines et au peuple de la Grande Bretagne suivies de l'extrait de leurs resolutions . . .* (London, 1775).

4. Jacques Abbadie, a French Huguenot clergyman, wrote a defense of the Glorious Revolution published in 1692; a lecture on sovereign power by Gerard Noodt, rector of the University of Leyden, was printed in 1707. Dumas sent a recent amalgam of the two, *Les Droits de Dieu, de la nature et des gens, tirés d'un livre de M. Abbadie . . . . On y a ajouté un discours de M. Noodt sur les droits des souverains . . .* (Amsterdam, 1775).

pas encore finies d'imprimer. L'une vous intéresse, Monsieur, particulierement: on continue à Leide les recherches que vous avez
commencées sur le phénomene de l'huile répandue dans l'eau; et
il a paru là-dessus une brochure in 8vo en Hollandois, dont la
Compagnie des Indes et l'Amirauté ont ordonné que tous les Capi-
taines de Vaisseaux emporteroient un Exemplaire en partant pour
leurs voyages, et feroient des expériences avec l'huile. On m'a prié
de mettre cela en François: ce que j'ai fait, en y ajoutant quelques
notes critiques de mon cru.[5]

L'autre Piece est un court Exposé de ce qui s'est passé entre la
Cour Br. et les Colonies depuis la paix de 1763 jusqu'à présent.
Cela n'est pas de moi: je ne suis pas assez instruit pour un pareil
ouvrage; mais le Manuscrit m'a passé par les mains; et j'en ai
conseillé la publication, en attendant que, tous ces troubles finis,
quelque Tacite moderne Américain nous donne tout cela en
détail.[6] Alors ce sera l'un des morceaux de l'Histoire du monde les
plus importants, les plus saillants, les plus féconds à peindre avec
des traits de maître. Le beau champ pour un grand génie! Les vices
aux prises avec les vertus! Le crépuscule d'une révolution totale
dans le monde! Sept ou huit *Etats nouveaux* appellés par la Providence à nous retracer les beaux âges de l'ancienne Grece! Monu-
mens éternels d'Admiration et de reconnoissance à ériger aux
généreux défenseurs de la liberté et de la patrie, que le fer parricide
a consumés, auxquels convient si bien cette belle Epitaphe des
Spartiates tués aux Thermopyles: *Passant, va annoncer à Lacédémone
que nous sommes morts ici pour obéir à ses Loix!*[7]

Le départ du Vaisseau ne me permettant pas de mettre ces deux
brochures dans le paquet, je les garderai pour une autre fois, dans
l'espoir que vous voudrez bien me permettre, Monsieur, de cul-
tiver toujours l'honneur de votre correspondance.

L'Impôt exorbitant mis en France il y a 4 ou 5 ans sur l'entrée
des Livres étrangers, en rebutant les Libraires forains d'imprimer
pour ce Royaume, m'avoit fait mettre de côté ma Traduction

5. For Dumas' translation see above, XXI, 519–20 n.

6. "Précis des différents survenus entre la Grande Bretagne et ses colonies,"
Jour. des sçavans, LXXXI (June, 1775), [177–]223. Dumas mentioned it by title
in his letter below, April 30, 1776.

7. Dumas used the same passage, quoted by Herodotus (Book VII, chap.
228), in his introduction to Vattel.

d'Anderson. L'Impôt vient d'être aboli.[8] J'ai repris cette traduction; mais d'autres occupations ne me permettent d'avancer que lentement. Je n'aurai garde d'oublier en son temps, si Dieu m'accorde vie et santé, que vous m'avez permis, Monsieur, de la dédier à votre Province; et je ferai bien plus de cas de cet honneur, que de celui de la mettre sous les auspices (comme s'exprime l'infame et basse flatterie) de quelque Monarque que ce soit.

Soyez persuadé, Monsieur, du respect sincere et profond, qu'a pour vous et pour tous vos vertueux concitoyens Américains, Monsieur Votre très humble et très obéissant serviteur

C G F DUMAS

Dieu répande sa bénédiction sur tous les justes moyens de défense que vos braves Colonies opposent à l'oppression, et les couronne de succès, et d'une paix avantageuse et solide!

Je fais bien des voeux en particulier, pour votre santé et conservation, Monsieur, et pour la prospérité de votre chere famille.

Quoique je date de La Haie, j'écris à une Campagne de la Province. J'avois commencé une autre Lettre à Lahaie, que j'oubliai d'emporter pour la finir. On vient de m'envoyer le paquet où je l'avois laissée. Souffrez Monsieur que j'en transcrive ici le contenu.

J'ai pris la liberté, Monsieur, il y a quelques semaines, de vous recommander deux François avec leurs Epouses, qui n'étoient pas en sûreté ici où ils s'étoient réfugiés, étant menacés d'être réclamés par l'Ambassadeur de France, et par conséquent livrés en vertu d'un Concordat qui subsiste entre cette Monarchie et la République. Vous verrez, Monsieur, par ma Lettre qu'ils vous présenteront de ma part, que je les ai prévenus de ne pas s'attendre à être à charge en aucune manière à qui que ce soit, mais seulement à la bonté que vous voudrez bien avoir de les diriger par vos sages avis dans les mesures quils prendront pour se former un établissement, afin quils ne risquent pas d'être dupés dans l'acquisition que leurs petits fonds leur permettront de faire. Je sens, Monsieur, que cela ne laissera pas de vous causer quelque embarras; mais votre humanité me le pardonnera.

---

8. See Athanase J.L. Jourdan, *Recueil général des anciennes lois françaises* . . . (29 vols., Paris, [1821–]33), XXIII, 154. Ever since 1771 Dumas had been working on his translation of Adam Anderson, *An Historical and Chronological Deduction of the Origin of Commerce* . . . ; see above, XVIII, 61.

Je vous suis très obligé, Monsieur, du présent que vous m'avez fait de vos excellents Ouvrages, surtout dans leur langage original, toujours préférable à une traduction; comme aussi des pieces exquises de politique sorties de votre plume, que j'ai lues avec une admiration égale à l'interêt que je prends non seulement à ce qui touche votre personne mais aussi les dignes Colonies dont vous êtes l'honneur et l'ornement.[9] Les Gazettes Américaines aussi, dont vous avez eu la bonté de me ré[galer] m'ont fait passer des heures bien agréables.

Voilà donc la guerre civile déclarée. Je m'y attendois. Je craignois même qu'une trop longue patience et débonnaireté ne fût funeste, en donnant le temps aux ennemis de la liberté de se fortifier, et de semer la division parmi les Colonies alliées. Avec tout cela je fus frappé et ému à la Lecture de l'Action du 19 Avril dans nos Gazettes.[1] Tout nécessaire qu'est devenu le mal, il ne m'en parut pas moins terrible. Puisse-t-il n'être funeste qu'aux têtes atroces et aux coeurs corrompus qui ont réduit tant de braves gens à l'affreuse extrémité de tuer leurs freres ou d'en être tués. En attendant, les yeux de toute l'Europe sont tournés sur votre Continent; et à la réserve de quelques sordides rentiers interessés dans les fonds publics des tyrans de l'Amérique, tous les voeux de l'ancien monde sont en faveur des braves habitans du nouveau.

Endorsed: M Dumas

From Jonathan Shipley

Incomplete autograph copy: Yale University Library

Dear Sir   [June 1775]
I would give much more than I can afford for one hours friendly Conversation with You. Writing is a tedious dilatory Business and tis impossible to enter into those Details which go to the Essence and Marrow of the Subject and enable us to judge with clearness and confidence.

9. The "Ouvrages" he had already acknowledged in his May letter. The "pieces exquises" were, we presume, BF's two satires above, XX, 389–99, 413–18.

1. See the *Gaz. de Leyde ou nouvelles extraordinaires de divers endroits* (Leyden), no. XLVII, June 9, 1775.

Since my last the face of things is grown not only alarming but horrible. A civil War is begun; for whatever some of my Countrymen may do, I will never give the name of Rebels to Men who fight for their Liberties. You can hardly concieve the astonishment that was occasiond here by the commencement of hostilities. I own I had my share in it; for I flatterd myself that the present Ministers would either alter their measures, or shrink away from the Brink of the Precipice; or else that they would resign or be forcd to resign the direction of affairs in to abler Hands. But as yet no good Symptom of this sort appears. Our Deliverance from the Rocks and Shoals that surround us must depend upon their Wisdom, who have steer'd us into the midst of them. In this situation what can a Man do who loves his Country and is no Friend to Administration? For my own part I will lose no opportunity of bearing a publick Testimony against these violent and destructive measures. And I will endeavour within my own narrow Province to convince my Fellow Citizens that our Quarrel is not national, but ministerial; that the People of England have no real interest in the Contest, tho' they may be infinite Sufferers by the Event; and that We can hope for no Advantage but from a speedy and equitable Reconciliation. I insist upon it that the ministerial Language is not true, that the Sense of the People is [not?] with them. I know not one, not even among themselves, who approves of all their measures and very few who approve of any. Many I meet with who are warmly and heartily your Friends and some whose constant Toast is Success to the Americans, in which, to own the Truth, I cannot join. My Toast is, Success to neither Party, but Peace and Good Will to both.

The only point in which Administration seem to have the People on their side is in asserting the Sovereignty of the Mother Country. But this would be to engage two Nations in a civil War about the meaning of a metaphysical Term. If by Sovereignty is meant that Power describd in the declaratory Law of making Laws for You in all cases whatsoever; or that absolute unlimited Power which contrary to Sense and Experience is supposd by Civilians, who borrowd their Ideas from Schoolmen[2] to exist necessarily in every State; I take this to be a sort of Sovereignty which You will

2. Authorities on Roman or civil law, in other words, who borrowed from medieval theorists.

not submit to and no reasonable Englishman would wish to enforce. But if We mean by Sovereignty that just mixture of Power and Authority which is necessary to carry on the common Interest, and on great occasions to exert the Strength of the whole, and which ought to be applied most religiously to these Purposes, and to these only; such a Sovereignty as this I think may be fairly claimd by England, and would meet, I hope, but little opposition in America. And even this Sovereignty should be precisely quantum sufficit, neither more nor less. I would reduce it to what the Mathematicians call a Minimum. No Man can be intitled to any power over their Equals unless for very good purposes.

I consider Peace as a Good so necessary to both Countries, that I wish and recommend that any Proposal of Treaty might be listend to, and any tolerable Terms, that would not require the sacrifice of essential Rights, might be accepted. We have burnt our Fingers so throughly, that You need never apprehend such Flippancies from us again. Our Ministers who refusd so often to listen to your Petitions are now begging for them. Tho I do not love them yet rather than prolong our publick Dangers and Calamities I would give them the Honour of closing the Breaches they have made, and suffer them to continue the Abuse of their power in England as long as Heaven shall permit.

I have just read over a long 5 s. performance intitled Remarks on the principal Acts of the 13th Parliament &c. by Lind the Author of some sensible Letters on the present state of Poland.[3] He labours to decide our Controversies by the interpretation of Charters and Acts of Parliament, by Facts and Narratives and such Topicks, as furnish matter for endless Debate and lead to no certain Conclusion. The grounds of natural Right and publick Utility, which ought to determine every thing are totally omitted. He shows Cleverness in condemning some of the ministerial measures; but He approves the worst of them. It is a visionary Idea to accommodate matters by reserving to ourselves the right of taxa-

---

3. John Lind (1737–81), an ex-cleric who was now studying for the bar, had spent some time at the Polish court and made a name for himself by attacking the partition of the country in *Letters Concerning the Present State of Poland* . . . (London, 1773). He was a close friend of Jeremy Bentham, who claimed credit for the plan of Lind's *Remarks on the Principal Acts of the Thirteenth Parliament* . . . (London, 1775). *DNB*. The book is entitled the first volume, but no more appeared. Both works were published anonymously.

tion; but to limit that right by requiring from You only a certain moderate proportion of the publick Expences. If there is such a Proportion in nature, which I doubt much, I believe our Ministers would neither find it, nor know where to look for it. It would be unjust too not to let You use your own Judgment in the Disposal of your own Money. If You contribute this proportional Quota your Money like ours, may be sacrificd to ministerial Extravagance, to Projects You dislike, or Jobbs You detest. Why should We endeavour to alter the good old way of Requisition? I am confident an honest Minister will allways gain more by your Generosity than by any Smithfield[4] Bargain We can make at present.

The same Author asserts that all Property is derivd from the liberality of Government; that every thing in this Kingdom belongs to our Rulers, and that they are to divide the good things to their Subjects in what proportion they please, and that every Man ought to be thankful for what is left to him. This Doctrine is rare news for Ld. Sandwich and Rigby;[5] but indeed it has not the merit of Novelty; for it was taught by Hobbes long ago. I am not of an intolerant Spirit and yet I should think it no great Crime to hang the Teachers of such Principles.

There is another Ministerial Pamphlet in the form of a Letter to You from the People of England, written by Sr. J. Dalrymple, so well known by his Publications and the Abuse they have brought upon him. A Large Cargo of them I am told is sent to the Colonies.[6] It is written with Sense and Temper, it endeavours to coax

4. Shrewd or hard.

5. For Sandwich see above, X, 412 n; XXI, 581 n. Richard Rigby (1722–88) was a notorious placeman who, like the First Lord, strongly opposed conciliation. Namier and Brooke, *House of Commons*, III, 358.

6. Sir John Dalrymple (1726–1810) was a prolific and controversial writer; see the *DNB*. His *Memoirs of Great Britain and Ireland* . . . (3 vols., London, 1771), which covered the period 1681–90, had been attacked for libeling heroes of the Revolution; see for example A. Francis Steuart, ed., *The Last Journals of Horace Walpole* . . . (2 vols., London and N.Y., 1910), I, 179–80, 271–3, 294. A reviewer agreed with Shipley that the anonymous pamphlet, *The Address of the People of Great-Britain to the Inhabitants of America* (London, 1775), was written by Dalrymple and paid for by the government for distribution in America, "apparently to co-operate with a late conciliatory resolution of the House of Commons. It is replete with expressions of tender affection for the inhabitants of the Colonies, and paints the measures and intentions of government toward them in the softest and most pleasing colours . . . . " *Monthly Rev.*, LII (1775), 540.

and to terrify; but with all its smoothness I think it will hardly perswade You to allow that the late Acts You complain of were just and moderate measures. However it shows that Ministry has alterd its Disposition and its Stile. They have alterd them so much, that to my certain Knowledge some of those who encouragd the illiberal Treatment You met with, have expressed the highest opinion of your Wisdom and Integrity and hope that your great Talents, your Love of your Country and your high Character in America will all operate towards a general happy Reconciliation.

The Minstry I am confident wish for Peace; but the Party amongst them that has hitherto prevaild would risk the Ruin of both Countries rather than part with their places. There is no appearance here of a Tendency to Peace, tho every body wishes for it. The Stocks keep up in a manner that cannot be accounted for. Some Art may have been usd and We have had some favourable Accidents. A surprising Demand from European Markets has made us as yet not sensible of the Loss of our American Trade.[7] People in general judge from their feelings and they have not yet begun to feel.

I own for my part I long for Peace. Every Hour may bring on new Calamities and (what may be worse in its consequences) every new calamity may increase that national hatred which I fear on your side has already gone too far. Indeed it is not so with us. The Majority here neither hate nor blame You.

I almost think I could demonstrate that Union and Friendship between our two Countries would be of infinite advantage to both and of yet more to yours than our own. The wise and the good on both sides, I trust, will do the little they can to restore them. But the wise and good who would use Power well, are seldom fortunate or enterprizing enough to get it. Providence governs us by the rough discipline of Experience and chiefly by the Experience of Evil. We must be content to foresee and to suffer the Calamities We cannot prevent. It is however my most firm Belief and Com-

---

7. Horace Walpole agreed that art had been used: "The keeping up of the stocks was the inexplicable phenomenon of the year, and which, it is just to say, the Government managed with great address." Steuart, *op. cit.*, I, 477. For the "favourable Accidents" see Thomas S. Ashton, *Economic Fluctuations in England, 1700–1800* (Oxford, 1959), pp. 160–1.

fort that He who acts a virtuous part will be rewarded some where or other.

But these publick Scenes of Wrath and Distress are not the whole of our Misfortunes. We must hope no more to see You at Twyford to enjoy your Friendship and Society so improving to me, and so agreable to my Wife and Daughters. Nobody now will convey Philosophical truth to us in common Chit Chat and make us wiser without the trouble of learning. They all desire their Love to You (Georgiana insists on being particularly nam'd).[8] They have lost their good Friend and are sensible of their Loss.

But after all why should I indulge these desponding Thoughts? Our Miseries perhaps may bring us to our Senses. (Indeed that seems to be the only vehicle of Instruction that the present Administration can profit by). After serving and reconciling the Mother Country and her Colonies, why may You not return to be respected, honour'd, and consulted by the Greatest in this Country? Our Men of Place and Titles will then be forcd to own that a Private Man may be wiser than themselves.

I love my poor Country and pray for it's Peace and Liberty; and I wish a long continuance of Peace and Liberty to America, to America, that is, in my eyes, the fairest the noblest, the most promising Work of Providence. But while You hate and despise our Ministers, in which You differ but little from ourselves, forget not how much You owe to the Virtue and Moderation of our Ancestors.[9]

Notation: Copy of my Letter to Dr. Franklin June 1775 / [*In another hand:*] (Bp of St Asaph)

Four Pennsylvania Delegates in Congress to the Philadelphia Committee of Inspection and Observation[1]

DS: Historical Society of Pennsylvania

Philip Skene had made a protracted visit to England and Ireland. During it he had furnished information to the ministry, and been rewarded with

8. For the Shipley family see above, XVIII, 199–202 ns.
9. The Bishop presumably did not copy his complimentary close.
1. The predecessor of the committee to which BF was elected in August; see the headnote on the Assembly's instructions above, May 9. The committee's activities are described in Ryerson, *Revolution Is Now Begun*, pp. 94–6 *et seq.*

appointments as inspector of crown lands and lieutenant governor of Ticonderoga and Crown Point.[2] When he returned to America he landed in Philadelphia, where he was promptly arrested on suspicion that Whitehall had sent him to bribe delegates.[3] Congress appointed a committee to examine his papers, and on June 27 ordered him sent under guard to Connecticut; the Pennsylvania delegation was charged with handling the matter. On July 5 a companion of his by the name of Lundy was ordered to go with him.[4] The Pennsylvania delegates apparently began to carry out their commission on July 3 and then, when Lundy was added two days later, hastily revised their letter to make it apply to both men.

Philada. July 3[–5?]. 1775.[5]

By order of the Continental Congress The Committee of the City of Philada. are earnestly recommended Immediately to Convey Major Philip Skeene and Mr. Lundy and deliver thim[6] to the Committee of New York who are requested to Convey him to Hartford in Connecticut. There to Deliver thim and the Order of Congress to the Committee of that Town And that this be done in the most Effectual Manner and the utmost care taken that he does not Escape. The Expences Will be paid by Congress.[7]

B FRANKLIN
GEO: ROSS
JOHN DICKINSON
JAMES WILSON[8]

Endorsed: July 3d. 1775 B. Franklin George Ross J Dickinson and Jas Wilsons Order to convey Major Skeene & Mr Lundy to New York

2. Above, XXI, 207 n; *Dartmouth MSS*, II, 269.
3. Burnett, *Continental Congress*, pp. 72–3; Smith, *Letters*, I, 456 n, 471–2, 479–80, 484–5. See also Wharton to BF above, April 17.
4. *JCC*, II, 82, 86, 108–9, 126–7. See also Doris B. Morton, *Philip Skene of Skenesborough* (Granville, N.Y., 1959), pp. 38–40.
5. This line, at the end of the document, is in BF's hand; the text itself is in Ross's, and may have been written as early as June 27. The emendations to include Lundy must have been made on or soon after July 5.
6. Ross's text reads at this point "Skeene to The Committee of Trenton that they be desired to deliver him," etc. This was replaced by "and Mr. Lundy"; "him," here and in "Deliver him" below, was turned into "thim."
7. For these payments see *JCC*, III, 290, 315.
8. Ross and Wilson were prominent lawyers, one in Lancaster and the other in Carlisle, and were chairmen of their local committees and colonels in the

To William Strahan

ALS: Library of Congress; copy:[9] Pierpont Morgan Library

This famous letter was unquestionably not sent. The positive evidence is that the original remained with Franklin's papers. The negative evidence is that Strahan later gave no sign that he had received such a blast: when he responded on September 6 to a letter, now lost, from Franklin two days after this one, and when he wrote again on October 4, he showed the pain and sorrow that one friend reserves for the other's delusions, and also the implicit assumption that the relationship remained intact. On the rare occasions when Franklin lost his temper he was likely to recover it quickly.[1] This outburst was an example in point: it relieved his rage at what was happening, and went no further.

Mr. Strahan,   Philada. July 5. 1775

You are a Member of Parliament, and one of that Majority which has doomed my Country to Destruction. You have begun to burn our Towns, and murder our People. Look upon your Hands! They are stained with the Blood of your Relations! You and I were long Friends: You are now my Enemy, and I am, Yours,

B FRANKLIN

Notation: Letter to Mr Strahan July 5. 75.

From William Strahan

Copy:[2] Papers of the Earl of Dartmouth deposited in the Staffordshire County Record Office

London, July 5. 1775.

I wrote you the 7th of last Month by the Packet, to which I beg leave to refer. I have since by the Papers and by several of your

---

associators. Ross (1730–79) served with BF on the committee of safety; Wilson (1742–98), one of the outstanding legal scholars in the colonies, had recently published a pamphlet that attracted wide attention by denying Parliament's authority in America. For both men see the *DAB.*

9. The copy, which is in what appears to be a later hand, is of unknown provenance; it was inserted in a volume of BF letters formerly owned by Samuel Pennypacker, but was apparently not part of that collection. The wording differs from the ALS in minor details, as if the copy had been derived from an earlier draft.

1. For an example see above, XXI, 526–9.

2. See the note on Strahan's letter above, June 7, which explains how much of the correspondence in 1775 is extant and how much missing.

85

JULY 5, 1775

Friends, heard that you were safely arrived at Philadelphia, and
unanimously voted by the Assembly then sitting, one of their
Delegates to the Congress, then about to meet.[3] I make no doubt
but your Reception among your Friends was abundantly cordial,
and I hope you will avail yourself of the great Knowledge you
possess, respecting the Matters in dispute between your Country
and this, to bring about a speedy Reconciliation. I see all your
public Papers are filled with your Unanimity and Preparations for
War. All this, however, seems to make no Impression here, or to
have the least tendency to any Alteration of Measures. What Time
may produce, I will not pretend to say. To me, I own, it appears,
that after the Concessions lately made by Lord Dartmouth, and
which seem to be rather more explicit than Lord North's conciliatory Motion of Feb. 20th.,[4] there is little to be done till one Side
or the other become sensible of the pernicious Consequences that
must necessarily attend a Continuation of the Quarrel. If nothing
less than a total Renunciation of the Legislature, of all Authority
over the Colonies will satisfy them, God knows where the Dispute
will end; for I am perswaded this will never be given up here. At
least, I see no Tendency towards it. And if the Colonies should
actually succeed in their Struggle to be totally emancipated from
all Subjection to, or Connection with Britain, it will remain to be
seen whether their Liberty and Security will or will not be mate-
rially affected by it; Whether it may not throw them under the
Dominion of some enterprising Leader among themselves, or leave
them a Prey to some ambitious European Power, under whom
they may *really* experience all the Evils in the highest Degree, the
very appearance of which, and that a very distant one, they now
endeavour to avoid. These you may, perhaps, consider as idle and
groundless Speculations. I wish heartily they may prove so. But
without looking so far into Futurity, the Evils of a civil War, even

3. The news was in the *Public Advertiser*, June 23, and the *London Chron.*,
June 22–24, 1775; Strahan received it also from David Hall, Jr., and WF:
PMHB, XII (1888), 250; XXXV (1911), 453–4.
4. Dartmouth conceded nothing more than North had already done. The
American Secretary glossed the conciliatory resolution of Feb. 20 (above, XXI,
591–3) in a lengthy circular letter of March 3, and on April 15 he authorized
Gage to offer conditional pardons: Carter, *Gage Correspondence*, II, 187–9,
192–3. The letter and offer, although more explicit than the original motion,
merely spelled out what the government intended.

for a short Duration, are worthy some Consideration. Possibly these may still be avoided. *Now* seems to be the critical Moment for America to obtain some permanent Constitution, in perfect Union with the Mother Country, by which her Liberties may be secured and protected by the Laws and Power of the whole Empire, and rendered as permanent in one Corner of it as in another, and every Part of it prove a mutual Protection to each other. Whether this Course will be taken we shall soon see, when the Resolutions of your Congress are made public. You are a perfect Master of the Subject, and therefore it is happy that you have a Voice in that Assembly, when so much of the Happiness of their Constituents depends upon their Proceedings. But I am somewhat afraid the Voice of Moderation will not now be listened to, and that the Violence of some Men whose Views may not be truly so patriotic as they appear to be, will inflame the Quarrel beyond a Possibility of Accommodation. This I hope you will exert all your Prudence and Sagacity to prevent. For my own Part, I have no doubt of the Prevalence of this Country in the End, should hostile Measures be pursued for any Length of Time. But, good God! Where does Victory on either Side lead to? To the immediate Destruction of half, and the ultimate Ruin of the whole, of the most glorious Fabric of Civil and Religious Government that ever existed on this Globe. If after we are both weakened by the Struggle, it terminates in our final Separation, this must unavoidably be the Consequence. However, I still hope better Things, and that perfect Order will arise from the present Convulsions. We are here in a State of the greatest Tranquility. All our Murmerings and Opposition to Government appear only in our Newspapers. I believe the Ministry are quite determined in their Operations, and in the Prosecution of coercive Measures. I see everybody is learning the Use of Arms with You; but surely it will not be attempted to distress You by Land. Our Navy is our great Strength, and sorry shall I be to see it long exerted against You; tho' if no Steps are taken towards a Reconciliation, I am afraid that must be the Case. Is not this a Situation devotely to be avoided, if any human Means can be devised to prevent it? But I will not trouble You further on this Subject at present. Had I any material Facts to convey to You, I should have satisfied myself with a bare Recital of them, without any Reflections of my own, which to You can convey no kind of Information.

87

I was truly concerned to hear the other Day that You had ordered your Books &c. to be transmitted to You; but it looks as if you gave up all Thoughts of returning to us. I hope this is not the case; as upon the whole, You have much Reason to be pleased with your Reception in this Country, putting Politics out of the Question. But were You now even resolved to remain where You are for the rest of your Days, that Resolution, I trust, will soon be broken; and I shall expect to see You in the beginning of the Winter, invested with full Powers to put an End to all our Differences; for, as I observed above, if there is any Desire left among you for a Restoration of ancient Amity, *now* is the Time to procure it on safe and honourable Terms.[5]

So may I prosper, as I wish the Liberty and Happiness of all our Brethren with You, with the same Ardor as I do our own. In this Desire I am sure we are of one Mind, however we may, at present, differ about the Methods of promoting it. May we quickly be united in Sentiment again; and may your Labours be once more confined to promoting the Arts of Peace, and encreasing the Means of human Felicity. I am ever, with the warmest Respect and Esteem &c. WILL. STRAHAN.

Copy.

To Docr: Franklin.

Docketed: London, July 5. 1775. Copy of a Letter from Will. Strahan Esqr: to Docr: Franklin.

Editorial Note on the Declaration of the Causes and Necessity for Taking Up Arms

On June 23 Congress appointed a committee of five, Franklin among them, to draft a declaration to the world that Washington would publish when he reached camp outside Boston. The committee reported its draft the next day, and on the 26th Congress, after some debate, recommitted it and added John Dickinson and Thomas Jefferson to the committee. These newcomers between them composed a second version, which was

5. BF's possessions were sent to him, as he had ordered, at some time before mid-July: JW to James Kinsey, July 12, 1775, APS. Strahan's earlier letter of June 7 had expressed much the same hope that his friend would return with power to negotiate.

reported on July 6 and adopted with minor changes. The question of which man wrote the famous declaration has generated much controversy among historians.[6] But no one to our knowledge has suggested, and we have no reason to believe, that Franklin played any part in its composition.

From Arthur Lee

ALS: American Philosophical Society

Dear Sir. July 6th. 1775.

I write to you more to prove my remembrance of you, than for the importance of any thing I have to communicate.

The two defeats near Boston seem to have made little impression on the Ministry. They still talk of great things to be expected from their Generals and Troops when united. One of your judgment will draw more information from the single word *Rebels* usd in the Gazette,[7] than from any thing I can say. Far from retracting they mean to exasperate, in perfect confidense of being successful. It is the curse of fools to be secure; and I trust their fate will prove, that the end of the wicked is punishment.

Ld. G. Germaine, the Father of the military murder Bill, is Dictator in all the military operations against America. As Cowards are often confident, when danger is at a distance, this man is not only bold himself but inspires the King and his Ministers with equal confidense.[8]

The report is that Ld. John Murray's Regiment of Highlanders, and others to be raisd by Col. Fraser are to be sent over. The former I believe is true.[9] The Scotch will fight with ten times the

6. See Boyd, *Jefferson Papers*, I, 187–92.

7. The *London Gaz.* was the official government publication.

8. For the old charge that Germain was a coward see above, XXI, 185 n. Lee is accusing him of having fathered the Mass. Administration of Justice Act, which was designed to secure, *inter alia*, fair trial of royal officials and soldiers indicted for murder: *ibid.*, p. 192. Although he was scarcely the father of the act, he did support it; see Cobbett, *Parliamentary History*, XVII (1771–74), 1312. By midsummer his influence was rising, as Lee says; but he was not yet a minister, let alone "Dictator."

9. Gen. Lord John Murray (1711–87) was colonel of the Black Watch, or 42nd Highlanders; Maj. Gen. Simon Fraser (1726–82) raised the 71st or Fraser's Highlanders at the beginning of the war and was its colonel. *DNB*; Namier and Brooke, *House of Commons*, II, 470–2. Both regiments were in

rancour and not half the bravery of the english. I can not conceive them to be formidable foes if bravely opposd. Against timid or flying enemies they act heroically.

The dissatisfaction of the Public here certainly increases every day. Shortly it will arrive to that degree, at which an untoward event or national calamity will kindle a flame destructive to all those who have plannd these fatal measures. You will see by the proceedings of the Common Hall, what are the sentiments of the City of London.[1] I am much deceivd or the Nation in general will speak the same language in a little time. Happily however America is capable of working her own salvation, or the influence of corruption and dissipation here woud render her escape from the hand of tyranny extremely doubtful.

The Revolutions of great Empires have often been forc'd, by the follies of weak and wicked men; but never before I think, did the folly of man sin so obstinately against the evidence of accumulated instruction. An overruling Providence seems to employ their ignorance and rashness for purposes which wisdom woud forsee and shrink from.

It will be of great use in proving the propriety of our proceedings, to state the number of Petitions from all the Provinces, which have been presented in vain. Not being in possession of them, nor knowing how to get them but by the Speaker of each Province sending the part of their Journals which contains them, I must beg the favor of you to endeavor to obtain that for me. There will be a moment, I am sure, when stating the repeatedly rejected Petitions of America here, will bring down vengeance upon the heads of her inveterate enemies.

———

America in time to participate in the Battle of Long Island: Sir Henry Clinton, *The American Rebellion: Sir Henry Clinton's Narrative of His Campaigns* . . . (William B. Willcox, ed.; 1971 reprint), p. 42. Both colonels stayed at home.

1. On June 24 the mayor, aldermen and livery adopted a number of resolutions, one of which denounced whoever had advised the monarch not to receive on the throne any petition from them. At the same time they drew up such a petition; it protested British policy in America, praised colonial resistance, and called for the dismissal of an administration that had corrupted Parliament. When the King refused to receive this indictment in the way they had stipulated, they withdrew and published it. On July 4 they passed further resolutions that the sovereign's conduct had made the right of petition nugatory. The next day the resolutions of June 24 and July 4 were presented without the petition, and the King received them in silence. Force, 4 *Amer. Arch.*, II, 1071–4.

Some Gentlemen here have lately found by experiment, that man can bear 180 degrees of heat, and a dog 230, without injury for 30 minutes. The heat of the Dog's body examind immediately, did not exceed 130. This proves, what I long ago observd in some experiments on Frogs, that the animal Body, when living, was endued with a power of generating Cold as well as heat.[2]   A.L.

To [Joseph Priestley[3]]

Extract printed in Benjamin Vaughan, ed., *Political, Miscellaneous, and Philosophical Pieces . . . Written by Benj. Franklin . . .* (London, 1779), pp. 552–4.

Dear Friend   Philadelphia, 7th July, 1775.

The Congress met at a time when all minds were so exasperated by the perfidy of General Gage, and his attack on the country people, that propositions of attempting an accommodation were not much relished; and it has been with difficulty that we have carried another humble petition to the crown, to give Britain one more chance, one opportunity more of recovering the friendship of the colonies;[4] which however I think she has not sense enough to embrace, and so I conclude she has lost them for ever.

She has begun to burn our seaport towns;[5] secure, I suppose, that we shall never be able to return the outrage in kind. She may doubtless destroy them all; but if she wishes to recover our commerce, are these the probable means? She must certainly be distracted; for no tradesman out of Bedlam ever thought of encreasing the number of his customers by knocking them [on][6] the head;

2. Lee had been an F.R.S. for almost a decade (*DAB*), and on the same day that he wrote he must have heard a paper by Dr. Charles Blagden, "Further Experiments and Observations in an Heated Room': *Phil. Trans.*, LXV (1775), 484–94. Blagden was reporting work on animal heat done by Dr. George Fordyce and others: Thomas Thomson, *History of the Royal Society . . .* (London, 1812), pp. 130–1.

3. As with the other letters to Priestley printed from Vaughan (above, May 16, and below, Oct. 3, 1775), WTF added MS notes on a proof sheet of Vaughan's work (Library of Congress). In this case the additions were "To Dr. Priestly" at the head of the letter and BF's initials at the end.

4. See the editorial note on the petition below, July 8, 1775.

5. See above, BF to Sargent, June 27; to Strahan, July 5.

6. Brackets are in the printed text.

or of enabling them to pay their debts by burning their houses.

If she wishes to have us subjects and that we should submit to her as our compound sovereign, she is now giving us such miserable specimens of her government, that we shall ever detest and avoid it, as a complication of robbery, murder, famine, fire and pestilence.

You will have heard before this reaches you, of the treacherous conduct . . . to the remaining people in Boston, in detaining their *goods*, after stipulating to let them go out with their *effects*; on pretence that merchants goods were not effects;[7] the defeat of a great body of his troops by the country people at Lexington; some other small advantages gained in skirmishes with their troops; and the action at Bunker's-hill, in which they were twice repulsed, and the third time gained a dear victory. Enough has happened, one would think, to convince your ministers that the Americans will fight, and that this is a harder nut to crack than they imagined.

We have not yet applied to any foreign power for assistance; nor offered our commerce for their friendship. Perhaps we never may: Yet it is natural to think of it if we are pressed.[8]

We have now an army on our establishment which still holds yours besieged.

My time was never more fully employed. In the morning at 6, I am at the committee of safety, appointed by the assembly to put the province in a state of defence; which committee holds till near 9, when I am at the congress, and that sits till after 4 in the afternoon.[9] Both these bodies proceed with the greatest una-

7. Gage's handling of these goods was the subject of Williams' complaint above, June 19. A reference to the General was clearly what was deleted, though why it should have been worse than his perfidy, mentioned in the first sentence, we are at a loss to explain. But Vaughan was nervous about publishing this and other letters from BF in the middle of the war; see his footnote on p. 550.

8. BF was already thinking of it; see his resolutions on trade below, under July 21, 1775.

9. The principal concern of the Congress during June was the organization of the army, and BF played his part. On the 10th he was appointed to a committee for obtaining saltpetre, and on the 23rd to another to draft Washington's declaration on assuming command of the troops. *JCC*, II, 86, 105. His work as president of the Pennsylvania committee of safety was also focused on organizing the provincial forces; see the editorial note on the committee above, June 30.

nimity, and their meetings are well attended. It will scarce be credited in Britain that men can be as diligent with us from zeal for the public good, as with you for thousands per annum. Such is the difference between uncorrupted new states, and corrupted old ones.

Great frugality and great industry are now become fashionable here: Gentlemen who used to entertain with two or three courses, pride themselves now in treating with simple beef and pudding. By these means, and the stoppage of our consumptive trade with Britain, we shall be better able to pay our voluntary taxes for the support of our troops.[1] Our savings in the article of trade amount to near five million sterling per annum.

I shall communicate your letter to Mr. Winthrop, but the camp is at Cambridge, and he has as little leisure for philosophy as myself.[2] . . . Believe me ever, with sincere esteem, my dear friend, Yours most affectionately

To Jonathan Shipley

ALS: Yale University Library

Philada July 7. 1775

I received with great Pleasure my dear Friends very kind Letter of April 19, as it informed me of his Welfare, and that of the amiable Family in Jermyn Street. I am much obliged by the Information of what pass'd in Parliament after my departure; in return I will endeavor to give you a short Sketch of the State of Affairs here.

I found at my arrival all America from one End of the 12 united

1. On June 22 Congress authorized the emission of $2,000,000 in bills of credit, which the colonies were pledged to redeem. *JCC*, II, 103. Further emissions soon followed. Redemption of the bills was to be through taxation, which was "voluntary" in the sense that the colonial delegates agreed to it; Congress was to set the quota for each colony according to population: Smith, *Letters*, I, 525. The quotas themselves were not fixed until July 29, and then subject to revision: *JCC*, II, 221–3. See also Ferguson, *Power of the Purse*, pp. 5–26.

2. John Winthrop, like BF, was becoming absorbed in political affairs. He had served first on the Council and then in the provincial congress, and was one of those whom the Mass. delegates in Philadelphia recommended to Washington as reliable men. In July, when the General Court was reconstituted, Winthrop was appointed to the new Council. *Sibley's Harvard Graduates*, IX, 258–60; Smith, *Letters*, I, 534.

Provinces to the other, busily employed in learning the Use of Arms. The Attack upon the Country People near Boston by the Army had rous'd every Body, and exasperated the whole Continent; The Tradesmen of this City, were in the Field twice a day, at 5 in the Morning, and Six in the Afternoon, disciplining with the utmost Diligence, all being Volunteers. We have now three Battalions, a Troop of Light Horse, and a Company of Artillery, who have made surprizing Progress. The same Spirit appears every where and the Unanimity is amazing.[3]

The day after my Arrival, I was unanimously chosen by our Assembly, then sitting, an additional Delegate to the Congress, which met the next Week. The numerous Visits of old Friends, and the publick Business has since devoured all my time: for We meet at nine in the Morning, and often sit 'till four. I am also upon a Committee of Safety appointed by the Assembly, which meets at Six, and sits 'till near nine. The Members attend closely without being bribed to it, by either Salary, Place or Pension, or the hopes of any; which I mention for your Reflection on the difference, between a new virtuous People, who have publick Spirit, and an old corrupt one, who have not so much as an Idea that such a thing exists in Nature. There has not been a dissenting Voice among us in any Resolution for Defence, and our Army which is already formed, will soon consist of above 20,000 Men.[4]

You will have heard before this reaches you of the Defeat the Ministerial Troops met with in their first *Sortie*; the several small Advantages we have since had of them,[5] and the more considerable Affair of the 17th. when after two severe Repulses, they carry'd the unfinished Trenches of the Post we had just taken on a Hill near Charlestown. They suffered greatly however, and I believe are convinc'd by this time, that they have Men to deal with, tho'

3. BF had said much the same thing, in more general terms, to Hartley on May 8. For the volunteer units that he speaks of here see the *Pa. Gaz.*, May 3, 1775; J. Thomas Scharf and Thompson Westcott, *History of Philadelphia* . . . (3 vols., Philadelphia, 1884), I, 296; W. A. Newman Dorland, "The Second Troop Philadelphia City Cavalry," *PMHB*, XLV (1921), 259.

4. For BF's concern with the military see the preceding document. His expectation of a total force of more than 20,000 was widely shared; see for example Smith, *Letters*, I, 613.

5. Presumably BF had in mind the capture in May of Ticonderoga, Crown Point, and St. Johns by forces under Ethan Allen and Benedict Arnold.

unexperienced, and not yet well arm'd. In their way to this Action, without the least Necessity, they barbarously plundered and burnt a fine, undefended Town, opposite to Boston, called Charlestown, consisting of about 400 Houses, many of them elegantly built; some sick, aged and decrepit poor Persons, who could not be carried off in time perish'd in the Flames.[6] In all our Wars, from our first settlement in America, to the present time, we never received so much damage from the Indian *Savages*, as in this one day from these. Perhaps Ministers may think this a Means of disposing us to Reconciliation. I feel and see every where the Reverse. Most of the little Property I have, consists of Houses in the Seaport Towns, which I suppose may all soon be destroyed in the same way,[7] and yet I think I am not half so reconcileable now, as I was a Month ago.

The Congress will send one more Petition to the King, which I suppose will be treated as the former was, and therefore will probably be the last;[8] for tho' this may afford Britain one chance more of recovering our Affections and retaining the Connection, I think she has neither Temper nor Wisdom enough to seize the Golden Opportunity. When I look forward to the Consequences, I see an End to all Commerce between us: on our Sea Coasts She may hold some fortified Places as the Spaniards do on the Coast of Africa, but can penetrate as little into the Country. A very numerous Fleet extending 1500 Miles at an immense Expense may prevent other Nations trading with us: but as we have or may have within ourselves every thing necessary to the Comfort of Life, and generally import only Luxuries and Superfluities, her preventing our doing that, will in some Respects contribute to our Prosperity. By the present Stoppage of our Trade we save between four and five Millions per Annum which will do something towards the Expence of the War. What *she* will get by it, I must leave to be computed by her own political Arithmeticians. These are some of my present Ideas which I throw out to you in the Freedom of Friendship. Perhaps I am too sanguine in my opinion of our Abili-

6. British artillery in Boston fired Charlestown during, not before, the Battle of Bunker Hill; Howe ordered the town destroyed because it sheltered skirmishers who were harassing his troops. William B. Willcox, *Portrait of a General: Sir Henry Clinton in the War of Independence* . . . (New York, 1964), p. 49.

7. See the note on BF to Sargent above, June 27.

8. See the editorial note that follows.

ties for the Defence of our Country after we shall have given up our Seaports to Destruction: but a little time will shew.

General Gage we understand enter'd into a Treaty with the Inhabitants of Boston, whom he had confin'd by his Works, in which Treaty it was agreed that if they delivered their Arms to the Select Men, their own Magistrats, they were to be permitted to go out with their *Effects*. As soon as they had so delivered their Arms, he seiz'd them, and then cavil'd about the meaning of the word *Effects* which he said was only wearing Apparel and Household Furniture, and not Merchandize or Shop Goods which he therefore detains: And the continual Injuries and Insults they met with from the Soldiery, made them glad to get out by relinquishing all that kind of Property.[9] How much those People have suffered, and are now suffering rather than submit to what they think unconstitutional Acts of Parliament is really amazing. Two or three Letters I send you inclosed may give you some, tho' a faint Idea of it. Gage's Perfidy has now made him universally detested. When I consider that all this Mischief is done my Country, by Englishmen and Protestant Christians, of a Nation among whom I have so many personal Friends, I am ashamed to feel any Consolation in a prospect of Revenge; I chuse to draw it rather from a Confidence that we shall sooner or later obtain Reparation; I have proposed therefore to our People that they keep just Accounts and never resume the Commerce or the Union, 'till Satisfaction is made.[1] If it is refused for 20 Years, I think we shall then be able to take it with Interest.

Your excellent Advice was, that if we must have a War, let it be carried on as between Nations who had once been Friends, and wish to be so again. In this ministerial War against us, all Europe is conjur'd not to sell us Arms or Amunition, that we may be found defenceless, and more easily murdered.[2] The humane Sir

9. See JW to BF above, June 19.

1. We have found no record of such a proposal, which differs from his suggested reparation for closing the port (below, p. 125). At about this time he apparently prepared, but did not submit to Congress, a number of propositions that are now lost (below, p. 139). Even if this was one of them, it was not "proposed . . . to our People."

2. Whitehall's effort, directed primarily against the Netherlands, to stop the importation of arms into the colonies had begun the previous October: above, XXI, 412 n. In March, 1775, the States General put strict conditions on the

W: Draper, who had been hospitably entertain'd in every one of our Colonies, proposes, in his Papers call'd the Traveller to excite the Domestic Slaves, you have sold us, to cut their Master's Throats. Dr. Johnson a Court Pensioner, in his *Taxation no Tyranny* adopts and recommends that Measure, together with another of hiring the Indian savages to assassinate our Planters in the Back-Settlements.³ They are the poorest and most innocent of all People; and the Indian manner is to murder and scalp Men Women and Children. His Book I heard applauded by Lord Sandwich in Parliament, and all the ministerial People recommended it. Lord Dunmore and Governor Martin, have already, we are told, taken some Steps towards carrying one part of the Project into Execution, by exciting an Insurrection among the Blacks. And Governor Carleton, we have certain Accounts, has been very industrious in engaging the Indians to begin their horrid Work.⁴ This is making War like Nations who never had been Friends, and never wish to be such while the World stands. You see I am warm:

---

export of war materials: *Pa. Gaz.*, May 17, June 7, 1775; Friedrich Edler, *The Dutch Republic and the American Revolution* (Johns Hopkins University Studies in Historical and Political Science, XXIX, no. 2; Baltimore, 1911), pp. 25–7.

3. Sir William Draper (1721–87) had embarked on his American tour in 1770, and climaxed it by marrying a Delancey. *DNB*. In his *Thoughts of a Traveller upon Our American Disputes* (London, 1774) he suggested that freeing the slaves would force the colonists to sue for pardon. Samuel Johnson's pamphlet also advocated manumission, and then providing the freed slaves with arms and tools in their own settlements. His further suggestion of arming and training the Indians he advanced as a "ridiculous proposal." Edward L. McAdam *et al.*, eds., *The Yale Edition of the Works of Samuel Johnson*, (10 vols. to date, London and New Haven, 1958–), X, 452–3.

4. BF's suspicions of Dunmore and Martin, governors respectively of Virginia and North Carolina, were widely shared. See for Dunmore *Pa. Gaz.*, May 3, 1775; *Va. Mag. of History and Biography*, XIII (1906), 48–50; John P. Kennedy, ed., *Journals of the House of Burgesses of Virginia, 1773–1776* (Richmond, 1905), p. 234, 256; Benjamin Quarles, *The Negro in the American Revolution* (Chapel Hill, [1961]), pp. 21–2. For Martin see William L. Saunders *et al.*, eds., *Colonial and State Records of North Carolina* (30 vols., Raleigh, etc., N.C., 1866–1914), X, 43, 46, 118, and the frequent references in the same vol. to the disarming of blacks. Carleton, Governor of Quebec, was supposed to be inciting the Indians to a border war; this supposition became a major grievance of the Congress and a reason for the invasion of Canada. Smith, *Letters*, I, 369, 439, 542–4; *JCC*, II, 108–10, 152–3, 167; Jack M. Sosin, "The Use of Indians in the War of the American Revolution: a Re-assessment of Responsibility," *Canadian Hist. Rev.*, XLVI (1965), 105, 107–10.

and if a Temper naturally cool and phlegmatic can, in old age, which often cools the warmest, be thus heated, you will judge by that of the general Temper here, which is now little short of Madness. We have however as yet ask'd no foreign Power to assist us, nor made any Offer of our Commerce to other Nations for their Friendship. What another year's Persecution may drive us to, is yet uncertain. I drop this disagreeable Subject; and will take up one, that I know must afford you and the good Family, as my Friends, some Pleasure. It is the State of my own Family, which I found in good Health; my Children affectionately dutifull and attentive to every thing that can be agreeable to me;[5] with three very promising Grandsons, in whom I take great Delight.[6] So that were it not for our publick Troubles, and the being absent from so many that I love in England, my present Felicity would be as perfect, as in this World one could well expect it. I enjoy however, what there is of it while it lasts, mindfull at the same time that its Continuance is like other earthly Goods, uncertain. Adieu my dear Friend, and believe me ever, with sincere and great Esteem Yours most Affectionately   B FRANKLIN

My respectfull Compliments to Mrs. Shipley.

Your Health on this side the Water is every where drank by the Name of THE Bishop.

I send for your Amusement a Parcel of our Newspapers. When you have perused them, please to give them to Mr. Hartley of Golden Square.

Addressed: Lord Bishop of St. Asaph / [*deleted:* Jermyn Street / London / *In another hand:*] at Twyford / near / Winchester

Editorial Note on the Olive Branch Petition

By the beginning of June, 1775, the shadow of coming events lay over the delegates in Philadelphia. Boston was informally besieged, New York went in fear of British attack, and at any moment the colonies might find themselves at the point of no return. Moderates were appalled

---

5. A remarkable statement in view of his relations with WF, for which see the headnote to BF to Galloway above, May 8.

6. WTF and the two young Baches, Benjamin Franklin, now almost six, and the two-year-old William.

at the prospect, and recoiled from commitment to civil war until the last stone had been turned in search of compromise. They faced strong opposition in Congress, but eventually secured agreement, grudging in many cases, for a final appeal to the King. On June 3 a committee of five, including Franklin, was appointed to draw up a petition. On the 19th the committee submitted its draft, the work of John Dickinson, which the Congress adopted on July 8 with virtually no amendment, and which all its members signed as individuals. The petition was couched in generalities, as it had to be to secure approval. Although it professed deep loyalty, it offered no concessions and asked for none, except the repeal of unspecified statutes that distressed the colonies.[7] It left the whole problem of reconciliation to the ingenuity of Whitehall, and there it made small impression because, as William Knox pointed out, "not one profession of what they will submit to is contained in it."[8]

No evidence has come to light that Franklin played any part in framing the petition, or had any real hope for it. On its arrival, he was quoted as saying months later, "the Ministry might think best to relax a little but it was by no means to be trusted to."[9] During his negotiations in London the previous winter he had offered specific and uncompromising terms, and had not coated them with professions of American loyalty; his approach had been crisply practical. Even by that time he had lost all faith in petitioning as a method of redress, and he had seen Whitehall's studied neglect of the petition from the first Congress.[1] When he now concurred in this gesture from the second, the reason was presumably that he wanted every effort made, however hopeless, before accepting the alternative of war.[2]

To Mary Hewson

ALS: Yale University Library

My dear Friend   Philada. July 8. 1775
I thank you for your kind Letter of April 11th. It grieves me that the present Situation of publick Affairs, makes it not eligible for you to come hither with your Family, because I am sure you

---

7. For the history of the petition see Richard B. Morris *et al.*, eds., *John Jay, the Making of a Revolutionary: Unpublished Papers*, 1745–1780 (New York, 1975), pp. 147–52. The text may be found in *JCC*, II, 158–62 and, with bibliographical references, in Boyd, *Jefferson Papers*, I, 219–23.

8. Knox Papers, Clements Library, IX, 15. The petition went unanswered; see the note on BF to Hartley below, Oct. 3, 1775.

9. Smith, *Letters*, II, 123.

1. See above, XXI, 476, 497.

2. See BF to Shipley, above, May 15.

would otherwise like this Country, and might provide better here for your Children, at the same time that I should be made more happy by your Neighbourhood and Company. I flatter myself that this may yet happen, and that our public Disputes may be ended by the time your private Business is settled to your Mind, and then we may be all happy together.[3]

The Debt you mention of mine to Bolton remain'd unpaid thro' his own Neglect. I was charg'd by Mathews £10 for the Tea Kitchen;[4] but Bolton told me I ought not to pay so much; that he would see what it should be when he got home, and send me word, which he never did. I dunn'd him for it by Letters, as often as Mathews sent to me, but receiv'd no Answer.

I take it kindly of my Godson, that he should remember me; my Love to him. I am glad to hear the dear Children are all well through the Measles. I have much Delight in my Grandsons. Mr. and Mrs. Bache join in Love to you and yours. Ben, when I delivered him your Blessing, enquired the Age of Elizabeth, and thought her yet too young for him; but as he made no other Objection, and that will lessen every day, I have only to wish being alive to dance with your Mother at the Wedding.[5]

Temple was much oblig'd by your kind Remembrance of him. He is now very happy with his Father at Amboy near Newyork, but returns to me in September, to prosecute his Studies in our College.[6]

I am much pleas'd with the Contribution Letter, and thank you for your Share in it.[7] I am still well and hearty, and never went

3. In her missing letter of April 11 Polly must have discussed her dream— which came true eleven years later—of emigrating with her family to America. The private business that detained her, which had to do with her legacy, is discussed in her letter below of Dec. 12.

4. A large tea kettle or urn, probably the one that BF had sent WF in March, 1773: above, XX, 90. William Matthews, a London watch-maker, was Boulton's chief agent in the city, charged with soliciting orders, showing designs and samples, dealing with craftsmen who made parts, and collecting bills: Nicholas Goodison, *Ormolu: the Work of Matthew Boulton* ([London, 1974]), pp. 86–7. For Boulton, whom BF had known for years, see above, X, 39, and subsequent vols.

5. BF's godson was William Hewson, Polly's eldest. Elizabeth, her youngest, was approaching her first birthday and Benjamin Franklin Bache his sixth.

6. See BF to WTF above, June 13.

7. For the gifts from the Constitutional Society to relieve impoverished Bos-

thro' more Business than I do at present. God knows when I shall be permitted to enjoy the Repose I wish. Adieu my very dear Friend. Continue your pleasing Correspondence; and believe me ever Yours most Affectionately   B FRANKLIN

Mrs. Hewson

Notation: Phil July 9, 75

Three Pennsylvania Delegates in Congress to the Lancaster County Committee   ALS:[8] Library of Congress

⟨July 11, 1775: We have received your communication about the rifle company to which Captain Smith is appointed. You mention that James Ross has raised men from whom a good company may be formed; we immediately laid this matter before Congress, which approved their enlistment. Please certify the officers, as with the other company, and have the best men available prepared with the utmost dispatch to follow Captain Smith, who we suppose will have marched before this reaches you.

The Congress highly approves the generous bounty provided by the people of Lancaster County.[9] Signed by Franklin, George Ross, and James Wilson.[1]⟩

---

tonians see Lee to BF above, April 3. Polly, in her missing April letter, doubtless referred to the donation voted on March 21, and enclosed a copy of the request for contributions. She might, from BF's phrasing, have had a share in composing it; but he probably means that she had contributed.

8. In the hand of George Ross. For the full text see Smith, *Letters*, I, 621–2.

9. On June 14 Congress resolved that Pennsylvania, Maryland, and Virginia should raise between them ten companies of riflemen for the continental service, to join the army before Boston as soon as possible. The next day several Pennsylvania delegates sent a circular letter to five county committees urging them to comply; Lancaster was asked for a single company. It was recruited by Matthew Smith (1740?–90), a veteran of Bouquet's expedition, largely from Scots-Irish, and was one of the first to reach Cambridge. James Ross (*c.* 1754–1808), George's son, undertook to raise a second (the bounty referred to), and Congress accepted it. Meanwhile, on June 25, Pennsylvania's quota was increased by another two companies, and all those from the province were incorporated in a battalion. *JCC*, II, 89–90, 104, 173; Smith, *Letters*, I, 491–2, 625; Herbert C. Bell, *History of Northumberland County . . .* (Chicago, 1891), p. 548; John B. Linn, *Pennsylvania in the War of the Revolution . . .* (2 vols., Harrisburg, 1880), I, 305, 320, 674.

1. Both are identified above in a note on a letter they signed, July 3.

Endorsement of Legal Opinions on Land Titles Obtained from the Indians
ADS: Historical Society of Pennsylvania

The promoters of the Walpole Company in London had decided not to wait for confirmation of their grant before putting at least part of it on the market. They had obtained two legal opinions that their title to that part, the lands that the Indians had ceded at Fort Stanwix to the "suffering traders" was a valid one.[2] Franklin's involvement in their marketing plan in 1775 seems to have been minimal. Samuel Wharton had asked him to help Major Trent's lobbying among members of Congress,[3] but the only small sign of his support that has come to light is the endorsement below. What he endorsed were the opinions, which Trent had brought with him.[4] The first was from Henry Dagge, a counsel for and member of the Walpole Company; he argued that the right to property lay with the original Indian possessors, who were free to alienate as they pleased; their conveyance to the crown at Fort Stanwix had been for the sole use of the traders, subject only to the king's sovereignty over settlers as British subjects, and title rested with the grantees. The second opinion, by Sergeant Glynn, was to the same effect: the crown had proprietary rights in vacant and unappropriated lands, but not in those that had been ceded to the traders, whose title was good and sufficient and protected by the laws of England.[5] This subject was, as Franklin says, one to which he had given a great deal of attention. It was also, as he does not say, one on which he held more radical views that those of the two lawyers.[6] His interest in it went beyond a mere endorsement. One of his

2. See the headnote above, April 11.

3. To BF above, April 17.

4. Below his endorsement is another by Patrick Henry, also an ADS and dated July 29, concurring in the opinions "from principles which appear to me very clear." (The principles were also profitable, for Henry received a fee: Lewis, *Indiana Co.*, p. 160). We assume, with no proof, that Trent brought with him Wharton's MS draft of *View of the Title to Indiana . . .* , and had the pamphlet printed as soon as he obtained the endorsements. This assumption, if true, explains where and when the first edition appeared; it bears neither place nor date. It was designed to influence Congress, we are convinced, and was therefore published in Philadelphia, probably in the late summer. The abysmal typography suggests a printer working in haste, and haste is understandable. The promoters were trying to elicit a Congressional declaration that the Indians had full power to alienate their land, and by August a scheme was afoot to sell the traders' tract. See below, Bancroft to BF, Aug. 7, and WF to BF, Aug. 14, 1775.

5. For Dagge see above, XVI, 45 n, 168, and for Glynn XXI, 89 n. The legal issues involved in this application of the Pratt-Yorke opinion are discussed in XX, 116–17, 300–1.

6. *Ibid.*, pp. 302–4.

proposed articles of confederation, which he was presumably drafting at about this time, rested on the assumption that previous purchases from the Indians were valid.[7] In 1776 he was actively concerned in Trent's efforts to dispose of the land ceded to the traders.[8] He retained his shares in the Walpole Company, and in 1780 he and Wharton petitioned Congress to complete the grant.[9]

Philada. July 12. 1775

Having long since carefully studied these Points, I concur fully with Counsellor Dagge and Serjeant Glynn in their Opinions as above deliverd.   B FRANKLIN

Draft of a Resolution Proposed to Congress by the Pennsylvania Committee of Safety

AD:[1] Historical Society of Pennsylvania

Trade had bred controversy in the debates the previous autumn over the Continental Association, and controversy grew with the outbreak of war. The nonexportation agreement was to go into effect on September 19, 1775. After that date no commodities whatsoever, except rice destined for re-export, might clear for Great Britain, Ireland, or the West Indies.[2] The experiment was bold and dangerous, and the danger was becoming more and more apparent. Such an embargo would in the long run ruin American merchants, and in the short run starve the colonies of the arms and ammunition that they might otherwise obtain from the West Indies. As the September date grew closer, the question of how to supply the troops became more pressing. The Pennsylvania committee of safety, created on June 30, must have taken up this question as one of its first concerns. On July 14 it submitted through its president, Franklin, a proposal that Congress modify the nonexportation agreement to permit trading produce for war material. The delegates debated the proposal

7. Article XI: below, under July 21, 1775.

8. See the editorial note below, Jan. 19, 1776. A headnote on his letter to Walpole below, Jan. 12, 1777, traces developments after March, 1776.

9. Bigelow, *Works*, x, 346–71, where the petition is misdated 1779.

1. The draft and endorsement (except the date) are in BF's hand.

2. See above, XXI, 275–6 n. In August, 1775, Congress defined the West Indies as those islands in the possession of any European power: *JCC*, II, 239.

the next day, and adopted it with modifications that were more verbal than substantive.[3]

[On or before July 14, 1775.]
Resolved Whereas the Govt. of Great Britain hath prohibited the Importation of Arms and Ammunition to any of the Plantations, and endeavoured to prevent other Nations from supplying us, That for the better furnishing these Colonies with the necessary Means of defending their Rights every Vessel importing Gunpowder, good Muskets, Field Pieces, and other military Stores, shall be permitted to load here with Provisions to the Amount of the Value of such Stores,[4] the Non Exportation Agreement notwithstanding. And it is recommended to the Committees of the several Provinces, to inspect the military Stores so imported, and to allow a generous Price for the same according to their Goodness, particularly [40] Dollars per Barrel for good Gunpowder, during one Year from the Date of this Resolution.[5]

Endorsed: Copy of a Resolve proposed by the Committee of Safety to the Contl. Congress. [*In another hand*]: 1775

From Jane Mecom   ALS: American Philosophical Society

Warwick July 14, 1775
The Concern I knew my Ever Dear Brother would be in to know what was become of me made me take the first opertunity to write to him and twice since, but did not recve a line from you till the

3. *Ibid.*, pp. 184–5. The minutes of the committee of safety do not record the proposal, but the problem of procuring arms and ammunition had been to the fore since the committee first met on July 3. *Pa. Col. Recs.*, x, 282–6.

4. The *JCC* text reads "importing Gun powder, Salt petre, Sulphur, provided they bring with the sulphur four times as much salt petre, brass field-pieces, or good muskets fitted with Bayonets, within nine months from the date of this resolution, shall be permitted to load and export the produce of these colonies, to the value of such powder and stores aforesaid," etc.

5. The brackets are BF's. The *JCC* text reads "their goodness, and permit the importer of such powder and other military stores aforesaid, to export the value thereof and no more, in produce of any kind." Congress went on to order the text delivered to the Pa. delegates, who were to ask "the committee of this city to forward the same in hand bills to the West Indies and such places as they think proper, taking care that it be not published in the news papers."

day befor yesterday when I recd. yrs of the 17 June and this Day I have recd. the first you wrot, it had been Return'd from Cambridg and had lane 3 weeks in Newport Office.[6]

Your care for me at this time Added to the Innumerable Instances of your Goodnes to me gives me grat comfort under the Difeculties I feel with others but not in a grater Degree[7] for I am in want of nothing haveing mony suficent to soport me some time if I should go to board (which however Mrs. Green will not consent to) and I have with me most of the things I had to sell and now and then sell som small mater. I thought I had tould you I Brought out what I could Pack up in trunks and chists and I so contrived to Pack em in our wereing Aparil Lining and Beding that they Pas'd Examination, without discovery. This was not an unlawfull smugling which you would have reproved for they were not owed for, nor any won cheated of Duties.[8] I wish I could have brought all my Effects in the same maner but the Whol of my Household furniture Exept a few small maters [*interlined*: some wood, soap, &c. &c. &c.[9]] I put into my trunk I left behind, secured Indeed in the house with locks and bars but those who value not to Deprive us of our lives will find a way to brake throw them if they are premitted. My Daughters Goods are there two for tho she Board[ed in] the country some time before the Town was sh[ut up?] she din not Remove her furniture, what [remained?] of there [moveables?] Cousen Williams got out[1] [*torn*] but he ar[*torn*]n'd Estates with so [*torn*] man [*torn*] there to Liv [*torn*] Leter Pleased me much, shall convey it to them first opertunity. My Daughter foot Gone to Dunstable, she in a bad stat of helth, left there Goods in Boston. My son John's widow who mareyed Mr. Turner an Officer left them in Boston how it has faired with them Can not hear tho I wish them saif for He realy apeared a

6. Above, May 26.

7. She is aware of others' difficulties, she may mean, and hers are no worse than theirs.

8. She had not defrauded creditors or the customs in bringing her goods from Boston, in other words, but had only evaded Gage's restrictions, for which see the note on Williams to BF above, June 19.

9. Where she intended this interpolation is impossible to say; we have put it where it makes some sense. By "wood," we suspect, she means wooden utensils.

1. For Williams' flight to Worcester see his letter just cited, and for Jenny Collas' exile in Roxbury Mecom to BF above, May 14.

Good sort of man. O how horrable is our situation that Relations seek the Destruction of Each other.

Por Flagg tho He has used me very Ill I Deplore His Fate the more as there is two of my Daughters Children left.[2] I know not how they will be Provided for. His storey is two long, and two full of shocking sircumstances to troble you with, shall only tell you that in the winter He was taken in a fitt which terminated in Distraction and confined Him some time, but got so much beter as to go about His Bus[iness] and sent out His wife and children Intending to folow them but was soon After taken in the same maner as in winter and Died in a few days. My Good Mrs. Royal and famely that I lived so happyley with 2 year is Gone to worcester.[3] I have not recved the Invitation you say your son was so good as to send me[4] nor a Line from Him a long time tho I have wrot several by such hands as I know he must have recved. Cousen Coffen has Invited me to nantuckett which was sent to Boston and Return'd before the Resolves of the Congres.[5] I dont know if it would be P[ruden]t for me to go now, I cannot Determin what [course to?] take at Present. I wish you could Advise me, I am [anxious?] at being an Incumbrance to this good Famely as my [torn] is for me, but I strive all in my Power [to make my vis?]it as light as I can, when Mrs. [Green]e In a jocoos [way mention?]ed our mounting our [torn] and see you [torn] Remember [torn] should [torn Conn]eticutt at the [torn.] I am rejoyc'd that your Children and famelys are well. I have before heard of your young Hercules, my Neice was so good as to write me won long leter about the Children, and ben franklin won for Himself of which I

2. Daughter Foot was Ruth, Edward Mecom's widow, who after his death had married Thomas Foot. Catherine Mecom, John's widow, had married a British officer who, although Jane apparently did not yet know it, had been wounded at Lexington and again at Bunker Hill. William Flagg, once Sarah Mecom's husband, had died the previous June; his two children by her were a girl of approximately twenty, who was with her grandmother at the Greenes', and a boy of sixteen. Van Doren, *Franklin—Mecom*, p. 159; above, XXI, 348 n; I, lxi; Mecom to BF, May 14, 1775.

3. See *ibid.*

4. BF's letter of June 17 had mentioned WF's invitation.

5. Van Doren (*loc. cit.*) credits the invitation, with conviction but without giving evidence, to Keziah Coffin, for whom see above, X, 397 n. Congress had limited the islanders to importing from Massachusetts, and only what they needed for their own use. *JCC*, II, 70.

wrot you to England. You say nothing about *him* he apeard to me to be an Extrodnery child, I answred His leter but He does not contineu the corispondenc.

I could have wish'd you had been left to your own Option to have assisted in Publick Affairs so as not to fatigue you two much, but as your Talants are superour to most other men I can't help desiering your Country should Injoy the benifit of them while you live, but cant bare the thought of your going to England again as has been sugested hear and won sentance in your leter seemes to favour.[6] You Positively must not go, you have served the Publick in that way beyond what any other man can Boast till you are now come to a good old Age and some younger man must now take that Painfull service upon them. Dont go, pray Dont go, you certainly may do as much good hear as surcumstances are at present [and] posable the Congress may not think it proper to send since those late transactions of the Armey. I am so much at a lose to know whether the News I hear be trew or no that prehaps I had beter leve it to other hands. But my Daughter wrot me last week from Roxbury that on our Army's fiering Canon that reach'd in to the fortifiecation and kill'd six men Gen'l Gage sent out word we had beter not proceed to Extremeties for the King had sent for two of the men of war home. I left my Daughter in so much fear that she could not sleep on nights but she now writs me (from the same place) that she hopes all things, and fears nothing, the Reason she Imagins because she sees all about her in the same disposition.

The Famely h[ere are?] well and almost as numerous, Mrs. Greene says she will [write and?] I only add my love to all your Children and grand Chi[ldren and tha?]t I am as Ever your most Affectionat Sister   JAN[E MECOM]

6. The sentence in BF's letter of June 17, which expressed uncertainty about how long he would be in Philadelphia before being ordered elsewhere.

To Margaret Stevenson

ALS (draft): American Philosophical Society

My dear dear Friend, Philada July 17. 1775

All Trade and Business, Building, Improving, &c. being at a Stand here, and nothing thought of but Arms, I find no Convenience at present of putting out your Money in this Country, and therefore have concluded not to draw it over, but return it into your Hands; and accordingly inclose an Order for it on Messrs. John & Robert Barclay, Cheapside, with whom I left it. I send you also inclos'd an Order on Browns and Collinson for £260 more, supposing by the Sketch Mr. Williams made of our Accts. that I may owe you about that Sum: When they are finally settled we shall see where the Ballance lies, and easily rectify it. In the mean time you will be in Possession of a compleat £1000[7] which as a Friend I would not advise you to trust in your Stocks; for Britain having begun a War with us, which I apprehend is not likely soon to be ended, and may possibly draw on one with some European Power, there is great Probability of those Stocks falling headlong, as you remember the India did.[8] You had better therefore, I think, put your Money out on a good Mortgage of Land.

I received what you sent me per Major Trent, and since your kind Letter of April 24.[9] I rejoice to hear you are well and happy. I am well, and as happy as I can be under the Fatigue of more Business than is suitable to my Age and Inclination: But it follows me every where, and I submit. I am delighted with my little Family. Temple is with his Father. He has written to you, and to his other Friends. My Respects to Mr. and Mrs. Elphinstone when you see them. I shall write to them when I can, for I think we are much indebted to them for the Improvement of that fine Boy.[1] My

7. For Mrs. Stevenson's intention of investing in Pennsylvania, and the confusing record of the transactions that followed, see above, XXI, 539. With the present letter BF enclosed a draft for £740 on the Barclays, plus that for £260 on Browns & Collinson: Jour., p. 60; Ledger, p. 67.

8. In 1769, when the outbreak of war in the Carnatic and the rumor of impending French intervention drove down the Company's stock by almost 10%: Lucy S. Sutherland, *The East India Company in Eighteenth-Century Politics* (Oxford, 1952), pp. 190–1.

9. The letter, which is above, mentions but does not explain what she entrusted to William Trent.

1. James Elphinston had for many years been responsible for WTF's education,

Love to dear Polly and Dolly. I shall write to them by next Opportunity. I pray God to bless and preserve you, being ever, my dear Friend, Yours most affectionately   BF.

Mrs Stevenson

From Catharine Greene[2]   ALS: American Philosophical Society

My Dear Friend   [July 18?,[3] 1775]
    Your letter which had the Pleasure of Receiving gave me great Pleasure as it gave me a fresh Proff of your own Dear Self, and being once more on the Same Land with us. Your Dear good Sister Grew Very impatient till She heard from you and began to fear you was not Come. She was kind enough to Shew me her letter and you are fear full She will be trouble Some but be assurd that her Company Richly Pays as She goes along and we are Very happy together and Shall not Consent to Spare her to any body but her Dear Brother was he to Stay at home and Be Positive. But if you are to Journey we must have her for She is my mama and friend and I tell her we are Rich that we have a lot here and another there and have 3 or 4 of them and we Divert one another Charmingly. Do Come and See us Certain! Dont think of going home again. Do Set Down and injoy the Remainder of your Days in Peace have Just been enguagd in Somethin that Prevents my writeing as I designd to have done. I hope ne[xt time?] I write to be more my[self. My?] kind love to [torn Mr. and] Mrs. Beach and the D[ear Children. I?] hope your [torn] Sympathiss with you [torn ma]de up in them [torn] girl. So is mine [torn] of each other [torn jou]rney love to B[torn] him Nancy[4] [torn Your affe]ctionate friend as long as life   CATY GREENE

_____

which had included dancing, drawing, music, and "Tea in the parlor"; see the schoolmaster's bill, Jan. 4, 1775, in a collection of BF's bills and business memoranda, 1775–89, APS. The young man's identity had not been divulged in America or, at least formally, in Craven Street; see the note on BF to Mecom above, June 17. But the casual reference to him here suggests that the secret was out by the time he and BF left for home.
    2. Written on the last page of Jane Mecom's letter above, July 14.
    3. The date of her husband's note, the following document; hers follows immediately on the same page.
    4. Doubtless her one-year-old daughter Anne: above, X, 191 n.

From [William Greene[5]]

AL: American Philosophical Society

[July 18?, 1775]

Our Men have Taken [2?] Islan and[6] brought of Eaght hundred Sheep and Catle of One an Other five hundred Sheep and Catle of the other and a Manawars barge with fore Men. Col. Robenson has Taken long Island and brught of Two hundred Sheep and Some Catle and Eaght Men and One Young Lade with out the loss of a Man. Two of the Islands was taken last Week and the Other this week. July th 18. Sickly in Boston the Solders and Inhabatants Die fast. The names of the Other Islands Deer Island and Pet-teiks.[7]

From Jonathan Williams, Jr.

AL (incomplete) and draft:[8] American Philosophical Society

Dear and honoured Sir   London July 19. 1775

Yesterday being the Day appointed by Lord Dartmouth I waited on him, but he having a greater Number of Gentlemen at Levee than he could attend to, I was desired to call again to day: which I accordingly did.

On my entring he said, Mr. Williams I have only to tell you, I have delivered your Petition into the Kings hands, but Things are in such a State, no regular Agent here, and American Matters being wholly under the consideration of Parliament, His

---

5. Some differences from his usual handwriting may be explained by the fact that he crammed his note into a small space above his wife's, which is the preceding document. BF acknowledged both in writing to Jane Mecom below, Aug. 2, 1775.

6. The text, almost illegible at this point, appears to read "Taken [*torn*] Islan and and."

7. The islands were raided, not taken, to deplete British supplies; and two of them were attacked not "last Week" but six weeks earlier. The foray against Pettick's, west of Hull, was on May 31 and that against Deer Island, off Pulling Point, on June 2. Barns and a stock of hay were burned on July 13 on Long Island, at the entrance to the harbor. Richard Frothingham, *History of the Siege of Boston* . . . (4th ed., Boston, 1873), pp. 110, 225.

8. Differences between the two are inconsequential. We print the bulk of the letter from the AL and the remainder from the draft.

Majesty did not answer it. The Petition remains in His Majestys Possesion.[9]

I returned. Then my Lord I am to say, the Petition was presented, but His Majesty did not condesend an Answer.

He said I would not have you write anything that may make an unfavourable Impression on the Minds of the People of New Jersey. The King could not with propriety give an Answer, and I do not consider my Conversation with you as Oficial. I then Answered My Lord I shall not presume to be an authorised Agent for the Colony, nor as such write an Answer to the *Speaker* of the House; But I shall do it through Doctor Franklin, and leave the Mode of communication entirely to him.

He said very well, and I retired.

Since I returned from Lord D, I have seen Mr. Lee; who told me he received the first Petition, and Lord D— returned it to him without presenting it.[1] I am happy that my Endeavours have been more successfull, though in[2] Effect of as little Use. I have however some Satisfaction in having got [*it*] into the Kings hands altho' it is unanswered as it leaves a Possibility of its being again taken up for which Reason did ask [*for*] it again.[3]

Endorsed: to Doctr Franklin July 19. 1775

9. JW received the duplicate of the N.J. petition, enclosed in Kinsey's letter to BF above, March 26, and assumed that the original had been returned to America with BF's unopened mail. Earlier in the month, therefore, he tried to deliver the petition to Dartmouth, who made some difficulty about his lack of credentials and asked him to come back. JW to Kinsey, July 12, 1775, APS.

1. See the note on the letter, just cited, from Kinsey to BF.

2. The AL breaks off at this point.

3. A deleted sentence in the draft clarifies the meaning: "I did not think proper to demand it again as remaining with his Majesty it may be again taken up tho' I think there can be no probability that it will." It apparently was not. At the end of the year the N.J. Assembly appointed Dennis DeBerdt, Jr., as agent and instructed him to try to get an answer to the petition. Force, 4 *Amer. Arch.*, III, 1855, 1864–5. We have no evidence that he succeeded.

Intended Vindication and Offer from Congress to Parliament, in 1775[4]

Printed in *The Public Advertiser*, July 18, 1777.

This document has often been reprinted but, for good reason, never explained. When it appeared in the *Public Advertiser* in 1777, it was introduced with what purported to be an account of its origin: "The following Paper was drawn up in a Committee of Congress, June 25, 1775, but does not appear in their Minutes, a severe Act of Parliament which arrived about that Time having determined them not to give the Sum proposed in it. It is supposed to have been written by Dr. Franklin." Although much of this note is fanciful, it has kernels of truth. Franklin did draw up the paper and read it to a committee, but it was probably not a report from that committee. It came before Congress and was not acted upon, but for a quite different reason from the one the printer assigned.

The evidence for these conclusions, although reported in the 1780's, is persuasive. Silas Deane referred to the episode twice, once in a letter to Franklin in 1782 and again, with more circumstantial detail, in a pamphlet published in 1784. Both letter and pamphlet were attempts to exonerate himself from charges against him,[5] and may be considered suspect for that reason. But what he had to say about this document was irrelevant to the later charges; he therefore had no motive for twisting the facts, and the gist of his testimony appears to be reliable.

It does, however, contradict itself in some details. In 1782 he spoke of the paper as a report, drawn up by Franklin in a committee on which he and Deane served, and submitted to Congress a few days after passage of the Olive Branch Petition. The offers it contained were debated and had warm support, particularly from Richard Henry Lee and Roger Sherman, but did not come to a vote; they were put aside because of "the multiplicity, and confusion, of the important business at that time on hand."[6] In Deane's pamphlet the story changes. The paper was not drawn up in a committee or submitted by it. Franklin, Deane, and Richard Henry Lee were serving on one with a quite different assignment, which must have been to recommend policy on trade.[7] During a

---

4. Benjamin Vaughan apparently concocted the title when he printed the document; see *Political, Miscellaneous, and Philosophical Pieces . . . by Benj. Franklin . . .* (London, 1779), p. 357. He also added a number of footnotes, of which we do not take notice, on matters of detail.

5. For the nature of the charges see the *DAB*.

6. *Deane Papers*, v, 48–9.

7. The committee on trade was the only one that included those three members and was active at the time. It was appointed on July 12 and reported nine

pause while the recommendations were being transcribed, Franklin read this paper to the members. Lee approved, and asked to have the offers in it brought before Congress as an individual motion. When Franklin declined to act, Lee moved them the next day. "The proposals appeared no way disagreeable to the house," but were objected to as premature, and inconsistent with the request in the Olive Branch Petition that the colonies be restored to the status quo of 1763. If after that request Congress approved the present offers and made them official, Whitehall might raise its demands. Lee thereupon withdrew his motion, and no entry was made of it in the journals.[8] This second version of the story, though written even longer after the event, is much the more plausible. The first presupposes a committee and a report of which no record exists, and ends with the offers' being in effect overlooked. The second explains why the records are silent about the proposal and why it was withdrawn.

The offers are, in contrast to the generalities of the Petition, concrete and to the point. They consist of two alternatives. If Britain will accord the colonies the commercial status that Scotland acquired in the Act of Union, and allow them to trade freely with the rest of the world, they will pledge an annual revenue of £100,000 for the next century. If this proposal is declined, they will bind themselves in a covenant to recognize for the same period the right of Parliament to regulate their trade in the common interest. Remarkable offers at the best of times, and that July the times were not at their best. News of Bunker Hill had reached the delegates on June 22; soon afterward they learned that the New England Restraining Act had been extended to other colonies, and branded these statutes as unconstitutional.[9] The fact that they then seriously considered such dramatic terms of conciliation says much about their open-mindedness.

The bulk of Franklin's paper is a vindication of the colonies against charges of ingratitude, and the arguments used had long been part of his stock in trade. The offers, which appear almost as interpolations near the end, are also outgrowths of his earlier thinking. The first one, of a fixed revenue, goes back to the "Hints" that began his negotiations in London the previous December: he there made and then withdrew the suggestion that Britain give up her trade restrictions on the colonies in exchange for such a revenue, although the amount and duration were not stipulated. The germ of the alternative offer, a century-long covenant to accept the Navigation Acts, is in another provision of the "Hints," that

---

days later; see the headnote on the resolutions on trade below, under July 21, 1775.

8. *Deane Papers*, V, 260–2.
9. Smith, *Letters*, I, 532; *JCC*, II, 125.

those acts be embodied in colonial legislation; the covenant is simply such legislation in more lasting form. [10] Nothing about the document is surprising except that Congress gave it a sympathetic hearing at that time.

Why was it first printed in London two years later? Because Franklin, we strongly suspect, added a few footnotes[11] and the fictitious explanation of why the proposals were not adopted and then, either just before leaving America or just after arriving in France, sent the paper to his old friend Richard Price. By the beginning of 1777, if not before, it was in Price's hands. He thought it so important that he inserted a quotation from and brief description of it, along with the same explanation of its fate that the printer used later, in a work of his own that was then in press.[1] He may well have gone on to send the entire document to the *Public Advertiser* in July, which was a timely moment for propaganda. A small United States squadron had been raiding with impunity in the Irish Sea; the damage to British commerce had been great and the public outcry greater.[2] It would have been natural for Price, a stalwart champion of the Americans, to try to demonstrate how reasonable, even generous, their attitude had been two years before, and thereby underline how costly British intransigence had proved to be.

[Before July 21,[3] 1775]
Forasmuch as the Enemies of America in the Parliament of Great Britain, to render us odious to the Nation, and give an ill Im-

10. See above, XXI, 368, 366. During the negotiations it became abundantly clear that both suggestions were unacceptable in Whitehall. "The Monopoly of the American Commerce could never be given up," and the colonies' binding themselves to obey the Navigation Acts "imply'd a Deficiency of Power in the Parliament that made those Acts." *Ibid.*, pp. 562, 466. The idea of a hundred-year covenant appears in a rough note that BF made at some point after mid-March: *ibid.*, p. 538 n.

11. The four in our text were not, we assume, in the original; one could not have been because it mentions a later action by Georgia. All have BF's style of capitalization, and their content, even to an old resolution by the House of Commons that he liked to cite, suggests his handiwork.

1. *Additional Observations on the Nature and Value of Civil Liberty* . . . (London, 1777), pp. 258–60. He made no attribution, but BF's authorship was suspected at the time; see Vaughan to BF below, Jan. 27, 1777. Much of Price's volume was in print, according to him, by the time he made the insertion, and publication was announced in the *Public Advertiser* on Feb. 20.

2. See Clark, *Wickes*, chap. xv.

3. When the committee on trade made its report. We are accepting Deane's account in his pamphlet, mentioned in the headnote, that BF read his paper to the committee a few days at most before that date; when he composed it, and

pression of us in the Minds of other European Powers, have represented us as unjust and ungrateful in the highest Degree; asserting on every Occasion, that the Colonies were settled at the Expence of Britain; that they were at the Expence of the same protected in their Infancy; that they now ungratefully and unjustly refuse to contribute to their own Protection, and the common Defence of the Nation; that they aim at Independence; that they intend an Abolition of the Navigation Acts; and that they are fraudulent in their commercial Dealings, and purpose to cheat their Creditors in Britain, by avoiding the Payment of their just Debts:

As by frequent Repitition these groundless Assertions and malicious Calumnies may, if not contradicted and refuted, obtain farther Credit, and be injurious throughout Europe to the Reputation and Interest of the Confederate Colonies, it seems proper and necessary to examine them in our own just Vindication.

With regard to the first, *that the Colonies were settled at the Expence of Britain*, it is a known Fact, that none of the Twelve United Colonies were settled, or even discovered, at the Expence of England. Henry the VIIth indeed granted a Commission to Sebastian Cabot, a Venetian, and his Sons, to sail into the Western Seas for the Discovery of new Countries; but it was to be *suis eorum propriis sumptibus et expensis*, at their own Costs and Charges.[4] They discovered, but soon slighted and neglected, these Northern Territories, which were after more than a hundred Years Dereliction purchased of the Natives, and settled at the Charge and by the Labour of private Men and Bodies of Men, our Ancestors, who came over hither for that Purpose. But our Adversaries have never been able to produce any Record, that ever the Parliament or Government of England was at the smallest Expence on these Accounts; on the contrary, there exists on the Journals of Parliament a solemn Declaration in 1642, only 22 Years after the first Settlement of the Massachusetts, when if such Expence had ever been incurred,

---

whether the vindication and the offers were written at the same or different times, are matters of pure speculation.

4. [*BF's note:*] See the Commission in the Appendix to Pownall's Administration of the Colonies. Edit. 1775. [The letters patent were actually to John Cabot and his sons, of whom Sebastian was one: Thomas Pownall, *The Administration of the British Colonies. The Fifth Edition* . . . (2 vols., London, 1774), II, 151–4.]

some of the Members must have known and remembered it, "That these Colonies had been planted and established *without any Expence to the State.*"[5] New-York is the only Colony in the founding of which England can pretend to have been at any Expence; and that was only the Charge of a small Armament to take it from the Dutch, who planted it. But to retain this Colony at the Peace,[6] another at that Time full as valuable, planted by private Countrymen of *ours*, was given up by the Crown to the Dutch in Exchange, viz. Surinam, now a wealthy Sugar Colony in Guiana, and which but for that Cession might still have remained in our Possession. Of late, indeed, Britain has been at some Expence in planting two Colonies, Georgia[7] and Nova Scotia, but those are not in our Confederacy; and the Expence she has been at in their Name has chiefly been in Grants of Sums unnecessarily large, by Way of Salaries to Officers sent from England, and in Jobbs to Friends, whereby Dependants might be provided for; those excessive Grants not being requisite to the Welfare and good Government of the Colonies; which good Government (as Experience in many Instances of other Colonies has taught us) may be much more frugally, and full as effectually, provided for and supported.

With Regard to the second Assertion, *That these Colonies were protected in their Infant State by England*, it is a notorious Fact, that in none of the many Wars with the Indian Natives, sustained by our Infant Settlements for a Century after our first Arrival, were ever any Troops or Forces of any Kind sent from England to assist

5. [*BF's note:*] Veneris, 10 March, 1642. Whereas the Plantations in New-England have, by the Blessing of the Almighty, had good and prosperous Success, without any public Charge to this State, and are now likely to prove very happy for the Propagation of the Gospel in those Parts, and very beneficial and commodious to this Kingdom and Nation: The Commons now assembled in Parliament, &c. &c. &c. [For BF's previous references to this resolution see above, XVI, 244; XXI, 603 n.]

6. The Treaty of Breda, 1667.

7. [*BF's note:*] Georgia has since acceded, July 1775. [For BF's similar comments on the founding of the two colonies see above, XVII, 377, 398. Georgia had sent no delegates to the first Congress and only one, from a single parish, to the second in the early months. The whole colony chose a delegation in July, and it arrived in mid-September. Smith, *Letters*, I, xxvii; II, xvii; William W. Abbot, *The Royal Governors of Georgia, 1754–1775* (Chapel Hill, [1959]), pp. 169–70, 178.]

116

us; nor were any Forts built at her Expence to secure our Sea-ports from foreign Invaders; nor any Ships of War sent to protect our Trade till many Years after our first Settlement, when our Commerce became an Object of Revenue, or of Advantage to British Merchants; and then it was thought necessary to have a Frigate in some of our Ports, during Peace, to give Weight to the Authority of Custom-house Officers, who were to restrain that Commerce for the Benefit of England. Our own Arms with our Poverty, and the Care of a kind Providence, were all this Time our only Protection; while we were neglected by the English Government, which either thought us not worth its Care, or having no Good-will to some of us on Account of our different Sentiments in Religion and Politics, was indifferent what became of us. On the other Hand, the Colonies have not been wanting to do what they could in every War for annoying the Enemies of Britain. They formerly assisted her in the Conquest of Nova Scotia. In the War before last they took Louisbourg, and put it into her Hands. She made her Peace with that strong Fortress, by restoring it to France, greatly to their Detriment. In the last War it is true Britain sent a Fleet and Army, who acted with an equal Army of our's in the Reduction of Canada, and perhaps thereby did more for us than we in the preceding Wars had done for her. Let it be remembered, however, that she rejected the Plan we formed in the Congress at Albany, in 1754, for our own Defence, by an Union of the Colonies;[8] an Union she was jealous of, and therefore chose to send her own Forces; otherwise her Aid, to protect us, was not wanted. And from our first Settlement to that Time, her Military Operations in our Favour were small, compared with the Advantages she drew from her exclusive Commerce with us. We are however willing to give full Weight to this Obligation; and as we are daily growing stronger, and our Assistance to her becomes of more Importance, we should with Pleasure embrace the first Opportunity of shewing our Gratitude by returning the Favour in kind. But when Britain values herself as affording us Protection, we desire it may be considered that we have followed her in all her Wars, and joined with her at our own Expence against all she thought fit to quarrel with. This she has required of us; and would never permit us to keep

8. BF's misremembrance of what happened is discussed above, XX, 208 n.

117

Peace with any Power she declared her Enemy; though by separate Treaties we might well have done it. Under such Circumstances, when at her Instance we made Nations our Enemies, whom we might otherwise have retained our Friends, we submit it to the common Sense of Mankind, whether her Protection of us in these Wars was not our *just Due*, and to be claimed of *Right*, instead of being received as a *Favour?* And whether, when all the Parts of an Empire exert themselves to the utmost in their common Defence, and in annoying the common Enemy, it is not as well the *Parts* that protect the *Whole*, as the *Whole* that protects the *Parts*. The Protection then has been proportionably *mutual*—And whenever the Time shall come, that our Abilities may as far exceed hers, as hers have exceeded ours, we hope we shall be reasonable enough to rest satisfied with her proportionable Exertions, and not think we do too much for a Part of the Empire, when that Part does as much as it can for the Whole.

The Charge against us, *that we refuse to contribute to our own Protection*, appears from the above to be groundless; but we farther declare it to be absolutely false; for it is well known that we ever held it as our Duty to grant Aids to the Crown upon Requisition, towards carrying on its Wars; which Duty we have chearfully complied with to the utmost of our Abilities, insomuch that frequent and grateful Acknowledgments thereof by King and Parliament appear on their Records.[9] But as Britain has enjoyed a most gainful Monopoly of our Commerce, the same with our maintaining the Dignity of the King's Representative in each Colony, and all our own separate Establishments of Government, Civil and Military, has ever hitherto been deemed an Equivalent for such Aids as might otherwise be expected from us in Time of Peace. And we hereby declare, that on a Reconciliation with Britain, we shall not only continue to grant Aids in Time of War as aforesaid, but, whenever she shall think fit to abolish her Monopoly, and give us the same Privileges of Trade as Scotland received at the

9. [*BF's note:*] Supposed to allude to certain Passages in the Journals of the House of Commons on the 4th of April 1748, 28th January 1756, 3d February 1756, 16th and 19th of May 1757, 1st of June 1758, 26th and 30th of April 1759, 26th and 31st of March and 28th of April 1760, 9th and 20th January 1761, 22d and 26th January 1762, and 14th and 17th March 1763. [See above, XXI, 136 n.]

Union, and allow us a free Commerce with all the rest of the World, we shall willingly agree (and we doubt not it will be ratified by our Constituents) to give and pay into the Sinking Fund £100,000. Sterling per Annum for the Term of One Hundred Years; which duly, faithfully, and inviolably applied to that Purpose, is demonstrably more than sufficient to extinguish *all her present National Debt*, since it will in that Time amount, at legal British Interest, to more than £230,000,000.

But if Britain does not think fit to accept this Proposition, we, in order to remove her groundless Jealousies, *that we aim at Independence and an Abolition of the Navigation Act*, (which hath in Truth never been our Intention) and to avoid all future Disputes about the Right of making that and other Acts for regulating our Commerce, do hereby declare ourselves ready and willing to enter into a Covenant with Britain, that she shall fully possess, enjoy, and exercise that Right for an Hundred Years to come, the same being *boná fide* used for the common Benefit; and in case of such Agreement, that every Assembly be advised by us to confirm it solemnly by Laws of their own, which once made cannot be repealed without the Assent of the Crown.

The last Charge, *that we are dishonest Traders, and aim at defrauding our Creditors in Britain*, is sufficiently and authentically refuted by the solemn Declarations of the British Merchants to Parliament, (both at the Time of the Stamp Act, and in the last Session) who bore ample Testimony to the general good Faith and fair Dealing of the Americans, and declared their Confidence in our Integrity; for which we refer to their Petitions on the Journals of the House of Commons. And we presume we may safely call on the Body of the British Tradesmen, who have had Experience of both, to say, whether they have not received much more punctual Payment from us than they generally have from the Members of their own two Houses of Parliament.

On the whole of the above it appears, that the Charge of *Ingratitude* towards the Mother Country, brought with so much Confidence against the Colonies, is totally without Foundation; and that there is much more Reason for retorting that Charge on Britain, who not only never contributes any Aid, nor affords by an exclusive Commerce any Advantages to Saxony, *her* Mother Country; but no longer since than in the last War without the least Provocation, subsidized the King of Prussia while he ravaged that *Mother Country*, and carried Fire and Sword into its Capital, the fine City of Dresden.[1] An Example we hope no Provocation will induce us to imitate.

Proposed Articles of Confederation AD: National Archives[2]

These articles and Franklin's "Short Hints" for uniting the northern colonies in 1754[3] are the two occasions when he formulated his ideas of what an intercolonial constitution should be. Both formulations were developed in ways that he could not have anticipated. He and others reworked the "Hints" into the Albany Plan.[4] He never reworked the present articles, and they were never implemented; but they became part of the intellectual store from which the Articles of Confederation and even the federal constitution were derived. Where did Franklin's ideas come from? A natural assumption would be that he quarried them from the Albany Plan, altered to fit the new circumstances; and to some extent he did. But his principal source, it was argued years ago, was the New England confederation of 1643,[5] which some of his earlier "Hints" resembled as well. We have no other evidence that he was familiar with the confederation; it was already beginning to arouse interest as a precedent for union,[6] however, and his debt to it is unquestionable.

He showed his draft articles to Jefferson and others, some of whom approved while some disapproved. The plan appealed to those who had abandoned hope of reconciliation, and antagonized those who had not;

1. BF is paraphrasing his "Dialogue"; *ibid.*, p. 604.
2. The copies are extremely numerous, and to list them would be redundant because it has already been done: Boyd, *Jefferson Papers*, I, 179–80; Smith, *Letters*, I, 643–4. Our text of BF's draft is printed in *JCC*, II, 195–9 n, where his deletions are indicated, but his insertions between the lines and in the margins are silently incorporated in the text. We have omitted the deletions but noted those that are significant and, because of the importance of the document, have enclosed the insertions in brackets. All other brackets except the last one are BF's.
3. Above, V, 335–8.
4. *Ibid.* pp. 374–87.
5. Lois K. Mathews, "Benjamin Franklin's Plans for a Colonial Union, 1750–1775," *Amer. Political Science Rev.*, VIII (1914), 396–8, 401, 406–11. For the substance of the confederation see Hutchinson, *History*, I, 107–8.
6. See for example Silas Deane's references to it in writing Patrick Henry on Jan. 2, 1775, and his request to his wife on May 12 to send a copy to him in Philadelphia to "help me in an important matter": *Deane Papers*, I, 38, 49.

putting it to a vote would shatter the fragile consensus in Congress. Franklin, however, was looking ahead to a time when the majority would accept, as he already did,[7] the need for bold action. He therefore asked leave to lay his scheme on the table, so that the delegates might think about the subject and prepare themselves to act when they saw the need to. Leave was given, according to Jefferson, but only on condition that the plan should not appear in the journals of Congress.[8] On July 21, when the house resolved itself into a committee of the whole, Franklin read his articles and left them on the table and hence off the record. But they were disseminated through the colonies,[9] to work as they might upon men's minds.

The possibility of a federation came up again the following January, and Franklin argued for it. But the delegates were still not ready, and the issue was shelved.[1] Not until June, 1776, was a committee appointed to work on the question, and Franklin was not a member. Although some of his points, such as a common treasury and an executive council, were embodied in the draft that came out of the committee, many of the most important ones, such as proportional representation and the amendment process, were not; and the committee's handling of representation led Franklin to draft, but not deliver, a protest to Congress.[2] There matters rested for a time. Tracing his ideas through the later debates on the Articles of Confederation and then on the federal constitution would be beyond the scope of this note.

Franklin was far ahead of most of the delegates in his readiness to separate from Britain. Just as his resolutions on trade asserted America's economic independence, so these articles asserted its political sovereignty. They empowered the United Colonies to amend their individual constitutions as they saw fit; a common treasury was to administer funds raised by proportional taxation; Congress was authorized to initiate amendment of the articles, to settle intercolonial disputes, to create new colonies and admit established ones into the union, to negotiate with

7. See his remarks to Sargent above, June 27, and John Adams' comments, two days after these articles were read, on the boldness of BF's thinking: Butterfield, *Adams Correspondence*, I, 252–3.

8. Jefferson wrote this account many years later, and assigned the whole episode to early 1776 instead of the summer of 1775: Boyd, *Jefferson Papers*, X, 372–3. With that exception, however, we are inclined to trust his memory, for what he said coincides with everything that is known about the mood of Congress that July.

9. *JCC*, II, 195 n; Burnett. *Continental Congress*, pp. 91–2.

1. *Ibid.*, p. 92; Smith, *Letters*, III, 103.

2. Below, under August 20, 1776. For an analysis of the differences and resemblances between the committee's draft and BF's see Burnett, pp. 213–19.

the Indians, to make war and peace and form alliances, and to send and receive ambassadors.[3] This degree of autonomy was independence. The final paragraph of the plan, it is true, provided that the new government would lapse if Britain conceded all the points at issue and made reparation for damages; the colonies would then return to "their former Connection." If Britain did not surrender, on the other hand, America would remain permanently outside the authority of Parliament and the crown.

[On or before July 21, 1775]

Articles of Confederation and perpetual Union, *proposed* [*interlined:* entred into] by the Delegates of the several Colonies of New Hampshire &c. in general Congress met at Philadelphia, May 10. 1775.

Art. I. The Name of the Confederacy shall henceforth be *The United Colonies of North America*.

Art. II. The said United Colonies hereby severally enter into a firm League of Friendship with each other, binding [*interlined:* on] themselves and their Posterity, for [*interlined:* their common] Defence [*interlined:* against their Enemies, for[4]] the Security of their Liberties and Propertys, the Safety of their Persons and Families, and their mutual and general welfare.

Art. III. That each Colony shall enjoy and retain as much as it may think fit of its own present Laws, Customs, Rights, Privileges, and peculiar Jurisdictions within its own Limits; and may amend its own Constitution as shall seem best to its own Assembly or Convention.[5]

Art. IV. That for the more convenient Management of general Interests, Delegates shall be annually elected in each Colony to meet in General Congress at such Time and Place as shall be agreed on in the next preceding Congress. Only where particular Circumstances do not make a Deviation necessary, it is understood to be a Rule, that each succeeding Congress be held in a different Colony till the whole Number be gone through, and so in perpetual Rotation; and that accordingly the next [*interlined:* Congress] after the present shall be held at Annapolis in Maryland.[6]

Art. V. That the Power and Duty of the Congress shall extend

3. The copies that we have examined omit this last attribute of sovereignty.
4. The draft originally read "for Defence and Offence, the Security," etc.
5. The gist of this article was in the 1643 confederation and the Albany Plan.
6. The idea of rotating meetings mirrors the confederation and the "Hints," but not the Albany Plan.

to the Determining on War and Peace, to [*interlined*: sending and receiving Ambassadors, and] entring into Alliances, [the Reconciliation with Great Britain;] the Settling all Disputes and Differences between Colony and Colony [*interlined*: about Limits or any other cause] if such should arise; and the Planting of new Colonies when proper. The Congress shall also make such general Ordinances as tho' necessary to the General Welfare, particular Assemblies cannot be competent to; viz. those that may relate to our general Commerce [*in the margin*: or general Currency]; to the Establishment of Posts; and the Regulation of [*interlined*: our common] Forces. The Congress shall also have the Appointment of all Officers civil and military, appertaining to the general Confederacy, such as General Treasurer Secretary,[7] &c.

Art. VI. All Charges of Wars, and all other general Expences to be incurr'd for the common Welfare, shall be defray'd out of a common Treasury, which is to be supply'd by each Colony in proportion to its Number of Male Polls between 16 and 60 Years of Age; the Taxes for paying that proportion [*interlined*: are] to be laid and levied by [*interlined*: the] Laws of each Colony.

Art. VII. The Number of Delegates to be elected and sent to the Congress by each Colony, shall be regulated from time to time by the Number of [*interlined*: such] Polls return'd, so as that one Delegate be allow'd for every [5000] Polls. And the Delegates are to bring with them to every Congress an authenticated Return of the number of Polls in their respective Provinces, [*interlined*: which is] to be annually [*interlined in another hand*: triennially] taken, for the Purposes abovementioned.[8]

Art. VIII. [*In the margin*: At every Meeting of the Congress One half of the Members return'd exclusive of Proxies be necessary to make a Quorum, and] Each Delegate at the Congress, shall have a Vote in all Cases; and if necessarily absent, shall be allowed to appoint [*interlined*: any other Delegate from the same Colony to be his[9]] Proxy, who may vote for him.

7. The planting of new colonies and appointment of officers derive from the Albany Plan; the powers of Congress resemble those in the confederation. In the margin of this article BF wrote "Gen. officers as Treasurer Secry."

8. The provision for apportioning contributions according to the number of adult males is found in the confederation, but proportional representation only in the Albany Plan.

9. The draft originally read, "to appoint a Proxy, who may vote," etc.

Art. IX. An executive Council shall be appointed by the Congress [*interlined*: out of their own Body,] consisting of [12] Persons; of whom in the first Appointment [*interlined*: one Third, viz.] [4], shall be for one Year, [4] for two Years, and [4] for three Years; and as the said Terms expire, the vacancies shall be filled by Appointments for three Years, whereby One Third of [the] Members will be changed annually. [*In the margin*: And each Person who has served the said Term of three Years as Counsellor, shall have a Respite of three Years, before he can be elected again.][1] This Council [*interlined*: (of whom two thirds shall be a Quorum)] in the Recess of the Congress is to execute what shall have been enjoin'd thereby; to manage the general [*interlined*: continental] Business and Interests to receive Applications from foreign Countries; to prepare Matters for the Consideration of the Congress; to fill up (*pro tempore*) continental Offices that fall vacant; and to draw on the General Treasurer for [such] Monies as may be necessary for general Services, and appropriated by the Congress to such Services.

Art. X. No Colony shall engage in an offensive War with any Nation of Indians without the Consent of the Congress, or great Council above-mentioned, who are first to consider the Justice and Necessity of such War.[2]

Art. XI. A perpetual Alliance offensive and defensive, is to be entered into as soon as may be with the Six Nations; their Limits to be [*interlined*: ascertain'd and] secur'd to them; their Land not to be encroach'd on, nor any private [*interlined*: or Colony] Purchases made of them hereafter to be held good; nor any [*interlined*: Contract for Lands] to be made but between the Great Council [*interlined*: of the Indians] at Onondaga and the General Congress.[3] The Boundaries and Lands of all the other Indians shall also be [*in the margin*: ascertain'd and] secur'd to them [*interlined*: in the same manner]; and Persons appointed to reside among them in proper Districts, who shall take care to prevent Injustice in the Trade with them, [*in the margin*: and be enabled at our General Expence by occasional small Supplies, to relieve their personal

---

1. BF inserted here, then deleted, "The Appointments to be determined by Ballot."
2. This article resembles one in the confederation.
3. Here is a distinct echo of the Albany Plan.

Wants and Distresses.] And all Purchases from them shall be by the Congress for the General Advantage and Benefit of the United Colonies.

Art. XII. As all new Institutions may have Imperfections which only Time and Experience can discover, it is agreed, that the General Congress from time to time shall propose such Amendment of this Constitution as may be found necessary; which being approv'd by a Majority of the Colony Assemblies, shall be equally binding with the rest of the Articles of this Confederation.

Art. XIII. Any and every Colony from Great Britain [*interlined*: upon the Continent of North America] not at present engag'd in our Association, may upon Application [*interlined*: and joining the said Association,] be receiv'd into this Confederation, viz. [Ireland] the West India Islands, Quebec, St. Johns,[4] Nova Scotia, Bermudas, and the East and West Floridas: and shall [*interlined*: thereupon] be entitled to all the Advantages of our Union, mutual Assistance and Commerce.

These Articles shall be propos'd to the several Provincial Conventions or Assemblies, to be by them consider'd, and if approv'd they are advis'd to impower their Delegates to agree to and ratify the same in the ensuing Congress. After which the *Union* thereby establish'd is to continue firm till the Terms of Reconciliation proposed in the Petition of the last Congress to the King are agreed to; till the Acts since made restraining the American Commerce [*interlined*: and Fisheries] are repeal'd; till Reparation is made for the Injury done to Boston by shutting up its Port; for the Burning of Charlestown; and for the Expence of this unjust War; and till all the British Troops are withdrawn from America. On the Arrival of these Events the C[olonies are to[5]] return to their former Connection and Friendship with Britain: But on Failure thereof this Confederation is to be perpetual.

Notation: Sketch of Articles of Confederation July 75. This Sketch in handwritg of Doct Franklin

Read before Congress July 21. 1775

---

4. Renamed in 1798 Prince Edward Island.
5. Illegible and supplied from copies.

Resolutions on Trade Submitted to Congress

AD: National Archives; draft:[6] American Philosophical Society

News of the second Restraining Act infuriated and alarmed Congress. On July 12, 1775, it appointed a committee, of which Franklin was a member, to formulate a program for protecting the colonies' trade.[7] Three days later, on Franklin's motion, the nonexportation agreement was modified to permit paying in produce for imported war material;[8] but this concession solved only one of the problems that the agreement posed. The committee addressed the others in two closely similar sets of resolutions, reported on the 21st by Franklin and Richard Henry Lee. Both proposed opening American commerce to the world outside the empire.[9]

Franklin had long disapproved, both in practice and principle, of Parliamentary constraints on American trade;[1] he was ready for a clean sweep. The content of his proposals showed his daring, and the method of implementing them showed his moderation. The ports would not be opened if the Restraining Act was repealed at any time before July 20, 1776; once opened on that date they would remain so, come what might, for two years at the least. Just as Franklin had acquiesced in the Olive Branch Petition to explore the last hope of compromise,[2] so he now offered the British government a year in which to reconsider its course. His fellow delegates, however, were not yet ready to commit themselves, even conditionally and in the future, to a declaration of commercial independence. They had lived so long within the closed system of the Navigation Acts that few could envisage dispensing with it. The resolutions were shelved, and the idea that underlay them was not adopted until almost nine months later.[3]

6. On the verso of the draft BF made unrelated jottings. First are several columns of figures, apparently British currency. Second are the sketch and Latin mottoes reproduced below, for reasons explained there, in the editorial note on BF's design for currency, Feb. 21. Third are notes, apparently written in pencil and for the most part overwritten in ink: "Ready to receive Irish Woollens whenever they shall ascertain Methods of sending them, free of all Imposition. / Resolve Not to treat separately. / Resolve concerning the Power of Parliament to alter Constitutions. Lord Chatham's Resolution. / Difference has been whether we shall give our Money, or have it taken from us by Force, contrary to our Rights."

7. See *JCC*, II, 125, 177.

8. See the draft resolution above, July 14.

9. *JCC*, II, 200–1.

1. See above, XXI, 175–7.

2. See the editorial note on the petition above, July 8.

3. The proposal was debated in October, December, January, and February,

At some time during those months Franklin's resolutions were apparently reintroduced. Someone brought them up to date by adding to the AD, in an unidentifiable hand, an introductory clause about the abundance of grain after the harvest of 1775, and by making other minor changes. These have understandably confused modern editors about both the wording and the date of what Franklin submitted.[4] His draft, which except for a few phrases noted below is identical with our text, permits us to delete silently the words added later, and to supply in brackets those later effaced.

[On or before July 21, 1775]

Resolved, That from and after the 20th of July [1776 being one full Year after] the Day appointed by a late Act of the Parliament of Great Britain for restraining the Trade of the Confederate Colonies,[5] all the Custom-Houses therein (if the said Act be not first repealed) shall be shut up, and all the Officers of the same discharged from the Execution of their several Functions; and all the Ports of the said Colonies are hereby declared to be thenceforth open to the Ships of every State in Europe that will admit our Commerce and protect it; who may [bring in] and expose to Sale free of all Duties their respective Produce and Manufactures, and every kind of Merchandise, excepting Teas, and the Merchandize of Great Britain, Ireland, and the British West India Islands.[6]

Resolved, That we will to the utmost of our Power maintain and support this Freedom of Commerce for two[7] Years certain after its Commencement, any Reconciliation between us and Britain notwithstanding;[8] and as much longer beyond that Term, as the

---

1775–76; but it was not finally adopted until April 6, 1776, and then with the proviso that colonies might levy their own import duties. *JCC*, III, 457, 477–80; IV, 59, 62, 159, 258–9.

4. Worthington Ford printed the text in the *JCC*, already cited, under July 21 as if the alterations were then a part of it; they appear in comparing that text with ours. Burnett and Smith assigned the draft, which we are convinced preceded the final version, to 1776 when the resolutions were reintroduced in their altered form: Burnett, *Letters*, I, 364; Smith, *Letters*, III, 305.

5. The second Restraining Act, 15 Geo. III, c. 18, incorporated and expanded the first.

6. The comma after "Teas" obscures the meaning, which is that they and British merchandise are excluded. This paragraph would have closed, along with the customs houses, the loophole in the nonexportation agreement whereby rice could be cleared for Britain to be re-exported from there.

7. BF first wrote "one," then "three," before settling for two.

8. The draft omits this prepositional clause.

late Acts of Parliament for Restraining the Commerce and Fisheries, and altering the Laws and Charters of any of the Colonies, shall continue unrepealed.

Endorsed by Charles Thomson: a proposal for opening the ports of N.A. brot. in by Committee read. July 21. 1775, on motion postponed for future Consideration.

From [David Hartley]   Transcript:[9] Library of Congress

Dear Sir   Golden Square July 22d. 1775

I take the opportunity of writing a line to you by Capt. Read,[1] tho. I have not any thing now to say. We seem rather on this side the water to be expecters of news and events; more especially as to the proceedings and proposals from the Congress. As to my own opinion and wishes, they continue the same. I can only wish generally for peace, and for such measures on your side of the water, as woud most contribute to it. As long as our Bretheren in America continue to trust that it is not the nation, but only the ministry, with whom they are at war, so long I shall still hope for an amicable accommodation. The very jealousy, that this nation coud take so unjust a part as not to wait for the impartial hearing of both sides, but that they woud swallow implicitly the Ministerial charges and representations against America, woud be the only possible way to create a national disquiet against you; but a confidence in the liberality and justice of this nation, expressed in terms of reliance and affection, woud in the greatest degree captivate the heart of a free and generous people; which I hope and believe to be the characteristick of the English. An exposition of facts, founded in historical evidence of transactions, which have hitherto been partially stated to the publick, must I am sure have

9. In the same hand as the transcripts of Hartley's letters below, Feb. 24 and June 8, 1776.

1. Thomas Read, master of the *Aurora*, sailed in early August and reached Philadelphia some two months later: *London Chron.*, Aug. 3–5, 5–8; *Pa. Gaz.*, Oct. 11, 1775. He carried books for WTF and the second consignment of BF's possessions: Williams to BF below, Nov. 23. Read then abandoned merchantmen for warships, and eventually received a command in the American navy: *Naval Docs.*, II, 582, 654–5; IV, 1445.

the most favourable effect to cultivate a good disposition here. There is nothing that I can think woud do so much good, as a kind of affectionate expostulation with the people of England. Facts have been so much misrepresented, that unless they are otherwise stated by Authority, it seems very much like giving up the cause as a Matter of Justice, and trusting to the security of a distant situation and arms; and upon these suggestions, runners of the Ministry ground the false charge of a long [*blank in* MS] view of independence; As to my own sentiments, I have long seen the terms of parent state, over children &c., as very misleading in themselves; if we must have allegorical terms, let us change them for Bretheren and friends. The duties annexed to the terms of Bretheren and friends in private life, woud naturally had [lead?] us to the contemplation of these duties between Great Brittain and America; which woud make a firm and everlasting bond of affection and mutual interest; but the superictious[2] usurpation of authoratative parental rights, over those whom God has made our equals, cannot fail to pervert reason at the outset. It presupposes a parental affection which cannot exist, having no foundation in nature beyond natural parents. It presupposes a dispensation of our own private interests, in competition with that of our provincial children; the very contrary of which, constitutes in our estimation their only value to us; and under this false colouring, even respect and gratitude from our Colonies, is received as the payment of a debt, and not set to the Account of affection or merit. Let us be bretheren and friends, and the mutuality of good offices required in the very terms, will impress upon the mind all those dispositions of humanity and mutual Assistance, which fellow Creatures and fellow Subjects shoud sustain towards each other. I send you the petition of the City of London to the King, which in my opinion breaths wisdom, humanity, and affection to our bretheren in America. As to the Answer of the Minister, (for so it must be considered, like the kings speeches to the Parliament,) I have nothing to say but this, that it appears to me to be canvassing for the people of England, and seems to confess that their Sentiments are not with the Ministerial Measures; for if they were, they wou'd

2. The copyist unquestionably used this nonexistent adjective, which was perhaps a misreading of "supercilious."

hardly want to be so studiously informed, that *their rights and interests* are the only points, which the Ministry have in view.[3] The very pointing this out in the terms of an Apology for the conduct of the ministry, shews that the general sense of the nation is not convinced. I think the proposition of the City of London is not far from the propositions made in Parliament on the 27th of March, for requisitions to the Colonies, and a suspension of hostilities in the enterim.[4] I am Dear Sir with the greatest regard Yours &c.

G B

Address by Pennsylvania and Virginia Delegates in Congress to the Inhabitants West of Laurel Hill[5]

LS: Library of Congress

⟨Philadelphia, July 25, 1775: We are concerned about your continuing boundary disputes.[6] We do not inquire into their origins or merits but, as representatives of two of the colonies united to defend the liberties of America, have the duty to remove if we can every obstacle that prevents Americans from co-operating to that end. This is our motive for earnestly requesting you to turn your

3. For the fate of the earlier London petition see the note on Lee to BF above, July 6. On July 7 the mayor, aldermen, and livery composed another, which this time was presented to the King. It begged him to allow the colonists an opportunity to give freely what they refused to give when required by laws passed without their consent, by suspending the use of force until they could suggest terms of accommodation. While one group of his subjects defied constituted authority, the King replied, he owed it to the rest to take measures to safeguard their rights and interests. Force, 4 *Amer. Arch.*, II, 1601–3.

4. Hartley had suggested the previous December that the Coercive Acts be suspended to see whether the colonists would not contribute by requisitions, and on March 27 he moved to that effect: above, XXI, 511. After a warm debate his motion was defeated without a division. Cobbett, *Parliamentary History*, XVIII, 552–74; David Hartley, *Speech and Motions Made in the House of Commons, on Monday, the 27th of March, 1775* . . . (London, 1775); Gipson, *British Empire*, XII, 306–7.

5. Laurel Hill is not a hill but a range of mountains east of Pittsburgh.

6. The long and involved conflicts between Pennsylvania and Virginia for control of the area. For the full text of this letter and an exhaustive discussion of the disputes that evoked it see Boyd, *Jefferson Papers*, I, 234–6.

animosities as inhabitants of separate colonies into a common effort to preserve all that makes our country dear to us.

We are convinced that you, like us, wish to see this transformation. To that end we recommend that you disband all bodies of armed men maintained by either province, discharge all those who are in prison or under bail for their part in the contest, and until it is settled leave every one in peaceful possession; thus "the public tranquility will be secured without injury to the titles on either side." We are confident that the dispute, which has brought much mischief and no good, will soon be peaceably and legally determined. Signed for the Pennsylvania delegation by Franklin, John Dickinson, Charles Humphreys,[7] George Ross, and James Wilson, and for the Virginia delegation by Benjamin Harrison, P. Henry, Jr., Thomas Jefferson, and Richard Henry Lee.⟩

Amendment to Jefferson's Draft of the Congressional Response to Lord North's Conciliatory Resolution

AD: Library of Congress

On March 3, 1775, Dartmouth transmitted to the colonial governors Lord North's conciliatory resolution, introduced in the House of Commons on February 20 and passed on the 27th. The assemblies of New Jersey, Pennsylvania, and Virginia took the position that an answer must come from Congress, to which the New Jersey delegates transmitted the resolution on May 26. On July 22 Franklin, Jefferson, John Adams, and Richard Henry Lee were named as a committee to report on the matter, which they did three days later; on the 31st Congress adopted the report with few changes.[8] Jefferson, who was familiar with the questions at issue because he had drafted the response of the Virginia House of Burgesses, wrote the bulk of the committee's report. Franklin added part of one paragraph, in which he advanced much the same arguments against the resolution that he had expressed months earlier in his journal of the negotiations in London.[9] Jefferson accepted the addition, and with mi-

---

7. The only signer who is not in the *DAB*. Humphreys (1712–86) had been a member of the Pa. Assembly since 1763 and was a delegate to the first and second Continental Congress; he subsequently opposed independence and withdrew from political life in July, 1776. A. A. Humphreys, "Charles Humphreys," *PMHB*, I (1877), 83–5.

8. Boyd, *Jefferson Papers*, I, 229–30 n.

9. Above, XXI, 510, 594–5.

nor verbal changes it was embodied in the final resolutions of Congress.[1] We print Franklin's draft, with bracketed insertions at the beginning and end to set it in the context of the committee's report.

[On or before July 25, 1775]
[The resolution seems to have been intended to deceive the world into thinking] that there was no Matter in Dispute between us but the single Circumstance of the *Mode* of Levying Taxes, which *Mode* as they are so good as to give up to us; of course that the Colonies are unreasonable if they are not thereby perfectly satisfied: Whereas in truth our Adversaries not only still claim a Right of demanding *ad libitum*, and of taxing us themselves to the full Amount [*in another hand*: of their Demands] if we do not fulfill their Pleasure, which leaves us without any thing we can call *Property*; but what is of more Importance, and what they keep in this Proposal out of sight, as if no such Point was in Contest, they claim a Right of altering all our Charters and establish'd Laws, which leaves us without the least Security for our Lives or *Liberty*. The Proposition seems also calculated more particularly &c. [to lull the British public into a false sense of security.]

Notation by Jefferson: amendment by Dr. Franklin.

Editorial Note on the Founding of the Post Office

One of the first institutions to suffer from the colonists' rising hostility to Britain was the royal Post Office. As early as 1773 enterprising post-riders in New England were establishing routes of their own in defiance of the law. "It is next to impossible to put a stop to this practice," wrote a new surveyor general, "in the present universal opposition to every thing connected with Great Britain. Were any Deputy Post Master to do his duty, and make a stir in such matter, he would draw on himself the odium of his neighbours and be mark'd as the friend of Slavery and oppression and a declar'd enemy to America."[2] Soon after Franklin's dismissal as deputy postmaster general for North America in January, 1774, the system to which he had devoted so much time and energy began to fall apart. The old argument that postal revenue was a form of

1. For the resolutions as reported out of committee and as adopted by Congress see Boyd, pp. 225–33. A more meticulous text than ours of BF's contribution, with all his deletions and interlineations noted, is on p. 230.

2. [Frank H. Norton, ed.,] *Journal Kept by Hugh Finlay . . . Begun the 13th Septr. 1773 and Ended 26th June 1774* (Brooklyn, N.Y., 1867), p. 32.

taxation gained new force as the quarrel with the mother country inten-
sified.[3] A system independent of the crown was becoming imperative,
furthermore, if the colonists were to communicate without fear of interception. By the summer William Goddard's "constitutional post," a
replacement for the older one, was making headway from New England
to Virginia. In the autumn Goddard tried and failed to have the first
Continental Congress take over his creation. But by the time the second
Congress got down to business the whole situation had changed. Independent post offices were burgeoning, set up sometimes by towns and
sometimes by colonial assemblies.[4] The outbreak of hostilities increased
the need for reliable communication, and the sooner the better; improvi-
sations would no longer serve.

The delegates wasted no time. On May 29, nineteen days after they
convened, they appointed a committee of six, including Franklin, "to
consider the best means of establishing posts for conveying letters and
intelligence through this continent."[5] The committee deliberated for
almost two months, and on July 25 brought in its report. The next day
the draft was debated by paragraphs, and may or may not have been
revised. The form in which it was adopted became the charter of the new
Post Office. The head of the organization was the Postmaster General.
His office was to be in Philadelphia and his annual salary $1,000; he was
authorized to appoint a secretary and comptroller at a salary of $340,
and as many deputies as he thought necessary, who were to have twenty
percent of receipts up to $1,000 and ten percent of those above that
amount, and who were to account quarterly with the central office. The
Postmaster General was to account annually with the continental trea-
surers (who, if proceeds were less than outlay, were to make good the
difference), and was to establish postal routes from Falmouth (now Portland, Maine) to Savannah, with as many side routes as he thought fit.
Franklin was unanimously elected to the position on the day it was
created, July 26.[6] Soon afterward he appointed Richard Bache as secre-

3. See above, XXI, 161 n.
4. Ward L. Miner, *William Goddard, Newspaperman* (Durham, N.C., 1962),
pp. 131–5. See also John C. Fitzpatrick, "The Post Office of the Revolutionary
War," *Daughters of the American Revolution Mag.*, LVI (1922), 575–6; this article,
innocent of footnotes, is one of the few on the subject by a reputable historian.
5. *JCC*, II, 71.
6. *Ibid.*, pp. 203, 208–9. The postal rates were set at 20% less than those
established by Parliament (for which see Fitzpatrick, *op. cit.*, p. 576); two
months later, when BF realized that this regulation would preclude hiring the
necessary number of postriders, it was suspended indefinitely: Smith, *Letters*, II,
83. BF devoted his salary to helping disabled veterans: to Strahan below, Oct.
3, 1775.

tary and comptroller and Goddard as surveyor general.[7]

There the record ends. The crucial report from Franklin's committee has disappeared; neither his correspondence nor that of other delegates says anything about how the report was compiled or about the ensuing debate on it; all that remains is the bare outline of the actions Congress took. The same silence covers Franklin's activities during his term of office. Almost no evidence about them survives, and the little that does is trivial: six commissions as postmasters over his signature; a letter from Bache as his deputy asking a local committee to nominate to the office; expenses of one journey to Perth Amboy on postal business.[8] The question of whether the new system was primarily Franklin's creation or his subordinates' seems to be unanswerable. The Post Office was one of the solid achievements of the period, and the one about which the least is known.

7. RB's commission, dated Oct. 2, 1775, and retroactive to Sept. 29, is in the Hist. Soc. of Pa.

8. The commissions are: to Ebenezer Hazard for New York, Sept. 21, 1775 (APS); to Elias Beers for New Haven, Sept. 25, 1775 (Mrs. Norman H. Pearson, Hamden, Conn.); to RB for Philadelpia, Oct. 2, 1775 (APS); to John Langdon for New Hampshire, same date (Yale University Library); to Abraham Hunt for Trenton, N.J., Oct. 13, 1775 (Theodore Sheldon, Chicago); and to Shubel Burr for Warren, R.I., Nov. 13, 1775 (Baptist Church Benevolent Soc., Warren). RB's letter is to the Carlisle committee, Jan. 31, 1776 (Yale). For the Perth Amboy trip see BF's Memorandum Book (above, VII, 167–8), entry of Sept. 6, 1775. BF established post offices as he traveled to the conference with Washington: Smith, *Letters*, II, 85. The Post Office issued a broadside over BF's signature, *Table of the Port of All Single Letters Carried by Post in the Northern District, as Established by Congress* . . . [Philadelphia, 1775]. Another broadside, *Directions to the Deputy Post-Masters, for Keeping Their Accounts* . . . , is assigned to the same year in Charles Evans, *American Bibliography* (12 vols., Chicago, 1903–34), V, no. 14,587; but our predecessors, for what seem to us good reasons, printed it under the tentative date of 1753: above, V, 169–74. Most of the actions of Congress relating to the Post Office during BF's term are noted in three brief secondary accounts: Wesley E. Rich, *The History of the United States Post Office to the Year 1829* (Harvard Economic Studies, XXVII; Cambridge, Mass., 1924), pp. 48–50; Ruth L. Butler, *Benjamin Franklin Postmaster General* (Garden City, N.Y., 1928), pp. 162–6; Jennings B. Sanders, *Evolution of the Executive Departments of the Continental Congress, 1774–1789* (Chapel Hill, N.C., 1935), pp. 153–4.

Advertisement by the Pennsylvania Committee of Safety

Printed in *The Pennsylvania Gazette*, August 2, 1775.

Early in May the voluntary organizations of associators took form in Pennsylvania, and by the end of June the Assembly endorsed them, promised to arm and pay them, and created the committee of safety to supervise the working of the new system.[9] On July 18 Congress embodied in a series of resolutions a plan for organizing, supplying, and officering the militia in each colony. Responsibility for carrying out the plan was delegated to the local committee of safety when the assembly or convention was not sitting.[10] The Pennsylvania committee, in implementing the plan, worked in three main areas: the issuance of commissions; the rules and regulations for governing the associators; and the organization of the companies and battalions, the encouragement of enlistment, and the identification of those who refused to join. The first is the subject of the advertisement that follows. The other two are discussed in editorial notes below, August 19 and 26, 1775.

Three days after publishing its advertisement the committee agreed on the wording of the commissions for militia officers. The printed form opened with a paraphrase of the Congressional authorization, and left blanks for name, rank, etc., but none for the date. The form for naval officers, of vessels to defend the Delaware, was adopted on August 26.[1] Five commissions that Franklin signed as president of the committee have come to light.[2]

Committee of Safety, Philadelphia, July 28, 1775.

Whereas the Continental Congress have, by their resolves of the 18th instant, recommended, that all officers above the rank of a

9. See above, the note on BF to Hartley, May 8, and the editorial note on the formation of the committee of safety, June 30.

10. *JCC*, II, 187–90; see also the headnote below on the committee of safety to the Assembly, Sept. 29, 1775.

1. *Pa. Col. Recs.*, X, 295, 321–2. The vessels were for the most part galleys, for which see John W. Jackson, *The Pennsylvania Navy, 1775–1781* . . . (New Brunswick, N.J., [1974]), pp. 14–18.

2. Two are undated: to George Taylor as colonel and Christopher Hartzel as adjutant of the first battalion of Pa. associators in Northampton Co. (APS; Omaha Public Library). The other three are to John Hennessey as lieutenant and to Isaac Rotche (*i.e.*, Roach) and James Willson as first lieutenants, respectively, of the armed boats *Effingham*, Oct. 4, 1775, *Franklin*, Feb. 16, 1776, and *Congress*, March 6, 1776 (2 *Pa. Arch.*, I, 378; Hist. Soc. of Pa.; APS). Four other commissions that BF signed as president of the convention are listed in our editorial note below, July 15, 1776.

Captain be appointed by their respective provincial Assemblies or Convention, or in their recess by the Committees of Safety, appointed by said Assemblies or Conventions.

The Committee of Safety, appointed by the Assembly of Pennsylvania, do therefore request the Committees of the City and Liberties of Philadelphia, and of the several counties in this province, to make a return to the Committee of Safety at Philadelphia, of all the officers of the Military Association, in order that commissions may be made out for them, agreeable to the above resolve of the Continental Congress.

And the several Committees are further requested to make return to the Committee of Safety, of the number of the Associators, and also of the Non-associators within their respective districts.

Signed by order of the Committee. B. FRANKLIN, President.

A true Copy from the Minutes, W. GOVETT, Clerk C.S.[3]

From [David Hartley]   ALS: American Philosophical Society

Dear Sir   Golden Square July 31 1775

I am very glad to collect by a Phrase in the letter from the Congress to the Canadians, that they think once more of imploring the Attention of their Sovereign.[4] I can give you no information of the State of the Ministry, I should be one of the last to be informed of their counsels. The great fear that I entertain, is, least they should make things desperate with America, in order to screen themselves. I can easily foresee, that in a short time, we shall have very little communication or intelligence from America, but what the Ministry please to retail out to us, and that modified as they shall think proper. If they act the part of Gobetweens making mischief and can intercept the Communications between the two Countries, they may make each Country think

3. William Govett had been appointed clerk on July 3; in his note below under Nov. 9, 1775, he styled himself secretary. Congress subsequently named him clerk to the auditor general. *Pa. Col. Recs.*, X, 282; *JCC*, V, 620.

4. Congress had approved the address to "the oppressed Inhabitants of Canada" in the late spring, and had had it printed in French and English: *JCC*, II, 68–70, 88. On July 27–29 the *London Chron.* published the English version; in it was a suggestion that the King be implored in a joint petition to "forbid a licentious Ministry any longer to riot in the Ruins of the Rights of Mankind."

ill of the other, by a course of mutual misrepresentations. All the accounts that were laid upon the table of the House of Commons last year, were garbled just for the purpose of misleading our judgements;[5] And the same will probably allways be the Conduct of men who have an interest to foment a quarrel between the two Countries, with a view to justify themselves *ex post facto*, and upon subsequent acts of violence and ill blood, which are inseperable from a state of war, to deceive the people of England into a persuasion, that our brethren, in America, were from the first ill disposed to this Country. The ministry have the Command of the sea, and thereby of all Correspondence. They may permit none but the most violent libels against the Americans, to be sent over to you in order to make you believe that the Spirit of this Country is against you. They may, on the other hand, give to us just what accounts they please. Both Countries must be at their pleasure for the representation of things. For instance in the Gazette account of the 19th of April they say; *Such was the Cruelty and barbarity of the rebels, that they scalped and cut off the ears of some of the wounded men, who fell into their hands.*[6] The worst impressions must be expected to arise, upon the minds of the people of both countries, from such articles as these, which can only be calculated to foment ill blood. For these Considerations, I most earnestly entreat, that our brethren in America will not give credit to any unfavorable reports that may be sent over to them, when a free communication of intelligence is intercepted. Disbelieve all such reports, and trust to the generosity and justice of the minds of the people of England. You will certainly find the nation just, generous, and affectionate to you. The General sentiments and feelings of this Country have been greatly shocked by the Gazettes of blood,[7] not that of enemies, but of our brethren and fellow subjects. I hope

5. This charge held true in one instance, at the opening of the session in January, 1775, when Gage's views in letters laid before the House were systematically falsified by deletions; see above, XXI, 473 n and the reference cited there.

6. The account of the retreat from Concord was reprinted from the *London Gaz.* in the *London Chron.*, June 10–13, and the *Public Advertiser*, June 12, 1775. The American account had been received and published weeks before; see the note on the Mass. congress to BF above, April 26.

7. The phrase is quoted from the undelivered petition from the City of London discussed in the note on Lee to BF above, July 6.

that even these horrid events, will not turn off the General Congress, from making some proposals for accommodation. The people of England cannot be alienated from those of their own blood, their own brethren and friends in America if they still find you earnest for reconcilement. You know, that the heart of this Country was not alienated from you, when you left us. Your friends Messrs. Osborne Falconer and Read, bring you more recent intelligence;[8] being discreet and intelligent persons, they can judge of the temper of this Country, and they will tell you, that it is not unfavorable to you. Whatever you hear to the Contrary, believe it not. Rely on the Candour of the People of England, and State facts. I hear particularly of great remittances daily coming over. Shew us how scrupulous you have been to pay your debts, and collect if you can, an Estimate of the remittances made this year. Any pains and labour will be well bestowed, to vindicate yourselves, and your character, to this Country and to posterity. Passion may sway for a while but reason must prevail in the end. Let your friends here, have all possible materials, to do justice to your Cause. Votes of assemblies petitions addresses facts dates, and the historical evidence of all transactions from the very beginning of these unfortunate troubles. I fear that I shall repeat the same things over and over, in all my letters, till {I} weary you, but I am most earnest to leave no chance untried, and to exert every possible means of reconciliation. Let your friends here, have all possible materials to do justice to your cause, and to strengthen their endeavours, to restore harmony and Confidence between the two Countries. Let us strive to the last; Let us leave nothing undone. All is lost if we despair. I remain Dear Sir With the greatest respect to your person and Character Your much obliged friend   G B

To Doctor Franklin.

8. Peter Osborne, with whom BF had crossed in the *Pa. Packet*, was doubtless a friend by this time, and Nathaniel Falconer had been for years. We have no other evidence that BF even knew Capt. Thomas Read, for whom see the note on Hartley's earlier letter above, July 22.

Proposed Resolution by Congress

AD (draft): American Philosophical Society

This resolution, as Paul Smith has pointed out,[9] is impossible to date but may reasonably, if conjecturally, be ascribed to July, 1775. The preamble, cramped at the top of the page, seems to have been drafted after the resolution itself. The unexplained "as aforesaid" in both, and the note at the end, suggest that the draft was to be inserted in a longer set of propositions, now lost, which Franklin intended to submit to Congress. He mentioned in early July what might have been one of them, and it also had to do with reparations.[1] The subject of quitrents and purchase money was on his mind at the time, when his friends in the Walpole Company were attacking the crown's proprietary rights in lands obtained from the Indians;[2] and the course he is advocating would have robbed those rights of their value.

[July (?), 1775]

And whereas altho' the Conquest of Canada, and Louisiana [*insert cropped and illegible*] was effected as aforesaid by the said [?] Force and Expence of America with Britain, the latter hath seized the whole acquired Territory as its own, excluding us from any Share in the Property, without the least regard to Equity or Justice

Resolved, That in case such Satisfaction as aforesaid is refused, all the Lands in America claimed by the Crown, and all the Quit-rents now unpaid to the same, shall be considered as liable to an Appropriation for that purpose. And all Persons from whom such Payments of Quitrents are now due, or who have purchased Lands from the Crown, and have not yet paid the Purchase-money, are advised to withold the same; and all Persons wanting Lands are advised to forbear Purchasing of the Crown, till such Satisfaction shall be made; that if Heaven shall finally bless our Endeavours in this just War with Success, as much as possible may be saved towards such Indemnification.

between Pages 4 & 5

9. *Letters*, I, 688–89.
1. BF to Shipley above, July 7.
2. See the headnotes above, April 11 and July 12.

Promissory Note to Peter Reeve[3] from Members of the Pennsylvania Committee of Safety

DS: Historical Society of Pennsylvania

This document throws light on the impromptu methods of financing the war. The Pennsylvania Assembly, in creating the committee of safety, had authorized the emission of £35,000 in paper currency for the defense of the province.[4] But the funds were not immediately available to the committee. In mid-July a subcommittee, including Thomas Wharton, Jr., and Robert Morris, was directed to borrow if possible from the provincial treasurer "until the Money for this Board is Emited." On July 31 another subcommittee, also including Wharton and Morris, was directed to borrow as much as it could from the wardens of the port of Philadelphia.[5] This promissory note was the result; it makes no mention of the committee, and the signers appear to be contracting the obligation as individuals. Wharton and Morris discharged it after the committee, on August 10, had made £25,000 available to them to cover such commitments.[6]

⟨Philadelphia, August 1, 1775: A promise to pay Reeve on demand the sum of £3,500, signed by Franklin and nine other members of the committee.[7] An endorsement shows that £2,500 were paid by Thomas Wharton, Jr., on September 23 and the remaining £1,000 by Robert Morris on Oct. 16, 1775.⟩

3. A ship captain and merchant, who had at least once been associated with BF in a business venture: above, XI, 315.

4. See the citations in the headnote on the committee above, June 30.

5. *Pa. Col. Recs.*, X, 286, 295. Since 1766 Reeve and Robert Morris had been among the wardens, who were responsible for the administration of the port, and Reeve was their treasurer; the funds he administered came partly from fines and partly from grants by the Assembly. James T. Mitchell and Henry Flanders, eds., *The Statutes at Large of Pennsylvania from 1692 to 1801* (17 vols., Harrisburg, 1896–1915), VII, 19–27; VIII, 264–84, 423–8.

6. *Pa. Col. Recs.*, X, 300–1.

7. Those who attended the meeting on Aug. 1: *ibid.*, p. 296.

The York County Committee to the Pennsylvania Delegates in Congress

Reprinted from Samuel Hazard *et al.*, eds., *Pennsylvania Archives* (1st series; 12 vols., Philadelphia and Harrisburg, 1852–56), IV, 640–1.[8]

Gentlemen, York Town, Augt 1st, 1775.

Our County Committee met 28th ult., and after going through the other business they were called for, (which will be the Subject of another Letter herewith sent,) they proceeded to Consider in what manner the recommendation of the Assembly and the Continental Congress, touching those People (in this County) who Conscientiously scruple bearing Arms, shou'd be Carried into Execution.[9] It was expected that some offer wou'd have been made by those People, but as no such offer was made on their part, it was recommended, that they should be applied to in every Township in this County, to see if they wou'd voluntarily propose any mode of Contribution agreeable to the recommendations aforesaid. But since the breaking up of the County Committee, It has been suggested to the Committee of Corres'dence and observation, by some worthy People of that Persuasion, that all such Applications wou'd be fruitless, as those People equally scruple subscribing as bearing Arms, but apprehend, that if the Commissioners and Assessors[1] wou'd lay a reasonable sum as a Tax on those who refuse or cannot consistent with their Consciences bear Arms, that it would be submitted to without reluctance, and consequently requested the Comittee to recommend that step to the Commissioners and Assessors.

In so delicate an Affair, where on the one hand any harsh Mea-

---

8. Documents in this volume reprinted from the *Pa. Arch.* apparently exist only in that form. The MSS are no longer in the Pa. State Library at Harrisburg, and a search elsewhere has failed to locate them.

9. On June 30 the Assembly urged on the associators "a tender and brotherly Regard" for their fellow citizens who would not serve, and stressed those citizens' duty to assist the associators. On July 18 Congress admonished conscientious objectors to do all in their power to help their distressed brethren and their oppressed country. 8 *Pa. Arch.*, VIII, 7249; *JCC*, II, 189. The records do not mention that the issue of the nonassociators was raised at the meeting in York Co. on July 28–29: 1 *Pa. Arch.*, IV, 639–40; 2, XIV, 536–8.

1. The county officials whom the Assembly had directed on June 30 to supply the militia with arms and ammunition and to levy taxes to support a new issue of paper currency: 8 *Pa. Arch.*, VIII, 7245–6.

sures might tend to infringe the rights of Conscience, and be Construed to be taking money out of our brethren's Pockets without their consent; and on the other the impropriety of one part of the Community defending the whole, in a struggle where every thing dear to Freemen is at stake, added to this the danger of the Militia laying down their Arms, finding the Burthen so unequally born, and that others wont so much as touch it with their Little finger; others (they say) who have as much at stake, and are in many instances abler than themselves to Assist in the Publick Conflict.[2]

The Committee thought it of too much emportance for them to proceed without the direction of the Congress, or at least of the Delegates of this Province, more especially as the same difficulty must occur in every County of the Province; and we doubt not but the Subject has been thought of by those so much more Capable then the Committee, of Framing an expedient to avoid the Evils on the one hand and the other. That suggested to us wou'd be agreeable here, and the Committee wish that the same or some other might be speedily recommended, to quiet the minds of People here and prevent inevitable confusion. We are, Gentlemen, Your most obedient, humble Servants. JAS. SMITH, Chairman.[3]

(Signed by order of the Committee,)

Directed. To the Delegates of the Province of Pennsylvania in Congress at Philada. Favoured per Mr. Abra. Usher.

To Jane Mecom   ALS: American Philosophical Society

My dear Sister   Philada. Aug. 2. 1775

Last Night I received with great Pleasure your kind Letter of July 14. with the most agreable Additions from Mr. and Mrs. Green.[4] God bless those two good ones!

2. For BF's concern with this issue see his proposals for conscientious objectors and the report to the Assembly from the committee of safety, both below under Sept. 29, 1775.

3. For Smith (*c.* 1719–1806), a lawyer who was one of the leaders in the back country of resistance to both Britain and the dominance of the eastern counties, see the *DAB*.

4. The Greenes' additions are printed above as separate notes, July 18.

The Congress has adjourned this Morning to the 5th of September. I have now upon my Hands the Settling a new General Post Office, and a Treaty to be held with the Indians on the Ohio,[5] besides smaller Businesses, all to be transacted by the time the Congress meets again. Govr. Ward is just setting out, and I cannot send this by him if I enlarge.[6] My Love to your Friends, from Your affectionate Brother   B FRANKLIN

Sally and Mr. Bache send their Love and Duty. I think you had best come hither as soon as the Heats are over, i.e. sometime in September, but more of this in my next.

To / Mrs Mecom / at / The honble Judge Green's / Warwick / per favour of Govr Ward.

From William Strahan

Copy:[7] Papers of the Earl of Dartmouth deposited in the Staffordshire County Record Office

London, August 2. 1775.

Having wrote You April 8. June 7. and July 5. this is the Fourth Letter I have sent you since you left Us.[8] I have in Truth Nothing new to convey to you, and only write now in Consequence of my

---

5. For BF's appointment as postmaster general see our editorial note above under July 26. On the 12th Congress had defined geographically three departments of Indian affairs, and the next day had elected BF, Patrick Henry, and James Wilson as commissioners for the middle one, lying between the Six Nations and the Cherokees. Henry declined to serve and was replaced; BF could not attend the subsequent meeting with the Indians, and another went in his stead. *JCC,* II, 175, 183, 251. His only involvement as commissioner was apparently in disbursing money for presents and other costs of the meeting; see the entries in his Memorandum Book (above, VII, 167–8) for Aug. 4, 7; Sept. 16; Oct. 4; and Nov. 12, 20. For the conference, held at Fort Pitt in September and October, see Walter H. Mohr, *Federal Indian Relations 1774–1788* (Philadelphia, 1933), pp. 31–4. BF had little to do with a second conference held the next year; see the note on BF and Wilson to Yeates below, July 4, 1776.

6. Samuel Ward's report to BF on his trip is below, Aug. 12, 1775.

7. See the note on Strahan's letter above, June 7.

8. It was actually the fifth, as explained in the note just cited; Strahan must have forgotten his letter of May 5, mentioned in his below of Sept. 6.

Promise of doing so every Packet till your Return, which I still hope will be towards the Fall.

It was with the utmost Concern I heard the News of the late Battle at Boston,[9] not only on Account of the Loss on both Sides, but as it widens the Breach, and renders all Hopes of Reconciliation more difficult and more distant than ever. Here is now a civil War broke out in good earnest, the final Consequences of which nobody can pretend to ascertain. What Pity it is that no Means can be found to stop it's Progress. For after we have slaughtered and distressed one another till we are weary, the Contest must end either in a final Separation, which I believe neither Side wishes for, or in an Accommodation, which may as well be proposed now, as at the Conclusion of a bloody, expensive and unnatural Civil War. I have only therefore to repeat my earnest Sollicitations, that you will exert every Nerve to prevent the farther Effusion of Christian Blood, and to promote a final and just Settlement of our Differences, such as may leave America every Species of Liberty they can reasonably wish for, and Brittain the just Supremacy over her Colonies, to which you say yourselves she is entitled, and which equally tends to the Happiness and Protection of the whole Empire. But I am afraid this is not the Time for the Voice of Reason to be attended to. Moderation cannot indeed be expected to grow amidst such violent Convulsions; but I hope you will not cease to do your best to put a Period to the Distresses of your Native Country, which as it is the chief Seat of the War must suffer prodigiously, should it be much longer protracted.

Here I will not say we are unanimous, but nearly so, to carry on the War with the utmost Vigor. Great Preparations are making to send more Troops and more Ships with all possible Expedition. The Honor and Dignity of the Crown, as well as the Commercial Interests of this Kingdom are, in the Opinion of the most dispassionate and impartial, all at Stake, and merit our utmost Exertions. You will doubtless smile at our Credulity, and think that you are able to repel every Force we can bring against you. Perhaps you may; but not without paying dearly for it in a Variety of Ways, which may render ultimate Victory itself a dear Purchase. Every *Part* of the British Empire must sensibly feel, and be affected by

9. Gage's account of Bunker Hill appeared in the *London Gaz.*, July 25.

144

the weakening of the *Whole*, and whether Success leans to the one Side or to the other, we shall all, in the long Run be considerable Losers.

I hear the Congress are once more to address the King.[1] If they do, and they should propose such Terms as can be deemed in any Shape admissible, a Stop may still be put to this Carnage, and all may yet be well. But as this Address is like to be the last Overture to Accommodation, I hope You have taken Care that it is conceived in proper Terms. Doubtless it would be submitted to your Correction. You know full well the Temper of the People here, and you must be sensible that your Countrymen may have in many Instances mistaken the Voice of Faction for the real Sense of the Nation at large. Even a Change of Ministry, an Event which I still think at a very great Distance, would make no material Alterations in the Measures now pursuing. I hope therefore you will not much lean to this Conception. By no Means think of insisting upon Conditions to which the British Legislature cannot listen, but come over next October or November, when the Parliament will certainly meet, with such fair and equitable and moderate Proposals as will shew to all Mankind how desirous, how sollicitous, you are to put an End to the Quarrel. In this case you may depend on the zealous Support and Assistance of all good Men, in which Number I reckon our gracious Sovereign, as well as a very great Majority of His Servants, who I am certain as they have no Interest earthly in taking Part against you, are excellently well disposed to do every Thing in their Power in Consistence with what they conceive to be their indispensable Duty, to spread the Blessings of British Liberty in the fullest Extent, to the most remote Corners of their Master's Dominions.

I have not yet had the Pleasure to hear from you, but expect it soon. I am in Expectation of seeing you here before Winter, and that you will be the happy Instrument in the Hands of Providence

1. Congress had reached this decision on May 26 (*JCC*, II, 65), and news of it was distorted in crossing the Atlantic. "The Deputies of all the Provinces, except those of the four New England Governments, having declared their Resolution to petition the King," the *Public Advertiser* reported on July 15, "the *Minority* have left Philadelphia. This Dissention has left us no Foes but the Bostonians. . . ." See also above, the editorial note, July 8, and Hartley to BF, July 31.

of restoring Peace and Harmony and Unanimity to British Subjects every where.   WILL. STRAHAN.

To Dr. Benjamin Franklin.

Copy.

Docketed: London, August 2, 1775 Copy of a Letter from William Strahan Esqr to Dr Benjamin Franklin

Bond from David Weatherby[2]

Printed form with manuscript insertions: Yale University Library

⟨August 2, 1775: Weatherby, a Philadelphia linen printer, binds himself and his heirs to pay Franklin or his assigns £ 44 in Pennsylvania currency. If £ 22 in the same, with interest, is paid within a year the obligation will be void. Sealed and delivered in the presence of Richard Bache and James Bryson.[3]⟩

To Ebenezer Hazard[4]

ALS: American Philosophical Society

Sir,   Philada. Aug. 3. 1775

I received your Application to be appointed Postmaster of New York, and have seen a Recommendation of you by your Provincial Congress, to which I shall pay due Respect by appointing you accordingly as soon as Commissions and Instructions can be

2. Perhaps one of the artisans who had emigrated from England to Philadelphia in 1773 with John Hewson and Nathaniel Norgrove; see above, XX, 321.

3. The same two had witnessed BF's signature on Trent's power of attorney above, April 11.

4. Hazard (1744–1817), the son of a Philadelphia merchant and in his youth a close friend of Benjamin Rush, graduated from the College of New Jersey in 1762, moved to New York, and became a partner in the publishing firm of Noel & Hazard. In May, 1775, the New York committee of safety authorized him to reorganize the local post office, and in July the provincial congress recommended him as "a most careful, fit, and proper person" to be postmaster. Two months later his appointment was confirmed; see BF's letter to him below, Sept. 25, 1775. In the fullness of time he became postmaster general. *Journals of the Provincial Congress . . . of New York, 1775–1776–1777* (2 vols., Albany, 1842), I, 90; Lyman H. Butterfield, ed., *Letters of Benjamin Rush* (2 vols., Princeton, 1951), I, 6 n; James McLachlan, *Princetonians, 1748–1768 . . .* (Princeton, 1976), pp. 378–84; *DAB*.

printed, and things got in Readiness to carry the Post through. In the mean time I wish to receive from you an Account of the present State of its Management, as far as is within your Knowledge; and am, Sir, Your most obedient humble Servant   B FRANKLIN

Mr Hazard

Addressed: To / Mr Hazard / Postmr / New York / per favour of / Mr Lewis.[5]

Endorsed: Letter Dr. Benja. Franklin Augst. 3d. 1775

From "a Freeman and Associator"

ALS: Historical Society of Pennsylvania

In the summer of 1775, while a subcommittee of the Pennsylvania committee of safety was wrestling with the organization of the associators,[6] the rank and file of fledgling soldiers in Philadelphia were voicing three main concerns. Two of them, their pay and the treatment of those who refused to volunteer, are discussed in the headnote on the report of the full committee below, September 29, 1775. The third, military authority and discipline, is the subject of this letter. The committee has undertaken to formulate regulations for the associators, the author says; he is therefore writing after the subcommittee began its work on August 3. The latest date of the letter depends on what he means by the "Laws of War" in the first sentence. He describes them as arbitrary because they vest in the officers an absolute power over men's lives. This description does not fit the articles adopted by the committee on August 19 and, in virtually the same form, by the Assembly in November; they provided for courts martial composed of enlisted men as well as officers, and empowered to punish with nothing more than a fine or dismissal. The description does fit the articles for the continental army adopted by Congress the previous June.[7] The writer, it seems reasonable to assume, did not yet know what the committee would propose, but feared that it would use for Pennsylvania a Congressional model that was alien to the nature of "a free cival Constitution." If this assumption is correct, he was presumably offering his alternative plan at a time when it had the best

5. No doubt Francis Lewis, a New York delegate, for whom see the *DAB*.

6. For the function of the committee of safety and the regulations that it promulgated see the editorial notes above, June 30, and below, Aug. 19, 26.

7. For the Pa. articles as formulated by the committee and passed by the Assembly see, respectively, *Pa. Col. Recs.*, X, 308–12; 8 *Pa. Arch.*, VIII, 7375–80. For the Congressional articles see *JCC*, II, 111–22.

chance of a hearing, in other words while the subcommittee was at work on its draft. The plan itself has disappeared, but its purport can be conjectured from what he says about it.

Sir   [Between August 3 and 19?, 1775]
    As the laws of war are very arbitrary; and vest an absolute Power in the Hands of one Class of men, over the Lives of another who have no voice among them, and as the Association of freemen can and Ought to be conducted on the principles of freedom, the enclos'd plan is submitted to your Consideration and that of the Committee of Safety. The plan is partly that design'd for one of the Companies of this city before it was known that the Committee of Safety would undertake to form any plan, and it is now laid before you with the utmost humility and Deference, and without the most distant view or Desire of dictating or directing, but purely to lay before you a Plan which would be generally approv'd by the privates, and which is principally design'd to hint to you that the plan which would Approach nearest to that of a free cival Constitution would meet with the highest Approbation and be most likely to answer the ends of our Association.
    The Plan is neither perfect nor intended as such. It is laid before you more to shew you that Plans have been thought of and something of this kind Generally Approv'd as far as it has been talk'd of, than with any other view. Submitting to your Superior Wisdom and discernment, I beg leave to subscribe myself Your Most Obedient Humble servant   A FREEMAN AND ASSOCIATOR

To Mr. Benjn. Franklin Esqr. Present [President?]

Addressed: To / Benjn. Franklin Esqr. / Present

Endorsed: Proposals for Regulating Militia

From Samuel Chase[8]   ALS: Yale University Library

Dear Sir: Annapolis. Augt. 4th. 1775
    Colo. Harrison yesterday having informed Me that a Constitutional Post Office is now established, and that You are appointed

---

8. Chase (1741–1811) was a Maryland lawyer and politician, who since the days of the Stamp Act had been prominent in opposition to royal authority. He

the Head of that Department,[9] the present Deputies I doubt not will be removed, particularly in this City and Baltimore Town.

Give Me Leave to recommend Mr. York as a Rider from Philadelphia. I never heard an Imputation on his Character and We have experienced his Diligence Sobriety, Punctuality and obliging Behavior. Our Letters have been frequently trusted to his Care and always delivered, I cannot therefore but wish he may be employed. I am Sir with Respect Your Most obedient Servant SAML. CHASE

Addressed: To / Benjamin Franklin Esqr. / Philadelphia

Endorsed: Mr. Chace is one of the Delegates from Maryland.

From Edward Bancroft[1]   ALS: American Philosophical Society

Dear Sir   Downing street London Aug. 7th. 1775

I had lately the honour of acquainting you by Capt. Read with some particulars which I now confirm,[2] and although but little of importance has since occurred I am induced to trouble you again with a few suggestions respecting the Title of the different Indian Tribes of America to the property and Jurisdiction of their Territories. You will doubtless remember that our Friend Mr. Wharton had collected and put together some important Facts and Observations relating to this subject, and as his sentiments thereon were perfectly agreable to my own we composed and printed, soon after your departure, a small Pamphlet, in vindication of the Rights of

---

was a member of the colony's committee of correspondence and one of its delegates to the first and second Congress. *DAB*. BF's endorsement suggests that the two men were unacquainted at this time; seven months later they were thrown together as commissioners to Canada. We have found no trace of the man who was the subject of this letter.

9. For Benjamin Harrison (1726?–91), the father of the ninth President and a member with BF of the committee of secret correspondence, see *ibid.* BF's appointment as postmaster general is discussed in our editorial note above, July 26.

1. Bancroft had been BF's protégé for some time; see above, XVI, 224–5 n. This is the first extant letter in a long correspondence between them.

2. The letter, which has been lost, was sent by Thomas Read in the *Aurora*. She sailed on Aug. 6 and was at Philadelphia by Oct. 5: *London Chron.*, Aug. 5–8, 1775; Smith, *Letters*, II, 121.

the Aborigines of America; one of which, Mr. Thomas Wharton was desired to shew you;[3] and least that may have miscarried, another is herewith sent for your acceptance; not that I suppose any new arguments will be necessary for your Conviction on this Topic; being satisfied from the Liberality and extensive Circuit of your Reflections, as well as from particular Conversations with which you have favoured me, that you have long perceived the absurdity of all distinctions between the Temporal Rights of mankind founded on any supposed defect in their Religious Opinions, and have rejected those pretensions on which Former Popes availing themselves of the ignorance and Superstition then prevailing over all Europe, arrogantly assumed a right to dispose of the Persons and Countries of unbelieving Nations in Asia Africa and America;[4] a right which is now universally ridiculed by all whose minds are emancipated from the shackles of superstitious prejudice. And indeed the aborigines of America being the Primitive Occupiers of that Continent, and having obtained the possession of it, from the Creator and most rightful disposer of the Earth, without that injustice and violence by which other Nations have frequently acquired their Territories, were by the Laws of Nature and Nations justly intituled to the full and Absolute Dominion and Property of that Continent. Before America had been discovered, the Inhabitants could not possibly have owed any Allegiance or Subjection to any foreign state; and nothing could be acquired by a discovery of Countries previously inhabited and Possessed; and therefore the American Indians must still have an indisputable Title to the Jurisdiction and Property of all Parts of that Continent, which have not been obtained from them by Purchase,

3. [Samuel Wharton,] *Facts and Observations, Respecting the Country Granted to His Majesty by the Six United Nations of Indians* . . . (London, 1775). Wharton, writing to his brother Thomas on the same day as this letter, enclosed four copies of the pamphlet, with an injunction to give one to BF and the others only to those, even members of Congress, who promised to return them. He also enclosed a letter to BF, now lost. Thomas was to read and copy it, then seal and deliver the original; the copy was to be shown to delegates, but confidentially and without offending BF. The Doctor, however well disposed to the cause, was growing old; and with his concurrence Thomas and Trent must take the lead in lobbying. *PMHB*, XXIV (1900), 394–5.

4. The demarcation line of Alexander VI, agreed upon in 1493–94, divided the overseas possessions of Spain and Portugal.

Cession, or justifiable Conquest.[5] This Truth was indeed so well known, and so sensibly felt by the first Settlers in our Colonies, that tho' protected by Grants from the Crown they appear never to have relied on those Grants, nor to have considered them as any other *than Political Distributions* of Country, which gave them no title to the Soil until it should be fairly obtained from the Indians themselves. And the same maxims were likewise adopted by the Lords of Council, in their decision respecting the appeal of the Moheagan Indians against the Coloney of Connecticut;[6] and in truth the British Government on many occasions, and particularly in the Negociations with the Court of France in 1755, and in the Purchase of Lands on the Ohio, made in behalf of the Crown, from the six Nations in 1768 has publickly acknowledged and Confirmed the Title of the Indian Nations of America to their respective Countries.[7] The King has indeed from Political Views assumed a right of restraining the Indians from Conveying their Lands to any but those who may be authorized by the Crown to purchase them; every reason however, and every Principle of Justice, supporting the *Limited* right, which is thus allowed them, must operate as strongly, in favour of their *full* and *unlimited* Right over the Lands in question. For as the Property of the Indians in their respective Territories, is *original* and underived, except from the Divine Creator, it must by a necessary consequence be full, absolute, exclusive, and indefeasable. I write not indeed to Convince you of these truths, of which you are already satisfied, but to suggest to you a particular application of them. You know it

5. See the headnote above, July 12, on BF's endorsement of legal opinions and the references cited there. Bancroft was no more a lawyer than was BF.

6. Thomas Life described this appeal, which had been in litigation off and on since the beginning of the century, as "the greatest cause that ever was heard at the Council Board." Quoted in Joseph Henry Smith, *Appeals to the Privy Council from the American Plantations* (New York, 1950), p. 418. The case involved land grants to Connecticut by the Mohicans; the issue was not the Indians' original title, which as Bancroft says was undisputed, but their claim that the grants had been invalid. An order in council in 1773 upheld Connecticut's right to the land. *Ibid.*, pp. 422–42.

7. For the abortive Anglo-French negotiations in 1755, after the outbreak of hostilities, see Theodore C. Pease, ed., *Anglo-French Boundary Disputes in the West, 1749–1763* . . . (Ill. State Hist. Library *Coll.*, XXVII; Springfield, Ill., [1936]), pp. xli–lxi. The land purchase in 1768 at Fort Stanwix was at a cost to the crown of more than £10,000: above, XV, 277 n.

has been generally though unthinkingly beleived *here*, that the Lands on which our Colonies in America have been settled, were *before* such settlement, *The Property of the British State*, and that this has been assumed as a fundamental Proposition by almost every writer in favour of Parliamentary Supremacy, and that the dependance and subjection of the Colonies to the Legislature of Great Britain has been from thence most strongly, though erroneously infered and maintained. A Regard therefore to the Civil Rights of our Countrymen in America, as well as to that equal and Common justice which belongs to the Indians demands that this fundamental and pernicious Error should be speedily and Publickly Corrected and Exploded; which could not be so properly and effectually done as by that respectable Body the *Congress*, whose Declaration in support of the absolute right of the Natives to their Territories, would for ever exterminate this Error in America, and probably in Europe likewise. There is besides another Consideration which should, I think, induce the Congress to this proceeding. There can be no doubt, but if the present hostile invasion of the Colonies should be prosecuted, which there is every reason to believe will be the case, so long as their is any hope of success, and if the Forces to be sent from hence should be found unequal to this unnatural purpose, that endeavours will be used to excite the Indians of America, to butcher the Inhabitants of the Colonies, to the end, that by an accumulation of distress and Carnage, they may the sooner be reduced to submission. These execrable attempts however might I think be effectually frustrated and the Affections of the Indians unalterably secured if the Congress should publickly assert and maintain the full and Absolute Right of the Natives to Sell and Convey their Lands to such Purchasers as may offer the best Prices, without any of those restraints from the Crown, which have hitherto rendered this (almost the only) property of the Indians, of but little value to them. You know sir, how jealous the Natives have long been of our intentions towards them on this Subject and I think an Act of so much justice, and so essentially conducive to their most important Intrests, could not fail to Conciliate their Friendship to those, who should thus espouse their Cause, and Assert their Rights. This indeed is now rendered the more expedient by the pernicious Views of Government manifested in the Quebec Act, and in the expressions which lately escaped from the Ministerial Speakers against Lord Camden's Motion.[8] To bind all the future settlements of British America in Chains of Despotism appears to have been the design of that part of the Act which so enormously extends the Limits of Quebec; but the ministry being Conscious of the Rights of the Indians have cautiously worded this part of the Act; which declares "that all the Territories, Islands and Countries in North America *belonging to the Crown of Great Britain*, bounded" within the Limits therein described, shall "be annexed to and made part and parcel of the Province of Quebec." And therefore if it be proved, as may easily be done, that the Countries of the Indians within those Limits, *do not belong* to the Crown of Great Britain but, to the different Indian Nations by whom they are possessed and who have been often treated with as independant Allies, these Countries will then be detached from the Province of Quebec and rescued from the Despotism which must otherwise be imposed upon them and also from those Quit Rents and other Reservations which have lately accompanied all Royal Grants in America, and which are so frequently adduced to support the supremacy of Parliament, as has been already mentioned.

I shall however respectfully submit the justice of these Observations, the use to which they may be capable of being applied, and the time and manner of their application to your Superior Wisdom. And have only to add to the Communications of my former Letter that Five regiments, containing in all, about fifteen hundred men, are soon to proceed from Ireland to America.[9] I strongly hope however, that the ill success, which I am perswaded will attend all the attempts of the Army and Navy in America this summer, may at the commencement of next Winter, compel the present ministry to Quit the Helm, which they have so unwisely

8. The debates in the two houses on May 17–18 upon the bill to repeal the Quebec Act evoked nothing from the government benches, as far as we have been able to discover, that had to do with the Indians.

9. At the beginning of August the officers of the 17th, 27th, 28th, 46th, and 55th foot were recalled to their regiments in Ireland: *London Chron.*, Aug. 1–3, 1775. The troops, rumor had it, were destined for operations in the southern colonies: *Public Advertiser*, Aug. 3, 1775. The report was premature; planning for the southern expedition did not begin until mid-October, and involved different regiments. Eric Robson, "The Expedition to the Southern Colonies, 1775–1776," *English Hist. Rev.*, LXVI (1951), 539–40.

and wickedly conducted, and that they may be succeeded by others who will contribute to a permanent and equitable reconciliation between Great Britain and the Colonies. I shall be happy at all times to hear of your Welfare and to receive and execute any Commands with which you may think fit to honour me. I am with great Esteem and respect Dear Sir Your much Obliged and most Devoted Humble Servant   EDWD. BANCROFT

Dr. Franklin

From Benjamin Gale[1]   ALS: American Philosophical Society

This letter was apparently Franklin's first news of an invention that might, given a fair trial, have affected the course of the war. Until the entrance of France, Britain had virtually complete control of the sea; the Royal Navy supplied and reinforced British armies, and moved them at will along the coast. Any challenge to the navy's predominance would have had incalculable consequences, and the *Turtle*, the submarine described in this letter, was such a challenge in embryo. It was a threat only to a ship at anchor, but a British squadron supporting an army ashore had to have a safe anchorage.

The inventor developed and tested his prototype for a year after this description of it was written. He and his companions were not completely ready for action when the New York campaign reached its crisis at the end of August, 1776, but they attempted to destroy Lord Howe's flagship.[2] The attempt failed, as did later efforts, and the idea was discarded; more than a century passed before the submarine became an effective weapon. But the *Turtle*, crude as it was, first demonstrated the possibility of underwater attack, and so provided one of the intriguing *if*'s of history.

Honoured and Dear Sir   Killingworth 7 Augt 1775.

After so Long Absence I have been Impatient To Congratulate You on Your Safe return to America, at a Time when Your Councel is so much Wanted, but have denyd my self that Pleasure, on Acct. of the Important Business in which I knew You were engag'd. The Scituation of this Country is truly Alarming, my Expectations of Aid from our freinds in Brittain but small, but God

1. The Killingworth physician with an appetite for science was an old acquaintance; see above, XI, 183 n and subsequent volumes.
2. See the note on Howe to BF below, Sept. 10, 1776.

be praised the Machinations of those who should have been our Freinds to ruin us, have been in a Surprizing Manner frustrated, and on the Other hand our most Unpromising Enterprizes have been Crown'd with Success.

You[r Congress dou]btless have [heard? Intim]ations [of the Inven]tion of a [new Machine?] for the D[estruction of? Ship]s of W[ar. I now sit?] down to Give [you an] Acct of th[at Machine and?] what Exper[iments have] been Alr[eady made? wit]h it,[3] what I relate [you] may Intire[ly rely] upon to be fact. I will not at this Time attempt to Give You a Minute Description of the Form, as the Post is now Waiting. Thus Much, it doth not Exceed 7 feet in Length, and the Depth not more then 5½ feet, the Person who Navigates it, sits on a Bench in the Center of the Machine. The Person who Invented it, is a Student of Yale Colledge, and is Graduated this Year.[4] Lives within five Mile of me. I was the second Person who ever was permitted to see it, there being no other Workman but himself and Brother, Excepting what Iron Work is wanted, which was done by His direction. His Plan is to place the Cask Containing the Powder on the Outside of the Machine, and it is so Contrived, as when it strikes the Ship, which he proposes shall be at the Keil it Grapples fast to the Keil, and is wholly Disengag'd from the Machine. He then Rows off. The Powder is to be fired by a Gun Lock fixed within the Cask which is sprung by Watch work, which he can so order as to have that take place at any Distance of Time he pleases. The Experi-

3. The MS has two large holes. When the letter was published in *Naval Docs.*, I, 1088–9, the editor filled these gaps by inserting bracketed words taken from a similar description by Gale two months later, printed in *ibid.*, II, 953–6. The insertions sometimes do not fit the spaces, or tie into fragments of remaining words; and we have then substituted our own guesswork.

4. David Bushnell (1740–1824) entered Yale at the age of twenty-nine and graduated in 1775. The previous summer he and his younger brother Ezra had begun to experiment with a submersible boat to plant gunpowder beneath a ship; a year later, as this letter indicates, the prototype was ready for testing, and a way had been found to detonate the underwater charge. *DAB*; Frederick Wagner, *Submarine Fighter of the Revolution; the Story of David Bushnell* (New York, [1963]), pp. 14–38; Alex Roland, *Underwater Warfare in the Age of Sail* (Bloomington, Ind., and London, [1978]), pp. 67–79. BF stopped to call on Gale, presumably to see a demonstration of the submarine, on his way to or from Washington's camp in October. Gale to Silas Deane, Nov. 9, 22, 1776, *Naval Docs.*, II, 955, 1099.

ments that has as Yet been Made are as follows. In the Most Private Manner he Conveyd it on Board a sloop In the Night and went out into the sound. He then sunk under Water, where he Continued about 45 Minutes without any Inconveniency as to Breathing. He Can Row it either Backward or forward Under water about 3 Miles an Hour, And Can steer to what Poi[nt o]f Compass he pleases. He Can Rise to the [top of?] the Water a[t any Time?] when he Pleases to [obtain a? fr]esh supply o[f air wh]en that is Exhausted. [He has also?] a Machine [already prep?]ard by which he can [tell the? dep]th under w[ater and can then?] admit water if [it is needed?] to Bring [the Machin]e into a perfect [Equilibr]ium with [the water.] He has allso another Pair of Oars by which he Can Rowe it either up or Down, and a forcing Pump by which he Can free himself from the Water which he Admits to bring the Machine to a Proper Equilibrium with the Water. At the Top he has a pair of Glass Eyes by which he sees Objects Under Water. These Parts are all Compleat and these Experiments he has Already Made. I might add, he has an Anchor by which he Can remain in Place to Wait for Tide Opportunity &c. and again Weigh it at Pleasure. About 1000 Weight of Lead is his Ballast, part of which is his Anchor, which he Carries on the outside at Bottom of the Machine. This story may Appear Romantic, but thus far is Compleated and All these Experiments above related has been Actually Made, He is now at New Haven with Mr. Doolittle an Ingenious Mechanic in Clocks &c. Making those Parts which Conveys the Powder, secures the same to the Bottom of the Ship, and the Watchwork which fires it.[5] I every Minute Expect his return, when a full Tryal will be made. And Give me Leave to Say, it is all Constructed with Great simplicity, and Upon Principles of Natural Philosophy, and I Conceive is not Equall'd by any thing I ever heard of or saw, Except Dr. Franklins Electrical Experiments. He Builds it on his own Acct. He was Urgd to Ask some Assistance from the Goverment. Upon the Leiut. Govrs. seeing it they Offered him Assistance, but it was so Inconsiderable a sum he refusd it, and says he will go through with it at his own

5. Isaac Doolittle (1721–1800) was a bell-founder as well as clock-maker, and during the Revolution manufactured gunpowder. William F. Doolittle, *The Doolittle Family in America* . . . (7 vols., Cleveland, O., 1901–08), I, 104–6. His principal assignment was apparently to make the pump for forcing out the water. Roland, *op. cit.*, pp. 78–9.

Risque.[6] The Only Objections in my Mind from what I have seen of the Machinery of it is that he Cannot see under Water so Deep so perfectly as to fix it right, and w[hethe]r 100 Weight of Powder will force its way through the ship. I fear the Water will give way before the Bottom of the ship, and the force of the Explosion Eluded.[7] The Whole machine may be Transported in a Cart. I might have added he has made the Experiment of firing Powder Under Water after remaining there 15[?] Minutes. I have been Long Urging him for permission to Acquaint You with these facts. He at Length has Consented with this Condition that I request You would not Mention the Affair Untill he has made the Experiment. When Compleated, if Agreable I will Acquaint you with the Experiments he makes before he goes with it down to Boston. He is Quite Certain he Can Effect the thing and his reasoning so Philosophically and Answering every Objection I ever made that In truth I have great relyance upon it.

I Congratulate You on Your Appointment to Your Former Situation with regard to the Post Office by the Continental Congress, and Would beg Leave Just to Mention Coll. Saltonstal of N London to that Department In N London a Worthy Good Man, who has Met with some Misfortunes. I Conclude another will be Thought Necessary at N Haven. If that has not been Already Engag'd Dr. Leveret Hubbard Jur. of that Town Who Married a Daughter of Mine I beg Leave to Recommend to Your favourable Notice.[8] Better Regulations of the Office Most Certainly is

6. Lieut. Gov. Matthew Griswold (1741–99) inspected the submarine and reported favorably to Gov. Trumbull: Wagner, *op. cit.*, p. 38.

7. The fear proved groundless: later experiments convinced Bushnell that he could destroy the largest ship in the navy. *Naval Docs.*, II, 955–6.

8. Gurdon Saltonstall (1708–85), son of a governor of the same name, was Silas Deane's father-in-law, a colonel of the militia, and an important figure in the colony. See Franklin B. Dexter, *Biographical Sketches of the Graduates of Yale College* . . . (6 vols., N.Y. and New Haven, 1885–1912), I, 316–18. The Assembly had appointed him to a committee to establish postriders, and he had stipulated to whom the mail was to be delivered. His choice of recipient in Killingworth (now Clinton) involved him in a bitter squabble with some of the inhabitants, with which Gale was directly involved. See Charles J. Hoadly, ed., *The Public Records of the Colony of Connecticut* . . . (15 vols., Hartford, 1850–90), XIV, 416; Conn. Hist. Soc. *Coll.*, II (1870), 225, 231, 245, 294n. All we know of Leverett Hubbard are his dates, 1749–87: Donald L. Jacobus, *Families of Ancient New Haven*, IV (1927), 865. The postmastership went in fact to Elias Beers.

Greatly Necessary and would further Presume to Add Great Complaints have been Made of Some of the Post Riders. I ask Ten Thousand Pardons for presuming to Trouble You with this Long Acct. which I fear will Appear to You too Romantic to Obtain Beleiff, but have Endeavoured in the Strictest Sense to relate Facts Truly. You Will Excuse Incorrectness as the Post Waits the Writing of this and Believe that I am with Great Truth and Sincerity Your Most Obedient and Most Humble Servant   BENJA GALE

Endorsed: Dr Gale

The Pennsylvania Committee of Safety to a Commissioner and Three Assessors of Bucks County

Copy:[9] Pennsylvania State Library, Harrisburg

⟨August 8, 1775: In answer to your letter of July 29 the committee directs you to provide 300 stand of arms and accoutrements as voted by the Assembly.[1] We will provide you with patterns, which you will take care to have followed in the manufacture; we will settle your accounts and have the treasurer pay you. If any opposition develops, inform us and give us the names, so that measures may be taken against such enemies of their country's safety.[2] Addressed to Theosophilus Foulke, commissioner, and to James Chapman, Jno. Vandegrift, and Jacob Bidleman, assessors,[3] and signed by Franklin as president of the committee.⟩

9. The text is printed in 2 *Pa. Arch.*, I, 544.
1. These were for county associators called into active service: 8 *Pa. Arch.*, VIII, 7245–6.
2. This injunction was in response to a letter from the four men, either that of the 29th or an earlier one, informing the committee that a majority of the board of commissioners and assessors had refused to carry out the Assembly's instruction. On Aug. 3 the committee ordered the whole board to appear before it, but the next day suspended the order. On the 8th BF brought up a letter, presumably of the 29th, to which this was the reply: *Pa. Col. Recs.*, X, 298–9.
3. Vandegrift we cannot identify. All we know of the other three is that Foulke (1726–85) lived in Richland and was disowned by the local Quaker meeting because he took the oath of allegiance to the colonies, and that Beitleman, as he seems to have been spelled, and Chapman were members of the local committee of observation; up to this time Beitleman had attended only once and Chapman not at all. Howard M. Jenkins, *Historical Collections Relating to Gwynedd* . . . (Philadelphia, 1884), pp. 228–9; *PMHB*, XV (1891), 259, 262.

Major General Philip Schuyler

To Philip Schuyler[4]

ALS: Massachusetts Historical Society

Sir,   Philada. Augt. 8. 1775. 5 PM.

Your Letter to the President of the Congress, arrived here just now by an Express from Albany, and is brought to me, the Congress being adjourn'd and all the Members out of town but my self.[5] I have taken the Liberty of looking into it, to see if it required any Service from hence in our Power to render. I wish we had more Powder to send you as you desire: But all hitherto arriv'd is gone to Boston, and an Order is left here for sending 5 Ton more thither as soon as it comes in. I hope the second Parcel sent you from hence, which had been delay'd on the Road by some Mismanagement, has got safe to you before this time.[6] I shall immediately forward your Letter to the President who is now I

4. Schuyler (1733–1805), who belonged to a prominent Albany family of Dutch extraction, was by this time a seasoned politician and a fledgling commander. In his seven years in the New York Assembly he had attempted to follow a middle course, opposing both radicals and extreme conservatives, but the developing crisis forced his hand. In April he joined the extralegal convention, which chose him as a delegate to Congress. His service in Philadelphia was brief, for he received one of the four original appointments as major general. In June Washington gave him command of the northern army, whereupon Congress ordered him to clear Lake Champlain of the enemy and, if "it will not be disagreeable to the Canadians," to occupy Montreal and take such other measures as might secure the northern border, *JCC*, II, 99, 109–10. Schuyler soon realized that he had meager resources for an invasion. His letter of Aug. 2 to John Hancock, which BF is here acknowledging, reported that Ticonderoga was in its present condition defenseless. The troops were desperately short of powder, and without it the ships Schuyler was building on the lake would serve only as transports. Force, 4 *Amer. Arch.*, III, 11–12; see also *DAB* and Martin H. Bush, *Revolutionary Enigma: a Re-appraisal of General Philip Schuyler of New York* (Port Washington, N.Y., 1969), pp. 12–37.

5. Congress adjourned in the first days of August, and did not meet again until Sept. 13.

6. The five tons ordered to Boston were, Congress believed, already in Philadelphia: *JCC*, II, 238. The first consignment to Schuyler seems to have been from Connecticut; the second was entrusted to the Philadelphia committee and sent by way of New Jersey, where it arrived in mid-July: *ibid.*, p. 108; Force, *op. cit.*, II, 1674; Smith, *Letters*, I, 560, 568. An additional three tons from South Carolina had been sent to the northern army in late July, and was expected to bring its total to five tons. *Ibid.*, p. 180. As late as Aug. 10 BF had apparently not learned of this most recent supply, for another 2,200 pounds then started northward from Philadelphia. See below, BF to Schuyler, Aug. 10, and to the N.Y. congress, Aug. 19, 1775.

suppose in the Camp before Boston. Wishing you Success in your arduous Undertakings, and a safe Return with Health, Happiness and Honour, I am, very respectfully Sir, Your most obedient humble Servant   B FRANKLIN

Gen. Schuyler

Endorsed: Benja Franklin   August 8th   Recd. 14th

The Pennsylvania Committee of Safety to the Albany Committee

Copy: New York Public Library

⟨Philadelphia, August 10, 1775: You will receive herewith 2400 pounds of gunpowder, to be forwarded to General Schuyler at the earliest opportunity. We have heard that a great and "superfluous" quantity of lead, an article much needed here, was captured at Ticonderoga. If you have it, and can load a parcel of it on the returning wagon, we shall be obliged and accountable for it.[7] Signed for the committee by Franklin as president.⟩

To Philip Schuyler

ALS: New York Public Library

Sir,   Philada. Aug. 10. 1775

I did myself the Honour of Writing to you by the Return of your Express on the 8th Instant. Immediately after dispatching him, it occurr'd to me to endeavour the obtaining from our Committee of Safety a Permission to send you what Powder remain'd in our Hands; which tho' it was thought scarcely safe for our selves to part with it, they, upon my Application and representing the Importance of the Service you are engag'd in, and the Necessity you were under for that Article, was chearfully agreed to. Accordingly I this Day dispatch a Waggon with 2400 lb. weight which actually empties our Magazine.[8] I wish it safe to your Hands, and to your self every kind of Prosperity.

7. See the following document.

8. On Aug. 8 the Pa. committee of safety took possession of Philadelphia's entire stock of powder, which on BF's suggestion was forwarded, as he says, to Schuyler on the 10th; earlier shipments are mentioned in the note on BF to Schuyler above, Aug. 8. This consignment reached Albany by the 21st; see the note of that date from the Albany committee below.

We find on Enquiry that there is an extream Scarcity of Lead here; and our Committee recollecting that a superfluous Quantity was taken at Ticonderoga, request you would spare us what you can of it.⁹ With great and sincere Esteem, I have the Honour to be Sir Your most obedient humble Servant   B FRANKLIN

General Schuyler

Endorsed: Benjn. Franklin Augt. 10. 1775 Philadelphia

From Thomas Bromfield¹   ALS: American Philosophical Society

Dear Sir.   London 12th Augst: 1775.

With pleasure your friends received the agreable inteligence of your safe arrival and health.

Inclos'd I return a Letter for you directed to our care. From different accounts I am pleased to observe, the great unanimity that prevails thr'o the Continent; your advise was never more wantd, hope it will tend to restore that invaluable blessing to which our unhappy Colonies have been so long strangers. From the best accounts we can collect, think the Ministry still seem determined to pursue rigerous measures, more troops and Men of War are going, to protect those already there till the spring, when a large reinforcment of fresh ones are to accomplish all there designs, (little thinking) What we must naturaly suppose will happen before that period arrives, from a total stopage in the Trade to America; but supposing it possible to be otherways, it is my Opinion, there Attemps to inforce theese measures by the sword

9. More than nine tons of ball and shot had been captured at Ticonderoga and Crown Point: Force, 4 *Amer. Arch.*, II, 646. BF's request was on instruction from the committee of safety, which had discovered that there were only five hundredweight of lead in the city. In his letter below, Aug. 23, Schuyler promised to send "a considerable quantity."

1. Briefly identified above, XXI, 157 n. He and his brother Henry were Boston merchants, and Thomas had been in England for some time on their business. During the visit of Josiah Quincy, Jr., the two Americans were often together in London, and sometimes in the company of Jonathan Williams, Jr.: Quincy, *Memoir*, pp. 227–8, 335. Less than three months after writing this letter Bromfield was in France, where he established a business connection with Silas Deane and then departed with a cargo for America, apparently in January, 1777: *Deane Papers*, I, 350, 448. His nephew, young Henry, will appear in future volumes in connection with the same business, in England and in France.

is impracticable. It is evident they have got so far in the Mire as not to be able to return back with any degree of Credit to themselves, therefore seem determin'd to pursue, th'o it may terminate in the ruin of both Countrys. Since the battle of the 17 June our reproch of Cowardice however, is wiped off.[2]

The Publick papers woud inform you of the death of our poor freind Mr. Quincy, it was great concern to us; We lament him as an agreable acquaintance and a sincere freind to the Interest of his Country; had a satisfaction however to think his papers fell into the hands of the Congress.[3]

I sincerely wish a continuance of your unanimity. May Peace be established upon a firm and lasting Basis, so ardently Wishes Your sincere friend and Most Humble servant   THOS: BROMFIELD

Addressed: To / Doctor Franklin / In / Philadelphia / per Capt. Newman Who is desired to deliver this with his own hand[4]

Endorsed: Mr Bromfield Aug. 12. 75

From Martin Howard[5]   ALS: American Philosophical Society

Dear Sir.   Newbern 12th. Augst. 1775.

I recieved your favour by Mr. Caswel.[6] When I wrote and informed you that I had recieved your Money of Mr. Cooke, I did

2. News of Bunker Hill appeared in the London newspapers in late July.

3. As we said above, XXI, 513, Quincy's information was in his head and died with him. No papers of his are recorded in the journals of either congress, the Mass. provincial or the Continental; and we must assume that Bromfield was mistaken.

4. By autumn the Philadelphia newspapers were no longer publishing the names of ships' masters, so that we cannot identify the obliging Capt. Newman or tell when he arrived.

5. The erstwhile attorney in Newport, R.I., who had been forced to flee the colony during the Stamp Act disturbances. For his and John Cooke's debt to BF, which elicited this letter, see above, XI, 459 n; XVIII, 220–1 n. In 1766 Howard had been named chief justice of North Carolina, and served until the courts closed in the wake of the Coercive Acts. He then retired to his farm, whence he fled to New York in 1777 and eventually to England. Samuel A. Ashe, *Biographical History of North Carolina* . . . (8 vols., Greensboro, N.C., 1905–17), III, [210]–15. The money at issue presumably went with him.

6. Richard Caswell (1729–89), a surveyor turned politician and soldier, had commanded under Tryon at the Battle of Alamance and was now a North Carolina delegate to the Congress: *DAB*.

not tell you the Truth. Mr. Cook was largely indebted to me, and gave me a Mortgage of a small House which I believe is his whole Property but not equal in Value to half the Sum he owes me, I included your Debt in this Mortgage, and when I wrote you, doubted not from his as well as from my then prosperous Situation of paying it with Ease as soon as I should recieve your Directions, but soon after our Courts became shut and the succeeding Distresses of this and the other Parts of America have not passed by without affecting me, and in my present situation I cannot pay it. It is proper to acquaint you that Mr. Cooke did not recieve your Money as my Clerk, he acted as an Attorney upon his own Bottom and in 1765 when I was precipitately hurried to England he took charge of all Papers in my Possession and unhappily for me and many others made a very unfaithful Use of them.

I mention these Circumstances to you that you may acquit me in *foro Conscientiae*,[7] not with an Intention to evade paying you what I have incautiously made myself chargeable with, but merely to obtain your Indulgence till better Times. As soon as Order and Government is restored here I shall instantly pay you, in the mean Time the little I possess, if I am permitted to possess it, will but just keep myself and Family above Indigence. I am Sir Your most Obedient and humble Servant   M. HOWARD.

Addressed: To / Benjamin Franklin Esqr. / in / *Philadelphia.* / favored by Colo. Caswel. / Free R Cogdell[8]

Notation: New Bern 23d. Novemr. 1775

From Henry Tucker   ALS: American Philosophical Society

The imperial crisis, long before it erupted in war, began to affect parts of the empire that were remote from the quarrel; and one of them was Bermuda. The small island, with a population of only 12,000, was in danger of being crushed between the upper and nether millstone. The embargo that the Continental Association laid on trade with other British possessions promised, once it went into effect, to paralyze the islanders' commerce and cut off their provisions. Their only recourse, unwel-

7. *I.e.*, morally rather than legally.
8. Richard Cogdell was a tavern-keeper in New Bern and chairman of its committee of safety. *N.C. Hist. Rev.*, XX (1943), 306. He was apparently acting also as postmaster.

come as it was to the many Loyalists among them, was to reach some measure of accord with the Americans even at the cost of annoying the British. Colonel Henry Tucker, himself half-American and the head of one of the great Bermuda clans, undertook to organize the negotiations. He prepared the way by instructing his son St. George, who was practicing law in Virginia, to get the ear of some of that colony's delegates and suggest to them that Bermuda might be useful. Then in May, 1775, the Colonel arranged for the election of a group of representatives to carry the islanders' case to Congress. Meanwhile, as an earnest of good faith, Bermuda prohibited exports to the British West Indies.

In July the delegation, headed by Tucker, reached Philadelphia. On the 11th it presented Congress an address that expressed guarded sympathy with the colonial cause, but insisted that Bermuda was too insignificant to take sides in the struggle, and begged for some means of procuring food when the American embargo took effect. Congress, unimpressed, answered six days later; it asked for statistics on previous imports of provisions and enclosed a copy of the resolution, introduced by Franklin on the 14th, that exempted from the embargo ships exporting produce and returning with arms or ammunition.[9] This move forced Tucker to bargain. He knew that powder was on hand in the royal magazine at St. George, and he apparently agreed with Franklin to trade it for exemption from the embargo. The Colonel returned at once to Bermuda, and on August 15th he and his friends carried out his side of the agreement: the powder was seized and shipped to Charleston and Philadelphia.[1]

Dear sir   Bermuda Augt. 12th 1775

Your very Acceptable favours of the 18th and 25st July I reced and embrace the earliest opportunity to Return you my thanks (as also those of our Deputies) for the ready and obliging manner in which you were pleased to present our Address to the Congress and we flatter ourselves that through your Assistance and their own good disposition towards us we shall obtain our reasonable request, which we shall be extremely glad to be Confirm'd in as it wou'd in a great measure relieve us from that Anxiety of mind

9. *JCC*, II, 174, 184–5, 187.
1. This account, except as noted, is based upon that in Wilfred B. Kerr, *Bermuda and the American Revolution: 1760–1783* (Princeton, 1936), pp. 13–15, 39–40, 42–50. The author gives no citations for BF's bargaining with Tucker in Philadelphia, and we have found no supporting evidence; but this letter and the subsequent theft of the powder strongly suggest that some such bargain was made.

which at present prevails among us. I have agreeable to your request Sketch'd out a plan for supplying us with provissions which I think will effectually prevent any part of them being exported to the West India Islands,[2] but shou'd any thing more be required of us, We shall readily Comply with it.

[The] Resolve of the Congress that you enclosed will undoubtedly engage many people to attempt the Supplies of powder &c. but the great difficulty in obtaining it will make the Quantities but small, as there is not the least probability of geting any at the English Islands, and the Dutch and French (as we are inform'd) have laid such Severe penalties on those that shall carry any from their ports that it will be almost impracticable to put such a Scheme in Execution to any Considerable extent.[3] Whatever Quantity comes to this place I shall Endeavour to secure that it may be sent to America. My Son St. George Tucker (a Youth lately call'd to the Bar at Williamsburgh, but on Account of the Courts being stop'd is now here till times alters) informs me of a Letter he wrote to Mr. Randolph late President of the Congress and Mr. Jefferson one of the Delegates for Virginia, representing the State of this Island, and proposing to them whether a plan may not be concerted to the Advantage of America by making this Island a Medium for Trade of Non-enumerated goods between the American Collonies and Foreign Ports, as we are under no restriction in reshipping such goods to any parts:[4] this wou'd not only be a means of disposing of large Quantities of your produce but woud also open a Door for the obtaining Powder &c. for no Doubt so

2. Both of BF's letters have been lost. One of them apparently intimated that Congress would support the islanders as soon as it found a method to prevent their re-exporting provisions to the British West Indies. *Ibid.*, p. 50. Tucker's plan, enclosed with the present letter and now among BF's papers in the APS, sketched such a method. It had three parts: (1) confining the island to trade only with the mainland colonies; (2) preventing the re-exportation of American foodstuffs from Bermuda; (3) permitting the exportation to America, in return for provisions, of any powder or military stores imported into the island.

3. The resolve was doubtless BF's resolution of July 14, mentioned in the headnote, about exchanging powder for provisions. The export of war materials from the Netherlands to the West Indies had been narrowly restricted at the source; see the note on BF to Shipley above, July 7.

4. St. George's letters to Jefferson from Williamsburg, printed in Boyd, *Jefferson Papers*, I, 167–9, contained a number of questions clearly instigated by his father, and intended as background for a second letter from the young man on Aug. 12, outlined below.

soon as the Dutch and French Feels the want of provissions they will Suffer Powder to be exchanged for them. But shou'd this plan be adopted by the Congress it shou'd be conducted with great Prudence and Secrecy and committed to the transaction of a very few. I have wrote pretty full upon this Subject to Mr. Robt. Morris Chairman of your Committee of safety and have desired him to consult you, which I dare say he will do. My Son has also wrote to Mr. Jefferson and I flatter my Self if it is thought practicable it will be readily adopted;[5] and it will give me great pleasure in being any ways Instrumental in Assisting the General cause of America.

It has been intimated here by Capt. Trimingham[6] that the people of Phila. blamed us very much for laying a prohibition on provissions, but I am convinced if they knew the true Motives they wou'd approve of it. As soon as the Account of the Engagement at Lexington reach'd us a report prevailed that the Port of New York was Shut up and all the other ports of America were likewise to be so in a few days. This Occasion'd many people as well Natives as strangers imediately to be exporting provissions to the West Indies expecting a great Market there, which allarm'd the people that they Addressed the Governor to call the Legislature imediately which he did and in Consequence thereof a Law passed to prohibit the Exportation of provissions,[7] and I am fully Assured had not this been done [torn] we shou'd have been in a most distress'd Situation f[or at the?] time of passing the Law there did not exceed a Months supply of Corn in the Island. I was greatly Shock'd at hearing the great Carnage that was made in the late Battle and most Sincerely hope some Expedient will be found to Accomodate Matters and prevent the further effusion of Blood.

5. The father's letter to Morris, now lost, presumably duplicated what the son, now home from Virginia, proposed to Jefferson on the same day as the present letter: that Bermuda be the entrepot for a trade in nonenumerated goods between America and foreign countries, that local merchants be the ostensible consignees in order to evade the Restraining Act, and that precautions be taken against infringing the Continental Association. *Ibid.*, pp. 239–40.

6. We know nothing about him except that he is said to have brought one of the letters from BF mentioned in Tucker's opening sentence. Kerr, *op. cit*, p. 48.

7. The act temporarily forbade exportation of cereal grains, potatoes and yams, and bread and biscuit; it was disallowed the following year. Thomas M. Dill, ed., *Acts of the Legislature of the Island of Bermuda, 1690–1923* . . . (3 vols., London, 1923), III, 21.

166

Our Deputies desire their Compliments to yourself and Mr. Dickinson. Wishing You health and happiness I remain Dear Sir Your most Obedient humble servant   HENRY TUCKER

Benja: Franklin Esqr:

From Samuel Ward[8]   ALS: Library Company of Philadelphia

Dear Sir   Providence 12th. Augst. 1775

On my Return I found the People of Connecticut in Arms for sixty Miles, a Fleet of twelve Sail of Men of War and Transports had been at the Mouth of Newlondon Harbor, an Attack was expected from them but they only went to Fishers Island and got about 1000 Sheep and Lambs and 30 head of indifferent horned Cattle the only fat ones being brought off a few Days before; The Wretch who owns the Island sold this Stock undoubtedly for his Tenant had made yards down by the Sea and got his Sheep and Cattle ready for them before they landed, the People deeply resent his Behaviour: The Fleet then stood for Gardners Island but a Number of armed Men probably prevented their Landing for they got no Stock save at Fishers Island: Wallace and Ayscough a Part of this Fleet returned to Newport and again terrified the People by making every Preparation as if they intended instantly to fire upon them: They stopped the Ferry Boats strictly examined every Person and took down the Names. They had heard of my Return and expected I should have gone to Newport and were in Hopes of getting one Delegate into their Possession; They took the western Post Rider and propose to send the Mail to Boston. I hope no Letters of Consequence may be in it but however that may be this shews the Impropriety of the Posts passing those Ferries.[9] I wish

8. Former governor of Rhode Island, one of its delegates to Congress, and an old friend; see above, v, 504 n.

9. The fleet was largely from Boston, on a raid to collect livestock (hence the transports), and created great alarm on the shores of the Sound; see Freeman, *Washington*, III, 506 n; *Naval Docs.*, I, 1167. Capt. Sir James Wallace in H.M.S. *Rose* commanded a small flotilla, including Capt. James Ayscough's *Swan*, that had for months been making life miserable for the inhabitants of Rhode Island by commandeering supplies, taking prisoners, and threatening to bombard towns; see *ibid.*, *passim*, and David S. Lovejoy, *Rhode Island Politics and the American Revolution. 1760–1776* (Brown University *Studies*, XXIII; Providence, R.I., 1958), pp. 185–7. The capture of the postrider, Benjamin Mumford, is

the People in Warren Bristol and Newport all the Advantages of an easy and speedy Communication but every private View ought to submit to the general Good and that in my Opinion absolutely requires that our Mails shoud be untouched unless at the proper Offices; By going [by?] the Narragansett Road (and if a Man of War sh[ould?] be at Newlondon crossing the upper Ferry) the Danger would be avoided save for the Newport Letters and the People and their Correspondents should write nothing a Discovery of which would injure their Country. The principal Gentlemen in this Town desired Me to write to You and request You to direct the Posts for the future to resume the narragansett Road. I doubt not but You will take the Affair into Consideration and give such orders as the public Safety may require.

A Mr. Otis who in the Act of Assembly which I gave You was appointed Depy. Postmaster in Newport has moved out of Town and Mr. Solomon Southwick the Printer a sincere Friend to his Country is appointed by the Assembly in his Room whom I doubt not You will continue.[1]

I was at home one Night on my Way here. Nancy who is at Bror. Greene's is unwell.[2] I have a good Mind to take her with Me to Philadelphia [to] see whether a long Journey and an entire Change of Air will not restore her the rest of my Family were all

---

discussed in Cooke to BF below, Aug. 15, 1775. Intercepting letters crossing the bay was a favorite British pastime. In early August Ayscough seized some that were on their way by private courier from Philadelphia to Massachusetts; Washington was alarmed because he thought they were to him and Charles Lee. Fitzpatrick, *Writings of Washington*, III, 398–9.

1. The Assembly had appointed Nathaniel Otis (1755–1817): John R. Bartlett, ed., *Records of the Colony of Rhode Island . . .* (10 vols., Providence, R.I., 1856–65), VII, 352. The young man, who was the son of Jonathan Otis (1723–91), nephew of Col. James Otis, and cousin of the more famous James, was a friend of Ezra Stiles and prominent in the local militia; the father moved at the end of June to Middletown, Conn., and Nathaniel accompanied him. Horatio N. Otis, *A Genealogical and Historical Memoir of the Family of Otis . . .* (Boston, [1848]), pp. 8–9, 15; Cooke to BF below, Aug. 15, 1775. Solomon Southwick (1731–97) was a Newport merchant and printer: Isaiah Thomas, *The History of Printing in America . . .* (2 vols., Albany, N.Y., 1874), I, 196–201.

2. Nancy was his third child, Anna: Bernhard Knollenberg, *Correspondence of Governor Samuel Ward . . .* (Providence, R.I., 1952), pp. 101–2, 214–15. "Brother Greene" was Catherine's husband William (above, V, 502 n); he and Ward had married sisters.

well: Mrs. Mecom I had not the Pleasure of seeing. She was gone to Worcester with Mrs. Greene who was not very well. Bror. Greene and all the rest were well, your Letter I left at his house.

The Love of Liberty triumphs in this Town over all other Considerations, every thing for the common Defence is pursued with immense Ardor every Danger is despised and every Difficulty surmounted and at the same time they are thus attentive to the general Interest of America. They are taking more effectual Measures for their own immediate Safety; Batteries on each Side of the River are opened in such advantageous Situations as will easily destroy any Ships which may attempt to come near the Town. Make my Compliments to Mr. and Mrs. Beach and such of my Acquaintance as may ask after Me. I am Dear Sir Your most affectionate Friend and humble Servant   SAM WARD

Addressed: To / Dr. Benjamin Franklin / Postmaster General / in / Philadelphia

Stamped: FREE / N*YORK*AU:28

Endorsed: Govr Ward

From William Franklin   LS: American Philosophical Society

Honoured Father,   Perth-Amboy, Augst. 14, 1775

I wrote to you by the Stage on Thursday last since which I have not heard from you.

As you were so kind as to say that you had no objection to doing any thing for me that might be in your Power respecting the Lands in the Traders Grant from the Indians, I send you enclosed a Copy of a Letter on that Subject from Mr. George Morgan, together with my Answer open, which after Perusal, please to Seal and Deliver.[3] I should be glad of your Sentiments respecting the Contents as soon as your Leisure will permit.

3. WF's earlier letter to BF has been lost. The copy of Morgan's letter that he enclosed, dated Aug. 8 and now in the APS, concerned selling the land given the "suffering traders" at Fort Stanwix in 1768 (see the headnotes above, April 11 and July 12): the sale, it was hoped, would occur the following spring under the aegis of the government of Virginia; a land office would be opened, and trustees appointed to collect the receipts and divide them among those proprietors who did not wish to take their shares in land. WF's position, although his response to Morgan has been lost, is clear from what follows.

I have read Messrs. Walpole and Sargent's Letter to you, and observe that since you left England they have received the *strongest Assurances* that as soon as the present Great Dispute is settled *our Grant shall be perfected*; and that they request that their Plan of Possessing and Leasing the Lands contracted for with Government may be "kept *as private as possible*, for should it be known on their side of the Water it might rather prejudice us than do us any service." I think it proper therefore to suggest to you that, in my Opinion, it is hardly possible that such a Transaction will be kept so secret as they think necessary, and consequently that you and Major Trent ought to weigh well the Consequences before you adopt the Measure.[4] I wonder Trent should make as an Excuse for not clearing the Judgement to Tilghman, or paying the Jersey Debt for Croghan, that he has nothing of Croghan in his Hands, when by Croghan's Letter to me the Judgement to Tilghman was principally, if not solely for a Debt of Trent's *own*, and, by his Acct. against Trent, there is a Ballance due to him of about £17 or 1800. Mr. Bernard Gratz (your Neighbour) has the Acct. and a Power to receive the Ball. and to pay it to me. Do send for him and he will shew it to you and make you acquainted with the Affair of the Judgement. He lately promised to write to me as soon as he could get Trent's Answer. Do let him know that I have not yet had a Line from him.[5]

We are all well and join in affectionate Duty to you and Love to the Family. I am, Honoured Sir, Your ever dutiful Son

WM: FRANKLIN

4. In the absence of Walpole's and Sargent's letter the question at issue must remain conjectural, but we believe that WF is still referring to the cession made to the traders. Selling this tract without royal authorization, he seems to be saying, would imperil the Company's last chance of securing the twenty million acres for which the promoters still hoped. For subsequent developments see below, the editorial note, Jan. 19, 1776, and the headnote on BF to Walpole, Jan. 12, 1777.

5. The jungle of WF's land speculations is fortunately beyond our purview. He and others had made a loan to George Croghan, secured in part by a mortgage on the latter's Philadelphia property, only to discover that the property was subject to a prior judgment obtained by Samuel Tilghman. Croghan professed to know nothing of the judgment, and promised that the money due would be paid by his financial agent, Barnard Gratz (for whom see the *DAB*), out of Trent's debt to him. Both the speculators, Croghan and Trent, had perfected the art of evading creditors, and WF collected nothing. William H.

P.S. I should be glad to have a Line from you by the Post to let me know if I may expect to see you here, whether you approve of my coming to Philada, and when it will be proper Billy should be there in order to go to the College.[6]

The above and enclosed were copied by him.[7]

Addressed: To / Dr. Franklin / Philadelphia

Burlington 16th. August 1775 reced and forwarded the 17th By *Mr. Wright* By Sir your obedt. Nephew   J. F. DAVENPORT[8]

Endorsed: W F. Aug. 14 75.

From Nicholas Cooke[9]   ALS: American Philosophical Society

Sir,   Providence August 15th. 1775

I think it my Duty inform you that on Friday Morning last as Benjamin Mumford who rides Post from Newport to New London was crossing the Ferry to Newport he was taken by Capt. Wallace of the Ship Rose who broke open the Mails sent some of the Letters ashore and kept the Remainder in Order to send them to Boston. He detained Mumford until Yesterday.[1]

Mariboe, "The Life of William Franklin . . . " (doctoral dissertation, University of Pa., 1962), pp. 324–7, 343–4.

6. BF did visit his son in Perth Amboy at the end of the month, and returned with WTF to Philadelphia: WF to WTF, Sept. 14, 1775, APS; see also below, p. 186n.

7. The closing salutation and postscript are in WF's hand, the rest in WTF's.

8. For Davenport, WF's secretary, see above, XX, 56–7.

9. The news of Lexington and Concord precipitated a political upheaval in Rhode Island. Nicholas Cooke of Providence was elected deputy governor in May, and the Assembly refused to permit the Loyalist Governor, Joseph Wanton, to take the oath of office; Cooke acted for him until November and was then appointed to succeed him. David S. Lovejoy, *Rhode Island Politics and the American Revolution, 1760–1776* (Brown University *Studies*, XXIII; Providence, R.I., 1958), pp. 182–3. BF's reply to this letter is below, Aug. 27, 1775.

1. An account of the incident appeared in the *Pa. Gaz.* of Aug. 23 and in the *N.Y. Gaz.* of Aug. 21, 1775; the latter is printed in *Naval Docs.*, I, 1197. For several years past Benjamin and Peter Mumford had kept an illegal post office in Newport. In June the Assembly had appointed them postriders from Newport, Benjamin to New London and Peter to Providence, and had instructed them not to handle any letters from previously existing post offices in the colony. John R. Bartlett, ed., *Records of the Colony of Rhode Island . . .* (10 vols., Providence, R.I., 1856–65), VII, 352–3. See also [Frank H. Norton, ed.,]

As the Mails will always be in the Power of the Ships of War so long as the Post continues to cross the Ferries to Newport which will not only render all Intelligence precarious but may be the Means of giving such Informations as may be very prejudicial to the common Cause I take the Liberty of recommending that the Mails be brought through Narragansett directly to this Town instead of being carried to Newport; and that they be returned the same Way.

Mr. Ward informs me that he delivered to you a Copy of the Act of Assembly establishing Post-Offices and Post-Riders in this Colony. In that Act Mr. Nathaniel Otis was appointed Post-Master for Newport; who hath removed to Middletown in Connecticut. The General Assembly have since appointed Mr. Solomon Southwick in his Room.[2] I am with great Truth and Regard Sir Your most obedient and most humble Servant   NICHS. COOKE

B. Franklin

Notation: Lre to Benja. Franklin Esqr. Augt. 15th. 1775

The New York Provincial Congress to the Pennsylvania Committee of Safety

Text printed in Samuel Hazard *et al.*, eds., *Pennsylvania Archives* (first series; 12 vols., Philadelphia, 1852–56), IV, 643–4.

⟨New York, August 16, 1775: A ship we sent for powder some three months ago has not returned, and our small stock is exhausted by supplying the camp before Boston with 1655 pounds and Ticonderoga with 300; all we could procure in this city has gone to eastern Long Island.[3] We must ask for the loan of a ton or as much more as you can spare, which we will replace from the first we receive; we request that the powder be sent immediately, in a tight cask, in care of the Newark committee. Addressed to

---

Journal Kept by Hugh Finlay (Brooklyn, N.Y., 1867), p. 33; James G. Mumford, *Mumford Memoirs* (Boston, 1900), p. 73.

2. See the note on Ward to BF above, Aug. 12.

3. The congress had sent 200 pounds with Connecticut troops dispatched to repel a British foraging raid: Force, 4 *Amer. Arch.*, III, 523.

Franklin and the other members of the committee and signed by P. V. B. Livingston as president.[4]

From D[avid Williams][5]   ALS: American Philosophical Society

My dear friend   [Between August 16 and 31, 1775[6]]

As some relief to you in your present circumstances, I wish you could have seen with what pleasure your letter to me, was read Yesterday by our friendly Society. We are removed from Slaughters T. to the Swan at Westminster bridge.[7] We have made a valuable addition to our number in *Mr. Raspe* whom you have seen in Germany, and who has been here a few weeks. He seemed to join us most sincerely in every expression of regard for you; and in regretting the unhappy measures which have separated us. I expect him every moment with a little parcel which is to accompany this letter. Major Dawson is made Lieutenant Governor of the Isle of Man; and probably fixed there some time. We are not likely to have him soon amongst us but we rejoice he is not to be called upon to fight the Americans. Mr. Knott has not yet been heard of; at least amongst our acquaintance.[8] We consider all our absent members as belonging to us; we cherish that affection for them which seems to characterise our little Club; and will probably continue it as long as we live.

We are extremely out of humour with the measures which are

4. For Peter Van Brugh Livingston, the wealthy New York merchant who was about to resign his presidency of the congress, see the *DAB*. The answer of the Pa. committee is below, Aug. 19, 1775.

5. Identified from the handwriting as well as internal evidence. For the Welsh dissenting clergyman turned deist see above, XXI, 119–20.

6. Williams speaks of a letter from Congress, which appeared in the *Public Advertiser* of Aug. 16; he also refers to a parcel about to be sent to BF, which was actually sent on Aug. 31: Rudolph Raspe to BF, Aug. 14, 1777, APS.

7. The friendly society was the Club of Thirteen, for which see above, XXI, 119–20; for the two coffee houses, Old Slaughter's and the Swan, see Bryant Lillywhite, *London Coffee Houses* . . . (London, [1963]), pp. 421–4, 561.

8. For Rudolph Erich Raspe, the German academic lately turned thief, see above, XIII, 345 n, and subsequent volumes. Richard Dawson had first introduced BF to Williams; Knott, whom we cannot identify, had collaborated with the Welshman in attempting a defense of BF after the scene at the Cockpit: above, XXI, 119–20.

pursued; but fear there is not virtue or spirit in this Country to resist them. John Bull is become a meer Ass, and will bear till his back is broken. I was myself exceedingly affected by the last letter from the Congress to the people of England. It drew tears from me, and the company I read it to, several times.[9] I declare that I do not remember to have read in any language passages so truly pathetick and excellent as some parts of the letter but it was to the people here like the whistling of the wind. They are callous to all the best sentiments of the human heart and references to public Spirit, love of general liberty, and even friendship and Justice, might do for Romances; but must not be expected to influence their Actions.

Your venerable Assembly and I sincerely look upon it, as one of the wisest and best that was ever brought together, may make America happy, by securing it's [torn] cannot produce in [torn] the virtues which alone could save [torn.]

I have lett my house at Chelsea [torn] Park street Grosvenor Square; where [torn] your next letter. The Design of [torn] liturgy is revived [?], and by several [torn . . . pro]pose to introduce it, this Winter.[1] I [torn] Copy when it is ready. I shall certainly [torn] read it with the sincerity and warmth, with which I [wish?] you health, success, and happiness. I remain Dear Sir, most affectionately yours   D [WILLIAMS]

9. The letter from Congress mentioned above, published in the *Public Advertiser* of Aug. 16 and addressed to the British people; for the text see *JCC*, II, 128–57.

1. Williams' *Liturgy on the Universal Principles of Religion and Morality* (London, 1776), for which see Edward V. Lucas, *David Williams, Founder of the Royal
Literary Fund* (London, 1920), pp. 9–11. Lucas states that this was a joint composition by the author and BF; he gives no evidence, and we have found none.

The Pennsylvania Committee of Safety to the New York Committee of Safety
LS:[2] New York State Library, Albany

⟨August 17, 1775:[3] We request you to receive and forward to Washington's camp, as we have promised to do, the baggage of Major French and two other British officers on parole.[4] We will pay the charges if the Major has already passed through New York; otherwise he will. Signed by Franklin for the committee.⟩

The Pennsylvania Committee of Safety to George Washington
LS: Library of Congress

Sir   Philadelphia August 17th 1775

The Committee of Safety for this City and Province, being informed on saturday last, that a Ship from Cork had come up to Gloucester with some passengers, Officers of the Ministerial Army, and a Quantity of Cloathing for that Army at Boston, immediately sent down Capt: Bradford with thirty Men to take those Officers prisoners, and at the same time an Armed Boat, to bring up the Cloathing, both which orders were accordingly executed. The Officers we have enlarged upon their written Parole, to render themselves at your Camp; and two Soldiers taken with them, being their Servants, on the Parole of Major French the Principal Officer, Copies of which Paroles are enclosed. The Major requested when he signed the Parole that we would for his Justification give him a Certificate of his making a Claim in behalf of himself and the others, and that his Claim was not admitted. We gratified him in this, and a Copy of our Certificate is Also enclosed. They were allowed to take with them their own Baggage, but the Baggage of some other Officers now in Boston, which he also requested, was refused, on account of the detention of the Effects of our Friends there by General Gage. So this Baggage with the Cloathing (an Invoice whereof is also enclosed) which we understand is for two Regiments, is Stored, to remain for the

2. The MS has been through a fire, and part of each line is missing; we have summarized what is legible.
3. Penciled in the margin in a different hand from that of the text.
4. For the circumstances of their capture see the following document.

175

Direction and disposition of the Congress.[5] The Officers and Soldiers are to set out for your Camp on Tuesday the 22nd inst. accompanied by two respectable Gentlemen of this City Capt. Willing and Capt. Wharton, whom we beg leave to recommend to your notice, who will protect the Officers on the Road and forward their Journey.[6]

No more Gun powder is yet arrived here. On the 10th Instant we sent 2200 weight to General Schuyler, which was all we could possibly spare.[7] With great Esteem and Respect, we have the Honour to be, Sir, Your most Obedient humble Servant
By Order   B FRANKLIN, Presidt.

P.S. With this you will also receive a packet directed to an Officer of The Ministerial Army, which we have not open'd, but submit it to your discretion.

5. The *Hope*, Capt. George Curwin, had been captured and brought to Gloucester, on the Delaware below Philadelphia; from there the prisoners were escorted to the city by Capt. William Bradford, whom we have tentatively identified as the recipient of BF's letter above, May 16. They consisted of Major Christopher French, of the 22nd Foot, an ensign, a volunteer, and two privates. The Major claimed that he was no prisoner of war, because he had come to America unaware that war had started and had not been taken in arms; but he declared that if he joined his regiment he would follow orders, and his claim was then overruled. The names of his companions and the documents enclosed with this letter are printed in Force, 4 *Amer. Arch.*, III, 499–501. Gage's "detention of the Effects of our Friends," on which the committee based its refusal to forward baggage, is explained in Williams to BF above, June 19.

6. Richard Willing (1745–98) was a captain in the 3rd battalion of Pa. associators (2 *Pa. Arch.* XIII, 556); John Wharton may have been the younger brother of Thomas and Samuel, but we cannot positively identify him. The two had volunteered if their expenses were paid, and BF signed their letter of instructions: Force, *op. cit.*, pp. 500–1. Their assignment doubtless had its bad moments, for French was a difficult prisoner; Washington packed him off to Hartford, whence came a buzz of complaints from and about him. Fitzpatrick, *Writings of Washington*, III, 463–4, 518–19, 522–3.

7. See above, BF to Schuyler, Aug. 8, 10, and the Pa. committee to the Albany committee, Aug. 10.

The New York Provincial Congress to the Pennsylvania Committee of Safety

Text printed in Samuel Hazard *et al.*, eds., *Pennsylvania Archives* (first series; 12 vols., Philadelphia, 1852–56), IV, 644

⟨New York, August 17, 1775: The intelligence contained in the enclosed paragraph of a letter from General Washington should be communicated to the various Pennsylvania committees.[8] Addressed to Franklin and the other members of the committee and signed by P. V. B. Livingston, President.⟩

The New York Provincial Congress to the Pennsylvania Committee of Safety

Text printed in Samuel Hazard *et al.*, eds., *Pennsylvania Archives* (first series; 12 vols., Philadelphia, 1852–56), IV, 645–6.

⟨New York August 18, 1775: Reconsidering the paragraph of General Washington's letter that we forwarded yesterday[9] has given us too much reason to think that the British troops are bound for New York.[1] No pains should be spared to make the city as strong as possible, and we urge you to keep your militia ready to march at a moment's notice. Postscript: Another letter from General Washington has just arrived. The total inactivity of the British troops for the past four weeks suggests, in his opinion, that they intend to move elsewhere, and New York is generally given out as their destination.[2] Addressed to Franklin and the other members of the committee and signed by P. V. B. Livingston as president.⟩

8. The enclosure is printed in 1 *Pa. Arch.*, IV, 645, and the entire letter, addressed to the New York legislature and dated Aug. 10, in Fitzpatrick, *Writings of Washington*, III, 413–14. The intelligence was a rumor that some or all of the British troops in Boston were about to move and that New York might be their destination; see also the following document.

9. With the preceding letter.

1. On Aug. 21 the congress appointed a committee to ask Gov. Tryon whether he knew of such a move: Force, 4 *Amer. Arch.*, III, 540. The Governor's answer is not recorded, but the rumor had no foundation.

2. The congress quoted the two final paragraphs of the General's letter to it of Aug. 8, printed in full in Fitzpatrick, *Writings of Washington*, III, 407–8.

Editorial Note on the Pennsylvania Committee of Safety's Articles of Association, August 19, 1775.

In August the committee continued the work, begun in its advertisement on July 28, of implementing Congress' plan for the militia, and on August 3 appointed a subcommittee of seven, including Franklin, to draft rules and regulations for the associators and an admonition to nonassociators to enlist promptly. On August 17 the draft of the rules was submitted to the full committee, and after two days of discussion and amendment it was adopted.[3] It took the form of articles that the associators were to sign, and covered in detail the standards of deportment and the procedures for airing grievances, for enforcing discipline, and for trial and punishment by courts martial. The general subject of a voluntary militia had long concerned Franklin.[4] But we have no evidence that he contributed anything to the highly specific articles of the draft and the finished product.

The Pennsylvania Committee of Safety to the New York Provincial Congress

LS: New York State Library; copy:[5] Harvard University Library

⟨Philadelphia, [August 19,[6] 1775]: We have received your request for gunpowder.[7] After we had furnished all we could spare to the army and neighboring colonies, we heard from General Schuyler that he was in need and sent him 2200 pounds in care of the Albany committee.[8] We did not then know, as he probably did not when he wrote, that a huge quantity had arrived in New Jersey from South Carolina and been forwarded to him, so that our supply will be unnecessary. It has not in all likelihood gone

3. *Pa. Col. Recs.*, x, 297, 307–8; the full text is on pp. 308–12. For the difference in nature between these articles and those governing the continental army see the headnote above, under Aug. 3. The admonition to nonassociators is discussed in an editorial note below, August 26, 1775.

4. See the headnote on his proposals below, under Sept. 29, 1775.

5. The LS, like that to the New York committee above, Aug. 17, has been damaged by fire; the copy is complete.

6. Supplied from the copy, where the date is clear. According to the minutes of the committee, however, the letter was written on the 21st: *Pa. Col. Recs.*, x, 312–13.

7. Above, Aug. 16.

8. See BF to Schuyler above, Aug. 10.

beyond Albany and might, if you apply to him, be brought back for your use. Signed by Franklin as president.⟩

The Pennsylvania Committee of Safety to the New York Provincial Congress   LS: New York State Library, Albany

⟨Philadelphia, August 21, 1775: We are obliged for the intelligence from General Washington[9] and will communicate it to the committees down the river. "As possibly the Enemy may think of calling upon us," we must keep what little powder we have; but we will readily spare you part of any fresh supplies that arrive.[1] Signed by Franklin as president.⟩

The Albany Committee to the Pennsylvania Committee of Safety

> Text printed in Samuel Hazard *et al.*, eds., *Pennsylvania Archives* (1st series; 12 vols., Philadelphia and Harrisburg, 1852–56), IV, 646.

⟨Committee chamber, Albany, August 21, 1775: We have received yours of August 10 with a wagonload of powder, which we will forward to Gen. Schuyler at the first opportunity. We have heard of a large quantity of lead at Ticonderoga and Crown Point, but do not know that any has been sent down; we will furnish the General with a copy of your letter so that he may dispatch whatever can be spared. Addressed to Franklin as president of the committee of safety and signed by Abraham Yates, Jr.,[2] chairman.⟩

9. In the letters from the provincial congress above, Aug. 17 and 18.
1. The congress' request for powder on Aug. 16 had already been answered on the 19th. The committee soon redeemed the promise given here; see its letter below, Aug. 26.
2. For Yates (1724–96), one of the most colorful and independent New York politicians of the period, see the *DAB*.

From Philip Schuyler   ALS and transcript: National Archives

Sir,   Albany August 23d. 1775
    Yesterday I had the honor to receive your favor of the 15th.
Instant.[3] The powder which the Respectable Committee of your
city has sent is already arrived here. You, and they, Sir, are Equally
Intitled to my best thanks for this mark of attention. I shall with
great pleasure order a Considerable Quantity of Lead to be conveyed to Philadelphia Immediately.
    We have struggled thro: that Variety of Difficulties which is
ever attendant on a want of method and Regularity, and altho: we
had not Craft to move 200 men when I arrived at Tionderoga on
the 18th: of July, and had then to repair Mills and send for Carpenters to this place, it is with pleasure I can inform you 100 are
now able to move about 1300 with Twenty Days Provision, and
that we shall very soon make an attempt on St. Johns, weak as we
are in Artillery, which I suppose will not Exceed six nine pounders. I have two Flatt Bottomed Vessels amongst those we have
Built. They are sixty Feet long and capable of carrying Five Twelve
pounders Each, but I can unfortunately mount only one, as I have
no Carriages. I am Sir with the most respectful Sentiments Your
obliged obedient and very humble servant,   PH. SCHUYLER
The Hon: Benn Franklin Esqr

Editorial Note on the Pennsylvania Committee of Safety's
Regulations for Associators and Nonassociators, August
26, 1775.

The drafting subcommittee appointed on August 3, to implement Congress' plan for the militia, completed its work on the 25th. The next day
the full committee debated, revised, and adopted its report, which endorsed the Congressional plan, encouraged nonassociators to enlist, requested from the county committee lists of those who had and had not
joined, established rules for appointing officers and determining seniority, and set up guidelines for organizing companies and battalions.[4]

    3. BF's letter is missing, but see his above of Aug. 10.
    4. Pa. Col. Recs., X, 315–16; the full text of the report is on pp. 316–22.
For the background see the headnote above on the committee's advertisement,
July 28.

Again, as with the subcommittee's articles of association (above, August 19), we have no evidence that Franklin contributed to these regulations.

The Pennsylvania Committee of Safety to the New York Provincial Congress

LS: New York Public Library; LS (duplicate): New York State Library, Albany

⟨Philadelphia, August 26, 1775: A small additional supply of gunpowder has arrived this morning, and we have ordered a ton shipped immediately according as you requested.[5] We are getting our militia in order as fast as possible.[6] Signed by Franklin as president.⟩

Memorandum on the Use of Pikes

AD (draft): American Philosophical Society

The Pennsylvania committee of safety, almost immediately after its creation in June, 1775, began to consider arming the associators with pikes. In early July it asked to see models, and ordered a prototype made according to Franklin's design. His memorandum was approved on August 26 and soon bore modest fruit, for on the 30th the committee distributed the first of the weapons and the following February appropriated £100 for manufacturing more.[7] Pikes were also in use in Washington's nondescript army, from its earliest days through the summer of 1776.[8] They were signs, among many, of an improvised war, and slowly disappeared as the infantry acquired firearms.

5. On Aug. 16, above. The powder was sent but not delivered, for BF took on himself to countermand the order; see his letter to Livingston below, Aug. 29, 1775.
6. As the congress had urged in its letter above, Aug. 18.
7. *Pa. Col. Recs.*, x, 283–4, 322, 328, 482.
8. As weapons of the rank and file they first appear in general orders in July, 1775, and are last mentioned in August, 1776. Fitzpatrick, *Writings of Washington*, III, 338; V, 469.

26th Augt. 1775

It has been regretted by some great Soldiers, particularly by Marshal Saxe,[9] that the Use of Pikes was ever laid aside, and many
experienc'd Officers of the present Times agree with him in Opinion, that it would be very advantageous in our modern Wars to
resume that Weapon; its length reaching beyond the Bayonet; and
the compound Force of the Files, (every Man laying hold of the
presented Pike) rendring a Charge made with them insupportable
by any Battalion arm'd only in the common Manner. At this time
therefore, when the Spirit of our People supplies more Men than
we can furnish with Fire Arms, a Deficiency which all the Industry
of our ingenious Gunsmiths cannot suddenly supply; and our
Enemies, having at the same time they were about to send regular
Armies against undisciplin'd and half-arm'd Farmers and Tradesmen, with the most dastardly Malice endeavour'd to prevail on
the other Powers of Europe not to sell us any Arms or Ammunition; the Use of Pikes in one or two Rear Ranks is recommended
to the Attention and Consideration of our Battalions. Every Smith
can make these, and therefore the Country may soon be supply'd
with Plenty of them. Marshal Saxe's Direction is, that the Staff be
14 feet in Length, and the Spear 18 Inches, thin and light; The
Staff to be made of Pine, hollowed for the sake of lightness, and
yet to retain a degree of Stiffness; the whole to weigh not more
than 7 or 8 pounds.[1] When an Army is to encamp, they may (he
observed) be used as Tent Poles, and save the Trouble of carrying
them. The Committee of Safety will supply Samples, to those
Battalions who are dispos'd to use them. Each Pikeman to have a
cutting Sword, and where it can be procur'd, a Pistol.

9. Maurice, comte de Saxe (1696–1750), Marshal of France and the victor of
Fontenoy, wrote one of the best known military treatises of the 18th century,
Mes Rêveries (2 vols., Amsterdam, 1757); his disquisition on pikes is in I,
59–73.
1. The pike that Saxe actually recommended was of fir, slightly shorter, and
a great deal lighter.

To Nicholas Cooke

ALS: American Philosophical Society

Sir,   Philada. Augt. 27. 1775.

I received yours of the 15th Instant, acquainting me with the Loss of the Mail; and proposing a new Route for the Post, to prevent such Accidents hereafter. In that you will take the Advice and Direction of the principal People in your Government. The Comptroller will soon be along your Road, for the purpose of establishing all the Stages and Offices as he shall be advis'd and find best.[2] I would request your Care of the enclos'd; and am, Sir, Your most humble Servant   B FRANKLIN

Mr. Cooke

Addressed: To / Mr Cooke / Postmaster[3] / Providence / New England / Free

To Silas Deane[4]

ALS: Historical Society of Pennsylvania

Dear Sir,   Philada Augt. 27. 1775.

I am much oblig'd by your Favour of the 13th Inst. Mr. Goddard, Riding Surveyor to the Gen. Post Office is gone to the Southward, for Settling the new Post-Offices all along to Georgia. Mr. Bache, the Comptroller, is to set out next Week Northward on the same Business, who will take with him Directions from me

2. RB was not formally appointed comptroller until Oct. 2, retroactively to Sept. 29, 1775; see the editorial note on the Post Office above, July 26. He clearly assumed his duties earlier, but we believe that he did not make his projected trip through New England; see the note on the following document.

3. BF should have known, as postmaster general, but all the evidence we have indicates that he was mistaken. The postmaster from 1772 to 1792 was John Carter, the publisher of the *Providence Gaz.* and a former apprentice in BF's Philadelphia printing shop; BF commissioned him in September, 1775. See the *DAB* and John C. B. Woods, "John Carter," R.I. Hist. Soc. *Coll.*, XI (1918), 101–7.

4. This is the first extant correspondence between BF and the man who was to be his fellow commissioner and close associate in France. Deane (1737–89) had established himself in Wethersfield, Conn., as a prominent merchant and lawyer, and become a leader in the colony's resistance to the British. He had been a delegate to the first Continental Congress, as he was now to the second, where he and BF served together on several committees. The tone of this reply to a missing letter implies that the two were already on cordial terms.

to establish all the Officers in your Government that you recommend, and the new Offices and Stages that appear likely to support themselves.[5]

I am glad to hear that the Gunsmith's Business goes on so well with you.[6] We make great Progress in it here; but the Price is high. If we would acquire that Manufacture in Perfection, it must be by assuring the Workmen of a large Demand, for a Number of Years, and at a Price certain. Then they will be encourag'd to bring up Apprentices for different Parts of the Work, and also to make Tools and Machines for facilitating and expediting it, such as Suages[7] for Lock Plates and Cocks, Mills for grinding and boring the Barrels, &c. Those bred to Parts of the Work only, will dispatch more and do it better. And then I am confident Arms may be made as good and as cheap in America as in any Part of the World. I intend therefore to propose to our Assembly to give that Encouragement here, by engaging to take 2000 Muskets per Annum for Ten Years, at a good Price, which I doubt not will in that time establish the Manufacture among us; and an Arsenal with 20,000 good Firelocks in it, will be no bad thing for the Colony. As the Numbers of People are continually increasing, we can never be long overstock'd with the Article of Arms. And I wish the Congress may think fit to recommend the same Project to the other Colonies.

I congratulate you on the plentiful Year with you as well as with us.[8] It makes one smile to see in the English Papers, the Ignorance of some of their Political Writers, who fancy we cannot continue the Non Importation Agreement; because if we do it must starve us.

I lament with you the Want of a naval Force. I hope the next

5. The evidence suggests that RB's trip was postponed and that Goddard, immediately after returning from the south, took his place; see the note on BF to Hazard below, Sept. 25, 1775.

6. For the past three months Connecticut had been actively encouraging the manufacture of arms, had offered bounties for providing them to soldiers, and had attempted to procure damaged guns and barrels abandoned at Ticonderoga and Crown Point. Charles J. Hoadly, ed., *The Public Records of the Colony of Connecticut . . .* (15 vols., Hartford, 1850–90), XV, 17–18, 97–8, 110–11.

7. Swages, metalworkers' tools.

8. The harvest was so exceptionally good that it left a surplus of grain for export; see the opening phrase that was subsequently added to BF's resolution on trade, above, p. 127.

Winter will be employ'd in forming one. When we are no longer fascinated with the Idea of a speedy Reconciliation, we shall exert ourselves to some purpose. 'Till then Things will be done by Halves.[9]

Those you mention who seem frightned at finding themselves where they are, will by degrees recover Spirits when they find by Experience how inefficient merely mercenary the regular Troops are, when oppos'd to Freeholders and Freemen, fighting for their Liberties and Properties. A Country of such People was never yet conquer'd, (unless through their own Divisions,) by any absolute Monarch with his Mercenaries: But such States have often conquer'd Monarchies, and led mighty Princes captive in Triumph.

I shall be curious to hear more Particulars of your new mechanical Genius.[1] A Mr. Belton, who I fancy comes from your Province and is now here, has propos'd something of the kind to us; but is not much attended to.[2] With great Esteem, I am, Sir, Your most obedient humble Servant   B FRANKLIN

Honble. Silas Deane Esqr

Endorsed: Benja Franklin Esqr Lettr. Sepr. 1775

9. Deane was one of the chief Congressional advocates of a navy. Rhode Island and Connecticut had already enlisted armed vessels, and Massachusetts and Pennsylvania were following suit; but Congress had done nothing more than urge the same course on the other colonies. The idea of creating a continental navy went hand in hand with the idea of opening the ports, for free trade without protection was meaningless. Conservatives resisted both ideas as too provocative. William M. Fowler, Jr., *Rebels under Sail: the American Navy during the Revolution* (New York, [1976]), pp. 42, 44–6. The first move to open the ports failed on July 21; see the headnote on BF's resolution on trade above, under that date. The agitation in Congress for a navy was consequently languishing.

1. Undoubtedly David Bushnell; see Gale to BF above, Aug. 7.

2. Joseph Belton, a native of Groton, Conn., who had graduated in 1769 from the College of Rhode Island, was living in Philadelphia. He had recently submitted to the Pa. committee of safety his plan for a submersible, to carry one or more cannon with which he expected to hole a warship below the waterline. Reuben A. Guild, *Early History of Brown University* . . . (Providence, R.I., 1897), p. 90; 1 *Pa. Arch.*, IV, 650–2, 654. The committee seems to have ignored him, as suggested here, and a year later he went to New York in hopes of trying out his invention against the British fleet in the harbor; see BF to Washington below, July 22, 1776.

To Gurdon Saltonstall[3]

Paraphrased and quoted in Saltonstall to Silas Deane, September 7, 1775: Connecticut Historical Society, Hartford.

[August 27, 1775]
I have an esteemed favor of Doctr. Franklyn's dated 27. ulto. kindly acknowledg the receipt of mine you forwarded datd. 11th. ulto. condolg me on my misfortunes, and adds "shall be glad of any opertunity of doing what may be agreable to you. The Comptroler of the General Post Office will soon be along your road to settle the Offices and Stages,[4] by him I shall send a Commission to you as you desire, with directions to him to inform himself of anything that may be done for your Son." And thanks me for the Inteligence sent him.

To Robert Morris[5]   ALS: University of Pennsylvania Library

Dear Sir,   Brunswick, Augt. 29. 1775
Understanding since I came hither that 4 Waggon Loads of Gunpowder for New York, which had been landed at the Neversinks, pass'd thro' here last Friday, I have dispatch'd an Order to our Waggoner, whom I pass'd yesterday at Trenton, to return back with the Ton we spar'd, since it will not be wanted at New York, and may be wanted with us. I hope our Committee will approve

3. Deane's father-in-law, for whom see the note on Gale to BF above, Aug. 7.
4. The comptroller was RB; see BF to Cooke above, Aug. 27.
5. This is the first extant letter in the long correspondence between BF and the famous Philadelphia merchant. For Morris' previous career see the *DAB*; his later activities will appear in our subsequent volumes. His close association with BF, which soon became even closer, began as far as we know when the Pa. Assembly appointed them to its committee of safety. Before the year was out they were serving together on two crucial standing committees of Congress, the secret committee and the committee of secret correspondence, and by the autumn of 1776 the latter consisted only of Morris and BF; see the note on the committee's memorandum below, Oct. 1, 1776.
Morris was the second-ranking member of the Pa. committee of safety and chaired it in the President's absence, as mentioned in the editorial note above, June 30. Hence he was the natural person to inform of the decision that BF describes in this note. We publish it before the letter that follows because it was written earlier on the same day, while BF was crossing New Jersey to visit his son at Perth Amboy.

of this.[6] If not I ought to pay the Expence. With great Esteem, I am Sir, Your most obedient Servant   B FRANKLIN

Addressed: To / Mr Robert Morris / Mercht / Philadelphia

Endorsed: from Doctr. Franklin Brunswick 29th. augt: 1775 recd 31st. augt. 1775

Notation: Dr. Benjamin Franklin Signer of the Declaration

To Peter Van B. Livingston

ALS: Princeton University Library; LS: New York State Library

Sir,   Perth-Amboy, Augt. 29. 1775
    The Committee of Safety acquainted you by a Letter dated the 26th Instant, that we had ordered a Ton of Gunpowder to be sent you agreable to your Request. It left Philada. early on Sunday Morning, and yesterday I overtook the Waggon on the Road at Trenton, and left it proceeding on the Journey. But being informed this Morning at Brunswick that 4 Waggon-Load of Powder had passed thro' that Place on Friday Evening for your City, and supposing it to be the Powder which you mention'd as having been expected but not arrived, which occasioned your sending to us; and as we have still too little at Philadelphia; I thought it best to stop that Powder and send it back again,[7] and wrote accordingly to the Waggoner by a Person just setting out for Trenton. I write this therefore that you may not expect it at Newark in consequence of our Letter. With great Respect and Esteem, I am, Sir, Your most obedient humble Servant   B FRANKLIN

P. V. B Livingston, Esqr

6. The powder promised to New York by the Pa. committee of safety, in its letter above of Aug. 26, left Philadelphia the next morning; see the following document. The committee approved BF's decision, and the consignment was returned to the city magazine on Aug. 31: *Pa. Col. Recs.*, X, 328. The other shipment of powder, ordered by the N.Y. congress and mentioned in its letter above of Aug. 16, had been expected to come by sea and doubtless did. The Neversinks are highlands between Sandy Hook Bay and an inlet known as the Shrewsbury River, where the powder was presumably landed to be carried overland; in that case the waggons would have crossed the Raritan at Brunswick. They were in New York by Sept. 1: Force, 4 *Amer. Arch.*, III, 570.
    7. See the preceding document.

The Officers of Minutemen in York County to the Pennsylvania Committee of Safety

LS: Pennsylvania State Library, Harrisburg

⟨York, August 31, 1775: The committee and militia officers of the county, at a meeting on July 20, carried out the recommendation of the Assembly and Congress by ordering the formation of a least five companies of minutemen, and elected the undersigned as field officers.[8] Five companies are already raised and most of the officers chosen. Several of the companies are large, about 100 each, partly in order to be at full strength even if all the men cannot appear, and partly to permit removing whatever "improper Persons may push themselves in," as well as those who have no settled residence.

The men are in the prime of life and for the most part good marksmen. "They considred that all their Mustering was mere parade without they actually intended to step forth when called up." They have placed themselves under martial law and have been told that its penalties, designed for those who do not behave, are no threat to those who do; the regulations of the continental army might properly be adapted for them. They cannot be expected to muster frequently because of the expense and loss of time, but have agreed to meet more often than the rest of the militia. Unless they have six weeks' training "we could not prudently attempt to meet regular Troops in the Field, though we might do Execution if permitted to act as irregulars." Only those who have a settled residence in the county should be accepted, so as to be readily available in case of emergency; and there are plenty of these. If after they are trained they are not called to action, they may be used to support the militia. "Should they be wanted before the

---

8. The meeting was on July 28–9; see the York committee to the Pa. delegates above, Aug. 1. The recommendation of the Assembly was in the resolutions establishing the committee of safety, and that of Congress was in the plan for the militia adopted on July 18; see the editorial note above on the committee of safety, June 30, and the headnote on its advertisement, July 28. The Congressional plan stipulated that a quarter of the militia in any colony be selected from volunteers, formed into companies and battalions and given more intensive training than the rest, so as to be ready for action whenever and wherever they were required; these minutemen might withdraw after four months and be relieved by other volunteers from the militia. *JCC*, II, 188–9.

publick Arms are finished we are in Hopes they will be supplied by the Militia companies, tho their Arms will not be so good." A company of riflemen will be raised to act as light infantry for the battalion, and if the latter is too small it can be enlarged.

A man may hold a commission in the minutemen, the committee has decided, and also in the militia. Otherwise many militia officers would have to be replaced, and "nothing seems to cause more confusion in Companies than the changing of officers." The county has tried to fulfil the Assembly's wishes. "Should there by any Alterations necessary because of the Tardiness of other Counties, we hope no such alterations will oblige this County to raise Minute-Men over again. Such a proceeding might be difficult to be carried into Execution." Addressed to Franklin, John Dickinson, and the committee, and signed by Richard McCalister, Thomas Hartley, and David Grier.

P.S.: Mr. Swope (Swoope), the member of the committee of safety from the county, has seen this letter.[9])

9. The first three were colonel, lieutenant colonel, and major respectively of the battalion of minutemen; McCalister was also colonel of the third, and Hartley lieutenant colonel of the first, battalion of York associators. McCalister, or as he is often spelled McAllister (1724–95), one of the most prominent landholders in southern Pennsylvania, remained in active service through 1776. Thomas Hartley (1748–1800), a lawyer, commanded a Pennsylvania brigade at the Brandywine and Germantown, and was later an important political figure in the state. David Grier (1742–90), also a lawyer, had been in the French and Indian War; he subsequently took part in the Canadian campaign, rose to be a lieutenant colonel, was wounded in 1777, and served thereafter in the quartermaster's department at York. For the three men's commissions see 2 *Pa. Arch.*, XIV, 476–7. Michael Swoope, as he spelled it, (b. 1748) was a major in Hartley's battalion of associators and later became its colonel, was captured in 1776, and in 1778 was proposed as an exchange for WF (*PMHB*, XXXIX (1915), 394; instead, after brief parole, he spent the rest of the war in prison. For Hartley see the *DAB* and *PMHB*, XXV (1901), 303–6, and for the others George R. Prowell, *History of York County, Pennsylvania* . . . (2 vols., Chicago, 1907), I, 185–6, 195, 245, 807–8.

From Joseph Priestley

Extract reprinted from Horace Wemyss Smith, *Life and Correspondence of the Rev. William Smith* . . . (2 vols., Philadelphia, 1880), I, 519.

[August (?),[1] 1775]

I thank you for Dr. Smith's excellent Sermon. If it be not impertinent, give him my most respectful compliments and thanks. I think to get it printed.[2]

To Lord Le Despencer   ALS: Mr. Ben Hibbs, Philadelphia (1956)

Philada. Sept. 3. 1775.

I hope my dear Friend continues well and happy, with good Mrs. Barry and the little ones.[3] I had a short Passage hither, arrived safe, was made very welcome by my old Friends and Countryfolks, and have constantly enjoyed my usual Health and Spirits. As I flatter myself you still retain your former Regard for me, I suppose this small News concerning me, will not be unpleasing to you.

---

1. The sermon that is the subject of the extract was published, as noted below, in early July. If BF forwarded the pamphlet at the first opportunity, Priestley could not have received and acknowledged it before mid-August.

2. For William Smith, the provost of the College of Philadelphia and BF's old enemy, see above, IV, 467–9 n. On June 23, 1775, Smith preached a sermon in Christ Church, before a large congregation that included officers of the city associators and members of the Congress; he then published it, on request, under the title *A Sermon on the Present Situation of American Affairs* . . . ([Philadelphia, 1775]), with an explanatory preface. Horace Smith, immediately before the extract, quotes at length from both: pp. 507–19. The pamphlet was first advertised in Pennsylvania on July 5, and was subsequently reprinted there and in Delaware. The Dilly brothers brought out a London reprint later in the year, perhaps at Priestley's instigation, and twice reissued it; numerous other reprints appeared elsewhere in Britain. Thomas R. Adams, *American Independence: the Growth of an Idea* . . . (Providence, R.I., 1965), pp. 144–7.

3. Little seems to be known about Mrs. Barry. She presided over Le Despencer's household for almost eleven years before his death in 1781. Some of his relatives believed that there had been a secret marriage, and he supposedly intended to acknowledge their children when they grew up. The couple had at least two: a son, for whom the Baron provided handsomely in his will, and a daughter, for whom he did not. [Rachel Fanny Antonina Dashwood Lee,] *A Vindication of Mrs. Lee's Conduct towards the Gordons Written by Herself* (2nd ed., London, 1807), pp. 11–12, 15.

We have here a little musical Club at which Catches are sometimes sung, and heard with great Pleasure: But the Performers
have only a few old Ones. May I take the Liberty of requesting
your Lordship to send me half a Dozen of those you think best
among the modern? It would add to the Happiness of a Set of very
honest Fellows. With sincere Respect and Affection, I am ever,
my dear Lord, Your Lordship's most obedient humble Servant

B FRANKLIN

Lord LeDespencer

From William Franklin   ALS: American Philosophical Society

Perth-Amboy Septr. 6, 1775 Wedy. Morng.
Honoured Father,
I hope this will find you safe at Home, and that you met with
no Accident on your Journey.
Yesterday Evening Thomas found the Enclosed Letter for you in
the Bar of one of the Taverns in this Town.
Enclosed is a Copy of the Exposition of the Resolution of the
House of Commons which you requested. I also send you the
Minutes of the two last Sessions of the New-Jersey Assembly, in
which you will see what I have said to them respecting the present
unnatural Dispute between G.B. and her Colonies, and also what
passed between us respecting my Letter to Lord Dartmouth.[4]
The Bearer waiting impatiently I have but just Time to add
that Betsy joins me in Duty to you and Love to Mr. and Mrs.

---

4. Thomas was presumably WF's servant or slave; about the letter we dare not
conjecture. The exposition was of North's conciliatory resolution (above, XXI,
592) in a lengthy circular letter from Dartmouth; see the note on Strahan to BF
above, July 5. WF embodied the letter, with minor changes, in the opening of
his speech to the Assembly when it convened on May 16: *Minutes of the Provincial
Congress and the Council of Safety of the State of New Jersey* (Trenton, 1879), pp.
119–23. On the same day an extract of WF's letter to Dartmouth of Feb. 1,
1775, was laid before the House, which two days later asked the Governor
whether it was genuine. He denied that it was, and arraigned the Assembly for
insulting him. *Ibid.*, pp. 130–1, 133–4, 144–7. In fact, however, the extract
was completely accurate; see 1 *N.J. Arch.*, X, 537.

Bache, Master William, and the Children. I am ever Your dutiful
and affectionate Son   WM: FRANKLIN

Addressed: To / Dr. Franklin / Philadelphia

Endorsed: W F Sept. 6.

From William Strahan

ALS: American Philosophical Society; extract:[5] Papers of the Earl of Dartmouth deposited in the Staffordshire County Record Office

Dear Sir   London Sepr. 6. 1775.

I have your Favour of July 7th. acknowleging the Receit of
mine of April 8th. and May 5th.[6] and am very sorry you seem to
think Matters are now gone so far as to be past all Accommodation. But as you tell me that *Words and Arguments are now of no Use,*
I shall not trouble you with many; only permit me to express my
Surprise and Concern at your saying, *all tends to a Separation.*
Perhaps the wisest Heads and honestest Hearts on your Side the
Water do not see all the Consequences of such an Event; for it
cannot be denied, that you have attained to your present Strength,
Riches and Consideration by your Connection with us and the
Protection you have received from the formidable naval Power of
this Country. Nobody can say what will be your situation when
that Protection is not only withdrawn, but that very Force exerted
against you. We may not indeed *recover you for Customers,* and in
that Case I hope we shall, as we do now, find other Markets for the
Commodities we can spare, but it should not be forgotten on your
Part that at the Commencement of our Commercial Intercourse,
and for many Years after, the Merchants of this Country supplied
you with a Variety of Goods which were then absolutely necessary
to your Subsistence and Comfort, (and what perhaps you cannot
yet well do wholly without) at no inconsiderable Risque, and with

5. See the note on Strahan's letter above, June 7. The extract contains the
first paragraph through the sentence ending "Force exerted against you," the
penultimate paragraph before the signature, and the postscript. Words missing
in those sections of the ALS we have silently supplied from the extract.

6. Strahan's letters have disappeared; so has BF's reply, which presumably
contained the italicized phrases that follow. Strahan omitted his May 5 letter in
listing on Aug. 2 those he had sent by that time. But the reference here is too
explicit to be a slip, and the date fits the monthly schedule he had set himself.

a Liberality of Credit, which probably no other European Nation would or could afford tó give you. It has indeed turned out to be a very beneficial Commerce to Britain as well as to you. But does she not deserve it? Surely she does. As for the Colonies *paying their Debts*, nobody here seems to give themselves any Concern on that Head. Whatever be the Convulsions of States, private Men will always discharge their just Debts, if they are honest and able. Of your Integrity we have had long Experience, and of your Ability there can be little Doubt when you can make such a Sacrifice of present Interests and such expensive Preparations for Resistance, when you think the sacred Voice of Liberty calls for it. Certain it is, that the Parliament were ignorant of your present Opulence when, at the Conclusion of the late War, they refunded you a large Sum, which they conceived you had expended beyond your Ability:[7] But this, while it discovered how little they knew of your real Wealth, shewed at the same time how little disposed they were to fleece or oppress you. Nor should this be altogether forgotten.

I own the Unanimity and Firmness you discover in the Prosecution of this Quarrel exceeds my Expectation. But this is not much to be wondered at, when one considers, how easy it is for a few violent Men with you (countenanced and encouraged as they were by the Clamors of the Opposition here) to spirit up the great [mass?] of the People under the specious Pretence that they have no [other altern]ative but *to die Freemen or to live Slaves*. This howe[ver, as you] well know, is by no means the Case. You know [that?] your [deman]ds have been constantly increasing ever since the Repeal of the Stamp Act; in particular, you will remember the Distinction you then made between *external* and *internal* Taxes, the former of which you admitted we had a Right to impose, and which was precisely the Case of the *Tea Duty*, now so odious with you.[8] So that at length you have brought the Matter to this simple Question; "Shall the British Colonies remain any longer a Part of

7. One of BF's reiterated points (see for example above, XXI, 136–7), which Strahan is trying to turn against him.

8. BF made his distinction when examined before the House of Commons in 1766. By 1769, when answering Strahan's queries, he had abandoned the distinction and advanced to challenging the principle of Parliamentary taxation behind the Townshend duties, of which the duty on tea was a part. Above, XIII, 139, 156–7; XVI, 244–5.

the British Empire?" This is the single Point you have now drawn
the Sword to decide: For not to talk of *Taxation* and *Representation*
of which I see no End, I believe there is no Precedent of the
Inhabitants of any Province, however distant, belonging to a
State, having, as you have, the same Privileges with those born in
the Mother Country, and enjoying the Protection of its Laws and
its Power, not being subject to the Legislature of that State. In
what manner our Legislature could best exercise their Power in
taxing you; in consistence with the Principles of the Constitution,
which more amply than in any other State upon Earth provides for
and guards the Liberty of the Subject, it might perhaps be still no
difficult Matter to discover, were you seriously disposed to acknowledge that the Parliament of England has *any Right at all* to
make Laws to bind you; a Right, which tho you have hitherto
submitted to the Exercise of, in a Variety of the most essential and
important Acts of Legislation, you now wholly renounce and disclaim.

You see how soon I have forgot that *Words and Arguments are out
of the Question*; but I have insensibly drawn out this Letter to a
Length which I did not intend when I begun it; as I purposed to
imitate yours, at least, in point of Brevity. You will for this once
forgive me. Perhaps these may be my *last Words* to you upon this
Subject; and should they turn out to be *my last* in every Sense, I
can truly say they come from an unprejudiced Mind, always open
to better Information, and from a Heart sincerely disposed to
promote the Happiness of my Fellow Creatures.

I am glad you are this Year blest as we [are] with [a boun]tiful
Harvest. Corn has been of late a very benefi[cial ar]ticle [of
com]merce to you (for the Benefits of Commerce are al[ways uni-
vers?]al.) [As?] you have generally much more than is necessary
for [your ho]me Consumption; but as it is a Commodity that will
not keep [with?] you, and one from the Produce of which your
Farmers are enabled to purchase all the other Necessaries of Life,
will not the present Obstruction to their Exportation of it be
severely felt by that useful Part of the Community? The Evils of
War are extensive and innumerable. May the present, and all Wars
(if Wars there must be) terminate so as to leave the greatest possible Numbers of human Beings free and happy. In this Particular
I am sure we are of one Mind.

There is nothing new here nor can there be, till the Parliament reassembles which will be the 26th. of next Month.[9] I shall then, as I have done always, have my Ears open to all that is said *pro* and *con*. I hope still (for I never cease to hope even in the greatest Extremities) that something may be luckily hit on to stop the Progress of this unnatural and destructive Quarrel; which I must own the *Declaration of the Congress* you inclosed to me, seems more calculated to perpetuate than any of your Publications I have yet seen.[1] They say, among other Things, *That Foreign Assistance, if necessary, is undoubtedly attainable.* Alas! do you consider the Danger of calling in Foreign Assistance? Where is the Foreign State you can with Safety and Propriety apply to? How many Nations have been ruined and enslaved by calling in Foreign Assistance! But I suppose this is only thrown out *in terrorem* and was never meant to be seriously put in Practise.

I am very happy to hear from yourself, that you are well and hearty. That you are busier than ever I can easily believe. I flatter myself you will live till the Peace and Liberty and Happiness of your native Country are established upon the surest and most lasting Foundations; and that you will not have the unspeakable Mortification to leave it in the State of Anarchy in which it is now involved. More has it already suffer'd, and much more it is likely to suffer in a few Years from this Contest, than the Amount of all the Taxes the British Parliament (always considering themselves as the Representative of every British Subject) would probably have imposed on them for a Century to come. My Family are all well and desire to be [kindly?] re[membered?] to you. I am Dear Sir Your affectionate humble Servant   WILL: STRAHAN

Since writing the above, I have read the last Petition of the Congress to the King, to which your name is annexed.[2] It appears to me to be couched in very loose Terms, neither making any Conces-

9. Parliament had been prorogued in May, and did reconvene on Oct. 26: *Commons Jours.*, XXXV (1774–76), 395–7.

1. In his missing letter of July 7 BF must have enclosed the declaration by Congress, passed the day before, of its reasons for taking up arms. The text is in *JCC*, II, 140–57.

2. The Olive Branch Petition (above, July 8) with the signatures of the delegates, BF among them, appeared in the *Public Advertiser*, Sept. 5, and the *London Chron.*, Sept. 2–5.

sions, or pointing out any feasible Plan of Reconciliation. It plainly appears, indeed, to be written *after* you was convinced that *Words and Arguments were of no Use*. I dare say, none of the Persons who sign it, expected it could have any Effect here, tho' it may have a good deal with the ignorant Part of your Provincials. By the way, may it not be justly apprehended, that the People of Property in America, after having put Arms into the Hands of the inferior Class, and taught them the Use of them, will one Day find it no easy Matter to perswade them to lay them down again? In my Opinion, you have much more Reason to dread being enslaved by some of your own Citizens, than by the British Senate. You will smile at my Folly, perhaps, but I am fully perswaded that this Contest will not only give a deadly Check to your growing Power and Prosperity, but greatly endanger those very Liberties you have now taken up Arms to defend.

To David Hartley

AL (draft): Library of Congress

Dear Sir,   Philada. Sept. 12. 1775

I have this Day received your Favours per Capt. Falconer, of which more in my next.[3] With this I send you a number of Newspapers and Pamphlets, by which you will see Things are become serious here.[4] Your Nation must stop short, and change its Measures, or she will lose the Colonies for ever. The Burning of Towns, and firing from Men of War on defenceless Cities and Villages fill'd with Women and Children: The exciting the Indians to fall on our innocent Back Settlers, and our Slaves to murder their Masters; are by no means Acts of a legitimate Government: they are of barbarous Tyranny and dissolve all Allegiance. The Insolence of your Captains of Men of War is intolerable.[5] But we suppose they know whom they are to please. I shall endeavour to

3. Falconer sailed from Deal on July 16: *Public Advertiser*, July 18. The favors were therefore not Hartley's letters above of July 22 and 31, but earlier ones that have disappeared. BF's "next," of Oct. 3, 1775, survives only in an extract.

4. The only enclosure that can be identified with any assurance is Duché's pamphlet, *The Duty of Standing Fast* . . . , for which see the note on the first of Hartley's letters below of Nov. 14.

5. For the burning of Charlestown and the inciting of Indians and slaves see BF to Shipley above, July 7. Since then British men-of-war had fired on Gloucester, Mass., New York, and Stonington, Conn. The "Insolence" of their captains

procure the Petitions so that you may have them against Winter: they cannot be collected suddenly. With the highest Esteem, I am Yours most affectionately

Pray present my Respects to Mr. Burke, to whom, and to you I shall write fully by the first safe hand.[6]

Addressed: To / David Hartley Esqr / Golden Square / London

Endorsed: from Dr F

To Jonathan Williams, Jr.
ALS: Yale University Library

Dear Jonathan,   Philada. Sept. 12. 1775.

I this Day receiv'd yours per Capt. Falconer, and am vastly oblig'd by your Industry in Packing and Dispatching my Things. Their Arrival makes me very happy; tho' they are not yet come on shore. I have not before written to you, imagining you would hardly be found there; but now I find by Mr. Alexander's Letter (to whom my best Respects) that he advises you to stay, for the Chance of something turning up to your Advantage.[7] I have lately heard from your Father. He has made a temporary Exchange of Houses and Furniture with a Mr. Putnam of Worcester, who now resides at your House in Boston, and your Family at his House in Worcester, where they were all well about two Weeks since.[8] My Sister is at Warwick with Mrs. Greene. She left her House lock'd up with the Furniture in it, but knows not whether she shall ever see it again.[9] I like your Conduct with Respect to the Jersey Petition. The first Copy had indeed been presented before, by Mr.

---

was illustrated by the treatment of Benjamin Mumford described in Cooke's letter to BF above, Aug. 15.

6. If BF wrote again to Edmund Burke after May 15, 1775, his letter or letters vanished.

7. William Alexander may already have had wind of the possibility, which later materialized, of a business arrangement with Walter Blunt; see JW to BF below, Nov. 23.

8. "A" Mr. Putnam was James, Sr. (1726–89), one of the outstanding lawyers in America, the teacher of John Adams, and too outspoken a Loyalist to be safe outside Boston; hence the exchange was for both householders a security measure. Williams subsequently complained, however, that Putnam had made off with furnishings of the Boston house. *Sibley's Harvard Graduates*, XII, 57–64.

9. See Jane Mecom to BF above, July 14.

Lee, but that you could not know.[1] If you determine to stay in England, I shall do what I can to throw Business in your Way: But whether America is ever again to have any Connection with Britain either Commercial or Political is at present uncertain. All depends upon that Nation's coming to its Senses. Here we are preparing and determined to run all Risques rather than comply with her mad Demands.

Mr. Fergusson, who will deliver this, is a Gentleman of amiable Character in this Country, who visits England on some Business of his own. If you can do him any Service, you will oblige me by it. I recommend him warmly to your Civilities: and likewise Mr. Stockton who goes over with him intending to study Law in the Temple.[2]

I desire to be affectionately and respectfully remembered to Mrs. Hewson, Miss Dolly Blunt, Mrs. Falconer,[3] Mrs. Barwell and all our other Female Friends. I am hurried and can now only add that I am ever Your affectionate Friend and Uncle

B FRANKLIN

I shall write to you fully, and to Mr. Alexander by next Opportunity.

Deliver the inclos'd yourself. I have given you a little Recommendation to the good Bishop.[4]

[*On the verso:*] miss'd finding M[r. Fergus]son to give him this. Enquire for him at the Coffee house.

Addressed: To / Mr Jonathan Williams / at Mrs Stevenson's / Craven street / London / per favour of Capt. Loxley

1. See above, Kinsey to BF, March 26; JW to BF, July 19.
2. Fergusson was undoubtedly Henry Hugh, the Scottish husband of Elizabeth Graeme Fergusson (above, VII, 177 n); he went to England at the time and returned two years later: DAB under his wife. We have no evidence that Samuel W. Stockton (1751–95) enrolled in any of the Inns of Court, although that was his purpose. He carried two letters of introduction from Benjamin Rush, who soon afterward married his niece; copies of the letters are in the University of Virginia Library. Stockton's correspondence with BF will appear in subsequent volumes when the young man was secretary to William Lee, the American commissioner to Vienna and Berlin, and his career is sketched in James McLachlan, *Princetonians, 1748–1768* . . . (Princeton, 1976), pp. 622–5.
3. Mrs. Magnus Falconar, William Hewson's sister; see the note on Mary Hewson to BF below, Dec. 12.
4. In the following document.

[*In Loxley's hand:*] Mr. Shakespeare please deliver the enclos'd to Mr. D. Barclays care opposite Bow Church and will obloige yours &c   B L
Chapeside 108
Endorsed: Doctor Franklin Phila 12th Sept. 1775. recvd Decr 1.

To Jonathan Shipley   ALS: Yale University Library

My dear Friend   Philada. Sept. 13. 1775.

I write but seldom to you, because at this time the most innocent Correspondence with me may be suspected, and attended with Inconvenience to yourself. Our united Wishes for a Reconciliation of the two Countries, are not I fear soon to be accomplished; for I hear your Ministry are determin'd to persevere in their mad Measures, and here I find the firmest Determination to resist at all Hazards. The Event may be doubtful, but it is clear to me that if the Contest is only to be ended by our Submission, it will not be a short one. We have given up our Commerce; our last Ships, 34 Sail, left this Port the 9th Instant: And in our Minds we give up our Sea Coast (tho' Part may be a little disputed) to the barbarous Ravages of your Ships of War; but the internal Country we shall defend.[5] It is a good one and fruitful. It is, with our Liberties, worth defending, and it will itself by its Fertility enable us to defend it. Agriculture is the great Source of Wealth and Plenty. By cutting off our Trade you have thrown us *to the Earth*, whence like *Antaeus* we shall rise yearly with fresh Strength and Vigour.

This will be delivered to you by Mr. Jonathan Williams, a Nephew of mine, whom I left in my Lodgings. Any thing you think fit to send me, may be safely trusted to his Care and Discretion. He is a valuable young Man, having, with great Industry and excellent Talents for Business, a very honest and good Heart. If he should stay in London, I beg leave to recommend him to a little of your Notice.

5. Exportation to Great Britain and the West Indies had been permitted under the Continental Association until Sept. 10, 1775; on that date complete nonintercourse, except for rice, went into effect. *JCC*, I, 77; II, 238–9. BF had long been expecting the destruction of American ports; see above, XXI, 584; BF to Sargent, June 27, to Strahan, July 5, and to Priestley, July 7, 1775.

I am here immers'd in so much Business that I have scarce time to eat or sleep. The Winter I promise my self will bring with it some Relaxation. This Bustle is unsuitable to Age. How happy I was in the sweet Retirement of Twyford, where my only Business was a little Scribbling in the Garden Study,[6] and my Pleasure your Conversation, with that of your amiable Family! With sincere and great Esteem and Respect, I am ever, my dear Friend, Your affectionate and most obedient humble Servant   B FRANKLIN

Lord Bp. of St. Asaph

The Perfidy of General Gage in breaking his Capitulation with Boston and detaining their Effects.[7]

The Firing of Broadsides from Men of War into defenceless Towns and Villages fill'd with Women and Children.[8]

The Burning of Charlestown wantonly without the least Reason or Provocation.[9]

The encouraging our Blacks to rise and murder their Masters.[1] But above all,

The Exciting the Savages to fall upon our innocent Outsettlers,[2] Farmers, (who have no Concern in, and from their Situation can scarce have any Knowledge of this Dispute) especially when it is considered that the Indian Manner of making War, is by surprizing Families in the Night, and killing all, without Distinction of Age or Sex!*

These Proceedings of Officers of the Crown, who it is presumed either act by *Instruction*, or know they shall *please* by such Conduct, give People here a horrid Idea of the *Spirit* of your Government.

6. In other words working on the first part of his autobiography; see *Autobiog.*, pp. 22–3.

7. See Jonathan Williams, Sr., to BF above, June 19. This list of American grievances, on a separate sheet from that containing the letter, seems to have no intrinsic relationship to it. But the watermark, divided between the two sheets, proves that they were originally one.

8. In August the British had fired on Stonington, Conn., and the Battery on the tip of Manhattan.

9. See BF to Priestley above, July 7.

1. *Ibid.*

2. *Ibid.*

*What would be thought of it, if the Congress should hire an Italian Bravo to break into the House of one of your Ministers, and murder him in his Bed? All his Friends would open in full Cry against us as *Assassins*, *Murderers* and *Villains*, and the Walls of your Parliament House would resound with their Execrations! Of these two damnable Crimes which is the greatest?

The York County Committee[3] to the Pennsylvania Committee of Safety

Text printed in Samuel Hazard *et al.*, eds., *Pennsylvania Archives* (2nd series; 19 vols., Harrisburg, Pa., 1879–93), XIV, 539–40.

⟨In committee, York, September 14, 1775: We return you the number of associators whose names we have received, 3,349; there are others whose names we do not know. We cannot list precisely the nonassociators, but will do so as soon as possible. Those of them whose names we have, like the associators known to us, "are chiefly taxable".

We enclose the proceedings of the committee and officers of the county militia companies. The divisions or battalions were formed, and the seniority of each was set, by unanimous vote according to the date when the majority of its companies associated. We, who are members of one or another battalion, are aware that fixing seniority by lot would create confusion and injure the cause, and therefore hope that commissions will be granted according to the regulations adopted. The convenience of the county and the men was considered in forming the battalions, which as you will see from the enclosed papers are of unequal numbers but none of less than five hundred. The first three are large enough for regiments, but give them whatever name you think proper. We send you the names of the officers to be commissioned according to seniority, as agreed in their battalions. Although one battalion

3. Apparently supplemented by militia officers, who may well have continued as ad hoc members of the committee after their meeting with it in July, for which see their letter above, Aug. 31. All but five of the signers had been elected to the committee at its formation the previous December, and we have found no record of a new election until the autumn of 1775. 2 *Pa. Arch.*, XIV, 475, 531–2, 541.

has but five companies, each is large enough to act as a grand division until it can be divided according to the men's wishes; the field officers, when commissioned, will be of great help, and attention must be paid to the townships of each battalion.

Those appointed officers the people generally find acceptable. Captain James Dill and his company officers and some others, we are told, are dissatisfied with Matthew Dill as colonel of the fifth battalion, and have written to you about a new election.[4] The Colonel was chosen fairly, without dispute, and a second election would merely encourage faction, "which we happily avoided in this county".

We enclose the names of officers of minutemen, those in the county who are prepared to be the first called into service.[5] Determining their order of call by lot would be inexpedient, because the companies vary in their discipline, length of training, and active complements; and the lot might fall on those upon which the community cannot rely. Minutemen should therefore be chosen on an individual basis.

"There are nearly 100 persons associated in Germany Township, but as there is some little confusion concerning their offices, we shall defer sending their names for some time." Addressed to Franklin and the committee and signed with seventeen names "and others".⟩

4. We can throw no light on this altercation except that the charges collapsed before the month was out; see the letter from York below, Oct. 4. Matthew Dill (1726–1812) was a lawyer, who had been a justice of the peace and judge of common pleas; he served as assemblyman in 1777–79, and after the Revolution as presiding justice of common pleas: George R. Prowell, *History of York County* . . . (2 vols., Chicago, 1907), I, 254; Rosalie J. Dill, *Matthew Dill Genealogy* (3 vols., Spokane, Wash., 1934–35), III, 1–2. The complaining captain may have been his son, but the few references we have found to an officer of that name are contradictory.

5. For the minutemen see the note on the letter of Aug. 31 from the county militia officers.

From John Foxcroft

ALS: American Philosophical Society

My Dear Friend   New york Septr. 15th. 1775

By Mr. Dashwood[6] who arrived Yesterday in the Harriott Packet Captn. Lee I rec'd a most Friendly and Polite Letter from our mutual good Friend Ld. Le Despencer wherein He approves of every step I have taken in those troublesome times, which if I mistake not will give you pleasure. I am very sorry to find by a Letter from your Son that some People has had the Curiosity to pry into our Correspondence. There was nothing of Politicks. I told you that whenever business would permitt you to comply with your promise that you would make the Family at Bellview Happy perticularly your Daughter,[7] you would have oblijed me by a Line on your intented Visit to amboy. I would have met you if I had been able but I believe I was confined to my Room about that time and for upwards of three Weeks with a constant Fever and Ague, it has pull'd me down but I can bear it. Inclosed you have his Majestys Answer to the City Address.[8] Ld. Le Despencer concludes his Letter as follows. "Whenever you write to Dr. Franklin assure him of my Sincere good will and Esteem. I fear much I shall not see him here so soon as he assured me I should." Mr. Dashwood begs his Compliments. I am and ever shall be Your assured Friend and oblijed humble Servant   JOHN FOXCROFT

To Benjn: Franklin Esqr

Addressed: To / Benjamin Franklin Esqr. / at / Philadelphia / J: Free: Foxcroft

Endorsed: J. Foxcroft

---

6. Francis Dashwood (d. 1793), a relative of Le Despencer, had been appointed Foxcroft's secretary, and in 1776 was imprisoned with him in Philadelphia; Dashwood was paroled and then exchanged, and spent the war in New York. He was later deputy postmaster general of Jamaica, where he died. [Whitfield J. Bell, Jr.,] *Benjamin Franklin at West Wycombe Park* . . . ([Philadelphia,] 1977), pp. 24–5.

7. The old joke about Foxcroft's wife Judith; see above, XVII, xxviii n.

8. The petition from the City of London protested the use of force against the Americans; the King replied that he must continue to use it while his authority was defied, in order to protect the interests of his other subjects. *Public Advertiser*, July 15, 1775; the petition and answer were reprinted in the *Pa. Gaz.*, Sept. 13, 20, 1775.

203

Editorial Note on the Secret Committee

On September 18, 1775, Congress established what became one of its principal institutions for waging the war, the secret committee.[9] Its nine members, Franklin among them, were elected the next day. Their chief responsibility was to obtain arms and ammunition, and the methods of doing so had been worked out some months earlier. Nonexportation had been relaxed to permit produce, with a few exceptions, to be carried abroad whenever the ship returned with war material of equivalent value; and Congress had made contracts with individual merchants to import gunpowder at a set commission.[1] The committee thus moved into a sphere of action in which the rudiments of procedure had been established.

Two-thirds of the original members were delegates who were also active merchants, but this mercantile majority shrank somewhat when the membership was enlarged.[2] Meetings usually consisted of the bare quorum, five. The chairman, Samuel Ward, was the most assiduous attender until his death from smallpox in March, 1776. In that period the next most faithful member was Franklin; of the thirty-seven meetings when those present were recorded, from the inception of the committee until his departure for Canada in late March, he was at twenty-nine. After his return in June, however, he seems to have given up attending.[3]

The documents that survive from the six months in which he was

9. *JCC*, II, 253.

1. See the resolutions on trade above, under July 21, and for an early contract *JCC*, II, 210–11. See also Jennings B. Sanders, *Evolution of Executive Departments of the Continental Congress, 1774–1789* (Chapel Hill, N.C., 1935), p. 78.

2. John Alsop and Philip Livingston of New York, Thomas Willing of Philadelphia, Silas Deane of Connecticut, Samuel Ward of Rhode Island, and John Langdon of New Hampshire. The three who were not merchants were BF and John Dickinson of Pennsylvania and Thomas McKean of Delaware. Dickinson soon resigned and was replaced by Josiah Bartlett, a New Hampshire physician, Archibald Bulloch, a Georgia lawyer, and Francis Lewis, another New York merchant. In December Robert Morris replaced Willing, his partner, and more changes were made in January, 1776.

3. He did sign, with others, two letters from the committee (below, Sept. 13 and 27, 1776), but the minutes of its meetings make no mention of him after March. These minutes, copied by Richard Henry Lee, are published with some omissions in Smith, *Letters*, II–V, *passim*. They do not always list the members present, and when they do are at times confusing: in two cases BF is recorded as both present and absent, which we take to mean that he was there part of the time.

active are few and far between. They consist of one letter from the committee that he did not sign, one to it that he probably did not see, an export licence, and six contracts, some of which he signed; a much greater number of contracts, which were the committee's central business, are minutely described in its minutes but have since disappeared. We summarize those extant documents with which Franklin was clearly connected, and omit the others.[4] His exposure to contracts, whether we print them or not, must have been educational in the ways in which merchants competed with each other and pulled strings in Congress. After Franklin arrived in France he asked, when it suited his purposes, to be "excus'd from any Concern in Matters of Commerce, which he so little understands."[5] But no one who had served on the secret committee was so innocent as he implied about the business side of conducting a war.

To Ebenezer Hazard　　　　　ALS: American Philosophical Society

Sir　　　　　　　　　　　　Philada Sept. 25. 1775

It seems the more necessary to establish speedily a Post to Albany, as we have an Army on your Frontiers. I hope you have found a Rider willing to go on more reasonable Terms than those mention'd in yours of the 6th. appear to be, compar'd with what is given to the New London Riders.[6] But if there are Reasons why he should have more, of which you can best judge, agree with him and let him proceed as soon as possible.

Mr. Goddard is expected in a few Days from the Southward, where he went to settle those Offices. As soon as he returns we shall open the Office here, and proceed regularly Northwards. By

---

4. The omissions are: a contract of Oct. 9, 1775, drawn at a meeting from which he was absent; letters to the R.I. and Va. committees of safety of Jan. 29 and Feb. 13, respectively; a letter to Schuyler of Feb. 21, signed by Ward for the committee, and a letter from Nicholas Brown to the committee, written in Providence on March 20, 1776, only six days before BF left for Canada. The texts of these documents may be found in *Naval Docs.*, II, 383; III, 1262–3; IV, 419–20; Smith, *Letters*, III, 166, 293.

5. Smyth, *Writings*, VII, 154.

6. The letter, now missing, was presumably in answer to BF's above of Aug. 3.

him I shall send your Commission and Instructions.[7] I am Sir
Your most humble Servant   B Franklin

I request your Care of the Enclos'd, and a Packet with the same
Direction

Mr Hazard

Addressed: To / Mr E. Hazard / Postmr / New York

Endorsed: From B Franklin

From Joseph Reed[8]   Copy: Library of Congress

Sir   Camp at Cambridge Sept. 25. 1775
    After congratulating you upon an Appointment[9] which is but
a small Acknowledgement of the many signal Services you have
rendered your Country, I beg leave to mention to you that by some
Accident or Misconduct in the Offices the Generals Letters for
these 2 Months past to his Family and Friends in Virginia have
miscarried. Some very important Business as well respecting his
own Estate as another committed to his Care has suffered in Consequence so much that he is exceedingly uneasy, and would take it
as a particular Favour if such Regulations were immediately made
as would prevent the like in future. He apprehends this Failure is
between Philad. and Alexandria. Besides the Vexation and Dis-

7. Goddard must have returned from the south a few days after this letter
was written, for on Oct. 10 RB announced the opening of a Philadelphia post
office and the schedule for riders to the south and to New York. *Pa. Gaz.*, Oct.
11, 1775. Almost immediately Goddard left for New England, to judge by the
references to his journey below in BF to RB, Oct. 19, and to Greenleaf, Oct. 26.
Hazard's commission, dated Sept. 21, is in the APS.
    8. Reed last appeared in this series as a N.J. lawyer in 1770, when he carried
documents to BF in London: above, XVII, 85, 89. Since then his career had
greatly changed. After returning to America he had moved to Philadelphia,
established a practice there, and involved himself in politics. In May, 1775, he
became an officer of militia, and in early July was appointed military secretary
to Washington. He left that post soon after writing the present letter, and
subsequently served, like BF, in Congress and as president of the Pa. Supreme
Executive Council. John F. Roche, *Joseph Reed, a Moderate in the American Revolution* (New York, 1957), pp. 60, 66; James McLachlan, *Princetonians,
1748–1768* . . . (Princeton, 1976), pp. 200–4.
    9. As postmaster general.

appointment attending this Circumstance there may be Danger of there being made an ill Use of at such a Time as this.

We have had no Occurrence of any Consequence in this Camp for several Days. There was a very heavy Cannonade upon Roxbury last Saturday Morning but with no Effect. In the mean Time a Number of Flat bottom Boats are building that if a favourable Oppor[tunit]y should present we may be ready to embrace it.[1] I am &c.   J REED

B. Franklin, Esqr.

The York County Committee to the Pennsylvania Committee of Safety   LS: Pennsylvania State Library, Harrisburg

⟨York, September 27, 1775: Two months ago the York committee started searching for some one to make saltpetre and found two men, Baltzer Moody and George Garver, who began the work in August. They dug in stables, outhouses, etc.; and the committee lent them money. Yesterday they delivered the 117 pounds of saltpetre that accompany this letter: they would have had more if the recent storm had not injured their earth. Mr. Owen Biddle is requested to settle the bill. The saltpetre is perhaps as good as that imported from Europe, and the bounty or price will presumably be the same.[2] "A Quantity of earth is now Collecting, and we hope to see the Business prosecuted with Spirit."[3] Addressed to Franklin, Biddle, and the committee of safety and signed by Thomas Hartley, David Kennedy, and John Houston.[4]⟩

1. Washington had consulted his generals on the advisability of attacking Boston in conjunction with an assault on the enemy's lines at Roxbury; a council of war on Sept. 11 had rejected the plan (Fitzpatrick, *Writings of Washington*, III, 483–5), but it was apparently held in reserve.

2. Presumably the price established by the Assembly on June 30: 8 *Pa. Arch.*, VIII, 7246–7. For Owen Biddle see above, XV, 262 n and the references there.

3. The York committee thought so well of the saltpetre men that it sent Moody (by then called Monday) to Philadelphia to ply his trade and instruct any who wished to learn: 1 *Pa. Arch.*, IV, 668.

4. For Hartley see the letter from York above, Aug. 31. The only references we have found to Lieut. Col. David Kennedy are uninformative: 2 *Pa. Arch.*, XIV, 475, 503, 541; *PMHB*, XXXII (1908), 489. John Houston (1743–1810)

Proposals for Conscientious Objectors: Two Drafts

AD: Historical Society of Pennsylvania

The outbreak of hostilities created political problems in Pennsylvania that continued to vex the province for a year or more.[5] Compulsory military service was unknown, and the inauguration of voluntary service on a larger scale than ever before raised the acute question of what to do about those who would not serve. Franklin had confronted that question in both the previous wars, when he had been one of the chief advocates on the one hand of a volunteer militia, and on the other of the right of those with religious scruples to stand aloof.[6] By 1775 the situation had changed drastically from that of twenty years before. The crisis was far graver, and the need for all to support the war effort in some way was far more imperative. The Quakers no longer had the political power, furthermore, to maintain the absolute constitutional rights that Franklin had once assigned them. His views were changing with the times but, it turned out, not so fast as public opinion.

The proposals are two drafts in his hand of documents that he believed conscientious objectors might sign; one applied to all of them, the other to Quakers alone. They are attempts, like his suggestions about the Moravians in his letter above of June 2, to find a compromise between religious scruples and the need to support the military. We presume, with no concrete evidence, that both proposals were drawn up for discussion in the committee of safety, or perhaps in the subcommittee charged with admonishing nonassociators to enlist.[7] If so they were written during the summer, when the issue of religious scruples was much to the fore,[8] and prior to Sept. 29, when the Assembly received the report from the committee of safety that is the following document; for that report contains, over Franklin's signature, a much harsher pro-

---

was a local physician who became an army surgeon: George R. Prowell, *History of York County* . . . (2 vols., Chicago, 1907), I, 519–20.

5. See the headnote on the following document.

6. In 1747 BF had pointed out that a Quaker government was unlikely to provide for defense, and had argued for a voluntary organization that allowed freedom to the pacifist conscience. Above, III, 199–213. In 1755 his militia bill created Pennsylvania's first official military system, but also prohibited any regulations in conflict with religious scruples against bearing arms. Soon afterward he answered the same question that was being raised in 1775, why Quakers should neither be compelled to muster nor pay a fine for their absence, by arguing that they were exempted by the charter and laws of the province. Above, VI, 266–272, 301–2; see also *Autobiog.*, pp. 182–6, 237–8.

7. See the editorial note above, Aug. 26.

8. See the York committee to the Pa. delegates above, Aug. 1.

posal than these: that nonassociators be taxed. The idea of asking them for voluntary assistance was out of date by then, as the associators' anger mounted against those who neither served nor paid.

[Before September 29, 1775]
We whose Names are hereunto subscribed, being conscienciously scrupulous of bearing Arms, and of taking away the Life of Man by the Use thereof; but desirous by all peaceable Means in our Power, of preserving as much as may be the Lives of our Fellow Citizens who are about to expose themselves to danger for the common Benefit of our Country; and understanding that there are many Services necessary and highly useful which may well be performed by Persons of our consciencious Persuasion; do hereby engage with each other, and with our Countrymen, that we will not in any time of danger, attempt separately to secure ourselves our Families and private Property, by withdrawing them from Situations of Danger, while others are engag'd in the common Defence; nor take any Measures for such purpose but in Concert with the Publick: but we will attend if in Cities or Towns with Fire Engines, Buckets, &c. to extinguish Fires; with Carriages or Boats to remove Women, Children and sick Persons; and if in the Field, with Spades and Mattocks or Wheelbarrows to cast up and remove Earth for the Purpose of Defence, or with Litters for carrying off wounded Men to places where they may receive Assistance: And we confide in the Equity and Generosity of our Countrymen, that they will allow us to have fulfill'd by these willing Services the Duty of good Citizens.

We the Subscribers, being of the People called Quakers do hereby declare, That our forebearing to associate in Arms with the Regiment of this City, is not owing to any Want of Loyalty to our King or Love to our Country, or Affectionate Regard for our Fellow-Citizens; And being thankful for the Indulgence shown to us by the Law, and willing to manifest our Readiness to do what Service we can towards the common Security, do agree as follows.
  1. That in case of any Alarm, we will not till it is thought generally necessary attempt to leave the City, nor carry off our Families and Effects while others are generously employ'd in its Defence; but will abide therein and share the Fate of our Fellow Citizens, range our selves with the Regiment, and take such Posts

as shall be appointed us by the Colonel or Commanding Officer, in order to perform the following Services; viz. To extinguish Fires in the City, whether kindled by the Enemy from without, or by traiterous Inhabitants within; To convey Intelligence as Expresses or Messengers. To suppress Insurrections of Slaves or disaffected Persons during an Attack. To carry off in time of Engagement the Wounded from the Batteries, Wharffes, or other Places of Action, into some Place of Security and take Care of them. To assist in constructing Breastworks and other Cover against the Enemies Shot, for preserving Life. To carry Refreshments to such as are on Duty. To assist in conveying away to such Place of Safety as the Colonel shall appoint the Women Children Sick aged and infirm Persons of the City: And at other Times when there is no Alarm To join in securing the Powder House, and relieving the Regiment in Watching and Guarding the same.

The Pennsylvania Committee of Safety: Report to the Pennsylvania Assembly

Printed in *Votes and Proceedings of the House of Representatives of the Province of Pennsylvania. . . , 1774–75* (Philadelphia, 1775), pp. 660–1.

During the summer the associators were growing more and more restive.[9] Those of the city of Philadelphia took exception in July to Congress' plan for the militia, and later to the plan formulated by the committee of safety.[1] By the beginning of autumn they were focusing on two grievances, that they were insufficiently compensated for their sacrifice of time and the hardship entailed for their families, and that the obligation to serve was not universal. On September 27 the privates of more than thirty companies, in an address to their officers, argued that the Assembly had no right to delegate to the committee of safety, or the committee to exercise, the power of legislating for them, and that they would not submit to any military law of the Assembly unless it applied to the community as a whole.[2] The officers forwarded this address to the house on the same day, along with a memorial of their own in which they asked for legislation "to oblige every Inhabitant of the Province either with his Person or Property to contribute towards the general

---

9. For an illustration see above, under Aug. 3.
1. These regulations are described in our editorial notes above, Aug. 19, 26.
2. *Pa. Gaz.*, Oct. 11, 1775.

Cause."[3] Two days later the committee of safety submitted the report below.

The Assembly referred this call to action to its successor, and then adjourned. The new legislature debated the matter for more than a month, and on November 15 finally adopted a program for the militia. It contained rules and articles of association similar to those that the committee of safety had drafted earlier, but with two crucial additions. First, provision was made for paying the soldiers when on watch or called to active duty, and for supporting their families when in need. Second, for the first time in provincial history a tax was imposed, as suggested here, on all able-bodied men of military age who refused to serve.[4]

[September 29, 1775[5]]

To the Honourable the Representatives of the Freemen of the Province of Pennsylvania, in General Assembly met, The Memorial of the Committee of Safety,

Respectfully sheweth,

That the said Committee, in Obedience to the Orders of the House, have taken upon them the Execution of the important Trust committed to them, and have proceeded to such Measures as appeared to them necessary to effectuate the Purposes for which they were appointed; the Minutes of their Transactions, together with an Estimate of the Expences incurred for the putting of this Province into a proper State of Defence, are with great Deference submitted to the Consideration of the House. From these it will appear, that the Sum of Money, granted by the House at their last Sessions, has been either wholly expended or remitted for the Purchase of Arms and Ammunition;[6] and that a considerable Sum is still necessary to fulfil the Engagements already made for the above Purposes, and for the Paying and Victualling of the Men in the Service.

3. 8 *Pa. Arch.*, VIII, 7259.
4. *Ibid.*, pp. 7263, 7369–84; see also Ryerson, *The Revolution Is Now Begun*, pp. 126–8, 133–4, 138–44.
5. A drafting committee had been appointed on Sept. 16 to deal with some of the issues covered here, but the memorial was drawn up in final form and presented on the 29th: *Pa. Col. Recs.*, X, 338, 348.
6. The orders of the house were those establishing the committee; see the editorial note above, June 30. The sum initially issued was £35,000, and the estimate of expenses came to £87,237: 8 *Pa. Arch.*, VIII, 7247–9; *Pa. Col. Recs.*, X, 350–1. See also the headnote above, Aug. 1.

It must be obvious to the House, that much yet remains to be done to accomplish their salutary Intentions, particularly if the British Ministry should obstinately persist in their present arbitrary Measures. Should this be the Case, (which from the present Appearance of Things seems but too probable) this Opportunity may perhaps be the only one we shall be possessed of to prepare the necessary Means for the Defence of our just Rights; for there can be no Doubt that vigorous Exertions will be made to intercept future Supplies. The Committee therefore apprehend it to be their indispensable Duty earnestly to recommend it to the House to grant such further liberal Aids, at their present Sessions, as may in their Wisdom be judged adequate to the Exigencies of the Province at this very important Crisis. They beg Leave also to represent to the House that there appears to be an immediate Necessity for constructing a Magazine or Magazines to receive the Powder already in the Province, and such as may arrive hereafter; large Quantities are shortly expected, and there is no Place where it can be stored with Safety, or any way guarded against Accidents, which that Article from its Nature must be exposed to, and which it is of considerable Moment to prevent.

The Committee having thus laid before the House the Steps they have already taken, and their Opinion of some Measures which appear proper to be adopted, beg Leave, before they conclude this Report, to submit to the House a Matter interesting to the public Welfare: The Military Association entered into by Numbers of the good People of this Province, has received the Approbation of the House,[7] and undoubtedly deserves every Encouragement, as a Body of Freemen, animated by a Love of Liberty, and trained to the Use of Arms, afford the most certain and effectual Defence against the Approaches of Slavery and Oppression. It is wished therefore that this Spirit could have been more universally diffused; but the Associators complain, and, with great Appearance of Reason, that whilst they are subjected to Expences to accoutre themselves as Soldiers, and their Affairs suffer considerably by the Time necessarily employed in acquiring a Knowledge of the military Art, very many of their Countrymen, who have not associated, are entirely free from these Inconveniences; they conceive that where the Liberty of all is at Stake,

7. On June 30: 8 *Pa. Arch.*, VIII, 7245.

every Man should assist in its Support, and that where the Cause is common, and the Benefits derived from an Opposition are universal, it is not consonant to Justice or Equity that the Burdens should be partial. The Committee therefore would submit it to the Wisdom of the House, whether, at this Time of general Distress and Danger, some Plan should not be devised to oblige the Assistance of every Member of the Community; but as there are some Persons, who, from their religious Principles, are scrupulous of the Lawfulness of bearing Arms, this Committee, from a tender Regard to the Consciences of such, would venture to propose that their Contributions to the common Cause should be pecuniary, and for that Purpose a Rate or Assessment be laid on their Estates equivalent to the Expence and Loss of Time incurred by the Associators. A Measure of this Kind appears to be founded on the Principles of impartial Justice, calculated to appease the Complaints which have been made, likely to give general Satisfaction, and be of Course beneficial to the great Cause we are engaged in.

Your Committee beg Leave to represent, that it will be necessary to appoint a Commodore or Commander in Chief of the armed Boats, which has been delayed hitherto out of Respect to your Honourable House.[8] Signed by Order of the Committee,

B. FRANKLIN, President.

8. On Oct. 20 the Assembly assigned the nomination of a commodore to the committee; it named Capt. Thomas Read, for whom see the note on Hartley to BF above, July 22. The commanders of the other armed boats objected, and the appointment was not made; the following January the committee, when the Assembly was in recess, appointed Capt. Andrew Caldwell. *Pa. Col. Recs.*, x, 379, 456; John W. Jackson, *The Pennsylvania Navy, 1775–1781* . . . (New Brunswick, N.J., [1974]), p. 31.

From Robert Rogers[9]

ALS: Historical Society of Pennsylvania

Much respected Sir,   New York 29th. Sepr 1775.

Between Burdin Town[1] and West Amboy in my Way to this City Unfortunately lost my Pockett Book which I cannot as yet recover tho' have taken every the most expedient means; Amongst other papers of Consequence to myself only, Was the Copy of my Parole with the Committees permission for my going to New Hampshire or where else I had Occasion. I have acquainted the Committee of Safety in this City with the Accident and am by them desired to remain here till I can procure another from Your Committee, and as the uncertainty of recovering my Pockett Book is great and my Finances low must request Your kind favour in presenting the Matter to the Committee and remitting me a Copy of that permission by the most imediate Opportunity under Cover to the Committee of safety here for till then I cannot go forward, trusting to your Consideration of my present situation for this imediate favour remain Sir Your most humble Servant

ROBERT ROGERS

Addressed: Doctor Franklin, / Chairman of the Committee of Safety / at / Philadelpa.

Endorsed: from Major Rt. Rogers New York 29h. Septr 1775 rec'd Octr 3. 1775.

---

9. When Rogers last appeared in this series, he was seeking BF's support for his scheme to find the Northwest Passage; see above, XIX, 80. All that his solicitation brought him was a sop: in the spring of 1775 he was given a major's half-pay and funds to return to America. He landed in Maryland and started north in search of a land grant. As he was passing through Philadelphia on Sept. 22 he was arrested; his case came before Congress, which released him on parole not to take up arms against the Americans. The Pa. committee of safety permitted him to go on toward New York, and the present letter secured him a copy of the parole that he had lost. He continued his travels and, wherever he went, found himself regarded with deep suspicion. John R. Cuneo, *Robert Rogers of the Rangers* (New York, 1959), pp. 255–60; *Pa. Col. Recs.*, X, 342–3, 354; *JCC*, III, 259.

1. Bordentown.

From Charles Moore[2]

AL: D. A. F. H. H. Hartley Russell, on deposit in the Berkshire Record Office (1955)

October 1st. 1775

Chas. Moore presents his Complements to Doctor Franklin, and sends the inclosed Papers to him by Order of the Assembly, to be transmitted by the next Packet, to Mr. Hartley, the Member for Hull, some of the Colony Agents, or such other Friends to America, as the Doctor may think most proper.[3]

Notation: Mr Moore Philad: Oct 1/75

To a Friend in London[4]

Extract printed in *The London Chronicle*, December 5–7, 1775.

[October 3?, 1775.[5]]

Tell our good friend, Dr. P——e,[6] not to be in any pains for us, (because I remember he had his doubts) we are all firm and united. As I know he is a great calculator, I will give him some data to work upon: ministry have made a campaign here, which has cost two millions; they have gained a mile of ground; they have lost

---

2. The clerk of the Pa. Assembly: above, XXI, 471 n.

3. In his letter of Sept. 12 BF promised to comply as best he could with Hartley's request, in a letter now lost, for petitions from the colonies. He apparently forwarded that request to the Pa. Assembly, which appointed a committee to search the records for its attempts since 1763 to secure redress of American grievances. The result was "the inclosed Papers," which were: copies of a petition on paper currency and of thanks for repeal of the Stamp Act, 1766; three petitions against the Townshend revenue act in 1768, and one in 1771 against continuing the tea duty. These documents are also in the Berkshire Record Office. BF doubtless transmitted them, along with Moore's covering note, in his letter to Hartley below, Oct. 3, which survives only in an extract.

4. So entitled by the printer. The extract is closely similar to that from the letter to Priestley below, Oct. 3, 1775. But significant differences in wording persuade us that this one came from another letter. The recipient, a mutual friend of BF, Price, and Priestley, cannot be identified.

5. BF was in the habit of devoting a day to correspondence, and on Oct. 3 wrote to Hartley, Priestley, and Strahan; it is reasonable to assume that the letter from which these sentences were taken was part of the same day's work.

6. Price; see the letter to Priestley just cited.

half of it back again,[7] they have lost fifteen hundred men, and killed one hundred and fifty Yankies. In the mean time we have had between sixty and seventy thousand children born. Ask him how long it will take for England to conquer America?

To David Hartley

Extract printed in Benjamin Vaughan, ed., *Political, Miscellaneous, and Philosophical Pieces . . . Written by Benj. Franklin . . .* (London, 1779), pp. 555–6; copy: D. A. F. H. H. Hartley Russell, on deposit in the Berkshire Record Office (1955); copy: Library of Congress[8]

Philadelphia, Oct. 3, 1775.

I wish as ardently as you can do for peace, and should rejoice exceedingly in co-operating with you to that end. But every ship from Britain brings some intelligence of new measures that tend more and more to exasperate; and it seems to me that until you have found by dear experience the reducing us by force impracticable, you will think of nothing fair and reasonable. We have as yet resolved only on defensive measures. If you would recall your forces and stay at home, we should meditate nothing to injure you. A little time so given for cooling on both sides would have excellent effects. But you will goad and provoke us. You despise us too much; and you are insensible of the Italian adage, that *there is no little enemy.*[9] I am persuaded the body of the British people are our friends; but they are changeable, and by your lying Ga-

---

7. See *ibid.*

8. We normally print the earliest version of a document, but this is an exception. In a speech in the House of Commons on Dec. 5, 1777, Hartley mentioned that he had read BF's letter to the House a few days after receiving it, presumably late in 1775, and that it had been ignored; he then quoted this extract. Cobbett, *Parliamentary History*, XIX (1777–78), 553. His copy of it, incorporated in the draft of his speech (Berkshire Record Office), is the earliest surviving version. The other copy, in the hand of C.-G.-F. Dumas, is headed by a note that it was derived from the speech as printed in *The London Evening-Post* of Jan. 20–22, 1778. Our text differs slightly and inconsequentially from these versions, and is likely to be more authentic because BF was in touch with Vaughan while the edition was taking form.

9. The adage, which was French rather than Italian, appeared in *Poor Richard* in 1733: above, I, 316.

zettes[1] may soon be made our enemies. Our respect for them will proportionally diminish; and I see clearly we are on the high road to mutual enmity, hatred, and detestation. A separation will of course be inevitable. 'Tis a million of pities so fair a plan as we have hitherto been engaged in for increasing strength and empire with *public felicity*, should be destroyed by the mangling hands of a few blundering ministers. It will not be destroyed: God will protect and prosper it: You will only exclude yourselves from any share in it. We hear that more ships and troops are coming out. We know you may do us a great deal of mischief, but we are determined to bear it patiently as long as we can; but if you flatter yourselves with beating us into submission, you know neither the people nor the *country*.

The congress is still sitting, and will wait the result of their *last* petition.[2]

To Joseph Priestley[3]

Extract printed in Benjamin Vaughan, ed., *Political, Miscellaneous, and Philosophical Pieces . . . Written by Benj. Franklin . . .* (London, 1779), pp. 365–6.

Dear Sir,　　　　　　　　　Philadelphia, 3d Octob. 1775.

I am to set out to-morrow for the camp,[4] and having but just heard of this opportunity, can only write a line to say that I am

1. Perhaps a reference to "Gazettes of blood" in Hartley's letter above, July 31.

2. The petition discussed above, July 8. Dumas' copy has a note here that must be his own; it is not in the text in the *Evening-Post* or in Vaughan: "This result has been, That no answer should be given." The result was not known in Philadelphia until November: *Pa. Gaz.*, Nov. 1, 1775. Dumas may have learned it from a newspaper enclosed in BF's letter below, Dec. 9, 1775, or may have seen the announcement in the London papers that an answer to a legally nonexistent body was "thought beneath the dignity of government." *London Chron.*, Aug. 22–24; *Public Advertiser*, Aug. 25, 1775.

3. WTF again identified the recipient, as in the letters to Priestley above of May 16 and July 7, in a MS note on a proof sheet of *Philosophical Pieces*, Library of Congress.

4. Vaughan here added a note to explain BF's visit to Washington, for which see the minutes of the conference below under Oct. 18, 1775.

well and hearty. Tell our dear good friend . . . ,[5] who sometimes has his doubts and despondencies about our firmness, that America is determined and unanimous; a very few tories and placemen excepted, who will probably soon export themselves. Britain, at the expence of three millions, has killed 150 Yankies this campaign, which is £20,000 a head; and at Bunker's Hill she gained a mile of ground, half of which she lost again by our taking post on Ploughed Hill.[6] During the same time 60,000 children have been born in America. From these *data* his mathematical head will easily calculate the time and expence necessary to kill us all, and conquer our whole territory.[7] My sincere respects to . . . , and to the club of honest whigs at. . . .[8] Adieu. I am ever Yours most affectionately,   B. F.

To William Strahan   Copy: Public Record Office

Philadelphia, October 3, 1775.

Since my Arrival here I have received Four Letters from you, the last dated August 2.[9] all filled with your Reasonings and Persuasions, and Arguments and Intimidations on the Dispute between Britain and America, which are very well written, and if you have shewn them to your Friends the Ministers, I dare say, they have done you Credit. In Answer I can only say that I am too fully engaged in actual Business to write much; and I know your Opinions are not easily changed. You wish me to come over with Proposals of Accommodation. Your Ministers have made that impracticable for me, by prosecuting me with a frivolous Chancery Suit in the Name of Whately, by which, as my Sollicitor writes me, I shall certainly be imprisoned if I appear again in England.[1] Never-

5. Here WTF, in another MS note, identified the friend as Dr. Price.

6. In August the British were supposedly preparing to occupy Ploughed Hill in order to control the low ground between it and Bunker. On the 26th the Americans forestalled them, and erected a battery that could dispute the ground with the enemy: Freeman, *Washington*, III, 519.

7. For a variation on these data, also intended for Richard Price, see the extract of BF's letter to a friend in London above, under Oct. 3.

8. The London Coffeehouse: above, XI, 98 n.

9. See the note on Strahan's letter above, June 7.

1. See the note on BF to Life above, June 5. Life's warning was presumably in his missing letter of April 5.

theless, send us over hither fair Proposals of Peace, if you choose it, and no body shall be more ready than myself to promote their Acceptation: For I make it a Rule not to mix personal Resentments with Public Business. They have voted me here 1000. Dollars per Annum as Postmaster General, and I have devoted the whole Sum to the Assistance of such as have been disabled in the Defence of their Country, that I might not have, or be suspected to have the least interested Motive for keeping the Breach open. My Love to Mrs. Strahan and Peggy. I am ever Dear Sir, your affectionate humble Servant B. FRANKLIN.

Present my respectful Compliments to my dear Friend Sir John Pringle; and to Mr. Cooper when you see him. I am to set out for the Camp tomorrow.[2]

Copy.

To William Strahan Esqr.

Docketed: Philadelphia, October 3. 1775. Copy of a Letter from Dr. Benjn. Franklin to William Strahan Esqr.

The York County Committee to the Pennsylvania Committee of Safety LS: The Rosenbach Foundation

⟨York, October 4, 1775: "Your Favour of the 29th ult. . . . by Mr. Swope" (Swoope) has been received, with its gratifying approval of what the county has done.[3] But the order for delivering 500 pounds of powder and 1250 pounds of lead alarmed the inhabitants until they understood that the ammunition would soon be replaced, which we beg you to do as soon as possible.[4]

2. Peggy was Margaret Penelope, the Strahans' younger daughter; Sir John Pringle and Grey Cooper, secretary of the Treasury, were old London friends. How was Strahan supposed to know that "the Camp" was Washington's headquarters, and that BF was going there as a member of a committee of Congress? Perhaps from information in the accompanying letter, now missing, sent in Strahan's care to Mrs. Stevenson and mentioned in hers below of Nov. 16.

3. For Swoope see the letter from the York militia officers above, Aug. 31. He carried a letter from the committee of safety, now lost, signed by Owen Biddle (*Pa. Col. Recs.*, x, 351); for that reason, presumably, Biddle is included in the address of this letter.

4. In late September the committee of safety had ordered the purchase of the county's powder and lead, to become part of the provincial stock, and the next

When the charges against Matthew Dill were laid before you by some officers of the fifth battalion, you recommended a new election.[5] The battalion officers met on September 30; judges were appointed, who examined the accusations and found them false "and propagated by the Faction with the Design of injuring the Man," whereupon the field officers previously chosen were re-elected: Dill colonel, William Rankin lieutenant colonel, Robert Stevenson and Gerhart Graeff (Graff) majors. We again request commissions for these men.[6] Addressed to Franklin, Owen Biddle, and the committee of safety, and signed for the York committee by James Smith, chairman.)

From William Strahan

Copy:[7] Papers of the Earl of Dartmouth deposited in the Staffordshire County Record Office

London October 4. 1775.

Though I have nothing new to communicate yet as this is the last regular Packett that is to sail from hence for some time at least,[8]

---

day had assigned the quantity mentioned to Westmoreland Co. for defense of the frontiers: *ibid.*, pp. 344, 346. On Oct. 20 the York committee acknowledged that the ammunition was provincial property, but lamented its use in an intercolonial quarrel: 1 *Pa. Arch.*, IV, 668. The quarrel was undoubtedly that with Virginia, for which see the letter from the Pa. and Va. delegates above, July 25.

5. For this dispute see the York committee's letter above, Sept. 14.

6. William Rankin, an English-born Quaker and justice of the peace, was later a member of the Pa. convention; in 1780 he was accused of treason, imprisoned, escaped, and fled to England. William H. Egle, "The Constitutional Convention of 1776," *PMHB*, IV (1880), 228–9. Stevenson appears in the records as a major and Gerhard or Garret Graff, as he is spelled there, as a captain through 1776: 2 *Pa. Arch.*, I, 427; XIV, 477.

7. See the note on Strahan's letter above, June 7.

8. The end of the weekly packets was a stage in the disintegration of the British colonial post. On Sept. 28 the General Post Office announced in all the London papers that the mails for New York and Charleston would leave for the last time on Oct. 4; thereafter regular service would stop. The reason, according to the *London Chron.* of Sept. 28–30, was that the colonial committees of safety had taken it upon themselves to open letters. Packets were continued only to Halifax; ships liberated from other routes were armed and put at the disposal of the War Office: William Smith, *The History of the Post Office in British North*

I do not choose to let it go without dropping you a Line. I see
with Concern that you have accepted of the Place of Postmaster
from the Congress, a Step of itself which sufficiently indicates
your Opinion, that *a Separation will take Place*; the Consequences
of which, sagacious as you are, you yourself cannot foresee in their
full Extent.[9] That *a Separation* has long been meditated and intended by some People on your Side the Water appears now to a
Demonstration, from the great Preparations that have been made
for it, from the gross Misrepresentations of your Committees of
Correspondence of what is done on this Side (particularly a long
circular Letter in the Carolina Gazette of the 18. July, which now
lies before me[1]) from the violent and arbitrary Measures that are
taken to *compel* People to sign your Associations, and from the
unwarrantable Persecution of all those who hesitate or refuse, or
who discover the least Symptoms of Attachment to the British
Government. It was indeed no difficult Matter for You to prophecy
in the year 1769. much of what has since happened, as you had it
so much in your own Power to fulfill that Prophecy.[2] But I am
greatly afraid you have carried Things too far, and I am persuaded
you will find it so ere long. You are now, I am very sorry to see it,
in the Evening of Life embark'd in the most arduous, most dangerous and most uncertain Task that ever Man engaged in, where
Difficulties will of course succeed Difficulties; where various Interests will clash against one another, perhaps unseen; where the

America, 1639–1870 (Cambridge, 1920), p. 67. This development released
Strahan from his promise, mentioned in his letter above of Aug. 2, to write by
every packet.

9. BF's appointment was announced in the *Public Advertiser*, Sept. 18, and
the *London Chron.*, Sept. 16–19. He agreed that his new office implied a breach,
and for that reason refused a salary; see his letter to Strahan above, Oct. 3. The
absence of the other letters to which Strahan replied precludes any guess about
how far BF had gone in predicting independence. Strahan, writing on Sept. 6,
quoted his remark that *"all tends to a Separation,"* and may have extrapolated
from that the more positive statement in this sentence.

1. The letter, from the Charleston committee of intelligence to local committees, was printed in the *S.C. Gaz.; and Country Jour.*, and is reprinted in
Robert W. Gibbes, ed., *Documentary History of the American Revolution . . .* (3
vols., New York and Columbia, S.C., 1853–57), I, 107–16. It indicted ministerial policy, including North's conciliatory resolution, cited British opposition to that policy, and called on South Carolina to prepare for war.

2. The prophecy was at the end of BF's answers to Strahan's queries above,
XVI, 248–9.

Humours of a great Body of People are to be attended to, and if possible, reconciled to the great Plan of Operations; and where the Ambition of a single Individual may, at length, in one Moment overturn that System of Liberty you are now contending. All these you may say are the idle Fears of a Man who has not Judgment or Capacity of Mind to judge of so vast an Undertaking. It may be so, and therefore I shall not trouble you farther upon the Subject than just to tell you once more after all that is past, that I am still of Opinion, that the Ministry of this Country was never disposed to fleece or oppress you, that this unnatural Civil War has been chiefly, if not wholly, occasioned by our wicked Factions at Home, whose Struggles for Places and Power have by degrees carried them such daring Lengths, as have induced and encouraged you to encrease your Demands much beyond what you at first dreamt of. I know not whether you now consider the present Temper of this Country, or indeed deem it worth your Consideration. If however it should turn out that they are unanimous in carrying on this unhappy Contest with the utmost Vigour (as I am apt to think they will) your Labour will be greatly encreased; and even if you should finally prevail, that may not happen till your Country has suffered more than half a Century can recover. In short I see no End to the Publick Calamities attending this Quarrel, tho' your present Unanimity may seem to you to promise a speedy Issue to the Dispute.

I have lately seen many worthy Men who have been forced to abandon their Homes in almost every part of the Continent, to avoid Confinement, Confiscation of Goods, and even Corporal Punishment. These are uniform and consistent in their Accounts of the Tyranny and Oppression of the leading Powers with you, and give a most lively and striking Picture of the Miseries of Anarchy which every where prevails among you, to which any Form of Government (almost) is infinitely preferable. How to quell that domineering Spirit among those who are now invested with the Reins of Government, or to wrest the Sword out of the Hands of the Military when the Business is done, *Hic Labor, hoc Opus est*,[3] and is in my Mind one of the greatest Difficulties that now lie before you.

3. Freely rendered, "this is the stumbling block." Strahan reversed the clauses: Ovid, *Ars Amatoria*, I, 453; Vergil, *Aeneid*, VI, 129.

I own I never thought of seeing what I now see, or that Things would come to this pass. You have doubtless weighed every possible Event in your Mind, with all the Consequences that can possibly follow, otherwise you had not at this late Hour of the Day, *personally* embarked in the Cause, instead of passing the Remainder of your Days in the Exercise of those Studies, and in the Company of such Men, as best suit your Philosophical Turn of Mind. I own I wish your great Talents had found other Employment. But *Dis aliter visum est*,[4] and there is at present no Remedy. When the Parliament meets, I shall probably send you some Account of their Proceedings, if Opportunity offers; but perhaps you are now upon the Brink of disregarding every Thing that passes here, and think no more of being guided by any of their Determinations. However you may depend on hearing from me, as I do on hearing from you, when you have Time to write, and when you think it can eventually answer any good Purpose. I am sorry to differ from you, *toto cælo*,[5] in this great Political Dispute; but I can nevertheless subscribe myself with great Truth, Dear Sir, Your affectionate humble Servant   WILL: STRAHAN

To Dr. Franklin,

Copy.

Docketed: London October 4 1775. Copy of a Letter from Will: Strahan Esqr to Dr. Franklin

To Jane Mecom   ALS: American Philosophical Society

Head Quarters, Camp at Cambridge. Oct. 16. 1775.
My dear dear sister
    I arrived here last Night with two other Delegates of the Congress. I suppose we may stay here about a Week. In order to take you home with me, I purpose quitting their Company, purchasing a Carriage and Horses, and calling for you at good Mrs. Greene's.[6] But let me hear from you in the mean time, and acquaint me with

4. "The gods decreed otherwise": *ibid.*, II, 428.
5. By the width of the heavens.
6. The postscript of BF's letter above, Aug. 2, had contained the invitation to join the Philadelphia family; his preparations for the journey indicate that Jane had accepted in a letter now missing.

223

any thing you would have me do or get towards the Convenience of our Journey. My Love to that hospitable Family, whom I hope soon to have the Pleasure of seeing. I am ever Your affectionate Brother   B FRANKLIN

Mrs. Mecom.

Addressed: To / Mrs Mecom / at the honble. Judge Greene's / Warwick / B Free Franklin

Minutes of the Conference between a Committee of Congress, Washington, and Representatives of the New England Colonies

ADS: Library of Congress; three ADS, one incomplete: National Archives; incomplete DS: Massachusetts Historical Society[7]

As summer wore on into autumn, Washington's troubles increased. His impromptu army was short of everything it needed, clothing, provisions, ammunition, and the money to buy them. Officers were disgruntled; privates threatened to mutiny if their wages were cut. Enlistments were about to expire, and the prospect of renewal was uncertain. The articles of war were in need of overhauling. Variations existed in the rate of pay; some regiments had more than their allotted number, furthermore, and Washington did not think himself authorized to pay the extra men. He could not obtain clothing or blankets, and now saw "Winter fast approaching upon a naked Army."[8] In a long letter on September 21, followed soon afterward by others, he laid his difficulties before the delegates in Philadelphia. They alone, he made clear, could keep the army from disintegrating.[9] They acted as soon as his first letter reached them on September 29, by appointing a committee of three to confer with him and representatives of the New England colonies "touching the most effectual method of continuing, supporting and regulating a continental Army."[1] On the 30th the members were chosen, Franklin,

7. The ADS in the Library of Congress, which we print, is the cleanest text. The three other ADS, like the first one, are in Joseph Reed's hand and signed by him. One appears to be his reworking of his original minutes, with alterations that he incorporated in our text. The incomplete ADS covers Oct. 23–4, whereas that in the Mass. Hist. Soc., attested by Edmund Randolph as Washington's aide-de-camp, ends with Oct. 22.

8. Fitzpatrick, *Writings of Washington*, III, 512.

9. *Ibid.*, III, 505–13, 526–7; IV, 9–13, 22–5.

1. *JCC*, III, 264–5.

Thomas Lynch, and Benjamin Harrison; and another committee was appointed to draw up their instructions. These, debated and approved on October 2, authorized the Commander in Chief to attack Boston before the end of the year, provided that success appeared likely, and to call in minutemen if need be to swell his numbers. They directed the committee to devise means of prolonging enlistments, to examine in detail the requirements for raising and maintaining the new army, to explore the other problems that Washington had raised and such new ones as might emerge from the conference, to determine the expenses already incurred and estimate those for the coming year, and to report their findings.[2] Congress envisaged a national army free of provincial distinctions, and the central task of the committee was to suggest how such a force could be raised, supplied, organized, and controlled. The three men left on October 4th, and arrived in Cambridge late on the 15th; by the 19th Franklin had become their chairman.[3] The conference began on the 18th and met for seven days. On the 24th the minutes that appear below, together with the committee's covering report, were dispatched to Philadelphia.

October 18[–24,] 1775
Minutes of a Conference held by the Delegates of the Hon. Continental Congress with General Washington

October 18th. 1775.
Minutes of a Conference of the Delegates of the Hon. Continental Congress, the Deputy Govirnours of Connecticut and Rhode Island, the Committee of Council of Massachusetts Bay with General Washington begun at Head Quarters Cambridge October 18th. 1775 and continued to the 22d. of the same Month.

Present His Excelly. General Washington

The Hon. Depy. Govr. Griswold ⎫
Nathaniel Wales Esqr.   ⎭   Connecticut.

The Hon. Depy. Govr. Cooke   Rhode Island.

The Hon. Thomas Lynch ⎫
Dr. Benj. Franklin   ⎬   Delegates from Congress
Col. Benj. Harrison   ⎭

---

2. *Ibid.*, pp. 266–7, 270–2. The details of the instructions will be apparent from the minutes.

3. Above, BF to Priestley, Oct. 3, and to Jane Mecom, Oct. 16; Fitzpatrick, *op. cit.*, IV, 35.

OCTOBER 18–24, 1775

The Hon. James Bowdowin ⎫
Col. Otis   ⎪   Committee of Council of
William Sever   ⎬   Massachusetts Bay
Walter Spooner[4]   ⎭

The Credentials of the Several Members of this Conference for Connecticut and Massachusetts Bay were then read.

The Presidt. of the Provincial Convention of New Hampshire not yet attending General Sullivan was desired to attend this Conference and took his Place accordingly.[5]

The Members of the Conference then proceeded on the Instructions from the Congress which were read through and then separately. And it was considered.

First. To cause proper Methods to be taken for continuing the Connecticut Troops now near Boston in the Continental Service

4. For Matthew Griswold, deputy governor for fifteen years from 1769, see the *DAB*. Nathaniel Wales had resigned as a collector in Windham at the time of the Stamp Act; he attended the conference as a member of the group, formerly the committee of safety, that advised the governor on military matters. Oscar Zeichner, *Connecticut's Years of Controversy* . . . (Chapel Hill, 1949), p. 52; Christopher Collier, *Roger Sherman's Connecticut* . . . (Middletown, Conn., 1971), p. 88 n. For Nicholas Cooke see his letter above, Aug. 15. Bowdoin, who needs no introduction, was the first member appointed by the provincial congress to the new executive council. *DAB*. James Otis, (1702–78), a colonel of militia and father of the more famous James, had served for years in the legislature and been chief justice of common pleas. Horatio N. Otis, *A Genealogical and Historical Memoir of the Family of Otis* . . . (Boston, [1848]), p. 7; William Tudor, *The Life of James Otis* . . . (Boston, 1823), pp. 6–7; *DAB* under James Otis, Jr. William Sever (1729–1809) had also been in the House, and was the senior member of the newly created council. *Sibley's Harvard Graduates*, XI, 575–8. Walter Spooner (1720–1803) had been a member of the old council as well as the new, and had recently served on a provincial committee sent to examine the situation of Ticonderoga and Crown Point. Thomas Spooner, *Memorial of William Spooner* . . . (Cincinnati, 1871), pp. 98–100, and *Records of William Spooner* . . . (Cincinnati, 1883), pp. 106–109.

5. For Matthew Thornton, president, see the *DAB*. Illness in the family detained him, and two days were lost before it was decided to start with a substitute; see the committee's report below, Oct. 24, 1775. The attack on Fort William and Mary the previous December (above, XXI, 413 n) had been led by John Sullivan; he was appointed a brigadier general the following June and joined Washington in July. *DAB*.

upon the same Terms as they are at present untill the last Day of next December.

Resolved that it is the Opinion of the Members of this Conference that the General immediately direct the Field Officers of the Connecticut Troops, that they consult with their Inferiour Officers and Men and endeavour to learn what Number of them will continue in the Service to the last Day of December next upon the present Terms and that as soon as possible.

The third Instruction was then read by Paragraphs containing the following Articles, to wit. First what Number of Men the new Army before Boston should consist of?

The Committee having been informed that this Question had been lately agitated in the Council of General Officers[6] desired the Result might be communicated: by which it appears that it was their unanimous Opinion that the new Army intended to lay before Boston should not consist of less than 20,372 Men. In which Opinion on a Consideration of all Circumstances this Committee unanimously concurs.

2d. What should be the Pay of the Officers and Privates that of some of the former in the present Army being it is apprehended too low and that of the latter too high?

That of the Privates unanimously agreed cannot be reduced and agreed by a Majority that raising the Pay of the Officers would be inconvenient and improper. It was also unanimously agreed that under the present Circumstances the Proposition of lowering the Pay of the Troops would be attended with dangerous Consequences.[7]

---

6. The general officers, aside from Washington, were Major Generals Horatio Gates, Charles Lee, Israel Putnam, and Artemas Ward, and Brigadier Generals Nathanael Greene, William Heath, Joseph Spencer, John Sullivan, and John Thomas. The council had been held on Oct. 8; its findings, summarized in Fitzpatrick, *Writings of Washington*, IV, 7–8 n, differed slightly from those reported here, and many of the subsequent minutes deal with questions not mentioned in that summary but by their nature within the province of military men. We assume that in such cases the committee was confirming recommendations that the generals had already approved.

7. Congress, on Nov. 4, approved most of these recommendations: *JCC*, III, 321–5.

October 19. 1775.

The Members of the Committee to confer with General Washington met.

Present as yesterday.

Mathew Thornton Esqr. President of the Convention of New Hampshire attending took his Seat this Day.

1. It was proposed for Consideration what Number each Company and how many Companies each Regiment should contain?

Agreed Unanimously that each Regiment consist of 728 Men (including Officers) that it be divided into Eight Companies, each Company to consist of One Captain, 2 Lieutenants, One Ensign, 4 Sergeants, 4 Corporals, 2 Drums or Fifes, 76 Privates.

2. Of what kind and Quality of Provisions a Ration should consist?

Resolved That it be as follows

One Pound of Beef or ¾ lb Pork or one Pound of Salt Fish

One Pound of Bread or Flour per Diem.

Three Pints of Pease or Beans per Week or Vegetables equivalent at 6s. per Bushel for Pease and Beans.

One Pint of Milk per Man per Day or at the Rate of 1d. per Pint

One half Pint of Rice or one Pint of Indian Meal per Man per Week

One Quart of Spruce Beer or Cyder per Man per Day or 9 Gallons of Molasses per Company of 100 Men per Week.

Three Pounds of Candles to 100 Men per Week for Guards &c.

Twenty four lb. of soft Soap or 8 lb hard Soap for 100 Men per Week.[8]

3. What is the best Method of providing Arms for the Troops to be engaged in the new Army?

Agreed that it be recommended to the several Assemblies or Conventions of the respective Colonies to set and keep their several Gunsmiths at Work to manufacture good Firelocks with Bayonets, each Firelock to be made with a good Bridle Lock, ¾ of an Inch in the Bore and of good Substance at the Breech, the Barrel to be 3 feet 8 Inches in Length and a Bayonet of 18 Inches in the Blade, with a Steel Ramrod the upper Loop to be trumpet

---

8. The conference was confirming the definition of rations in Washington's general orders of Aug. 8. The price of vegetables since then had risen by 1 s. Fitzpatrick, *op. cit.*, III, 409.

mouth'd. The Price to be fixed by the Assembly or Convention or Committee of Safety of each Colony. And to import all that can be procured.

Also that the good Arms of all such Soldiers as leave the Service be retained on a Valuation made of them.

Friday October 20. 1775.
The Committee met present as before.

It was now proposed to the Consideration of the Members what will be the best Method of providing Cloathing for the Troops which are to compose the new Army.

Agreed that the Cloathing be provided by the Continent and paid for by Stoppages out of the Soldiers Wages at 10s. per Month, that as much as possible of the Cloth for this Purpose be dyed brown and the Distinctions of Regiments made in the Facings.

Also that a Man who brings a good new Blanket into the Camp should be allowed two Dollars therefor and take it away with him at the End of the Campaign.

2d. What is the best Method of getting Provisions for the Army?

Agreed that the best Method of procuring Salt Provisions will be to drive the Cattle and Hogs at proper Seasons to the Camp there to be cured and that the New England Colonies can fully supply the Army with these Articles.

That in the Article of Flour and Bread the Commissary proceed in the Way he has done for some Time past, that appearing to be both safe and frugal.

3d. By whom the Officers should be chosen and recommended and how the best Officers and Men in the present Army may be engaged for the next making a complete Arrangement of the whole?

Agreed that such Officers as have served in the present Army to Approbation and are willing to stay be preferred; if there are more of these than are necessary for the new Army the General to distinguish such as he deems best qualified.

Agreed upon a Representation from the General that the Committee recommend to the Continental Congress that proper Authority may be given him to impress Carriages Vessels, Horses and other Things necessary for the Transportation or March of the Army, or any Part of it, or on any other Emergency, and that this

Power may be deputed in Writing under the Hand of the General to the Quarter Master Gen. or to any Inferiour Officers, who are to be accountable for any Abuse thereof.

October 21. 1775

The Members of the Conference met, present as before, except General Sullivan.

It appearing on a full Discussion and Consideration of all Circumstances that any Attempt to reduce the present Pay would probably prevent the Soldiers reinlisting and that the Advancement of the Season does not admit of any Delay in forming a new Army, Agreed that it be proposed to the Officers now serving in the present Army that they signify in Writing as soon as possible which of them will continue to serve and defend their Country and which of them will retire. And that such Officers as propose to continue in the Service and are approved by the General proceed to inlist their Men into the Continental Service upon the same Pay and Allowance of Provisions as is now given. The Service to continue to the last Day of December 1776, subject to be discharged at any Time by the Continental Congress as has been heretofore practised in the like Cases.

Agreed that if upon Tryal it should appear that the Number of 20,372 Men before resolved on cannot be raised out of the present Army: that then the Officers appointed for the new Army, recruit their several Regiments and Companies to their full Complement. And in Case the Necessity of the Service should require it, the General be impowered to call in the Minute Men or Militia from this or the neighbouring Colonies according to the Nature and Exigence of the Service.

The Rules and Regulations of the Continental Army were then taken under Consideration[9] and the following Alterations proposed.

1. All Persons convicted of holding an unwarrantable Correspondence with or giving Intelligence to the Enemy shall suffer Death or such other Punishment as a Genl. Court Martial shall think proper.[1]

9. Congress, after considerable debate, had adopted these articles of war on June 30; the text is in *JCC*, II, 111–22. We note below the changes recommended in them.

1. Article 28 permitted a court martial to impose for this offense whatever punishment it thought fit, but Article 51 prohibited the death penalty except

October 22. 1775.

The Members of the Conference met.

Present as yesterday.

The Rules and Articles of the Continental Army were again considered. Agreed

That it be recommended to the several Legislatures of the Colonies or Conventions to enact some Law or pass an Ordinance inflicting the following Punishment on Persons harbouring Deserters knowing them to be such, viz. A Fine upon all such Offenders not less than 30 or more than 50 Dollars. And in Case of Inability to pay the Fine to be punished with Whipping not exceeding 39 Lashes for each Offence.

That any Person who shall apprehend a Deserter and bring him to the Regiment to which he belongs upon a Certificate thereof by the Colonel or commanding Officer of such Regiment be intitled to receive 5 Dollars from the Continental Paymaster General which is to be deducted out of the Pay of such Soldier.

2d. That all commissioned Officers found guilty by a General Court Martial of any Fraud or Embezzlement shall forfeit all his Pay be ipso facto cashiered and deemed unfit for farther Service as an Officer.[2]

3. That all non commissioned Officers or Soldiers convicted before a Regimental Court Martial of stealing embezzling or destroying Ammunition, Provisions, Tools or any Thing belonging to the publick Stores (if a non commissioned Officer) to be reduced to the Ranks and punished with whipping not less than 15 nor more than 39 Lashes, at the Discretion of the Court Martial, if a private Soldier with the same corporal Punishment.

That it be recommended to the several Legislatures of the Colonies to impower the Commander in Chief or the Officer commanding a Detachment or out Post to administer an Oath and swear any Person or Persons to the Truth of any Information or Intelligence or any other Matter relative to the publick Service.

That in the Punishment of cashiering an Officer for Cowardice or Fraud it be added that the Crime, Name, Place of Abode and

---

when specifically authorized in previous articles. The amendment of Article 28 was precipitated by the case of Benjamin Church, and was duly adopted; see below.

2. This was a broadening of Articles 58–9 and 61–2, which dealt only with specific forms of fraud.

Punishment of the Dilinquent be published in the News Papers in and about the Camp and of the Colony from which the Offender came and where he usually resides after which it shall be deemed scandalous for any Officer to associate with him.

That the 3d. Article of the Rules &c. be amended by making the Punishment refer to the 2d. instead of the 1st. Article.[3]

That the 5th. Article be amended by making the Offence punishable with Death or otherwise at the Discretion of a General Court Martial.[4]

That the 8th. Article be amended to make Deserters to the Enemy who may afterwards fall into our Hands punishable with Death or otherwise at the Discretion of General Courts Martial.[5]

That Article 20. and 21. be amended by punishing the Offences therein specified in the following Manner viz. An Officer offending be cashier'd and drumm'd out of the Army with Infamy, a private Soldier to be whipp'd not less than 20 Lashes nor more than 39 according to the Nature of their Offence.[6]

That the 17th. Article be amended by expressing the Punishment following viz. The Officer be mulcted in one Months pay for 1st. Offence, Cashiering for the second. A Soldier to be confined for 7 Days on Bread and Water for the 1st. Offence, for the second the same Punishment with a Forfeiture of one Weeks Pay.[7]

That the 25th. Article be amended by leaving out the Word *immediately* and after the Word *Death* substituting the Words *"by any Person on the Spot."*[8]

That the 29th. Article be amended by making the Embezzlement of the Stores therein mentioned punished as the like Offence

3. Some one must have misread the article, which did refer back to Article 2.

4. The offense was exciting or joining in a mutiny.

5. The article covered desertion or absence, and prescribed no specific penalty.

6. The articles covered any one drunk on duty, and sentries who fell asleep or left their posts; the amendment stiffened the penalties or made them more precise.

7. The amendment again defined the penalty, which was for leaving camp without permission.

8. The offense was abandoning under fire a post committed to one's charge, or inciting others to do so.

upon the Stores &c. mentioned in the 15th. Article of the Rules and Regulations of the Army.[9]

That the 30th. Article be amended by making the Offences punishable as the Breach of the 20th. and 21st. Articles together with the Forfeiture of all Share of Plunder taken from the Enemy.[1]

That the 55th. Article be amended by expressing the Punishment viz. cashiering and mulcting of his Pay.[2]

That the 57th. Article be amended so as to include all Surgeons and their Mates and make the Offence of giving a false Certificate of Health punishable as a false Certificate with respect to Absence.[3]

It appearing that both General and Special Orders are not duly obeyed agreed that it be recommended to the Honble. Congress to form a new Article by which Officers and Soldiers wilfully or negligently disobeying such Orders be punished at the Discretion of a Regimental Court Martial when the Offence is against a Regimental Order by a General Court Martial when the Offence is against Orders given by the Commander in Chief or of any Detachment or Post and such General Court Martial can be had.[4]

The Committee then proceeded to the Consideration of such Matters as have been mentioned in the Generals Letters to the Congress upon which no Order had been made.

First. What Steps are necessary to be pursued with Regard to Dr. Church? If guilty, the Articles for the Government of the Army point out a very inadequate Punishment, and to set him at Liberty must be exceedingly dangerous?

9. The stores were those captured from the enemy. The punishment for a noncommissioned officer in Article 15 was loss of rank, and for a private was left to the court martial.

1. The offense was leaving in the face of the enemy to hunt for plunder; the punishment was that prescribed by the earlier articles as amended.

2. The article made a commanding officer responsible for mustering his men when so instructed.

3. The article gave the commanding officer sole responsibility for certifying absentees at a muster and the length and cause of absence.

4. This new article, and all the amendments proposed above to existing articles (except the third), were adopted by Congress on Nov. 7. The only substantial change in the conference's proposals was in Article 29: Congress extended it to cover commissioned officers, and the penalties were stiffened. *JCC*, III, 331–4.

Upon a Discussion of all Circumstances it was agreed to refer Doctor Church for Tryal and Punishment to the General Court of Massachusetts Bay: But that no Procedure be had hereupon untill the Pleasure of the Congress be known on the late Application made by the General.[5]

2. What Distinctions are necessary to be made between Vessels and Cargoes taken by the armed Vessels in the Pay of the Continent and those taken by Individuals? Should not the fitting out of Privateers by Individuals be done under some Authority and Accidental Captures subject to some Regulations to prevent Piracies and other capital Abuses, which may arise?

Agreed that the General Court ought properly to take Cognizance of all armed Vessels fitted out by Individuals in this Province and that Commissions should be granted in such Cases; at least that Captures be made under some Authority. That Captures made by armed Vessels in the Pay of the Continent be disposed of by the General for the publick Use untill the Continental Congress give farther Direction.

The Delegates then proposed to the Consideration of the Members what Number of effective Men it may be expected that the Colonies of New Hampshire, Massachusetts Bay, Connecticut and Rhode Island could and would furnish by the 10 March next and on what Terms.

The Massachusetts Gentlemen were of Opinion that 20,000 effective Men might be raised in this Province to serve the next Campaign if absolutely necessary on the Terms of the present Army viz. A Coat, 40 s. per Month, one Months Wages being advanced, and a greater Number to come on a special Emergency.

The Connecticut Gentlemen were of Opinion that 8000 Men may be raised in their Province to serve the next Campaign on the Terms of the present Army viz. 40 s. per Month and 40 s. Bounty.

5. Dr. Benjamin Church (1734–77?), a member of the Mass. House and one of the colony's Congressional delegates, was director general of the army hospital at Cambridge. He had been detected in correspondence with the enemy. A council of war on Oct. 4 had agreed unanimously that his conduct had been criminal, but because of the wording of the 28th and 51st articles of war had agreed that his punishment must be left to Congress. On the 5th Washington had requested its direction in the matter. Church was subsequently examined before and expelled by the House, and Congress ordered his imprisonment. Freeman, *Washington*, III, 544–52; Fitzpatrick, *op. cit.*, IV, 9–11; Force, 4 *Amer. Arch.*, III, 958.

The President of New Hampshire Convention gave his Opinion that his Colony could furnish 3000 Men for the next Campaign at the Rate of 40 s. per Month without a Bounty unless a Bounty was given by the adjoining Colonies, in which Case they would expect it.

The Governor of Rhode Island gave his Opinion that Province could not go farther than they had done this Campaign viz. to raise 1500 Men on the same Terms.

Upon considering the additional Instruction[6] it was unanimously agreed that the Number of Forces necessary for the Northern Department depended so much on Events and particularly the Success of the present Expedition against Canada that no probable Calculation can be made at this Time. Therefore deferred.

It was then deliberated what should be done with Tory Property; how is it to be applied or treated? Some of the Tories have Estates near the Camp at Cambridge, which have Wood upon them and other Articles wanted for the Army ought they to be meddled with?

Agreed that the Determination of this Matter be referred to the Congress.

The General then proposed the following Question

Should there not be a reasonable Price fixed upon Wood, Hay and other Articles wanted for the Army to prevent Imposition and Extortion?

Agreed that if it be indispensably necessary, such Articles should be valued and taken at such Valuation for the Use of the Army and that a Regulation corresponding herewith be recommended to the General Court of Massachusetts Bay.

The Conference then broke up with the several Governours of Connecticut Rhode Island and the President of the Convention of New Hampshire and the Committee of Council for Massachusetts Bay.

October 23d. 1775

The Delegates now proceeded to confer with General Washington as well on sundry Matters mentioned in his Letters to the Congress upon which no Order has been made as also upon other Matters occurring in the Course of this Business, and

6. *JCC*, III, 276.

First. In the new Establishment of the Army should the General Officers be allowed Regiments and the Field Officers Companies?

Agreed in the Negative unanimously.

Secondly. The Affairs of the Hospital require a Director General if Doctor Church is adjudg'd unworthy of continuing in that Office. Lt. Col. Hand late a Surgeon in the Army and Dr. Foster are the only two who have made Application for the Office to the General.

Agreed that it be referrd wholly to the Congress.[7]

3. In what Light are Vessels which are made Captives of with their Cargoes to be considered? that is what Part is to be assigned the Captors in the Pay of the Continent and whose Vessels are fitted out at the publick Expence and how is the Residue of the Vessel and Cargo to be disposed of?

The Instructions given by the General to the armed Vessels now out being considered were approved (except that one third of the whole Capture be allowed the Officers and Men without any Reserve).[8]

4. What is to be done with Prisoners taken in Transports by Vessels either in the Continental Pay or others? are they to be detained as Prisoners or released? if the former what Distinctions are to be made between those taken by the Continental Vessel and others (In Respect to the Generals Cognizance of them is meant)?

Agreed that all Persons taken in Arms on Board any Prize be deemed Prisoners at the Disposal of the General as well such Prizes as are taken by Vessels fitted out in the Pay of the Continent as others. That all Vessels employed merely as Transports and unarmed with their Crews be set at Liberty upon giving Security to return to Europe but that this Indulgence be not extended longer than to the 1st. April next.

5. In what Manner are Prisoners to be treated? What Allowance made them and how are they to be cloathed?

Agreed that they be treated as Prisoners of War but with Hu-

---

7. BF's old acquaintance, Dr. John Morgan (above, IX, 374 n), had already been appointed by Congress: *JCC*, III, 297. For Drs. Edward Hand and Isaac Foster see respectively the *DAB* and *Sibley's Harvard Graduates*, XIV, 262–8.

8. Washington had raised this question with Congress on Oct. 5, and on the 22nd had authorized the commander of a sloop to divide among the ship's complement a third of any captured cargo, with the exception of military and naval stores. Fitzpatrick, *op. cit.*, IV, 11–12, 38–9.

manity. And the Allowance of Provisions to be the Rations of the Army. That the Officers being in Pay should supply themselves with Cloaths, their Bills to be taken therefor and the Soldiers furnished as they now are.

6. Suppose Troops should be landed at New York is it expected that any Part of the Army before Boston be detached whilst the ministerial Troops remain there?

Agreed That the Number of Men in the new Army being calculated to oppose the Army at Boston, It is not expected that the General should detach any Part of it to New York or elsewhere unless it appears to him necessary so to do for the common Safety.

7. Ought not Negroes to be excluded from the new Inlistment especially such as are Slaves? All were thought improper by the Council of Officers?[9]

Agreed, that they be rejected altogether.

[8.] How often should the Troops be paid? The General Officers were divided on this Point some were for a Payment per Month and others every three Months?

Agreed, That they be paid monthly.

9. Are the Rations which have been allowed the Officers, and have been issued an Account thereof given to the Congress and now laid before the Committee agreeable?

Agreed That the present Allowance be continued as being usual and necessary.

10. Is it adviseable to propose an Exchange of Prisoners? Should any of the Officers and Soldiers in the Army or Navy now in our Power be given up for any except the Officers and Soldiers of the American Army?

Agreed that the Exchange will be proper, Citizens for Citizens, but not Officers and Soldiers of the regular Army for Citizens.

11. A Proposition has been made in Behalf of Ensign Moland to go and reside among his Friends in Pennsylvania giving his Parol.[1] Would this be disagreeable?

9. The council on the 8th had decided unanimously against slaves, and by a great majority against any blacks. Fitzpatrick, *op. cit.*, IV, 8 n.

1. Undoubtedly Joseph Moland (c. 1753–87), an ensign in the 26th Foot and one of the many sons of John Moland, who had been a leader of the Pennsylvania bar. Charles P. Keith, *The Provincial Councillors of Pennsylvania* . . . (Philadelphia, 1883), pp. 417–19 of second pagination. We have found no record of the ensign's capture, but one company of his regiment was taken at Ticonderoga: Carter, *Gage Correspondence*, II, 690.

Agreed that under all Circumstances it is best he should remain where he is.

12. Artificers of different Sorts have been employed on the best Terms they could be got, but may nevertheless appear high, none having less than 1 *s.* extraordinary for every Day they work, Some £4 10 *s.* per Month and with great Difficulty got on those Terms, is this agreeable?

Agreed that it is and that the General go on upon the present Agreement as being the best that can probably be made.

13. The Riffle Companies have exceeded their Establishments in Point of Numbers, but have nevertheless been paid as they had no more Officers than were allowed by Congress. Is this right?

Agreed, That the General pick out from each Company such as are not Marksmen and dismiss them in such a Manner as may be safest with an Allowance of Pay to go Home, and in the mean Time that all recieve their Pay.

14. Very unhappy Disputes prevail in the Regiment of Artillery. Col. Gridly is become very obnoxious to that Corps and the General is informed that he will prove the Destruction of the Regiment if continued therein. What is to be done in this Case?

Agreed that as all Officers must be approved by the General if it shall appear in forming the new Army that the Difference is irreconciliable Col: Gridly be dismiss'd in some honourable Way, and that the half Pay which he renounced by entering into the American Army ought to be compensated to him.[2]

15. Artillery of different Kinds will be wanted how is it to be got and where?

Agreed, That what can be spared from New York and Crown Point be procured.

16. Engineers also much wanted where can they be got?

Agreed to recommend to the Congress Henry Knox Esqr. and Lieut. Col. Puttnam who have Skill in this Branch as Assist. Engineers with suitable Pay and Rank as Lieut. Colonels, the present Pay of Assistant Engineers being deemed too small.[3]

2. For the military career of Richard Gridley, then in his late sixties, see the *DAB.* In early November the council of officers unanimously recommended his dismissal; Congress concurred, on the ground of age, and indemnified him for the loss of pay. Fitzpatrick, *op. cit.,* IV, 74; *JCC,* III, 358–9.

3. Henry Knox and Rufus Putnam were beginning their rise to fame. Congress commissioned Knox colonel of artillery on Nov. 17; Putnam did not

17. Several Indian Chiefs of the St. Francis, Penobscot Stockb[ridge] and St. Johns Tribes have been to offer their Services and told they would be called for if wanted and dismiss'd with Presents. Ought they to be called if a Necessity for them should appear and is the giving them Presents proper?

Agreed That these Indians or others may be called on in Case of real Necessity and that the giving them presents is both suitable and proper.

18. Would it not be adviseable to have Expresses posted along the Roads at different Distances Persons of Character for the Purpose of conveying early and frequent Intelligence?

Agreed that such a Regulation is highly necessary but that the Mode of carrying it into Execution be left to the Congress.

19. Lead and Flints are much wanted where and in what Quantities can they be procured?

Agreed that as much Lead as can be spared from the Northern Department and is wanted here should be sent down from Ticonderoga and all other Supplies of the Articles attended to.

20. Several issuing Commissaries and Clerks are necessarily employed under the Commissy. General:[4] For whom no Provision is made. Several Assists. Quarter Masters are also employed in order to discharge that Duty. A Clerk is and allways has been found necessary to assist in the Office of the Adjut. General. What Pay should be allowed them?

The Commissary being sick and unable to explain the Duty of these Commissaries Clerks &c. Agreed that he draw up a Memorial to the Congress stating the Ranks, Duties &c. of the several Officers under him: that the Quarter Master Genl. do the same to inable the Congress to fix the Proportion of Pay to be allowed them. That these Memorials be first shewn to the General and by him transmitted to the Congress.

21. Six Vessels (armed) are now fitted out and fitting upon the best Terms to intercept the Enemys Supplies, will this be agreeable to the Congress?

---

receive his colonelcy until the following August, and soon resigned to command a Mass. regiment. *DAB.*

4. Col. Joseph Trumbull, son of the Governor of Connecticut, had held this position since July. *DAB.*

Agreed that this Committee approve the Scheme and recommend it to the Congress.[5]

October 24. 1775.

The Committee proceeded in their Conference on the Generals Queries.

When the Army receives such Supplies of Powder as to be enabled to spare some to the Country, how and upon what Terms is it to be done?

Agreed that it be sold them at a reasonable Price.

2d. Tents, if the Army should have Occasion to take the Field next Spring will be indispensably necessary for both Officers and Men, how are they to be provided and are the Officers to be allowed any?

Agreed that it be recommended to the Congress to pay an early Attention to this Article and if the Pay of the Officers is not considerably increased that Tents be allowed them.

The General informed the Committee that he had given particular Orders that all the Tents now in Use should be carefully pack'd up in proper Places during the Winter.

The Council of War lately held having in Consequence of an Intimation from the Congress deliberated on the Expediency of an Attack upon Boston and determined that at present it was not practicable, The General wishes to know how far it may be deemed proper and adviseable to avail himself of the Season to destroy the Troops who propose to winter in Boston by a Bombardment, when the Harbour is block'd up or in other Words whether the Loss of the Town and the Property therein are to be so considered as that an Attack upon the Troops there should be avoided when it evidently appears the Town must of Consequence be destroyed?

The Committee are of Opinion this is a Matter of too much Consequence to be determined by them therefore refer it to the Hon. Congress.[6]

5. The committee did so, and the small squadron played a role of some significance. See William M. Fowler, *Rebels under Sail: the American Navy during the Revolution* (New York, [1976]), pp. 21–31, 37–8, 57.

6. On Dec. 22 Congress, after considerable debate, came to a decision: if Washington and his officers believed that the British troops might be successfully attacked, the attempt should be made even at the risk of destroying the town. *JCC*, III, 444–5.

The General then requested that the Committee would represent to the Congress the Necessity of having Money constantly and regularly sent and that some Regulations upon this Head should be made as soon as possible.

Also that the Congress would be pleased to establish or recommend it to the Legislature of this Colony to establish some Court for the Tryal and Condemnation of Vessels taken from the Enemy, so that they may be distinguished from those of a different Character and all Abuses prevented as much as possible.

A true Copy of the Minutes of the Conference held by the Delegates from the Continental Congress with General Washington.

Jos: REED Secretary

To Richard Bache   ALS: Bristol, R.I., Historical Society

Dear Son   Cambridge Head Quarters, Oct. 19 [–24]. 1775.

We hear you have had an Alarm at Philada. I hope no ill consequences have attended it.[7] I wonder I had no Line from you. I make no doubt of our People's defending their City and Country bravely, on the most trying Occasions.

I hear nothing yet of Mr. Goddard, but suppose he is on the Road.[8] I suppose we shall leave this Place next Week. I shall not return in Company with the other Delegates, as I must call for my Sister, and we shall hardly be able to travel so fast, but I expect to be at Philada within a few Days of them.

There has been a plentiful Year here as well as with us: And there are as many chearful Countenances among those who are driven from House and Home at Boston or lost their All at Charlestown, as among other People. Not a Murmur has yet been heard, that if they had been less zealous in the Cause of Liberty

7. On Oct. 6 the Pa. committee of safety arrested Dr. John Kearsley (above, XXI, 516) and others for hatching a plot against Philadelphia. The conspirators had written Dartmouth promising that five thousand Loyalists would turn out if the same number of regular troops appeared, and had also sent a map of the Delaware on which they marked the location of the chevaux-de-frise. Smith, *Letters*, II, 151–3; see also William Duane, ed., *Extracts from the Diary of Christopher Marshall* . . . (Albany, N.Y., 1877), pp. 45–6; *Pa. Col. Recs.*, X, 357–61.

8. See BF to Greenleaf below, Oct. 26.

they might still have enjoy'd their Possessions. For my own Part tho' I am for the most prudent Parsimony of the publick Treasure, I am not terrified by the Expence of this War, should it continue ever so long. A little more Frugality, or a little more Industry in Individuals will with Ease defray it. Suppose it £100,000 a Month or £1,200,000 a Year: If 500,000 Families will each spend a Shilling a Week less, or earn a Shilling a Week more; or if they will spend 6 pence a Week less and earn 6 pence a Week more, they may pay the whole Sum without otherwise feeling it. Forbearing to drink Tea saves three fourths of the Money; and 500,000 Women doing each threepence Worth of Spinning or Knitting in a Week will pay the rest.* I wish nevertheless most earnestly for Peace, this War being a truly unnatural and mischievous one: but we have nothing to expect from Submission but Slavery, and Contempt. I am ever Your affectionate Father   B F

Love to dear Sally and the Children.

*How much more then may be done by the superior Frugality and Industry of the Men?

P.S. Oct. 24. We purpose setting out homewards tomorrow. Here is a fine healthy Army, wanting nothing but some Improvement in its Officers, which is daily making.

This Letter should have gone by last Post, but was left by Accident. You may publish the Part of it that is mark'd[9] mentioning no Name. We have just receiv'd Advice of the burning of Falmouth Casco Bay; and are assur'd that Orders are come over to burn, ravage and destroy all the Sea Coast;[1] such is the Government of the best of Princes! If the People of Philadelphia, to be more at their Ease in defending the City should think fit to remove their Families, and some of their Goods, do you after taking Care of Sally and the Children, remember to secure my Account Books and Writings which are in the Glass Desk and two Trunks in my

9. BF made no marks.
1. For accounts of this episode see *Naval Docs.*, II, 500–2, 513–16, 590–2. The British commander reportedly informed a committee of townsfolk, before the bombardment, that orders had been received to destroy all the seaports on the American coast that would not deliver up their arms and give hostages. *Ibid.*, p. 595.

Library. I hope too that the Library may be sav'd; but we must run all Risques, that being to bulky to be remov'd.

Addressed: To / Mr Richard Bache / Postmaster / Philadelphia

The Settlement with Franklin for His Massachusetts Agency
DS and copy: Massachusetts Archives

Ever since Franklin's appointment in 1770 as agent of the Massachusetts House of Representatives, he had served his constituents without pay. They had authorized his salary time and time again, but the Governor had always refused, on instruction, to give his assent;[2] and the agent conducted the colony's business at his own expense. His principal outlay was for lawyers' fees, in the Chancery suit that grew out of the affair of the Hutchinson letters and in the proceedings before the Privy Council on the petition from the House to remove the Governor and Lieutenant Governor; minor items were for printing pamphlets designed to further the colony's cause.[3] Franklin was philosophical about the situation. "If I serve my Constituents faithfully tho' it should be unsuccessfully," he had written the Speaker in 1773, "I am confident they will always have it in their Inclination and sometime or other in their Power to make their Grants effectual."[4] Now the time had come when they had the power, and at long last he was reimbursed.

[October 23, 1775]
A state of the Account between The Honble. Benjamin Franklin Esqr. late agent for this colony in Great Britain and the colony.

The sum of the last Grant made by the House of Representatives to the said Franklin and concurred by the Honble. Board being for his services at the court of Great Britain from Octo. 31st 1770 to Octo. 31st 1773. --------------------- £1100[5] : — : —

2. See above, XVIII, 153–4 n, 242 n; XIX, 209–10 n; XX, 284 n.
3. BF submitted the detailed bills, receipted; they are printed in the Mass. Hist. Soc. *Proc.*, LVI (1922–23), 104–20.
4. Above, XX, 284.
5. We find the total incomprehensible except on the assumption that the salary was £400 per annum for two years and £300 for one; yet as late as June, 1773, the House and Council tried to pay him £800 for two and two-thirds years: *ibid.*, n. We said earlier (XVIII, 242 n) that the settlement was for four years' salary at £400; we should have said that BF's accounts in 1774 indicate

The Interest of that sum from Octo. 31st 1773.
to Octo. 31st 1774 ---------------------------- 66 : — : —
    For his services from Octo. 31st 1773 to
Octo. 31st 1774 ------------------------------- 300 : — : —
    For his Services from Octo. 31st 1774 to the end
of his agency being 4. Months ----------------- 100 : — : —
    His Account of Sundry disbursements of Money
in the Service of this colony -------------------- 285 : — : —

In the House of Representatives Octo. 23d 1775. Resolved that there be granted and paid out of the publick treasury of this colony to The Honble. Benja. Franklin Esqr. late agent for the House of Representatives of the said colony in Great Britain in full for his Services and disbursements in his said agency from Octo. 31st 1770, to the first day of March 1775 when his agency determind the sum of Eighteen hundred and fifty one pounds Sterling and that Henry Gardner Esqr. Treasurer of this colony be and he is hereby directed to wait on the said Benja. Franklin Esqr. now at Cambridge and pay the said sum to him taking his receipt for the same. Sent up for Concurrence   J WARREN Spkr

In Council Octr. 23d. 1775. Read and Concurred PEREZ MORTON Dpy Secrt

Consented to[6]
JAMES OTIS	JAMES PRESCOTT
W SEVER	M FARLEY
B GREENLEAF	S HOLTEN
CALEB CUSHING	MOSES GILL
J WINTHROP	JABEZ FISHER
B CHADBOURN	B WHITE
JOSEPH GERRISH	JOHN WHETCOMB
JEDH: FOSTER	

that he believed that sum was due him. We cannot resolve this conflict of evidence.

6. For Henry Joseph Gardner, treasurer and receiver general of Massachusetts, see the *DAB*. BF was not at Cambridge and, by his figures, was owed only £1835 5s. 3d. "This Acct. was settled and paid in full," he wrote, "by the Assembly of Massachusetts when I was at Watertown 1775." Ledger, p. 57.

Joseph Hawley[7] to the Committee of Conference of Congress

ALS: American Philosophical Society

Gentlemen   Cambridge Octr. 23d. 1775.

To give you full Satisfaction that what was granted and paid in the last War to the Non commission officers and private Soldiers by this colony was in the whole much more than the whole which has been engaged to the Non commissiond officers and privates in the present service by the late Congress of this colony. Col. Warren and the Subscriber have bro't for your inspection the Journals of the house for 1758 and 1759. and beg you to inspect the establishment for each of those years. The one is in page 350. of 1758. The other is Page 335. of Journal for 1759.[8] As We are so unhappy as not to find your Honours at Head Quarters, Mr. Randolph[1] will do us the favour to present the said Journals to you for inspection. We are with great respect Your Servants JOSEPH HAWLEY for himself and Mr. Warren

P:S: from the perticular Circumstances of this Colony we are unable to avail ourselves of the Journals containing [*illegible*]ishments

To The Honble the Comtee of the General Congress of the American United Colonies

Addressed: To / The Committe of / The Continental Congres / att / Head Quarters

---

7. A member of the Mass. House for almost a decade: above, XX, 481 n. His letter is the only one we have found to the committee.

8. Congress had instructed the committee to determine the pay of officers and men (*JCC*, III, 271), and the matter had been discussed in the conference on Oct. 21; see the minutes above, under Oct. 18. The committee must have requested information about the comparative rates as established in Mass. by the provincial ("the late") congress and in the French and Indian War. Hawley and James Warren (1726–1808), the speaker of the new House of Representatives and paymaster general of the army, produced the information in the *Mass. House Jour.*

1. The name seems to be misspelled, and only "dolph" is legible. For Edmund Randolph, Washington's aide-de-camp, see the *DAB*.

The Committee of Conference: Report to Congress

DS: National Archives

Sir   Cambridge Octo 24. 1775

We arrived at this place on the 15 and shoud have proceeded immediatly to perform the Duty imposed by the Congress, but the President of the Congress of New Hampshire was detained by the Illness of his Family from attending, after waiting two days for him it was determined to call in General Sullivan to represent that Colony. The president joined us next day, and we have been constantly employed in the Consideration of the many important Matters with which we are charged, all of which we hope will be finished today.[2]

We enclose you a Copy of the Several Determinations of this Meeting on those Heads on which the Governors of Rhode Island and Connecticut, the Council of this Province the President of the Congress of New Hampshire together with the General were directed to be consulted, by Which you will see that they were unanimously of Opinion not only, that any Reduction of pay was absolutely impracticable but that a bare proposal of this Nature woud cause such Discontents, if not Mutinies as woud perhaps prove the Ruin of the Army. We are sorry to find this Opinion too much confirmed, by the Difficulty that occurs in prevailing on the Troops of Connecticut to enlist for the Month of Decembre only, according to the Directions of Congress.

Under these Circumstances we thought it our Duty to consent that the General shoud immediatly proceed to a new Inlistment of the present Army for the next Year without waiting for the Directions of Congress, being convinced by the Opinion, not only of the Gentlemen, we were directed to consult, but of every Officer we conversed with on the subject that every Moments delay was big with Danger. We have however reserved, in the terms of the new Inlistment a Right in Congress to disband at Pleasure without mentioning the Months additional pay Voted the Soldiers in Case they had listed at 5 Dollars per Month.

Last Night we received the Melancholy Account of the burning the Town of Falmouth, by some Ships Sent for that Purpose by

2. See the minutes of the conference above, Oct. 18. They were enclosed with this report, and included the two final days after the New England representatives had withdrawn.

Admiral Graves, the commanding officer of which declared he had orders to destroy every Seaport between that and Boston[3] it is easy to conceive what Effects this must produce in this Camp, every Soldier who came from Falmouth insisting on Leave to go and take care of his Family and to find a place for them where they may be covered from the inclemency of the approaching Winter, indeed 'tis too reasonable a Request, to be refused, shoud the same Fate fall to the share of Many such Towns, tis easy to foretell what must happen to the army especally shoud it happen before the new Army is inlisted, this we hope will not only excuse our conduct, but induce Congress to hasten their Determinations upon this Matter.

One more Reason for despatch is that Men may much more probably inlist before; than after they feel the hardships of a Winter Campaign.

Upon examining the Journals of assembly it appears that the Men raised in the Years 1758 and 1759 by this Colony received fourteen pounds bounty and had thirty six Shillings per month pay,[4] which, as their Engagements were for Six Months only, was much higher Terms than the present when no other Bounty is allowed than a Coat to each Man. We are with great Respect Sir your most Obedient   THOS LYNCH
                                                    B FRANKLIN
                                                    BENJ HARRISON

Addressed: To / The honble / John Hancock Esqr / President of the Continental / Congress at / Philadelphia

Endorsed: N.B. Letter from Comm. of Conference. Cambridge 24 Oct. 1775 Recd. & read Novr. 2. with 2 reports from sd Comm.

---

3. Adm. Graves had been ordered to take steps to suppress the rebellion, and had sent out a small squadron to attack a number of ports on the Mass. and N.H. coast. The officer commanding, however, contented himself with destroying Falmouth (now Portland, Me.), and Graves abandoned his policy of destruction before it had a chance to be effective. BF to RB above, Oct. 19; William M. Fowler, Jr., *Rebels under Sail: the American Navy during the Revolution* (New York, [1976]), pp. 33–4.

4. See the preceding document.

To Joseph Greenleaf[5]

ALS: American Philosophical Society

Sir, Head Quarters, Cambridge, Oct. 26. 75

I intended to have called upon you yesterday at Watertown, but was prevented by other Business.[6]

Mr. Goddard, appointed Riding Surveyor to the General Post-Office, is on his Way, settling the Post-Offices from Philadelphia Eastward. He will probably be here in a few days, and has Instructions for Regulating everything relating to them.[7] I think it will be right for the Committee to receive and pay all to the End of the last Quarter; and let the present Quarter, commencing with this Month, be on Account of the General Post-Office. I should be glad however to know from you, the *Amount* of the Receipts, and of the Disbursements, while the Offices were under the Direction of the Committee; which if you please you may send me at your convenient Leisure. I am very respectfully, Sir, Yours and the Committee's, most obedient humble Servant   B FRANKLIN

I do not recollect that I received the Letter you mention to have sent me in August last.

I return homewards this day.

Jos. Greenleaf Esqr

Addressed: To / Joseph Greenleaf Esqr / Wa[tertown]

Endorsed: Letter from Dr. Franklin Octr. 26. 1775.

5. Greenleaf (1720–1809) emerged in 1771 as a propagandist for the colonial cause in his contributions to the *Mass. Spy*, and the following year joined the Boston committee of correspondence. In 1774 he was advocating an independent postal system and in May, 1775, was named to a committee appointed by the provincial congress to establish such a system. William Lincoln, ed., *The Journals of the Provincial Congress of Massachusetts in 1774 and 1775* . . . (Boston, 1838), pp. 208, 222–4; James E. Greenleaf, *Genealogy of the Greenleaf Family* . . . (Boston, 1896), pp. 77–8; Richard D. Brown, *Revolutionary Politics in Massachusetts* . . . (Cambridge, Mass., 1970), pp. 181–4. This committee, we assume, was the one to which BF refers in the second paragraph.

6. At least a part of which was settling his accounts as Mass. agent; see the note on that settlement above, Oct. 23.

7. Either Goddard was further delayed, or he spent a long time in the Boston area, for Ezra Stiles met him at Wrentham on Nov. 21: Franklin B. Dexter, *The Literary Diary of Ezra Stiles* . . . (3 vols., New York, 1901), I, 635.

From Horatio Gates[8]

ALS: American Philosophical Society

Dear Sir   Head Qrs: 7th[–8[9]]: November 1775

Thursday last I had the pleasure to send a Copy of General Lee's Letter to Lord Thanet, and on Monday [another of?] one to General Howe, both these I suppose you received[1] [*torn*.] I made strickt inquiry as you directed me after [*torn*], and find he died, and was buried about a Week before [*torn* Cam?]bridge, the Ten Dollars you paid into my Hands [*torn* sha]ll be disposed of to your Order. The Letter I shall [put in the?] Fire (if you think proper). Some Deodands[2] has come to Us since you left Cambridge. A ship from your Port with One Hundred and Eighteen Pipes of Wine is wrecked to the Eastward, the Wine and Crew saved. She was bound into Boston. The Captain and Crew, are prisoners, and will be here in a Day or Two, when they arrive, you shall know who were the Shippers of This Cargo. A Vessel bound from Boston to Nova-Scotia with Dry Goods, is taken by Fishermen from Beverley and Carried in there. The letters found on board and brought hither are full of Commissions for Fresh Meat Forrage, and Fire wood to be sent at any price to Boston. A Sloop from the West Indies is taken by One of our Cruizers. She was bound to Boston, had Rum, Sugar, and Fruit on board, so Wine, and Punch will

8. BF had met the erstwhile British major and future American general, perhaps for the first time, at a dinner party in London in 1768: above, XV, 78. We have no evidence that the acquaintance ripened between then and 1772, when Gates yielded to the urging of his old friend Washington and emigrated to become a Virginia planter. Soon after the outbreak of war Congress commissioned him a brigadier general, and he joined Washington's army as adjutant general. See the *DAB* and Paul D. Nelson, *General Horatio Gates . . .* (Baton Rouge, La., [1976]), pp. 34–45. During BF's recent visit to the camp, it is clear from this letter, he and Gates renewed contact; and they kept it alive by a correspondence that went on intermittently until 1785.

9. The letter was not completed until the next day, when some of the news in it reached Cambridge and the courier mentioned in the last sentence left for Philadelphia. *Naval Docs.*, II, 913 n.

1. Sackville Tufton, Earl of Thanet (1733–86), had been Charles Lee's patron for years. A copy of the letter to him, dated Oct. 20 and explaining the General's reasons for joining the American army and his expectation of what would overtake the British if they continued the war, is among BF's papers in the APS. The letter to Howe, if our guess at the missing words is correct, we have been unable to locate.

2. Free use of the medieval term, which denoted an object responsible for a death and hence given to God, via the crown, for charitable purposes.

not be wanting to the Sons of Liberty. Let the Sons of Slavery get them how they can; One of Our Arm:d Vessells brought in on Fryday, a la[rge?] Sloop, and a Schooner, bound from Nova-Scotia to Bo[ston and?] full Freighted with Cattle, Sheep, Hoggs Poultry, Po[tatoes and?] Fire Wood;[3] our Squadron are now at Sea and I [hope I shall?] have more news to send of their Success next P[ost. I shall?] recommend the Fitting of Arm'd Vessells to every [torn] how does the pulse of the Polliticians beat, since [the burn]ing of Falmouth, and Lord Dumores intrenching himself at Gosport?[4] I shall never be able to write you a Line without half a dozen interruptions, an Ambassador from the Committee of safety at Marblehead will not allow me one moments peace but must this Instant have an Order for two Barrells of Powder for the defence of that Port. Capt. Macphersons[5] horse is at the door and he s impatient to be gone. Adieu yours most truly

HORATIO GATES

Addressed: To / The Honble. / Doctor Benjamin Franklin / Philadelphia

3. The sloop from Philadelphia was the *Monmouth*, commanded by Perkins Allen and wrecked at Eastham en route to Boston. The capture by Beverly men was the sloop *North Briton*, bound to Annapolis Royal. The West India sloop we have not identified. The schooner from Nova Scotia was the *Polly*, captured along with the schooner *Industry* by Capt. William Coit. *Pa. Packet*, Nov. 20; *Pa. Gaz.*, Nov. 22, 1775; *Naval Docs.*, II, 870–1, 879–81, 904.

4. For the news about Falmouth see BF to RB above, Oct. 19. Lord Dunmore had taken refuge on a man-of-war, which lay in the Elizabeth River off Gosport, and he soon amassed a small flotilla with which he made desultory raids on the coast. *DNB*.

5. John Macpherson, a Philadelphia merchant and ex-privateer, had gone to Cambridge with Congressional approval of his plan for an explosive torpedo to use against ships at anchor. Washington persuaded him to return to Philadelphia on Nov. 8 to explain his proposal further to the delegates. Smith, *Letters*, II, 28; Fitzpatrick, *Writings of Washington*, IV, 76.

The Pennsylvania Assembly: Instructions to Its Delegates in Congress

Printed in *Votes and Proceedings of the House of Representatives of Pennsylvania* . . . , VI (Philadelphia, 1776), 647; AD (draft): Historical Society of Pennsylvania.

In May the Pennsylvania Assembly had committed its delegates to military resistance, colonial union, and a continued search for compromise.[6] After the elections in October the new Assembly chose a new Congressional delegation, again including Franklin, and in early November drafted its instructions. By then the news had come that the King had refused to receive or answer the Olive Branch Petition and had proclaimed the colonies in rebellion, and at the same time Congress urged two colonies to establish revolutionary governments.[7] The possibility of settling the crisis within the old constitutional framework was steadily growing fainter. But John Dickinson, the chief spokesman for majority opinion in the Assembly, continued on the moderate course set the previous spring. The drafting committee, appointed on November 7, reported two days later; the instructions that it submitted for the delegation were largely Dickinson's handiwork, and seem to have been adopted without amendment.[8] The first two paragraphs differed little from those of May, but the third was quite different: it attempted to buttress the status quo by forbidding the delegates to vote for independence or for a change of government. This position proved to be untenable. By the following spring the advocates of change swept away first the instructions and then the Assembly itself.[9]

Gentlemen,   November 9, 1775.
The Trust reposed in you is of such a Nature, and the Modes of executing it may be so diversified in the Course of your Delibera-

6. The instructions are above, May 9.
7. Smith, *Letters*, II, 285, 291, 320 n, 321; *JCC*, III, 319, 326–7.
8. 8 *Pa. Arch.*, VIII, 7350, 7352. We assume that Dickinson's draft, the AD cited in the source identification and published in Smith, *Letters*, II, 319–20, was the one that he submitted to the committee, which slightly reworked it into the version that we print.
9. See the headnote on the Assembly's instructions below, June 14, and for the background Ryerson, *The Revolution Is Now Begun*, pp. 124–47; David L. Jacobson, *John Dickinson and the Revolution in Pennsylvania, 1764–1776* (University of Cal. *Pubs.* in History, LXXVIII; Berkeley and Los Angeles, 1965), pp. 87–100.

tions, that it is scarcely possible to give you particular Instructions respecting it.

We therefore, in general, direct, that you, or any Four of you, meet in Congress the Delegates of the several Colonies now assembled in this City, and any such Delegates as may meet in Congress next Year; that you consult together on the present critical and alarming State of public Affairs; that you exert your utmost Endeavours to agree upon, and recommend, such Measures as you shall judge to afford the best Prospect of obtaining Redress of American Grievances, and restoring that Union and Harmony between Great-Britain and the Colonies so essential to the Welfare and Happiness of both Countries.

Though the oppressive Measures of the British Parliament and Administration have compelled us to resist their Violence by Force of Arms,[1] yet we strictly enjoin you, that you, in Behalf of this Colony, dissent from, and utterly reject, any Propositions, should such be made, that may cause, or lead to, a Separation from our Mother Country, or a Change of the Form of this Government.

You are directed to make Report of your Proceedings to this House. Signed by Order of the House, JOHN MORTON, Speaker.

From William Govett[2]   ALS: American Philosophical Society

[Between November 9 and 25, 1775[3]]

The Committee of Safety meet tomorrow Morning at 9 oClock And attend the Committee of Assembly at 10. On Wednesday Morning 9 oClock the Board meet and go into the Consideration of the appointment of a Commodore, at which times the Members are Requested to meet Punctually.   WM. GOVETT Secry

To Benja. Franklin Esqr.

1. Dickinson's draft substituted for this clause an injunction to avoid any measures that would tend to prevent reconciliation with Britain.

2. See the note on the committee's advertisement above, July 28.

3. The dates derive from the mention of a commodore. This matter was referred to the committee on Oct. 20; see the note on its report to the Assembly above, Sept. 29. Govett, we assume, knew that BF was out of town in late October on his visit to Washington's camp, and would not have written him. The dates we assign are the only ones thereafter, until a commodore was appointed in January, when BF was in Philadelphia and the committee and the Assembly were both in session.

From Catharine Greene
ALS: American Philosophical Society

Westerly monday noon [November 13, 1775[4]]

My Dear Friend

I have Some days Past Plast [Placed] you at home happy with your Dear Children and Sister. I am not able to find Words to tell you how Pleasd I am to have our Boy with you[5] I wish he may Deserve Such Goodness God Will Reward you. Thank you for your Kind letter from New haven I Shall write you as Soon as I get home am Just going.[6] I write to Ray but the letter is got So soild would write Another if I was not in Such hast you will excus it. The family here all Desire there love and would been Glad it had been Convenient for you to Calld upon them. I am with true affection your Friend   CATY GREENE

Did you travill as fast after you got by Springfield? how does it go on?

Addressed: To / Doctr. Franklin / Philadelphia

From William Greene
ALS: American Philosophical Society

Dear Friend   Westerly Novr: 13th: 75

On my Coming here I found Your Favor from Newhaven, it gives me great pleasure To hear You was so far on Your journey well, hope before this You have Arriv'd safe home. My little son who You have Taken with You how shall I enough express my Gratitude, I was much at a loss what to Doe with him. I had three Years past a good writing master so that he learn't Very fast since he has been To an Indifferent school when not Otherways Ingag'd, but he being Very handy to go of Errands and upon the Farm, that he has had Very little Advantages that I really am at a loss what may be his Genius. If he has a Turn for learning shall give it him freely if not I shall be glad of Your Advice in regard to his Genius

4. See the following letter, which was sent with this one.
5. Young Ray Greene, at ten, had left home with Jane Mecom and BF to attend the Academy of Philadelphia; see *ibid.*, Mecom to Greene below, Nov. 24, and above, V, 502 n.
6. The Greenes were visiting Caty's sister and brother-in-law, Anna and Samuel Ward, at the Ward farm in Westerly.

as I have a great Desire that he may be a useful member of Society.[7] His Mamma has wrote him. My love to him Your Children and in perticular manner to Mrs. Meacome and except a share of the same from Your Sincear and much Oblig'd Friend.   WM. GREENE

From [David Hartley]

ALS: Public Record Office;[8] copy: Clements Library

Hartley's cast of mind was similar to that of the peace negotiators with whom Franklin dealt during his last months in England. All of them regarded reconciliation as a problem to be analyzed, ordered, and reduced to rational terms from which a rational solution might emerge. Barclay and Fothergill pinned their hopes on negotiating by emissary. Hartley, as a member of Parliament, pinned his on legislative actions that would close the breach. The previous March he had suggested a system of requisitions to settle the financial dispute.[9] He was now preparing a more ambitious plan, which embodied that system and went beyond it to provide for repealing the initial Coercive Acts and—the key to his scheme—passing a statute that the colonial assemblies would be willing to enroll and thereby acknowledge, with a minimum of pain, the principle of Parliament's authority to make laws for them. He expected that the British, once their honor had been thus salvaged, would allow the principle of supremacy to become a dead issue. He was soon disillusioned: after he amended some details of the plan outlined here, he brought it before the House of Commons on December 7; and it was resoundingly defeated. So ended, stillborn, his attempt to legislate away a revolution.

7. Young Ray fulfilled his father's desire. After schooling at the Academy of Philadelphia and Gov. Dummer Academy in Mass., he graduated from Yale, studied law, and was eventually elected to the U.S. Senate. Franklin B. Dexter, *Biographical Sketches of the Graduates of Yale College* . . . (6 vols., N.Y., 1885–1912), IV, 339–40; William G. Roelker, ed., *Benjamin Franklin and Catharine Ray Greene: Their Correspondence* . . . (Philadelphia, 1949), p. 59.

8. Hartley's other letters in November, of the 14th and the 23rd, and Robert Crafton's two to BF about the plan, of the 15th and 22nd, are in the same repository. We have no evidence that BF received them, and suspect that they were intercepted and sequestered.

9. Above, XXI, 511–12. Hartley's reference below to making this suggestion "last year" must have been a slip for "last session."

Dear Sir   London November 14 1775

I have recd your Letter and packet of the 12th of September and am much obliged to you for them. I am very anxious to hear more fully from you, as you are so good as to give me reason to expect. Before this can reach you, you will certainly have seen the Kings Speech. I heartily wish that that or any thing else may put the contending parties into a disposition of reconcilement. On the Debate of the Address, Lord North said with great emotion, to this effect. Would to God that all things were as they were in 1763, if the Authority of this country could likewise be replaced in to the same state that it was in, in the year 1763, but that an unconditional repeal of all the acts since 1763, without some honourable satisfaction to the authority of this Country would leave this Country much disgraced. Then follow as of course angry accusations of America, as meaning nothing but independence and insult to this Country.[1] Your friend Mr. Hartley who offered last year a draught of a letter of requisition as a plan of settlement and accomodation desired to offer a proposition to Ld. N upon the new ground that he had taken, for Ld. N had declared that we were not now at war for a revenue, but in support of our Authority resisted. The Substance of Mr. H's proposition was that if there was any sincere desire for peace[2] he would endeavour to join issue with Ld. N and to offer such terms of accommodation, by which, if ministry would consent to replace America to the year 1763 he should on the other part propose that America should give full satisfaction to the point of honour. That he thought himself founded to engage for every thing that could in reason be required from the Americans under that declaration in their petition to the King, that they did not wish even for reconciliation, notwithstanding all their distresses, upon terms inconsistent with the dignity of Great Britain. That taking his ground from this decla-

---

1. The King's speech manifested no "disposition of reconcilement" unless the colonies returned to obedience. North's speech in the debate on the reply ("the Address") seems to have been equally intransigent, but it was briefly reported. Cobbett, *Parliamentary History*, XVIII (1774–77), 695–7, 770–1.

2. From here to the sentence below, "This is the substance of Mr. Hartley's proposal," the text is a draft of part of his speech in the House on Dec. 7 (*ibid.*, cols. 1048–9), except that he later deleted the parenthesis about Duché's pamphlet.

ration, he should propose a recognition, not in words but in fact, which should effectually replace the Authority of this Country (be it more or less without any invidious line drawn) where it was in 1763. The test proposed was the enrolling some act of parliament by the assembly of each province, supposing that the act of Parliament in view should be formed upon principles of justice and such as the Colonies would have received with a silent and thankfull Compliance in 1763. All recognitions in words being unavoidably both invidious and insidious, that, therefore a test bringing no line of Authority or of obedience into Question was the only safe proposition. You Americans shall be as you were in 1763 if you will likewise admit an act of test, such as you would not have had the least scruple to have admitted in 1763. We will throw a veil over all the theoretical disputes of rights of subjects either as Colonists or men at large. We will not discuss the rights reserved or supposed to be reserved at your emigration whether tacitly or explicitly. We wish that mutual concessions on both sides should bring the two parties together. We will on our part replace you where you were in 1763, if you will admit and register in your assemblies such an act of Parliament, as you yourselves shall confess that you would have admitted in 1763. It is not an unreasonable request to make to America, that they should treat an act of Parliament flowing from general principles of humanity and justice, with a different reception, to what has been given to acts of grievance. It is certainly dangerous to disturb questions of the extent [of] Empire or obedience because after that, even acts of acquiescence may be construed to involve hazardous concessions, supposed to be included in the principles which have been brought under contest. But in the State of human affairs we must not always be too scrupulous. Something must be given up for peace. A Civil war never comes too late. Take your situation as it was in 1763, for better and for worse. In the present miserable prospect of things, I conceive that to be a fair and equitable bargain. The object of the act of Parliament to be proposed to you, may be perhaps in the event the abolition, but at present can only be considered as the first step to correct a vice, which has spread thro the continent of North America, contrary to the laws of God and man, and to the fundamental principles of this Constitution, from which yours are derived. That vice is slavery. It would be infinitely absurd to send over to you, an act to abolish slavery in one word, because however repugnant the practice may be to the laws of morality or policy, Yet to expell an evil which has spread so far and which has been suffered for such length of time, requires information of facts, and circumstances, and the greatest discretion to root it out. (Upon this subject pray look to a note in Mr. Duche's sermon on July 7 1775 before the Battalion of Militia p 16 17³) And moreover the unavoidable length of settling such a point, would defeat the end, of its being proposed as an act of compromise to settle the present unhappy troubles. Therefore the act to be proposed to you as a auspicious beginning, to lay the first stone of universal liberty to mankind, should be what no American could hesitate an instant to comply with, viz that every slave in America should in all cases be entitled to his trial by jury. Will you not receive and enroll such an act as this, and thereby reestablish peace and harmony with your parent state? Let us all be reunited in this as a foundation to extirpate slavery from the face of the earth. Can they who seek justice and liberty for themselves refuse to give justice and liberty to their fellow creatures? This is the Substance of Mr. Hartley's proposal. The first step in the execution would be to suspend the Massachusets charter act, by which means every colony would be in a full competence to enroll the required act. The Plan therefore would be

1st To Suspend The Massachusetts charter act
The Boston port act
The act for removing trials.⁴
2dly
To pass an act to establish the right of trial by jury to all Slaves in America and to annull all Laws in any Province repugnant

---

3. The sermon was preached before the Philadelphia associators and published at their request: Jacob Duché, *The Duty of Standing Fast in Our Spiritual and Temporal Liberties* . . . (Philadelphia, 1775). The page reference for the note indicates that Hartley used the American edition, not the London one published in late October (*Public Advertiser*, Oct. 31, 1775); hence we assume that he had received the pamphlet with BF's letter above, Sept. 12. In the note Duché laid the origin of the slave trade at Britain's door, and contended that the trade could be abolished only through Britain's control of imperial commerce. For Hartley's deep concern with the subject see George H. Guttridge, *David Hartley, M.P., an Advocate of Conciliation, 1774–1783* (University of Cal. *Pubs.* in History, XIV, no. 3; Berkeley and London, 1926), pp. 327–30.

4. The Mass. Administration of Justice Act. By Nov. 23, when he wrote again on the subject, Hartley had dropped this and the Boston Port Act.

thereto, and to require the enrollment of the said act by the respective assemblies of each Province in North America.
3dly

To pass an act to establish a permanent reconciliation between Great Britain and its dependencies in North America, and to restore his Majesty's Subjects in North America, to that happy and free condition, and to that peace and prosperity, which they enjoyed in their constitutional dependence upon Great Britain, before the Commencement of the present unhappy troubles.
4thly

To pass an Act of Oblivion.[5]

The great Misfortune in proposing any terms, is the distance and the length of time between us. Ministry say upon any proposal for mutual concessions, Who can give us assurance that such or such terms will not be rejected in America? Then they catch at some hasty or ambiguous phrase from America, or talk in the high strain of supremacy, against those whom they charge with a view of independence, and by such means all equitable propositions of peace are quashed. In short a majority is not to be convinced by reasoning. They will put what constructions they please. If the Ministry should declare for peace, then the most favorable construction would be put upon every phrase, but in the Contrary case every thing is turned against America; every hasty phrase is a settled plan of independence, and even silence in any points upon the most prudent motives is construed into secret views of independence. As to the late petition to the King that is said to be very decent indeed but to mean nothing. With regard to the offers from parliament of the last year, It has been said both to Mr. Burke and to Mr. Hartley, The Americans have very explicitly

5. The steps that Hartley proposed to take were more clearly explained in his speech. The first one, omitted here, was to end hostilities. The second was to suspend the Mass. Government Act, so as to induce the inhabitants to elect a legislature. The third was to pass the slave act, which the colonies would then enroll. The fourth was to establish "a permanent reconciliation between Great Britain and its dependencies" by an act to restore those dependencies to their condition before the present troubles. The healing process, when it had reached that point, was to be marked by an act of oblivion. The final step, also omitted here, was to legislate the system of requisitions. At the end of his speech Hartley proposed the first step as a motion, which was overwhelmingly defeated. He then proposed the other five in a single motion, with the same result. Cobbett, *op. cit.*, cols. 1050–2, 1056.

refused Lord North's proposition, but they have been totally silent as to the proposals of their own friends. They have taken notice of *Delenda est Carthago*, which was a private incident in debate, but they have not added to their exceptions to Ld. Norths plan, that, if any proposition had been sent to them conformable to some plan proposed by their friends, they would have acceded to such an one.[6] Thus by the intervention of jealousies and misconstructions, The time of accommodation is lost, and anger is augmented into fury. I have consulted several American Gentlemen, who have all expressed themselves as confident that America would not hesitate to comply to the act of Jury to slaves, if they could be assured by their compliance with such an act of parliament, that they could secure to themselves restoration to their condition in 1763. It would be a satisfaction to receive some respectable or authentic opinion from America upon that subject. If some authentic sentiments either upon that or upon any similar plan of mutual concession, could be communicated in the course of the spring, so as to be here in february or March or April (that is to say before the prorogation of Parliament) It might give some chance of preventing blood. A Supply upon requisition, would, like the case of Ireland,[7] effectually exclude any other possible idea of taxation, and open the way to very desirable relaxations of restrictions in trade, and, taxation once out of the question, this country could not have a motive to harrass America with needless or vexatious acts of legislation, more especially if Supply were reserved to the Americans, as being the Constitutional ballance to defend the Subjects in any state from grievous legislation. Then will you

6. The "late petition" was the Olive Branch discussed above, July 8. The "private incident in debate," over the Boston Port Bill on March 23, 1774, was in a speech by Charles Van, in which he advocated destroying the town if reparation were not forthcoming: Namier and Brooke, *House of Commons*, III, 572. The exceptions to North's plan were taken by Congress; see BF's contribution to them above, under July 25.

7. Hartley put store by this analogy: Cobbett, *op. cit.*, cols. 1046, 1356. But it scarcely bore on the American dispute, because the Irish Parliament had little autonomy, financial or otherwise. Although in practice it responded to requisitions, in principle the Westminster Parliament had asserted its own complete authority in the Declaratory Act of 1719, 6 Geo. I, c. 5, which was the equivalent for Ireland of the later Declaratory Act for the empire. Thus the Irish were constitutionally subordinate to a degree that the colonists would no longer have tolerated.

strike the bargain? A supply upon reasonable estimates to be laid before you for your free compliance. The enrollment of an act for trial by jury to slaves, or of some other act of justice and humanity of a similar nature, and for you to receive a general redress of grievances since 1763. With respect to the idea of putting a final end to slavery in North America, It should seem that when this country had led the way, by the act for jury that each colony knowing best their own peculiar circumstances, should undertake the work in the most practicable way, and should endeavour to establish some system, by which slavery might in a certain term of years be abolished. Let the only contention henceforward between Great Britain and America be, which can exceed the other, in zeal for establishing the fundamental rights of liberty to all mankind. Compliments to Messrs Falconer Read and all friends, I am Dear Sir Your most affectionately   G B.

Addressed: To Dr Franklin / Philadelphia

From [David Hartley]   ALS: Public Record Office

Dear Sir   London Nov 14 1775
    I send you a copy of the petition from the County of Berks for lenient measures with America, which my Brother[8] and I have signed with about a thousand others. Some time ago the ministerial agents began to move for vindictive addresses, and got many from boroughs, several of them by surprize and management, as I have been informed by public newspapers. All these *addresses* are printed in the Gazettes, but none of the *petitions* for Lenient measures. Probably the Gazettes will be sent to America, to convey the idea that this country is in a most vindictive temper towards America. As far as I can judge the body of the people are cold, and uninformed, but since these addresses have been set on foot, the spirit of petitioning has been roused thro the Country. Sir G Savile has presented a petition from Halifax with 1800 hands, and an-

---

8. Winchcombe Henry Hartley (1740?–94), M.P. for Berkshire from 1776 to 1784, was a large landholder there and in Gloucestershire: Namier and Brooke, *House of Commons*, II, 594; Frank O'Gorman, *The Rise of Party in England: the Rockingham Whigs, 1760–82* (London, [1975]), p. 439.

other from Newcastle with 1200. The Addressers began in general. At Halifax the addressers began, and got perhaps 40 or 50 hands. The petitioners who otherwise perhaps would not have moved yet, amounted to 1800. It was just the same case with the County of Berks; The Address was brought ready drawn, but when proposed at an open meeting was voted down ten to one, however no one can hinder a few addressers from signing their address. The addressers in Berkshire have made so lamentable a figure that they could not have made any tolerable show as *freeholders*, therefore their address is entitled from *freeholders* and inhabitants. As for inhabitants of a county you may pick them up as you walk the streets of any town, But freeholders make the respectable body of any County.[9]

You know my opinion as to this unhappy dispute. I do not think that it is the people of England, but the ministry, who have been the aggressors, and I take that to be the cause chiefly, which makes the people of England so cold. They are not conscious of any ill designs in themselves, and do not know the aggressions of the ministry, or the conduct of Governors, judges, custom house officers, and placemen in America, and above all they are deceived by the misrepresentations of ministers at home. They do not know the history of the year 1768, and of the first introduction of troops into Boston &c. &c. &c. &c. Therefore not being conscious of evil towards America themselves, and being in the dark as to the conduct of ministry towards america, they do not know what is to be said in justification of America. Ninety nine in the hundred are quite in the dark. But I hope the people of England will not be nationally alienated from America, and tho ministers may keep us asunder for a time, I hope that we shall some day or other come to a good understanding with each other. I write in great haste. My

9. At the Berkshire meeting, to take the sense of the county on the American question, the sheriff introduced the address in favor of the government. A local peer, supported by other magnates, introduced an opposing petition, which was endorsed by a great majority of the freeholders, in other words the voters. It and the address were then circulated in the county for signatures. James Townsend, ed., *News of a Country Town: Being Extracts from 'Jackson's Oxford Journal' Relating to Abingdon* . . . (Oxford, etc., 1914), p. 83. For the text of the Halifax petition see the *London Chron.*, Nov. 7–9, 1775; for the texts of the other petitions and addresses that Hartley mentions see Force, 4 *Amer. Arch.*, III, 1201–2, 1261–2, 1383–4, 1549–50.

Brother joins with me in the most earnest wishes for restoration of peace, and of health and prosperity to yourself. I am Dear Sir yours most affectionately   G B

Addressed: To Dr Franklin / Philadelphia

From Robert Crafton[1]   ALS: Public Record Office

My good Sir,   London Novr. 15. 1775.

I can't excuse myself from troubling you at this critical Juncture, having a very momentous Affair to communicate, with my poor Sentiments on it; and when a proper Conveyance offers, I should be glad of yours in return.

A Peace and Union between G. Britain and America, is certainly worth some Sacrifice on each Part; and if a middle Line could be drawn; tho' it should not come up to the sanguine Ideas of either, it might perhaps be Wisdom to adopt it.

Such a Plan is now in contemplation, and I am not without Hopes, that it will be carried into Execution; so far at least as concerns Government here; it originates with a worthy Member in the lower House, who is zealous in the great Cause of Conciliation; and as he will explain himself fully to you, by this very Conveyance; I shall not weary you with a Repetition, of what will come so much better, from his Pen than mine.

My whole Design, is to assure you, that I have consider'd his Plan, as minutely as I am able; and am of Opinion, that it is highly eligible, and worthy the Attention of America; and tho' it may, and must appear a Degree of Presumption in me; unequal as I am, to pronounce on Questions of such magnitude; yet I trust that my known Zeal and Integrity, will afford some Apology; and as our Friend here, has flatter'd me so far; as to consult me on the Occasion; I am in hopes to escape without any severe Censure.

I wish this may meet yourself and Family in good Health; and permit me to assure you, that among other happy Advantages, that will flow from this Reconciliation; that of your probable

1. A London merchant who was an old acquaintance of BF and a member of one of his clubs: above, XIV, 120 n; XVIII, 59. Hartley was in correspondence with Crafton, two of whose letters in the fall of 1775 are in the Hartley papers, Berkshire Record Office; the plan discussed here is that outlined above in the first of Hartley's letters to BF of Nov. 14.

Return to England, will not be thought the least, by your many Friends here; and I must be vain enough, to thrust myself into that Circle. Interim I salute you and yours and remain your assured humble Servant   ROBT. CRAFTON

Addressed: Benjamin Franklin Esqr. / Philadelphia

Notation: 15 Novr 1775

From Margaret Stevenson   ALS: American Philosophical Society

My Dear Sir   Nobr. 16 75 Northumberland Court[2]
    I hope you and all your Dear family ar weel as to my Self, i am, in tolerable health but Confind to my Roome on acont my Leg wich is vere panfull a nights, but ho [oh? know?] if i could geat to America i should be hapey; but that is such a distant prospict that i fear never will be, so I shall never see you my Dearst freind, but only thinke and wish that I may be onse more be so hapey. In this Court I have a kind freind, Mr. Lechmoen he comes and seats with me and talkes of you with a hiy regard and friendship. Mr. Alxander, he is as you know, by Mr. Willimas,[3] so I need say noe moer of him. Mr. and Mrs. Viny was to visit me and I wod mention them with Love and Regard for thar dear Dot [Doct?] and thar Girlls,[4] and maney moer of your friends that Comishion me to say all Love and frindshipe but dar not Name thar Names. Indede i

2. At some time between spring and autumn Mrs. Stevenson left Craven St., for reasons unknown. This letter may have been in the packet that BF did not receive for more than a decade; see below, the endorsement on JW to BF, Sept. 3, and the note on Polly's letter, Dec. 12. Only after BF arrived in France did he learn that his friend was in lodgings in Northumberland Court, off the Strand, and commented that he did not expect her to be comfortable there. To Polly Hewson below, Jan. 26, 1777.

3. Mrs. Stevenson's almost illegible hand makes us unsure we read "Lechmoen" aright, but we suspect that he was the "Mr. Lichmer" of her letter below, Sept. 3. If so she was referring to Charles Lechmere (died 1791), on whom the house in which she was living had been entailed years before: *Gent. Mag.*, LXI (1791), 491; *Survey of London . . .* , XVIII (1937), 19. The next sentence means, we believe, that BF will know from JW about William Alexander. The banker had been imprisoned for debt in August, and a commission in bankruptcy had been issued against him in October: Price, *France and the Chesapeake*, II, 698.

4. Thomas Viny, as far as we know, had only sons; and we have no information about the children of his brother John.

feer poor scrible will be opond and maby never rich you. I have
pad Mr. Matthuss Ten pound for the Tea Uern the furst Bill was a
£[. .⁵] 10s: 0d. You hase not orderd me to Pay Mr. Elfston nor he
has not askst for it but thinke it will be excptable. I shall aske for
his Bill and pay him, he is dising [designing? desiring?] to leve of
Scool at Christmass and Lett his Hous furnishd.⁶ I wish he may to
advantage I have a Regard for him on my Dear Temples sacke.
Pray my Love to him, I hope he will not forgete me. I cant write
to him, but beg you will say from this Letter every thing in
behalfe of my affetiont Regard to him I shall be Glad to Read a
letter from him. I know how to Convay you the news papers. Mr.
Temple I fear will think the packit to Large⁷ as thar is few oppir-
tutys [to] send I wish when you writ next say if i continu to take
them in. Yours Oct. the 3 cam safe by Mr. Stharn [Strahan] Came
safe he cald on me and Read your letter to and he was sorry to difer
from you but he acted upon Princple.⁸ Mr. Fergson and Mr. Stock-
don ar wel and kind in visting moste wensdays for your⁹ as i cant
afoord to keep too feiers i see my frinds ones a week so your to
under stant i keep my Visiting day I have none come but what ar
your friends so we Chate and lamant your absanes. All most hartly
wish for a Recocilishon with both Counitrys also. God G[r]ant it
soon. Mr. Steele has sent a Bock for me to send,¹ but i doe not
expect to Mr. Temple to take it [unless I?] cut the news papers to
make them less Bulcke, if thar opind [opened] Shur I am thay will
by pussld to Read this letter.

5. The figure, if indeed it is one, is illegible. For William Matthews and the
trouble in settling for the urn see the note on BF to Polly Hewson above, July 8.

6. For WTF's schooling under James Elphinston see above, XIII, 443; XVI,
170 n. Elphinston did give up his school; see Mrs. Stevenson's letter below,
Sept. 3, 1776.

7. This was doubtless William, John Temple's brother, who sailed for New
York the following January; see the note on BF to JW below, March 29.

8. Strahan's differences in principle are clear from BF's letter to him above,
Oct. 3; the accompaning letter to her has been lost.

9. "Sake" was perhaps omitted. For Fergusson and Stockton see BF to JW
above, Sept. 12.

1. For Joshua Steele see above, XX, 312 n. He was doubtless sending *An
Essay towards Establishing the Melody and Measure of Speech* . . . (London, 1775),
and the book did arrive; it is a presentation copy, with a few notes by BF, and is
now in the Yale University Library.

I only wish my Dearst friend to know wil'st stop[?] the vieys of Eng i shall be glad of every oppertunty to tell you I have the warm wishs for your heath and hapynss I am Dear Sir Your most affesntly

MARGT STEVENSON

My Love to Mr. and Mrs. Bache and Dear Boys i wish to Live to kiss them fair well God allmity Bless you and yours Amen.

The Pennsylvania Committee of Safety to the Lancaster County Committee

LS: Library of Congress

In Committee of Safety, Philadelphia November 17th 1775
Gentlemen

We have considered your respectful answer to our application for the public Arms in the County of Lancaster,[2] and are fully satisfied with the reasons you assign for retaining them for the use of the poor Associators in said County, and have only to acknowledge your Zeal in the Public Cause and to desire you will send to us, the names of the persons in whose hands the Arms are left, that it may be known where to apply for them on any Emergency, and that the public property may be taken care of. We also acknowledge your care in carrying our Resolves, respecting Kearsley and Brooks into execution,[3] and we are, Gentlemen Your most obedient humble Servants

Signed by Order of the Board   B. FRANKLIN Presidt.

To the Committee of Lancaster County

2. In early October the committee of safety had requested that the county send at once to Philadelphia all the arms belonging to the province. On Nov. 9 the county committee replied that the weapons, left over from the previous war, had proved to be in bad condition. Many of them had been repaired by poor associators, nevertheless, who would lose their martial spirit if deprived of their arms. *Pa. Col. Recs.*, X, 356; 2 *Pa. Arch.*, XIII, 296–8.

3. For Kearsley's conspiracy, in which James Brooks was involved, see the note on BF to RB above, Oct. 19. On Oct. 23 the committee of safety resolved to move the two prisoners to jails outside the city; both were sent to Lancaster, where Brooks remained while Kearsley was taken to York. 2 *Pa. Arch.*, XIII, 298, 503–4; *Pa. Col. Recs.*, X, 373, 378, 380–1, 385, 773.

NOVEMBER 17, 1775

Addressed: To / Jaspar Yeates Esq'r[4] / chairman of the Committee / Lancaster

Endorsed: 17th. Novr. 1775

From Robert Crafton

ALS: Public Record Office

My good Sir,   London Nov. 22d. 1775.

Tho' I have already addressed you by this Conveyance;[5] yet as my Mind is not quite clear, I must trouble you again; and I trust to your Friendship and Candour, to impute my Presumption to the best Motives.

Always sanguine in my Ideas, I am already looking forward; and supposing, that the fair and equitable Terms, which our Friend will offer to the House on Monday next;[6] will produce a lasting Peace and Union, between the contending Parties; I have therefore turned my Thoughts, towards the Consequences of this happy Æra.

The old Mode of Requisition, is undoubtedly the most eligible; but I imagine that I foresee an Evil, that may even arise out of this; and which should I think be provided against in Time; and I think farther, that no Time is so proper as the present; now that the Congress is sitting, and that such implicit Obedience, is paid to all their Mandates.

If the Requisition for future Supplies, is made by the Minister, to each particular Assembly; it is possible (nay probable) that some may be for complying, and others for refusing, or limitating; this may create Jealousies among yourselves; and the Ministry taking Advantage of your Dissensions, may by cajolling and favouring the more pliant Assemblies, effectually disunite you.

But if the Congress should now take it into Consideration, to establish the proportionate Quota of each Colony; so that the Supply required, might be furnished in a collective Manner, by

4. For Yeates (1745–1817), already a prominent lawyer-politician in Lancaster, see the *DAB*. He had been elected chairman on Nov. 8: 2 *Pa. Arch.*, XIII, 294.

5. Above, Nov. 15.

6. On Monday, Nov. 27, another member introduced a motion aimed against the government's American policy, and perhaps for that reason Hartley postponed his until Dec. 7.

266

the whole Continent it would be in my humble Opinion, the Means to cement you more closely; indeed I could wish, that all Supplies might be furnished by a Congress, to be held at certain stated Periods; and I believe that something of that kind, would be best for both Countries.[7]

I am aware that it will require great Abilities and great Application, to investigate and settle this complex Business; but I confide, that the present Congress, are fully competent to it; and tho' it will assuredly appear, that some Colonies can more readily supply Men, others Money, and others again Provisions; yet it might surely be adjusted and proportioned, by the Wisdom and Patriotism of the present Delegates.

I shall trespass no farther on your Time and Patience; than only to recommend, an earnest Consideration of our Friend's Proposal, and a speedy Answer; and I must confess that I think it of such Importance, as to deserve a special Messenger. I salute you most respectfully and am your assured Friend and Servant

ROBT. CRAFTON

Addressed: Benjamin Franklin Esqr / Philadelphia.

Notation: 22 Nov 1775

From [David Hartley]   ALS: Public Record Office

Dear Sir   London November 23 1775.

Some American friends have desired to have an account drawn out of Mr. Hartleys proposition for terms of accommodation, drawn up with a view to send it to some of their friends in America for their opinion, therefore an account of the plan of those motions which are to be actually moved in the house next week has been drawn up from part of the letter which was sent to you a few days ago.[8] I dont know to whom this account will be sent but if you should meet with it you may perhaps observe some slight differences from the account which was sent to you. Ld North moved

7. Hartley's plan, as he subsequently moved it in the House of Commons, provided for requisitions on individual colonies: Cobbett, *Parliamentary History*, XVIII (1774–77), 1056. Crafton's amendment would have meant Parliamentary recognition of Congress as a permanent fixture.

8. Hartley's first letter above of Nov. 14.

on monday the repeal of the Boston port bill and the restraining bills of last year as being partial bills to make way for a general bill including all America, and as I hear to make prizes of all American vessels that can be catched.[9] Mr. H's proposals will stand thus: To suspend the act taking away the Massachusets charter and to suspend hostilities. To pass the act for Jury to slaves in all criminal cases. To pass an act replacing America to 1763. To pass an act of oblivion.[1] Yours most sincerely   G B.

Addressed: Doctor. Franklin

Endorsed: 23. Nov 1775

From [Jonathan Williams, Jr.]   AL: Public Record Office

Dear and honored Sir   London Nov. 23 1775.

I have already written to you by this Ship, since which I have come to a Conclusion with Mr. Blunt and shall engage in my new Business next Week.[2] The Terms are to be as follows. I am to be 'till next July on probation; at the End of that Time I shall be able to judge of the Advantages and Disadvantages of the Connection. We are then to begin our Partnership, my share of the Capital to be the ¼ part of £20,000 for which I am to allow 4 per Ct Interest,[3] and to have ¼ part of the Net Profits of the Business for

9. On Nov. 20 North had moved to bring in what became on Dec. 22 the Prohibitory Act, 16 Geo. III, c. 5. It repealed the Boston Port Act and the Restraining Act, banned all trade with the colonies while the rebellion lasted, and legalized the confiscation of captured rebel shipping; it also authorized the crown to appoint commissioners to grant pardons, and to restore commercial relations with any colony that chose to submit. Gipson, *British Empire*, XII, 346–9.

1. Hartley's original proposals are in his letter of Nov. 14 cited above. By now he had for some reason dropped suspension of the Mass. Administration of Justice Act, and North had taken care of the Boston Port Act.

2. JW's earlier letter, which has not survived, was presumably the one in September to which BF replied below, March 29. Walter Blunt and his brother Sir Charles (above, XIX, 151 n) were London sugar-refiners: *Kent's Directory* . . . (London, 1775). Their firms, although at different addresses, were apparently connected; for William Alexander referred to JW as being "very agreeably Setled with the Blunts." To BF below, Dec. 22, 1776.

3. Blunt, in other words, was assigning him a quarter interest at 4%.

my Labor and Care. Taking the darkest side of the Matter Mr. Blunt says the Business yields from 10 to 12 per Ct, and in Case of War or other Cause of Demand it will yield much more: he says he has made 30 per Ct. However reckoning at the Worst, I suppose it may produce about 11 per Ct, which, deducting the 4 I allow, will leave me 7 per Ct on £5000 equal to £350 per annum; and for this I shall be dependant only on my own Industry, which will yield me more satisfaction than double the Sum gained by fawning, and held at the Caprice of a haughty Superior, whose Vanity must be gratified at the Expence of Truth to insure a Continuation of his Favour. I will endeavour to get Mrs. Stevensons Money placed as you reccommend.[4]

I thank you most sincerely for your Offer of Service. Mr. Alex[ander] interprets it to be (according to what he wrote) an Intention to get me the Agency if an Accommodation should be brought about.[5] I am not to say what you intend, or what I deserve. You know what is best for me, and I acquiese.

Knowledge is always usefull whether applied or not. I shall therefore employ all my Leisure Time, and am determined to make myself master of every thing that can possibly relate to the Colonies. I hope I need not add, that I am attached to their Cause and interested in their welfare.

When I have a reputable thriving Business I shall think of my wished Connection, which I have often written to you about, and a reasonable Assistance at the same Time will greatly forward my Views: If Mr. A has it in his Power, and I succeed with the Lady, I know his assistance will be reasonable.[6]

The mention of Politics in these unhappy Times is almost sufficient to prevent a Letter from arriving safe in America, but there surely can be no harm in writing, what is not designed to be

4. See BF's letter to her above, July 17.

5. BF had promised in his letter above of Sept. 12 to do what he could, if JW stayed in England, to throw business his way; and William Alexander interpreted this vague statement to mean a colonial agency.

6. This is the first extant reference to JW's courting Mariamne Alexander, whom he eventually married. His acquaintance with the family had obviously ripened fast since their first meeting little more than a year before, for which see above, XXI, 272–3. His confidence of improving his prospects by the match is surprising in the circumstances, for the banker's fortunes were at their nadir; see the note on Margaret Stevenson to BF above, Nov. 16.

secret, and no Man can disapprove of Sentiments that tend to Peace and Reconciliation.[7]

You will see by the Papers that a Bill is to be brought in to cut off all Intercourse with the Colonies, and to repeal some of the late Acts. The Principle upon which this is founded I am told is, That as America has declared She will not trade with Britain, this Country is determined she shall not trade with any other Power if it can be prevented. That the Boston Port Bill and others were intended as a Punishment on that Colony, as being then the most refractory one; since that Time, all have come into the same Measures, therefore all are equally culpable, it is therefore they say unjust to make a Distinction and they propose by repealing these Bills to put them into one Situation and then to punish them all.

I am inclined to believe that the M[inistr]y are sick of this Business, and as to the Nation in general those who have the Liberty of thinking for themselves must see the fatal Consequences of the Controversy, and of Course wish for a Reconciliation. The Question then only is how this can be effected. I know not the Powers of the proposed Commissioners, nor the real Intention in sending them; but I am told that the former are very extensive, and that the Latter is to finish the Dispute.[8] If the Design is founded on a Wish to settle with Justice to both Sides, and the Men are as good, and as honest, as the Trust will be great, I hope Peace and Happiness will succeed to War and Distress; but if there is any artfull Intention, cloaked under a specious appearance, and the Measure should turn out to be a Trick of State; America knows her Rights and her Ability to defend them. I have therefore only to add my Wish, that Virtue and Justice may be always [?rewarde]d with deserved Success. I am most dutifully and affectionately Yours &c.

I received my good Friend Billy T Franklins Letter and feel myself Happy in the Appelation of Kinsman which he gives me.[9]

7. The present location of the letter suggests that its sentiments did not keep it from being intercepted. BF's letter below of March 29 made no mention of it.
8. What he had been told of the commission authorized by the Prohibitory Bill was unduly optimistic; see the note on the preceding document.
9. See the note on BF to Jane Mecom above, June 17.

I beg my Love to him. He will receive his Books by Read with the second parcell of your Things.[1]

My best Respects to the Govr Mr. and Mrs. Bache and all Friends.

Addressed: Doctor B Franklin / Market Street / Philadelphia / Favoured by Capt Hunter via Virginia

Notation: 23 Nov 1775

From [Jonathan Williams, Jr.]   AL: Public Record Office

London Nov. 23. 1773 [*i.e.*, 1775[2]]

Since writing the Inclosed, I have had some Conversation with a Gentleman relative to the proposed Bill, which he assures me is to look Back to all the Seizures made by the Kings Ships in America, and make them as well as all future ones legal Prises. The Bills proposed to be repealed are only the two fis[hing?] ones, and they intend to have as large a F[leet?] in America as they can raise and cut [off?] commercial Intercourse.

I am desired to give you this as [certain?] Information,[3] to which I shall only add that I am as ever most dutifully and affectionately Yours.

Addressed: To / Doctor B Franklin / Market Street / Philadelphia

Notation:[4] 23 Nov. 1773

1. For Read and what he carried see the note on Hartley to BF above, July 22.

2. This line has been added at the bottom by some one else, who clearly mistook the year; JW was adding a postscript to the "Inclosed," the preceding letter. But he could scarcely have enclosed that letter, for each has its own address; we assume that they were mailed separately and intercepted together.

3. The information about the Prohibitory Bill, as in his preceeding letter, was a mishmash of true and false.

4. The same as that of the notation on the address of the preceding letter, and different from that of whoever added the place and date of this one.

Jane Mecom to Catharine Greene

ALS: American Philosophical Society

Philadelphia Novr. 24 [–December 2] 1775

My Dear Mrs. Green

Asure your self the Epethet of Daughter which you seem to like to use cannot be Disagreable to me would to God I had such a won all the Alurements of this Place my Brother Exepted should not seperate me from her. I write not this in Disparagement of my own Daughter for she is a good woman but Provedence does not Premit us to be to gather and as to sons I have nothing but miserey in those that are left Boath of them Distracted and I have heard of the Death of Poor Josiah since I came hear but by what means I am not Informed.[5] God grant I may make a proper Use of all His Dealings with me.

I thank you for your very kind and perticular leter of the 12 of this month you know it will be allways agreable to me. I am sorry you were so Afflicted in your Jurny to westerly. My seat was Exeding Easey and Jurney very Pleasant. My Dear Brothers conversation was more than an Equivelent to all the fine wether Emaginable but I mett with won mortification on the Rhoad. We had Apointed to Dine at wethersfeald where mrs. Hancock is[6] and had conciderable talk about it but we being Engaged at that time in other conversation the Postilion Drove a mile or two beyond before we discovered it and I could not prevale with him to go back so we did not Dine till we put up for the night. I Expected Master Ray would have Given you som Discription of what he saw on the Jurny Espeshally at Governer Franklins house which was very magnificent and we shew him it all over but I percive he did not in his last and He now thinks it not proper as the small Pox is out on him tho I dont beleve He could Infect any body he has so litle we cant number more than ten that I am afraid he will not have won pit for a Recipt. He has had no Illnes but won Day a litle shivery and feverish so much as to say he was in no hurry for His

5. The daughter was Jane Collas. Of the sons, Benjamin and Peter were insane; Josiah had enlisted and soon afterward died, and the cause of death is still unknown. Van Doren, *Franklin—Mecom*, p. 164.

6. Lydia Hancock, the widow of John Hancock's uncle Thomas, had attended her nephew's recent wedding in Fairfield, Conn., where she apparently stayed until her death. Why she was in Wethersfield at this moment we have no idea.

coffe. We thought it not proper to make his cloaths till we saw how it would fare with him but now shall have them made with all Expedition. He is very tractable and hear is a young gentleman who setts him a compleat Example of good maners and Politenes,[7] and my Brother will give Proper Directions about his Scooling. He will write him self as soon as he thinks it saif. I have not seen Mr. Mumford tho I Desiered your Brother woud to Ask him to come but I am a going out to look for him and shall finish my leter when I come back.[8]

Since the Above I have rec'd yours of the 21 and am Glad to find there is won in the world so free from Giult. Your crime was unnoticed that you might have kept your own secrit and absolved your self. Ill be Ansurable for your Husband that He shall not Beat you. Ray Behaves as well as can be Expected Inded very well, and he will now be able to Injoy himself without fear. I shall have no use for my Gownd this winter and I dont give my self the least concern about it. I Dont know that I got cold with my Jurny but I have had a bad fit of Astme, am now as well as Usal have not had the c—l—k [colic] but do not sleep well on nights. Mrs. Bache is not yet a bed. She is as well as can be Expected. I am so happy as to have my choice of places of worship so near that the wether need not hinder me from going. Remember my kind love to Mr. Greene to Dear litle Samey to Mr. and Mrs. Gouch and your mother,[9] and respect to all Inquiering friends and beleve me to be your most faithfull and obliged frind   JANE MECOM

Saterday Dec'r 2. I have not seen Mr. Mumford supose He is gone so Jenny must [go?] without her silk till a nother opertunity. Ray is abroad and [hale?] and harty, Mrs. Beach was Last night Delivered of a fine Gorl.[1] My Brother Remembers his love to you.

Addressed in Franklin's hand: To / The honble. William Greene Esqr / Warwick / Rhodeisland / B Free Franklin

7. Ray Greene's model was undoubtedly WTF, who had recently entered the College of Philadelphia.

8. Perhaps Benjamin or Peter Mumford, the two postriders who had established an extra-legal post office in Newport; see Cooke to BF above, Aug. 15.

9. For the Gooches see Jane's letter above, May 14. "Samey" was Caty's son Samuel, and her "mother" was her mother-in-law and widow of the Governor, Catharine Greene (1698–1777).

1. For Jenny, Jane's granddaughter, see *ibid.* The new Bache daughter was named for her mother.

Song: "The King's Own Regulars."

Printed in *The Boston Gazette*, November 27, 1775.[2]

The King's own REGULARS;
And their Triumphs over the *Irregulars*.
A New SONG,
To the Tune of,
*An old Courtier of the Queen's, and the Queen's
old Courtier.*

Since you all will have singing, and won't be said, nay,
I cannot refuse where you so beg and pray;
So I'll sing you a song—as a body may say.
'Tis of the King's Regulars, who ne'er run way.
  O the old Soldiers of the King, and the King's own Regulars.

At Preston Pans we met with some Rebels one day,
We marshall'd ourselves all in comely array:
Our hearts were all stout, and bid our legs stay,
But our feet were wrong headed and took us away.
  O the old soldiers, &c.

At Falkirk we resolv'd to be braver,
And recover some credit by better behaviour;
We would not acknowledge feet had done us a favour;
So feet swore they would stand, but—legs ran however.
  O the old soldier, &c.

2. The song was also published in the *Pa. Evening Post*, March 30, 1776, and the *Constitutional Gaz.*, April 6, 1776; we have supplied readings of some illegible words from the former. Charles Carroll, on his way to Canada with the other commissioners in the spring of 1776, sent a MS copy to his wife; it was, he said, "a song made by Dr. Franklin. I think it abounds with good wit." April 15, 1776, Md. Hist. Soc. In the MS the stanzas are numbered after the first six, and for some reason the fourteenth, beginning "Says our General," is omitted. The wording differs throughout in many small details from our and the other printed texts; we therefore assume that BF quoted from memory to his traveling companion. We cannot tell what tune he had in mind. Sheet music for the famous Caroline ballad that was his model was published about 1710, but the only copy we have located, in the Folger Library, is for flute alone. When he wrote the song is anyone's guess. Ours, based on the place and time of first publication, is that he composed it to relieve the tedium of the long conferences at Cambridge in October, 1775.

No troops perform better than we at reviews;
We march and we wheel, and whatever you chuse.
George would see how we fight, and we never refuse;
There we all fight with courage—you may see it in the news.
    O the old soldiers, &c.

To Monongehela with fifes and with drums
We march'd in fine order, with cannon and bombs:
That great expedition cost infinite sums;
But a few irregulars cut us all into crumbs.
    O the old soldiers, &c.

It was not fair to shoot at us from behind trees:
If they had stood open as they ought before our great Guns we should
    have beat them with ease.
They may fight with one another that way if they please;
But it is not regular to stand and fight with such rascals as these.
    O the old soldier, &c.

At Fort George and Oswego, to our great reputation,
We shew'd our vast skill in fortification;
The French fired three guns, of the fourth they had no occasion;
For we gave up those forts, not thro' fear—but mere persuasion.
    O the old soldiers, &c.

To Ticonderoga we went in a passion,
Swearing to be revenged on the whole French nation.
But we soon turned tail, without hesitation
Because they fought behind trees, which is not the[3] fashion.
    O the old soldiers, &c.

Lord Loudon he was a fine regular General, they say;
With a great regular army he went his way
Against Louisbourg, to make it his prey;
But return'd without seeing it, for he did not feel bold that day.
    O the old soldier, &c.

Grown proud at reviews, great George had no rest,
Each grandsire, he had heard a rebellion supprest.

    3. The text in the *Pa. Evening Post* adds "regular," which also appears in the MS version.

He wish'd a rebellion, look'd round and saw none,
So resolv'd a rebellion to make of his own—
  With the old soldiers, &c.

The Yankees he bravely pitch'd on, because he thought they would not
    fight,
And so he sent us over to take away their right,
But least they should spoil our review clothes, he cried braver and
    louder,
"For God's sake, brother kings, don't sell the cowards any powder."
  O the old soldiers &c.

Our General with his council of war did advise,
How at Lexington we might the Yankees surprise.
We march'd—and we march'd—all surpriz'd at being beat;
And so our wise General's plan of surprise was complete.
  O the old soldiers &c.

For fifteen miles they follow'd and pelted us, we scarce had time to pull
    a trigger;
But did you ever know a retreat perform'd with more vigour?
For we did it in two hours, which sav'd us from perdition,
'Twas not in *going out* but in *returning* consisted our *expedition.*
  O the old soldiers, &c.

Says our General, we were forced to take to our arms in our own defence:
(For *arms* read *legs,* and it will be both truth and sense.
Lord Percy (says He) I must say something of him in civility,
And that is, I can never enough praise him for his great—agility.
  O the old soldiers, &c.

Of their firing from behind fences, he makes a great pother,
Ev'ry fence has two sides; they made use of one, and we only forgot to
    use the other.
That we turn'd our backs and ran away so fast, don't let that disgrace us;
'Twas only to make good what Sandwich said, "that the Yankees would
    not face us."
  O the old soldiers, &c.

As they could not get before us, how could they look us in the face?
We took care they should not, by scampering away apace;

That they had not much to brag of, is a very plain case.
For if they beat us in the fight, we beat them in the race.[4]
 O the old soldiers of the King, and the King's own Regulars.

From George Ross[5]

Extracts and paraphrase: Parke Bernet sale catalogue, May 16, 1967, p. 40

⟨November 27, 1775: I am sending you, as president of the Pennsylvania committee of safety, a copy of the minutes of the local committee that relate to provincial arms, for which money is in short supply. No public funds are available, and the workmen ask to be paid for repairing the weapons.⟩

Contract Between the Secret Committee and Thomas Mumford[6] for Supplying Gunpowder

Owner anonymous; transcript furnished by courtesy of Dr. Joseph E. Fields, Joliet, Ill. (1957)

Less than a month after the creation of the secret committee Silas Deane, one of its members, wrote his friend Thomas Mumford to suggest that he come to Philadelphia to find out what profit could be made under the committee's aegis. The letter seems to have crossed one from Mumford, who explained that two of his captains had already contracted for fifty tons of gunpowder in St. Eustatius; he was working through the Gov-

4. BF was going through a roster of actions in which the regulars failed, or in one case failed to act: the Battles of Prestonpans and Falkirk in the Jacobite rising of 1745–46, Braddock's defeat on the Monogahela in 1755, the loss to the French of Fort William Henry on Lake George ("Fort George") in 1757 and of Fort Oswego in 1756, the repulse of Abercromby at Ticonderoga in 1758, Loudoun's failure to attack Louisbourg in 1757, and the retreat from Concord that was covered by a relief force under Lord Percy.

5. For Ross see the letter from him and others above, July 11. He was then writing as a member of Congress to the Lancaster Co. committee; he is here writing as chairman of that committee.

6. A wealthy merchant and ship-owner living in Groton, and its representative in the Assembly. Mumford (1728–99) had been instrumental in financing the expedition against Ticonderoga, and later played a major part in New London's privateering business. James G. Mumford, *Mumford Memoirs . . .* (Boston, 1900), pp. 192–5.

ernor and the Connecticut delegation to secure from Congress permission to export goods sufficient to purchase the powder.[7] Mumford presumably went to Philadelphia as Deane suggested, for the negotiations culminated in the document summarized below.

⟨Committee chamber, Philadelphia, November 28, 1775: The undersigned, a quorum of the committee of secrecy, contract with Thomas Mumford of New London, merchant, for a voyage or voyages to procure speedily fifty tons of good gunpowder or, if so much cannot be obtained, sufficient saltpetre and sulphur to make up that amount. The United Colonies will charter the vessel or vessels required, freight to be paid on their return, and will insure them against capture. The owners assume the risk of the sea, will employ prudent and skilful supercargoes, and will receive a 5% commission on the purchase. $28,500 in continental currency will be advanced to Mumford, for which he will render account to the United Colonies. The powder will be landed in the colonies at a safe and convenient place east of Chesapeake Bay, and the location will be revealed as soon as possible to a quorum of the committee. Signed by Samuel Ward, Franklin, Thomas Willing, Josiah Bartlett, Francis Lewis, and Thomas Mumford.⟩

From Catherine Meed

ALS: American Philosophical Society

This letter is the first appearance of a niece whose existence Franklin seems to have forgotten. He had doubtless not seen her for many years, and she lived in a remote part of Pennsylvania. All we know of her first brief effort to refresh her uncle's recollection of her is in the present letter and another below, December 16. She had written him on his return from England, with no response; here she is trying again. The second attempt elicited a reply. Although it has disappeared, it was clearly a baffled one: who was she? In December she explained, and then the extant correspondence breaks off for a decade.[8]

7. *Naval Docs.*, II, 464, 521.

8. This reconstruction has to be conjectural because the present letter is not dated by year. It has been assigned to 1785: I. Minnis Hays, *Calendar of the Papers of Benjamin Franklin* . . . (5 vols., Philadelphia, 1908), III, 287. But all the small signs associate it with the letter of December, 1775: both are addressed to "Dear Uncle" and signed "Affectionate Cousin" and ask to be remembered to Sally, whereas the two letters of 1785 and 1786, cited below, are

She was unquestionably a niece of sorts. Her father was John Croker, who was the second husband of Deborah Franklin's sister Frances. Three children of that marriage are recorded, and Catherine was not among them.[9] After Frances' death in 1740 the widower remarried and moved to Staten Island; in 1745 he and his new wife sold to Franklin their interest in some Philadelphia property left by Deborah's mother.[1] Thereafter the whole family disappeared from view except for Joseph Croker, Catherine's brother or uncle, who died in 1758.[2] We are inclined to think that Catherine herself was her father's daughter by his second wife rather than by Deborah's sister, in which case her relationship with Franklin was tenuous enough to explain his bafflement. Where she grew up, whom she married, and why she moved to the frontier are questions without answers. She exists only in four brief notes, two of them in 1775 and the other two ten years later.[3]

Dear Uncle   Sunbury Shemokin[4] Nov the 28 [1775?]

When I heard of your arrival nothing Ever made me So happy. I wrote Directly to you, but when I was not Honored with A line from you, I Could not help Crying, for your all the uncle I have in the world by my Poor Father. I thought you would not write to A Poor little Country Girle, but Every body Says you have no more Pride than A Child and that has incouraged me to write to you again. I often think if Could See you and Cousin Sally I would be the Happiest woman in the world, but I live A great way off.

addressed to "Honored Uncle" and signed "Affectionate Niece" and say nothing of Sally.

9. *PMHB*, xv (1891), 356.

1. Above, III, 44 n; see also the White genealogical chart above, VIII, [140].

2. BF's "Cousin Josey" seems to have been quite young when he died. He was a stone mason and carved the epitaph to Josiah and Abiah Franklin; BF tried to get him to England to ply his trade, but he was killed by Indians. Above, VII, 218 n, 229, 367. Our predecessors never fully identified him, and we can only conjecture. He could scarcely have been a son of John Croker's second marriage, unless he developed his stone-carving skill at a startlingly early age. He might have been an unrecorded child of John and Frances Croker, but it seems more likely that he was John's younger brother.

3. On BF's second return, from France in 1785, she wrote him a letter similar to this one; he apparently answered as before by asking who she was, and again she told him: to BF, Oct. 27, 1785; Feb. 14, 1786, APS.

4. Sunbury had been laid out in 1772 on the site of the Indian village of Shamokin, at the confluence of Shamokin Creek and the upper Susquehanna. See Herbert C. Bell, *History of Northumberland County* . . . (Chicago, 1891), pp. 444–5.

NOVEMBER 28, 1775

Pleas to Give my [love?] to Cousin Sally and Except the Same
from your Affectionate Cousin   CATHERINE MEED

Addressed: Honl. Benj Franclin / in / Philadelphia

Endorsed: Catherine Meed

The Committee of Secret Correspondence to [Arthur Lee]

Copy:[5] University of Virginia Library

On November 29, 1775, Samuel Chase brought before Congress a proposal to send ambassadors to France. John Adams seconded the motion,
and a vehement debate ensued. A number of alternatives were advanced,
and one finally gained approval: to appoint a five-member committee of
secret correspondence for the purpose of opening communication with
friends of America in Great Britain and elsewhere. The committee's
expenses were to be paid, along with those of such agents as it saw fit to
appoint. The members were Franklin, John Dickinson, Benjamin Harrison, John Jay, and Thomas Johnson.[6] From this small beginning developed the American diplomatic service.

The first person to whom the committee wrote was the obvious one.
Only Franklin, Bollan, and Lee, of all the active colonial agents in
London, had associated themselves with the first Continental Congress.[7]
Bollan, "a cautious exact Man," was unlikely to be of use, and did in fact
wash his hands of Congress. Lee, on the contrary, was more active than
ever.[8] He had inherited the Massachusetts agency, and had recently acted
without credentials for the New Jersey Assembly.[9] When Congress sent
the Olive Branch Petition by Richard Penn, Lee was one of the four
London agents charged with presenting it, and the only one who acted.
He and Penn delivered the petition and, after an answer was refused,

5. Apparently in the hand of Richard Henry Lee; if so he made the copy after
his subsequent election to the committee. He also appended a long note, in
the course of which he identified his brother as the recipient: Smith, *Letters,* II,
410 n.

6. John Adams to Chase, July 9, 1776, and to Benjamin Rush, Sept. 30,
1805: Charles Francis Adams, ed., *The Works of John Adams* . . . (10 vols.,
Boston, 1856), IX, 421; I, 200–1; see also *JCC,* III, 392. For Johnson see the
note on Gates to BF below, Dec. 5.

7. Above, XXI, 338.

8. *Ibid.,* p. 586; Jack M. Sosin, *Agents and Merchants: British Colonial Policy
and the Origins of the American Revolution* . . . (Lincoln, Neb., 1965), p. 224.

9. See above, Kinsey to BF, March 26; JW to BF, July 19.

saw to its publication; Congress had recently received their report of its reception.[1] Lee, then, was the natural choice for a correspondent.

He did not accept the assignment in any normal way. His distrust of two members of the committee prevented his answering this letter; instead he sent intelligence to individuals, whom he addressed by names not their own, and whose identity is often beyond guesswork.[2] He may have written the committee while Franklin served on it, but the only direct communication of which we have record was the verbal report of a messenger.[3] During Franklin's term, in short, there is no evidence that Lee played a significant role as the committee's agent.

Sir,   Phila. 30 Novr. 1775

We have the honor to be appointed by the Congress a Committee of Correspondence with the friends of America on the other side of the ———. Our institution is with design to preserve secresy, and thereby secure our friends, who we suppose may be endangered and alarmed by the late proclamation.[4] It is considered as of the utmost consequence to the cause of Liberty, that an intercourse should be kept up, and we shall be obliged by your sentiments of the most probable and secure method of effecting it. If any should be certainly resolved on which you may think much concerns America to be apprised of, we shall consider it within the power of our appointment to pay the expence of an Express Boat, if you can provide one under proper cautions. We are Sir your most obedient servants.

Notation: Committee of Correspondence letter to A.L. 30 Novr. 1775

1. The covering letter from the President of Congress was to Penn, Bollan, Burke, Garth, and Lee. Richard Henry Lee, *Life of Arthur Lee* . . . (2 vols., Boston, 1829), I, 46–8. Penn's and Lee's report was entered on Nov. 9: *JCC*, III, 343.

2. See the headnote on Lee's ostensible letter to BF below, Feb. 13.

3. See the committee's memorandum below, Oct. 1. A letter from Lee to the committee, not delivered until years later, is discussed in the headnote below on Deane to Morris, June 23. In October, 1776, Jay mentioned another letter, now unidentifiable: Wharton, *Diplomatic Correspondence*, II, 165. It may or may not have been one of those discussed in the headnote on Lee to BF below, Feb. 13.

4. See the headnote above, Nov. 9.

To Israel Pemberton[5]

AL: American Philosophical Society

Thursday Nov. 30. 75.

Dr. Franklin presents his Respects to Mr. Pemberton, and is willing to take the Ground Rent propos'd to him; but hopes Mr. Pemberton will abate of the Price mention'd, as he hears some have lately been sold at 15 Years purchase.

Notation: To Israel Pemberton Esq.

A Public Notice by Franklin and Robert Morris

Printed in *The Pennsylvania Gazette*, December 6, 1775.

Philadelphia, December 5, 1775.

Mrs. Brodeau, from England, Takes this Method of acquainting her Friends and the Public in general, that she has opened a Boarding School, in Walnut-street, near the Corner of Fourth-street, where young Ladies will be genteely boarded, and taught to read and speak the French and English Language, the Tambour, Embroidery, and every Kind of useful and ornamental Needle-Work.

Mrs. Brodeau hopes to prove by her Assiduity and Attention to the Morals and Behaviour of those Ladies entrusted to her Care, that she in some Measure merits the Recommendation she has been favoured with from her native Country.[6]

5. Pemberton, one of the most prominent Quakers and civic leaders in Philadelphia, has appeared often but peripherally in earlier vols.; see in particular V, 424 n, and also *PMHB*, LXVII (1943), 282–5. The subject of this letter, the ground rent reserved on property that BF had purchased in 1764, is explained above, XI, 319–21. BF's negotiation to buy the rent succeeded, but the evidence does not indicate whether Pemberton lowered his price. See the summary of the deed below, Dec. 13.

6. We have no information about this venture, or how Morris and BF came to sponsor it. All that is known about Mrs. Brodeau in 1775 is that her first name was Ann or Anne, and that she had an infant daughter. Her husband, if he ever existed, seems to have left no record, and one theory is that her baby's father was the Rev. William Dodd, an English clergyman who in the summer of 1777 was hanged for forgery; see the annotation of Dodd to BF below, Jan. 29, 1777. Her school was a great success. In 1783 Sally Bache mentioned to her father that "Mrs. Brodeau who was recommended to you when you were last at home, has made a hand[some] fortune." (June 1, 1783; APS.) By 1785 the school had

DECEMBER 5, 1775

Any Person desirous of Information concerning the Character and Recommendation of Mrs. Brodeau, may apply to either of us, ROBERT MORRIS, B. FRANKLIN.

From Horatio Gates

ALS: American Philosophical Society

Dear Sir   Head Quarters 5th December 1775

For this Week past Fortune has Smiled upon Us from All Quarters, and last Night, word was brought out of Boston by some Inhabitants who left it Yesterday, that a Vessel was Just arrived there from Quebeck. The Master of which Declared that Our Troops, Assisted by near 6000 Canadians, took Possession of that Capital a day or Two After the Middle of November; that thereupon all the Ships belonging to the Ministerialists Slip'd their Cables, and push'd Down the River, thus is the whole Province of Canada most Gloriously Added to the United Colonies.[7] You will in your Wisdom, no Doubt immediately let them take their Places accordingly. I wish Two or Three Battallions could be sent from them this Way, and the like Number of Ours replace theirs to Garrison Quebeck which with the Earliest of the Spring should be Fortified in the very best Manner.

Burgoyne Sails this Day from Boston in The Boyne Man of War for England, pretty Accounts he will carry his Tory Friends in Parliament, where I think he will be examin'd, and Cross ex-

---

apparently moved to Lodge Alley, and was still there six years later. In 1790 her daughter, supposedly aged sixteen, married Dr. William Thornton, the inventor and architect who had a part in designing the new Capitol; the Thorntons achieved some prominence in Washington society, and Mrs. Brodeau often visited them. [John McPherson], *Macpherson's Directory for the City and Suburbs of Philadelphia* . . . (Philadelphia, 1785); Clement Biddle, *The Philadelphia Directory* . . . (Philadelphia, 1791); *DAB* under Thornton; Allen C. Clark, "Doctor and Mrs. William Thornton," *Records of the Columbia Historical Society*, XVIII (1915), 144–208.

7. The report confused Quebec with Montreal, which Montgomery had captured on Nov. 13 after Gov. Carleton, hopelessly outnumbered, had sailed down river with his few men and his most valuable stores. On Dec. 9 a report from Providence, supposedly emanating from American headquarters, announced the capture of Quebec on Nov. 17: *Pa. Gaz.*, Dec. 20, 1775. In fact the assault occurred at the end of the year and was a disaster.

amin'd, til he Sweats. If there is an honest Mob left in England, Gage and He, cannot ride the Streets of London in Safety.[8]

Our Success by Sea you will hear enough of in Congress, but pray have no Doubts about Condemning the Glasgow Ship, as we want ever Tittle of her Cargoe for the Cloathing of The Troops, and other Publick Service.[9] In the Mean Time my Voice shall be, Use what we want; if you like that best, your High Mightyness's may pay for it Afterwards.

We have lately had some trouble to retain the Connecticut Troops and with Difficulty prevail'd upon them to consent to remain only to the 10th: Instant when the Legislature of this Colony have engaged to supply us with 5000 Militia to make good the Gap occasion'd by the Discharge of the Five Connecticut Regiments and The Absentees upon the Recruiting Service.[1]

I look with Earnest Eyes towards Canada, and wish You and my Worthy Friend T. Johnston, could have been spared to have Assisted the Committee sent to Montreal.[2] Indeed after the Fatigue you had just endured, it could not be expected from you. I hope

8. Before Burgoyne's departure from England the King and Lord North had agreed that he should return and report on the situation. Gage had been ordered home, and had turned over the command to Howe and sailed on Oct. 11. Sir John Fortescue, ed., *The Correspondence of King George the Third* . . . (6 vols., London, 1927–28), III, 203–4; John R. Alden, *General Gage in America* . . . (Baton Rouge, La., 1948), p. 283.

9. The *Concord*, out of Glasgow laden with dry goods and coal worth more than £3600, had been captured by Capt. John Manley and brought into Marblehead on Dec. 3. Washington, in a letter to Congress on Dec.7, echoed Gates's opinion that the army must have the cargo. *Naval Docs.*, II, 1245, 1258, 1322.

1. The Connecticut militia had enrolled on seven- and five-month terms, which were expiring at the beginning of December. The men's insistence on returning home was not apparent until late November, and they had to be kept until Massachusetts and New Hampshire had furnished replacements; otherwise the enemy, it was assumed, would overrun the lines. They were kept, against their will, until the new levies began to arrive. Freeman, *Washington*, III, 569–80.

2. In early November Congress appointed a committee of three to confer with Schuyler. Thomas Johnson was a Maryland delegate and BF's colleague on the committee of secret correspondence. The ad hoc committee was not "sent to Montreal," but was expected to go into Canada. It reached Ticonderoga, went no farther, and urged that another committee be sent when travelling conditions were better. *JCC*, III, 317, 339–41, 350, 447, 451.

there is Brains and Language sufficient in those upon that Delegation, to influence the Canadians to support all our Measures.

The Brilliantcy of General Montgomerys Character, will be the Admiration of Our Friends, and the Astonishment of Our Enemies. Colonel Arnolds resolute and persevering behaviour, even after 300 of his Command had left him, is a most meritorious Example.[3] These Two Men should be held in High Estimation, and reward Accordingly. Col. Arnold begun with Taking Ticonderoga, and the Vessell then at St. Johns.[4]

In case General Carleton, and Lord Pit Fall into your Hands, as I cannot but think they will, you will consider well how to dispose of them, That Capt. Allan taken at Montreal of the Connecticuts, should be directly return'd; or Mr: Carleton should go to Gaol.[5]

My Compliments to Messieurs Johnston, and Chace. They never write to me, I want to know if the Serjeants and Corporals of the Regulars that I sent Chace ever deliverd him my letters of Recommendation (for that was all they contain'd). Our Arm'd Vessells are at Sea, I hope soon to send you further Accounts of their Success. A Play House is establish'd in Boston, as Mr. Hancock can inform You. They have Open'd with a Tragedy—it's very probable they may conclude with One: The Fine Brass 13 Inch Mortar which we have got to Cambridge, looks as if he could Play his Part to perfection.[6] I am ever Affectionately Yours

HORATIO GATES

3. In late October 300 men had withdrawn without authorization from Arnold's expedition against Quebec; a court martial had acquitted their commanding officer the day before Gates wrote. Freeman, *Washington*, III, 562–65, 567, 574–5; Christopher Ward, *The War of the Revolution* (John R. Alden, ed.; 2 vols, New York, 1952), I, 175–6.

4. After the capture of Ticonderoga in May Arnold set out with fifty men for the fort at St. Johns, which he captured and then evacuated; part of the booty was a seventy-ton sloop.

5. Lord Pitt has appeared briefly above, XXI, 518 n; he was serving as an aide to Carleton. Ethan Allen had joined Montgomery's expedition and been captured the previous September.

6. For Chase, like Johnson a Maryland delegate, see his letter to BF above, Aug. 4. The first performance of Aaron Hill's *Zara*, organized by Burgoyne and with his own prologue and epilogue, was announced for Dec. 2 in Faneuil Hall: *Mass. Gaz.*, Nov. 30, 1775. The mortar was part of a cargo of military supplies in an ordnance brig captured by Capt. Manley, and was christened the "Congress." *Naval Docs.*, II, 1247, 1261, 1284.

My best respects to Mr: Allen Senior[7] and Mr: Bob Morris, to whom I have not Time to write, but if you please You may shew them this.

From Horatio Gates

ALS: American Philosophical Society

Sir   Head Qrs: 7th: December 1775

I did myself the Pleasure to write you upon Monday by Express. I now inclose to you, a Copy of General Lees Letter lately sent to General Burgoyne which if you approve of it may be publish'd in the News paper.[8] I long to send you Lees and my Opinions of the measures to be pursued in Consequence of the Conquest of Canada, that is the Military Measures, somany Solons, cannot but execute to perfection the Civil Ones, we are inform'd, that your Hight Mightynesses are together by the Ears about independentcy, do not immitate the Dog in the Fable, who by snapping at the Shadow, lost the Substance, let Us first Establish'd our Freedom, when that is done, it will be time enough to Wrangle about Forms of Government. Perhaps this moment the Legislature of G. Britain has determined to endeavour to Force Us to a Slavish Dependance. When you hear that, you have only an independant Freedom to resolve upon! Glorious and Successfull as the Continental Arms have been, let us not Tarnish Them, nor by a Timmid Conduct draw down the Vengance of Providence upon our Ingratitude. You want none of this reasoning to stimulate *you* to Action, can not you inforce it with better of your Own into The Farmer, &c. &c. &c.?[9] I am ever Your Faithfull Humble Servant

HORATIO GATES.

7. William Allen (1704–80), the Philadelphia merchant and, until 1774, chief justice of Pennsylvania, has appeared frequently in earlier volumes; for his career see the *DAB*.

8. Gates's Monday letter is the preceding document. Charles Lee and Burgoyne were old comrades in arms. Lee had declined Burgoyne's proposal of a meeting, but they had exchanged letters. The most recent one, to which Gates refers, was of Dec. 1 when Burgoyne was about to return home; Lee urged him to do all in his power to end the war before it forced independence on the Americans and ruin on the British. *Lee Papers*, I, 222–5. The letter was published in the *Pa. Gaz.*, Dec. 20, 1775.

9. Gates's rhetoric obscures his meaning, but he is clearly urging BF to embolden the timid. John Dickinson, "The Farmer," was staunchly opposed to

To Charles-Guillaume-Frédéric Dumas

Reprinted from *The Port Folio*, II (1802), 236–7; extracts: American Philosophical Society; Archives du Ministère des affaires étrangères, Paris; Algemeen Rijksarchief, the Hague.[1]

DEAR SIR,   Philadelphia December 9, 1775.

I received your several favours, of May 18, June 30, and July 8, by Messrs. Vaillant and Pochard;[2] whom, if I could serve upon your recommendation, it would give me great pleasure. Their total want of English is at present an obstruction to their getting any employment among us; but I hope they will soon obtain some knowledge of it. This is a good country for artificers or farmers, but gentlemen, of mere science in *les belles lettres*, cannot so easily subsist here, there being little demand for their assistance among an industrious people, who, as yet, have not much leisure for studies of that kind.

I am much obliged by the kind present you have made us of your edition of Vattel. It came to us in good season, when the circumstances of a rising state make it necessary frequently to consult the law of nations. Accordingly, that copy which I kept, (after depositing one in our own public library here, and sending the other to the college of Massachusetts Bay, as you directed[3]) has been continually in the hands of the members of our congress, now sitting, who are much pleased with your notes and preface,

---

independence; see the note on the instructions from the Pa. Assembly above, Nov. 9.

1. The APS extracts are both by the same copyist, and contain only the sentence relating to the bill for £100 that the committee sent him. The fullest extracts are those in Paris and at the Hague; both are accompanied by a French translation, and the portions extracted are not the same. The English text in the former is in an unidentifiable hand and the translation in Dumas', whereas in the latter both are in Dumas'. The capitalization and punctuation of these MS versions have clearly not followed verbatim the missing ALS, and we have therefore adhered to those of the printed text.

2. The first two are above, the earlier one in a draft dated May 17; the third is missing. For the baffling change in the bearers' names see the note on the May letter, and for the subsequent adventures of Alexandre Pochard and what little we know about his friend Vaillant see Pochard to BF below, Oct. 11.

3. Dumas left the choice of where to send the third copy to BF, who was in the habit of making such gifts to Harvard. The College's acknowledgment is below, Sept. 30.

and have entertained a high and just esteem for their author. Your manuscript *Idee sur le gouvernment et la royauté*, is also well relished, and may, in time, have its effect.[4] I thank you, likewise, for the other smaller pieces, which accompanied Vattel. *Le court exposé de ce qui s'est passe entre la cour Br. et les colonies, &c.* being a very concise and clear statement of facts, will be reprinted here, for the use of our new friends in Canada.[5] The translations of the proceedings of our congress are very acceptable. I send you herewith what of them has been farther published here, together with a few newspapers, containing accounts of some of the successes providence has favoured us with. We are threatened from England with a very powerful force, to come next year against us. We are making all the provision in our power here to oppose that force, and we hope we shall be able to defend ourselves. But as the events of war are always uncertain, possibly, after another campaign, we may find it necessary to ask aid of some foreign power. It gives us great pleasure to learn from you, that *toute l'Europe nous souhaite le plus heureux succes pour le maintien de nos libertes.*[6] But we wish to know whether any one of them, from principles of humanity, is disposed magnanimously to step in for the relief of an oppressed people, or whether if, as it seems likely to happen, we should be obliged to break off all connection with Britain, and declare ourselves an independent people, there is any state or power in Europe, who would be willing to enter into an alliance with us for the benefit of our commerce, which amounted, before the war, to near seven millions sterling per annum, and must continually increase, as our people increase most rapidly. Confiding, my dear friend, in your good will to us and our cause, and in your sagacity and abilities for business, the committee of congress, appointed for the purpose of establishing and conducting a correspondence with our friends in Europe, of which committee I have the honour to be a member, have directed me to request of you, that as you are

4. A MS note in the copy of Vattel that found its way to Harvard; the idea in it was that society should be ruled by the eldest landholders. For the text see Denys P. Myers, "A Franco-American Memento," *Harvard Alumni Bulletin*, XXI (1918), 105.

5. If we correctly identified this article in our note on Dumas' letter above, June 30, BF is citing it not by title but as described there. We have found no trace of an American reprint.

6. Doubtless quoted from the missing letter of July 8.

situated at the Hague, where ambassadors from all the courts reside, you would make use of the opportunity that situation affords you, of discovering, if possible, the disposition of the several courts with respect to such assistance or alliance, if we should apply for the one, or propose the other. As it may possibly be necessary, in particular instances, that you should, for this purpose, confer directly with some great ministers, and show them this letter as your credential, we only recommend it to your discretion, that you proceed therein with such caution, as to keep the same from the knowledge of the English ambassador, and prevent any public appearance, at present, of your being employed in any such business, as thereby, we imagine, many inconveniences may be avoided, and your means of rendering us service, increased.

That you may be better able to answer some questions, which will probably be put to you, concerning our present situation, we inform you . . . [7] that the whole continent is very firmly united . . . the party for the measures of the British ministry being very small, and much dispersed . . . that we have had on foot, the last campaign, an army of near twenty-five thousand men, wherewith we have been able, not only to block up the king's army in Boston, but to spare considerable detachments for the invasion of Canada, where we have met with great success, as the printed papers sent herewith will inform you, and have now reason to expect that whole province may be soon in our possession . . . that we purpose greatly to increase our force for the ensuing year; and thereby we hope, with the assistance of well disciplined militia, to be able to defend our coast, notwithstanding its great extent . . . that we have already a small squadron of armed vessels, to protect our coasting trade, who have had some success in taking several of the enemy's cruisers, and some of their transport vessels, and store ships. This little naval force we are about to augment, and expect it may be more considerable, in the next summer.

We have hitherto applied to no foreign power. We are using the utmost industry in endeavouring to make salt-petre, and with daily increasing success. Our artificers are also every where busy in fabricating small arms, casting cannon, &c. Yet both arms and

7. This and the following ellipses in the paragraph are probably a printer's vagary. The extract at the Hague appears to give the full paragraph, with no sign of omissions, and agrees with our text.

ammunition are much wanted. Any merchants, who would venture to send ships, laden with those articles, might make great profit; such is the demand in every colony, and such generous prices are and will be given; of which, and of the manner of conducting such a voyage, the bearer, Mr. Story, can more fully inform you.[8] And whoever brings in those articles, is allowed to carry off the value in provisions, to our West Indies, where they will probably fetch a very high price, the general exportation from North America being stopped. This you will see more particularly in a printed resolution of the congress.

We are in great want of good engineers, and wish you could engage and send us two able ones, in time for the next campaign, one acquainted with field service, sieges, &c. and the other with fortifying of sea-ports. They will, if well recommended, be made very welcome, and have honourable appointments, besides the expenses of their voyage hither, in which Mr. Story can also advise them. As what we now request of you, besides taking up your time, may put you to some expense, we send you, for the present, enclosed, a bill for one hundred pounds sterling, to defray such expenses, and desire you to be assured that your services will be considered, and honourably rewarded by the congress.

8. This was undoubtedly Thomas Story, about whom we know little. The committee of secret correspondence was sending him on a mission to France, the Netherlands, and England; in mid-December BF had advanced him £50 for the committee. The note on the committee's memorandum below, Oct. 1; Memorandum Book (above, VII, 167–8), entry of Dec. 13, 1775. He was an Irishman established in Philadelphia, according to Dumas' later accounts, who sailed from the Delaware to Le Havre and then, on his way to the Netherlands, amused himself for several weeks in Paris on the excuse that he had never seen the opera. When he finally met Dumas in April, 1776, he explained that he had brought with him drafts on the British government and was impatient to be off to England to collect. "Je le laissai aller, sans profiter de ses connoissances, qui me parurent médiocres, et sans oser mettre à l'épreuve sa loyauté dans une affaire de cette conséquence." "Lettres et Mémoires pour servir à l'Histoire des Et. Un. d'Amérique" (Algemeen Rijksarchief), p. 2. Soon after Story reached London he was ready to return to America, and tried and failed to get a berth on the *Richmond*; his testimony in the prize case that resulted from her capture immediately preceded BF's below, Oct. 14. When Story did sail somewhat later, he brought with him the oral report from Arthur Lee that is embodied in the committee's memorandum just cited. Either this Story or another of the same name was later charged with treason, but eventually released: *Pa. Col. Recs.*, XL, 494; 1 *Pa. Arch.*, X, 258; 6 *Pa. Arch.*, XIII, 477.

We desire, also, that you would take the trouble of receiving from Arthur Lee esquire, agent for the congress in England, such letters as may be sent by him to your care, and of forwarding them to us with your dispatches. When you have occasion to write to him to inform him of any thing, which it may be of importance that our friends there should be acquainted with, please to send your letters to him, under cover, directed to Mr. Alderman Lee, merchant, on Tower Hill, London: and do not send it by post, but by some trusty skipper, or other prudent person, who will deliver it with his own hand.[9] And when you send to us, if you have not a direct safe opportunity, we recommend sending by way of St. Eustatia, to the care of Messrs. Robert and Cornelius Stevenson, merchants there, who will forward your dispatches to me.[1] With sincere and great esteem and respect, I am, Sir, your most obedient, humble servant. B. FRANKLIN.

Mons. Dumas.[2]

Philadelphia Dec. 12. 1775.
We the underwritten, appointed by the american congress a committee of foreign correspondence having perused the above Letter, *Written at our Request*, do approve and confirm the same.
(Signed) JOHN DICKINSON
JOHN JAY

9. Dumas took this caution to heart. He did not trust Story with important letters to William Lee, Arthur's brother, and one that he did give him was confiscated in England; see Dumas to BF below, April 30.

1. The firm was engaged in the American trade; see the secret committee to Ross below, Sept. 27. Our little information about Cornelius Stevenson is in the annotation of his letter below, Aug. 22, with which he forwarded the two packets from Dumas.

2. What follows, omitted in the printed version, is supplied from the extract at the Hague. The letter and this attestation, as John Adams pointed out years later, were the only credentials Dumas ever had: Boyd, *Jefferson Papers*, VIII, 340. The lack of a formal commission made trouble when he sought reimbursement.

From Charles Lee[3]

ALS: American Philosophical Society

Dear Sir, [Before December 10, 1775[4]]

I am very happy that my letter to Lord Thanet meets with your approbation. I send you here some crude notions of what ought be adopted.

1st A solemn league and covenant defensive and offensive to be taken by every man in America, particularly by those in or near the Sea Port Towns; all those who refuse, to have their estates confiscated for the public use, and their persons remov'd to the interior par[t of] the Country with a small pension res[erved?] for their subsistance.[5]

2dly New York to [be] well fortify'd and garrison'd or totally destroy'd.

3dly No Regiments to be rais'd f[or any?] particular local purposes, but one general g[reat?] Continental Army adequate to evry purpose. South Carolina may be excepted from its distance and peculiar circumstances.

4thly. The Regiments to be exchang'd those who are rais'd in one Province to serve in another rather than in their own, viz. the New Englanders in New York the N. Yorkers in New England and so on. This system will undoubtedly make 'em better Soldiers.

3. This is the first extant letter from Lee to BF since what we assume was their initial meeting in London in 1768 (above, XV, 78, 93–4). After the Englishman came to America in 1773 he toured the country, made many friends among colonial leaders, devoted his pen to their cause, and quickly acquired the reputation of a military expert. He was proposed for the command in chief in 1775, and was the second major general commissioned as Washington's subordinate. John R. Alden, *General Charles Lee, Traitor or Patriot?* (Baton Rouge, [1951]), chaps. iv–v; *JCC*, II, 97. BF had presumably renewed his acquaintance with Lee, as with Gates, during his recent visit to headquarters.

4. In his letter of Dec. 10, the following document, Lee asks whether his "propositions" have reached BF; these are undoubtedly the eight listed here. Gates had forwarded to BF Lee's letter to Lord Thanet, referred to in the first sentence, with his above, Nov. 7; and BF's missing reply, which voiced his approbation, had reached Lee before he began this letter. Hence its most likely date is late November or the first days of December.

5. Lee recapitulated the first, second, and seventh of his "crude notions" in a letter to Richard Henry Lee of Dec. 12, which here clarifies his meaning: the pensions were to be taken out of the confiscated estates. *Lee Papers*, I, 229.

5thly. A general Militia to be establishd and the regular Regiments to be formd by drafts from the Militia or their substitutes.

6thly. A certain portion of lands to be [assign]ed to evry Soldier who serves one campaign [a d]ouble portion to him who serves two, and so on.

7thly. A strong flying camp to be kept about Hampton Bay, another about Annapolis and Charles Town in S. Carolina to be well watch'd and guarded.[6]

8thly. The greatest [pains?] to be taken and no expence to be spar'd in securing the Indians to our interest.

These measures may appear bold but I am sure they will be efficacious and decisive decision is the onset[?][7] of success. I wish I had time to write a longer letter, and I wish my pen was better to be more legible. I am, Dear Sir Yours most sincerley

CHARLES LEE

From Charles Lee   ALS: American Philosophical Society

Dear Sir,   Camp Dec'r the 10th 1775

I find that Gates has sent you a copy of my letter; I hope that is correct as I am desirous it shou'd be printed, on condition it meets with your approbation. The other too (Ld. Thanet) you may likewise publish, but I cou'd wish that his Lordship's name shou'd be omitted and that the title shou'd be General Lee's letter to a noble Lord.[8] We are all here a good deal surpriz'd, and not a little shock'd, at the proceedings of your Assembly. We conceive that the injunction laid by these Gentlemen on their delegates to dissent from any resolve leading to independence is ill-time'd impertinent and impolitic, for as the question has not been agitated We can see no good effects from it, and apprehend many bad ones.[9] It is indeed doing the busyness of Government better than any of

6. A flying camp was a mobile reserve with no fixed station. By Hampton Bay we assume Lee meant Hampton Roads. Charleston was attacked the following June, and Lee defended it.

7. The word appears to be "onsent."

8. Lee's two letters, to Burgoyne and to Thanet, are discussed in Gates to BF above, Dec. 7 and Nov. 7 respectively.

9. See the instructions above, Nov. 9.

their hireling writers; these Creatures in order to prejudice the People at home against you have labour'd to spread the opinion that independence is what you aim at, and they seem to have labour'd without success, but this accursed injunction will now give a solidity to their assertions which before they were destitute of. It also betrays some symptoms of timidity than which at a crisis like the present, nothing can be more pernicious. I am myself inclin'd to think that America is not yet ripe for independance, nor am I sure as men's minds are now dispos'd that it wou'd be for their advantage but at the same time I am persuaded that if you loudly proclaim that nothing shall induce you to break the bands You risk the total loss of your liberties. A declaration of this kind will encourage and enable the Ministry to stand their ground or at least to procrastinate the issue. In short I am conceited enough to wish the Continent wou'd adopt the sentiments and language of my letter to Burgoyne, that is, if you chuse to declare great affection for the Mother Country, to assure 'em that unless they give up immediately the Ministry and Ministerial system you are determin'd to dissolve the connection. I am much mistaken if this is not the line You ought to pursue. Have you receiv'd my propositions, and do you approve of 'em? I wish you wou'd send some Man who has the reputation of being a Soldier to Virginia. I think Virginia is our weak vulnerable part. I have the highest opinion of Mr. Henry, but it is inconceivable how necessary it is in order to inspire the Common People with confidence that a reputed Soldier shou'd be at their head. They cannot be perswaded that a Man who has seen no service (altho of the first abilities) shou'd lead them to victory. This, I know, is folly and superstition; but it is a folly and superstition You must give way to. I really believe that the dullest Adjudant with the base reputation of having seen many battles and receiv'd one or two wounds has a better chance of effecting great things at the head of a raw People than a Man possess'd of all the attributes of Marshal Turenne himself if the latter was suppos'd not to have seen service. They never will think themselves safe under his auspices.[1] I had a ri-

1. Marshal Turenne (1611–75) was one of the great commanders of the *ancien régime*. In August the Virginia convention had elevated Patrick Henry to titular command of the colony's militia, but also created a committee of safety that progressively eroded his authority; the following February he resigned in disgust. *DAB*. Lee was not the only one to emphasize so early in the war the

diculous instance of this truth here. A grave Citizen from N. Haven one day visited plow'd hill[2] with me. A shell was thrown by the Enemy. This wise Person immediately seiz'd me by the arm. I happen'd not to stoop when the shell was seemingly over our heads. My Companion held himself erect, altho the rest fell flat on their faces. As soon as He had recover'd breath He told me He was sure I must act right, and that He was perfectly safe by doing just as I did. I mention this as an instance as a proof of bigotry which must be indulg'd. Upon the whole, I must repeat, that I think Virginia in danger and that you ought to take your precautions. We were for some time uneasy at the backwardness the Men shew'd in inlisting [?] for the new Army, but the tide has turn'd, and the affair goes on most swimmingly.[3] Our Army will be soon compleat. Give us Powder and Boston shall be yours. You wou'd much oblige me by the present of a few lines from time to time. Adieu, Dear Sir, Yours most sincerely,   CHARLES LEE

From George Ross   ALS: Amherst College Library

Dear Sir   Lancaster: Decr: 10th: 1775

I am told that the Congress have determined to raise four more Battalians in the Province.[4] And as a member of the committee of Safety have been applyed to by several Gent who will be glad to enter into the Service.

Among others Mr: Thomas Hartly of York Town a Gent of the Law of distinguished Zeal in the Cause he is generally known to the Genl: [Gentlemen] who are members of the Committee of

---

importance of Virginia. Gen. Clinton, Howe's second in command, was making the same point at the same time: William B. Willcox, *Portrait of a General* . . . (New York, 1964), p. 63.

2. See BF to Priestley above, Oct. 3.

3. See the note on Gates's letter above, Dec. 5. The "new" army was the product of the reorganization by Congress after the Cambridge conference; see the headnote above, Oct. 18.

4. In June Congress formed Pa. rifle companies into a battalion for continental service; see the note on the committee of safety to the Lancaster Co. committee above, July 11. In October Congress requested another battalion, and in early December ordered four more and instructed the committee of safety to recommend field officers. In the first days of 1776 the province was called upon for a seventh battalion. *JCC*, III, 291, 418, 429; IV, 29.

Safety And I think would fill the Office of Lieutn: Col: with Honor.[5] When you have leisure (if such a thing be possible) you Don't know how much pleasure a line from you would give me.

I am forced to write and keep the paper steady with the same hand having the Gout in my left hand and Elbow. And tho' I should be glad to get rid of his Company yet I have so much of the Christian Spirit I use him kindly and with the greatest tenderness. Yet I own could I by any means bring about *a seperation* between the Gout and me I should do it, Non Obstante any Instructions even from the Assembly of Pennsylva.[6] I am with real Affection Your Much Obliged and Obedient Humble Servant   GEO: ROSS

Doctor Franklin

Notation: Thomas Hartly Lieut. Colonel Recommended by Geo: Ross

The Committee of Secret Correspondence to [Arthur Lee[7]]

ALS:[8] Maine Historical Society

Sir,   Philada. Dec. 12. 1775

By this Conveyance we have the Pleasure of transmitting to you sundry printed Papers, that such of them as you think proper may be immediately published in England.

We have written on the Subject of American Affairs to Monsieur C. G. F. Dumas, who resides at the Hague. We recommend it to you to correspond with him, and to send through his Hands any Letters to us which you cannot send more directly. He will transmit them via St. Eustatia. When you write to him direct your Letter thus, *A Mons. Monsr. C. G. F. Dumas chez Made. le Ve.*

5. Hartley held the same commission in the minutemen and the first militia battalion; see the letter from the York committee above, Aug. 31. He became lieut. col. of the 6th Pa. on Jan. 10, 1776: Heitman, *Register of Officers*, p. 212.

6. The separation from Britain precluded by the Assembly's instructions to its delegates above, Nov. 9. A violent attack of gout killed Ross in 1779 at the age of forty-nine: *DAB*.

7. A tear at the bottom of the second page obliterates what once was apparently there, "Arthur Lee, Esq."; see Richard Henry Lee, *Life of Arthur Lee . . .* (2 vols., Boston, 1829), I, 54.

8. In BF's hand.

Loder, à la Hague;[9] and put it under Cover directed to Mr. A. Stuckey Merchant at Rotterdam.

Mr. Story may be trusted with any Dispatches you think proper to send us.[1] You will be so kind as to aid and advise him.

It would be agreable to Congress to know the Disposition of Foreign Powers towards us, and we hope this Object will engage your Attention. We need not hint that great Circumspection and impenetrable Secrecy are necessary. The Congress rely on your Zeal and Abilities to serve them, and will readily compensate you for whatever Trouble and Expence a Compliance with their Desires may occasion. We remit you for the present Two Hundred Pounds Sterling.[2]

Whenever you think the Importance of your Dispatches may require it, we desire you to send an Express-Boat with them from England, for which Service your Agreement with the Owner there shall be fulfilled by us here.

We can now only add that we continue firm in our Resolutions to defend ourselves, notwithstanding the big Threats of the Ministry. We have just taken one of their Ordnance Store Ships, in which are abundance of Carcasses and Bombs intended for burning our Towns.[3] With great Esteem, we are Sir, Your most obedient humble Servants   B FRANKLIN

JOHN DICKINSON

JOHN JAY

Committee of Correspondence

9. See BF's letter to Dumas above, Dec. 9, written in the name of the committee. The printed papers enclosed in that letter were presumably the same as those with this one. Mme. Loder was in fact Mme. Dumas, a widow whom he had married some years before: J.W. Schulte Nordholt, "Dumas, the First American Diplomat," in Owen D. Edwards and George Shepperson, *Scotland, Europe and the American Revolution* (Edinburgh, 1976), p. 18.

1. Story carried the letter to Dumas and, we assume, this one as well.

2. Congress had just put $3,000 at the committee's disposition. *JCC*, III, 423.

3. Along with the great mortar that Gates mentioned in his letter above, Dec. 5. Carcasses, or shells filled with combustibles, were ammunition for the mortar.

To Don Gabriel Antonio de Bourbon[4]

Copy: Library of Congress; letterpress copy:[5] Yale University Library

Illustrious Prince   Philadelphia Decr: 12. 1775

I have just received through the Hands of the Ambassador of Spain, the much esteemed present your most serene Highness hath so kindly sent me, of your excellent Version of Sallust.[6]

I am extreamly sensible of the honor done me, and beg you would accept my thankful acknowledgements. I wish I could send from[7] hence any American Literary Production worthy of your perusal; but as yet the Muses have scarcely visited these remote Regions. Perhaps however the Proceedings of our American Congress, just published, may be a subject of some Curiosity at your Court. I therefore take the Liberty of sending your Highness a Copy, with some other Papers which contain Accounts of the successes wherewith Providence has lately favoured us. Therein your wise Politicians may contemplate the first efforts of a rising State, which seems likely soon to act a part of some Importance on the stage of human affairs, and furnish materials for a future Sallust. I am very old and can scarce hope to see the event of this great Contest: but looking forward I think I see a powerful Dominion growing up here, whose interest it will be to form a close and firm alliance with Spain, (their Territories bordering[8]) and who being united, will be able, not only to preserve their own people in peace, but to repel the Force of all the other powers in Europe. It seems therefore prudent on both sides to cultivate a good understanding, that may hereafter be so useful to both; towards which a fair Foundation is already laid in our minds, by the well founded popular Opinion entertained here of Spanish Integrity and Honour. I hope my presumption in hinting this will be pardoned. If in any thing on this side the Globe I can render either service or pleasure to your Royal Highness, your commands will make me

4. Infante of Spain; see Williams to BF above, June 7.

5. Lacking the address at the end; otherwise the two copies differ only in picayune details.

6. The "just received" should be taken with a grain of salt. Williams sent the volume by a Capt. Miller, who arrived in Philadelphia in mid-August: *Pa. Gaz.*, Aug. 16, 1775.

7. "From," and "Franklin" in the signature, have been deleted in what appears to be a different ink; both are present in the Yale copy.

8. The new American state, in other words, will stretch to the Mississippi.

298

happy. With the utmost esteem and veneration I have the Honour to be Your serene Highness's most obedient and most humble Servant   BN. FRANKLIN

To His most Serene Highness Dn Gabriel of Bourbon. on receiving his Version of Sallust.[9]

From Mary Hewson   ALS: American Philosophical Society

My dear Sir   Kensington Dec. 12. 1775

By not being inform'd in proper time I have miss'd several opportunities of writing to you, which I regret because I wish to live in your memory, and to convince you that you are in mine. Do not sigh at the addition I make to the packet, for I ask no return, you have enough to do without scribbling to me, and my letters you may lay by till you have a few minutes to spare for relaxation.[1]

My mother I suppose writes by the same conveyance so you will have what she has to say from herself. What I have to say of her is not so pleasing as I could wish, the disorder she had in her leg last summer is return'd, which, as it prevents her activity, lowers her spirits. I and my little ones are well. William is grown very bookish, I cannot say he reads yet, but he is an excellent speller, the words he has learnt he does not forget, and when he attempts to spell those he is acquainted with only by sound he manages very well according to the miserable rules of the present orthography; rules that are so perpetually violated, that now my attention is call'd to it I am astonish'd at the power of memory which enables us to read and write. As I reckon you are soon to be sovereigne, and lawgiver in the Empire of America, I pray you establish your

9. There follows "(Insert it above)", and at the head of the letter is "(Insert here the Title below)."

1. The letters were laid by for more than a decade before BF saw them. They were in a packet which JW did not mail until September, 1776 (safe conveyances must have been few and far between), and which did not reach Philadelphia until after BF left for France. The packet contained two more letters from Polly, those of Sept. 5 and 8 below, along with others, and RB kept it. BF wrote her on May 7, 1786 (Morristown National Historical Park) that he had only just received her three letters, and referred to the contents of each. For the others in the packet see the note on JW to BF below, Sept. 3.

alphabet[2] that my grandchildren may attain the rudiments of learning more easily.

My son Tom is a genius that steps out of the common way of learning, he takes up a book and gives names to the letters, U. he calls bell and P. he calls bottle. He begins to chatter now and has some phrases of his own, a handkerchief he call a nose kitpi. I find that by our alphabet I can convey a new sound to you with precision, which it would be impossible to do by the common rule of spelling, so my *uncommon* learning is useful.

As to my daughter I cannot say much of her mental qualities at present, but her personal charms improve, I fancy she grows handsome; to give you some idea of her countenance I must tell you that I trace in it a strong resemblance of my aunt Rooke, whom you us'd to call *your lovely*.[3] She is a jolly girl, and as her shape is suffer'd to take it's natural form I believe her waist would measure nearly equal to that of a grown up fashionable lady, in circumference I mean. I hope your countrywomen will be too wise to adopt our present preposterous modes. I long to be in America, fancying that I there may appear without distortion. Perhaps you may think our heads were come to their full size before you left our island, but I assure you their magnitude is encreas'd this winter. A stranger would suppose the women were to carry burthens upon their heads, for they wear a cushion of hair almost as large as a porter's knot.[4]

My fortune is not yet settled tho' Mr. Mure appointed a day for meeting my friends, and Mr. Henckell, Mr. Williams and Mr. Walter Blunt went and spoke for me. However Mr. M. was very polite and offer'd to settle the affair to my satisfaction, agreeing to all their demands, which he acknowledg'd to be reasonable, but referr'd them to Mr. Atkinson as he was more acquainted with the

2. The phonetic alphabet that he had taught Polly seven years before: above, xv, 173–8.

3. About Mrs. Rooke, who has appeared with Mrs. Tickell in earlier volumes, we know virtually nothing.

4. The mid-seventies were the period when waists were most tightly corseted and headdresses most extravagant. The latter were structures built over wire frames and filled out with wool and false hair, and sometimes simulated such things as ships or windmills. See Emily Ashdown, *British Costume during XIX Centuries* . . . (London, 1910), pp. 323–9; Iris Brooke and James Laver, *English Costume from the Fourteenth through the Nineteenth Century* (New York, 1937), pp. 316–21.

affairs than himself. Mr. A. postpon'd the looking into the affairs for a few weeks as he was much engag'd in business, which he said was a national concern, contracting with government to supply them with sheep and hogs to feed—the fish in the channel. M & A. do not contract for the arrival of the stock at Boston, the place it was destin'd for by government, so they will be paid for it, and the real destiny of the chief part is what I mention'd, and most probably the rest will go into the Atlantic.[5] The fish are our friends so I may be allow'd to rejoice at their having a feast rather than our enemies.

Mr. Williams no doubt will inform you of his situation with Mr. Blunt.[6] Lady Blunt has at length produc'd a boy. I have a niece.[7] Dolly Blunt is still with her sister who is in a deep decline.[8] So the world goes on; it is a wonderful mixture, and I think my letter resembles it. One good thing I have always found in the

5. The fortune was her inheritance from her aunt, Mrs. Tickell. Henckell may have been either James, the father of Dolly's friend Elizabeth, or the T. Henckell who had been part of BF's and Polly's circle in 1768; Williams was JW, and Walter Blunt was Dolly's brother (above, XIX, 152 n; XV, 237). Mure was Hutchinson Mure (1711?–95), a partner of Thomas Tickell (who we assume was Polly's uncle) until the latter's death in 1755, and since 1767 a member of Mure, Son & Atkinson. For Mure see the *Gent. Mag.*, LXIV (1794), 771, and for Richard Atkinson see Namier and Brooke, *House of Commons*, II, 32. In the fall of 1775 the firm provided shipping and provisions for the army, but the victualing fleet was scattered by disastrous storms: R. Arthur Bowler, *Logistics and the Failure of the British Army in America, 1775–1783* (Princeton, [1975]), pp. 53–5. Even if the partners were not liable for the resultant losses, paying a legacy at that moment out of assets may have given them pause. They eventually settled for £7,000 in bonds, less than Polly thought due her; see her letter below, Sept. 5. But she said years later that the inheritance brought her into easy circumstances and took care of educating her children: George Gulliver, ed., *The Works of William Hewson* . . . (London, 1846), p. xiv.

6. He already had; see his letter above, Nov. 23.

7. Charles, the son of Sir Charles and Lady Blunt, was born on Dec. 6: *Burke's Peerage*, p. 330. Polly's niece was undoubtedly born to her husband's sister, Mrs. Magnus Falconar, the wife of a young anatomist whom William Hewson had intended to be his successor: Thomas J. Pettigrew, *Memoirs of the Life and Writings of the Late John Coakley Lettsom* . . . (3 vols., London, 1817), I, 146 of second pagination. Falconar married Hewson's sister five months after the Doctor's death; most of the Craven Street circle attended the wedding, and BF gave away the bride: Polly to Barbara Hewson, Oct. 4, 1774, APS. Falconar completed and published the final part of Hewson's *Experimental Inquiries* in 1777, but died the next spring at the age of twenty-four: Gulliver, *op. cit.*, p. xlvi.

8. She died before the end of the month: *Burke's Peerage*, p. 330.

world that is Friendship, and amidst all my folly you will find that in my letter; nay I flatter myself that my medley may amuse you. God bless you! and prosper your undertakings. The blessing I dare to pray for, the subsequent part of the sentence I must only wish, for tho' I believe your cause is just I am too pious to pray for prosperity. I am with sincere regard My dear Sir Your faithful and affectionate humble Servant   MARY HEWSON

Deed from Israel and Mary Pemberton Discharging Ground Rent

> Copy of abstract: Department of Records, Recorder of Deeds, City of Philadelphia

⟨December 13, 1775: Israel Pemberton, merchant of Philadelphia, and his wife Mary, in consideration of £350 on lawful Pennsylvania money, release and confirm to Benjamin Franklin the annual ground rent of fifteen Spanish pistoles, or the equivalent in Pennsylvania currency, due from James Pearson to Pemberton by deed of sale of June 6, 1760, for a lot on the south side of Jones's Alley, commonly called Pewter Platter Alley, in Philadelphia, thirty-eight feet in breadth[9] and sixty feet in depth, bounded on the east by a house and lot of the late Thomas Ryles, on the south by lots of Thomas Hyne and John Lynn, on the west by a house lately owned by Robert Grace, and on the north by the alley. The Pembertons warrant Franklin's title and their own power to convey it. Signed by them, witnessed by Jno. Ord and W.P. Gibbs, and acknowledged the same day before Jno. Ord, justice of the peace. Recorded May 25, 1776.⟩

9. BF had bought the lot from Pearson in 1764 and assumed the ground rent due Pemberton: above, XI, 319–21. When BF's real estate was divided among Sally Bache's heirs on Jan. 14, 1812, this property went to her daughter Sarah (D.3.8); by then a more recent survey had pared three inches off the breadth. Department of Records, Recorder of Deeds, City of Philadelphia, Book IC, 19, pp. 12, 19.

"Bradshaw's Epitaph": a Hoax Attributed to Franklin

Printed in *The Pennsylvania Evening Post*, December 14, 1775.

The newspaper that printed this epitaph introduced it with a sentence explaining that the lines had been deciphered three years earlier on a cannon near where the famous regicide's ashes were buried in Jamaica. Franklin has been widely accepted as the author. The only evidence is a copy in Jefferson's hand, which came to light in 1828 and has since disappeared, but of which a transcript is extant. The copy was headed 1776, contained the explanatory sentence and text from the *Evening Post*, and concluded with a note by Jefferson that there was reason to think the inscription "was written by Dr. Franklin, in whose hand [hands?] it was first seen."[1] Whether this attribution was correct must remain an open question; even if the paper Jefferson saw was in the Doctor's *hand*, rather than hands, Franklin might have copied it. He was certainly struck by it, for he made it the last line of the motto for his proposed great seal of the United States.[2]

STRANGER,
Ere thou pass, contemplate this CANNON,
Nor regardless be told
That near its base lies deposited the dust of
JOHN BRADSHAW,
Who, nobly superior to all selfish regards,
Despising alike the pagentry of courtly splendor,
The blast of calumny, and the terrors of royal vengeance,
Presided in the illustrious band of heroes and patriots,
Who fairly and openly adjudged
CHARLES STUART,
Tyrant of England,
To a public and exemplary death,
Thereby presenting to the amazed world,
And transmitting down, through applauding ages,
The most glorious example

1. Boyd, *Jefferson Papers*, I, 677–9.
2. Jefferson worked with BF on the committee to design that seal; see the headnote below, under Aug. 14. It seems reasonable to conjecture that at that time the Doctor showed his young colleague the epitaph and Jefferson copied it.

Of unshaken virtue, love of freedom, and impartial justice,
Ever exhibited on the blood-stained theatre of human action.
O, reader,
Pass not on till thou hast blessed his memory
And never — never forget
THAT REBELLION TO TYRANTS IS OBEDIENCE TO
GOD.

From Catherine Meed   als: American Philosophical Society

Dear Uncle   Sunsbury Shemokin Der 16 1775
    I Recevd your kind Condesenging letter,[3] and think myself
happy to Inform you who I am—the Daughter of John Croker. I
was once at your House when Very little. I am not Very Bigg yet
but I am Sure I am at least A head taller Since you honered me
with A letter. I hope I Shall never grow so proud but allways
Endeavour to Deserve the Notice of so good and worthy an uncle.
Pleas to give my love to my Dear Cousin Sarah and Except the
Same from your Affectonate Cousin   CATERINE MEED
Notation: Catharine Meed

The York County Committee to the Pennsylvania
Committee of Safety   ls: National Archives

⟨York, December 23, 1775: By last night's post came the newspaper account of Congress' resolve that Pennsylvania should raise
four battalions, and that the committee of safety should appoint
the company officers and recommend field officers to the Congress.[4] The time set was January 2, 1776, when the York County
member of the Pennsylvania committee cannot attend. The
county committee therefore recommends the following appointments: Thomas Hartley as lieutenant colonel of one of the battalions; David Grier, John McDowel and William Nicholls as captain, lieutenant, and ensign of one company, and Moses McClean,

3. It has not survived. See the headnote on her earlier letter above, Nov. 28.
4. See Ross to BF above, Dec. 10.

Lewis Bush, and Robert Hopes of the other.[5] If a third company is raised in the county, Bernard Eichelberger should be "Captain or Leiutenant as you may think best."[6] The committee will do all in its power to fill the rolls quickly, with the best men and at the least expense. Addressed to Franklin, Robert Morris, and the committee of safety, and signed for the York committee by James Smith as chairman.⟩

From [Edward Bancroft]   AL[7]: American Philosophical Society

Dear Sir   London Decr. 23d. 1775.
   The difficulties and Dangers attending all American Correspondence have for sometime suspended those Communications which Friendship would have inclined me otherwise to make you. I am however several Letters in advance with you and of which you have not acknowledged the Receipt. This will be Delivered by Mr. Wrixon a Gentleman who was formerly a Field Officer in the Kings Service, but who has lately applied himself to the Study of the Law. He confessedly possesses a distinguished Share of Millitary Knowledge and of personal Bravery. He has given many decisive Proofs of the Integrity of his Political Principles, and from an intimate acquaintance I am Convinced that he is a Gentleman of Good Understanding, respectable Talents, and the strictest Honour; and as such I beg leave to recommend him to your friendly Acquaintance and Assistance. He will explain to you the nature of his Wishes, and considering his valuable Qualifications, I have no Doubt but the services which he may receive from you

5. All the men were eventually appointed, but to an additional battalion that was raised in January: *Pa. Col. Recs.*, X, 444, 450–1; *JCC*, IV, 29, 47. For Hartley and Grier see the officers' letter above, Aug. 31. The military careers of the others, one of which was brief and two of which were fatal, may be found in outline in John B. Linn and William H. Egle, *Pennsylvania in the War of the Revolution* . . . (2 vols., Harrisburg, 1880), I, 74, 167, 185, 188, 330, 402 n, 572, 602, 780; Heitman, *Register of Officers*, pp. 110, 227, 280, 309; 2 *Pa. Arch.*, XIV, 476, 512; *PMHB*, XX (1896), 508, 511. McDowel was also spelled McDowell, Nicholls Nichols, McClean McLean, and Bernard (Eichelberger) Bernet.
   6. He declined to serve; see the committee's letter below, Jan. 29.
   7. The signature has been cut off or torn off.

will be the means of his becoming eminently useful to those for whose Intrests we are both sollicitous.[8] The work of which we have formerly Conversed on, is now gone to the Press; it contains many new important and Decisive Facts, and I will contrive somehow or other to furnish you with a Copy or two soon.[9] Your old Friend the Dean has of late repeatedly transgressed and is now about to receive a *most Severe* Chastisement—you will guess from whom.[1] With regard to Political Matters, I must for many reasons refer you for information respecting them to the Bearer. The Game is now grown Desperate, and on *this side* is desperately Played. And yet nothing would perhaps be more agreable than a Compromise on any terms which would permit certain Folks to keep their Seats and Save their Credit, which however I think impossible. Lord Howe has been undoubtedly in Treaty with the Minister, respecting a Conciliatory visit to America. I beleive his intentions are good and that he would Gladly go with such Powers as are necessary to restore peace, but not without them. He however is Slightly disgusted by the Promotion of Sir H. P—and is gone to the Country to wait and see whether the Ministry *can* gratify his Demands respecting the Marines, and whether they *will* sufficiently extend his Powers.[2]

After the Present recess I think opposition will increase and act with Vigour. Adieu Dear Sir and be assured that under every

8. Elias Wrixon, before turning to the law, had served in Germany during the Seven Years' War. He was in Philadelphia by March, 1776, when he was examined by a Congressional committee, on which BF served, and offered the position of chief engineer in Canada with the rank of colonel; but he declined the commission. *JCC*, IV, 219, 242, 275, 316. He had his strong supporters in Congress, of whom John Adams was one, and his equally strong critics. He returned to Europe, disgruntled and convinced that the American cause was doomed. Butterfield, *John Adams Diary*, III, 382, and *Adams Correspondence*, I, 361–2; Taylor, *Adams Papers*, IV, 148, 467; Smith, *Letters*, III, 420, 440; Wharton to BF below, Jan. 17, 1777.

9. We have found no pamphlet attributed to Bancroft or Samuel Wharton published in London at this time.

1. We dare not guess. Dean Tucker published three pamphlets in 1775.

2. In the late autumn, while Howe was being considered for peace commissioner and the extent of his powers was under discussion, a naval sinecure that North had promised him, the lieutenant generalcy of marines, went instead to a junior rear admiral, Sir Hugh Palliser. Howe threatened to resign, and then retired to the country to negotiate with the government through a go-between. Gruber, *Howe Brothers*, pp. 63–6.

Vicissitude and in every Place, I shall always Continue Your most faithful, Affectionate and Devoted Servant,

From [Samuel Wharton³]   AL: American Philosophical Society

Dear Sir   London December 23. 1775
    The Bearer hereof Mr. Wrixon, a Gentleman of Character and good Connexions in Ireland, I beg leave to introduce to your Frindship, Civility and protection. Major Trent is well acquainted with Mr. Wrixon, and knows his useful Qualifications, and I dare say, will, with great Pleasure mention Them to You; and give Me leave to add, That Mr. Wrixon has not been an indifferent Spectator of the unhappy Dispute, between this Country and America, as his late Publication will shew. If you can render Mr. Wrixon any acceptable Services, and particularly with Respect to his Views in America (Which He will amply explain to You) I flatter myself you will chearfully do it, and Thereby, much Oblige, Dear Sir Your most Obedient and affectionate Servant.

I dare not say a Word on publick affairs, Neither is it Necessary, as the Bearer will fully and faithfully represent Them to you. He carrys the restraining Act with Him.⁴

From George Ross   ALS: Historical Society of Pennsylvania

⟨Lancaster, December 26, 1775: Pardon my asking your support in obtaining for my son James, now a captain in a company of the rifle battalion, a majority in one of the four battalions about to be raised.⁵ I shall be obliged for your friendship in the matter.⟩

3. Identified by the handwriting.
4. For Wrixon see the preceding letter. John Adams called his publication "a Pamphlet under the Title of the Rights of Britons": Butterfield, *Adams Correspondence*, I, 361; we have had no more success in identifying it than Butterfield had. The statute that Wrixon brought with him was the Prohibitory Act, which had become law on Dec. 22: *Public Advertiser*, Dec. 23, 1775.
5. For James Ross's rifle company see Pa. delegates to the Lancaster County committee above, July 11, and for the new battalions his father's letter above, Dec. 10. Young Ross was apparently not nominated. He retained his rank in the rifle battalion, which was reorganized the following January and renamed the first continental infantry, and attained his majority in it on Sept. 25, 1776.

To Philip Mazzei[6]

ALS: Dartmouth College Library

Dear Sir,   Philada. Dec. 27. 1775

It was with great Pleasure I learnt from Mr. Jefferson, that you were settled in America; and from the Letter you favour'd me with, that you like the Country, and have reason to expect Success in your laudable and meritorious Endeavours to introduce new Products. I heartily wish you all the Success you can desire, in that, and in every other Undertaking that may conduce to your comfortable Establishment in your present Situation.

I know not how it has happened that you did not receive an Answer to your Letter from the Secretaries of our Society. I suppose they must have written, and that it has miscarried. If you have not yet sent the Books which the Academy of Turin have done us the Honour to present us with, we must, I fear, wait for more quiet Times before we can have the Pleasure of receiving them, the Communication being now very difficult.[7]

I can hardly suspect Mr. Walpole of the Practise against you which you mention, especially as he was then expecting to have Lands of his own in America, wherein the Productions you were about to introduce must have been beneficial. I rather suspect a Person whom you may remember was frequently with him, I

He was promoted to lieut. col. the next year, transferred to the 8th Pa., and played a role of some importance in the Battle of the Brandywine. Heitman, *Register of Officers*, p. 351; Freeman, *Washington*, IV, 475, 477, 487.

6. This is the first surviving letter in a correspondence that continued throughout the war. Mazzei (1730–1816) was a jack of all trades. He had been born and educated in Italy, practised medicine in Smyrna, and been for years a wine merchant in London. There he had been asked to obtain two Franklin stoves for Grand Duke Leopold of Tuscany (above, XX, 330 n); BF had helped him find them, and had later advised him to go to America. He did so in 1773 and, with the help of Thomas Jefferson, settled near Monticello with the intention of establishing viticulture. See his *Memoirs of the Life and Peregrinations of the Florentine Philip Mazzei* . . . (Howard R. Marraro, trans.; New York, 1942), pp. 165, 189–93; Boyd, *Jefferson Papers*, I, 158–9; *DAB*.

7. Mazzei's letter, of Dec. 7, 1773, informed the APS that he had received from the Turin Academy four volumes of its proceedings as a gift to the Society. Not until 1779 did the APS ask for delivery of the books; the request was apparently unsuccessful, for the copies now in the APS library, volumes II–V of the *Mélanges de philosophie et de mathématique de la Société royale de Turin* (1760–73), were purchased from BF's library. APS, *Early Proc.* . . . (Philadelphia, 1884), pp. 86, 102, 315.

mean Martinelli.[8] I rejoice that you escap'd the Snares that were laid for you, and I think all America is oblig'd to the Great Duke for his Benevolence towards it, in the Protection he afforded you, and his Encouragement of your Undertaking.

We have experienc'd here that Silk may be produc'd to great Advantage. While in London I had some Trunks full sent me from hence three Years successively, and it sold by Auction for about 19*s.* 6*d.* the small Pound, which was not much below the Silk from Italy.[9]

The Congress have not yet extended their Views much towards foreign Powers, and particularly not to those of Italy, who are so distant. They are nevertheless oblig'd by your kind Offers of your Service, which perhaps in a Year or two more may become very useful to them. I am myself much pleas'd that you have sent a Translation of our Declaration to the Grand Duke;[1] because having a high Esteem for the Character of that Prince, and of the whole Imperial Family, from the Accounts given me of them by my Friend Dr. Ingenhauss and yourself, I should be happy to find that we stood well in the Opinion of that Court.

Mr. Fromond of Milan, with whom I had the Pleasure of being acquainted in London, spoke to me of a Plant much used in Italy, and which he thought would be useful to us in America. He promis'd at my Request to send me some of the Seeds, which he has accordingly done. I have unfortunately forgotten the Uses, and know nothing of the Culture. In both those Particulars I must

8. In Mazzei's *Memoirs*, cited above, he purported to explain this paragraph (pp. 219, 249): While in London he refused to join a project for having European textile designs executed in China, but when next in Italy he found the whole scheme blamed on him as a result, he learned later from Thomas Walpole, of a letter from a Florentine writer living in London, Vicenzo Martinelli. This explanation has no apparent bearing on BF's reference, which is to some charge against Walpole himself.

9. Mazzei envisaged producing silk, as well as wine and oil, in the back country of Virginia. Grand Duke Leopold helped this project by permitting him to take with him a group of skilled Tuscan farmers. *Ibid.*, pp. 182, 184–5; Richard C. Garlick, *Philip Mazzei, Friend of Jefferson . . .* (John Hopkins Studies in Romance Literatures and Languages; extra vol. VII; Baltimore, etc., 1933), pp. 27–9, 45–7. The sale of Pa. silk in London figures prominently in our earlier vols., particularly XVIII and XIX.

1. The Declaration of the Causes and Necessity of Taking up Arms, a note on which appears above, July 6. Jefferson had a copy of what was presumably the same translation: Boyd, *Jefferson Papers*, I, 218 n.

beg Information and Advice from you. It is called *Ravizzoni*.[2] I send Specimens of the Seed inclosed.

I received from the same M. Fromond Four Copies of a Translation of some of my Pieces into the fine Language of your Country.[3] I beg your Acceptance of one of them, and of my best Wishes for your Health and Prosperity. With great Esteem and Regard, I have the Honour to be, Dear Sir, Your most obedient and most humble Servant   B FRANKLIN

M. Mazzei.

Endorsed: D. Franklin dated Phil. 27: Dec: 1775 Rec'd 8. Feb. 1776 Answered.

Achard de Bonvouloir to the Comte de Guines: Extract[4]

Extracted from AL[5]: Archives du Ministère des affaires étrangères, Paris

The committee of secret correspondence had been in existence less than a month when it was approached by the Chevalier de Bonvouloir, an agent of the French court. The discussions that ensued, which this letter reports, set in train major developments on both sides of the Atlantic. At Versailles Bonvouloir's report strengthened the hand of the foreign minister, the Comte de Vergennes, in pressing for arms and ammunition for the American rebels.[6] In Philadelphia Congress responded to the

2. For Fromond see above, XX, 354. Ravizzoni is winter rape, extensively grown in Europe as forage for sheep.

3. Fromond doubtless transmitted the four copies, which were a gift from the translator, Carlo Campi: above, XXI, 250–1.

4. For Adrien-Louis de Bonnières de Sousastre, Comte de Guines (1735–1806), who since 1770 had been ambassador to St. James's, see Larousse, *Dictionnaire universel*. Julien-Alexandre Achard de Bonvouloir et Loyauté (1749–83), cadet of an aristocratic Norman house, had emigrated in the early 1770's to the French colony of St. Domingue. For his career see Joseph Hamon, *Le Chevalier de Bonvouloir* (Paris, 1953).

5. The remarkable spelling and punctuation persuade us that the document is an AL rather than a copy. The letter is repetitious, and we have omitted roughly half of it. The complete text, with the French corrected and modernized, is in Doniol, *Histoire*, I, 267–9, 287–92, and in English translation in *Naval Docs.*, III, 279–85.

6. See Dubourg to BF below, June 10. For Charles Gravier, Comte de Vergennes (1717–87), a former ambassador who since 1774 had been secretary of state for foreign affairs, see Orville T. Murphy, "Charles Gravier de Vergennes: Portrait of an Old Regime Diplomat," *Political Science Quarterly*, LXXXIII (1968),

agent's visit by appointing Silas Deane, the following March, to go to France for the committee of secret correspondence and act as its agent there.[7]

The background of Bonvouloir's mission was a tour of American cities that he had made before the outbreak of hostilities. In Philadelphia he had been in touch with members of the first Continental Congress and believed he had acquired information of value; he had then gone to London in hope of putting it to use. There he met de Guines, the French Ambassador, who was in the process of persuading Vergennes that an agent should be sent to America, and who now proposed the young man's name.[8] In August, 1775, Bonvouloir was dispatched on his mission. It had, according to Vergennes' instructions, two objectives. The first was innocuous, to observe and report. The second was less so, for it marked a departure from strict neutrality: the agent was to assure the Americans that France had no designs on Canada, wished them well, and would be glad if circumstances permitted their ships to use French ports.[9]

Bonvouloir was back in Philadelphia by mid-December. Through contacts made during his earlier visit he gained access to the committee of secret correspondence, and under cover of night had three meetings with it in Carpenters' Hall.[1] By a strange coincidence the secret committee, of which Franklin was also a member, met at almost the same time with two other Frenchmen, of whom Bonvouloir had heard only a rumor. They were merchants, Pierre Penet and Emmanuel de Pliarne, who came from St. Domingue; a ship dispatched there for gunpowder brought them to Rhode Island on December 10. They offered to supply the colonists with arms, and cultivated the impression that they were agents of their government, which in fact they were not. Governor Cooke sent them to Washington, who in turn sent them—expenses paid—to Congress. Penet returned to France with a list of American requirements, just when Bonvouloir's report was on its way to Versailles. The list gave body to the report, and by another coincidence reached the

---

400–18. In strict parlance a secretary was the administrative head of a department of state, such as foreign affairs or the marine, whereas a minister, who might be either a secretary or without portfolio, was a member of the *conseil d'état*, the most important of the king's formal advisory councils. We use minister and secretary interchangeably, however, as they were used in Britain.

7. See the committee's instructions to Deane below, March 2.

8. See de Guines to Vergennes, July 1, 28, 1775: Doniol, *Histoire*, I, 128, 154–5.

9. *Ibid.*, pp. 155–6. See also Hamon, *op. cit.*, pp. 15–34.

1. William Jay, *The Life of John Jay with Selections from his Correspondence . . .* (2 vols., New York, 1833), I, 39–41.

court just after the King had decided, the following May, to furnish the rebels with military supplies.[2]

Bonvouloir had only this moment on stage. He subsequently went to Canada, where the British captured and imprisoned him. By the time he returned to France the time had long passed, if it had ever existed, for capitalizing on his mission, and he turned to Franklin for help in furthering his fortunes.[3] Failing there, he secured a naval commission and went with his ship to India, where he died.

P[hiladel]phie le 28 Xbre 1775

Jai trouvé, Comme je m'y étais attendu, Ce pais Cy Dans une agitation inconcevable. Les Confoederés font Des preparatifs immances pour Le printems prochain et malgré La Rigeur De La saison, ils Continuent La Campagne. Ils ont assiegé mont-Real qui a Capitulé, et sont acctuellement sous quebec, qui, je pense, en fera Bientôt autant: ils se sont emparés De quelques Vaisseaux De Roy, Chargés De provisions De guerre et De Bouche: ils sont parfaittement Retranchés sous Boston, ils se font même une petite marine: ils ont une ardeur et une Bonne Volonté incroyable: il est vrai qu'ils sont Conduits par De Bonnes tetes.

Trois choses importantes Leur manquent, une Bonne marine, Des provisions et De l'argent: ils en sont Convenus avec moy. Je vais Vous Rendre Compte mot pour mot De trois Conversations particulieres, que jai eues avec Mr. frankelain et trois autres Bonnes tetes qui Composent Le Conseil privé.[4] Je suis entré Comme *particulier* Dans Leur intimité, par Le Canal Dun honnête français, Du quel je suis sur, et qui a acquis une Bonne part Dans La Confience Des Deputés. Ce français se nomme Daymons, je

2. Penet will appear prominently in later volumes. For his and Pliarne's reception in America see *Naval Docs.*, III, 55–7, 94–5, 324; Price, *France and the Chesapeake*, II, 702. Bonvouloir's report reached de Guines after the ambassador had been recalled from London and was en route to Versailles; he arrived there on March 2 (Doniol, *Histoire*, I, 394) and presumably transmitted the report to Vergennes. For ensuing developments see the headnote on Dubourg's letter below, June 10.

3. His letter to BF [August?, 1778] is in the APS.

4. Bonvouloir concocted this name for the committee, we assume, because he considered it the American executive. Its membership was reduced to four by the absence of Thomas Johnson, who was in Maryland: Burnett, *Letters*, I, xlvi.

Vous Le Reccommande, il est Bibliotequaire De La Ville.[5] Tout Ce que Vous me ferez passer, Viendra a son addresse, et mes pacquets seront marqués A.B. et ils me seront Rendus.

Je ne Leur ai fait aucuns offres absolument aucuns, Leur promettant *seullement*, De Leur Rendre tous Les services qui *Deppenderaient De moy* sans me *Compromettre*, et sans me Rendre *garant* Des *evennements* en *aucune façon*, et Le tout par Le moyen De mes *Connoissances* et sans Leur faire aucune Confidance. Ils mont Demmande si La france Les aiderait, et à quel prix; je Leur ai Repondu; que je *Croyais*, que La france Leur *Voullait* Du *Bien*; qu'elle Les aiderait; que Cela *pourait Bien etre*; sur quel pied; que je n'en *sçavais* Rien mais que si Cela arrivait se serait toujours à Des Conditions justes et equitables, que Du Reste, *s'ils* Le *jugeaient* a *propos*, ils fissent Leurs propositions, que j'avais De Bonnes Connoissances, que je me Chargerais De *presenter* Leurs Demmandes, sans *Rien plus*. Ils m'ont Demmande si je Croyais, qu'il fut prudent a eux Denvoyer un Deputé plenipotantiere en france. Je Leur ai Dit que je mimaginnais, que Cela serait precipité, même hasardeux, que tout se sçavait De Londres en france, et De france a Londres; et que Le pas serait glissant à La barbe [des] anglais, que sils me Chargeaint De quelque Chose, *peut-etre* auraige Des Reponses qui pouraient Dessider De La Conduite qu'il faudrait tennir: que Du Reste je ne Les Conseillais en aucune espece De façon, que jetais un particulier, Voyageur Curieux; mais que je serais Charmé si par Le moyen De mes *Connoissances*, je pouvais Leur Rendre quelques services, que je ne Les exposerais pas ny moy ny *personne*, que Des affaires De Cette consequence étaient trop Delicates pour y être etourdy, surtout nayant aucun *droit* ny aucun *pouvoir*, que je *netais garant* que D'une Chose, s'etait De ne pas trahir Leur Confiance. Ils ne sont que Cinq Dans Le Conseil privé Dont je Vous dirai Les noms à La fin de ma Lettre: tout Ce qu'ils font est Bien fait et à force sans La sanction Du Congrés, qui est tres nombreux, et ou il

5. Francis Daymon was born in Paris and moved to Philadelphia; he married an American woman and ran a store in the city. He also tutored in French, and Congress employed him in 1776 to translate army regulations into French for use in Canada. He was librarian of the Library Co. from 1774 to 1777, when he resigned and devoted himself to the business of privateering. Hamon, *op. cit.*, pp. 26–7; *Dunlap's Pa. Packet*, Dec. 19, 1776, March 11, 1777; *JCC*, IV, 168; Library Co. minutes; *PMHB*, XXVI (1902), 146–7.

s'est glissé Des feaux freres, ils en ont Decouvert un Ces jours qui a evité sa peinne par La fuite.[6] Jai souvent avec Eux Des entrevues Comme particulier: chaqu'n se Rend Dans L'obscurité, par Des Routes Differantes Dans un Lieu marqué. Ils m'ont Donné Leur Confiance; après Leur avoir Dit que je ne *promettais, noffrais* et ne *Repondais* De Rien, et Les avoir averti *plusieurs* fois que jagirais Comme *particulier Benevole.*

Voici Le Resultat De nos entrevués, Dont eux même m'ont engagé De faire part a mes *Connoissances*, De même que De toutes Celles que nous aurons Dans La suite, et De L'état même De Leurs affaires, sans me Demmander à qui, ni Comment, ny ou je m'addresserais me Regardant Comme homme privé, et Dans Lequel ils ont De La Confiance. . . .[7]

Ils sont persuadés qu'ils ne peuvent se soutennir sans une nation qui Les protege par mer: que Deux seulles puissances sont en état De Les secourir, La france et Lespagne; mais qu'ils scavent faire La Difference De L'une a L'autre. Je Leur ai fait encore sentir adroittement La superiorite en tout genre que Le Roy mon maitre a sur Lespagne, et ils en sont Convainqus. Ils sont même je pense Resollu, peutetre meme Depuis Longtems, De Recclamer sa majesté, mais jentrevois, qu'ils Veullent attendre que La Campagne soit ouverte, parceque Dans Ce pais Beaucoup De gens tiennent encore au Roy, qui ne Leur a pas fait encor assez de mal; ils Verraient peut etre avec inquietude une nation etrangere se mêler De Leurs affaires. Ils Veullent gagner Les esprits, et Leur faire sentir Le Besoin qu'ils ont Dêtre aidés: en Cela je pense qu'ils sont prudents. Ils s'attendent D'avoir Leurs Villes Detruites, et Leurs maisons Brulées, Ce qui achevera De Leur faire abhorrer Les Leopards. Ils ont envoyé, *sans mon Conseil*, un Brigantin a nantes nommé *john*, ou la st. *jean* Capitaine Charles forest addressé a Mr. jean-daniel schweighoẅser.[8]

6. Perhaps a reference to Benjamin Church, although he had not fled; see the note above on the proceedings of the Cambridge conference, under Oct. 18.

7. The omitted passage dealt optimistically and inaccurately with American affairs.

8. This is the first appearance of a man with whom BF, when he arrived in France, had extensive dealings in supplies. Schweighauser (*c.* 1714–81), a Swiss by birth, was an important Protestant merchant in Nantes. We do not know how the committee made contact with him so soon, but by the following

Ce Vaisseau portera ma lettre. Jembarque moy même un homme Dont je suis sur sans Cela je me servirais d'une autre Voye pour Vous ecrire; mais il est important qu'aucun mot ne Vous echape. Voici Les Demmandes qu'ils me prient De presenter pour eux. Le Batiment est Chargé De farine et autres productions du païs, qu'ils ont envie D'echanger Contre d'autres effets, Dune autre nature; Comme La Carguaison D'importation excedera peut être Celle Dexportation, ils prient quon Remplisse Le Chargement, qu'on Leur permette Den faire passer Lexcedant a st. Domaingue, aux Lieux et personnes quon Leur indiquera, et qu'on en Reçoive Le payement en Denrées Du pais n'ayant pas De numeraires. Sil y avait moyen De Leur faire passer La même espece De marchandise en differents endroits De st. Domingue, mes Correspondants Ly iraient Chercher à Leurs *perils* et *Risques*: ils Voudraient Deux hommes Capables De Conduire Des fortifications. Sil en Vient ils irraient Les Chercher au Cap francais qui est La plus sure Route pour Les faire parvennir ici, parceque si par malheur ils etaient pris ils ne Risqueraient Rien, Les habitans De Ces Brulantes Contrées Vennant ici souvent pour Reparer Leur santé. Voici pour Le present Leurs demmandes se Chargeant Des frais, et ils mont prié De Les faire sçavoir a mes Connoissances. Je Leur offrirais Bien mes petits talens pour Le genie, mais je ne peux etre sedantaire, etant obbligé De Courir tous Les jours. . . .[9]

Je ne Leur ai Rien Dit qui peut Leur faire Croire que j'aye Des Correspondances avec Le M[inistr]e, et j'agis Comme particulier, mais je Crois et jen ai de fortes preuves qu'ils simaginnent que je ne suis point Vennu Directement Deurope[1] Dans L'hyver sans de fortes Raisons, ils n'en ont que plus De Confiance en moy et me marquent Des egards on ne peut pas plus flatteurs. Je Vais Vous faire part dun petit Billet que Le Conseil privé ma envoyé Ce matin par Desmonds [Daymon], homme sur et qui mest singulierement utile; j'y ai fait La Reponce que Vous Verrez; après Leur

---

summer it had provided him with funds for military purchases; see Penet to BF below, Aug. 3.

9. The omitted passage stressed further the importance of his role and how well he was performing it, and asked for baggage that he had left behind in Europe.

1. Doniol misread the phrase as "d'Anvers," and "Anvers" reappears in the translation cited above.

avoir *Dit* que Cecÿ se passait Comme De particulier a particulier, et avoir Reçu Les plus fortes assurances, qu'ils ne Le faisaient que pour me Communiquer Leurs doutes et me prier de Les ecclairer Le plus que Le peut faire un homme qui ne se mêle ny ne Connait Les affaires d'état.

Je scai tout Ce qui se passe De plus secret et Leurs Deliberations me sont Communiquées, et en Les flattant et Leur Lachant un peu La main jen ferai Ce que je Voudrai.

Ils m'ont tous dit qu'ils Combattaient pour etre Libres et qu'ils Le seraient à quelque prix que se fut, qu'ils étaient Liés par serment, et quils se feraient hacher plutot que de seder. Qu'ils sçavaient Bien qu'eux seuls ne pouvaient se soutenir par mer, et qu'il ny avait que La france en état De proteger Leur Commerce, sans Le quel Leur pais ne serait guers florissant: quils ignoraient si en cas que Cela en vint aux propositions, La france se Contenterait d'avoir Chez eux pendant un tems limité un Commerce exclusif pour L'indamniser Des frais que Lui occasionnerait Leur Cause, qu'ils ne pouraient pas payer D'une neutralité même D'un peu De secours en Cas de guerre entre Les deux nations, et D'un attachement inviolable, Choses auxquelles ils ne manqueraient jamais.

Jai Repondu que Cela ne me Regardait point, qu'ils etaient prudents et sages; qu'ils Discuteraient Leurs Interests mais que quand L'on demmande on ne fait pas toujours La Loy. Ils sont plus puissants que L'on ne pense, Cela passe même L'Imagination, et vous en seriez surpris. Rien ne Les epouvante. Reglez vous Ladessus.

Le bruit Court, qu'il est arrivé au Camp Deux officiers français Chargés De faire Des propositions,[2] on m'a demmandé Ce que jen Croyais; jai Repondu que je n'en sçavais Rien que Cela me paraissait etrange, que La france etait Bien puissante, et que Loin d'offrir elle n'accordait même pas toujours Ce quon Lui demmandait. . . .[3]

Voici Le Billet que je Viens De Vous annoncer, Dont je garde L'original en anglais Ecrit de La main de Ces Mrs.

Mr. De B . . . est prié De La part de Mrs. Du Conseil privé De

2. Washington paid Penet's and Pliarne's expenses, as mentioned above, but his letters gave no indication that he considered them more than private individuals. *Naval Docs.*, III, 94, 95.

3. The omitted passage contained further self-praise and brief mention of his hardships on the voyage to America.

Considerer et Repondre aux propositions suivantes. Le tout sans tirrer a Consequence et Comme de particulier a particulier. Scavoir.

1°. peut il nous informer Des dispositions De La Cour De france a L'egard des Colonnies Du Nord De L'amerique, si elles sont favorables, et De quelle maniere on en peut avoir une authantique assurance.

2°. Pouvons nous avoir en france Deux habiles ingenieurs surs et Bien Reccommandés, et quelles demarches Devons nous faire pour nous Les obtennir.

3°. Pouvons nous avoir directement en france Des armes et autres provisions De guerre, en Echange Des productions du pais: et nous accordera-t-on une libre entrée et sortie Dans Les ports français.

Mr. De B. peut etre assuré, que, si par Le moyen De ses soins nous pouvons etre eccoutés favorablement nous aurons en Lui toute La Confiance, que Lon puisse Donner à un homme De Distinction, Dont la Bienveuillance pour nous, na pas encore Reçu une marque sure, De notre Recconnoissance.

Voici ma Reponce. Si Cela Reussit ils ont Dit a quelqu'n (de qui je sçai tout Ce qui se passe) qu'ils me Regarderaient Comme un de Leurs membres et ne feraient Rien sans mon Conseil, *ils me Regardent* Comme Leur liberateur.

Reponce De Mr. De B . . . au Billet De Mrs. du Conseil privé.

Je Reponderai, Mrs. a Ce que Vous me faites l'honneur De me demmander Le plus positivement possible, et Vous instruirai, autant, que peut être instruit lui même un homme particulier qui na point de part aux affaires du M[inistè]re. Mais je Vous Reponderai suivant mes Conjectures, La Voix publiques, et quelques avis de mes Connoissances.

1°. Vous Demmandez quelle est L'intention De La france a L'egard Des Colonnies du Nord De L'amerique, je ne Crois point trop avancer, en vous disant quelle Vous Veut du Bien, et quelle na point eu je *Crois* Dautres sentiments pour Vous que De La Bienveuillance. Du Reste pour s'assurer authentiquement des Volontés de quelqu'un il faut si addresser directement. Le pas est scabreux, et demmande Bien des menagements. Je ne Vous donne D'avis ny pour ni Contre. Je ne Le prendrai pas sur moy. L'affaire est trop delicatte.

2°. La france est Bien en etat De Vous Fournir Deux Bons ingen-nieurs, même plus. La seulle demarche, Cest de Les Demmander. Je Lai fait pour Vous, *Mrs.* sans me Rendre garant de La Reussite, quoique je L'espere ayant de Bons Correspondants.

3°. Si Vous pouvez Vous procurer, Des armes et autres munitions, directement en france, en echange de Vos Danrées. Comme Cecy est affaire De marchant a marchant je ne Vois pas De grands incon-venniants De La part de La france. Je Vous addresserai, Même a D'assez Bons Correspondants, sans Me Rendre Responsable de Rien. Vous pouvez L'entreprendre à Vos perils et Risques. Car peut etre L'angleterre ne Vous Laissera pas tranquiles; et Vous ne Devez pas esperer detre deffendus. Du Reste je ne Vous Conseile pas denvoyer tout au Même port. Cela pourait faire du bruit. Jignore si L'on Vous donnera une libre entrée et sortie dans Les ports francais, se serait se declarer ouvertement pour Vous et la guerre pourait sensuivre. Peutetre fermera t'on Lesieux [les yeux], Cest Ce qu'il Vous faut. Jai L'honneur De Vous Repeter, *Mrs.* que je ne Reponds De Rien; je suis Bien peu De Chose, jai de Bonnes Connoissances C'est tout. Si je suis assez heureux pour Reussir je serai trop paye par L'honneur De Votre Confiance, et Le plaisir De Vous servir. Je suis Votre, etc.[4]

Notation: M. de Bonvouloir

The Cumberland County Committee of Correspondence to the Pennsylvania Committee of Safety

Text printed in Samuel Hazard *et al.*, eds., *Pennsylvania Archives* (1st series; 12 vols., Philadelphia and Harrisburg, 1852–56), IV, 693.

⟨Carlisle, December 29, 1775: We understand that troops are to be raised in this province, and believe that we can recruit a complete battalion in this county; we enclose a list of officers whom we recommend.[5] Having officers and men acquainted, when a corps is raised in a small district, serves the common cause and prevents discord, "too often prevalent amongst promiscuous

4. A long postscript, which we have omitted, gave American news, some of it preposterous, and further testimony to the high regard in which Bonvouloir was held.

5. The list immediately follows in the *Pa. Arch.*

Crowds of men." Addressed to Franklin as president of the committee and signed by John Armstrong, Jno. Byers, Robert Miller, John Agnew, and James Pollock, the committee of correspondence of Cumberland County.[6])

George Ross to the Pennsylvania Committee of Safety

ALS: Historical Society of Pennsylvania

⟨Lancaster, December 29, 1775: The bearer, Samuel Atlee, was the eldest captain in the Pennsylvania service when the troops were disbanded at the end of the last war. He told me this morning that he intended to ask the committee of safety to recommend him for command of one of the battalions to be raised on order of the Congress. His character as a gentleman is good among us; his conduct as an officer I have heard well spoken of, and Colonel Miles, with whom he served, knows it well.[7] I recommend him as one who, if appointed, will do honor to the nomination. Many members of the committee are well acquainted with him, and I should not bring any one to their attention unless I were fully satisfied that he deserved it. I am so recently recovered from the

6. For John Armstrong (1717–95), who had acquired a military reputation in the previous war and soon rose to be a general in the current one, see the *DAB*. John Byers (1735–88) was a landholder, justice of the peace, and judge of common pleas in Cumberland Co.: *PMHB*, II (1878), 230–1; III (1879), 240. Robert Miller (*c*. 1724–95) was also a justice of the peace and had been a member of the committee since the summer of 1774; John Agnew, a former prothonotary, was later appointed a justice of the peace. 2 *Pa. Arch.*, IX, 808; *History of Cumberland and Adams Counties* . . . (Chicago, 1886), pp. 27, 78–9, 95 of second pagination; Henry J. Young, *The Spirit of 1775* . . . (Carlisle, Pa., 1975), pp. 12, 14. For James Pollock (d. 1800) see the *PMHB*, LXXIV (1950), 451 n.

7. Samuel J. Atlee (1739–86) and Samuel Miles (1739–1805) were not only of an age but had interconnected careers. Both emerged from the French and Indian War as captains, when Atlee retired to a farm near Lancaster and Miles became an Assemblyman. In March, 1776, they were both commissioned as colonels of Pennsylvania units, Atlee of a militia battalion and Miles of a continental rifle regiment. Both were captured at the Battle of Long Island, and remained prisoners until 1778. Atlee then served in Congress. Samuel W. Pennypacker, "Samuel John Atlee," *PMHB*, II, (1878), 74–84. W. A. Newman Dorland, "The Second Troop Philadelphia City Cavalry," *ibid.*, XLVI (1922),

gout that traveling would be dangerous in this severe weather;[8] otherwise I should attend the committee on Tuesday next. Addressed to Franklin as president of the committee.)

From Israel Gilpin[9]

ALS: American Philosophical Society

Sir   Wilmington Decmr the 29d 1775

My kinsman Doct. George Gilpin[1] informs me that Severil of the manufactorys is like to Suffer for want of Stone or ground Coal Such as the glass work and blacksmith who is imployd in making Iron work for the Coloneys Ships &c. I think it is very provible if Strict Sarch and inquiry was made Coal mout bee had but am not sirtin but prohaps it wold Not bee a mis for the Congres or Committy to give som Direccions to som pirsons who the may think proper. I know of Severil plasis whar I have Saw Coal but for the quontity I Cant Say I Saw Coal Dug out of tusseys hill not three miles from heer and one mill [mile] from Delawa river. I have offen found Coal in Chester county neer whair I was born ten miles from the river. Inqure of Thomas Gilpin mirchant in Phila if he has no Coal by him that was sent him from Elk by his brother[2] or if occasion I wil goe down and See. I am apt to think their is plenty 12 miles from Christiana crick. Inquire of Robart Lewis mirchant of phila if he knows of aney Coal [in?] his Land in

---

72–3. For Atlee see also *Biographical Directory of the American Congress* . . . ([Washington,] 1971).

8. See his earlier letter above, Dec. 10.

9. Information about Gilpin (1740–1834) is fragmentary. He moved with his family in the early 1760's from Birmingham, Pa., to Christiana Hundred, Del., and by this time was living in Wilmington and was an officer in the Delaware militia. After the war he went to Kentucky, where he died. Gilbert Cope and Henry G. Ashmead, *Historic Homes and Institutions . . . of Chester and Delaware Counties, Pennsylvania* . . . (2 vols., New York and Chicago, 1904), I, 177; J. Thomas Scharf, *History of Delaware* . . . (2 vols., Philadelphia, 1888), II, 686; George P. Perkins, *The Kentucky Gilmans* (Washington, D.C., 1927), pp. 34–38; National Soc. of the Daughters of the Amer. Revolution, *Lineage Book*, CLVII (1937), 191.

1. Perhaps the George Gilpin of Birmingham who was read out of the Chester meeting in 1775: Geneal. Soc. of Pa., *Pubs.*, XIII (1941), 131.

2. Thomas Gilpin has appeared a number of times in these volumes; see in particular above, XVI, 31–2. For his brother Joseph see Thomas Gilpin, Jr., "Memoir of Thomas Gilpin," *PMHB*, XLIX (1925), 290.

Newlin township Chester County.[3] I was informd by a gentilman
who livs neer his Land that there was Coal their. As the Congres
is now a promoting Every yousful art and sians as well as prosirv-
ing our Libarteys and properteys I have thaught it mout bee of
youse to imploy Som honist Scilful men to make Sarch for Sulfer
Coal &c. as it mout bee of immediate youse and sirvis and if a
raconsileacion Shold take plase thees things wold bee of infinate
youse to our posterity. From your most obediand Sirvant
ISRAEL GILPIN

Addressed: To / Doct: / Bengemin Franklin / Philadelphia

From Robert Strettell Jones[4]

ALS: Library of Congress

Sir,   30th. Decr 1775
   Col. Lewis of Lower Dublin has ordered the Bearer to deliver
these Prisoners to me as Secretary of the Committee of this City
and Liberties; but apprehending them to fall more properly under
the Notice of the Committee of Safety I have taken the Liberty of
referring to you for your Orders being Sir Your most obedient
humble Servant   R STRETTELL JONES

Addressed: Honble: Benjamin Franklin Esqr / President of the /
Committee of Safety.

---

3. For the little that is known about Lewis (1714–90) and his land see
Thomas A. Glenn, *Merion in the Welsh Tract* . . . (Baltimore, 1970), p. 237;
Pennsylvania Genealogical Magazine, XVI (1948), 62; J. Smith Futhey and Gilbert Cope, *History of Chester County, Pennsylvania* . . . (Philadelphia, 1881),
pp. 189–90, 635.

4. He has appeared frequently in earlier volumes as a member of the Library
Company; see for example XVIII, 18. He appears now as secretary of the Philadelphia committee of inspection and observation, to which he had been elected
the previous August: *Pa. Gaz.*, Aug. 23, 1775. The committee of safety was
much concerned with prisoners at the time, but its minutes do not identify this
particular group or Col. Lewis. Lower Dublin is in Philadelphia Co.

To Robert Morris

AL:[5] Library of Congress

[On or after December 30, 1775]

Mr. Franklin presents his Compliments to Mr. Morris, and not knowing what was done by the Committee with regard to the other Prisoners, requests Mr. Morris would direct what is to be done with these.

Addressed: To / Robt Morris Esqr

Proposed Preamble to a Congressional Resolution

AD (incomplete draft): American Philosophical Society

The nature of this fragment is clear enough: it is to introduce a resolution, undoubtedly by Congress, authorizing some action against the crown. But what action is impossible to say. The preamble was not adopted and hence not recorded in the *Journals*, and its language is too general to identify the measure it was intended to justify. One possibility is the resolutions that sanctioned privateering in March, 1776. They began with a recital of the colonists' grievances, and an amendment was offered "wherein the King was made the Author of our Miseries instead of the Ministry." The amendment did not carry.[6] The description of it, vague as it is, does not seem to fit the present document; in 1776, furthermore, Franklin had in mind another preamble, and, although he might conceivably have been considering two at once, this appears implausible. The one that we know he composed at that time stressed the Prohibitory Act, which lay behind the Congressional resolutions, and laid the blame for it on the British nation.[7] The statute is not mentioned here, where the argument is quite different: allegiance becomes void when the King is demonstrably responsible for hostile acts. The fact that the acts mentioned, burning towns and inciting the Indians, were all ones that were much on Franklin's mind in late 1775 is our reason for guessing that the draft belongs to that period.

---

5. BF penciled this note at the bottom of the preceding one, then crossed out his own name on the address and penciled in Morris'. By now BF had withdrawn from the committee of safety, although he attended a few meetings in January, and Morris had taken his place; see the editorial note on the committee above, June 30.

6. Smith, *Letters*, III, 427; *JCC*, IV, 229–30.

7. See BF's draft below, under March 23.

[1775?]

And whereas whenever Kings instead of Protecting the Lives and Properties of their Subjects as is their bounden Duty, do endeavour to perpetrate the Destruction of either, they thereby cease to be Kings, become Tyrants, and dissolve all Ties of Allegiance between themselves and their People; we hereby farther solemnly declare, that whenever it shall appear clearly to us that the King's Troops or Ships now in America, or hereafter to be brought there, do *by his Majesty's Orders*, destroy any Town or the Inhabitants of any Town or Place in America, or that the Savages have been by the same Orders hired to assassinate our poor Outsettlers, and their Families [*torn*] that time renounce all Alleg[iance *half-line missing*]tain, so long as that King's [*half-line missing*] submit to him or any of his [*remainder missing*.]

Export License from the Secret Committee

DS: University of Pennsylvania Library

⟨Philadelphia, January 9, 1776, to the New Hampshire committee of inspection: The secret committee, as empowered by the Congress, authorizes John Langdon of New Hampshire[8] to export to the amount of $10,000 the produce of the colonies, in their service and according to the Continental Association;[9] horned cattle, sheep, hogs, and poultry are excepted. Signed by Samuel Ward, John Alsop, Josiah Bartlett, Robert Morris,[1] and Franklin; attestation by John Hancock that the signers are a quorum of the committee and have the requisite authority.⟩

8. Langdon (1741–1819) was a merchant and politician and member of the Continental Congress: *DAB*.

9. As amended by BF's resolution above, under July 14.

1. Morris had succeeded Thomas Willing as a member of the committee. For John Alsop (1724–94), the only signer not in the *DAB*, see *Biographical Directory of the American Congress* . . . ([Washington,] 1961), p. 475.

Contract between the Secret Committee and Oswell Eve and George Losch[2]

Text printed in Samuel Hazard, *et al.*, eds., *Pennsylvania Archives* (1st series; 12 vols., Philadelphia and Harrisburg, 1852–56), IV, 696.

⟨January 11, 1776: It is agreed between the undersigned members of the committee and Oswell Eve and George Losch, of Philadelphia County, that Eve and Losch will manufacture all the saltpetre delivered to them by the committee during the next year into good gunpowder, provide the necessary sulphur and charcoal at their own expense, refine the saltpetre and carry it to the powder mills, and deliver the powder to Philadelphia as the committee directs; that they will be paid eight dollars for each hundred-weight of good powder so delivered; and that they will provide good, seasoned barrels, half-barrels, and quarter-barrels as directed and receive half the cost thereof. Signed by Franklin, Joshua Bartlett, Silas Deane, Thomas McKean, Robert Morris, and Samuel Ward for the committee, and by Oswell Eve and George Losch.⟩

From Catharine Greene   ALS: American Philosophical Society

My Dear Friend   Warwick Jany the 13th [1776]
    I Some times feel quite Bashfull Scribling a way to you So much but when troublesom a hint will do. But now I think of it it will Relax you for a moment from hard Study. How do you do Methinks Rather low Spirited. I have every letter Sayd or inquerd after Ray but Never of you of My Dear good Friend your Sister. Is

2. Eve was, we assume, the sea captain who had forwarded a story that much interested BF about a house struck by lightning in Jamaica: above, XX, 4. We said there that he returned "temporarily" from the Caribbean in 1774 and then left for the Bahamas, but he was in Pennsylvania much longer than that implies. He established the celebrated Frankford powder mill near Philadelphia, and maintained it throughout the British occupation; the result was a charge of treason, which doubtless explains his departure. 1 *Pa. Arch.*, XI, 494; "Extracts from the Journal of Miss Sarah Eve," *PMHB*, V (1881), 19–20; David L. Salay, "The Production of Gunpowder in Pennsylvania during the American Revolution," *ibid.*, XCIX (1975), 423–6, 429–30. George Losch or Lush was a powder-maker in Germantown: Edward W. Hocker, *Germantown, 1683–1933* (Germantown, Pa., 1933), p. 117.

324

She not extreem low Spirited for her? Dear Lady what Continued Sceenes of Misfortunes She has waded throw enough to have buried Seeverial Such as your friend.[3] Mr. Greene is most all the while gone but Comes home with a Smile and I Smile again. Is not that as you used to tell me? I impute Great Part of the happiness of my life to the Pleasing lessons you gave me in that Journey.[4] For those and all favors allow me to Subscribe my Self your most obligd friend   CATY GREENE

Addressed: To / Doctr Franklin / Philadelphia

Editorial Note on the Reorganization of the Indiana Company, January 19 to March 20, 1776

The Indiana Company, which represented the claim of the "suffering traders" to whom the Indians had ceded land at Fort Stanwix in 1768, contained a number of Americans who were not traders, William Franklin and Joseph Galloway among them. When the Company was absorbed into the Grand Ohio or Walpole Company at the end of 1769, the claim of the former became part of the grant for which the latter was negotiating in London.[5] For the next five years and more the senior Franklin, as far as we know, had no concern with the Indiana Company as such; he was focused on the vastly larger Walpole scheme. Then in the spring of 1775 the promoters in London, through William Trent as their agent, moved to put parcels of their land on the American market before the crown had confirmed their grant. What parcels they had in mind is not clear, but those that they believed they had legal ground for selling were within the Indiana claim.[6] Perhaps as a consequence, the Indiana Company began to re-emerge as a separate entity; its shareholders held meetings, first in western Pennsylvania and then in Philadelphia, to consider their prospects.[7]

Franklin apparently became involved for the first time in December, to safeguard his son's interests. He attended a meeting in Philadelphia

3. For her son Ray see William Greene to BF above, Nov. 13. Jane Mecom's troubles are explained in her letter to Caty of Nov. 24.
4. From Boston to Westerly in December, 1754: above, v, 502–3.
5. Above, XVI, 163; XVII, 8; XX, 304 n.
6. See the headnotes above, April 11 and July 12.
7. Lewis, *Indiana Co.*, pp. 164–7, 169–70; Sewell E. Slick, *William Trent and the West* (Harrisburg, Pa., 1947), p. 161; Thomas Wharton to William Trent, Nov. 8, 1775, Thomas Wharton letterbook, Hist. Soc. of Pa., pp. 173–4.

just after Christmas, at which were discussed plans that Galloway had made for reorganizing the company.[8] The discussions continued into the new year, and Franklin seems to have played a part in them.[9] They produced five documents in January that he signed as agent for his son: to appoint three trustees for the company, to convert it into a joint-stock enterprise, to define the rights of shareholders and set a date for a meeting in March that would name a president and vice-president, to appoint a secretary and receiver general, and to appoint a surveyor general; the proceedings of the March meeting Franklin also signed.[1] He subsequently paid his son's share of costs incurred in the reorganization.[2] This caretaking may seem odd at a time when he and the Governor were thoroughly estranged, but it probably stemmed from concern for the family. The old man was finding in his grandson a replacement of sorts for the son he had lost, and William's claim to potential riches would be part of Temple's legacy.[3]

Contract between the Secret Committee and John Brown[4]

Copy with DS by Nicholas Brown: John Carter Brown Library

⟨[Before Jan. 20, 1776]: Agreed between John Brown on the one part and members of the committee on the other that a voyage or

8. Thomas to Samuel Wharton, Jan. 1, 1776, *ibid.*, pp. 185–8.

9. To judge by a few obscure references in another letter of Thomas to his brother, Feb. 25, *ibid.*, pp. 196–7.

1. The documents, in copy and dated Jan. 19, 20, 25, and March 20, are in a volume of the company's deeds and indentures in the Hist. Soc. of Pa.; they are summarized in Lewis, *op. cit.*, pp. 185–8, 190–2. See also Albert T. Volwiler, *George Croghan and the Westward Movement, 1741–1782* (Cleveland, O., 1926), pp. 298–300; Max Savelle, *George Morgan, Colony Builder* (New York, 1932), pp. 81–7. We have found no evidence for Savelle's statement on p. 86, plausible as it is, that BF played a major part in settling differences.

2. Memorandum book (above, VII, 167–8), Oct. 2, 1776.

3. WF was confirmed, thanks to his father, in more than 5,000 shares of the roughly 80,000 in the reorganized company: Lewis, *op. cit.*, p. [316]. In 1785, when BF met his son in England, he witnessed an agreement by which WF made over half his shares to WTF; the other half he conveyed in his will. Vanderpoel Papers, New York Public Library.

4. For Brown (1736–1803), one of the four brothers who made up the internationally known house of Nicholas Brown & Co., see the *DAB*. The firm had an entrée to the committee through Samuel Ward, also a Rhode Islander, and contact with Penet and Pliarne, and became a major American mercantile link with France. The present contract, printed in extenso in *Naval Docs.*, III, 879–80, grew out of the Congressional resolutions of Jan. 3 empowering the

voyages will be undertaken to procure thirty-six tons of gunpowder (or, failing that, sufficient saltpetre and sulphur to make up
the same amount), 1,000 stand[5] of good arms, 1,000 gun locks,
twenty tons of lead, and 1,000 bolts of canvas. If the arms are
unprocurable their value will be put into gunpowder or its ingre-
dients, if they also are unprocurable into linen goods, and if none
of these is procurable into gold and silver. Freight will be paid on
the vessels' return; they will be chartered for the use of the United
Colonies, which will insure them against British capture while
the owners will run the risk of the sea. Brown will employ competent crews, and will receive a 5% commission for buying new
cargoes abroad. He will be advanced $20,000 in continental cur-
rency, for which he will render an account to the United Colonies,
who will bear the whole risk[6] of the adventure. The returning
ships will be unloaded east of Chesapeake Bay and the committee
notified as soon as possible of the location. Signed "the Day and
Year aforesaid"[7] by Brown and by Franklin, Josiah Bartlett,
Thomas McKean, Robert Morris, and Samuel Ward for the committee.

Providence, Jan. 20, 1776: An acknowledgment by Nicholas
Brown[8] that he has received from John Brown $4,666⅔; that sum
together with $2,000 sent to Nantucket to buy oil make up his
one-third share in the contract, for which he will be accountable
to the committee.⟩

Notes for a Report from the Committee of [Secret] Correspondence
Two ADs:[9] National Archives

The arrival of captives taken in Canada, and the camp followers who
were with them, created a new set of problems for the towns where the

---

committee to import dry goods as well as arms and ammunition: *JCC*, IV,
24-5.
    5. A stand was equipment for a single soldier.
    6. In other words the profit or loss involved.
    7. The contract is nevertheless undated.
    8. The eldest brother (1729-91), for whom see the *DAB*. The whole ac-
knowledgment is in his hand.
    9. BF's two sets of notes, which we have numbered, are separated in the
papers of the Continental Congress, although they must have been written at
virtually the same time.

uninvited guests were billeted. Local authorities, hard pressed to house and feed the new arrivals, took their difficulties to Congress, which followed its usual practice of referring such matters and others to standing or ad hoc committees. The Congressional *Journals* are often uninformative about why these committees were given particular assignments, and the referral to which Franklin is responding here is a case in point. On January 25, 1776, Congress asked what it designated as the committee of correspondence to report on four letters.[1] One was from a local committee, one from a captured surgeon, one from a group of British officers in custody, and one from General Washington. Those letters had one thing in common: they were not the business of the standing committee appointed the previous November, which later came to be known as the committee of secret correspondence; its rubric was to maintain contact with friends of America abroad.[2] But Congress seems to have been so busy improvising a workable system that it ignored its own rubrics and used that committee, at least in its early months, for other kinds of correspondence.[3] Franklin and his fellow members had a Pandora's box of problems.

I.   [After January 25, 1776]

The Committee to whom the Letter from the Committee of Trenton was referred, are of Opinion,

That the Receipt thereof be acknowledged, and the Thanks of the Congress express'd for the Readiness with which its Orders relating to Gen. Prescot and Capt. Chace had been executed.[4]

1. *JCC*, IV, 87, 90–1.
2. See the headnote on the committee's letter to Lee above, Nov. 30.
3. A better substantiated example is the report to Congress below, Feb. 14, which dealt with a matter that was again outside the committee's rubric. The writers there refer to themselves, as far as we know for the first time, as the committee of secret correspondence; the adjective did not appear in the *JCC* until May: IV, 345.
4. The letter of Jan. 23 from the Trenton committee (National Archives) acknowledged an order from Congress the day before to send the two prisoners to Philadelphia. Brig. Gen. Richard Prescott had been captured in Canada; he was kept in close confinement, until ill health brought him relief, as reprisal for the way he had treated Ethan Allen as a captive in Montreal, and was later exchanged for Gen. Sullivan. Robert Chase had commanded the *Gaspée*, the brig on which Carleton had tried to reach Quebec, and had been captured with her in November; he was eventually returned to Trenton, paroled, and then sent to York, Pa. *JCC*, IV, 23, 78, 101, 112; Richard Cannon, *The Historical Record of the Seventh Regiment, or the Royal Fusiliers . . .* (London, 1847), p. 108; Chris-

The Same Committee on considering Dr. Huddlestone's Letter, are of Opinion

That he be immediately set at Liberty on the Terms he mentions. And that a verbal Proposition be sent by him to General Carleton to enter into a Stipulation on both sides, not only to release all Physicians and Surgeons; but that if by the Fortune of War, the Hospital of either Army should fall into the Power of the other, the same Subsistence and Supplies should be afforded to the Sick and Wounded as if Friends; and that neither they nor the Attendants of the Hospital should be considered or detain'd as Prisoners. And it is farther the Opinion of the Committee, that if Govr. Carleton should not agree to the mutual Release of Surgeons Dr. Huddlestone is to be on his Parole to return immediately hither.[5]

Notation: Report on Letter from Come. of Trenton and on Dr. Huddleston's Letter Pospon'd 1776

II.

Agreed to set Dr. Huddlestone at Liberty on the Terms he mentions. And send by him a Proposition to Gen. Carleton, that it be Stipulated on both Sides, not only to release all Surgeons; but that if by the Fortune of War, the Hospital of either Army should fall into the Power of the other, the same Care should be taken of the Sick and Wounded as if Friends, and that nether they nor the Attendants of the Hospital should be considered as Prisoners. And if Govr. Carleton should not agree to the mutual release of Surgeons, Dr. Huddleston is to be on his Parole to return immediately.[6]

------

topher Ward, *The War of the Revolution* (John R. Alden, ed.; 2 vols., New York, 1952), I, 260; 2 *Pa. Arch.*, I, 410.

5. On Jan. 23 Richard Huddleston, the surgeon of Prescott's regiment, explained in a dignified letter to Congress (National Archives) that he had given all the assistance he could to sick American soldiers retreating from Canada, and asked to be sent back because Quebec needed surgeons. They were friends to both sides, he argued, and by the rules of war might not be made prisoner; he promised if returned to carry no intelligence.

6. This repetitive paragraph, we conjecture, was BF's draft of a resolution on which Congress did not act.

Officers Answer at Lancaster

1. To be left on the Footing it was plac'd on in our Letter of the 18th.[7]

2. Resolve related merely to the Officers at Trenton, no Complaint having been received of those at Lancaster.[8]

3. 2 Dollars per Week was the Allowance of Congress, the Officers may refuse it or add to it on their own Acct as they please.

4. Enquire the meaning[9]—High Accounts from Trenton.

5. See the Resolution of Congress—express Stronger than before what relates to Gen. Schuyler's Promise.[1]

6. We shall be extreamly sorry to be reduc'd to the Necessity of confining them in Prison if they cancel their Parole.

7. Cloathing ordered by us. Their Cloathing ordered to be brought up.[2]

8. Provided for in our former Letter.[3]

9. and 10. It is not desired to remove any Officer to the Prejudice of his Health. Directions given in former Letter relating to the Women and Children.[4]

7. The Lancaster committee had reported difficulties with the British officers in custody there, and on Jan. 18 Congress had sent advice on how to handle the problems: *JCC*, IV, 66–7. The committee replied on Jan. 22, enclosing the officers' answer to that letter: National Archives. BF's notes are on points raised in the answer, in this case a query whether bills that the officers drew for their support would be honored.

8. On Jan. 12 Congress had castigated the officers for their extravagance, and limited captured officers to a weekly allowance of two dollars: *JCC*, IV, 51–2.

9. The officers explained that they were billeted in taverns, which were expensive.

1. This was an old issue. The officers had complained that the paroles they had given were conditioned on Schuyler's promise not to separate them from their men. The Congressional letter of Jan. 18 pointed out that the General had said nothing about such a promise and had no authority to make it; the officers' answer insisted that it had been made and confirmed by Congress.

2. The private soldiers, according to their officers, had too little clothing to cover themselves.

3. The officers contended that when the baggage arrived they had to be with their men to insure a fair distribution. The letter of the 18th allowed two to be present for the purpose of paying the soldiers.

4. The officers explained that they could not change quarters because they were short of baggage and many were in bad health. Their answer closed by thanking Congress for promising, in its letter, to repay the Lancaster committee for the food it was distributing to the women and children.

Gen. Washington's Letter

All the Tent Cloth to be got, shall be forwarded. Some arrived in Maryland.

No Arms to spare here. Write to the Assemblys &c. to strengthen G. Washington's Application.[5]

The Carlisle Committee of Correspondence to the Pennsylvania Committee of Safety

Text printed in Samuel Hazard *et al.*, eds., *Pennsylvania Archives* (1st series; 12 vols., Philadelphia and Harrisburg, 1852–56), IV, 706.

⟨Carlisle, January 26, 1776: We have received your request of the 11th to send people to Philadelphia to learn the method used at the saltpetre works there and communicate it on their return. We recommend Jonathan Kearsley, who already has some knowledge of the process; he is willing, and will be able both to manufacture and to instruct others.[6] In response to your letter of the 12th we have appointed Robert Miller to receive the saltpetre manufactured in the county.[7] Addressed to Franklin as president of the committee of safety and signed by William Irvine, Ephraim Blaine, John Byers, and John Montgomery.[8]⟩

5. In his letter, Jan. 14, Washington requested tents. He also stressed the shortage of arms; he was asking the assemblies of Mass. and adjacent colonies for whatever weapons could be spared. Fitzpatrick, *Writings of Washington*, IV, 237–9.

6. Kearsley (1718–82) came from Scotland and was a druggist in Carlisle: [Elmer L. White,] *The Descendants of Jonathan Kearsley* . . . (n. p., 1900), pp. [3]–6. He reported to the committee of safety in March that he was making no headway in the manufacture: 1 *Pa. Arch.*, IV, 727–8.

7. Miller was a signer of the Cumberland Co. committee's letter above, Dec. 29.

8. Irvine was later captured at Trois Rivières; see Wayne to BF below, June 13, 1776. For Ephraim Blaine see Smith, *Letters*, III, 673 n., and for John Montgomery *PMHB*, LXXIV (1950), 451 n., and above, XII, 94 n. All three were Irish by birth. Byers, like Miller, was a signer of the Cumberland Co. committee's letter above, Dec. 29.

The York County Committee to the Pennsylvania
Committee of Safety
LS: Amherst College Library

⟨York, January 29, 1776: The committee's recommendation of officers was made, because the time was so short, without consulting them. Personal affairs prevent Barnet Eichelberger from serving; he has given his reasons in writing, and they are valid.[9] His letter deals partly with private matters and is not enclosed; his lieutenant colonel will return the commission to Philadelphia. In his place John Edey (Edie) is recommended as first lieutenant; he is well behaved, well qualified, and so well connected that "he will have the greatest Influence in raising Men." Please obtain the commission from the Congress and send it by the Lancaster post "or some safe hand." Addressed to Franklin, Robert Morris, Owen Biddle, and the committee of safety and signed by James Smith, Chairman, and Michael Swoope.[1]⟩

Memorandum Concerning the Snow *Dickinson*
AD: American Philosophical Society

On December 26, 1775, the secret committee contracted with Bayard & Jackson of Philadelphia to spend $15,000 on flour and other produce to be exchanged at Nantes for gunpowder, arms, and cloth. The firm had had earlier dealings with Montaudoüin et frère of Nantes, to whom it entrusted the new transaction.[2] The ship selected was the *Dickinson* or

9. For the recommendations see the committee's letter above, Dec. 23, 1775. Eichelberger's commission was issued, nevertheless, on Jan. 9; and his resignation became effective on Feb. 5. Heitman, *Register of Officers*, p. 165.

1. John Edie had been commissioned as a second lieutenant on Jan. 9 and was promoted to first on Feb. 5, presumably in Eichelberger's place. He was wounded and captured during the retreat from Canada and exchanged almost two years later. *Ibid.*, p. 164. For Smith and Swoope see the letters from York above, respectively, Oct. 4 and Aug. 31.

2. *Lee Family Papers*, roll 2, frame 541. The brothers, Arthur Montaudoüin and Jean-Gabriel Montaudoüin de la Touche, were among the greatest merchants in Nantes and were sympathetic to the American cause. Jean-Gabriel (1722–81), who later became closely associated with BF, was a writer as well as a merchant, and a correspondent of the Académie royale des sciences. *Index biographique des membres et correspondants de l'Académie . . .* (Paris, 1954), p. 365; Jean Meyer, *L'Armement nantais dans la deuxième moitié du XVIIIe siècle* (Paris,

Dickenson, Capt. William Meston. Pierre Penet had intended to return on her with his list of American requirements, but changed to a faster vessel before the snow sailed in the latter part of January.[3] The shift was lucky for him and the American cause, for the *Dickinson* never reached Nantes: when she was at sea her crew, learning the purpose of the voyage, mutinied and carried her in to Bristol. This contretemps caused great embarrassment to the French government as well as to the Montaudoüins.[4]

Penet and his partner, Emmanuel de Pliarne, appeared before Congress on December 30 and were referred to the secret committee.[5] Franklin must have written this memorandum for the committee at some time after that and before he knew that Penet was not returning by the *Dickinson*; early January seems the most likely date.

[January, 1776]

The Proof to be inserted[6]
Mr. Penet to give us his Address
We are to give him the Address of Mr. John Daniel Schweighauser
   Mercht. at Nantes.[7]

The Snow Dickinson; Capt

Charter Party between the Secret Committee and Joseph Harper and James King   DS: The Rosenbach Foundation

⟨February 1, 1776: The agreement is between members of the committee and James King and Joseph Harper, Philadelphia merchants and owners of the brigantine *Cornelia* of approximately 100

1969), *passim*; Gaston Martin, "Commercial Relations between Nantes and the American Colonies," *Jour. of Economic and Business History*, IV (1932), 821–2.

3. For Penet's list see the headnote above, Dec. 28, and for his change of plan *Naval Docs.*, IV, 1025. The *Dickinson* sailed after Jan. 18, for she carried a letter of that date from Bayard & Jackson: *Lee Family Papers*, roll 2, frame 541.

4. Smith, *Letters*, II, 523; *Naval Docs.*, III, 771–2; IV, 1023–5, 1058–9, 1074–5; Crout, "Diplomacy of Trade," pp. 104–9. Jean-Gabriel, nevertheless, was for a time Vergennes' choice as forwarding agent for the funds that the King planned to furnish the Americans in secret: Doniol, *Histoire*, I, 372.

5. *JCC*, III, 466.

6. Bayard & Jackson's contract stipulated only that the gunpowder should be good; see the *Lee Family Papers, loc. cit.* BF presumably meant that the committee should stipulate the quality with more precision.

7. See the note on Bonvouloir to de Guines above, Dec. 28.

tons,[8] Thomas Genn master, to hire her for a voyage to France. She is to sail to a port in South Carolina to be subsequently designated, there to be loaded with rice, indigo, or whatever the committee's agents select; she is to deliver her cargo at Nantes, replace it with whatever the committee's agents there may choose, and return to a port between Virginia and New Hampshire and deliver her goods to the order of the committee. She will be in good condition and well provisioned and manned. The owners will pay all the expenses, and the crew will give the customary assistance in loading and unloading and diligently performing their duties.

The committee will pay £120 Pennsylvanian per month for the hire of the ship, from the date of the charter party until the day after she returns to Philadelphia or the day when she is sunk or captured. If she is captured, the committee will also pay her assessed value of £650 Pennsylvanian. Each party binds itself, if it defaults, to pay the other £2,000 Pennsylvanian. Signed by Harper and King and by Franklin, Josiah Bartlett, Joseph Hewes, Thomas McKean, Robert Morris, and Samuel Ward for the committee.⟩

From Trevor Newland[9]   ALS: New-York Historical Society

Sir   Stafford 5th. Feby. 1776.

Immediately after I had waited upon you at Philada. I proceeded to N. York, and finding much difficulty in pursuing my Intended journey, I deliver'd your Dispatches to Mr. Lewis, by

8. She was registered in September, 1773, as thirty tons. *PMHB*, XXVIII (1904), 477. For an annotated text of the contract see Smith, *Letters*, III, 184–5.

9. We are almost sure that he was the same man who had written BF from Wiltshire in 1765 and about whom our predecessors drew a blank: above, XII, 105. The handwriting of the two letters is not identical, but the eleven-year interval between them may account for the slight differences. In 1765 Newland was engaged in unsuccessful recruiting, and hence was beyond doubt an army officer; this letter harps on his twenty-eight years of varied military experience "both abroad, and at home, during both the late wars." At some time between 1765 and 1770 he moved to America, for in the latter year he was appointed a justice of the peace in Monmouth Co., N.J.: *N.J. Arch.*, XVIII, 177–8. Stafford, from which he writes, was then in that county, and the meeting at Freehold to which he refers was at the county seat. He seems to have obtained some

Direction of Mr. Van B. Levingston, and wrote to you at my return acquainting you therewith.[1] I have not wrote to you so frequently as I would do Immagining that your time might be Employ'd better in Matters of Greater moment to the publick, and where publick Utility is in question apologys become un-necssary, please therefore to accept the following hints from one who has seen service. I'm amazed at a ship or two laying at N. York for some time past in open Violation of the United Provinces, I never saw two Vessels that lay in more danger were they At-tack'd, and they as well know it, the Asia lay long in the North River and refused to go into the Sound, until Parker a Senr. Capt. was sent with a ship to reinforce him, with positive orders from the Admiral to go in,[2] it may also be seen by their writing to the Mayor,[3] and by Parkers treatning, and bullying the Town. There is three ways of taking or destroying them, could it be kept secret, first by boarding for as the Asia must Ground at low water the springs upon her Cabels would be of no use, and I apprehend that her lower Guns could not range over the wharf when a Ground, therefore, a few guns with Grape shot run down upon the Wharfs upon her bow and quarter, would efectually sweep and Clear her decks while the people Boarded. Secondly if there was mortars or even Guns to through combustable matter on the decks, into the Riging, to stick on her sides, with grape as before, to prevent extinguishment, the guns with the grape would be out of the power of her Guns while a ground. The 3d and best method as I

military appointment, because he subsequently left for Quebec; see his wife's letter below, Aug. 12. We have found no later record of him.

1. The disappearance of his letter to BF leaves us in the dark about the dispatches that he carried to Francis Lewis, who was one of the New York delegates to Congress; see the DAB. For Peter Van Brugh Livingston see the letter from the N.Y. provincial congress above, Aug. 16.

2. H.M.S. Asia, a ship of the line, had been at New York since the previous May. H.M.S. Phoenix, a heavy frigate under the command of Capt. Hyde Par-ker, Jr. (1739–1807; see the DNB), had been commissioned the previous sum-mer to replace a ship of the line on the American station. On Dec. 20 the two vessels moved from an anchorage off the Battery to one in the East River, where they remained. Naval Docs., I, 541, 1322; III, 195, 1125, 1137, 1217–18. Vice Adm. Molyneux Shuldham commanded on the station.

3. The previous August, when New Yorkers had removed the guns from the Battery, the Asia had opened fire to try to dissuade them. A correspondence ensued between her captain and Mayor Whitehead Hicks: ibid., I, 1221–7.

immagin, I would undertake myself with a reasonable person to Command the detachment, as second in Command or Ingineer, or Conductor of the Works, or as I told you, in any Character so that I might be servisable to the Cause. The method I will here lay down as well as I can, there is Long Island and Nutten Island[4] well situate'd to place Guns, and I immagin three or four hundred men would be Sifficient to Compleat all the works that would be Necessary in one night, the greatest difficulty would be to get Cannon to Nutten Island, but they might come from the Narrows by night in flats, it would be Imposible to point out either the facilitys, or difficultys, of the undertaking in the Course of a letter, the greatest difficulty will be to keep it sacred [secret] from the people of N. York. It occur'd to me when they went to quel the Torys upon Long Island that it would be a good time, but there might be a divertion of the like kind, and on the same or on any other that might keep it Secret from the people of Stattan Island, Long Island, and N. York, whome I look upon to be Very rotten, and to have done much hurt. If this matter is not soon put in execution, they will be reinforced or they will fall into the N. River,[5] but if there was a lodgment with some Guns upon Nutten Island, with the Town Battery to Assist, the Could not get out without runing a Ground. As soon as the Batterys upon Long Island, and Nutten Island, begin to play there should be some of the Connecticut men, or some others, ready to run down upon the wharfs with some few Guns a head and a Stern, with grape, to Clear the decks, and fire into the ports while loading.[6] The batterys will have this advantage, that they Can play by night if Clear, this method will so harres and disable them that they must strike quicly, or they will be boarded, when this affair is finished the men Should Immediately march to the Narrows, and Erect a battery that would keep all out, and all In. 20 Guns would Sink any Vessel that would dare attempt to go up properly disposed of, and would be out of the range of all shot from shiping, your Crusers would find Shelter and a good harbour, had this been done last summer, our Enemies at Boston would Starve e'ar this.[7] There

4. Now Governor's Island.
5. The ships, that is, will fall back to the Hudson.
6. While the guns, inboard for loading, left the ports open.
7. Perhaps he means that a safe anchorage at the Narrows would have permitted cruisers to raid British supply ships bound for Boston.

336

should be a Camp formed there early in the Spring, and two Strong Forts Erected with retrenchments to Cover them, for you may depend upont there will be a Vigorous push made early to get up the north river, works upon each[?] Side would greatly retard and delay their Opperations, and I doubt not but defeat the design of the Campaign. To attack both, they must divide their Army, which would greatly harres them, and if they wait to attack them one after another the Campaign is lost, besides the Attacks made upon them at Landing within the Vicinity and perhaps under cover of these forts, and retrenchments, also the attacks on their rear, while they are attacking the works. In short we have every thing in our favor to defeat the Ensuing Campaign, if we only begin in time and conduct matters properly, you want nothing but experianc'd Officers 500 at least. But to return to the men of War, that, I find so much intimidates the people of this Country, is a well Constructed floating Battery, formidable and powerfull in her own Element at sea, no doubt, but when Opposed to the land but an Eggshell, Batterys and Guns properly placed will soon silence them. I will here describe as well as I can the batterys of late made use of against shiping, the old batterys in our ports and harbours at home found almost useless as they are built, they are all built simular or like that at N York, Verry low and near the water, whereby the Vessel has all the power over them that she Could wish, not only from her great Guns, but small arms, where as quite the reverse aught to be the Case, the batterys should be fixed at a distance from the Water and Vessel, no nearer then 200 yards if the Ground will admit, from the Channel or where the Vessel is to Anchor or sail, and upon ground high enough to be out of the range of her shot. If such ground can not be found, take the highest you can get, and sink or let in your platforms and guns upon the top or Summit of the hill, the muzels of the guns as it were peeping out of the hill, thus the men will work their Guns when thus situated with facility and safety and out of the reach of all shot. There is no ship in the world that would dear offer to Attack or pass such a battery, if 20 Guns was mounted, these are the kind of batterys that I would prepose for all attacks upon Vessels, and what I would make use of upon Long Island, and Nutten Island, and tho the land is not so high as may be wished, yet the sinking and leting in the Guns into the firm and highest Ground will answer the purpose no doubt. Ships fire verry

337

slow, and fire at randum, neither can it be Immagin'd, that men can stand to their Guns, where shot, and Splinters, is Continualy flying, much less level and point Guns Accurately, inshort the must do as the french did on board 4 sail of the Line at Lewisburgh,[8] in a Short time the must Strike, or jump into the Hold, Notwithstanding we never had more than two Guns playing upon any Ship at a time. Twelve Guns would be sufficient, Six upon long Island, and Six upon Nutten Island, and 12 pounders would be heavey enough as the distance is but short, and less then 3 lb. of powder would be sufficient for a Charge there aught to be two men to each Gun, that understand loading and fireing, the rest may be raw. I would Immagin that Lord Sterling would be a verry proper person to Command the detachment, and would readily accept the Command I make no Doubt,[9] the troops might keep moveing some at the Narrows some at the ferry at York some even might go to jamaica flat bush &c. until Guns and Matters are in readiness, the Command Officer and Ingineer at the ferry, off and on, to reconnoiter the Ground, and View the position of the Vessels. I have here thrown a few matters togeather in a rough maner however I shall not Needlessly make any apology for troubling you, as the Intention is Good. I can asure you that these hints as I call them, are no whim, or production of my own, but from real practice and Experiance, which I have often seen and help'd to execute in Rivers, Lakes, and Harbours. I would not offer to Impose any thing of My own fraiming, And inshort I have seen somuch of War fair during 28 years service, and as Experiance is allow'd to be the best master, if I follow only that which I have seen, and executed, there Can be no rom in me left for Invention. I cannot dismis the Narrows yet, tho I need not inform you, that that part should be much attended to, let the York people be Torys or what the will, the Enemy should not be allow'd to slip into the heart of the Countery, without Gaining it by Inches. The Narrows are Centrical, and the people thereabouts disposed to be troublesom, it is a most desirable situation for an Army, as they can Act either to the Easward, or Westword togeather, or seperate, and supplys can come from all quarters either by land or Water.

8. For this episode in 1758 see Gipson, *British Empire*, VII, 204.

9. The day before, whether Newland knew it or not, Col. William Alexander, Lord Stirling, and his N.J. regiment had received orders to join Gen. Lee in New York: Alan Valentine, *Lord Stirling* (New York, 1969), pp. 163–4.

My acquaintance friends to the Cause have frequently attack'd me with respect to my Inactivity in this affair. I told them frequently that I had offered my services to you, and said that no doubt but I should be call'd upon when Wanted, this appeased them for some time, but at our County meeting at Freehold, they threw out several Innuendos, purporting, that I never had Offer'd my Services signafying that it appear'd to them Imposible, or Verry Strange, that an Experanced Officers Service at such a juncture could be refused by any Prince, or Potentate. I beg therefore that you'd offer my services to the Honble. the Congress and send me something to shew that I have done so, otherways notwithstanding, I belong to all their Committees and Councils (but they look upon that as Trifling in a Millitery man) yet I expect to be look'd upon as a rank tory in a short time, without you send me something to shew them. They have attack'd Morris Violently, they look upon all who is, or have been, Connected with Goverment with an eye of distrust especially Officers that is not Employ'd.[1] A battery plac'd as before mentione'd, has great power and Command of Shiping, one shot fire'd in this Angular maner from an eminence, will do more Execut[ion?] then 20 fire'd Horizontally, for if the Shot strike the Vessel on one side, between wind and Water, they will come out on the othersid some feet below Water, inshort their powder room and all is in danger, nor will the mens lying flatt upon the decks Screen them. I have had experiance of this, acting as a marine Officer on board men of War, you Want as I have said before experianc'd Officers, who have explor'd the Countery rivers, Lakes, and difficult passes, inshort that know every Inch of Ground, that have drub'd, and been Drub'd, for drubing brings them to reason, and reflexion, and will Oblige them to think, those that know the people on the Opposite side, when and wh[ere to] attack, and when not, that know when they have gain'd an advantage and how to keep it (Amherst's advice to his Officers at Table, and upon all ocasions, was never to loos an Inch of Ground gain'd, and use'd to say, that

1. Probably John Morris, of Shrewsbury, who had been a half-pay lieutenant in the British army. He returned to his old allegiance, and by the beginning of 1777 was a colonel or lieutenant colonel in the British service. E. Alfred Jones, *The Loyalists of New Jersey* (Newark, N.J., 1927), pp. 147–8; Dennis P. Ryan, ed., *A Salute to Courage: the American Revolution as Seen through Wartime Writings of Officers of the Continental Army and Navy* (New York, 1979), p. 60.

a thousand gain'd, nay a Millian, would not compensate for one foot lost, he mov'd so slow and so Cautiously, that he never lost an Inch, or met with a Check, by which he acquir'd the name of Snail from the Volatile) that know all their Manuvers, and how they Carry on their Works and duty, both by day, and by night, that know the meaning of every tap of their drum, such as these Would be thought Inestimable in any service that ware opposed to England. You may remember Sir that Mr. Swan was recomended last War in your Regiment For an Adjutant because he fought the Blacks in Jamaica.[2] I can without exaggeration (and I'm sure there is none that will be hardy enough to denigh it) say that there is not one Officer this day in America that has seen more service then I have, both abroad, and at home, during both the late wars, I have serv'd both in horse, foot, and marines, I have acted as Inginer at several siege's, and in several other departments not Regimental. It cannot be that they have seen more, from this reason, I know them all and the service they have seen, there is none of them much older, if any, and I'm sure I went as early into the service as any of them, and I'm positive that I met with as much approbation and Applause from my Superior Officers as any man ever did upon all ocasions, and yet there is no[thing?] could prevail with me to engage again, but the present Cause, my all is now at Stake the dye is thrown I must Conquor or dye. I have the honor most respectfully to be Sir, Your most Humble and most Obedient Servant   TREVOR NEWLAND

P.S. I do not know that I have the Honor to be acquainted with many of the Honble. the delegates of the Congress, I think that you, and Mr. Clinton,[3] must be the first and earliest acquaintance I have in that respectable body. The matter I have here prepos'd I would undertake, as director, or Ingineer, of the works, with a reasonable man to Command the men, I wish Lord Sterling would

2. Swan was perhaps a son of Richard Swan, the Philadelphia hatter; BF's regiment of militia existed briefly from February to October, 1756. Above, IV, 206 n; VI, 409–12.

3. George Clinton (1739–1812), delegate from New York, was one of the few political leaders with military experience; he had served in the French and Indian War and been on Bradstreet's expedition against Fort Frontenac in 1758. *DAB*.

accept it, he serv'd the Campaign of 56 with us as Secretary.[4] I
hope you'l excuse this long Epistle and Impute it to the Implse I
feel for the Cause.

Honble. Doctr. Franklin

copied

Contract between the Secret Committee and John and Nicholas Brown[5]
Copy: John Carter Brown Library

⟨Philadelphia, February 6, 1776: The Browns will procure in
Europe 10,000 good blankets at approximately 4s. 6d. to 5s.
sterling apiece; 9,200 yards of blue and brown broadcloth for
uniforms and 800 yards of different colors for facings, most of the
cloth, being for privates, at about 4s. sterling per yard and the
rest, for officers, at 6s.; ten tons of lead; 250 stands of good arms
such as are used by French infantry; and fifty 100-pound barrels of
good gunpowder. Gov. Cooke will value the vessels and estimate
their hire or the freight to be paid on the goods exported and
imported.[6] The Browns are hereby advanced \$24,000 for which
they will be accountable to the committee. Signed for the Browns
by Josiah Hewes, who has their power of attorney, and for the
committee by Franklin, John Alsop, Josiah Bartlett, Joseph
Hewes, Francis Lewis, and Samuel Ward.⟩

4. This is the only concrete information about Newland's military background: he had served under Gen. Shirley during the expedition against Fort
Niagara in 1756, when Alexander was Shirley's secretary; above, VI, 244 n.

5. See the previous contract above, under Jan. 20.

6. We omit the other terms, which are the same as those of the contract just
cited. For the text of this one see *Naval Docs.*, III, 1153–4.

The Cumberland County Commissioners to the Pennsylvania Committee of Safety

Text printed in Samuel Hazard *et al.*, eds., *Pennsylvania Archives* (first series; 12 vols., Philadelphia and Harrisburg, 1852–6), IV, 713.

⟨Carlisle, February 9, 1776: We received yours by John Montgomery[7] and in response inform you that we have workmen under bond to finish the full complement of muskets by April 1 next. Gun locks are not available at any price, but we will do our best to have the work completed by then. The cartouche pouches and belts are done, but no cloth is to be had for knapsacks; please order them made in Philadelphia. Addressed to Franklin as president of the committee and signed by James Pollock and Samuel Laird.[8]⟩

To Charles Lee

ALS: Justin G. Turner, Los Angeles (1959)

Dear Sir,   Philada. Feb. 11. 1776

The Bearer Monsr. Arundel is directed by the Congress to repair to Gen. Schuyler, in order to be employ'd by him in the Artillery Service. He purposes to wait on you on his Way, and has requested me to introduce him by a Line to you. He has been an Officer in the French Service, as you will see by his Commissions; and professing a Good Will to our Cause, I hope he may be useful in Instructing our Gunners and Matrosses.[9] Perhaps he may advise in Opening the nail'd Cannon.

7. A member of the Carlisle committee of correspondence; see the letter to it above, Jan. 26.

8. Pollock was a member of the county committee of correspondence; see its letter above, Dec. 29. Samuel Laird (*c.* 1732–1806) was a lawyer who was subsequently treasurer and then a trustee of Dickinson College. *PMHB*, III (1879), 235; Charles F. Himes, *A Sketch of Dickinson College* . . . (Harrisburg, Pa., 1879), p. 139; Charles C. Sellers, *Dickinson College* . . . (Middletown, Conn., [1973]), pp. 120, 484.

9. Louis O'hickey d'Arundel was an Alsatian, though obviously of Irish descent, who had been a lieutenant of artillery in St. Domingue; he was fluent in German and French, and knew a little English. Archives Nationales, E 325 Colonies. On Feb. 5 he had been recommended to Congress, which sent him to Schuyler to be examined and, if qualified, taken into service. He was later reassigned to Lee and made a captain of artillery retroactive to Feb. 8. *JCC*, IV,

I receiv'd the enclos'd the other day from an Officer, Mr. New-land, who served in the two last Wars, and was known by Gen. Gates, who spoke well of him to me when I was at Cambridge. He is desirous now of entring into our Service. I have advis'd him to wait upon you at New York.[1]

They still talk big in England, and threaten hard; but their Language is somewhat civiler, at least not quite so disrespectful to us. By degree, they may come to their Senses, but too late I fancy for their Interest.

We have got in a large Quantity of Saltpetre 120 Ton, and 30 more expected.[2] Powdermills are now wanting. I believe we must set to work and make it by hand. But I still wish with you that Pikes could be introduc'd; and I would add Bows and Arrows.[3] Those were good Weapons, not wisely laid aside.

1. Because a Man may shoot as truly with a Bow as with a common Musket.

2. He can discharge 4 Arrows in the time of charging and discharging one Bullet.

3. His Object is not taken from his View by the Smoke of his own Side.

4. A Flight of Arrows seen coming upon them terrifies, and disturbs the Enemy's Attention to his Business.

5. An Arrow sticking in any Part of a Man, puts him *hors du Combat* 'till 'tis extracted.

6. Bows and Arrows are more easily provided every where than Muskets and Ammunition.

Polydore Virgil speaking of one of our Battles against the French in Eduard the 3d's reign, mentions the great Confusion the Enemy were thrown into *Sagittarum nube* from the English; and concludes, *Est res profectò dictu mirabilis, ut tantus ac potens Exercitus a solis ferè Anglicis Sagittariis victus fuerit; adeò Anglus est*

111–12, 243. The following summer, while commanding the Virginia artillery, he was killed by the explosion of a wooden mortar that he had invented. E.M. Sanchez-Saavedra, *A Guide to Virginia Military Organizations in the American Revolution, 1774–1787* (Richmond, Va., 1978), p. 98. Matrosses were gunners' assistants.

1. See Newland's letter above, Feb. 5.

2. Two days earlier Congress had learned of the arrival of the saltpetre and directed the secret committee to purchase it. *JCC*, IV, 53, 124.

3. See BF's draft above on the use of pikes, Aug. 26.

Sagittipotens, et id genus armorum valet.[4] If so much Execution was done by Arrows when Men wore some defensive Armour, how much more might be done now that is out of Use.

I am glad you are come to New York; but I also wish you could be in Canada.

There is a kind of Suspense in Men's Minds here at present, waiting to see what Terms will be offer'd from England. I expect none that we can accept; and when that is generally seen, we shall be more unanimous and more decisive. Then your propos'd solemn League and Covenant will go better down; and perhaps most of your other strong Measures adopted.[5]

I am always glad to hear from you, but I don't deserve your Favours being so bad a Correspondent. My Eyes will now hardly serve me to write by Night; and these short Days have been all taken up by such Variety of Business, that I seldom can sit down three Minutes without Interruption.

God give you Success. I am, with the greatest Esteem Yours affectionately   B FRANKLIN

Addressed: To / The honourable Charles Lee, Esquire / Lieut. General of the Continental / Army / New York / per Monsr. Arundel

Notations in different hands: Dr: Franklyn Feby 11 1776 / copied.

To the Committees of Trenton, Brunswick, and New York
ALS: Williams College Library

Gentlemen   Philada. Feb. 13. 1775 [*i. e.*, 1776]

The Bearer John Grace has the Care of a Ton of Gunpowder sent by the Congress to the Committee of Safety at New York.[6] If he

---

4. *Anglicae historiae libri vigintiseptem* . . . (Basel, 1570), p. 375. The Latin may be rendered as "by a cloud of arrows." "It is assuredly a wonderful thing that such a large and powerful army was conquered by nothing more than English archers; so the Englishman is arrowstrong, and this kind of weapon prevails."

5. See Lee to BF above, before Dec. 10.

6. Grace was apparently a Philadelphian, and was styled a wagon master: 6 *Pa. Arch.*, I, 517. The powder was consigned to Gen. Charles Lee, and was sent in response to a warning from him that New York was threatened with

should need any Advice or Assistance on the Way you will be so good on his Application to afford it to him. I am, Gentlemen, in Behalf of the Committee here,[7] with much Respect Your most obedient humble Servant   B FRANKLIN

Directed. To the Gentlemen of the Committees of Trenton Brunswick and New York.[8]

Endorsed in different hands: A Letter from Benjamin Franklin Esqr. of Philadelphia With one Ton of powder / Benjamin Franklin.

From [Arthur Lee]

AL:[9] National Archives; copies: National Archives; copy: University of Virginia Library

This is the first time that we have printed a letter addressed to Franklin but not meant for him. Our reason is that he eventually received it, contrary to the writer's intent. The whole episode remains to this day, thanks to the character of Arthur Lee, in Winston Churchill's phrase "a riddle wrapped in a mystery inside an enigma." Only parts of the surface are visible, and they do not reveal much.

In early February Lee received a letter, dated November 30, informing him that the committee of secret correspondence had been appointed and that he was expected to co-operate with it. The letter was clearly from a member of Congress, for no outsider would have known that the committee had been created the day before and was at the moment composing its letter to Lee above, November 30; the likely author was Richard Henry Lee.[1] Arthur sent two long answers, dated February 13 and 14 and addressed for some unknown reason to Cadwallader Colden,

---

attack: *JCC*, IV, 127–8. The threat was illusory; on Feb. 4 Howe's second in command, Gen. Clinton, had arrived in the harbor with transports on his way to a rendezvous on the Cape Fear with a force sent from Britain. See William B. Willcox, *Portrait of a General: Sir Henry Clinton in the War of Independence* (New York, 1964), pp. 66–7, 69–70.

7. The secret committee.

8. "Directed" and "Gentlemen of the" have been added in another hand.

9. Perhaps in Lee's hand, but if so he disguised it with unusual consistency. The address may or may not be in the same hand as the letter.

1. All that is known of this letter is Lee's reference to it in his answers: Wharton, *Diplomatic Correspondence*, II, 72, 76. Whoever wrote it was violating, at the risk of expulsion, the secrecy that members of Congress had just imposed upon themselves: *JCC*, III, 342–3.

Lieutenant Governor of New York. That of the 13th was enclosed in the covering note printed here; that of the 14th apparently had with it a similar note to R.H. Lee.[2] In both his answers Arthur refused to co-operate until the committee's membership was changed and the two men whom he most distrusted were replaced by confidants of his.[3] He sent all these documents, again for some unknown reason, by an American prisoner of war who had been captured in Canada and was being returned there. The man escaped and made his way to New Hampshire, where a local committee opened his letters and forwarded them. They reached General Washington, who after some hesitation sent the letter of the 13th and its covering note to Franklin and the other to R.H. Lee.

This strange story seems to justify two conclusions. The first is that Lee's letter of the 14th was in fact to his brother, as Washington believed it was.[4] The other is that the present note and the letter enclosed were not designed for Franklin's eyes, which were quite keen enough to identify the two committee members of whom the writer expressed particular distrust; Lee, even at his most erratic, could scarcely have intended that result. Then why use Franklin's name? And why, the following March, did he address a long intelligence report to a "dear friend" on whom we do not believe he had ever laid eyes, Sarah Bache?[5] The answers remain his secret.

London 13 Feb. 1776.

The Inclosed will easily explain itself. The intelligence you should observe and take measures accordingly; A fund for necessary expences should be fix'd here, in such hands as can be confided in.[6] You know who is to be trusted. From Experience I can say (tho' without any connection or commerce with them,) the New England Men are fittest to be trusted in any dangerous or important

2. Washington, in forwarding the latter to R.H. Lee the following May, referred to it as "the one directed to you," as distinct from that to BF. Wharton, *op. cit.*, II, 74–5; for the whole episode, with the texts of the enclosures and details of how they reached Philadelphia, see pp. 71–8. The copies of the present note in the National Archives explain that it covered Lee's letter of the 13th. BF received both the note and the enclosure, as witness Washington's letter to him below, May 20, and his reply of June 21.

3. Wharton assumes (p. 72 n) that the two whom Lee distrusted were BF and Jay, and even with no concrete evidence we accept the assumption.

4. Wharton suggests (pp. 75–6) that it was actually to Colden; we disagree, although it does contain a number of references designed to bolster that impression.

5. March 19, followed on April 15 by his third and last communication addressed to Colden: *ibid.*, pp. 80–4.

6. The committee had already done so; see its letter to him above, Dec. 12.

enterprize. Show this, *only to R.H.L.* of Virginia, and he will *guess* from whence it comes.

The Intelligence if it gets to hand in time, should be communicated as soon as possible to every part of America, that she may be prepared.[7]

Addressed: To / Doctor Benjamin Franklin / Philadelphia

Notation: Letters of Intelligence from London

From Joseph Priestley

ALS:[8] American Philosophical Society

Dear Sir   London 13 Feby. 1776.

I lament this unhappy war, as on more serious accounts, so not a little that it renders my correspondence with you so precarious. I have had three letters from you, and have written as often; but the last, by Mr. Temple, I have been informed he could not take.[9] What is become of it I cannot tell.

This accompanies a copy of my second volume of *Observations on air* and of a *pamphlet*, which may perhaps make you smile. Major Carleton, brother to the Governor of Quebec, has undertaken to convey the parcel to you.[1]

7. The intelligence, about British military plans, was only slightly more accurate in the first quasi-Colden letter of the 13th than in the second one the following day.

8. The signature has been torn away except for a fragment of the "P."

9. Presumably a letter in November, when William Temple returned to Mrs. Stevenson and her daughter letters of theirs that he was supposed to take; see their explanations to BF below, Sept. 3 and 5, and for Temple BF to JW, March 26, 1776.

1. The second volume of *Experiments and Observations on Different Kinds of Air* . . . (3 vols., London, 1774–77) was published in 1775; the pamphlet we cannot identify. The bearer of the parcel was Thomas Carleton (1735–1817), who had returned to England in 1775 after a visit with Gen. Henry Clinton to the Russian army in the Balkans. Gov. Carleton appointed his brother quartermaster general and, although Germain gave the plum to another man, the Major was eventually confirmed. He was expected to leave for Canada in late February, 1776, but the expedition actually sailed in early April. William B. Willcox, *Portrait of a General* . . . (New York, 1964), pp. 32–5; Wharton, *Diplomatic Correspondence*, II, 73; *Public Advertiser*, April 6, 1776; A. Francis Steuart, ed., *The Last Journals of Horace Walpole* . . . (2 vols., London, etc., 1910), I, 528; A.L. Burt, "The Quarrel between Germain and Carleton," *Canadian Hist. Rev.*, XI (1930), 203–4; see also W.O. Raymond, "A Sketch of the

By the same hand you will receive a most excellent pamphlet by Dr. Price, which, if anything can, will, I hope, make some impression upon this infatuated nation. An edition of a thousand has been nearly sold in two days. But when Ld. G. Germaine is at the head of affairs, it cannot be expected that anything like *reason* or *moderation* should be attended to. Every thing breathes *rancour* and *desperation*, and nothing but absolute impotence will stop their proceedings. We therefore look upon a final separation from you as a certain and speedy event. If any thing can unite us, it must be the open immediate adopting of the measures proposed by Ld. Shelburne, and mentioned in Dr. Prices pamphlet.[2]

As, however, it is most probable that you will be driven to the necessity of governing yourselves, I hope you have wisdom to guard against the rocks that we have fatally split upon, and make some better provision for securing your natural rights against the incroachment of power, in whomsoever placed.

Amidst the alarms and distresses of war, it may perhaps give

Life and Administration of General Thomas Carleton, First Governor of New Brunswick," New Brunswick Hist. Soc. *Coll.*, VI (1905), 439–74.

Priestley sent his parcel by way of the St. Lawrence because postal service to the colonies had been discontinued. His hope in his postscript that the Major would "fall into your hands" may have been half-serious, for at the time a rumor of the fall of Quebec was gaining ground in London; news of the American repulse did not arrive for another ten days. *Public Advertiser*, Feb. 12, 22, 23, 1776. Carleton eventually found means to forward the letter from Canada; it reached Philadelphia, with or without the rest of the parcel, in September. BF to Priestley below, Jan. 27, 1777.

2. Publication of Richard Price's *Observations on the Nature of Civil Liberty, the Principles of Government, and the Justice and Policy of the War with America . . .* (London, 1776) was announced in the *Public Advertiser* of Feb. 12, and before the end of the year many editions were printed on both sides of the Atlantic: Thomas R. Adams, *American Independence: The Growth of an Idea . . .* (Providence, R.I., 1965), pp. 172–7. The pamphlet's stress on the ruinous cost of war alarmed financial circles, according to Horace Walpole, as no previous writings had: Steuart, *op. cit.*, pp. 529–30. Price commented (pp. 104–9) on a recent speech of Shelburne, which we assume was that of Nov. 10, 1775 even though it is differently reported in Cobbett, *Parliamentary History*, XVIII (1774–77), 920–7. The Earl, according to Price, proposed repealing the obnoxious acts, suspending hostilities, limiting the authority of Parliament in America to the regulation of trade, and obtaining imperial revenue from the colonies' voluntary contributions.

you some pleasure to be informed that I have been very successful in the prosecution of my *experiments* since the publication of my second volume. I have lately sent to the Royal Society some *observations on blood* (which I believe have given great satisfaction to my medical friends) proving that the use of it in respiration is to discharge phlogiston from the system, that it has the same power of affecting air when congealed and out of the body, that it has when fluid and in the body, and acts thro a bladder and a large quantity of serum, as well as in immediate contact with the air. In pure air it becomes of a florid red, and in phlogisticated air black; and the air to which it has been exposed is affected in the same manner as it is by respiration, the calcination of metals, or any other phlogistic process.[3]

I am now in a very promising course of experiments on *metals*, from all of which dissolved in spirit of nitre, I get first nitrous air as before, and then distilling to dryness from the same materials *fixed air*, and dephlogisticated air. This proves that fixed air is certainly a modification of the nitrous acid.[4] I have, however, got no fixed air from gold or silver. You will smile when I tell you I do not absolutely despair of the transmutation of metals.

In one of your letters you mention your having made a valuable discovery on your passage to America, and promise to write me a particular account of it.[5] If you ever did this, the letter has miscarried, for which I shall be sorry and the more so as I now almost despair of hearing from you any more till these troubles be settled.

The club of *honest whigs*, as you justly call them, think themselves much honoured by your having been one of them, and also by your kind remembrance of them.[6] Our zeal in the good cause is not abated. You are often the subject of our conversation.

Not to burden my friend too much, I give him only one copy of

3. Priestley's paper had been read on Jan. 25, 1776, and was published as "Observations on Respiration, and the Use of the Blood," *Phil. Trans.*, LXVI (1776), 226–48.

4. For earlier experiments of his involving "nitrous air" (nitric oxide) and spirit of nitre or "nitrous" (nitric) acid see above, XIX, 173, 201–2.

5. The promise was in BF's letter above of May 16; the particular account was begun but never finished, we believe, and is above at the end of May.

6. BF had sent his greetings to the Club in the letter above, Oct. 3, that Priestley is answering.

my book; but I hope you will communicate it to Professor Win-throp, with my most respectful compliments. I am, as ever, truly yours [J PRIESTLEY]

P.S. Lord Shelburne and Colonel Barré were pleased with your remembrance of them, and desire their best respects and good wishes in return. The best thing I can wish the friendly bearer of this letter is that he may fall into your hands, as I am sure he will meet with good treatment, and perhaps have the happiness of conversing with you, a happiness which I now regret. Your old servant, Fevre often mentions you with affection and respect. He is, in all respects, an excellent servant. I value him much both on his own account, and yours. He seems to be very happy.[7] Mrs. Stephenson is much as usual. She can talk about nothing but you.

Addressed: To / Doctor Franklin

The Committee of Secret Correspondence: a Report to Congress   AD:[8] National Archives

The invasion of Canada, authorized by Congress in June, 1775, had begun in August under Major General Philip Schuyler. Because of his ill health the command almost immediately devolved upon his subordinate, Brigadier General Richard Montgomery, who by November had captured the forts at Chambly and St. Johns and the city of Montreal. Governor Carleton escaped to Quebec with the remnants of his force. Meanwhile Benedict Arnold was advancing through Maine for a junction with Montgomery, which occurred near Quebec on December 3. The siege of that fortress lasted through the month, and culminated on the 31st in an assault in which Montgomery was killed and Arnold wounded. The siege continued in a desultory fashion, and the fate of the expedition now depended as much on political as on military factors.

Everything hinged on the attitude of the inhabitants, for until reinforcements arrived from Britain neither side had enough troops to decide the issue. The invaders were few in number and had long supply lines to

7. The Frenchman, Lewis or Louis Fevre, had been BF's clerk in London since 1772 and at some point, presumably when his employer returned home, joined Lord Shelburne's household: above, XIX, 438 n.

8. In BF's hand.

guard; the British regulars, the backbone of the defense, were even fewer. American success was probable if the Canadians were welcoming, possible if they held aloof, and out of the question if they remained loyal to the crown. The great landowners and the Roman Catholic hierarchy, as this document makes clear, were satisfied with British rule; and they carried influence with the mass of the people. What carried even more was success in the field, backed by effective persuasion. Washington did what he could from a distance, by an address that painted the troops as liberators and appealed for Canadian support in securing freedom for all.[9] But addresses were not enough. What were needed were victories and the political leadership to exploit them.

General Montgomery was well aware of the political need. As his army moved toward Quebec he twice urged General Schuyler, who had remained at Ticonderoga, to ask for a Congressional committee to act as a council in Canada.[1] Schuyler forwarded the request, and Congress appointed a committee to confer with him. It did not go beyond Ticonderoga, however, and contented itself with reporting on the situation there and suggesting that another committee be sent when the weather became better for traveling.[2] Months passed and nothing happened. During the siege that followed the failure to storm Quebec, the invasion hung by a thread. The sort of council that Montgomery had had in mind, capable of seizing the initiative when opportunity offered, was as important as reinforcements.

A factor in precipitating Congressional action was the arrival of a French Canadian with an urgent appeal. Preudhome La Jeunesse lived in Montreal, and all we know about him before his appearance in Philadelphia is contained in this report.[3] Its impact was immediate. It was read to the delegates on February 14, and next day they appointed a committee of three, Franklin among them, to go to Canada.[4]

[On or before February 14, 1776]

The Committee of secret Correspondence report that they have conferr'd with the Person just arriv'd from Canada, and find that

9. Freeman, *Washington*, III, 536–7.

1. Force, *4 Amer. Arch.*, III, 840–1, 1694–5.

2. See above, Gates to BF, Dec. 5.

3. He soon returned to Canada, carrying BF's letter to Schuyler below, March 11, but was back in Philadelphia in August. By then he could not go home, and petitioned Congress to be allowed to raise a corps of French Canadians for the American army. Force, *5 Amer. Arch.*, I, 1093–4. The request was granted, and he was reimbursed for past services: *JCC*, IV, 163; V, 646, 692.

4. *Ibid.*, IV, 148–9, 151–2.

he was furnish'd with a Passport from Gen. Wooster,[5] containing Orders for his Travelling at the Publick Expence; with another Pass from Gen. Schuyler to the same Purpose, and one from the Committee of Kingston, who sent a Guide with him hither. That he has been engag'd in the American Service ever since the Appearance of our Forces in that Country, of which he is a Native; and being as he says well acquainted with the Sentiments and way of Thinking of his Countrymen, his Intention in undertaking this Journey was to give the Congress true Information on that Subject. He says that when the Canadians first heard of the Dispute they were generally on the American side; but that by the Influence of the Clergy and the Noblesse, who have been continually preaching and persuading them against us, they are now brought into a State of Suspence or Uncertainty which Side to follow.[6] That Papers printed by the Tories at New York have been read to them by the Priests assuring them that our Design was to deprive them of their Religion as well as their Possessions. That the Letters we have address'd to them[7] have made little Impression, the common People being generally unable to read, and the Priests and Gentry who read them to others, explain them in such a Manner as best answers their own purpose of prejudicing the People against us. That he therefore thinks it would be of great Service if some Persons from the Congress were sent to Canada, to explain vivâ voce to the People there the Nature of our Dispute with England, which they do not well understand, and to satisfy the Gentry and Clergy that we have no Intention against their Interests, but mean to put Canada in full Possession of Liberty, desiring only their Friendship and Union with us as good Neighbours and Brethren. That the Clergy and Gentry might he thinks by this means be brought over, and would be follow'd by all Canada. And unless some such Measure is taken he is of Opinion our Affairs there will meet with continual Difficulty and Obstruction.

5. Brig. Gen. David Wooster (1711–77), a veteran of the French and Indian War, had been left in command of Montreal. *DAB*.

6. For the inflexible opposition of the clergy, which extended to refusing absolution to those who supported the Americans, see Gustave Lanctot, *Canada and the American Revolution, 1774–1783* (Margaret M. Cameron, trans.; Cambridge, Mass., 1967), pp. 51–3, 124.

7. The first and second Continental Congress had addressed letters to the inhabitants of Quebec, urging them to support American resistance to tyranny: *JCC*, I, 105–13; II, 68–70.

He left Montreal the 20th past; says our Troops continued to invest Quebec; that he had heard of no Sally made by the Garrison; but was inform'd by an Ecclisiastick who came out of that Town 15 Days before, that the Inhabitants were in great Distress for Fewel, and reduc'd to one Fire for 6 or 7 Families. That Flesh and Flour was also scarce; but they had plenty of Corn, which not having Means to grind they boil'd to subsist on. That on his Route he met several Parties of our Reinforcements marching toward Canada. That Lake Champlain is frozen and passable but Lake George not yet. He adds that there is great Jealousy in Canada, of our Paper Money.

He offers to carry safely any Dispatches the Congress may have to send into that Country.

Notations in different hands: Feby 14. 1776 No. 1. Report of the Comee of Correspondence apptd to confer with a gentleman from Canada. Read Feby 14. 1776. Referred for consideration till tomorrow. / Monsr. Pruxdent la Jeunesse & [*illegible*]

Charter Party between the Secret Committee and Joseph Hewes

Copy (microfilm): University of North Carolina Library, Chapel Hill[8]

⟨February 14, 1776: The agreement is between members of the committee[9] and Joseph Hewes of North Carolina, merchant, one of the owners of the brigantine *Fanny* of approximately 150 tons, now in the York River, to hire her for a voyage to Europe. She will be in good condition and well provisioned and manned. The owners will pay all the expenses except port charges noted below, and the crew will give the customary assistance in loading and unloading and diligently perform their duties. The ship will receive from

8. Hayes Collection, microfilm in the Southern Historical Collection made from MSS owned by John Gillam Wood, Hayes Farm, Edenton, N.C.

9. The copy omits the signatures, but the opening sentence designates the parties as Hewes and, for the committee, BF, Robert Alexander, John Alsop, Josiah Bartlett, Francis Lewis, Thomas McKean, Robert Morris, and Samuel Ward. The complete text is in *Naval Docs.*, III, 1285–7. For Alexander, a Maryland delegate who a few months later joined the British, see *Biographical Directory of the American Congress* . . . ([Washington, D.C.,] 1961), p. 467.

the committee's agent a cargo of tobacco and other produce of Virginia, and will sail to the destination he provides. After the cargo is delivered she will load a new one, either at the port of delivery or at any other in the world to which she is directed, and will return, again as directed, to some American port between Connecticut and North Carolina. The committee will pay $400 Spanish per month for her hire, from the day loading begins in Virginia until the day after her unloading (or, if in ballast, her arrival) at the American port or the day when she is captured or sunk, and port charges at any port other than those where she loads and unloads in America and Europe, and her assessed value, if she is captured, of $4,600 Spanish. Each party binds itself, if it defaults, to pay the other £3,000 Pennsylvanian.⟩

Contract between the Secret Committee and Silas Deane and Others

Copy: South Carolina Historical Society; copy: Connecticut Historical Society

We normally summarize contracts of the secret committee signed by Franklin, but this one is important enough to be printed in full because it was the initial reason for Deane's going to France. Soon after he lost his seat in Congress in October, 1775, and thereby his membership in the secret committee,[1] he began to negotiate as a merchant about doing business with that committtee. On January 11, 1776, he and his brother contracted to purchase goods in the West Indies.[2] On the 20th, he said later, the committee approached him about buying in Europe £40,000 worth of presents for the Indians.[3] He thereupon formed a consortium for that purpose with the four other merchants listed here, all of them members of Congress and all except Livingston members of the secret committee. The conflict of interest seems to have disturbed no one.

The result of the negotiations was this contract, which is unusual not only in the large sum involved. Comparison with the committee's two contracts above with John and Nicholas Brown, January 20 and February 14, shows that this one is much less detailed in its specifications and more generous in its terms: such contractors as go to Europe receive

1. Smith, *Letters*, II, 192 n.
2. *Ibid.*, III, 82.
3. *Deane Papers*, V, 245. A Congressional resolution of Jan. 27 empowered the committee to act: *JCC*, IV, 96–8.

twice John Brown's commission for selling and buying there. Deane, in the event, was the one selected to go. He received his authorization from the other partners on March 1, in a letter that included the contract.[4] His simultaneous negotiations with the committee of secret correspondence culminated the next day in his commission and instructions as its agent in Europe.[5]

[February 19, 1776]

Be it remembered, that it is agreed by and between John Alsop, Francis Lewis and Philip Livingston of the City of New York Merchants and Silas Deane of the Colony of Connicticut Merchant and Robert Morris of the City of Philadelphia merchant of the one part, and Samuel Ward, Benjamin Franklin, Thomas Mc.Kean, Joseph Hewes, Josiah Bartlett, and Robert Alexander Esqrs., Members of the Committee of Secrecy appointed by the Honorable Continental Congress of the thirteen United States[6] in North America of the other part; as follows, to wit.

That the sum of 200,000 dollars Continental money now advanced and paid by the said Committee of secrecy to the said John Alsop, Francis Lewis, and Philip Livingston, Silas Deane and Robert Morris, shall be laid out by them in the produce of these colonies and shipped on board proper vessels to be by them chartered for that purpose, to some proper port or ports in Europe (Great Britain and the British Isles excepted) and there disposed of on the best terms.

And the neat proceeds of such cargoes laid out in the purchase of such goods, wares or merchandize as the said Committee of Secrecy shall direct and shipped for the said United Colonies to be landed in some convenient harbour or place within the same, and notice thereof given as soon as conveniently may be to the said Committee of Secrecy.

For which the said John Alsop, Francis Lewis, Philip Livingston, Silas Deane and Robert Morris, shall be allowed five per ct. for purchasing the cargo here, and also to such of said contractors

4. For their letter, mislabeled as from the secret committee, see the *Deane Papers*, I, 116–18, and for Deane's various references to the genesis of his mission III, 381; IV, 156; V, 384–5. The contract was in fact never carried out; see the headnote on BF to Deane below, Dec. 4, 1776.

5. See the headnote on his instructions below, March 2.

6. This term also appears in the copy in the Conn. Hist. Soc., reprinted from the *Deane Papers* in *Naval Docs.*, IV, 11–12.

as shall go personally to Europe to execute and superintend this business, exclusive of the charges of selling the produce and manufactures of these colonies to be exported as aforesaid, and for shipping the remittances, besides the duties, a clear commission of five per ct on the original costs of such remittances in Europe; the said United Colonies running the whole risk of the said adventure, being for their benefit and advantage, and also insuring such vessels against all British seizures or captures.

Witness our hand this 19th. Day of Febuary in the year of our Lord, one thousand, seven hundred and seventy six.

At Philadelphia
Witness JOHN LEGG.

JOHN ALSOP.	SAMUEL WARD.
for self and	BENJAMIN FRANKLIN.
PHILIP LIVINGSTON.	THOMAS MCKEAN.
FRANCIS LEWIS.	JOSEPH HEWES.
ROBERT MORRIS.	JOSIAH BARTLETT.
SILAS DEANE.	ROBERT ALEXANDER.

Copy. Examined. JOS: PENNELL

Copy of the Contract.

To Charles Lee

One page reproduced in facsimile in Samuel T. Freeman sales catalogue, February 17, 1947, p. 7; full text reprinted from *The Lee Papers* (4 vols., New York, 1871–74), I, 313.[7]

Dear Sir,   Philada Febry. 19, 1776.

I rejoice that you are going to Canada. I hope the Gout will not have the courage to follow you into that severe Climate.[8] I believe

7. We have found no trace of the ALS since it was advertised for sale. From the facsimile, which begins with the end of the sentence "to us or our Cause," we have amended the punctuation of the printed version. That version, the facsimile indicates, is closer to the original than the first printing of the letter, which also lacks the postscript: Edward Langworthy, *Memoirs of the Life of the Late Charles Lee* . . . (London, 1792), pp. 249–50.

8. Lee had been sounded out as Montgomery's successor, and had hesitated because he was suffering from both gout and rheumatism: *Lee Papers*, I, 280. Congress ordered him to Canada on Feb. 17, countermanded the order on the

you will have the Number of Men you wish for: I am told there will be 2,000 more: but there are always Deficiencies.

The Bearer, Mr. Paine, has requested a Line of Introduction to you, which I give the more willingly, as I know his sentiments are not very different from yours. He is the reputed, and I think the real Author of Common Sense, a Pamphlet that has made great Impression here.[9] I do not enlarge, both because he waits, and because I hope for the pleasure of conferring with you face to face in Canada. I will only add, that we are assured here on the part of France, that the Troops sent to the W. Indies, have no inimical views to us or our Cause. It is thought they intend a War without a previous Declaration.[1] God prosper all your Undertakings, and return you with Health, Honour and Happiness. Yours most affectionately   B Franklin

Martinico and Cape Francois, by the last Advices, are now fortifying with immense Diligence and great Expence.

To The Honble General Lee at New York.

Editorial Note on the Design of Continental Paper Currency

On June 22–23, 1775, Congress authorized the issuance of $2,000,000 in bills of credit, and Franklin was on a committee to superintend the printing. In November came a further issue of three million, in denominations of one dollar and more. The designs of the bills remained the same, and some of them were adapted from older ones, available in

---

28th, and the next day appointed him to command in the south. *JCC*, IV, 157, 175, 180–1.

9. A few weeks earlier Lee, in writing to Washington, had characterized *Common Sense* as "a masterly, irresistible performance," which had convinced him that independence was a necessity. *Lee Papers.* I, 259–60.

1. In the summer of 1775 Versailles had decided to reinforce its West Indian possessions for fear that the war might spread. Since December the American papers had been filled with much exaggerated reports of French troops and ships of the line arriving in the Caribbean. Uncertainty about their purpose persisted through the spring; in May Congress instructed the committee of secret correspondence to try to fathom French designs. *JCC*, IV, 366; Dull, *French Navy*, pp. 27, 377; James H. Hutson, "The Partition Treaty and the Declaration of American Independence," *Jour. of Amer. History*, LVIII (1972), 887–8. See also the instructions to Bingham below, June 3.

volumes that we know were in Franklin's library; this fact suggests that
he had a hand in the adaptation. On February 17 and 21, 1776, Congress authorized another four million, and included for the first time
bills for four fractions of a dollar, ranging from one-sixth to two-thirds.
These fractional bills were to have a new design,[2] which has particular
numismatic significance because it became, with slight modification,
that of the first coin issued by the United States, the so-called Fugio
Cent of 1787. Franklin has been widely credited with being the original
designer.[3] The drawings reproduced here persuade us that he was responsible at least for the back of the bill.

The first drawing indicates rays emanating from the central circle, as
they did on the bill; the second drawing contains the same legend as that
on the bill. The remaining question is whether those two designs were
Franklin's or merely found their way into his papers. Here the sketch on
the back of his draft resolutions on trade assumes importance.[4] It was his
beyond any doubt, and the Latin legend appears to be in the same hand
as the English legend on the second drawing; if so both were his. When
these bits of evidence are put together, the conclusion is hard to escape
that Franklin was the designer.

From William Goforth[5]   ALS: American Philosophical Society

Sir   Three Rivers 22d.[-23] Feb. 1776.
I have been informd that it is a Custom in the polite world
when about to address a Stranger to Apoligize for so doing. But

2. *JCC*, II, 103, 105–6; III, 390, 398; IV, 157, 164–5. The new design was
ordered on Feb. 21.

3. See in particular Eric P. Newman, *The Early Paper Money of America*,
(Racine, Wis., 1967), pp. 32–3.

4. The sketch was one of a number of jottings unrelated to the draft itself;
see the note on the resolutions above, under July 21.

5. Goforth (1731–1807) had been a New York artisan and radical leader.
Bernard Mason, *The Road to Independence: the Revolutionary Movement in New York,
1773–77* (Lexington, Ky., 1966), pp. 39 n, 72n; Carl Becker, *The History of
Political Parties in the Province of New York, 1760–1776* (reprint with foreword
by A.M. Schlesinger; Madison, Wis., 1968), pp. 132, 168; Staughton Lynd,
"The Mechanics in New York Politics, 1774–1788," *Labor History*, V (1964),
239. Four companies of Goforth's regiment had been dispatched to Ticonderoga
the previous summer: Justin H. Smith, *Our Struggle for the Fourteenth Colony:
Canada and the American Revolution* (2 vols., New York and London, 1907), I,
256. He himself explains his position at Trois Rivières, where he remained
until April; and he was in the battle there the following June. The next month
he resigned from the army, after being promoted to major in another regiment

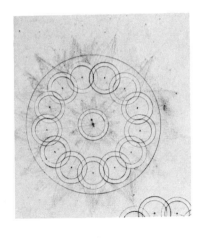

Franklin's Design of Continental Paper Currency

Top, two drawings on a loose sheet among Franklin's papers; *bottom, left and right*, sketch and motto on the verso of his resolutions on trade (see above, p. 126 n), and the back of one of the fractional Continental bills.

in order to Evade the Necessity of Such Tedious Business I have only to prove that I am perfectly well acquainted with you, which I Shall Evince by assureing you that a Number of years ago when in Providence and looking out of a window I Saw you Pass by.[6] But Perhaps you may notwithstanding my good Acquaintence and the great right I have to the freedom ask why it is that I write. I answer because I understood you are a great man that you Can Turn the Common Course of nature that you have power with the Gods and Can Rob the Clouds of their Tremendious Thunder. Rouse once more my old Trojan Collect the Heavey Thunders of the United Colonies and Convey them to the Regions of the North and Enable us to Shake the Quebec walls or on the other hand inform us how to Extract the Electric fire from the Center. Then Perhaps we may be able to draw a Vein athwart their Magazene and Send them upwards Cloathd as Elijah was with a Suit of fire. One or the other of these must be done or we shall be drove to the Necessity of another Frolick of boarding the Town.

As this is now the third time that I have been sent forth after the Tories in this Province the which has gavin me a Small View of the Situation of the Country as also of the Circumstances Condition and Disposition of the people An Idea of which I would fain Coney [Convey] you therefore would Just Say I Apprehend their Disposition is to be for freedom their Condition and Circumstances in General very poor being not opulent and very Unlearnt. As to their Situation it is distress'd and Pitiable for Notwithstanding the Breathings that they and all the Human Race must have for freedom yet from a fear that we Shall either be forced out of the Province by the Ministerial Troops on the one hand or that we Shall leave them to fall a Sacrifice on the other when we have Carried our point with great Britain they are reduced to the greatest distress. That they may be releived from Slavery I hope we Shall Soon be in Possession of Quebec and they have members in the Congress and a Civil Government Established. I would think it an Excellent Expedient in order to open their Eyes and raise

under officers whom he considered his juniors. Richard B. Morris, ed., *John Jay: the Making of a Revolutionary* . . . (New York, 1975), pp. 218 n, 248–52, 293 n; Daughters of the American Revolution, *Lineage Book* . . . , LXXXI (1910), 266.

6. Presumably in July, 1763, when BF visited Providence on business of the Post Office: above, X, 278.

their Appetite for freedom that twenty or thirty Protestant Clergymen of Different Denominations Should be Sent into the Province who were orthordox both in Religion and Liberty and whose greater Concern would Rather be to promote the Church of Christ and to Cloath Human Nature with happiness than to gain Customers to Support any Sectarian Purpose. I am of Opinion many of them might get modorate liveings from the people but what do you think of a few missionaries? Should you Imploy any Show no Respect to denominations. As to forms I think the people have as good a right to Compose now as in Past ages and if you think that George the third has Sinned the Unpardonable Sin Race his name out of the Common prayer book and put in the name of the Congress which I Suppose is as much Connected with Episcopacy as he is, and instead of giveing them a Sallery from the Society in England give them a Sallery from the Society in Philadelphia and I'll warrent they will promote Whygism. As the Canadians bestow but little Learning on their Sons I would beg leave to Recommend the Sending to this province forty or fifty discreet young men as Schoolmasters. The Consequence will be that the Protestants Sons will be qualified for places of Profit and Honour and by a very natural Consequence fall into them. Doctors also are much wanted and might be usefull in the Same way. This will be Proselytezing without Persecution. The Regalor Officers are Violent in abuseing the Canadians because they were not true to Tyranny. Our People Seem in Some measure to be quite out of humour with them because Some have Changed Sides but of this I think no man will think Strange who is in the least acquainted with the history of the Cevil wars in England. However I think it will be necessary from a number of Considerations to have at least an army of ten thousand men in this Province to Secure the Province to ourselves and Releive the People from their fears.

Since I began this letter I have understood that Messers Walker and Price from Montreal have Gone to the Congress who Can give you the last [best?] information of this Province. Mr. Walker has been maimd for dareing in these Corrupt times to be an honest majistrate[7] and his property burnt for dareing to be a friend to the

7. Thomas Walker (c. 1718–85) and James Price were Montreal merchants. The former, who was also a justice of the peace, ardently supported the Americans and eventually left with them. He had been "maimd" by having his ear cut off in a dispute over billeting British troops. W. Stewart Wallace, *The Macmillan*

United Colonies. Sir I am afraid I have tired your Patience and therefore Shall Conclude wishing you when your time Comes a Pleasant and Easy Passage into the other world as I Imajine by the Pursers Books that it Cant be long before you will be under way.

WILLIAM GOFORTH

Captain in the first Batalion of the Newyork Forces Commander of three Rivers and Father of the Solid Boys in the Northern Army.

Perhaps Sir you will Say you dont know me. I Cant help that it is none of my fault if you had looked into the window as I looked out perhaps your accquaintance might have been Simelar to mine. However I must be at you again I am not without my fears that the Northern Department will yet be neglected (as it has from the begining of the Champain in Every Respect Except that of provisions for which the Congress must have Credit) as I have the Command at this place it is natural to Suppose I must know what forces are Come to our assistance. Since the defeat at Quebec which I Can assure you notwithstanding the Bustle you perhaps think you have made does not amount to more than * Exclusive of the Garrisson which were at Quebec and Some of which have been moveing towards the Scene of action. See the inclosed note.[8] The lakes Sometimes is Impossible [*until?*] 20th [?] march. If we have not the heavey apparatus for a Seige nor men Enough to Storm we shall Soon be in very pretty way in this part of the world. 23d feb in the morning.

Addressed in another hand: To / Doctor Benjamin Franklin / Member of the Continental / Congress at / Philia / from the Northern army

---

Dictionary of Canadian Biography (3rd. ed., rev.; London and Toronto, 1963), p. 779. Price, who had already been on a mission to Philadelphia as an informal representative of his fellow merchants, repeatedly lent money to support the invading army, and had recently been made its deputy commissary general. The two men were southward bound to discuss with Congress the Indian trade in Canada. Smith, *op. cit.*, I, 206; II, 160, 235, 351, 364–5.

8. Without the missing note we cannot explain what he meant by "the Garrison that were at Quebec," where the siege still continued, or by "the Scene of action."

From Horatio Gates

ALS: American Philosophical Society

Dear Sir   Head Quarter's 23 Febry 1776

This will be deliverd to you by The Baron de Woedtkee, who appears to be a Gentleman, and a Veteran Charectors you will esteem him for he has with him other recommendations to your Notice, from some of your Paris acquaintance; if I had never fallen out with Royalty for any other reason, I should detest it, upon the poor Barons account, for the Tyrannical treatment he has received from The King Prussia: may he enjoy in This Land of Freedom that Comfort which has been denied him in Germany; and may this Land continue to Embrace with her wonted Cordiality, every Oppress'd Subject from every other Quarter of The Globe.[9]

Last Night our People surprized a Corporal, and Two Sentrys of the Enemys, and brought them this morning to head Quarters, they declare General Clinton took with Him when he Saild from Boston a considerable Quantity of Artillery, and Artillery Men; besides The Detachment of The Troops; this convinces me that he design'd to take post at New York from whence, as I hinted to you in my last Letter, I am satisfied the Enemy meant to commence their Summer Opperations:[1] as The Baron goes by Providence, and that way to New York, I shall not write any thing Further to day. A few days will probably furnish matter for an Express, when you may expect to hear further From Dear Sir Your most Affectionate Humble Servant   HORATIO GATES

Mine and Mrs. Gates's best respects wait Upon Mr. and Mrs. Bache and your Fire side.

---

9. Frederick William Baron de Woedtke had been a major in the Prussian service and a captain and inspector of cavalry in the French. His brother, Lieut. A.M. de Woedtke, to BF, March 10, 1781, APS. Soon after the Baron's arrival in Philadelphia he was appointed a brigadier general, given an advance of $750, and ordered to go to New York and then accompany the commissioners on their journey to Canada. *JCC*, IV, 209–10, 226. BF said later that he was responsible for the appointment, and that the General received $600 and promptly squandered it: to A.M. de Woedtke, April 13, 1781, Library of Congress. It is not clear how far the Baron traveled with the commissioners, but a few weeks later he joined the army; by early July he was writing BF from Crown Point, where he died soon afterward. *Ibid.*; his letters below, July 3, 4.

1. A letter now lost. The British were in fact planning to seize New York as a base for the coming campaign but not with Clinton's force, which had been detached for an expedition to raise the Loyalists in the Carolinas.

Addressed: To / Doctor Benjamin Franklin / Member of The Continental / Congress / Philadelphia

[*In another hand:*] At Pater [St. Peter's?] Parish Corner of Race Street and Second Street.[2]

From [David Hartley]

ALS: American Philosophical Society; transcript:[3] Library of Congress

Dear Sir   Lond feb 24 1776

It is so long since I have had the pleasure of hearing from you that I fear the administration has but too effectually stopt the Channel of Communication between this Country and its colonies.[4] I have allways dreaded this event as fatal and final to the prospect of national reconciliation. When in any contention the parties are not only studiously kept assunder but mischief-making go-betweens exert every art and practise every fraud to inflame jealousies animosities and resentments between them, It is but too obvious to fear that your own prophetic words should be accomplished, that instead of that cordial affection that once and so long existed, and that harmony so suitable to the happiness, safety, strength and wellfare of both Countries, an implacable malice and mutual hatred, such as we see subsisting between the spaniards and Portugueze, the Genoise and Corsicans, should fatally take root between the parent state and its Colonies. These fears are not abated by the Consideration of the incessant injuries, which have been and which continue to be heapt upon our unhappy fellow subjects in America. These injuries are indeed brought upon them by the administration, who usurp the personality and authority which they pretend to derive from the people,

2. If this was a forwarding address, BF must have been visiting; the location is some blocks northeast of his house.

3. The transcript omits the place and the day of the month, and the final salutation; otherwise it conforms closely to the original. The margins of the ALS are badly frayed, and we have silently supplied from the transcript missing words and parts of words and in one case, indicated by bracketed italics, two words that Hartley omitted and the transcriber interpolated. The transcript also contains a long passage, given below, that is not in the ALS.

4. This may be true of Hartley's letters. See the note on the first of the two above of Nov. 14.

but from the distance between us and our american brethren, and the false evidence mutually transmitted from one to the other by a treacherous administration, I greatly fear that national resentments will become indiscriminate. It is inseperable from human nature that the mind under any grievous suffering, especially injury, will be distracted and broken from its nearest and most affectionate connexions which may happen to be but accidentally and collaterally involved. The affection of States to each other consists of the combination of personal affections parentage and intercourse; when blood is shed, and the parent weeps for his son, the widow for her husband, brother for brother an inextinguishable resentment arises; the Appeal for blood. Those unfortunates who have lost their relations and friends become furious, and in those who have them yet to lose, horrors and fears take place of, and drive out affection, the bonds of attachment are let loose and all the tumultuous passions are set afloat. I know that you are as sensible of these consequences as any one can be; you have foreseen them afar off, You have predicted them; You have done every thing in your power to soften animosities, and to put off the evil day. I hope still that you will not despair. Your age, experience, character, humanity and example of moderation in disregarding those injuries and insults which have been offered to yourself, give you the best title to plead with your countrymen, to suspend their resentments, to discriminate those who have not injured them, and to remember the ties of affection between them and their fellow subjects in England. I see the influence of your Counsels in the Congress. I see the distinction clearly made between the ministry and the people of England but I fear that at the same time the seeds of jealousy are struggling to break out. The Address from the Congress to the assembly of Jamaica speaks of the people of England as dissipated and corrupt.[5] The people of England are far otherwise. They are just and generous and if it were put to the sense of the people of England, you would not be left in any doubt whether it was *want of will or want of power* to do you justice. You know the blot of our Constitution by which to our disgrace, and to your misfortune, a corrupt ministry, sheltered by parliamentary influence, are out of our immediate Controul. A day of account

5. And in no uncertain terms. For the text of the address, adopted on July 25, 1775, see *JCC*, II, 204–6.

may come, when the justice of the nation may prevail, and if it comes not too late, it may prove a day of reconciliation and cordial reunion between us and America. The trial is with you, to suspend your resentments from becoming indiscriminate, and a great trial it is, in which the assistance and guidance of good men like yourself [*may contribute?*] to abate popular fury, but, unexampled as the forbearance of America has hitherto been, Believe me that fury which among nations is inseperable from accumulated injury is rising. You must exert all your discretion, to take at least the chance of keeping it down till the fiery trial may abate. I cannot tell you what Efforts the ministry have in their malicious purpose to try. I am amazed at their desperate and headstrong hardiness to proceed in an undertaking, which gives them so little prospect of Success and such certainty of the severest responsibility to this Country when they rouse themselves to the enquiry. The only machinery of the administration which is to be feared, is, least the course of their injustice and tyranny in America should throw your Countrymen into fury beyond the bounds of forbearance, by cruelties exciting an implacable hatred, and upon that hatred so raised by themselves, to attack the view of the people of England thereby to keep off enquiry from themselves. They are masters of all communication, and consequently of the representation of facts to their own purposes. They will send false accounts to you of the disposition of the people here towards you, and if they can drive you by any means to acts of irreconciliation they will endeavour to raise that implacable disposition on this side of the water, upon the false suggestion of which they are now endeavoring to urge you on. We who are friends to both countries wish to prevent such fatal jealousies and misunderstandings.[6]

6. Here the transcript interpolates the following passage: "The disposition of the bulk of the people I think is very little altered since you left us a twelve month ago. The Ministry were very assiduous to get addresses in the beginning of the winter and our lying gazettes would convey that to you as the sense of the nation by suppressing all the petitions. Many of the addresses were carried by surprize. Many are from very inconsiderable places and signed with a few hands, and many even of the addresses [addressers?] did by no means intend to give countenance to sanguinary Measures but were taken in by the pretexts which have been thrown out of supporting parental authority &c. But the Ministry range all addressers as promoters of sanguinary Measures which was very far I believe from the intentions of any of them. And for the petitions for peace and reconciliation they have been secreted from your knowledge at least they have

Many of your best friends in England regret that the Congress has not made some specific and definite proposition, upon which the sense of the people of England might have been consulted. A people at large cannot enter into historical details, especially when facts are so studiously confounded and misrepresented, but still they could judge of a simple proposition. If any such had been made, I think it would have been the most likely method to have captivated the good will of the nation. While the propositions of the Congress are generall and indefinite, the ministry treat them as general words meaning little or nothing in fact. But I think the further prosecution of hostile measures could not be supported by the ministry, if they were to refuse any definite and equitable offer of accommodation made on the part of America. If it be possible let the two countries be once more reunited in Affection. It is not simply peace that we ought to strive for, but reconciliation which is more than peace. We may have peace with foreign states, but it must be reconciliation alone that can reunite us as one people. However forlorn the prospect may be, Let not the common friends slacken their endeavours. Constancy is our only hope. All is lost if we despair. I am Dear Sir With the greatest regard and esteem very affectionately yours   G B

To Dr Franklin Philadelphia

Endorsed: G.B. Feb. 24. 1776.

———

been suppressed out of the Gazettes, but I conceive the Number of the petitioners to be ten to one to the addressers. Newcastle 3 or 4000 Dublin 4000 Berkshire near 1000 petitioners to 2 or 300 addressers, Hampshire 1900 petitioners to about 250 or 300 addressers and so of many other places. The petitions from London Halifax Newcastle Dublin County of Berks and Hampshire have above 10,000 hands to them."

This interpolation, to judge by the reference in the first sentence, must have come from another letter, now lost, written in late March, 1776. The subject matter is closely similar to that in the first of Hartley's two letters above, Nov. 14.

To the Speaker of the Pennsylvania Assembly

Printed in *Votes and Proceedings of the House of Representatives of the Province of Pennsylvania* . . . , VI (Philadelphia, 1776), 189.

On February 15, 1776, Congress named Franklin as one of the commissioners to Canada.[7] This appointment crystallized discontent over his position as a member of the Assembly, to which he had been elected in October.[8] On the 24th the Philadelphia committee of inspection and observation, to which he had just been re-elected but which he apparently never attended, took the matter under advisement. In that time of crisis, it concluded, the city was entitled to full representation in the house; Franklin had never taken his seat and "will probably go abroad soon in the service of the united colonies." A deputation from the committee was instructed to wait upon him, ask him whether service in the Assembly was consonant with his other public responsibilities, and if not to ask for his resignation.[9] The question was rhetorical and the answer obvious.

Sir,   February 26, 1776.

I am extremely sensible of the Honor done me by my Fellow-Citizens, in chusing me their Representative in Assembly, and of that lately conferred on me by the House, in appointing me one of the Committee of Safety for this Province, and a Delegate to the Congress. It would be a Happiness to me if I could serve the Public duly in all those Stations; but aged as I now am, I feel myself unequal to so much Business, and on that Account think it my Duty to decline a Part of it. I hope therefore that the House will be so good as to accept my Excuse for not attending as a Member of the present Assembly, and, if they think fit, give Orders for the Election of another in my Place, that the City may be more completely represented.[1]

I request also that the House would be pleased to dispense with

7. *JCC,* IV, 151–2.
8. See the headnote above on the Assembly's instructions to its delegates in Congress, May 9.
9. Copy of the committee's minutes, APS. The city's other representative, Thomas Mifflin, was also an absentee because he was Washington's quartermaster general: *DAB*; Ryerson, *Revolution Is Now Begun,* p. 137.
1. The letter was received and read on Feb. 27, when the house vacated BF's seat and ordered a new election. It was held on March 2, and David Rittenhouse was returned. 8 *Pa. Arch.,* VIII, 7411, 7428.

my further Attendance as one of the Committee of Safety.[2] With the greatest and most sincere Respect to yourself and the House, I have the Honour to be, Sir, Your most obedient and most humble Servant,   BENJAMIN FRANKLIN

To the Honourable John Morton, Esq.

From Jonathan Williams, Sr.

ALS: American Philosophical Society

Honored Sir   Worcester march 1st. 1776
    Agreeable to your desire I now inclose your Acct. Drawn in the best manor I now Cane tho' not So partecular as I Could wish as Some of my Old books and papers were Consumed Last may in my werehouses[3] but I belive it is nearly right. I received an acct. of yours from England drawn by Jonathan in which was Some omitions the £50. paid your niece on her marage with the many repairs of your House and £18.8s.5d. Difficience in Reiley rent Which you Order'd me to Charge Your Acct. with &c.[4] My Wife Joines in duty to you and Love to your Children. I am Your Friend and Nephew   JONA WILLIAMS

PS Please to Let Us know if you hear from Our Son.

Addressed: To / The Honble. Benjamin Franklin Esqr / In / Philadelphia / per Post

Franked: Free William Ellery[5]

2. He had himself dispensed with attendance for some time past; see the note on the committee above, June 30.
    3. See his letter to BF above, June 19.
    4. For JW's account and the one that his father enclosed with this letter see above, X, 354–61. The former actually included the wedding present to Jane Mecom's daughter Jane, and the costs of repairing the house on Unity Street and the sum left unpaid by its tenant, James Reilly.
    5. A Newport merchant and lawyer, who two months later became one of the Rhode Island delegates to Congress. *DAB.* We have no idea why a letter from Worcester to Philadelphia should have passed through his hands, or in what capacity he franked it.

The Committee of Secret Correspondence: Certificate for Silas Deane[6]

DS: Connecticut Historical Society; DS: Library of Congress; copy: South Carolina Historical Society; copy: Yale University Library[7]

[March 2, 1776]

We the underwritten, being the Committee of Congress for secret Correspondence, do hereby certify whom it may concern, that the Bearer, the Honourable Silas Deane Esquire, one of the Delegates from the Colony of Connecticut, is appointed by us to go into France, there to transact such Business, commercial and political, as we have committed to his Care, in Behalf and by Authority of the Congress of the thirteen united Colonies. In Testimony whereof we have hereunto set our Hands and Seals at Philadelphia, the second Day of March 1776.

B FRANKLIN
BENJA HARRISON
JOHN DICKINSON
JOHN JAY
ROBT MORRIS

The Committee of Secret Correspondence: Instructions to Silas Deane

Copy: Connecticut Historical Society; copy: Yale University Library; copy: South Carolina Historical Society[8]

These instructions, which were probably drafted by Franklin,[9] are the first to an American agent in a foreign country. They mark an important

6. See the headnote on the following document.

7. In both copies the certificate, along with the instructions, is included in the minutes, also copied, of the committee's meeting on March 2; the texts vary inconsequentially from those we print. In these copies the certificate is unsigned; that in the S.C. Hist. Soc. leaves Deane's name blank in the certificate and in the instructions.

8. The second and third copies were included in the minutes of the committee meeting on March 2; see the note on the preceding document. Both are dated at Philadelphia on the 2nd; the copy we print, or one from which it was copied in turn, was presumably made the next day and so dated.

9. See Edward Bancroft's narrative, Aug. 14, 1776: *Deane Papers*, I, 178.

step toward the assumption of sovereignty, and the committee of secret correspondence seems to have taken that step on its own initiative. The committee had been created to keep in touch with the European friends of America, and had been authorized to pay "such agents as the said Committee may send on this service."[1] Whether that rubric covered appointing a resident agent in France to transact its commercial and political business may be questioned. Yet the committee did so, and apparently did not communicate to Congress what Deane's instructions were.[2]

His mission was a sign of changing times. The publication of *Common Sense* in January and the arrival in February of news of the Prohibitory Act, aimed at the destruction of American trade, altered the views of many delegates.[3] On February 29 Congress debated such fundamental questions as opening that trade to the outside world, declaring independence, and contracting foreign alliances. Although no action was taken, the prospect of it drew nearer.[4] Deane's appointment, if it did not reflect majority opinion at the time, did anticipate the direction in which opinion was moving.

The committee had never construed its mandate as merely corresponding with friends. Its first letters had inquired about how foreign powers were disposed, and whether any would consider a commercial alliance; its discussions with Bonvouloir in December had suggested that France might be one that would.[5] The question was how to explore this overture, and Deane soon began to emerge, through another connection, as the man for the purpose. His commercial partners selected him to go to Europe as their representative in carrying out their large contract with the secret committee. One of those partners was Robert Morris, who joined the committee of secret correspondence on January 30. When that committee sought an agent to buy army supplies and open communications with Versailles, Deane was ready to hand.[6] His mission was thus two-sided. He was the agent of, and partner in, a private firm that had a contractual relationship with the secret committee; at the same time he represented the committee of secret correspondence, and was

1. *JCC*, III, 392.

2. *Deane Papers, loc. cit.*

3. See the note on Hartley to BF above, Nov. 23.

4. Smith, *Letters*, III, 307–8, 311–12, 416–17.

5. See above, BF to Dumas, Dec. 9; the committee to Lee, Dec. 12; and Bonvouloir to de Guines, Dec. 28.

6. On March 1 his partners formally authorized him to go to Europe as their agent; see the headnote on the contract above, Feb. 19. The details of his two assignments must have been worked out simultaneously in the preceding weeks.

therefore closer than any one before him to being an accredited ambassador from the United Colonies.

Philadelphia March 3rd. [*i.e.*, 2,] 1776

On your arrival in France, you will for some time be engaged in the business of providing goods for the Indian trade. This will give good countenance to your appearing in the character of a merchant, which we wish you continually to retain among the French, in general, it being probable that the court of France may not like it should be known publickly, that any agent from the Colonies is in that country. When you come to Paris, by delivering Dr. Franklin's letters to Monsieur Le Roy at the Louvre, and M. Dubourg, you will be introduced to a set of acquaintance, all friends to the Americans.[7] By conversing with them, you will have a good opportunity of acquiring Parisian French, and you will find in M. Dubourg, a man prudent, faithful, secret, intelligent in affairs, and capable of giving you very sage advice.

It is scarce necessary to pretend any other business at Paris, than the gratifying of that curiosity, which draws numbers thither yearly, merely to see so famous a city. With the assistance of Monsieur Dubourg, who understands English, you will be able to make immediate application to Monsieur de Vergennes, *Minister des Affairs Etrangeres*, either personally or by letter, if M. Dubourg adopts that method, acquainting him that you are in France upon business of the American Congress, in the character of a merchant, having something to communicate to him, that may be mutually beneficial to France and the North American Colonies; that you request an audience of him, and that he would be pleased to appoint the time and place. At this audience if agreed to, it may be well to shew him your first letter of credence, and then acquaint him that the Congress, finding that in the common course of commerce, it was not practicable to furnish the continent of America with the quantity of arms and ammunition necessary for its defence, (the Ministry of Great Britain having been extremely

7. Jean-Baptiste LeRoy had had quarters at the Louvre since at least 1772: above, XIX, 84. BF's letters to him and Dubourg have since disappeared, but one and presumably both were presented; see Dubourg to BF below, June 10. Deane complained, however, that neither Frenchman proved to be in a position to help him: *Deane Papers*, V, 388.

industrious to prevent it) you had been dispatched by their authority to apply to some European power for a supply. That France had been pitched upon for the first application, from an opinion, that if we should, as there is a great appearance we shall, come to a total seperation from Great Britain, France would be looked upon as the power, whose friendship it would be fittest for us to obtain and cultivate, That the commercial advantages Britain had enjoyed with the Colonies had contributed greatly to her late wealth and importance. That it is likely great part of our commerce will naturally fall to the share of France; especially if she favours us with this application, as that will be a means of gaining and securing the friendship of the Colonies; and that as our trade was rapidly increasing with our increase of people, and in a greater proportion, her part of it will be extremely valuable.[8] That the supply we at present want, is clothing and arms for twenty-five thousand men with a suitable quantity of ammunition and one hundred field pieces. That we mean to pay for the same by remittances to France or through Spain, Portugal, or the French Islands as soon as our navigation can be protected by ourselves or friends; and that we besides want great quantities of linins and woollens, with other articles for the Indian trade, which we are now actually purchasing, and for which you ask no credit, and that the whole, if France should grant the other supplies, would make a cargo which it might be well to secure by a convoy of two or three ships of war.

If you should find M. de Vergennes reserved, and not inclined to enter into free conversation with you, it may be well to shorten your visit, request him to consider what you have proposed, acquaint him with your place of lodging, that you may yet stay sometime at Paris, and that knowing how precious his time is, you do not presume to ask another audience, but that if he should have any commands for you, you will upon the least notice immediately wait upon him. If at a future conference he should be more free, and you find a disposition to favor the Colonies, it may be proper to acquaint him, that they must necessarily be anxious

8. This expectation, which was widespread in the colonies, bred the hope of French support even at the risk of war; see James H. Hutson, "Intellectual Foundations of Early American Diplomacy," *Diplomatic History*, I (1977), 1–19.

to know the disposition of France, on certain points, which, with his permission, you would mention, such as whether if the Colonies should be forced to form themselves into an independant state, France would probably acknowledge them as such, receive their ambassadors, enter into any treaty or alliance with them, for commerce or defence, or both? If so, on what principal conditions? Intimating that you shall speedily have an opportunity of sending to America, if you do not immediately return, and that he may be assured of your fidelity and secrecy in transmitting carefully any thing he would wish conveyed to the Congress on that subject. In subsequent conversations, you may, as you find it convenient, enlarge on these topics, that have been the subject of our conferences with you, to which you may occasionally add the well known substantial answers, we usually give to the several calumnies thrown out against us.[9] If these supplies on the credit of the Congress should be refused, you are then to indeavor the obtaining a permission of purchasing those articles, or as much of them as you can find credit for. You will keep a daily Journal of all your material transactions, and particularly of what passes in your conversation with great personages; and you will by every safe opportunity, furnish us with such information as may be important. When your business in France admits of it, it may be well to go into Holland, and visit our agent there, M. Dumas, confering with him on subjects that may promote our interest, and on the means of communication.

You will indeavor to procure a meeting with Mr. Bancroft by writing a letter to him, under cover to Mr. Griffiths at Turnham Green, near London, and desiring him to come over to you, in France or Holland, on the score of old acquaintance.[1] From him you may obtain a good deal of information of what is now going

9. BF, if he wrote the instructions, presumably had in mind the answers in his "Vindication" above, under July 21.

1. Our note on Edward Bancroft above, XVI, 224–5 n, does not mention that Deane, while teaching in Hartford before he turned to the law, had young Bancroft as a pupil. Julian P. Boyd, "Silas Deane . . . ," 3 *W&MQ*, XVI (1959), 176–7. His trip to France is discussed in the headnote below on Deane to Morris, June 23. Ralph Griffiths was the proprietor and publisher of the *Monthly Review*, in which Bancroft often contributed from 1774 on. *DNB*; Benjamin C. Nangle, *The Monthly Review . . . Index of Contributors and Articles* (Oxford, 1934), p. 3.

forward in England, and settle a mode of continuing a correspondence. It may be well to remit him a small bill to defray his expenses in coming to you, and avoid all political matters in your letter to him. You will also indeavor to correspond with Mr. Arthur Lee, agent of the colonies in London.[2] You will indeavor to obtain acquaintance with M. Garnier, late *Chargé des Affairs de France en Angleterre*, if now in France, or if returned to England, a correspondence with him, as a person extremely intelligent and friendly to our cause.[3] From him, you may learn many particulars occasionally, that will be useful to us. Signed B. FRANKLIN

BENJ. HARRISON
JOHN DICKINSON
ROBERT MORRIS
JOHN JAY.

Instructions to Silas Deane.

From the committee of secret correspondence to Silas Deane.

To Charles-Guillaume-Frédéric Dumas

Reprinted from *The Port Folio*, III, (1803), 214.

Dear Sir,   Philadelphia, March 22, [*i.e.*, 2[4]], 1776.
I wrote to you lately by Mr. Story, and since by another convey-

2. Deane did write to Lee, by a courier whom Vergennes furnished: *Deane Papers*, I, 204. For Lee's response see the headnote below on the memorandum of the committee of secret correspondence, Oct. 1.

3. Charles-Jean Garnier, chargé d'affaires of the French Embassy, was regarded as an expert on British affairs: Doniol, *Histoire*, I, 67. BF had known him well enough by 1772 to get him to translate his letter of acceptance to the Académie royale des sciences: above, XIX, 294. Deane suggested to Garnier that they correspond, in a letter that he sent to London by Bancroft: *Deane Papers*, I, 206. Garnier considered that doing so directly would be undiplomatic, but agreed to furnish Bancroft with such information and advice as were consistent with duty to his King; Bancroft in turn furnished him with intelligence from America. Bancroft to American Commissioners, Oct. 3, 1777, APS. This instruction to Deane, in other words, opened by mischance a channel of communication with the French court through Bancroft; and by the time it was opened the go-between had become a British agent.

4. Dumas dated the letter the 2nd (to BF below, Aug. 4) and must have been right because it went by Deane, who left Philadelphia on the 8th and was in Delaware Bay on the 16th: *Deane Papers*, I, 126–7.

ance.[5] This line will be delivered to you by Mr. Deane, who goes over on business of the Congress, and with whom you may freely converse on the affairs committed to you, in behalf of that body. I recommend him warmly to your civilities. Mess'rs. Vaillant and Pochard continue close at their new business, and are already able to subsist by it: as they grow more expert, they will be able to make more money.[6]

Mr. Deane will inform you of every thing here, and I need not add more, than that I am, with esteem and respect, Dear Sir, Your most obedient, And most humble servant,   B. FRANKLIN.

From the Pennsylvania Committee of Safety

LS: National Archives

Sir   In Committee of Safety Philada. 4th March 1776

In order to carry into execution the Resolve of Congress for the manufacturing Fifty Tons of Salt Petre into Powder the Committee of Safety have purchased a seat for erecting a Powder Mill which they intend to build in such manner as to manufacture about four tons per Week,[7] and they are of opinion it will be necessary to build a magazine for the secure keeping the Powder as it is made at a suitable distance from the Mill. This being a proper Season for Erecting the same and those Gentlemen who have the superintendance of the Mills will be able at the same time [to] oversee the building the Magazine.

The Committee request you will please to take the opinion of the Congress relative to the Erecting such Magazine.[8] By Order of

5. The letter by Story is above, Dec. 9; the other has disappeared.

6. We have no idea what the business was; BF had doubtless explained it in his lost letter. He clearly had not heard that Pochard was about to leave for Canada, whence he went to England while Vaillant remained in Philadelphia; see Pochard to BF below, Oct. 11.

7. The directive to send the saltpetre to the committee was adopted on Feb. 12, 1776; four days later the committee authorized construction of the powder mill. *JCC*, IV, 128; *Pa. Col. Recs.*, X, 488.

8. The request was presumably made of BF as a member of the secret committee. Supplying gunpowder, as explained in the editorial note on that committee above, Sept. 18, was one of its responsibilities. BF did as he was

the Committee I am Sir: your most Humble Servant

GEO: ROSS Chairman

Addressed: Doctor Franklin

Notation: No. 11 Letter from Comee. of safety of Pensylvania respecting erecting a Magazine. 4th March 1776

Proposed Alterations in William Smith's Oration on General Montgomery   AD: Historical Society of Pennsylvania

On February 19, 1776, William Smith, Provost of the College of Philadelphia and Franklin's old antagonist, delivered in one of the city churches an oration that Congress had requested on General Montgomery and the other Americans killed in the attack on Quebec.[9] Smith was anything but a revolutionary, and still longed to see the quarrel peacefully settled; he felt in honor bound, furthermore, to express his views. As a result his oration was frostily received. When William Livington subsequently moved that Congress thank the Provost for it and have it printed, so many objections were raised that the motion was withdrawn.[1] Smith then went ahead himself to have the speech published, but first showed the manuscript to Franklin and Livingston and asked for their criticisms.[2] They suggested a number of minor changes, most of them stylistic, and urged him to omit one long passage in which he most clearly expressed his hope of reconciliation. He seems to have accepted the changes, or eliminated the need for them by rephrasing his

---

requested; the letter was read before Congress on March 4 and deferred for consideration the next day: *JCC*, IV, 184. No record of action has survived.

9. For Smith see above, IV, 467–9 n. BF seems to have been responsible for arrangements at the church, for Congress subsequently reimbursed him to the tune of almost $100. *JCC*, IV, 200.

1. Smith, *Letters*, III, 294, 304; see also Butterfield, *Adams Correspondence*, I, 346, 361, 400–1.

2. In January Congress had constituted them and another man a committee to arrange a tribute to Montgomery. Soon afterward Smith was commissioned to give the oration, and at the same time BF was charged with obtaining from France a monument to the dead hero. *JCC*, IV, 78, 89–90. Hence the two delegates were natural men for Smith to consult, particularly if he did so before Congress refused to print the oration.

baroque prose. The deletion he refused to make; he let the original stand, and added a defensive footnote.[3]

Franklin's draft of his and Livingston's suggestions is frequently unintelligible, because the manuscript to which it refers has disappeared. We confine ourselves to noting in brackets, where possible, the pages of the printed pamphlet to which the suggestions may have applied, and to explaining them where the pamphlet gives ground for explanation.

[Before March 6, 1776.[4]]

[Pag]e. 3 [3]	Beyond *the usual Place of Oblivion*, an Expression obscure. Same Page. And the Performance &c. read. And this solemn Office was perform'd before the Great Assembly of the People, omitting their most renown'd Oretors.[5]
4 [3]	*Fames.* Fame
[4]	Relicts of publick Contest.[6]
11 [10]	Fields Theology: Query. Mythology?
14 [12]	What is placed, &c: the Meaning or Application seems obscure.
19 [16]	*Creation*, will not be clear to many Readers. breathe out his *last* is at *last*.
20 [17]	. . . in vain . . . investigate. Should it not be . . . attempt, or endeavour, to investigate?
21 [18–19?]	I speak not this, my Country men, &c. as far as, I feel, we think better omitted.
23–24. [20]	*Pomp* of War and *Pride* of Conquest had no other Charms, than . . . : Would it be better to say, War and Conquest had, &c.?

3. William Smith, *An Oration in Memory of General Montgomery and of the Officers and Soldiers, Who Fell with Him, December 31, 1775, before Quebec . . .* (Philadelphia, 1776), p. 29 n.

4. The date when the oration was published: *Pa. Gaz.*, March 6.

5. Smith was referring to Athenian funerals for those who had died for their country.

6. Smith was using Thucydides' quotation from the funeral oration by Pericles: "future relicts of those who may fall in the public contests."

those generous Americans who stood . . . . :
who *then* stood.

25. [21] Instead of enable them to give us Peace, and protect us: Would it not be better to say, to obtain Peace for them and us, and Security in the Enjoyment of our common Liberty? For Gratitude: Affection.

Part. 2. Page 6. [28–30]. Had he evidenced, &c. to page 8, as far as Principles and Consistency: In our Opinion had much better be omitted.[7]

Page 11. for nothing except: nothing but

17. [37] instead of *deserted*, &c. say were compell'd perhaps by hard Necessity to return home.[8]

20 [40] Pennsylvanian.

21 recorded to their perpetual honour: omit *perpetual*.

In another hand: The foregoing in the Handwriting of Dr. Franklin, were the Amendments and Alterations proposed by Him and Wm. Livingston, Esqr., on perusing the Mss. Oration on Gen. Montgomery before it went to the Press.

To Daniel Roberdeau[9]   ALS: University of Indiana Library

Dear Sir   Wednesday March 6. 76

The Congress desire a Return to be made to them of the Powder the Committee of Safety have lent them, that it may be known

---

7. Montgomery had gone on the expedition, Smith contended, still hoping for reconciliation; otherwise he himself could not have given the oration and remained true "to my own principles and consistency."

8. Smith was referring to the men who had left Arnold at the beginning of his expedition against Canada; see Gates to BF above, Dec. 5. The printed text still depicted these men as in effect deserters, but again a defensive footnote was added.

9. A prominent Philadelphia merchant who has often appeared before; see for example above, XVII, 81–90, 237–9. He served with BF on the Pa. committee of safety, and the following July was promoted to brigadier general of Pa. militia. *DAB*.

how much is due. I am very respectfully Dear Sir Your most obedient humble Servant   B FRANKLIN

A Copy of the Order for Replacing the Arms was given 2 Days since by Mr. Thomson to the Commissary Mr. Towers.[1]

Col. Roberdeau

Addressed: Col. Roberdeau / at the / Committee of Safety / Lodge

Endorsed: Doctr. Franklin 6th Mar: 1776

To Philip Schuyler   ALS: New York Public Library

Sir   Philada. March 11. 1776

The Congress have appointed three Commissioners to go to Canada, of which Number I have the Honour to be one. We purpose setting out some day this Week.[2] I take the Liberty of mentioning this, as possibly a little previous Notice may enable you more easily to make any Preparation you shall judge necessary to facilitate and expedite our Journey, which I am sure you will be kindly dispos'd to do for us. A Friend with us will make our Company Four, besides our Servants. We shall either come in Carriages directly to Albany, or by Water, if the River is open, from N York.[3] Hoping soon for the Pleasure of seeing you I now

1. BF is writing, we assume, for the secret committee, which had been ordered by Congress in February to return to the Pa. committee of safety two tons of the powder that the latter had furnished and the arms that had been borrowed; a further order to return powder was issued on the day of BF's note. *JCC*, IV, 124, 168, 187. Charles Thomson was secretary of Congress and Robert Towers commissary of the committee of safety, which on March 8 ordered him to apply for the arms and powder. *Pa. Col. Recs.*, X, 508, 511.

2. They were delayed by the debate over their instructions, for which see the headnote that follows. On the 26th BF bought a new saddle and left Philadelphia: entries of that date in his Memorandum Book described above, VII, 167-8. Congress, however, provided a carriage as far as New York: *JCC*, IV, 271.

3. The friend was Father Carroll, for whom see the headnote just cited. The company turned out to be five. On March 16 Congress commissioned Baron de Woedtke a brigadier general and ordered him to go with the party from New York; see the notes on Gates to BF above, Feb. 23, 1776, and on BF to Alexander below, March 27. The river was in fact open, and BF asked for a sloop: *ibid.*

only add, that I am, with the sincerest Esteem and Respect, Sir, Your most obedient humble Servant   B Franklin

P.S. The Bearer M. Le Jeunesse has been considered by the Congress as a Friend to the American Cause, and he is recommended to your Protection in his Return to Canada.[4]

Honourable General Skuyler

Endorsed: Philadelphia March 11th: 1776 From Dr. Benj: Franklin

Instructions and Commission from Congress to Franklin, Charles Carroll, and Samuel Chase for the Canadian Mission.

> I: Copy,[5] National Archives; II: DS, Yale University Library; copy, National Archives.

On February 15, in response to the report the day before from the committee of secret correspondence, Congress resolved to send a committee of three as its commissioners to Canada. Two of the members were to be delegates, and Franklin and Samuel Chase were chosen. The third member was Charles Carroll of Carrollton, a prominent and wealthy Maryland Roman Catholic who had been educated in France; and he was asked to persuade John Carroll, his cousin and a priest, to accompany the mission.[6] On the 17th a three-man committee, on which John Adams served, was appointed to draft the instructions for the commissioners. Then followed weeks of inaction. On March 11 and 12 the instructions were debated; on the 19th the committee submitted

---

4. See the headnote above on the report to Congress from the committee of secret correspondence, Feb. 14.

5. We have been unable to locate the original MS. The copy, with two exceptions noted below, differs only in capitalization and punctuation from the text in the *JCC*, IV, 215–19, and is in the same hand as the copy of the commission.

6. *Ibid.*, pp. 151–2. For Chase see his letter above, Aug. 4, and for the two Carrolls the *DAB*. Charles Carroll's *Journal* is the best single source for the mission. Father Carroll, although he agreed to go, was extremely pessimistic about the chance of success; see Thomas O'Brien Hanley, ed., *The John Carroll Papers* (3 vols., Notre Dame, Ind., and London, 1976), I, 46. John Adams, by contrast, was extremely optimistic: BF's knowledge of French and of France, his experience, wisdom, prudence, and "engaging Address," and his devotion to the American cause made him the best possible man for the undertaking; Chase was active, eloquent, and capable; and the Carrolls were qualified by their background and religion as well as by their abilities. Smith, *Letters*, III, 275–6.

some new ones, and on the 20th others were offered from the floor, adopted, and incorporated in the final form of the document as it appears below. At the same time the commission, introduced by the committee in draft on the 19th, was also debated by paragraphs and adopted.[7]

The long pause between taking and implementing the decision to send the mission may seem puzzling. The need to seize the initiative in Canada had long been apparent, and grew steadily more pressing.[8] The commissioners in fact arrived too late to accomplish anything; why then were they so slow in leaving Philadelphia? One reason was no doubt the weather: the journey in winter, particularly for a man of Franklin's age, would have been awesomely hazardous, and even by April he was not sure he would survive it.[9] A more fundamental reason, John Adams said years later, was political. The principal charge to the commissioners was to form a union with the people of Canada, who were to be instructed in American ways of self-government so that their province might become an harmonious part of the whole. When the United Colonies made this proposal, they took a major step toward declaring their own independence; and this fact, according to Adams, gave the delegates pause. At the time the great objective of Adams and his partisans was to have Congress recommend the establishment of new governments in the colonies—precisely what the instructions recommended for the Canadians, and what aroused opposition in Philadelphia. Acceptance of the instructions, Adams concluded, was "a strong proof of the real determination of a Majority of Congress to go with Us to the final Consummation of our Wishes."[1]

I

Gentlemen,   In Congress March 20th. 1776.

You are with all convenient Dispatch to repair to Canada, and make known to the People of that Country the Wishes and Intentions of Congress with Respect to them.

Represent to them that the Arms of the United Colonies having been carried into that Province for the Purpose of frustrating the Designs of the British Court against our Common Liberties, we expect not only to defeat the hostile Machinations of Govr. Carlton against us, but that we shall put it in the Power of our Canadian Brethren to pursue such Measures for securing their own Freedom

---

7. *JCC*, IV, 159, 197–8, 213, 215–19.

8. See the headnote on the report from the committee of secret correspondence above, Feb. 14.

9. BF to Quincy below, April 15.

1. Butterfield, *John Adams Diary*, III, 372.

and Happiness, as a generous Love of Liberty and sound Policy shall dictate to them.

Inform them that in our Judgment their Interest and ours are inseparably united. That it is impossible we can be reduced to a servile Submission to Great Britain without their sharing in our Fate; and on the other Hand, if we obtain, as we doubt not we shall, a full Establishment of our Rights, it depends wholly on their Choice, whether they will participate with us in those Blessings, or still remain subject to every Act of Tyranny, which British Ministers shall please to exercise over them. Urge all such Arguments as your Prudence shall suggest to enforce our Opinion concerning the mutual Interests of the two Countries and to convince them of the Impossibility of the War being concluded to the Disadvantage of the Colonies if we wisely and vigorously co-operate with each other.

To convince them of the Uprightness of our Intentions towards them, you are to declare that it is our Inclination that the People of Canada may set up such a Form of Government, as will be most likely, in their Judgment, to produce their Happiness; and you are in the strongest Terms to assure them, that it is our earnest Desire to adopt them into our Union as a Sister Colony, and to secure the same general System of mild and equal Laws for them and for ourselves, with only such local Differences, as may be agreeable to each Colony respectively.

Assure the People of Canada that we have no Apprehension that the French will take any Part with Great Britain, but that it is their Interest, and we have Reason to believe their Inclination, to cultivate a friendly Intercourse with these Colonies.

You are from this, and such other Reasons as may appear most proper to urge the Necessity the People are under of immediately taking some decisive Step to put themselves under the Protection of the United Colonies. For expediting such a Measure, you are to explain to them our Method of collecting the Sense of the People and conducting our Affairs regularly by Committees of Observation and Inspection in the several Districts, and by Conventions and Committees of Safety in the several Colonies. Recommend these Modes to them. Explain to them the Nature and Principles of Government among Freemen, developing in Contrast to these, the base, cruel and insidious Designs involved in the late Act of

Parliament for making a more effectual Provision for the Government of the Province of Quebec. Endeavour to stimulate them, by Motives of Glory as well as Interest, to assume a Part in a Contest, by which, they must be deeply affected: and to aspire to a Portion of that Power by which they are ruled, and not to remain the mere Spoils and Prey of Conquerors and Lords.

You are further to declare that we hold sacred the Rights of Conscience, and may promise to the whole People solemnly, in our Name, the free and undisturbed Exercise of their Relegion, and to the Clergy the full, perfect, and peaceable Possession and Enjoyment of all their Estates, that the Government of every Thing relating to their Relegion and Clergy shall be left entirely in the Hands of the good People of that Province, and such Legislature as they shall constitute: provided however that all other Denominations of Christians be equally entituled to hold Offices and enjoy civil Privileges and the free Exercise of their Relegion and be totally exempt from the Payment of any Tythes or Taxes for the Support of any Relegion.

Inform them that you are vested by this Congress with full Powers to effect these Purposes; and therefore press them to have a compleat Representation of the People assembled in Convention with all possible Expedition to deliberate concerning the Establishment of a Form of Government and an Union with the united Colonies. As to the Terms of the Union insist upon the Propriety of their being similar to those on which the other Colonies unite. Should they object to this, report to this Congress those Objections, and the Terms on which alone they will come into our Union. Should they agree to our Terms you are to promise in the Names of the united Colonies that we will defend and protect the People of Canada against all Enemies in the same Manner as we will defend and protect any of the united Colonies.

You are to establish a free Press and to give Directions for the frequent Publication of such Pieces as may be of Service to the Cause of the United Colonies.[2]

2. Congress had already commissioned Fleury Mesplet (1735–94), a French printer who had emigrated from Lyons to Philadelphia via London, to ply his trade in Canada: *JCC*, IV, 168, 173. He left Philadelphia on March 18 and set up a press in Montreal the following May; when the Americans retreated the British briefly imprisoned him. Aegidus Fauteux, "Fleury Mesplet: une étude

You are to settle all Disputes between the Canadians and the Continental Troops, and to make such Regulations relating thereto as you shall judge proper.

You are to make a Strict and impartial Enquiry into the Cause of the Imprisonment of Col. Du-fee Lt. Col. Nefeu, Major Saint George Du pree, and Major Gray Officers of Militia and of John Frazer Esquire late a Judge of Police at Montreal, and take such Order concerning them as you shall judge most proper.[3]

In reforming any Abuses you may observe in Canada, establishing and enforcing Regulations for Preservation of Peace and good Order there, and composing Differences between the Troops of the United Colonies and the Canadians, all Officers and Soldiers are required to yield Obedience to you.

And to enforce the Decisions that you or any two of you may make, you are empowred to suspend any military Officer from the Exercise of his Commission, till the Pleasure of the Congress shall be known, if you or any two of you shall think it expedient.

You are also empowred to sit and vote as Members of Councils of War in directing Fortifications and Defences to be made, or to be demolished,[4] and to draw Orders upon the President for any Sums of Money not exceeding one Hundred Thousand Dollars in the whole to defray the Expence of the Works.

Lastly, you are, by all the Means you can use, to promote the

---

sur les commencements de l'imprimerie dans la ville de Montréal," Bibliographical Soc. of America, *Papers*, XXVIII (1934), 165–8.

3. The inquiry was into allegations that Gen. Wooster's military government of Montreal was arbitrary. Col. Dufy-Desaulniers, Lieut. Col. Neveu-Sevestre, and Maj. Saint-Georges Dupré had been chosen by Carleton to organize French and British militia units in the town. Wooster ordered them to surrender their commissions and, when they refused, sent them to Chambly as prisoners. Gustave Lanctot, *Canada and the American Revolution, 1774–1783* (Margaret M. Cameron, trans.; Cambridge, Mass., 1967), pp. 57, 79, 114. Wooster demanded some papers from John Fraser, paymaster of the British garrison and a judge of common pleas and member of the legislative council; when Fraser declined, the General had him arrested and deported to Albany. *The MacMillan Dictionary of Canadian Biography*, (3rd ed., rev.; London, New York, Toronto, 1963), p. 246; Hilda M. Neatby, *The Administration of Justice under the Quebec Act* (Minneapolis, Minn., 1937), pp. 56–7; Fraser's memorial to Congress, read Feb. 9, 1776, National Archives. See also Fraser to BF below, Aug. 24, Oct. 15.

4. The *JCC* text here adds "by land and water."

Execution of the Resolutions now made or hereafter made in Congress.

Additional Instructions

You are empowred and directed to promote and encourage the Trade of Canada with the Indian Nations, and grant Passports for carrying it on as far as it may consist with the Safety of the Troops and the Public Good.[5]

You are also directed and authorized to assure the Inhabitants of Canada, their Commerce with foreign Nations shall in all Respects be put on an equall Footing with, and encouraged and protected in the same Manner as the Trade of the United Colonies.

You are also directed to use very wise and prudent Measure to introduce and give Credit and Circulation to the Continental Money in Canada.[6]

In case the former Resolution of Congress respecting the English American Troops in Canada[7] has not been carried into Effect, you are directed to use your best Endeavours to form a Battalion of the New York Troops in that Country; and to appoint the Field and other Officers out of the Gentlemen who have continued there during the Campaign according to their respective Ranks and Merit: And if it should be found impracticable, you are to direct such of them as are provided for in the four Battalions now raising in New York to repair to their respective Corps. To enable you to

5. Trade with the western Indians was of great concern to the merchants of Montreal. When the town fell to Montgomery, one of the articles of capitulation stipulated that the trade should continue as before and that passports should be issued for the purpose. The Indians in general, however, were tied to the British, and might be turned against the Americans by agents posing as traders. For this reason Gen. Wooster, when he assumed the command at Montreal, prohibited its merchants' carrying on the trade. They petitioned Congress to be allowed to reopen it. George F. G. Stanley, *Canada Invaded, 1775–1776* (Toronto, 1973), pp. 117–18; Donald Creighton, *The Empire of the St. Lawrence* (Toronto, 1956), pp. 64–5; Robert McC. Hatch, *Thrust For Canada: The American Attempt on Quebec in 1775–1776* (Boston, 1979), p. 196.

6. As early as the previous December Montgomery has complained that the inhabitants would not take American paper money except at a discount; he had suggested sending sutlers with goods that the troops would buy, and so gradually establishing local confidence in the currency. Force, 4 *Amer. Arch.*, IV, 464–5.

7. Congress had resolved in January to maintain nine battalions in Canada and to reinforce them with all possible speed: *JCC*, IV, 39–40, 70–1.

MARCH 20, 1776

carry this Resolution into Effect, you are furnished with blank Commissions by the President. By Order of Congress.

JOHN HANCOCK President

Instructions to Benjamin Franklyn, Saml. Chase, and Charles Carrol Esquires.

II

[March 20,[8] 1776]

The Delegates of the united colonies of New-Hampshire, Massachusetts-bay, Rhode-island, Connecticut, New-York, New-Jersey, Pennsylvania, The three counties on Delaware, Maryland, Virginia, North Carolina, South Carolina, and Georgia in Congress assembled.

To Benjamin Franklin Member of the Royal Academy of Sciences at Paris FRS &c. &c. one of the delegates of the province of Pennsylvania, Samuel Chase Esquire, one of the delegates of the colony of Maryland, and Charles Carroll of Carrolton in the said colony of Maryland Esquire Greeting.

Know ye, that we reposing especial trust and confidence in your zeal, fidelity, abilities and assiduity do, by these presents, constitute and appoint you or any two of you Commissioners for and on behalf of us and all the people of the united colonies, whom we represent, to promote or to form an union between the said colonies and the people of Canada according to the instructions herewith given you and such as you may hereafter receive and to execute all such matters and things as you are or shall be directed by your said instructions. And we do require all officers soldiers and others, who may facilitate your negotiation or promote the success thereof to aid and assist you therein. And you are from time to time to transmit and report your proceedings to Congress.

This Commission to continue in force until revoked by this or a future Congress. By order of the Congress

JOHN HANCOCK President

Attest. Chas Thomson secy.

8. The *JCC* text (IV, 219) has a final line that is missing in ours: "Dated at Philadelphia, this [*blank*] day of [*blank*]." It also omits the signature and attestation. We assume that Hancock signed the document, as he did the instructions, on the day it was approved by Congress.

From Samuel Cooper ALS: American Philosophical Society

My dear Sir, [March 21, 1776⁹]

It is too long since I wrote to any of my Friends your way, being you know a dilatory Correspondent, but not I hope a forgetful Friend. The Relish of the Conversation at Mr. Bowdoin's last Fall is not quite gone off yet.¹ Have you been well ever since? "Accidents of Health, Sir Wm. Temple some where says, are often Accidents of State."² I esteem America not a little interested in your Life and Health; and while these Remain I shall hope my Country will do well. You will hear before this reaches you that the British Troops and Fleet have left Boston: They have retir'd with Disgrace from before the General and Forces of the united Colonies. I congratulate you on this Honor to our Country. Should the War continue, prepar'd as we now are, we should have been well contented they had remain'd here. The Bombardment and Cannonading from our Lines, reaching all Parts of Boston, was unexpected, and troubled their Host; our taking Possession of Dorchester Hills in so judicious and masterly a Manner compleated their Constirnation, and left them no Time to deliberate. They embarqu'd with Trepidation; and most of them I am just told sail'd this Morning. Where they are bound remains a Secret; whether to Hallifax, or the Southwards or to both in Divisions.³ Boston stands, to the Surprize of many, but much plunder'd. I am a Sufferer among a Multitude of Others. My House was let to a Capt. Cochran⁴ of the British Army upon written Engagements. He had the Use of all my Furniture, but has not left a Bed, Coverlid, Sheet, or any Pewter, China, or Crockery, many other Things of great Value carried off or destroy'd. This is a small

9. See Cooper's diary, *Amer. Hist. Rev.*, VI (1900–01), 338.

1. On Oct. 26, 1775, Cooper went to Washington's headquarters to meet BF, Bowdoin, and John Winthrop and his wife; Mrs. Cooper joined them, and they spent two nights with Bowdoin. BF left them on the morning of the 29th to return home. *Ibid.*, p. 323.

2. We have not traced the quotation; for its author (1628–99) see the *DNB*.

3. The British evacuated Boston on the 17th, and sailed on the 21st. They were expected at New York, which was being hastily fortified against them; see BF to Todd below, March 29. In fact they went to Halifax, to await the large reinforcement coming from England, and met it off New York in midsummer.

4. Doubtless Capt. the Hon. Charles Cochrane (1749–81), for whose American career see the Mass. Hist. Soc. *Proc.*, 2nd ser., VI (1890–91), 433–42.

Specimen of the Perfidy and Villainy of British Officers and Soldiers. I esteem it however an Honor in such a Cause to suffer with
and for my Country. Shall we have a Negotation this Summer?
Must we return to the mild and gracious Governm't of Britain?
How is *Common Sense* relish'd among you; it is eagerly read and
greatly admir'd here. The Inability of our Enemies to subdue us
by Force is more and more apparent; I doubt not our Councils will
avail themselves of this and evr'y Circumstance. I am dear Sir with
the greatest Esteem and Affection Your obedient humble Servant

SAML COOPER.

Dr Franklin.

Addressed: Benjn. Franklin Esqr. LLD / Member of / the Continental Congress / Philadelphia

Franked: Free Wm. Ellery[5] New York

Proposed Preamble to a Congressional Resolution on Privateering

Copy: Library of Congress

On March 23, 1776, in response to petitions from merchants, Congress
passed a set of resolutions to authorize privateering.[6] The move was an
answer to the Prohibitory Act of the previous December, which declared
the colonies in rebellion and provided for confiscation of their shipping.
That act was prominent among the grievances in the preamble that was
actually adopted, as it is in this one. During the debate on the resolutions Franklin gave his opinion that they ought to be preceded by a
declaration of war,[7] and the tone of this draft is certainly bellicose.
William Temple Franklin referred to the preamble as "not passed,"[8]
which may imply that it was offered and turned down. Or Franklin may
have withheld it because he concluded that the language was stronger
than the Congressional market would bear.

[Before March 23, 1776]

Whereas the british Nation, through great Corruption of Man-
ners, and extream Dissipation and Profusion both private and
publick, have found all honest Resources insufficient to supply

5. See the note on Williams to BF above, March 1.
6. *JCC*, IV, 180, 200, 210–13, 225–7; the text is on pp. 229–32.
7. Smith, *Letters*, III, 387.
8. WTF, *Memoirs*, I, 288.

their excessive Luxury and Prodigality, and thereby have been driven to the practice of every Injustice which Avarice could dictate or rapacity execute, and wheras, not satisfied with the immence plunder of the East, obtained by sacrificing Millions of the human Species, they have lately turned their Eyes to the West, and grudging us the peaceable enjoyment of the Fruits of our hard Labour and virtuous Industry, have for Years past been endeavouring to extort the same from us under Colour of Laws regulating trade; and have thereby actually succeeded in draining us of large sums to our great Loss and detriment, and wheras impatient to seize the whole they have at length proceeded to open Robbery, declaring by a solemn Act of Parliament that all our Estates are theirs and all our Property found upon the Sea divisible among such of their armed plunderers as shall take the same; and have even dared in the same Act to declare that all the Spoilings, Thefts, burnings of Houses and Towns, and murders of innocent People perpetrated by their wicked and inhuman Corsairs on our Coasts, previous to any War declared against us were just Actions, and shall be so deemed, contrary to several of the Commandments of God, which by this Act they presume to repeal, and to all the Principles of Right and all the Ideas of Justice entertained heretofore by every other Nation Savage as well as Civilized thereby manifesting themselves to be *hostes humani generis*: And whereas it is not possible for the People of America to subsist under such continual Ravages without making some Reprisals: therefore Resolved

Notation: Introduction as proposed to a Congress Resolution

To James Bowdoin

ALS: Massachusetts Historical Society

My dear Friend,   Philada. Mar. 24. 1776.

Inclos'd is an Answer to the Request from the Inhabitants of Dartmouth.[9] I have comply'd with it upon your Recommendation, and ordered a Post accordingly.

I have put into Mr. Adams's Hands directed for you, the new

---

9. Since the previous October Bowdoin had been serving as president of the executive council of Massachusetts: *DAB*. In that capacity he must have requested the establishment of a post office in Dartmouth, now New Bedford.

Edition of Vattel. When you have perus'd it, please to place it in your College Library.[1]

I am just setting out for Canada, and have only time to add my best Wishes of Health and Happiness to you and all yours. Permit me to say my Love to Mrs. Bowdoin, and believe me ever, with sincere and great Esteem, Yours most affectionately B FRANKLIN

James Bowdoin Esqr

Addressed: To / The honourable / James Bowdoin, Esqr / Middleborough / Massachusetts Bay / B Free Franklin.

Endorsed: Dr. Benja. Franklin's Letter Phila. March 24. 1776. abt a Post & Vattel.

From Jacques Barbeu-Dubourg   Extract: National Archives

This paragraph extracted and translated from Dubourg's letter,[2] the original of which has disappeared, introduced a man who played a considerable role in the first two years of the war. The Chevalier Gilles-Jean Barazer de Kermorvan (1740–1817) was the scion of a Breton family. He entered the French army at eighteen, but five years later his corps was disbanded; he then took service with the Ottomans during their war against Russia, and rose to be a brevet colonel of engineers.[3] The end of the war left him unemployed, and by March of 1776 he was in Paris. A fellow officer introduced him to Dubourg, who concluded after one conversation that Kermorvan was "un zelé defenseur, un preux Chevalier qui ne craint point de franchir les monts et les mers, pour chercher de glorieuses aventures, et combattre pour la liberté des hommes comme les anciens Preux pour l'honneur des Dames." The Chevalier was leaving the next day, Dubourg added, to offer his services to America.[4] He reached New York in June and, as one of the first French volunteers, attracted immediate interest. Washington supplied him with a letter of introduction to Congress, and Gates with one to Franklin. He was cordially received in Philadelphia, and within a few weeks was put to work.

1. See above, Dumas to BF, May 17, June 30, and BF's reply of Dec. 9. Harvard's acknowledgment of the gift is below, Sept. 30.

2. On BF's instructions; see his note to Rush below, June 26.

3. Lasseray, *Les Français*, I, 120–2.

4. Dubourg to Benjamin Rush, March 24, 1776, printed in Lyman H. Butterfield, "Franklin, Rush, and the Chevalier Kermorvan: an Episode of '76," APS *Library Bulletin*, 1946 (Philadelphia, 1947), pp. 34–5.

By late July he was outlining to Franklin his ideas for defending the coast.[5]

[March 24. 1776.]
I very seriously think that the Chevalier de Kermorvan is one of the best Men your Country can acquire, he has already embraced its sentiments, and neither demands nor has the ambition of obtaining any Rank, untill his Zeal and talents have been experienced. He is even willing to devote himself to all dangers as a simple Volunteer with as good and Chearfull a Will as if he had the cheif Command, besides he appears to me well instructed in the Military Art of which our Foibbles hardly know the Name. &ca.

Extract of a Letter from Mr. Dubourg to Doctor Franklin Dated Paris March 24. 1776.

Notation: Extract 24th. June 1776 Lre from Monsr Dubourg at Paris to Dr Franklin recomending Monsr Kermovan reced 28th. June before Bd of War

To William Alexander[6] ALS: New-York Historical Society

My dear Lord, Brunswick, March Wedny. 27. 1776
I received your obliging Letter some Days since at Philada. but our Departure from thence being uncertain, I could not till now acquaint your Ldp. when we expected to be at New-York. We move but slowly, and think we shall scarce reach farther than Newark to-morrow, so that we cannot have the Pleasure of seeing you before Friday. Being myself from long Absence as much a Stranger in N York as the other Gentlemen, We join in requesting you would be so good as to cause Lodgings to be provided for us, and a Sloop engaged to carry us to Albany. There are five of us,

5. *Ibid.*, pp. 35–7; below, Gates to BF, June 23; BF to Rush, June 26; Kermorvan to BF, July 26.
6. Known as Lord Stirling, and an old acquaintance: above, XIX, 191 n. He had been commissioned colonel the previous November and a major general in the continental army on March 1, and was in charge of preparing the defense of New York against the expected British attack. *DAB.*

and we purpose staying in New York two Nights at least.[7] With great and sincere Esteem and Respect, I have the Honour to be, My Lord, Your Lordship's most obedient and most humble Servant
                                                    B FRANKLIN

Rt. Honble Lord Stirling

To Anthony Todd[8]

ALS: Public Record Office; copy; American Philosophical Society

Dear Sir,   New York, March 29. 1776
    Being here in my Way to Canada and understanding that your Packet sails to-morrow, I take the Opportunity of sending a Line or two to some Friends; among the rest give me leave to salute you with my warmest Wishes for your Health and Prosperity.
    I shall write Politicks to none of them but to you. How long will the *Insanity* on your side the Water continue? Every Day's Plundering of our Property and Burning our Habitations, serves but to exasperate and unite us the more. The Breach between you and us grows daily wider and more difficult to heal. Britain with-

7. The five were the three commissioners, Father Carroll, and Baron de Woedtke, who joined them that day at New Brunswick—to the considerable amusement of the priest. "Though I had frequently seen him before," John Carroll wrote his mother, "yet he was so disguised in furs, that I scarce knew him, and never beheld a more laughable object in my life. Like other Prussian officers, he appears to me as a man who knows little of polite life, and yet has picked up so much of it in his passage through France, as to make a most awkward appearance." Thomas O'Brien Hanley, ed., *The John Carroll Papers* (3 vols., Notre Dame, Ind., and London, 1976), I, 47. We have found no mention of the Baron as part of the group after April 8: *Journals of the Provincial Congress . . . of New York*, 1775–1776–1777 (2 vols., Albany, 1842), I, 402. Achard de Bonvouloir, the young French agent whose report is printed above, Dec. 28, is said to have accompanied the party because BF had persuaded him to try to sway the French seigneurs as Father Carroll was to sway the clergy: Joseph Hamon, *Le Chevalier de Bonvouloir* (Paris, 1953), pp. 60–1. The author cites no evidence, and we have found none.
    The stay in New York was longer than BF expected, and in the letter just cited Father Carroll characterized it as disagreeable. The party sailed on the afternoon of April 2: Carroll, *Journal*, p. [37].
    8. This is the first surviving letter, since BF's return from England, to his old acquaintance in the Post Office; and it shows more than any previous one the relationship between them.

out us can grow no stronger: Without her we shall become a tenfold greater and mightier People. Do you chuse to have so increasing a Nation of Enemies? Do you think it prudent by your Barbarities to fix us in a rooted Hatred of your Nation, and make all our innumerable Posterity detest you? Yet this is the Way in which you are now proceeding. Our Primers begin to be printed with Cuts of the Burnings of Charlestown, of Falmouth, of James Town, of Norfolk,[9] with the Flight of Women and Children from these defenceless Places, some Falling by Shot in their Flight. Allen and his People, with Lovell, an amiable Character and a Man of Letters! all in CHAINS on board your Ships;[1] [*in the margin*: Is any body among you weak enough to imagine that these Mischiefs are neither to be paid for, nor revenged?] while we treat your People that are our Prisoners, with the utmost Kindness and Humanity. Your Ministers may imagine that we shall soon be tired of this, and submit. But they are mistaken, as you may recollect they have been hitherto in every Instance in which I told you at the time that they were mistaken. And I now venture to tell you, that tho' this War may be a long one, (and I think it will probably last beyond my Time) we shall with God's Help finally get the better of you. The Consequences I leave to your Imagination.

I hope your dear little Girl is well, and that you continue happy. Pray present my most affectionate Respects to my good Lord Le Despencer: and my Love to Mrs. and Mr. Jackson.[2] With sincere Esteem and Regard, I am ever, Dear Sir, Your most obedient humble Servant   B FRANKLIN

I do not trouble you with the enclos'd in order to frank them. Be so good as to wafer, charge and forward them: By that means they will go safe.

9. Charlestown had been burned on June 17, 1775, during the Battle of Bunker Hill, Falmouth (now Portland, Me.) on Oct. 18, Jamestown, R.I., on Dec. 10, and Norfolk by Lord Dunmore on Jan. 1, 1776.

1. Ethan Allen had been captured in Canada the previous September. James Lovell (1737–1814), the first orator to commemorate the Boston Massacre, had been arrested for spying after Bunker Hill, and in 1776 was sent to Halifax. *DAB.*

2. His daughter was Eleanour, then a teen-ager; Charles Jackson was comptroller of the Post Office. See Kenneth Ellis, *The Post Office in the Eighteenth Century* . . . (London, 1958), pp. 105–6, 144.

P.S. Since writing the above I have been riding round the Skirts of this Town to view the Works; they are but lately begun, but prodigiously forward, all Ranks of People working at them as Volunteers with the greatest Alacrity, and without Pay, to have them ready for the Reception of Gen. Howe, who having finish'd his Visit to Boston is daily expected here.[3]

What will you do with this Spirit? You can have no Conception of Merchants and Gentlemen working with Spades and Wheelbarrows among Porters and Negroes: I suppose you will scarce believe it.

Antho Todd, Esqr

Notation: Original Letter from Doctor Franklyn to Mr Todd communicated by Mr Todd

To Jonathan Williams, Jr. ALS: American Philosophical Society

Dear Nephew, New York, March 29. 1776.

I have not written to you for some time, partly from the Difficulty of Corresponding, and partly because I understood from yours of September last that you purposed a Voyage to the West Indies, and I expected to hear of you from thence. Mr. Wm Temple who arrived lately in the Packet, tells me, that you are settled down in England for Life, and have no Thoughts of ever again visiting America.[4] Are you married to that sweet Girl? Or are you satisfy'd with the Sweets of the Sugar House which he tells me

3. See the note on Cooper to BF above, March 21.

4. The disappearance of the September letter leaves us in the dark about the trip to the Caribbean. William Temple (1735–86), John's brother, was a friend of Benning Wentworth, Governor of New Hampshire, and had served for a time on his council. Jere R. Daniell, *Experiment in Republicanism: New Hampshire Politics and the American Revolution* . . . (Cambridge, Mass., 1970), p. 18; Temple Prime, *Some Account of the Temple Family: Appendix* . . . (New York, 1899), p. 117; Ogden Codman, *Index of Obituaries in Boston Newspapers* . . . (3 vols., Boston, 1968), III, 448. Temple sailed on Jan. 10 and arrived in New York in early March: *Pa. Gaz.*, March 13, 1776. He went on at once to Philadelphia, where he created a stir in Congress by producing two letters from Arthur Lee: Smith, *Letters*, III, 384, 409. Temple presumably brought BF news of Mrs. Stevenson as well as of JW, and perhaps the large parcel that she had mentioned in her letter to BF above, Nov. 16.

you are engag'd in?[5] Or are you turned Tory? When you have an Opportunity, if there is ever to be another, let me know that you are well and happy; which will be a great Pleasure to Your affectionate Uncle   B FRANKLIN

[*In the margin:*] I write this upon New York Paper. Look thro' it and you will see the Stamp.

I am here in my Way to Canada: Quite well and hearty. My best Respects to Mr. Alexander &c.

Addressed: To / Mr Jonathan Williams / at the New England / Coffeehouse near the 'Change / London

Endorsed: Doctr. Franklin N York 29 Mar. 1776.

From David Barclay   ALS: American Philosophical Society

This letter was written, a modern scholar has suggested, at the initiative of the man who is the subject of it, Admiral Lord Howe.[6] The suggestion is plausible: Barclay and Howe were not well acquainted, as far as is known; but in the circumstances their common friendship with Lord Hyde might have been enough to elicit this testimonial. Franklin's Quaker friend was as anxious for peace as the Admiral, and had worked hard for it the year before.[7] Howe was now about to embark on a peace mission for which he needed all the help he could get. The government had decided that he and his brother should be at the same time commanders in chief for waging the war in America and peace commissioners for ending it. The details of their instructions were still being negotiated, and the letters patent did not issue under the great seal until May 6. But the general outline had already been settled.

The Prohibitory Act of the previous December had authorized the King to appoint commissioners to restore peace. The plan worked out in Whitehall provided for two stages of pacification. In the first stage the rebellion would cease: illegal bodies that had usurped power would be dissolved and the legitimate royal officials restored to their functions; all armed bodies acting under this usurped authority would be disbanded and all fortifications held by them surrendered; the old assemblies would

5. See JW to BF above, Nov. 23. We believe that that letter was intercepted; if so he must have said much the same thing in his missing September letter.

6. Gruber, *Howe Brothers*, p. 78.

7. For Barclay's, Hyde's, and Howe's involvement in these negotiations see above, XXI, 360 *et seq.*

reconvene, to provide assurances of loyalty and to petition for release
from the restrictions of the Prohibitory Act. At that point the act would
be suspended, pardons would be issued at the commissioners' discretion,
and the colonies that had returned to their allegiance would be declared
at peace.

In the second stage a variety of readjustments would be made. The
commissioners would insist on compensation for those who had suffered
in the rebellion. A system of raising revenue would be arranged along
the lines of North's conciliatory resolution of February, 1775.[8] The colonists would be assured that judges would receive tenure, that the freedom of legislatures would be maintained by revision of instructions to
the governors, and that any act of Parliament which was considered a
grievance would be reconsidered. The government of Connecticut, and
particularly of Rhode Island, would be altered so as to bring these colonies into proper dependence upon Great Britain.[9] The Quebec Act was
excluded from discussion. Any actions taken by the commissioners were
subject to review in London.[1]

If Barclay knew the limits of Lord Howe's authority, and still believed
that his qualities might bring him success in his mission, the wish was
father to the thought.

London 31st. 3d/Mo. 1776

I could not with any satisfaction avoid informing My Friend Doctor Franklin that Lord Howe continues as *respectable* a Character at
this hour, as when we last parted—a Hint, that I thought, in every
point of view, consistant for me to comunicate to my respectable
Friend, at this critical Conjuncture; with this addition, that whatever the Mission of Lord Howe may prove, I am firmly persuaded,
that, it will *not* be for want of *Inclination* in him, should the Ollive
Branch not rise superior to the direful Din of War. In this Sentiment, I am not alone, as my much valued and able fellow Labourer

8. For the resolution see *ibid.*, p. 592.
9. This was an old intention: *ibid.*, p. 473.
1. We have been unable to find the instructions in print, and have used the
MS copy in the Knox Papers (Clements Library), IX, 19; additional instructions
are in the Hist. MSS Commission, *Sixth Report . . .* (London, 1877), pp.
400–1. The most modern account of the genesis and political ramifications of
the government's proposals is in Gruber, *op. cit.*, pp. 33–8, 73–9. See also
Weldon A. Brown, *Empire or Independence: a Study in the Failure of Reconciliation,
1774–1783* ([Baton Rouge,] La., 1941), pp. 109–15; Troyer S. Anderson, *The
Command of the Howe Brothers during the American Revolution* (N.Y. and London,
1936), pp. 153–6.

Lord Howe

in the desireable Work of *Peace*,[2] most cordially joins me and however the M:D: and myself differ in Opinion from others, we daily have the satisfaction of hearing from *all* Parties Approbation of the Man, who, we have wish'd, should wear the Laurels, by *reuniting* the Colonies to the Mother Country—an Achievement deserving of *more Honours*, and which, must be productive of more *heartfelt Satisfaction* to a *Good* Man, than the Destruction of an *Armada*. I am Thy respectful Friend,　　　DAVID BARCLAY.

Doctor Benjamin Franklin in America

The Commissioners to Canada to [William Heath[3]]

ALS: National Archives

Off Constitution fort[4] April 5th. 1776.
On Board The Rhode Island packet

Sir,

We this Evening arrived here, and from Curiosity Mr. Chase and Mr. Carroll went ashore,[5] and found the State of the fort as

2. Barclay's fellow negotiator the year before, Dr. John Fothergill, who also praised Howe to an American friend and expressed high hope for his mission. Betsy C. Corner and Christopher Booth, eds., *Chain of Friendship: Selected Letters of Dr. John Fothergill* . . . (Cambridge, Mass., 1971), p. 467.

3. The letter, in Chase's hand, does not indicate the addressee, whom Carroll identified as Heath: *Journal*, pp. 40–1. The Major General (1737–1814) had been ordered to New York on March 19, to take command if he found no senior officer present. Fitzpatrick, *Writings of Washington*, IV, 409. In fact, as noted below, it was Gen. Putnam who received and forwarded the letter.

4. The only fort in the Highlands at the time, on what had been Martelaer's Rock and was coming to be known as Constitution Island; it is across from West Point at the narrowest part of the river. The party had left New York late on April 2, and been delayed by a severe storm and a split mainsail: *Journal*, pp. 38–9.

5. Their curiosity was doubtless not idle, for the fortification had become a matter of controversy. On Feb. 15 Congress had stopped construction, although the existing works were to be garrisoned, and had ordered a new battery erected to the east of the island and another, which developed into Fort Montgomery, below it on the west bank at the confluence of Popolopen Kill. *JCC*, IV, 152–3. In June work was resumed on Fort Constitution; see H. Crampton Jones, "History of Constitution Island," *New York History*, XXXIII (1952), 280–5.

follows: 3 Companies of Minute Men, Captain Moffats, Capt. Raymonds, and Capt. Woshons, Consisting of 5 Lieutenants, 6 Serjeants, 8 Corporals, 2 Drummers, a fifer and 102 privates. Mr. Seth Marvin 1st. Lieutenant of Capt. Moffats Company has now the Command.[6] On the South Bastion are 13 6 [pounders] and 1 9 pounder mounted. On the East Bastion are 7 9 [pounders] and 1 6 pounder mounted; there are 81 Quarter Barrells and 1 whole Barrell of powder; about one half of the privates are armed and about 60 Bayonets among them. In the block House are 8 double fortified 4 pounders mounted. The Fort on the Land-Side is intirely open. There is not one Gunner or Artillery Man in the fort. Nothing but pork, Beef and flour, no Vegetables; no Barrack Master. The Minute Men work about 6 Hours in the Day and that with great Reluctance.

We are informed by Capt. Bondloe that at Pooplopens Kill there are 180 Troops under the Command of Lieutenant Lee,[7] that 6 32 pounders, and all other Necessaries for Cannon, except powder, arrived there the 3rd Inst. The fortifications directed by Congress 15 Feby, and laid out by Mr. Smith, remain wholy neglected.[8]

Hearing of the Arrival of part of the fleet at the Hook We thought it proper to give You this Information by Express.[9] You

6. Thomas Moffatt and Samuel Raymond were captains of minutemen in Orange County and "Woshon" was, we presume, Ebenezer Woodhull, captain of light horse and adjutant; the three were apparently fellow townsmen in Bowling Grove. Seth Marvin had just been nominated for a captaincy. *Public Papers of George Clinton* . . . (10 vols., New York and Albany, 1899–1914), I, 266–7; V, 679; James A. Roberts, *New York in the Revolution* (2nd ed., Albany, 1898), p. 253; Force, 4 *Amer. Arch.*, V, 252.

7. "Bondloe" was William Bedlow, one of the commissioners appointed by the New York provincial congress, on orders from the Continental Congress, to supervise the fortification of the Highlands. Thomas Lee was a lieutenant in the continental line. Jones, *op. cit.*, pp. 280–1; Heitman, *Register of Officers*, p. 261.

8. Captain William Smith was chief engineer at New York under Gen. Lee, who had a high opinion of him. In late February Smith had briefly inspected the area and mapped out fortifications, and his report went to Congress. *Lee Papers*, I, 356; Dave R. Palmer, *The River and the Rock: the History of Fortress West Point, 1775–1783* (New York, [1969]), p. 51.

9. The letter was delivered to Gen. Putnam, who had just assumed command at New York; he did not forward it by express because the report about the enemy fleet proved to be unfounded. Force, 4 *Amer. Arch.*, V, 811.

will be pleased to communicate the Substance of the above to Congress. We are Sir Your obedient Servants

B FRANKLIN
SAML. CHASE
CH. CARROLL of Carrollton

Notation: Letter from Franklin Chase and Carrol enclosed in general Putnams of the 7th April. 1776

From Philip Schuyler[1]   ALS and copy: National Archives

Dear Sir: Fort George 13th Apr. 1776.

The lake is open in so many places that I am of opinion you may set out for this place as Early as you can. I have received some dispatches from Canada which I Inclose you and by which you will see the necessity of sending a large reinforcement. Please to bring up with you the papers I Inclose as I have no Copies of them.[2]

The Bearer goes Express to Congress and to Gen: Washington. I am Dear Sir Your most Obedient Humble Servant,

P SCHUYLER.

Dr. Franklin

1. We print this letter before the one that follows because we believe that BF received it before writing Hancock. If so the General's messenger covered the more than twenty-five miles between Fort George, from which Schuyler wrote, and Saratoga, from which BF wrote, in a single day. In the conditions then prevailing this seems possible. The snowfall on April 12 produced, as BF told Hancock, a strong current in the Hudson that would have accelerated passage down river. Several days later the commissioners, making the reverse journey encumbered by baggage and fighting the same current, spent an extra night en route but otherwise would have arrived in a day and a half. Carroll, *Journal*, pp. 46–9.

2. The dispatches were, we assume, the gloomy ones from Montreal and Quebec printed in Force, 4 *Amer. Arch.*, v, 868–71. Some of them were long. When they arrived in the late afternoon of the 12th Schuyler, to judge by his covering notes to Congress and to Washington (*ibid.*, cols. 868, 871–2), had copies made for each; his messenger left early on the 13th. The General apparently sent BF the originals in order to save making second copies.

To John Hancock

ALS: National Archives

Sir   Saratoga, April 13. 1776.

We have been here some Days waiting for General Schuyler's Orders to proceed, which we have just received, and shall accordingly leave this Place to morrow.[3] Tho' by the Advices from Canada communicated by him to us, and as we suppose sent forward to you, I am afraid we shall be able to effect but little there. We had a heavy Snow here yesterday and the Waters are so out, as to make Travelling difficult by Land, and there is a strong Fresh in the River against the Boats, but we shall endeavour to get on as well as we can. We join in Respects to the Congress, and to yourself in particular. I have the Honour to be, Sir, Your most obedient humble Servant   B FRANKLIN

To the honble John Hancock Esqr

Endorsed: Col Lee Mr J. Adams Mr J. Jay Mr W Braxton Mr. Johnson[4]

Letter from Doct B Franklin Saratoga April 13. 1776 22 April Copied

To Josiah Quincy, Sr.

ALS: Historical Society of Pennsylvania

Dear Sir,   Saratoga, April 15. 1776

I am here on my Way to Canada, detain'd by the present State of the Lakes, in which the unthaw'd Ice obstructs Navigation. I begin to apprehend that I have undertaken a Fatigue that at my Time of Life may prove too much for me, so I sit down to write to a few Friends by way of Farewell.

I congratulate you on the Departure of your late troublesome Neighbours. I hope your Country will now for some time have Rest, and that Care will be taken so to fortify Boston, as that no Force shall be able again to get Footing there.

3. His "Orders" to proceed to Fort George were the information in the preceding document. The commissioners had left Fort Constitution in the evening of the 5th, reached Albany on the 7th, and gone on the 9th to Schuyler's country seat at Saratoga; in fact they did not start north again until the 16th. Carroll, *Journal,* pp. 39–46.

4. Congress referred this letter, along with others, to an ad hoc committee of Lee, Adams, Jay, Carter Braxton, and Thomas Johnson. *JCC,* IV, 298.

Your very kind Letter of Nov. 13. inclosing Lord Chatham's Speech and Lord Camden's, I duly receiv'd. I think no one can be more sensible than I am of the Favours of corresponding Friends, but I find it impracticable to answer as I ought.[5] At present I think you will deem me inexcusable, and therefore I will not attempt an Apology. But if you should ever happen to be at the same time oppress'd with Years and Business, you may then extenuate a little for your old Friend.

The Notes of the Speeches taken by your Son (whose Loss I shall ever deplore with you) are exceedingly valuable, as being by much the best Account preserv'd of that Day's Debate.[6]

You ask, "When is the Continental Congress by general Consent to be formed into a supreme Legislative, Alliances defensive and offensive formed, our Ports opened, and a formidable naval Force established at the Public Charge?" I can only answer at present, that nothing seems wanting but that "general Consent"; The Novelty of the Thing deters some, the Doubt of Success others, the vain Hope of Reconciliation many. But our Enemies take continually every proper Measure to remove these Obstacles, and their Endeavours are attended with Success, since every Day furnishes us with new Causes of increasing Enmity, and new Reasons for wishing an eternal Separation; so that there is a rapid Increase of the formerly small Party who were for an independent Government.

Your Epigram on Lord Chatham's Remark, has amply repaid me for the Song.[7] Accept my Thanks for it; and for the charming Extract of a Lady's Letter contain'd in your Favour of Jan. 22d.

I thought when I sat down to have written by this Opportunity to Dr. Cooper, Mr. Bowdoin and Dr. Winthrop; but I am interrupted. Be so good as to present my affectionate Respects to them,

5. Quincy's letter of Nov. 13, 1775, and that mentioned below of Jan. 22, 1776, had clearly gone unanswered. Both are missing.

6. This was undoubtedly the enclosure mentioned in the first sentence of the preceding paragraph. For the English mission and death of Josiah Quincy, Jr., see above, XXI, 513. He attended the Lords on Jan. 20, 1775, when Chatham moved to withdraw the troops from Boston; so did BF: *ibid.*, pp. 575–8. The young man's account of the debate was copied, we assume, from his MS journal, and may be found in Quincy, *Memoir*, pp. 318–35.

7. The epigram is lost with the letter. The song was in all likelihood BF's, "The King's Own Regulars": above, under Nov. 27.

and to your good Ladies. Adieu, my dear Friend, and believe me ever Yours most affectionately   B FRANKLIN

Endorsed: Dr. Franklin

To Philip Schuyler   AL:[8] New York Public Library

Dear Sir   At Mr. Wyng's. April 17. 76
    We are all concern'd to hear of your Indisposition, and join in requesting you earnestly to take care of your self. We purpose staying here as you advise in your kind Note of this Morning. We left all well at your House: The Sergeant has a Letter that I brought for you: Mrs. Schuyler requests that you would send him back as soon as may be. I return inclos'd the Papers you favour'd us with. Our Respects to Mr. Chase: I desire him to send back my Mare by the Sergeant.[9] Our best Wishes attend you. I am, Dear Sir

We have sent forward Mr. Chase's Bed and Portmanteau Trunk, on a Supposition that he intends not to return hither.

Gen. Schuyler

Endorsed: April 17th: 1776   From Dr Franklin

John Hancock to the Commissioners to Canada

ALS (draft): National Archives

Gentlemen,   Philada. April 26th. 1776.
    The late Disturbances in Canada, owing to an Insurrection of a Number of the Inhabitants, have, for some Time, occupied the most serious Attention of Congress. In Pursuance of which they

8. The closing salutation and signature appear to have been cut or torn off.

9. Five days earlier the General had been suffering from scurvy; by the time the commissioners joined him it had given way to or was accompanied by ague, from which their medicines cured him. Force, 4 *Amer. Arch.*, V, 872, 1098. On the 17th, when they were en route to Fort George from Fort Edward, he sent a message that the lake was not yet open, and suggested that they stop at Wing's tavern, midway between the two forts; this they did, except for Chase, and continued their journey the next day. Carroll, *Journal*, pp. 48–9. By the messenger BF returned the dispatches that Schuyler had enclosed with his letter above of April 13. Why Chase went with the messenger is not clear.

have come into sundry Resolves calculated both to increase our military Force in that Country, and to allay the Fears and Apprehensions of the People. Of this latter Kind is the Resolve I herewith transmit by order of Congress to you. In Addition to the four Battalions now on their March to Canada, the Congress have, since the Receipt of Genl. Schuyler's last Letter, ordered six[1] more to be sent there as soon as possible.[2] With sincere wishes for your Health, and Success, in your important Engagements I have the Honour to be, with every Sentiment of Esteem and Regard, Gentlemen, your most obedient and very humble Servant

J H. Prest.

To the Honble B. Franklyn, Saml. Chase, & Charles Carrol Esquires, Commissioners in Canada

Charles-Guillaume-Frédéric Dumas to the Committee of Secret Correspondence

AL and copy: National Archives; letterbook draft: Algemeen Rijksarchief, the Hague.[3]

Monsieur   Utrecht 30e Avril [-May 9] 1776
J'ai reçu le 6e de ce mois à La Haie, des mains de Mr. Tho. Storey, les dépêches dont vous l'aviez chargé pour moi en date du 9e Xbr. 1775.

1. The draft originally read "four."
2. On April 1, after Gen. Wooster had left for Quebec, the commander of the garrison in Montreal reported at length to Schuyler on the gloomy situation: the Canadians around Quebec were taking up arms for the British, and those around Montreal were only waiting to do the same; American mismanagement had achieved what Carleton never could have. Force, 5 *Amer. Arch.*, IV, 869–70. Schuyler forwarded this report to Philadelphia; see his letter above, April 13. Congress expressed thanks for the information, appropriated $300,000 for the army in Canada, instructed the commissioners (presumably the resolve Hancock enclosed) to apologize for the troops' behavior and remedy the Canadians' grievances, and ordered six additional battalions sent north from the army at New York. *JCC*, IV, 301–2.
3. The draft, which is in a letterbook entitled "Lettres et Mémoires pour servir à l'Histoire des Et. Un. d'Amérique," omits a considerable portion at the end of the AL, and has frequent small differences in phrasing; we note only those that substantially affect the meaning. Bracketed passages in the AL are in code; the decoding has been interlined on the MS. In the present letter and later ones

Je suis touché, pénétré jusqu'au fond du coeur, de l'honneur que me fait et de la confiance que me témoigne le Committé nommé par le Congrès général pour la Correspondance des Provinces unies Américaines avec l'Europe, dont vous êtes, Monsieur, l'un des dignes membres. Je mourrai content si ce qui me reste de vie peut être utile à une cause si belle et si juste; et je trouve plus noble et plus glorieux de partager, en la servant dans le secret et dans le silence, ses craintes et ses espérances, que d'être le Ministre titré de la Puissance qui veut vous la faire perdre. J'accepte donc avec joie, Messieurs, la commission dont vous me chargez, et toutes celles que vous jugerez à propos de me donner à l'avenir, et vous promets une bonne volonté, un zele à toute épreuve: puisse seulement ma capacité justifier de son côté l'idée favorable que vous avez prise de moi. Cette promesse de ma part est un vrai serment de fidelité que je prête entre vos mains au Congrès de mon propre mouvement[4]; recevez-le, Messieurs, comme tel.

Après cette déclaration, et ces protestations faites une fois pour toutes, je commence, Messieurs, par observer, qu'il est absolument nécessaire que nous établissions un chiffre entre nous, afin que si quelques-unes de nos Lettres sont interceptées dans le trajet, nos secrets n'en restent pas moins cachés. Je vous épargnerois volontiers la peine de faire ce chiffre, en vous envoyant copie de celui que j'ai déjà dressé à cet effet pour mon usage: mais si cette Lettre ici par malheur ne vous parvenoit pas, et cette copie et mon original seroient inutiles; il faudroit en faire un autre, et je ne pourrois pas m'en servir dès à présent. Les paroles sur lesquelles je l'ai composé sont dans le Livre que je vous ai envoyé dernierement, dont je suit l'éditeur, et au-devant duquel j'ai écrit sur un feuillet blanc mon idée sur le *Gouvernement et la Royaute*, dont vous me marquez qu'elle n'a pas déplu.[5] Je vous le désigne assez, je pense.

Dumas used "Monsieur" and "Messieurs" interchangeably, in other words made no distinction between BF and the committee; we have arbitrarily designated such communications as to the committee. This AL went by way of St. Eustatius, and was in Philadelphia by Oct. 1. See below, Stevenson to BF, Aug. 22, and BF to Dumas, Oct. 1.

4. The draft here inserts "et par choix."

5. His edition of Vattel's *Droit des gens*, discussed in his letters above of May 17 and June 30 and in BF's reply of Dec. 9. The committee apparently had tables made for encoding in this cipher; copies are in the APS and the National Archives.

Vous trouverez ces paroles dans ma Lettre à Mr. *** qui suit
immédiatement le titre page III, IV et V. savoir
page III. les 3 dernieres lignes du texte.
page IV. les 7 lignes du texte.　　　　　} en tout 13 lignes.
page V. les 3 premieres lignes du texte.
La premiere Lettre de la 1e de ces 13 lignes est 1. et la derniere 57
La derniere Lettre de la 2e Ligne est ------------------------- 114
--------------------de la 3e ------------------------------- 168
--------------------de la 4e ------------------------------- 223
--------------------de la 5e ------------------------------- 278
--------------------de la 6e ------------------------------- 335
--------------------de la 7e ------------------------------- 394
--------------------de la 8e ------------------------------- 445
--------------------de la 9e ------------------------------- 499
--------------------de la 10e ------------------------------ 555
--------------------de la 11e ------------------------------ 612
--------------------de la 12e ------------------------------ 666
--------------------de la 13e ------------------------------ 682

　　Tout a son nombre là-dedans, même les ' ou apostrophes, les-ou
traits d'union, les virgules, les points, les & et les renvois ou (*).

　　Pour vous rendre cette opération plus facile, j'ai fait imprimer
une série de passé 1000 nombres, dont voici quelques feuilles. Il
n'y a qu'à prendre une de ces feuilles, et écrire le long des colonnes,
depuis 1 jusqu'à 682, (qui est un point) les lettres ou caracteres
des 13 lignes indiquées, chaque caractere à côté de son nombre, et
comme vous aurez besoin en m'écrivant de *k* et de *w*, dont on ne
se sert pas en françois, il n'y a qu'à en mettre 5 ou 6 de chacun à
côté d'autant de nombres qui suivent le 682e; ou, ce qui vaudra
encore mieux, faire servir les c du chiffre, indifféremment pour
des *c* ou pour des *k*, et les *v* pour des *v* ou pour des *w*. Cela ne
m'embarrassera point en déchiffrant. Pour prévenir tout mal-en-
tendu, vous trouverez ci-joint un modele de chiffre sur d'autres
paroles, qui vous servira d'exemple pour la méthode de construire
celui dont nous nous servirons, et dont je vous ai indiqué les
paroles ci-dessus. Vous pourrez cependant garder ce modele pour
des cas imprévus, par exemple si l'autre chiffre etoit découvert. En
attendant nous l'appellerons le petit chiffre, pour le distinguer du
grand. J'en garde aussi copie ici.

　　Pour commencer, je vous dirai, Messieurs, en me servant du
grand chiffre des 13 lignes, que quand je vous ai dit dans ma

405

derniere lettre que *toute l'Europe vous souhaite le plus heureux succès pour le maintien de vos libertés,*[6] j'entendois le public Européen impartial, équitable, humain, en un mot les citoyens de la Société universelle, les hommes en général; et qu'il faut excepter de ce nombre les Rentiers intéressés dans les fonds publics [anglois et celles des cours europeennes qui s'entendent avec la cour d'Angleterre]. Loin de vous [secourir,] elles vous [sacrifieroient] à leurs [interets] ou à leur [peur. Des alliés qui vous] conviennent dans cette conjoncture [, c'est la france et l'espagne,] car leur interêt est que vous [soyiez libres et independants de l'angleterre] dont [l'enorme puissance maritime les] inquiete. Je me suis donc [ouvert a un ministre de france[7]] et la copie et traduction de [vos demandes, et lettre de creance] à mon sujet, sont depuis quinze jours au moins [entre les mains du ministère] et par conséquent [du roi de france.] Dans la conversation [que j'ai eue avec ce ministre,] j'ai bien pu [remarquer que] les [voeux] de sa [nation] sont pour [vous. Il m'a] seulement [fait une difficulte] contre les [secours qu'on pourroit] donner aux [colonies] c'est que, si [elles se reconcilient] avec les Anglois, [elles se reuniront avec eux contre] la puissance qui les [aura secourues] et imiteroient ainsi [les chiens de la fable.] Je n'eus rien de bon à répliquer, sinon que s'agissant ici d'êtres raisonnables, s'ils voyoient qu'on ne venoit pas [pour leur ravir la liberte pour laquelle] ils se battoient, mais plutôt [pour la leur assurer] ils ne seroient pas assez méchants pour [se liguer contre leurs bienfaiteurs] avec ceux qui vouloient leur [arracher cette liberté.] Enfin il a voulu savoir de moi positivement ce que je demandois [a sa cour] pour [les colonies?] Je lui ai répondu que vous desiriez de savoir *Primo*: si [le roi de france voudroit] bien, [par humanité et magnanimité, interposer sa me-

6. In the lost letter of July 8, 1775, which BF acknowledged in his of Dec. 9.

7. The abbé Desnoyers, a Jesuit who was the chargé d'affaires of the French embassy; the Ambassador had been recalled, and his replacement did not arrive until the end of the year. Dumas has left an amusing account of their interview. He began it by asking the chargé to forward to Vergennes a letter of crucial importance. Desnoyers consented if he could see the contents and, when the other hesitated, assured him that he would treat it as if it were under the seal of the confessional. Dumas answered that he never confessed. What, then, was his faith—Jewish? Quaker? "Je n'appartiens à aucune secte." The abbé then read the letter, agreed on its importance, and promised to let him know when an answer came from Versailles: the letterbook cited in the first note, pp. 2–3.

diation en faveur des peuples opprimes, et menager une reconciliation qui leur conservat toutes leurs libertés dont ils jouissaient
auparavant]. *Secundo*, au cas qu'une telle [reconciliation ne puisse
avoir lieu,] si les [nations soumises à la maison de bourbon voudroient accepter l'alliance des colonies avec le benefice d'un commerce immense?] Il goûta beaucoup la premiere de ces propositions, [d'offrir a son jeune roi la gloire de rendre la paix aux sujets
des autres comme aux siens?] L'autre proposition ne lui déplaisoit
pas non plus, sans [l'horrible guerre qui s'ensuivroit en europe.]
Je lui remis donc, avec l'Extrait de votre Lettre, un petit Mémoire,
où j'insinue combien il importe [a la france de ne pas laisser sub-
juguer les colonies.] Le tout a été envoyé à [sa cour] il y a quinze
jours environ; et quand la réponse tarderoit, il n'y a point de mal:
en attendant j'ai toujours gagné que l'ouverture est faite, et qu'elle
ne peut que bien disposer [la france pour vous, et l'engager a
tolerer, a favoriser meme sous main les secours que vos vaisseaux
peuvent tirer de france, d'espagne et des iles.] Voilà pourquoi j'ai
copié exactement, dans l'Extrait, ce que vous me marquez avoir
[le plus besoin, comme ingenieurs, armes, munitions.]

Tout cela je l'ai exécuté avec le plus profond secret, comme vous
me l'enjoignez avec raison. La personne dont je viens de vous
parler l'a aussi exigé de ma part, et promis de la sienne. Ainsi
personne, en ce pays, que lui et moi, n'en sait mot: et c'est aussi
le meilleur pour votre service et pour [ma surete, que je ne sois
point connu pour etre charge de vos affaires.]

Mr. Storey, en partant pour l'Angleterre, n'osant y porter deux
Lettres, l'une to Arthur Lee Esqr., l'autre to Mistr. Hannah Phi-
lippa Lee,[8] me les laissa en dépôt, et fit bien; car par deux Lettres
que j'ai reçues depuis de Mr. Arthur Lee, en date du 20e. et 23e.
Avril, j'apprends qu'on a pris à Mr. Storey, à sa descente en Angleterre, une Lettre dont je l'avois chargé pour Mr. Lee. Heureusement elle n'étoit pas signée de mon vrai nom, et la lettre même ne
pouvoit rien apprendre à vos adversaires; ainsi ils ont fait cette
vilainie de plus à pure perte. J'ai envoyé ces Lettres à un ami à
Rotterdam, selon les desirs de Mr. Arthur Lée; et cet ami me
marque en date du 3e. May[9] d'avoir expédié le paquet par un

8. William Lee's wife.
9. The draft adds that he sent the letters on April 30; by this point he was
writing in early May.

Capitaine de Sloep de ses anciens amis, et qui lui a promis de le rendre en main propre, c'est-à-dire à l'adresse que j'y ai mise par ordre de Mr. Lee. Le départ subit des Vaisseaux m'empêchera de vous apprendre qu'elles ont été bien rendues. Ce sera donc par quelque vaisseau suivant. J'ai joint au paquet un chiffre pour Mr. A. L. dans le goût de ceux que je vous envoie, mais sur d'autres paroles, afin que nous puissions nous communiquer nos secrets en toute sûreté. Je l'ai averti aussi que j'aurois l'honneur de vous écrire fréquemment, afin qu'il m'envoie ses lettres, s'il n'a pas de meilleures voies.

Nos Gazettes nous apprennent qu'un Vaisseau Américain, nommé *le Dickenson*, chargé de farine, bougies de spermaceti, cire et douves, pour le compte de Messrs. Bayard Jackson & Compe. de Philadelphie, et adressé à Messrs. Montandouin & freres Marchds. à Nantes, Capitaine W. Meston, a éte conduit par ce miserable et par son équipage, qui se disoit engagé par force, à Bristol, pour gagner la prime proposée par le Parlement. L'ordre écrit de Messrs. Bayard Jackson & Compe. à ce coquin de Cape. est imprimé tout du long dans ces Gazettes. Ces malheureux ont déclaré qu'il y avoit encore plusieurs autres Vaisseaux en route pour la France, tous destinés, comme le leur, à charger en retour des armes et munitions de guerre.[1]

Je sai un Ingénieur, âgé de 50. ans passés, très habile, très expérimenté, très excellent non seulement dans le Génie mais dans toutes les parties de l'art de la guerre, enfin très grand Capitaine, mais très mal récompensé. Je ne pourrai m'aboucher avec lui que dans quelques semaines d'ici. Je lui proposerai le service des Colonies. Mais comme il est veuf, peu à son aise, avec plusieurs enfants, s'il accepte, il lui faudra vraisemblablement quelques avances pour pouvoir se rendre chez vous. Je vous rendrai compte en son temps de l'entretien que j'aurai eu avec lui.[2]

Ce n'est qu'aujourd'hui que j'endosse à l'ordre de Mr. Rey, Libraire à Amsterdam,[3] votre Lettre de change de £100 St. De

1. The draft adds: "J'ai cru bien faire de vous faire part de cela Messieurs, car il se peut que ma lettre vous parvienne avant que cette nouvelle vous soit annoncée d'ailleurs." For the loss of the snow *Dickinson* see the headnote above at the end of January.

2. Dumas' later letters refer to this man but never name him. By June 9 he had declined an offer, and Dumas wrote him at length to try to reverse the decision: the letterbook cited in the first note.

3. See above, XXI, 34 n.

bonnes raisons m'ont détourné de le faire plutôt, et sur toute autre place qu'Amsterdam. Puisse l'emploi conscientieux que je ferai de ce fonds justifier parfaitement vos vues et la confiance dont vous m'honorez. Du reste je suis persuadé de la générosité du Congrès, et je prie le Ciel de mériter par mes services d'en être l'objet un jour, lorsque Dieu aura béni ses travaux pour le salut et la félicité des Colonies, soit par une bonne et solide réconciliation, soit par le succès de vos armes justes et pieuses: en attendant croyez, Messieurs, qu'il n'est rien qui pût me consoler, si les choses ne tournoient pas aussi favorablement pour vous que je le desire. Au fond j'espere beaucoup plus que je ne crains à cet égard. La sagesse si constamment soutenue du Congrès, l'union et la concorde parfaite qui y regne, me rassurent de plus en plus. Par cette union rare, heureuse, admirable, bien plus sûrement encore que par toutes les alliances du monde, vous êtes et vous serez finalement supérieurs à vos cruels et mercenaires ennemis, quelque redoutables qu'ils paroissent et qu'ils puissent être. *Concordia res parvae crescunt, discordia maximae dilabuntur.*[4] Puissent cette grande vérité et le sublime mot de Thémistocle à Eurybiade levant la canne sur lui dans le Conseil, *frappe, mais écoute,*[5] être constamment présents à vos esprits et dans vos coeurs, ainsi que dans ceux de tous vos constituants! Quelle force alors pourra tenir contre la vôtre? Pardonnez la liberté de cette apostrophe à l'enthousiasme[6] qui m'anime pour votre Union, le plus bel édifice que la liberté se soit jamais élevé: en lui se concentre tout ce que le spectacle du monde politique peut encore avoir d'attraits pour moi.

Je vous remercie, Monsieur, de vos bontés paternelles pour les deux françois. Ils sont jeunes; et par conséquent ils doivent s'interdire jusqu'à l'idée d'être un instant à charge à personne, et un poids inutile à la Société.[7]

4. "Harmony makes small states grow, while discord undermines the mightiest empires." John C. Rolfe, ed. and trans., *Sallust* . . . (London and N.Y., 1931), p. 149.
5. Bernadette Perrin, ed. and trans., *Plutarch's Lives* . . . (11 vols., N.Y. and London, 1914–26), II, 33.
6. In the draft the rest of this sentence reads: "de celui de tous les Spectateurs de la tragédie qui prend le plus vif intérêt à vos travaux pour le plus bel édifice que la liberté se soit jamais élevé, et qui verroit crouler avec lui tout ce que le Spectacle du monde politique peut encore avoir d'attraits à ses yeux."
7. In the draft this paragraph reads: "Je suis bien aise que les Sieurs Vaillant et Pochard soient arrivés et se soient appliqués à apprendre l'Anglois pour être

Je suis charmé que le *Précis des différents entre la G.B. et les Colonies* ait été approuvé au point de le faire imprimer pour l'instruction de vos amis les Canadiens. Voici la seule suite qu'ait eu cet Ecrit, car l'Imprimeur ne débitant pas assez de son Journal pour y faire d'autres frais que ceux de l'Impression, a discontinué de salarier l'Auteur de ces pieces.[8] Je me suis fait donner son adresse, pour lui proposer de m'aider à réfuter le Juif[9] Pinto dont la plume vénale s'est émancipée contre les Américains d'une maniere insolente. Quelqu'un que vous savez, Monsieur, est faché de s'être laissé éblouir par son système de finance jusqu'à l'approuver sans réserve dans une lettre ou avis à la tête du Traité de la circulation.[1] Car encore qu'il y ait du bon par-ci par-là, ce quelqu'un est revenu depuis longtemps sur bien des faux-brillants que ce Juif y débita pour bons, selon la coutume constante de sa nation de tout temps.[2]

---

utiles et gagner leur vie de quelque manière que ce soit: ils sont jeunes; ainsi l'idée même d'être un instant à charge à personne doit leur être interdite; et, dans leur situation, je n'aurois pas honte de manier la beche ou de porter le mousquet, plutôt que d'être un poids inutile à la société." BF's most recent surviving letter, that of Dec. 9, had not mentioned that the young men were learning English. That news was doubtless in BF's missing letter mentioned in his above of March 2.

8. "Qui lui a fait aussi," the draft adds, "quelques Extraits de Livres Anglois." For the "Précis" see above, Dumas' letter of June 30 and BF's reply of Dec. 9. What Dumas now enclosed was doubtless "Continuation du précis des différens survenus entre la Grande Bretagne et ses colonies septentrionales d'Amérique," *Jour. des Sçavans*, LXXXIV [*i.e.*, LXXXIII] (Oct., 1775), 222–51.

9. The draft reads "proposer de me faire quelque chose sur le même sujet que je voudrais ajouter à divers autres pieces destinées à la refutation du Juif," etc.

1. The some one was Dumas, who had had the treatise published: above, XXI, 36. Isaac Pinto (1715–87), after a period when he had been influential in the counsels of the Stadholder, lived in Paris and London. His *Lettre . . . au sujet des troubles qui agitent actuellement toute l'Amérique septentrionale* (the Hague, 1776), and a sequel the same year, disturbed the friends of America. See Leon Hühner, "Isaac de Pinto: Noted European Publicist and Defender of Great Britain's Policy during the American Revolution," Amer. Jewish Hist. Soc., *Pubs.*, XIII (1903), 113–26.

2. The draft ends here with a concluding paragraph: "Après vous avoir prié Monsieur de vouloir bien assurer de mon plus profond respect et parfait dévouement le Congrès général et tous ceux qui le composent en particuliers; souffrez que j'ajoute ma vive reconnoissance pour les membres du Comitté des affaires étrangères, pour vous Monsieur, pour Mr. Dickenson et pour Mr. Jay, du grand honneur que vous m'avez fait par l'opinion favorable que vous avez de

Quant à l'idée sur le Gouvernement et la Royauté, je vois avec joie qu'elle a plu, et que peut-être le temps viendra où l'on y fera encore plus d'attention. Cette idée me rend heureux et glorieux, plus que si j'avois fait l'Iliade: car je pense comme Phedre, *nisi utile est quod facimus, stulta est gloria.*[3] C'est un grain que j'ai cru devoir semer dans votre terre, la seule du monde connu où il soit possible de le faire germer. Au reste, je crois cette idée, de plus en plus, vraie et praticable, et de tous les systêmes politiques le plus à l'épreuve des objections. Elle n'a besoin que d'être développée. Dieu veuille que nous puissions bientôt le faire en paix et à loisir. Je vous prierai alors, Monsieur, avec l'estimable et savant Auteur du *Fermier de Pensylvanie*, de correspondre avec moi sur cette matiere pour la mettre en évidence, sinon pour les contemporains, au moins pour la postérité.

Je vous remercie, Monsieur, du Journal des Actes du Congrès du 10e. May jusqu'au 1er. Aout 1775, que vous avez la bonté de m'envoyer.[4] Mais daignez, je vous en supplie, me completter cela, en m'envoyant tout ce qui a précédé et suivi: car nous n'avons ici rien d'authentique de votre part. Tout ce que nous savons de vous, nous le tenons des gazettes, imparfaitement, par lambeaux, d'une maniere vague et variable, le faux mêlé parmi le vrai.

Pour revenir au chiffre, lorsque vous aurez mis les 13 lignes lettre par lettre (y compris les apostrophes, virgules, points &c.) en colonne sur une des feuilles que voici (car c'est par-là qu'il faut commencer) pour déchiffrer facilement et vite tout ce qui est chiffré dans ma lettre, il n'y a qu'à avoir la feuille en main et écrire sur chaque nombre de ma lettre le caractere que vous trouverez à côté du même nombre sur la feuille. Je fais cette opération assez rapidement seul et sans aide, quoique pour la premiere fois de ma vie.

Vous comprenez, Monsieur, pourquoi je ne signe point mon nom.

---

moi: continuez moi Messrs. vos graces tant que je m'en rendrai digne par mon zele à remplir vos vues."

3. "Unless our deeds bear fruit, their fame's but foolishness." Phaedrus, *Fables*, III, 17:12: Thomas B. Harbottle, *Dictionary of Quotations (Classical)* . . . (London, 1897), p. 166. For Dumas' idea see the note on BF's letter above, Dec. 9.

4. *Journal of the Proceedings of the Congress, Held at Philadelphia, May 10, 1775* (Philadelphia, 1775).

Quant aux Lettres que vous m'écrirez à l'avenir, ne mettez rien autre dessus sinon ces trois mots *pour Mr. Vryman*; et là-dessus une Enveloppe à l'adresse de *Mr. M. M. Rey Libraire à Amsterdam*, si vous vous servez de la voie de St. Eustache; ou à l'adresse de *Mr. A. Stuckey Mercht. à Rotterdam,*[5] si vous m'écrivez en droiture de Philadelphie, ou par la France. De cette maniere vos Lettres me parviennent surement.

Utrecht 9e. May *1776*

Dans ce moment, Monsieur, je reçois la lettre suivante sans signature:[6] "Vous serez peut-être tenté, Monsieur, de venir voir {la foire de la haie] j'aurai l'honneur de vous y renouveller les sentimens d'une sincere estime. [Je serai a vos ordres tous les jours a midi, ou plutot,] si vous voulez bien m'écrire un mot de votre logement, pour me faire savoir l'heure qui vous sera la plus commode. Nous pourrons {philosopher quelques momens sur des objets que nous avons deja traites. S'il me reste peu de choses a vous dire,] ce sera avec une vérité et une candeur que je me flatte que vous approuverez."

Je ferai ce voyage Samedi pendant la nuit, pour revenir ici la nuit du dimanche au Lundi; ne pouvant autrement. Quant à la présente Lettre, je dois l'envoyer aujourdhui à Amsterdam, autrement on me menace que les vaisseaux partiront sans elle. Ce sera donc dans une autre Lettre, soit par le même Vaisseau, soit par un autre, que je vous rendrai compte Messieurs de la conversation. Je suis faché de devoir vous laisser en suspens sur une chose si intéressante.

Recevez ici, Monsieur, pour tous les membres du Congrès en général, et pour vous, Mr. Dickenson et Mr. Jay en particulier, les assurances sinceres de mon profond respect.

Endorsed: April 30 1776 From Mr. Dumas

5. Vryman was presumably Dumas' alias in his new career. The committee had instructed Lee, in its letter above of Dec. 12, to write to him via Stuckey.

6. From Desnoyers.

The Commissioners to Canada to John Hancock

LS:[7] National Archives

Sir   Montreal 1st. May 1776

After some difficulty and delay in getting thro' the ice of Lake George, we arrived here on monday last and were very politely received by General Arnold who at present commands in this Post.[8]

It is impossible to give you a just idea of the lowness of the Continental credit here from the want of hard money, and the prejudice it is to our affairs. Not the most trifling service can be procured without an assurance of instant pay in silver or gold. The Express we sent from St. John's to inform the General of our arrival there, and to request carriages for La Prairie, was stopt at the ferry, till a friend passing changed a Dollar for him into silver, and we are obliged to that friend (Mr. M'Cartney[9]) for his engagement to pay the Caleches, or they would not have come for us. The general apprehension, that we shall be driven out of the Province as soon as the King's troops can arrive, concurs with the frequent breaches of promise the Inhabitants have experienced, in determining them to trust our people no farther. Therefore the utmost dispatch should be used in forwarding a large sum hither

7. The first paragraph is in the hand of Charles Carroll and the remainder in that of John Carroll.

8. The party left Fort George on the afternoon of April 19 and spent the next day contending with the ice. The passage of Lake Champlain consumed more than three days, and the travelers did not reach St. Johns, on the Richelieu, until the afternoon of the 27th. There, while waiting for carriages from La Prairie to carry them to the St. Lawrence, they stayed for two nights at a house belonging to Col. Hazen, which had been thoroughly pillaged. They had to lie on the floor, Charles Carroll remembered later, and sleep was out of the question; Chase complained of his back, while BF entertained them with stories. They left on the 29th and apparently reached Montreal the same day. Arnold received them, and they were put up at Thomas Walker's house, which Charles Carroll considered the best built and probably best furnished in town. Carroll, *Journal*, pp. 52–75; for the stay at Hazen's house see Bernard U. Campbell, "Memoirs of the Life and Times of the Most Rev. John Carroll," *U.S. Catholic Mag. and Monthly Rev.*, III (1844), 175.

9. Probably William McCarty, a Montreal merchant sympathetic to the American cause; Chase and Carroll later recommended his appointment as deputy quartermaster general. Gustave Lanctot, *Canada and the American Revolution* (Margaret M. Cameron, trans.; Cambridge, Mass., 1967), p. 140; Force, 4 *Amer. Arch.*, VI, 588.

(we believe twenty thousand pounds will be necessary); otherwise it will be impossible to continue the war in this Country, or to expect the continuance of our interest with the people here, who begin to consider the Congress as bankrupt and their cause as desperate. Therefore till the arrival of money, it seems improper to propose the federal union of this Province with the others, as the few friends we have here, will scarce venture to exert themselves in promoting it, till they see our credit recoverd, and a sufficient army arrived to secure the possession of the Country.[10]

Yesterday we attended a Council of war, the minutes of which we inclose. The places proposed are proper to prevent the further progress of the Enemy, in case they should oblige us to raise the siege of Quebeck. The plank and timber for the Gondolas is all prepared and ready at Fort Chamblee, and some of the Carpenters are arrived from New York; others are to be engaged here:[1] and as hard money is necessary for these, we have a need to advance some out of what the Congress put into our hands for our own subsistance; to be replaced when cash shall arrive.

We understand that the Troops now before Quebeck have not ten days provision; but hope, as the lakes are now open, supplies will soon reach them.[2]

We have directed the opening of the Indian Trade, and granting passports to all, who shall enter into certain engagements to do nothing in the upper Country prejudicial to the Continental interests.[3]

We hope to morrow to obtain an account of our debts, that ought instantly to be paid. If besides what is necessary for that purpose, we had a sum to manage by opening a bank for exchanging continental bills, it is supposed that we might thereby give a circulation to those bills. The twenty thousand pounds above mentioned will, we think, answer both these purposes.

We are told that not less than the eight thousand orderd by

10. Congress had already acted; see the note on Hancock's letter above, April 26, 1776.

1. The places to be fortified were the falls of the Richelieu and the post at Jacques Cartier on the St. Lawrence; the gondolas, or flat-bottomed barges, were to be armed with cannon. Force, 4 *Amer. Arch.*, v, 1166–7.

2. This information came from Arnold: *ibid.*, cols. 1099, 1104.

3. See the commissioners' instructions above, March 20.

Congress will be a sufficient army for this quarter. As yet there are but about three thousand, including those now passing down to Quebeck, who are just come over the lakes. The small pox is in the army, and General Thomas has unfortunately never had it.[4] With great respect to yourself and Congress we have the honour to be, Sir Your most obedient humble Servants

> B FRANKLIN
> SAMUEL CHASE
> CH: CARROLL of Carrollton

Honble. John Hancock Esqr

Endorsed: Letter from the Comrs. in Canada dated Montreal May 1. 1776 read 16th.

The Commissoners to Canada to Philip Schuyler

ALS: Robert B. Gillespie, Lake Forest, Ill. (1973)[5]

Dear Sir,   Montreal, May 1. 1776

We arrived here on Monday last, and have proceeded to Business, as you will see by the enclosed Letter to Congress,[6] which we leave open for your Perusal, and request you will seal and forward it.

We are deeply impress'd with a Sense of the many Civilities we received from you and your good Family,[7] and your kind Attention to every thing that might render our Passage over the Lakes as convenient to us as possible. Accept our thankful Acknowledgements, and make them acceptable to Mrs. Schuyler. With the

---

4. Congress had promoted John Thomas to major general in March and ordered him to take over from Wooster the command in Canada. He reached Quebec on May 1, and was forced to improvise a precipitate withdrawal; see his letter to the commissioners below, May 7. A few weeks later he died of smallpox. *DAB.*

5. The MS, in BF's hand, is now in the Dallas Public Library.

6. The preceding document.

7. The civilities extended over a ten-day period. Schuyler met the commissioners at Albany on April 7 and took them to dinner with his wife and two attractive daughters. The next day they all left by carriage, with Gen. Thomas, for the Schuylers' country seat at Saratoga, where the commissioners remained until the 16th. Carroll, *Journal,* pp. 42–6.

greatest Esteem and Respect we have the Honour to be Dear Sir, Your most obedient humble Servants

B FRANKLIN

SAML. CHASE

CH. CARROLL of Carrollton

Mr. John Carrol joins in Compliments and best Wishes.

Honble. General Schuyler

From Ebenezer Hazard[8]   ALS: American Philosophical Society

Sir,   New York May 3d. 1776

We have no News here, except that the last Phila. Post brought Advice that the Roebuck of 44 Guns was on Shore on the East Bank of Brandywine, and that eight Row Gallies, the Province Ship and Reprisal were gone down to take her.[9] The Phila. Post is not arrived today, and we are not yet informed whether they have been successful.

Mr. Measum writes me that the Genl. has ordered him to frank Soldiers Letters.[1]

Yesterday a Detachment of Troops sailed for Albany.[2] I enclose Holt's Paper[3] and am Sir your very humble Servant

EBEN HAZARD

8. The New York postmaster. See the note on BF's letter to him above, Aug. 3.

9. H.M.S. *Roebuck*, ordered to open the Delaware, ran aground on April 28 on Brandywine Shoal. Capt. Wickes in the Continental ship *Reprisal* and Capt. Thomas Read in the provincial ship *Montgomery* were ordered to attack her, but she got afloat before they arrived. Clark, *Wickes*, pp. 9–10; *Naval Docs.*, IV, 1315–16.

1. George Measam, a Montreal merchant sympathetic to the American cause, was postmaster of the province during the occupation and fled with the retreating army. Force, 5 *Amer. Arch.*, I, 725–6; see also BF to Adams below, Aug. 28.

2. The six battalions that Congress had ordered Washington to send. They were commanded by Maj. Gen. John Sullivan. Fitzpatrick, *Writings of Washington*, V, 7–8. Sullivan took over the command in Canada at the end of the campaign.

3. The *N.-Y. Journal*. For John Holt, the publisher, see the *DAB*.

P.S. Should any Thing remarkable happen in Canada I beg to be favored with a Line.

Addressed: Doctor Franklin / Montreal. / If not there, to be forwarded.

The Commissioners to Canada to Philip Schuyler

LS: Yale University Library

Sir   Montreal May 4th 1776
   Having orders from Congress to enquire into the case of John Fraser Esqr. now prisoner at Osopus, we have thought proper to direct the Commanding Officer there to allow him to repair hither, on his parole to present himself before us immediately on his arrival.[4] We desire you to give the necessary orders for this purpose. We are with great regard, Sir, Your most obedient humble Servants   B FRANKLIN
                                      CHARLES CARROLL of Carrollton
                                      SAML. CHASE

Philip Schuyler Esqr. Major Genl.

Addressed: On the service / of the United Colonies / To / The Honorable Philip Schuyler Esqr. / Major General of / the Continental Forces / Tionderoga / *Franked:* Free

Endorsed: Montreal May 4th: 1776 From Commissioners. Benj. Franklin.

The Commissioners to Canada to [John Hancock]

LS and copy: National Archives

Sir   Montreal, May 6th 1776.
   In our letter of the 1st. instant, we informed you of the lowness of the Continental credit in this Province and the necessity of a

4. For Fraser see the commissioners' instructions above, March 20. The commander whom the commissioners addressed at Esopus (Kingston, N.Y.) was probably Col. Cornelius D. Wynkoop. He had been in charge of officers captured at Montreal until Congress had them removed to New Jersey, and was still at Kingston in late April. *JCC*, IV, 81; Force, 4 *Amer. Arch.*, V, 1053. The

speedy supply of hard money: unless this very essential article arrives soon, our forces will suffer exceedingly from the want of many necessaries, particularly flour, which might be laid in much cheaper here than it could be supplied from New York, provided gold or silver could be procured to purchase it. It is very difficult to keep soldiers under proper discipline without paying them regularly. This difficulty increases in proportion to the distance, the troops are removed from their own country: the want of money frequently constrains the Commanders to have recourse to violences in providing the army with carriages, and other conveniences, which indispose and irritate the minds of the people. We have reason to conclude that the change of sentiments, which we understand has taken place in this colony, is owing to the above mentioned cause, and to other arbitrary proceedings.[5] If hard money cannot be procured and forwarded with dispatch to Canada, it would be adviseable, in our opinion, to withdraw our army and fortify the passes on the lakes to prevent the enemy, and the Canadians, if so inclined, from making irruptions into and depredations on our frontiers. We have given orders for the return of Mr. Frazer to this city, and we now have under consideration the confinement of the other Gentlemen particularised in our instructions.[6]

At Fort George we had an interview with the Deputies of the seven Indian tribes of Canada to the great council of Onandaga: they were on their return home from this council. They informed us that the result of their deliberations was to maintain a perfect

commissioners' directive was apparently not carried out because of the American retreat, and Fraser was eventually transferred to Reading, Pa. See his letters below, Aug. 24, Oct. 15.

5. On May 9 Schuyler acknowledged receipt of the $300,000 that Congress had appropriated for the troops: Force, 4 *Amer. Arch.*, VI, 417; *JCC*, IV, 301; neither source indicates the kind of currency. It was probably paper, for on April 29 the New England governments were asked to collect as much hard money as possible and send it to the General: *ibid.*, pp. 318–19. BF advanced Gen. Arnold and others £343 in gold out of his own pocket, he claimed near the end of his life, and Congress repaid him in paper: Smyth, *Writings*, IX, 696; draft of BF to Charles Thomson, Dec. 29, 1788, APS. The settlement of his account as recorded in July, 1776, however, mentions only a much smaller loan to Arnold: *JCC*, V, 557.

6. See above, the instructions of March 20 and the commissioners to Schuyler, May 4.

neutrality during the present contest: that they had received the hatchet from Colonel Guy Johnson; but being a sharp weapon and liable to wound their bosoms, they were resolved no longer to keep it, but to deliver it up to us.[7] Since our arrival in this city, we have had another conference with the same Deputies, which terminated in a confirmation of their former promises not yet complied with, but delayed only to give time for the assembling of all their tribes, that the hatchet may be given up with the consent of the whole, and with greater solemnity. We judged it expedient to make them a small present, and we think it will be necessary to make them another more considerable, when the hatchet is deliverd up.

We are informed that our debts in this Colony amount to ten thousand pounds, exclusive of what is due to Mr. Price: we have hitherto obtained a list amounting only to between three and four thousand. It will be necessary to appoint persons to settle these accounts.[8] With great respect to Yourself and the Congress we have the honour to be, Sir, Your most obedient humble Servants

B. FRANKLIN
SAMUEL CHASE
CHARLES CARROLL of Carrollton

Endorsed: Letter from the Commissioners in Canada May 6. 1776[9]

7. For an account of the council at Onondaga see Force, 4 *Amer. Arch.*, V, 1100–04. Guy Johnson, Sir William's son-in-law, had been a chief organizer of Indian support for the British until his departure for England the previous winter; see the *DAB*.

8. For Price see Goforth to BF above, Feb. 22. Congress repeatedly authorized payments to the deputy commissary general in April, and on the 22nd empowered the commissioners to have his accounts settled. *JCC*, IV, 298–9; see also pp. 240–1, 250–1, 274–5, 284, 288, 303.

9. The endorsement of the copy provides the further information that the letter was read on May 18 and referred to William Livingston, Thomas Jefferson, "etc.," meaning John Adams. The three men had been designated on May 16 a committee to consider this and other letters received. *Ibid.*, p. 359.

The Commissioners to Canada to Philip Schuyler

LS: New York Public Library

Dear Sir   Montreal May 6th. 1776.

General Arnold thinking the publick interest would be better promoted by appointing Colonel Hazen to command at St. John's and Chambly, in the room of Colonel Buel, has orderd the latter to repair to the Camp before Quebeck, where the General is of opinion his services will be more wanted. Colonel Hazen speaking the French language, and having a considerable influence over the people in the neighbourhood of S. John's and Chambly, and being as active and zealous in the service, and as intelligent as Colonel Buel, induced us to concur with Genl. Arnold in approving the appointment of Colonel Hazen.[1] As we are convinced that you wish only, and seek how best to promote the publick service, so are we satisfied that this arrangement will meet with your approbation. We are informed by General Arnold that the army before Quebeck is only victualled up to the 15th or 20th instant at farthest. We need not point out to you the necessity of keeping our forces in this country well supplied with provisions, as, excepting flower, none can be procured here, and that not without hard money. The army is entirely without surgeons: Dr. Stringer receives 30 *s.* a day: his assistance is much wanted at the Camp; and the Congress, no doubt, expects, when they pay for services,

1. Hazen, while commanding at Montreal, had sent the report discussed in a note on Hancock to the commissioners above, April 26, 1776. The Colonel (1733–1803) had been a half-pay officer in the British service. He owned land near the border, and his allegiance wobbled when hostilities began, with the result that he was briefly imprisoned by both sides and both plundered his property. *DAB.* After he joined the Americans he claimed compensation for his losses; the accounts he submitted were considered excessive, and Congress instructed the commissioners to look into the matter. They do not seem to have made a formal report, but he was subsequently compensated. *JCC,* IV, 73–4, 192, 198–9; V, 812; VI, 900; Carroll, *Journal,* p. 73. Meanwhile his zeal was called into question. After Arnold complained of his conduct he was court-martialed and acquitted, and subsequent inquiries upheld the verdict. For a fuller account of this phase of his career see Allan S. Everest, *Moses Hazen and the Canadian Refugees in the American Revolution* (Syracuse, N.Y., 1976), chap. iii. Lieut. Col. Nathaniel Buel had been commanding at St. Johns; his complete ignorance of French was Arnold's reason for transferring him: Force, 4 *Amer. Arch.,* V, 1155.

to have them performed.[2] We desire to be respectfully rememberd to your family, and are with great esteem, Dear Sir, Your most obedient humble servants   B FRANKLIN
                                               SAMUEL CHASE
                                               CH. CARROLL of Carrollton

Genl. Schuyler.

Endorsed: Montreal May 6th: 1776 From Commissioners of Congress. B. Franklin and others.

John Thomas[3] to the Commissioners to Canada

Reprinted from Peter Force, ed., *American Archives: Consisting of a Collection of Authentick Records, State Papers, Debates, and Letters and Other Notices of Publick Affairs* . . . (4th series; 6 vols., [Washington, D.C.,] 1837–46), VI, 451–2.

Head-Quarters, Point Deschambault, May 7, 1776.
Gentlemen:
Immediately on my arrival at the camp before Quebeck, which was on the 1st instant, I examined into the state of the Army, and found, by the returns, there were one thousand nine hundred men, only one thousand of whom were fit for duty, including

2. Samuel Stringer, a medical officer in the previous war and later the leading doctor in Albany, was Schuyler's friend and probably his family physician, and had been appointed the previous September to head the medical service of the northern department: George R. Howell and Jonathan Tenney, *Bi-centennial History of the County of Albany* (New York, 1886), p. 205. The implication in this letter that the Doctor was neglecting his duty was, if true, soon remedied: by mid-June he was at St. Johns, trying to deal with a vast number of sick and wounded. Force, 4 *Amer. Arch.*, VI, 1039.

3. The new commander in chief; see the final note on the commissioners to Hancock above, May 1. The siege of Quebec had persisted into the spring, maintained by the ice that blocked the St. Lawrence; a large relieving force from Britain had been waiting down the river, and its arrival at the city turned the orderly retreat that Thomas was planning into a near rout. The Americans withdrew to Sorel, and then attempted and failed to mount a new offensive; see the headnote on Wayne to BF below, June 13.

officers; the rest were invalids, chiefly with the small-pox.[4] Three hundred of those effective were soldiers whose inlistments expired the 15th ultimo, many of whom refused duty, and all were very importunate to return home. There were several posts to be supported with this small number, at such distances from each other that not more than three hundred men could be rallied to the relief of any one, should it be attacked by the whole force of the enemy, by means of rivers and other obstructions. In all our magazines there were but about one hundred and fifty pounds of powder, and six days provisions. The French inhabitants were much disaffected, so that supplies of any kind were obtained with great difficulty from them.

Considering these and many other disagreeable circumstances, I thought it expedient to call a council of war; and the council, consisting of Brigadier-General Wooster and all the Field Officers in camp, after mature deliberation, were unanimously of opinion, that as, upon the first arrival of any reinforcement to the enemy, all communication by the river would inevitably be cut off by their armed vessels, it was absolutely necessary, for the safety of the invalids, immediately to remove them in batteaus to the Three Rivers; and to collect the artillery and other stores, in order to remove them and the Army farther up the river, as soon as it could conveniently be done, for the purpose of securing some important posts, where there would be a prospect of resisting with success. This was on the 5th instant, and in the evening of the same day I received certain intelligence of fifteen ships being forty leagues below Quebeck, making up the river. Early next morning five of them appeared in sight, and the wind and tide being favourable, they soon arrived before the city.[5] We were employed at this time in carrying the sick, artillery, &c., on board the batteaus; the enemy, in landing their troops, and, as the event shows, in preparing to make a sally. Our movements were retarded by the change the arrival of these vessels had produced in the dispositions of the inhabitants; for they would neither furnish us with teams nor in any way afford us assistance, but kept themselves concealed.

About one o'clock a considerable body of the enemy attacked

4. The disease was as dangerous an enemy as the British. It had ravaged the troops before Quebec, and continued to kill or incapacitate a large part of the army throughout the ensuing retreat.

5. The vanguard of the relief expedition.

our sentinels and main-guard, in consequence of which I instantly ordered the troops under arms, and detached a party to support the main-guard, which was now coming off in good order. By the best judgment I could make, the enemy were one thousand strong, formed into two divisions, in columns six deep, supported with a train of six pieces of cannon. The most that we could collect at this time on the plains to oppose them did not exceed one-quarter of that number, with only one field-piece.

This being our situation, by advice of the Field Officers present I gave orders for the Army to march up the river to this place, where the greater part came up this day. On my arrival I without delay called a council of war; a copy of the determinations of which I have enclosed, as I have of that held in camp before Quebeck.[6] The result of this council is, as you will see, to advance still farther up the river, and is founded on many reasons, some of which I will suggest: The ships of war were hastening forward with all possible despatch, and had already got up as far as Jacques Cartier; we had no cannon to prevent their passing the falls of Richelieu; and if cannon could have been procured, we had no ball, and not more provision than would subsist the Army for two or three days. We should therefore be under the same disadvantages at Point Deschambault as before Quebeck. They could run above us with their men-of-war and cutters, intercept all our resources, and oblige us to decamp. I am, very respectfully, your most obedient, humble servant,   JOHN THOMAS

To the Honourable Committee of Congress.

From Richard Bache   ALS: American Philosophical Society

Dear and Honored Sir   Phila: 7th: May 1776

I am favored by yours of the 18th. Ultimo from Lake George; this I hope will find you well at Montreal. Yesterday the Alarm Guns were fired, which put the Town into some Consternation for a short time, the Alarm was on Account of three Men of War which were at the Capes, coming up the Bay, we *now* suppose for Water; should they attempt to come up the River we are ready to

6. The minutes of this and the earlier council of war are in Force, 4 *Amer. Arch.*, VI, 454.

receive them. The Roebuck, which by my last I informed you was ashore in the Bay got off again without sustaining any Damage; Capt. Barry is return'd from his Cruize, having sprung his foremast.[7] You will see by the Papers What a formidable Armament we are daily to expect, 45,000, *Commisioners* at least, of different Nations that is to say Hessians Hannoverians &c. &c. Commanded by Lord How, it is said. We are all well and send our joint Love and Duty. I am Dear sir Yours Affectionately RICH BACHE

Addressed: Benjn. Franklin Esqr. / Montreal[8]

The Commissioners to Canada to [John Hancock]

ALS:[1] National Archives

Sir   Montreal. May 8th. 1776

With this You will receive Copies of our two preceding Letters.[2] We find Ourselves obliged to repeat the Necessity of sending immediately the Supply of hard Money therein mentioned. We have tried in vain to borrow some here for the immediate Occasions of the Army, either on the public or our own private Credit. We cannot even sell Sterling Bills of Exchange which some of Us have offered to draw. It seems it had been expected, and given out by our Friends, that we should bring Money with Us. The Disappointment has discouraged every Body, and established an Opinion that none is to be had, or that the Congress has not Credit enough in their own Colonies to procure it. Many of our Friends are drained dry, others say they are so, fearing perhaps We shall never be able to re-imburse them. They show Us long Accounts, no part of which we are able to discharge, of the Supplies they have furnished to our Army, and declare that they have borrowed and taken up on Credit so long for our Services that they

7. Capt. John Barry, in the continental brig *Lexington*, had lost his foremast while being chased; he returned from his cruise on May 5. *Naval Docs.*, IV, 1415.

8. On the address sheet is a jotting in BF's hand: "Our Accts with Congress. What News from Johnson Hall." The accounts were presumably the commissioners' and Johnson Hall a synonym for British dealings with the Indians.

1. In Chase's hand.

2. Above, May 1, 6.

424

can now be trusted no longer even for what they want themselves. The Tories will not trust Us a Farthing, and some who perhaps wish Us well, conceiving that We shall thro' our own poverty, or from superior Force be soon obliged to abandon the Country, are afraid to have any Dealings with Us, least they should hereafter be called to Account for Abetting our Cause. Our Enemies take the advantage of this Distress, to make Us look contemptible in the Eyes of the Canadians, who have been provoked by the Violences of our Military in Exacting provisions and Services from them, without Pay; a Conduct towards a people, who suffered Us to enter their Country as Friends, that the most urgent Necessity can scarce excuse, since it has contributed much to the Changing their good Dispositions towards Us into Enmity, makes them wish our Departure; and accordingly We have daily Intimations of Plots hatching and Insurrections intended for Expelling Us, on the first News of the Arrival of a british Army. You will see from hence that your Commissioners themselves are in a critical and most irksome Situation, pestered hourly with Demands great and small that they cannot answer, in a place where our Cause has a Majority of Enemies, the Garrison weak, and a greater would, without Money, increase our Difficulties. In short, if Money cannot be had to support your Army here with Honor, so as to be respected instead of being hated by the people, We repeat it as our firm and unanimous Opinion, that it is better immediately to withdraw it. The Fact before your Eyes, that the powerful British Nation cannot keep an Army in a Country where the Inhabitants are become Enemies, must convince You of the Necessity of Enabling Us immediately to make this People our Friends. Exclusive of a Sum of Money to discharge the Debts already contracted, which General Arnold informs Us amounts to 14,000 besides the Account laid before Congress by Mr. Price,[3] a further Sum of hard Money not less than Six thousand pounds, will be necessary to reestablish our Credit in this Colony; with this Supply, and a little Success, it may be possible to regain the Affections of the People, to attach them firmly to our Cause, and induce them to accept a free Government, perhaps to enter into the Union, in which Case the Currency of our Paper Money, will we think follow as a certain

3. See the note on *ibid*.

Consequence. With great Respect to Yourself and the Congress
We have the Honor to be Sir Your Most obedient Servants
B FRANKLIN
SAMUEL CHASE
CHARLES CARROLL of Carrollton

Endorsed: Letter from the Commissrs. in Canada May 8. 1776 read
May 18.

The Commissioners to Canada to John Hancock

LS: National Archives

Sir   Montreal May 10th. 1776
By Col: Campbell, who arrived here early this morning from
Quebeck, we are informed that two men of war, two Frigates and
one Tender arrived there early on monday the 6th. instant about
eleven o'clock the enemy sallied out, to the number, as is supposed, of one thousand men. Our forces were so dispersed at
different posts, that not more than two hundred could be collected
together at Head Quarters; this small force could not resist the
enemy: all our cannon, five hundred muskets, and about two
hundred sick unable to come off have fallen into their hands. The
retreat, or rather flight was made with the utmost precipitation
and confusion; however Col: Campbell informs us, that he imag-
ines we have lost very few men except the sick abovementioned.[4]
Genl. Thomas was last Thursday evening at De Chambeau; at a
Council of war it was determined by eleven to three to retreat to
the mouth of the Sorel: this day Genl. Arnold goes down here;
and if he can get information of the enemy's real strength and it

4. Donald Campbell, deputy quartermaster general, took command of
Montgomery's column at Quebec when the General was killed, and ordered the
assault abandoned; it would have succeeded, according to one participant, without that order: Dennis P. Ryan, ed., *A Salute to Courage: the American Revolution
as Seen through Wartime Writings of Officers of the Continental Army and Navy* (New
York, 1979), p. 21. The colonel is said to have had a hearty manner and meager
intelligence. Arnold, when wounded at Quebec, resigned the command to him,
but had to resume it because his officers refused to serve under Campbell. Justin
H. Smith, *Our Struggle for the Fourteenth Colony: Canada and the American Revolution* (2 vols., New York and London, 1907), II, 115–16; George F. G. Stanley,
Canada Invaded, 1775–1776 (Toronto, 1973), pp. 98, 106.

should be found inconsiderable, perhaps a council of war on reconsideration, may think proper to march the army back to Dechambeau, which is now strengthened by Col: Gratton's, Burrels, and Sinclair's regiments.[5] Besides the above losses, one batteau loaded with powder, supposed to contain thirty barrels, and an armed vessel, which the Crew were obliged to abandon, were intercepted by one of the enemy's frigates. We are afraid it will not be in our power to render our Country any farther services in this Colony: if our army should maintain possession of any considerable part of this country, it will be absolutely necessary to keep some power to controul the military. With our respects to yourself and the Congress, we have the honour to be, Sir, Your most obedient humble Servants   B FRANKLIN
                                SAMUEL CHASE
                                CHARLES CARROLL of Carrollton

Honble. John Hancock Esqr Presidt of Congress

Endorsed: Letter from The Commissioners in Canada Montreal May 10. 1776 Read May 18.

The Commissioners to Canada to Philip Schuyler

LS: New York Public Library; copy: Library of Congress

Dear Sir   Montreal May 10th, 1776

Colo. Campbell arrived here early this morning from Quebeck; he informs that five ships of war arrived there last monday the 6th about sunrise, viz: two large ships, two frigates and a tender. The enemy made a sally on monday, between 10 and 11 o'clock, in a body supposed not to be less than a thousand. Our forces were so dispersed that not more than two hundred could be collected at Head Quarters. In this situation a retreat was inevitable and made in the utmost precipitation and confusion with the loss of our cannon on the batteries, provisions, five hundred stand of small

---

5. The regiments were those of John Greaton, Charles Burrall, and Arthur St. Clair; for Greaton and St. Clair see the *DAB* and for Burrall, commanding Conn. troops, Heitman, *Register of Officers*, p. 110. The antecedent of "which" must be "army" rather than "Dechambeau," for the letter following this one, written the same day, places Greaton's regiment at Sorel.

427

Arms, and a batteau load of powder going down with Colo. Allen.[6] Colo. Campbell believes the loss of men inconsiderable, except the sick in the respective Hospitals, amounting in the whole to about two hundred so ill, as not to be removed, who have fallen into the Enemy's hand.

Our army are now on their way to the mouth of the Sorel, where they propose to make a stand. Colo. Gratton's battallion is arrived there, and we expect the residue of the Brigade under the command of Genl. Thompson is arrived before this at St. Johns.[7] From the present appearance of things; it is very probable we shall lie under the necessity of abandoning Canada, at least all, except that part which lies on the Sorel. We may certainly keep possession of St. John's till the Enemy can bring up against that post a superior force, and an artillery to besiege it.

A farther reinforcement will only increase our distress; an immediate supply of provisions from over the lakes is absolutely necessary for the preservation of the troops already in this province. As we shall be obliged to evacuate all this country, except that part of it already mentioned, no provisions can be drawn from Canada; the subsistance therefore of our army will entirely depend on the supplies it can receive, and that immediately, from Ticonderoga.

We need not mention the propriety of immediately fitting out the vessels at that place to bring over provisions and the sending off batteaus, and constructing more for drawing the troops out of Canada, should we be constrained by superior force to take that

6. Campbell's report is also discussed in the preceding letter. Col. Allen must have been William Allen, lieut. col. of the 2nd Pa.; he was not drowned, for he reappears in Wayne to BF below, June 13. He was the son of BF's old political opponent, Chief Justice Allen (above, III, 296–7 n), and, like his father, was alienated by independence; soon after the Declaration he resigned, joined the British, and subsequently raised a Loyalist regiment. Sabine, *Loyalists*, I, 157–8; *PMHB*, IX (1885), 191.

7. William Thompson, who had commanded one of the first contingents of Pa. riflemen to arrive at the siege of Boston, had recently been promoted to brigadier general in command of reinforcements to Canada. He sailed from N.Y. on April 21 with four regiments and a company of riflemen and of artificers. Fitzpatrick, *Writings of Washington*, IV, 500. On May 13 BF, on his way back to Philadelphia, met him south of St. Johns: Force, 4 *Amer. Arch.*, VI, 448. A few weeks later Thompson's military career ended with his capture by the British. Wayne to BF below, June 13; *DAB*.

measure; and in the interim to bring them provisions. It is probable a considerable part of the batteaus now on the S. Laurence will be destroyed, or fall into the Enemy's hands. We mention this circumstance to shew the necessity of constructing more.

We can form no opinion of the force brought into Quebeck by the enemy. Col: Campbell mentions that the information received at our camp before Quebeck was, that fifteen sail of ships were in the river, tho' only five were come up, as before mentioned.

We received your Favour of the 2d Instant directed to BF. We are with great respect and regard Dear Sir, Your most obedient humble Servants   B FRANKLIN
                                       SAMUEL CHASE
                                       CH. CARROLL of Carrollton

Addressed: To / The honourable Philip Schuyler / Esquire, Major General / of the Continental Forces / Lake George

Endorsed: Montreal May 10th: 1776 From Commissioners Benj. Franklin and others.

The Commissioners to Canada to [Philip Schuyler]

LS: Château de Ramezay Museum, Montreal

Dear Sir   Montreal 11th. May 1776

We desire that you will shew to Mrs. Walker every civility in your power and facilitate her on her way to Philadelphia; the fear of cruel treatment from the enemy on account of the strong attachment to, and zeal of her husband in the cause of the united Colonies induces her to depart precipitately from her home; and to undergo the fatigues of a long and hazardous journey.[8] We are sorry for the occasion of writing this letter and beg your attention to alleviate her distress; your known politeness and humanity, we are sensible, without this recommendation from us, would prompt you to perform the friendly office. We are with great

8. Mrs. Walker's house was also the commissioners' during their stay; see the note on their letter to Hancock above, May 1. She traveled with BF as far as Albany; at Saratoga they were joined by her husband, for whom see the note on Goforth to BF above, Feb. 22. By the time that that journey was over, BF was thoroughly annoyed with both Walkers; see his letter to the other commissioners below, May 27.

MAY II, I776

esteem and sincere regard for yourself and family Dear Sir Your
affectionate humble Servants   SAML CHASE
                                    CH CARROLL of Carrollton
                                    B FRANKLIN[9]

From Charles Carroll and Samuel Chase[1]

Copy: Library of Congress

Dear Sir.   Montreal May 11th: 1776
    We are fully sensible of the great Risk of taking post at De-
chambeau. We have suggested in Writing the Difficulties and
Reasons which have occurred to us against that Measure to Genl:
Arnold. Our Army's remaining at Dechambeau will depend in
great Measure on the Strength of the Enemy's Land Forces, and
their Activity and Diligence in following up the Blow they have
already given our small and shattered Army.[2] Before this, no
Doubt General Thomas has received some Information of the
Enemy's Numbers and of their Motions. We are inclined to think
a Retreat will be made first to St. John's and then to the Isle aux
Noix. Our Letter to General Schuyler will give you all the Information we have in our power to give respecting the possibility of
subsisting our Army in Canada.
    We are of opinion that General Sullivan's brigade ought to be
stopped at Fort George, till General Schuyler, can send over with
them a sufficient supply of pork not only for the Subsistence of
that Brigade but of the Rest of the Army in Canada.[3] Flour we are

9. BF normally signed first. In this case he received the note, enclosed with
Father Carroll's below of May 11, and presumably added his signature.
1. After BF left his fellow commissioners on the 11th to return to Philadelphia, he sent them a note that has since disappeared. This letter was their reply.
See BF to Schuyler below, May 12.
2. The commissioners' letter to Arnold, if it exists, has eluded us; but its
purport was presumably the same as that of their letter to Schuyler: that a
garrison at Deschambault could easily be cut off by water and would have almost
no chance of retreating by land. Force, 4 *Amer. Arch.*, VI, 481.
3. Pork was the overriding necessity, the commissioners said in the letter
just cited; without it the men would either starve or eat each other. Sullivan's
brigade was the six regiments that had sailed from New York on May 2, as
Hazard had informed BF in his letter of the 3rd; see also the headnote on Wayne
to BF below, June 13.

in Hopes of procuring in sufficient Quantities to support the Army, at least for four Months, provided we can keep possession of the Country adjacent to the River Sorrel for the Space of three Weeks. We sincerely wish the perfect Re-establishment of your Health.⁴ Our Stay at this place is uncertain: we shall be cautious to retreat in Time to St. John's. We understand there is but a very small garrison there and exceedingly negligent. No Centries posted in the Night. This Information we had from Mr: Price, who was an Eye Witness of this Negligence. Do speak to Col: Hazen about it.⁵ We are with great Esteem Dear Sir Your affectionate humble Servants   CH: CARROLL of Carroll-Town
                                                        SAMUEL CHASE.

B. Franklin Esqr.

Notation: Copy Letter from Messrs. Chase and Carrol to Dr. Franklin

From John Carroll
ALS: Henry E. Huntington Library

Dear Sir   Montreal May 11th. 1776

Among the inclosed papers is an open letter to Genl. Schuyler in recommendation of Mrs. Walker, which your B[rothe]r Commissioners desire you would deliver to her.

If you can conveniently wait all tomorrow at S. Johns, you will oblige me much, as I am uncertain whether I shall not join you.⁶

4. See the note on Mecom to Greene below, June 1.
5. Hazen had just been transferred to the command of Chambly and St. Johns; see the commissioners to Schuyler above, May 6, 1776. If BF did speak to the Colonel about his negligence, the effect was nil. When a shipment of goods from Montreal arrived at Chambly soon afterward, Hazen refused to receive it, despite instructions, and it was pillaged. "This is not the first or last order Colonel Hazen has disobeyed," Arnold commented when he discovered the loss. "I think him a man of too much consequence for the post he is in." Force, 4 *Amer. Arch.*, VI, 797.
6. The note to Schuyler for Mrs. Walker is above, May 11. BF had decided to leave, according to Charles Carroll, partly because of his declining health and partly because of the grim prospect in Canada. *Journal*, pp. 75–6. Father Carroll left because his mission had proved hopeless. The Canadian clergymen whom he saw argued that they were better off under the British than they ever would be under the Americans, who were intolerant of Catholicism. In addressing the British people in 1774 Congress had called their faith, they reminded him, "a

Believe me, my Dear Sir, that no one can wish your welfare more ardently, or bear a greater regard for you than, Dear Sir Your affectionate and most obedient servant   J CARROLL

To Philip Schuyler   ALS: New York Public Library

Dear Sir   St. John's. May 12. 1776

The enclos'd from the other two Commissioners to me[7] is in answer to a few Lines I wrote them from the Ferry after I had taken leave of them, and had in the mean time convers'd with Mr. Price, who told me the other Regiments coming into Canada brought with them only 10 Days Provision. Paterson's I left at La Prairie, no Boats to take them over.[8] It was with the utmost Difficulty I got a Conveyance here, the Country being all afraid to be known to ass[ist us] w[ith car]riages. You will see the absolute Neces[sity from?] the other Papers of forwarding Provisions hither, [or?] the Army must starve, plunder, or surrender. I open'd the Letters to you, being refer'd to them by that to me. I proceed to day, having waited here 36 Hours, and now seeing no probability of the others joining me, since I understand they intend only to retire when the Garrison does. With the greatest Respect, I am, Dear Sir, Your most obedient humble Servant   B FRANKLIN

Honble General Schuyler

Addressed: On the Service of the United Colonies / To The honble. Philip Schuyler Esqr / Major General [of] the Continental / Army / Fort George / per Express

Endorsed: S John's May 12: 1776 from Dr Franklin.

---

religion that has deluged your island in blood, and dispersed impiety, bigotry, persecution, murder and rebellion through every part of the world." See Bernard U. Campbell, "Memoirs of the Life and Times of the Most Rev. John Carroll," *U.S. Catholic Mag. and Monthly Rev.*, III (1844), 244–6, and for the quotation *JCC*, I, 88. Carroll did join BF at St. Johns, and they traveled together to Philadelphia; see the note on BF to Carroll and Chase below, May 27.

7. Above, May 11.

8. For James Price see Goforth to BF above, Feb. 22. The Canadian's gloomy report on the provisions brought by Gen. Thompson may have been true, but within a few weeks the situation had vastly improved; see the headnote on Wayne to BF below, June 13. Col. John Paterson's regiment was the 15th continental infantry: *DAB*.

Charles-Guillaume-Frédéric Dumas to the Committee of Secret Correspondence

AL and copy: National Archives; letterbook draft:[9] Algemeen Rijksarchief, the Hague

Messieurs,   Utrecht 14e. May [-June 6,] 1776.

Après vous avoir donné ci-joint copie ou extrait de ce qu'il y avoit de plus essentiel dans ma premiere dépeche que je nommerai A pour la briéveté, je commence celle-ci, que je nomme B, en forme de Journal. Ayez la bonté, conséquemment, lorsque vous m'écrirez, de me marquer que vous avez reçu, ou non, la Dépeche A, la Dépeche B &c.

J'avois écrit le 9e. à la personne qui m'avoit écrit la Lettre du 6e.[1] dont je vous ai donné la copie, que si ce qu'il avoit à me dire pressoit j'irois et reviendrois deux nuits de suite pour être auprès de lui le jour du dimanche, 12e., qui est entre deux, mais que si l'entrevue pouvoit souffrir une semaine de délai, je pourrois faire le voyage un peu plus commodément et sans inconvénient. Voici ce qu'il me répondit le lendemain 10e. May.

"J'ai reçu, Monsieur, la Lettre que vous m'avez fait l'honneur de m'écrire. J'obéis dans l'instant à l'ordre que vous me donnez de vous répondre sur le jour où je pourrai avoir le plaisir de vous voir. Comme ce que j'aurai l'honneur de vous dire ne presse pas, vous pouvez, Monsieur, remettre au Samedi que vous me proposez, et qui sera de Samedi prochain en huit, c'est-à-dire, le 18 de ce mois, la visite dont vous me flattez, et qui est la plus intéressante que je puisse recevoir. Oserois-je vous prévenir [sur l'offre des fraix dans tous les cas ou vos bontes me seroient utiles? Car un homme tel que vous, par ses connoissances, n'est pas borne a un seul genre de bons offices.] Flatté, honoré de la connoissance que j'aurois faite avec vous, je serois au désespoir de vous être à charge et d'en abuser. J'ai l'honneur d'être bien respectueusement, Monsieur, à vos ordres."

Ne croyez pas, Messieurs, qu'une puérile vanité me fasse vous rapporter cette lettre, et m'attribuer réellement les douceurs qui

9. The draft omits the letter quoted in the third paragraph and the conclusion written on June 6 and has, like Dumas' first report as agent (April 30 to May 9, 1776), passages in code. They are the same as those in the AL, which we indicate as we did in the first report by placing them in brackets.
1. The abbé Desnoyers, French chargé d'affaires.

m'y semblent adressées. Je veux seulement vous faire remarquer combien [on caresse le serviteur pour l'amour du maitre.]

Mardi 21e. May 1776

Me voici, Messieurs, de retour de mon voyage, dont je suis fort content, parce que je crois que vous aurez lieu de l'être. Après nous être entretenus quelques instants de la grande nouvelle, et toute récente, de l'évacuation de Boston par vos ennemis, comme d'un nouveau trait de la sagesse de vos opérations Messieurs, Le Roi d'A. me dit notre homme (dont j'ai dû promettre de ne pas encore vous décliner le nom) ne s'oublie pas non plus de son côté comme vous voyez; et il me montra dans une Gazette un Edit prohibitif fort severe de l'Imperatrice Reine d'Hong. contre toute exportation d'armes et munitions de ses Etats pour l'Amérique.[2] Je l'avois déjà vu, et je lui dis: mais ce que vous ne savez pas, reprit-il, c'est que le roi a demandé cela à l'Impératrice par une Lettre écrite de sa propre main. Je lui fis connoître que j'espérois que sa Cour ne seroit pas si partiale. [Vous allez entendre,] me dit-il, vous avez de l'esprit; ainsi vous [me comprendrez bien.] Quant à votre premiere demande [, la mediation du roi ne peut avoir lieu tant que les colonies seront sujettes du roi d'angleterre, qui] d'ailleurs [ne l'accepteroit pas.] Quant à votre seconde demande [, le roi est vrai chevalier, sa parole lui est sacree, il l'a donnee aux anglois de vivre en paix avec eux, et il la tiendra.] Ainsi tant que [la france ne sera pas en guerre avec les anglois, il ne s'alliera point contre eux avec les colonies, et ne fournira point de secours a ces dernieres.] Mais d'un autre côté, et par-là même [les americains ont la meme protection] et [liberte que tout autre anglois, d'aborder en france,] et [d'en exporter, comme marchandise, des armes,] et [munitions de guerre,] sans pourtant [en former des magasins en france,] ce qui n'est permis chez aucune nation. Du reste, ajouta-t-il, [les colonies n'ont pas besoin] que [ni la france ni l'espagne se melent dans cette guerre, le commerce seul fournira] aux Américains tout ce dont ils auront besoin pour se bien défendre.

Je suis de son avis. Je crois même qu'il vous sera plus avantageux, et [a la france aussi, qu'elle ne se presse pas de se declarer ouvertement pour vous.] Encore une fois, Messieurs, votre union,

2. News of both these developments appeared in the *Supplément aux Nouvelles extraordinaires de divers endroits*, XXXVII (May 7, 1776), [3–4].

votre constant amour pour la liberté, votre courage à vous passer de tout ce qui sent le luxe et à le mépriser, votre haine pour la tyrannie et le despotisme, qui sont les tristes fruits du Luxe, enfin toutes vos vertus républicaines vous rendront supérieurs à vos ennemis et invincibles, même sans alliés. Ceux-ci cependant ne vous manqueront pas, soyez en sûrs: car il ne faut pas croire qu'avec ce qui se passe dans votre partie du monde la nôtre puisse longtemps demeurer en paix. Le temps viendra où vos amis se démasqueront, et où votre alliance sera non seulement acceptée, mais recherchée. En attendant vous avez fait un grand et sage coup de chasser vos ennemis de Bost. Ils publient qu'ils ont évacué la place exprès, par ordre et politique profonde; Le public en rit, et les siffle. Je finis, Messieurs, par vous souhaiter de toute mon ame la plus heureuse campagne, victoire [, Quebec, l'ile de Providence, independance,] et [a moi de vivre et mourir votre utile serviteur Dumas.] P.S. Postscript.

J'oubliois Messieurs de vous rapporter, que le personnage en question m'a offert de me rembourser les fraix de mon voyage; et que j'ai répondu qu'ils l'étoient déjà. Sur quoi il me dit de lui dire au moins en quoi l'on pourroit me faire plaisir? Je repartis que c'étoit en me mettant à même de rendre de grands services aux Américains. Enfin il m'a exhorté à correspondre de temps en temps avec lui; je m'y suis engagé, et je n'y manquerai pas. Ainsi il ne dépend plus que de vous, Messieurs, de rendre cette correspondance de plus en plus intéressante. De mon côté je serai vigilant à profiter de tous les événements, qui pourront faire quelque changement en Europe. Ceux qui arriveront en Amérique, exigeront sans doute que Vous, Messieurs, me donniez fréquemment de nouvelles instructions et ordres, munis toujours de Lettres de créance, ou du moins d'une, qui sera pour le temps que vous jugerez à propos. Je sai à qui m'adresser pour faire parvenir de vos nouvelles [Messieurs a la cour de france] et [avoir reponse en peu de jours.]

6e. Juin 1776

Voici copie d'une Lettre de Londres en date du 21e. May, vous comprenez bien de qui, Je lui avais envoyé, sous les enveloppes qu'il m'avoit indiquées, les deux lettres que Mr. Sto. m'avoit laissées en dépôt; et j'y avois joint un chiffre, dont il s'est déjà servi avec succès.

435

"Everything is safe. I shall write you fully next week by our frind Sto. [One Hortalez,] will apply to you on business that concerns our frinds. He has your adress. Be so good as to assist him."[3]

Je les attends avec impatience, et ferai tout ce qui dépendra de moi pour votre service, Messieurs, et le leur.

Je vous supplie, Messieurs, de me répondre toujours le plutôt possible, afin que je sache si mes Lettres vous sont parvenues. Je vous enverrai encore une autre fois copie générale de ma précédente Lettre A et de celle-ci B. pour remédier à la perte de l'une ou de toutes les deux, supposé que les vaisseaux qui les portent viennent à périr ou à être pris.

Il faut toujours m'écrire sous l'enveloppe de *Mr. M. M. Rey Libraire à Amsterdam*, si vous m'écrivez par St. Eustache; ou sous celle de *Mr. A. Stuckey Mercht. Rotterdam* si c'est en droiture ou par la France.

Quand j'ai promis au Ministre avec lequel je me suis entretenu de vos affaires, de ne pas vous le nommer, c'est en tant que vous n'exigiez pas expressément que je vous le fasse connoître; car en ce cas vous le saurez quand vous voudrez.

Dans environ huit jours je pars d'Utrecht pour une Campagne qui me rapproche de 7 lieues de la Haie, et où je compte de passer l'Eté.

J'espere que le temps viendra où je pourrai résider là où il vous plaira, messieurs, et ne plus travailler que pour vous.

Je ne sai si j'ai déja dit dans une de mes Lettres à Mr. Franklin, que depuis un an déjà, j'ai dans ma chambre son portrait gravé. J'y ajouterai le Portrait de Mr. Dickenson et de tous les Honorables Membres du Congrès, quand j'aurai le bonheur de pouvoir me les procurer. *Vos, Libertatis assertores, veri mihi patriae patres estis; vulgo reges nauci facio.*[4]

Endorsed: May 14 [?] 1776 From Mr. Dumas Utrecht

---

3. The letters that Story did not take to London are explained in Dumas' earlier communication cited above. In this note from Arthur Lee Dumas first encountered, we assume, the name of Hortalez, *i.e.*, Beaumarchais.

4. We have not traced the quotation. "You advocates of Liberty," it may be rendered, "are for me the true fathers of the country; I have no use for kings in general."

From Richard Bache

ALS: American Philosophical Society

Dear and Honored Sir   Phila. 14th. May 1776.

We have not had the Pleasure of a Line from you since I last wrote you. I wish I had time to give you a particular Account of the Action between our armed Boats and his Majesty's Ships the Roebuck of 44 Guns, and Liverpoole of 28 Guns, off Wilmington. I fully intended it this Morning, but have been so much employed, I find it impossible. I must therefore beg leave to refer you to the Acct. in Towne's Paper[5], shall only add that the Ships have got a severe drubing and are fairly drove away; some People that have seen them since their Retreat, say the Ships have suffered greatly. We are all Well, and with much Love and Duty join in wishing you a safe return to us. I am Dear sir Yours &c.

                                                      R BACHE

Addressed: Benjn. Franklin Esqr.

From George Washington

AL:[6] American Philosophical Society

Dear Sir,   New York May 20. 1776

I do myself the pleasure to Transmit you the Inclosed Letter, which I received yesterday with several others in the condition this is, and containing similar Intelligence;[7] the rest I forwarded to Congress immediately on receipt. They had passed thro the hands of some of the Committees in the Eastern Governments by whom they were opened.

On the morning of the 17 Inst. with much concern and surprize I received the melancholy account[8] of our Troops being Obliged

---

5. *Pa. Evening Post*, May 9, 11, 1776. The engagement occurred on May 8 and, despite newspaper accounts, apparently left the British ships almost undamaged: *Naval Docs.*, IV, 1470–1; V, 15–16, 18–19.

6. The text of this MS as printed in Fitzpatrick, *Writings of Washington*, V, 64–5 does not make clear that the closing salutation and signature have been torn away.

7. This was the long letter from Arthur Lee addressed to Cadwallader Colden, with the covering note addressed to BF and printed above, Feb. 13. Our headnote there gives the outlines of the baffling story.

8. In a letter from Schuyler of May 13, acknowledged on the 17th. Fitzpatrick, V, 52.

to raise the Seige of Quebec with the loss of their Cannon, a number of small Arms, Provisions &c.

I had hoped before this misfortune, that the Troops there wou'd have maintained their Posts, and on the Arrival of the two Brigades detached from hence, consisting of Ten Regiments (the last of which was at Albany under Genl. Sullivan when the Account came) the Blockade bravely kept up for a long time by a handfull of men against a victorious Enemy superior in numbers, wou'd terminate in a favourable and happy Issue, the reduction of Quebec and our consequent possession of the Important Country to which It belongs. To what cause to ascribe the sad disaster, I am at loss to determine, but hence I shall know the events of War are exceedingly doubtfull, and that Capricious fortune often blasts our most flattering hopes.

I feel this important and Interesting event, not a little heighten'd by Its casting up, just on your entrance and that of the other Honorable Commissioners in that Country. Tho your presence may conduce to the public good in an essential manner, yet I am certain you must experience difficulties and embarrasments of a peculiar nature. Perhaps in a little time, Things may assume a more promising appearance than the present is, and your difficulties in some degree be done away.

Wishing your Councils under the guidance of a kind providence and a tender of my respectfull Compli[ments] to the Gentlemen who accompany you [*torn*] I have the [*torn*]

Addressed: [*Torn.* Benjami]n Franklin / at / Montreal

John Hancock to the Commissioners to Canada

ALS (letterbook draft): National Archives

Gentlemen,   Philada. May 24th. 1776.

By the enclosed Resolves of Congress which I do myself the Honour of transmitting, you will perceive that every Step has been taken to procure hard Money that could be devised.

I have forwarded to Genl. Schuyler by this Conveyance the Sum of sixteen Hundred and sixty two Pounds one Shilling and three

Pence in hard Money, which was all that was in the Treasury.[9] Genl. Washington arrived here yesterday Afternoon in good Health, the Congress having requested his Attendance in order to consult him on the Operations of the approaching Campaign, and such other Matters as should be necessary. I have the Honour to be Gentlemen, your most obedient and very humble Servant

J H. Prst.

The Honble B. Franklyn Saml. Chase, and Charls Carrol, Commissioner in Canada

To Charles Carroll and Samuel Chase

ALS: New York Public Library

Dear Friends,   N York, May 27. 1776.

We arrived here safe yesterday Evening, having left Mrs. Walker with her Husband at Albany, from whence we came down by Land. We pass'd him on Lake Champlain; but he returning overtook us at Saratoga, where they both gave themselves such Liberties in taunting at our Conduct in Canada, that it came almost to a Quarrel. We continu'd our Care of her, however, and landed her safe in Albany, with her three Waggon-Loads of Baggage, brought thither without putting her to any Expence, and parted civilly tho' coldly. I think they both have excellent Talents at making themselves Enemies, and I believe, live where they will, they will never be long without them.[1]

9. On May 18 and 22 Congress ordered the immediate dispatch to Canada of some cash recently brought in by ship, of all that remained in the treasury, and of all that could be procured elsewhere. Schuyler was to be informed that, if the total sent him would not buy enough locally to maintain the army, more supplies would be purchased and shipped northward. *JCC,* IV, 365–6, 375–8. On the 26th BF, in or near New York, met two officers carrying specie to the commissioners; see the following document.

1. On the following day John Carroll wrote a letter to his cousin and Chase on the back of this one. BF, he said, "has given you but a faint idea of the impertinence of our fellow travellers. The lady had the assurance to tell us that the Commissioners had advised with and been governed by Tories." Mrs. Walker eventually settled in Boston and became acquainted with Jane Mecom and Jane Collas; after her husband's death she fell on bad times, and in 1788 requested BF, via his sister, to use his good offices in procuring the return of

We met yesterday two Officers from Philadelphia, with a Letter from the Congress to the Commissioners, and a Sum of hard Money.[2] I opened the Letter and seal'd it again, directing them to carry it forward to you. I congratulate you on the great Prize carry'd into Boston. Seventy-five Tons of Gunpowder is an excellent Supply; and the 1000 Carbines with Bayonets, another fine Article.[3] The German Auxiliairies are certainly coming:[4] It is our Business to prevent their Returning.

The Congress have advis'd the erecting new Governments, which has occasion'd some Dissension at Philada; but I hope it will soon be compos'd.[5]

I shall be glad to hear of your Welfare. As to my self, I find I grow daily more feeble, and think I could hardly have got along so far, but for Mr. Carroll's friendly Assistance and tender Care of me. Some Symptoms of the Gout now appear, which makes me think my Indisposition has been a smother'd Fit of that Disorder, which my Constitution wanted Strength to form compleatly.[6] I have had several Fits of it formerly.

God bless you and prosper your Councils; and bring you safe again to your Friends and Families. With the greatest Esteem and Respect, I am, Your most obedient humble Servant

B FRANKLIN

Honble. S. Chase and Chas Carroll, Esquires

Turn over.[7]

---

some small articles of plate that Charles Carroll and Chase had taken from her house on leaving Montreal. Van Doren, *Franklin—Mecom*, pp. 312–13.

2. The letter was Hancock's above, May 24, 1776.

3. The prize was a British ammunition ship brought into Boston: *Naval Docs.*, V, 134–5.

4. BF presumably heard this news from Washington, who had had the first report of the mercenaries in March, and had recently sent Congress copies of the British treaties with the rulers of Brunswick, Hesse-Cassel, and Hesse-Hanau. Fitzpatrick, *Writings of Washington*, V, 56–7; *JCC*, IV, 369.

5. For the action of Congress and the resulting dissension see the headnote below, June 14.

6. See the note on Mecom to Greene below, June 1. BF left New York with Father Carroll on the morning of the 28th and reached Philadelphia on the 30th at night. The Carroll letter cited in the first note; BF's entry of March 26 in the Memorandum Book described above, VII, 167–8.

7. For the letter from Father Carroll mentioned in the first note.

To Philip Schuyler

ALS: New York Public Library

Dear General, New York, May 27. 1776

We arrived here safe yesterday Evening, in your Post Chaise driven by Lewis. I was unwilling to give so much Trouble, and would have borrowed your Sulkey, and driven myself: but good Mrs. Schuyler insisted on a full Compliance with your Pleasure, as signify'd in your Letter, and I was oblig'd to submit; which I was afterwards very glad of, part of the Road being very Stoney and much gullied, where I should probably have overset and broke my own Bones, all the Skill and Dexterity of Lewis being no more than sufficient. Thro' the Influence of your kind Recommendation to the Innkeepers on the Road, we found a great Readiness to supply us with Change of Horses. Accept our Thankful Acknowledgements; they are all the Return we can at present make. We congratulate you on the very valuable Prize made at Boston. They threaten us with a mighty Force from England and Germany.[8] I trust that before the End of the Campaign, its Inefficacy will be apparent to all the World, our Enemies become sick of their Projects, and the Freedom of America be established on the surest Foundation, its own Ability to defend it. May God bless and preserve you for all our Sakes, as we[ll as] for that of your dear Family. Mr. Carrol joins me in every hearty Wish for Prosperity and Felicity to you and yours. With the highest Esteem and Respect I am, Dear Sir, Your obliged and most obedient humble Servant B FRANKLIN

Honble. Gen. Schuyler

Addressed: To / The honourable Philip Schuyler, Esquire / Major General of the Continental Army / Fort George

Endorsed: New York May 27th: 1776 From Dr. Franklin:

8. See the preceding document.

From Ebenezer Hazard

AL: American Philosophical Society

Tuesday morning [May 28?, 1776[9]].
Mr. Hazard's Compliments to Doctor Franklin. He will watch the Sloops from Albany, and forward the Doctor's Bedding by the first Stage after it comes to Hand.

Addressed: Dr. Franklin.

Jane Mecom to Catharine Greene: Extract

ALS: American Philosophical Society

Philadelphia 1st June 1776
My Dear Brother and the whol worlds freind is Returned; the cause and Circumstances are maloncholy but thank God he is again saif hear. He suffered many Difeculties in going was taken sick in a Day or two after His arival and has never had a well Day since.[1] The Raiseing the seige of Quebeck, the Ignorance of the Canadans, there Incapasity and Aversnes to have any thing to do in the war and his [?] Indisposition I beleve Affected His Spirets, but He seems [a] little chearfull this morning.[2] All that He himself says about it, is, it is a time of Life with Him to Expect Infermities but Docr. Bond says He will soon git well.[3] He has never layn by but won Day at Newyork in His Return to Rest. He Remembers His love to you all.

9. BF left that morning for Philadelphia; see the note on his letter to Carroll and Chase above, May 27. We assume that he asked the New York postmaster to look out for his bedding, and received this note before his departure.

1. He was suffering, to judge by his later accounts, from boils, edema, and what appears to have been psoriasis: to Ingenhousz, Oct. 17, 1777 (Oesterreichische Nationalbibliothek); Bigelow, *Works*, VII, 334. Almost as soon as he got home, gout incapacitated him. In the second and third weeks of June he was out of touch with what was going on in Philadelphia; he then left town for a friend's house, presumably to recuperate, and did not return until the end of the month: below, to Washington, June 21; to Rush, June 26.

2. He arrived on May 30; see the note on BF to Carroll and Chase above, May 27, 1776.

3. Thomas Bond, an old friend of the family, had attended DF on her deathbed: above, XXI, 401.

The Committee of Secret Correspondence: Instructions to William Bingham[4]   LS: Historical Society of Pennsylvania

These instructions were composed on the day that Congress authorized the secret committee to export to the West Indies enough goods to pay for the 10,000 muskets described in the second paragraph.[5] Bingham's mission to the Caribbean was similar to Deane's earlier one to Europe in that both went in a dual role. Each was the agent of the committee of secret correspondence, and was also doing business on his own. As Deane was representing a group of his partners who had contracted with the secret committee, so Bingham was under contract with Willing & Morris. His private assignment was to watch for the arrival at Martinique or St. Eustatius of gunpowder from Europe, a shipment in which he as well as the firm had a share, and to buy West Indian goods on credit and dispatch them to Philadelphia.[6] This business gave reality to the "Appearance of Commercial Views" with which the committee of secret correspondence instructs him to cover his activity in buying arms and gathering intelligence.

Sir   Philada June 3d 1776.

    You are immediately to repair on Board the Sloop Hornet Wm. Hallock Esqr. Comr. bound to Martinico;[7] On your Arrival deliver

---

4. Bingham (1752–1804) was the precocious scion of a prominent Philadelphia family. He graduated from the College of Philadelphia in 1768, owned some ships by the age of twenty, made the grand tour of Europe at twenty-one and established valuable commercial connections there, and in the fall of 1775 was appointed secretary of the committee of secret correspondence. He must have impressed its members, for he had just turned twenty-four when they gave him this major assignment. Robert C. Alberts, *The Golden Voyage. The Life and Times of William Bingham* (Boston, 1969), pp. 10–20; see also Margaret L. Brown, "William Bingham, Agent of the Continental Congress," *PMHB*, LXI (1937), 54–87. The *DAB* sketches his later career but is mistaken about his activities before his mission.

5. *JCC*, IV, 366, 414.

6. Alberts, *op. cit.*, p. 19.

7. William Hallock originally commanded a sloop in the infant colonial navy, and had been promoted to the *Hornet* the previous April. William B. Clark, "The Log Book of the Wasp," *Daughters of the Amer. Revolution Mag.*, LXIV (1930), 609–19; Hulbert Footner, *Sailor of Fortune: the Life and Adventures of Commodore Burney, USN* (New York and London, 1940), pp. 14, 18. The *Hornet* proved unseaworthy, and Bingham was transferred to Capt. Wickes in the *Reprisal: Naval Docs.*, V, 429, 454.

the Letter you are entrusted with to the General there and show him your Credentials.[8]

You are earnestly to endeavor to procure from him Ten Thousand good Musquets, well fitted with Bayonets; If he cannot or will not supply them, You are to request his Favor and Influence in procuring them in that or any other Island, if to be had. We propose to pay for them by remitting the Produce of this Country with all possible Dispatch to any Island that may be agreed on; You are to take especial Care, that the Musquets you send are good. We direct you to send 2500 of them by the Hornet on her Return and the Remainder in Parcels not exceeding 1000 in swift sailing well appointed Vessels, with Directions to the Masters to put into the first Port within the united Colonies, where they can safely land. We desire you to obtain from the General if possible a French Man of War or Frigate to convoy these Vessels so far that they may be out of the Course of the British Ships that are cruizing in the West Indies. You are carefully to publish all the Papers delivered to you by us for that Purpose and disperse them as much as you can throughout the Dutch English and French West Indies, having first obtained the General's Permission to do so in the Latter.

You must with the greatest Prudence endeavor to discover either by Conversation with the General or others the Designs of the French in assembling so large a Fleet with a great Number of Troops in the West Indies and whether they mean to act for or against America. You are to convey to us the speediest Intelligence of any Discoveries you may make on this Head.[9]

You are to continue at Martinico untill we recall you and are to cultivate an intimate and friendly Correspondence with the General and other Persons of Distinction there, that you may be enabled to procure all the usefull Intelligence you can. You are immediately on your arrival to inform Silas Deane Esqr. of it and desire him to address to you his Dispatches for us.

---

8. Robert d'Argout had replaced the comte de Nozières in March as governor and lieutenant general of Martinique. He was expected to be as well disposed as his predecessor to American trade. *Dictionnaire de biographie française*, III, 606–7; Crout, "Diplomacy of Trade," pp. 46–7.

9. See the note on BF to Lee above, Feb. 19.

Your Letters to him are to be directed under Cover to Mess. Saml. and J. H. Delap at Bourdeaux[1] or to Monsr. Dubourg at Paris. Whenever you obtain any Intelligence which you think of such Importance, that it ought to be immediately conveyed to us, You are to charter a fast sailing Vessel, if no other opportunity offers and Send her to this Continent, with such Directions to the Master as are herein before mentioned.

You are to observe the strictest Secrecy and not to discover any Part of the Business you are Sent upon to any Persons, but those to whom you are under an absolute Necessity of communicating it, in the Transaction thereof. It will readily occur to you that an Appearance of Commercial Views will effectually cover the Political; therefore you will make frequent Enquiries amongst their Merchants what Articles of this Country's Produce are most wanted in the Islands and You must consider yourself as authorized by the United Colonies to engage for the Payment of the 10,000 Musquets in Such Articles deliver'd at Martinico (or any other Islands they may fix on) as fast as they can be introduced; The Exports shall be made from the Continent on the first Advice of your having succeeded and as our Ships are liable to Capture, when one is taken another shall be dispatched untill the entire Payment is made agreable to your Contract.

When you write to Mr. Deane desire him to put his current Dispatches addressed to you, under Cover to the General, but when he has any particular Matters to communicate either to Congress, Yourself or to Us, that he thinks should not be risqued through that Channel for fear of Inspection let him procure a Mercht. in France to put such Dispatches directed for you under Cover to a Mercht. in Martinico with an express Injunction to deliver them into your own Hands, and when you have made

1. The firm of Samuel and J. H. Delap had been designated by Deane's partners as a house that would receive the proceeds of American goods sold for the purchase of arms, and on his arrival provided him with introductions. The Delaps, of Irish Protestant origin, were already involved in the American trade, and became an extremely important connection. L. M. Cullen, "The Irish Merchant Communities of Bordeaux, La Rochelle and Cognac in the Eighteenth Century," *Négoce et industrie en France et en Irelande aux XVIIIe et XIXe siècles* . . . (Paris, 1980), p. 55 and *passim*; Paul Butel, *Les Négociants bordelais, l'Europe et les îles au XVIIIe siècle* (Paris, 1974), pp. 162, 181, 287.

acquaintance with an established Merchant of good reputation in Martinico, you had best name him to Mr. Deane, that he may so address his Dispatches without the Intervention of a Merchant in France.

We shall from Time to Time furnish you with Intelligence of what is passing on this Continent in order that you may not only make good use thereof in the West Indies, but also transmit the same to Mr. Deane. It is of great Importance that He should be fully and frequently advised of what passes and as you may often have earlier and fuller Intelligence by means of News Papers and private Letters, than our Avocations will permit us to give, You will be on the Watch; send all Advices forward to Mr. Deane marking what you receive from us, what from private Letters, what from public Papers and what from Hearsay and always distinguishing between what you think can be depended on and what is doubtfull. In short sir, you are to be constantly on the Watch, and give to Mr. Deane and us every Information that you think connected with the Interest or that can be improved to the Advantage of the United Colonies.

You may possibly find it necessary or usefull to visit Guadaloupe, St. Eustatia or other foreign Islands. If you do always take Passage in Foreign Vessels and don't be long absent from Martinico at any one Time, as our Dispatches will be directed thither.

Should you at any time during your Stay in the West Indies have an opportunity to contract on reasonable Terms for Arms Ammunition or other Articles wanted here, give us Information thereof and you shall be instructed on that Head; in the mean time you will encourage as many private Adventurers as you can, by holding up the high Prices we give, the low Price of our Produce, and as we have Cruizers on this Coast to watch the Enemies Tenders Cutters &c., small Vessels have a good Chance of getting safe in and out of the Bays Rivers and Inlets on our Coast.

As we have already many Cruizers and are daily adding to the Number, you will take proper opportunities of sounding the Genl., and learn from him whether he could admit Prizes made by our Cruizers to be sent in and protected there untill proper Opportunities offered for bringing them to the Continent; But this being a Matter of great Delicacy you must introduce it as a

Thing of your own and not as any Part of your Instructions. Dated at Philadelphia, this 3d Day of June 1776.   B FRANKLIN
BENJA. HARRISON
JOHN DICKINSON
ROBT MORRIS

Endorsed: Instructions from Committee of Secret Correspondence June 3d 1776

The Committee of Secret Correspondence to William Bingham   LS: American Philosophical Society

Sir   Philada June 3d 1776
We deliver you herewith two Letters from the secret Committee of Congress, one directed to Messr. Adrian Le Maitre and Mr. Richard Harrison at Martinico, whereby they are directed to pay the Net Proceeds of a Cargo of Provisions Consign'd them per the Sloop Fanny Capt. Britton to our Order and We have endorsed on said Letter that the Payment is to be made to You; the other Letter is directed to Mr. Richd Harrison directing him to pay to our Order the Net Proceeds of another Cargo of Provisions Consign'd him per the Sloop Peggy Capt. Patton, which we have also endorsed to you.[2]
We hope both these Cargoes may arrive safe and thereby afford

2. The letters, each accompanied by one from this committee, immediately follow. Adrien le Maitre was a Martinique merchant with whom the secret committee and private individuals had been doing business since April. Richard Harrison, a young Baltimore merchant, was acting as agent in Martinique for Maryland and Virginia; he had taken a cargo of flour to the island to exchange for arms and ammunition, and in June formed a partnership with Abraham van Bibber, the Maryland agent in St. Eustatius. William Briton was a Philadelphia ship's captain and exporter to Martinique. Capt. Thomas Patton's sloop, in the convoy that Wickes was taking to the island, was captured with others off the Capes of Virginia. MS proceedings of the secret committee (Harvard University Library), p. 61; Smith, *Letters*, III, 543, 598–9; *Naval Docs.*, II, 1299, 1327; V, 648, 1134; Robert C. Alberts, *The Golden Voyage. The Life and Times of William Bingham* (Boston, 1969), p. 31; J. Franklin Jameson, "St. Eustatius and the American Revolution," *Amer. Hist. Rev.*, VIII (1902–3), 685; Crout, "Diplomacy of Trade," pp. 42–9; Clark, *Wickes*, p. 53.

you the intended Supply of Money. In that Case you must detain what may be sufficient for your present Expences and apply the Remainder to Payment for the Ten Thousand Stand of Arms you are directed to procure; but should things be so circumstanced that You cannot procure those Arms nor any Part of them, You may then only take up so much of the Money as may be necessary for your present Expences and direct the Gentlemen to whom the Cargoes are consigned to pursue the Orders they received from the secret Committee and to dispatch the two sloops as quick as they can under Convoy of Capt. Hallock in the Hornet; On the Contrary if you take up the whole Money and send the Muskets by the Hornet you may order the two Sloops to be sent away without any Goods or you may send a Part of the Muskets by each as you shall judge may be best. We are Sir Your obedient humble Servants

B FRANKLIN
BENJA HARRISON
JOHN DICKINSON
ROBT MORRIS

Wm Bingham Esqr

Addressed: To / Mr William Bingham

Endorsed: Com' of Secret Correspondence June 3d 1776

The Secret Committee to Richard Harrison and Adrien le Maitre
LS: American Philosophical Society

Gentlemen   Philada. June 3d. 1776

We wrote you the 2d Ultimo by the Sloop Fanny Capt. Wm Britton which we hope will get safe, at that time we directed how you were to dispose of the Net Proceeds of the Cargo Consigned you by said Sloop and probably you may have complied with those orders before this reaches you, if so its well, but if those orders are not executed and you remain possessed of the Net Proceeds of said Cargo when you receive this letter, We desire that in such case you may pay the same to the order of Benjn. Harrison, Benjn. Franklin, John Jay, Thos. Johnston junr., John Dickinson and Robt Morris Esquires or any three of them who are a Committee of Congress that send a young Gentleman [to] your Island on bussiness and [?we ex]pect he will have Occasion for the Money. You [are also?] to Comply with their instructions respecting the dispatch of the Sloop Fanny. We are Sirs Your obedient Servants

THOS M: KEAN
RICHARD HENRY LEE
B FRANKLIN
ROBT MORRIS
JOSIAH BARTLETT
JOSEPH HEWES[3]

Messrs. Richd Harrison and Adrien Le Maitre

Addressed: To / Messrs Adrien Le Maitre and Rd. Harrison / Merchants / Martinico.

The Committee of Secret Correspondence to Richard Harrison and Adrien le Maitre

LS: American Philosophical Society

Gentlemen   Philada. June 3d. 1776

In Consequence of the Annexed letter of order from the Secret Committee of Congress We desire you to Account with Wm. Bingham Esqr. the bearer hereof for the Amount of the Cargo mentioned therein and either pay him the whole or any part of the Money or do with it what he may desire for the Public Service of this Continent. We are sirs Your humble servants

B FRANKLIN
BENJA HARRISON
ROBT MORRIS
JOHN DICKINSON

Messrs. Adrien Le Maitre and Richd Harrison

Addressed: To / Messrs. Richd Harrison & / Adrien Le Maitre / Merchts / Martinico

Endorsed: Secret Committee of Congress. June 3d. 1776

3. For Hewes (1730–79), a N.C. delegate who had been put on the committee the previous January, see the *DAB*.

The Secret Committee to Richard Harrison

LS: Historical Society of Pennsylvania

Sir   Philada. June 3d. 1776

We have already wrote you of this date by the Sloop Peggy Capt. Patton and directed how you shou'd apply the Net proceeds of that Cargo unless you received other Orders from us.

But shou'd you receive this letter in time it will be delivered you by a Young Gentleman who will be Authorized by another Committee of Congress to receive and dispose of the Net proceeds of said Cargo, Therefore we hereby Authorize and direct you to pay the said Net proceeds to such person and in such manner as may be ordered by Benjn. Harrison Benjn. Franklin, John Jay, Thos. Johnston junr. John Dickinson and Robert Morris Esquires or any three of them and also to comply with their orders respecting the dispatch of the Sloop but if this letter does not arrive in time you will of Consequence follow the directions we have given. Sir Your humble Servants.

THOS M: KEAN
JOSIAH BARTLETT
JOSEPH HEWES
ROBT MORRIS
B FRANKLIN
RICHARD HENRY LEE

Mr. Richd Harrison

The Committee of Secret Correspondence to Richard Harrison

LS: Historical Society of Pennsylvania

Sir   Philada. June 3d. 1776

In Consequence of the annexed letter of order from the Secret Committee of Congress We desire You to Account with Wm Bingham Esquire the bearer hereof for the Amount of the Cargo mentioned therein and either pay him the whole or any part of that Money or do with it what he may desire which will oblige Sir Your humble servants

B FRANKLIN
BENJA HARRISON
ROBT MORRIS
JOHN DICKINSON

450

Mr Richd Harrison

Addressed: To / Mr. Richd Harrison / Mercht / Martinico

From [David Hartley]

Dear Sir   June 8. 1776

It is so many months since I have heard from you that I fear the Communication between the two Countries is but too effectually Stopt. I have writ to you from time to time letters which perhaps you have never received. My object is the same with yours viz. the restoration of peace. The Stoppage of communication between the two countries seems to have had the very worst of consequences as it has given the Ministry the opportunity of sending their own irritating information to America and of withholding the knowledge of all the good dispositions which there are in this Country towards their fellow Subjects in America.[4] Angry Addresses have been sent with all the parade of Authority to America while the petitions in favour of peace have not been Suffered to appear in the gazettes. I see the fatal Effect of all this. *Common Sense* says The last cord is broken the people of England address against us. Therefore we must look to our own Safety in independence.[5] If this question is to be determined by the general sense of the people of England that sense is in my Opinion full as favorable to America as it was a year and half ago when you left us. The Ministry have certainly not been able to raise any national Spirit of resentment against America. The generality of the people are cold upon the Subject. Nine Men in ten content themselves with an indolent wish for peace, but there are many Zealous and principled friends to America. The only bitter enemies are the Ministry and their dependents jobbers contractors &c. &c. quibus utile bellum.[6] Several propositions of conciliation have been offered this year as well

---

4. He had said this at the beginning of his letter above of Feb. 24. In much of what follows he also repeats, either that letter or the first of his two on Nov. 14, 1775, perhaps because he assumed that they had not reached BF.

5. [Thomas Paine], *Common Sense: Addressed to the Inhabitants of America . . .* (Philadelphia, 1776), especially pp. 59–60.

6. Freely rendered, "who make a good thing out of war."

as the last by the friends to peace.[7] The constant answer to all such propositions when they come from the friends to America is if we were to give a parliamentary Sanction to such or such an offer what reason have [we] to suppose that it would not be refused with contempt in America for the Americans have not taken any more favorable notice of propositions made by their friends then of any made by the Ministry? All propositions which can be made in a British Parliament must and ought to consult the dignity of this country as well as the Security of America. The Congress appear to be fully aware of [this] by their petition, which expresses that they do not wish even for reconciliation inconsistant with the dignity of Great Britain. Under these Circumstances their total Silence as to all propositions made by their friends without making some specific definite offer of their own has in my Opinion contributed to remove the hopes of peace to a great distance. The Ministry make great advantage of this to circulate a persuasion that the Americans keep to general professions from an unwillingness to peace upon reasonable and honorable terms to this country. I am aware that it is easy to reason like Philosophers to those who neither see nor feel the horrors of War. I make all allowances for the Sufferings of America. Yet still I think reconciliation and peace the best bargain to both sides. Security upon the articles of taxation and charters being provided which I shall allways consider as fundamentals lesser matters would drop of themselves. Time would secure and confirm all the rights of America. As to the Commissioners that are sent to America We know nothing of their instructions or powers.[8] Peace is the general wish of this country. I hope it is the same in America. It would give me great pleasure to hear of your being well in health and that you could see any prospect of accommodatioon and peace. I am &c.

Notation: David Hartley to Benjamin Franklin.

7. During the session, between November, 1775, and May, 1776, five such motions, one by Hartley, were advanced in the Commons and two in the Lords: Cobbett, *Parliamentary History*, XVIII (1774–77), 863–70, 910–36, 963–92, 1042–56, 1188–1228, 1247–86, 1352–62.

8. Whitehall had apparently not divulged the Howe brothers' powers, although Lord Howe did so as soon as he reached America. See the headnote on Barclay to BF above, March 31, 1776, and Howe to BF below, June 20.

From Jacques Barbeu-Dubourg

ALS: National Archives

This letter, if Franklin received it when we think he did, brought him the first news of developments in France that proved to be as momentous for his own future as for the United States. They grew out of Vergennes' cautious overture in 1775 through the Chevalier de Bonvouloir, whose report on the assistance that the Americans wanted reached Versailles at the beginning of March, 1776.[9] A few days earlier the King had received another report, from Caron de Beaumarchais in England. The playwright, who for some time had been pleading the American cause, had made contact in London with Arthur Lee, and received from him an ultimatum that France must either conclude a secret commercial treaty with the colonies or face disaster in the Caribbean.[1] Such wild talk could scarcely have impressed Vergennes, but he seems to have used it: on March 12 he presented to the King and an inner council of ministers a memorandum in which he urged aiding the Americans, in order to prolong the war and buy time for France to protect its West Indian possessions. Each minister was asked his opinion, and Turgot dissented in a long memorandum of his own.[2] The fundamental choice, he made clear, was whether to concentrate on domestic reform, as he had been

9. See the annotation of the report above, Dec. 28.

1. Lee took on himself to offer such an alliance. If Versailles refused it, he warned, the Americans would either force France into war against Britain, or come to terms with the mother country and join it in attacking the French West Indies. Beaumarchais took this nonsense in all seriousness. Brian N. Morton, ed., *Beaumarchais correspondance* (4 vols. to date, Paris, 1969—), II, 171–77.

2. Vergennes' memorandum is in Stevens, *Facsimiles*, XIII, no. 1316. The council, unlike the more formal *conseil d'état*, was an ad hoc inner group of the King's closest advisers. The members were Maurepas, Vergennes, Sartine, Saint-Germain, and Turgot. Jean-Frédéric Phélypeaux, comte de Maurepas (1701–81), had been recalled from exile in the country immediately after Louis' accession and become the King's unofficial first minister, although without portfolio. Claude-Louis, comte de Saint-Germain (1707–78), had been a soldier of fortune under many sovereigns before returning to France after the Seven Years' War. He became secretary of state for war in 1775 and set to work to reform the army, thereby helping to create the flood of applicants for service in America; his reforms led to his ouster in 1777. See Léon Mention, *Le Comte de Saint-Germain et ses réformes* . . . (Paris, 1884). Antoine-Raymond-Gualbert-Gabriel de Sartine (1729–1801) had been for years the head of the Paris police; he was appointed minister of marine and the colonies in 1774 and remained in office until 1780. Anne-Robert-Jacques-Turgot, baron de l'Aulne (1727–81), was at the end of his two years as *contrôleur général des finances*; for his appointment see above, XXI, 308, 312. He was dismissed on May 12, 1776, and thereafter the dominant triumvirate in the government was Maurepas, Vergennes, and Sartine.

doing, or to adventure in foreign affairs. The latter course was less controversial and more glamorous, and he alone among the ministers sensed its danger.

After some weeks Vergennes' arguments persuaded the King. On April 22 the first step was taken toward preparing the navy to meet any British threat, and on May 2 the crucial decision came: Louis agreed to provide the Americans with one million livres for arms. This commitment was not the concern of Versailles alone, for France was bound by the Family Compact to work in concert with Spain. Vergennes had already sounded out Madrid and learned that it wished to prolong the war, and he now communicated this new development. The result was that the Spanish government agreed to provide another million livres.[3]

On May 5, three days after King Louis' decision, Dubourg appeared at Versailles. He had with him Pierre Penet, who had met with the secret committee of Congress months before and brought with him a list of the rebels' military requirements.[4] Immediately after Vergennes won his fight to make funds available, in other words, he learned how the committee wanted them spent. He turned to Dubourg, who found that all the doors on which he knocked were opened to him. For a time, as he says here, he was in a whirl of unaccustomed and highly secret activity. But the whirl was brief. The physician and philosophe had nothing in his background, as he was dimly aware, to equip him for such operations; and the major reason that he was entrusted with them was that he happened on stage at the right moment. While he was writing his long report to Franklin, another actor was stealing his role. On May 24 Beaumarchais returned from London, and in the following weeks he and the court arranged to create in secret a trading firm, Roderigue Hortalez & Cie., which would be capitalized by government funds but of which Versailles would be officially ignorant; through the firm the playwright would buy arms from French arsenals and sell them to the Americans in return for tobacco and other commodities.[5] Once this decision was reached, Dubourg's days as principal procurement agent were numbered.[6]

Before his report reached Franklin, the Americans suffered their first military disaster in the Battle of Long Island. They needed heartening

3. Dull, *French Navy*, pp. 6–9, 31–3, 36–7, 44–9, 52–3; Doniol, *Histoire*, I, 345, 347–8, 369–72, 374–6, 484–5.

4. See the annotation of Bonvouloir's report cited above.

5. Doniol, *Histoire*, I, 482–4; Morton, *op. cit.*, II, 218–19; *Deane Papers*, I, 110–15.

6. Crout, "Diplomacy of Trade," pp. 124–9. At least one observer in Paris was well aware that Dubourg was out of his depth; see William Alexander to BF, May 24, 1777, APS.

news, and in mid-September they received it. We believe, although we cannot prove, that it was in this letter; no other encouraging report about developments at Versailles has come to light.[7] In any case two delegates wrote on the 16th about the glad tidings from France, and one of them added that Philadelphia was toasting King Louis and a speedy alliance.[8] Little more than a week later the United States took its first overt step toward that alliance, when Congress issued its instructions to Franklin and his fellow commissioners to France.

Mon cher Maitre   A Paris ce 10e juin [-July 2] 1776.

Après une longue privation, j'eus enfin le plaisir de recevoir de vos nouvelles directes le 4 may par M. Penet arrivant de Philadelphie. Il me dit que vous l'aviez chargé d'une lettre et de quelques papiers à me remettre, mais qu'il avoit laissé tous ses paquets à Roterdam dans la crainte qu'ils ne fussent interceptés en passant de hollande en france. Cela me donna dabord quelque inquietude; j'osois à peine m'ouvrir à lui; cependant toutes ses reponses à mes diverses questions me parurent si satisfaisantes que je n'hesitai plus à lui parler à coeur ouvert.

7. A possible exception is Deane's letter to Morris below of June 23, which we believe arrived by Sept. 12, and which did mention that France was well disposed and, with Spain, was arming. But this tidbit, because it was so vague and came from Bordeaux, could scarcely have generated intense excitement.

8. A translation of Dubourg's letter, misdated June 12, went to Washington and is among his papers; it is printed under its correct date in Force, 4 *Amer. Arch.*, VI, 771–82 n. It may well have been one of the enclosures sent the General on Sept. 16th and acknowledged, unnamed, on the 20th: Fitzpatrick, *Writings of Washington*, VI, 84. Benjamin Rush mentioned the toasts in writing to Dubourg on the 16th, and on the same day John Adams told his wife that good news from France, as well as from the French West Indies, gave him "great Reason to think they will not always remain inactive." Lyman H. Butterfield, ed., *Letters of Benjamin Rush* (2 vols., Princeton, 1951), I, 111; Butterfield, *Adams Correspondence*, II, 126. The good news from the West Indies came by Lambert Wickes, when he returned to Philadelphia from Martinique on the 13th: Clark, *Wickes*, pp. 64, 67–8. Although Wickes himself had no news from France, he may have carried a duplicate of Dubourg's letter. The ALS, as explained below, did not reach Philadelphia until mid-December. But at the end of his letter Dubourg speaks of two duplicates sent by other hands. A natural route, where ships were frequent, would have been via Nantes to Martinique; if this was Dubourg's choice, one duplicate or both might well have been delivered to Wickes in St. Pierre and carried north by him, and so arrived two months before the original. We have no evidence that this happened. Unless it did, however, the optimism about France immediately after Wickes reached Philadelphia remains inexplicable.

Il m'etonna beaucoup lorsqu'il me dit que non seulement le peuple des 13 Colonies unies, mais encore le Congrès, et Vous-même doutiez beaucoup des dispositions de la Cour de france à votre egard, et que vous apprehendiez ses liaisons avec la Cour de Londres.[9] Lorsque je l'assurai que tous les voeux de notre nation en general, et plus specialement encore ceux du Ministere actuel etoient en faveur des Insurgens, je vis sur son visage un epanouissement de joye si naturel qu'il acheva de me convaincre que je pouvois me confier à lui.

Le lendemain 5 may, je le conduisis à Versailles, afin de le convaincre à son tour que je ne m'etois pas fait illusion à moi même sur un objet aussi important. Je le fis parler à notre ami Du Pont, qui etoit, comme vous pouvez le savoir, le plus intime confident de M. Turgot, alors Controlleur general des finances, et qui nous dit entre autres choses que l'une de leurs plus grandes inquietudes etoit que le Congrès n'echouât dans ses operations faute d'argent. Il nous ajouta même qu'ils avoient revé ensemble par quels moyens ils pourroient, sans se compromettre, faire trouver du credit à ce peuple si malheureux et si interessant.[1] Cette seule conversation acheva de dissiper toutes les allarmes de M. Penet. En consequence il eut bientôt pris son parti, qui fut de continuer sa route jusqu'a Nantes, sans repasser même par Paris, si je voulois me charger du soin des affaires de l'Amerique tant à Paris qu'à la Cour, tandis qu'en correspondance avec moi, il se porteroit successivement dans tous les ports et les manufactures differentes où le bien du meme service l'appelleroit. Il m'avoit assuré dès le moment de son arrivée que vous lui aviez recommandé sur toutes choses de s'adresser à moi, de ne prendre confiance que dans les persones dont je lui repondrois, et de concerter, autant qu'il lui seroit possible, toutes ses operations avec moi.

J'etois bien disposé sans doute à le seconder en tout ce qui seroit de mon pouvoir, dans une cause à laquelle j'ai toujours pris un si

9. For the fear in Philadelphia that France and Britain planned to partition North America see James H. Hutson, "The Partition Treaty and the Declaration of American Independence," *Jour. of Amer. History*, LVIII (1971–72), 877–96.

1. In 1774 Turgot appointed du Pont de Nemours, BF's old acquaintance and Dubourg's friend for twenty years, as inspector general of commerce, and worked closely with him until the Minister was dismissed. Ambrose Saricks, *Pierre Samuel Du Pont de Nemours* (Lawrence, Kan., 1965), pp. 62, 67, 70.

vif interêt qu'il m'a attiré dans ce pays cy une espece de sobriquet dont je ne me tiens point pour offensé. Mais votre Envoyé exigeoit de moi bien plus que je ne croyois pouvoir lui promettre, puisqu'il vouloit me laisser seul chargé de toute la besogne en cette ville ainsi la conjoncture me paroissoit tres delicate.

Comment m'ingerer dans une longue suite d'affaires majeures et de negociations importantes sur la simple parole d'un inconnu, soi disant porteur de lettres qu'il ne sauroit representer? Comment m'annoncer moi même à quantité de gens en place, connus et inconnus, pour traiter avec eux des affaires d'un peuple etranger, sans la moindre lettre de croyance de sa part? Et en supposant même la necessité de m'abandonner au torrent des circonstances aussi essentielles que critiques; en supposant la possibilité de trouver partout un accès favorable, et d'etre même ecouté avec confiance de tous ceux avec qui j'aurois à traiter, quoique en m'y presentant sans titre et sans mission, comment remplir cet objet de surerogation sans negliger les devoirs que ma profession m'impose, et m'exposer à perdre entierement l'etat duquel je tire principalement ma subsistance? Ces reflexions me mettoient du noir dans l'esprit; mais mon attachement pour vous et pour vos respectables amis, ma reconnoissance pour les sentimens de bienveillance que vous avez inspirés à tous vos compatriotes en ma faveur, mon zele pour la cause de la justice, de la liberté et de l'humanité, enfin la necessité même des conjonctures où la Providence sembloit m'avoir specialement designé, au defaut de tout autre, pour un service si honnéte et si indispensable l'emporterent sur toutes les considerations particulieres, et me firent regarder comme un devoir sacré de me devouer sans reserve à ce qu'on me demandoit en votre nom. Et depuis cet instant je me suis regardé comme le depositaire eventuel de la confiance des Colonies unies de l'Amerique; j'ai tâché de remplir toutes les fonctions d'un Agent fidele et zelé; et je continuerai ainsi jusqu'à ce que leurs vrais Representans me désavouent. Je compare ma situation à celle de quelquun qui s'etant trouvé seul à portée de recueillir des effets precieux d'un naufrage, ou d'un incendie, veille plus scrupuleusement sur ce depôt forcé que sur ce qui se passe en ce moment dans sa propre maison.

Sachant que l'Amerique unie avoit un besoin urgent d'une certaine espece d'hommes et d'un certain genre de provisions, je me

457

suis empressé de lui procurer l'un et l'autre. J'ai frappé, pour ainsi dire, à toutes les portes pour cet effet; j'ai parlé vaguement aux uns, et enygmatiquement aux autres, j'ai fait des demiconfidences à plusieurs, et le moins qu'il m'a eté possible de confidences entieres à qui que ce soit, à l'exception des Ministres du Roi, et d'un Neveu dont je suis tres assuré, que j'ai fait venir exprès de sa province pour me seconder en tout.[2] J'ai eu la satisfaction d'etre accueilli de toutes parts, et de voir que personne ne me demandoit d'autres assurances que ma parole pour traiter avec moi des affaires de la plus grande consequence, et sur lesquelles je convenois de bonne foi n'avoir reçu ni plein pouvoir, ni même la moindre commission ou instruction de vive voix non plus que par ecrit. Des Ministres à qui je n'avois jamais fait ma cour, m'ont marqué dès la premiere entrevue la confiance la plus flatteuse, m'ont parlé sans détour ni mystere, ont discuté avec moi les matieres les plus graves, et deliberé ensemble sur le parti à prendre et les moyens de le remplir. Des particuliers isolés, negocians, militaires et autres, se sont prêtés sans tergiverser à prendre avec moi des arrangemens conditionels, promettant de les executer quand ils en seroient requis, quoique je leur eusse declaré que de mon côté je ne pouvois leur garantir positivement quoique ce soit.

D'un autre côté, j'ai eté quelquefois mal adressé et en risque de faire de mauvais choix, ou de mauvais marchés, si je ne m'etois tenu soigneusement sur mes gardes, et si je n'avois tiré sur chaque objet des informations de plusieurs endroits. Vous auriez peine à croire, par exemple, qu'un Ministre plein de bonne volonté m'ait indiqué et recommandé pour du salpetre, pour des fusils &c. des magazins, des fournisseurs chez qui le salpetre etoit trop cher, et les fusils defectueux. Aussi loin de trouver mauvais que j'aye pris des arrangemens tout differens, il m'a sçu gré de l'avis que je lui en ai donné.

J'ai fait six* differens voyages à Versailles depuis un mois, pour voir non seulement les Ministres, mais aussi tout ce qui les approche, ou les frequente, et sonder ou faire sonder les dispositions de chacun, car il ne faut pas croire qu'ils soient tous egalement

*et trois nouveaux dans le reste du mois de juin

2. His sister's son, Jean Lair de Lamotte; see Paul Delauney, *Vieux médecins mayennais, deuxième série . . .* (Laval, 1904), p. 58n. In the later years of BF's mission to France Lamotte served as his secretary.

bien intentionnés; cependant je voulois tâcher de tirer quelque parti de tous, et effectivement quoique j'aye plus à me louer des uns que des autres, il n'y en a aucun de qui je puisse me plaindre sans ingratitude.

J'ai obtenu entre autres choses, sous le nom de M. de la Tuillerie entrepreneur d'une manufacture d'armes, qu'il lui soit delivré incontinent des arsenaux du Roi quinze mille fusils à l'usage de l'infanterie suivant les modéles de 1763, pour etre employés dans son commerce, à condition de les *remplacer dans le courant* d'une année par un pareil nombre de nouveaux fusils de sa fabrique, en donnant bonne et suffisante caution pour ce remplacement; et on m'a agréé pour caution. Le premier envoi de ces fusils est deja en route pour Nantes, où M. Penet attend les vaisseaux que votre Comité secret doit y envoyer. J'espere que vos braves guerriers seront contens de ces fusils; mais il faut les avertir de ne pas trop se fier aux fusils ordinaires du commerce que l'on appelle fusils de traite, qui sont presque aussi redoutables aux amis qu'aux ennemis.[3]

J'aurois obtenu sans difficulté du canon de bronze aux mêmes conditions, si l'on n'avoit pas eté retenu par la consideration qu'ils portent les armoiries, ou les chiffres du Roy, qui les rendroient trop reconnoissables. Cependant si j'avois eté autorisé par le Congrès à insister fortement là dessus, il auroit eté possible d'enlever à la lime les L.L. et les fleurs de lys; mais tout cela ne pouvoit s'executer sans fraix, et qui est-ce qui en auroit fait les avances? M. Turgot, le seul Ministre de qui j'aurois pu attendre tant de faveur, a eté disgracié le 12 may; et tous les autres sont tellement harcelés aujourd'huy par les cabales extraordinaires de la Cour, que chacun est trop occupé du soin de se maintenir pour prendre sur son propre compte des affaires publiques qui ne sont pas absolument et uniquement de son ressort. Tous se preteront de bonne grace à une cause juste et honnête, mais aucun ne l'epousera avec chaleur. On a beau leur representer le grand interêt

3. This is the first appearance of the firearms that later became controversial enough to bear out Dubourg's words of caution. The question of where the weapons came from, and through whom, is discussed in our note (p. 464) on Carié de Montieu, whose successor in the arsenal at Saint-Étienne was M. Tuillerie or Thuilerie: L. Rouzeau, "Aperçus du rôle de Nantes dans la guerre d'indépendance d'Amérique . . . ," *Annales de Bretagne* . . . , LXXIV (1967), 230.

qu'a la france de ne pas manquer l'occasion d'enlever à l'Angleterre et d'attirer chez elle un commerce immense, et qui ne peut que s'accroitre encore d'année en année. Ils comprennent tres bien cela; mais la france oberee a besoin de la paix, et ils ont interêt de l'entretenir.

On m'auroit permis de tirer sourdement de l'arsenal même de Paris de la poudre, du plomb, du salpêtre &c., si nous n'en avions pas trouvé dans le commerce d'aussi bon et à meilleur compte, et même en plus grande quantité que M. Penet n'a ordre d'en charger.

J'ai obtenu des congés à longs termes pour des Officiers d'artillerie et autres; et on m'en a promis de semblables pour tous ceux qui nous seroient nécessaires, et que je pourrois faire entrer dans mes vues.

On m'offre de toutes parts quantité de bons Officiers, qui ne demandent pas mieux que de passer au service des Colonies Americaines, si j'etois autorisé à leur assurer un grade tel qu'ils le desirent (ou tel qu'on a coutume de l'accorder à ceux que l'on fait passer d'icy aux grandes Indes); mais je crois que c'est, pour ainsi dire, de quoi vous avez le moins de besoin, pour ne pas degoûter vos genereux compatriotes. J'ai cependant cru pouvoir promettre le grade de Capitaine, avec quelques petites avances, et le voyage defrayé, à M. fareli ancien Lieutenant d'infanterie, de ceux que l'on appelle Officers de fortune; la même chose, à l'exception du grade, à M. Davin ancien Sergent Major d'une grande distinction; et seulement le passage franc en mer à M. de Bois-Bertrand jeune homme plein d'honneur, de courage et de zele, qui a icy le brevet de Lieutenant-colonel, mais qui n'exige rien, et que vos Generaux placeront comme ils jugeront à propos pour le plus grand bien du service. J'ai regret de n'avoir pu rien promettre à un ancien Officier protegé de M. Turgot, et qui a eté employé sous M. son frere à Cayenne; mais surtout à deux Officiers Irlandois, Messrs. Geoghegan, l'un que je connois depuis longtems, a eté pendant les deux dernieres guerres Aide de camp d'un Officier general, aujourd'huy Marechal de france, qui en faisoit le plus grand cas, il n'a qu'un brevet de Lieutenant-colonel de Cavalerie, mais je le crois capable de tout; son Cousin a fait ses preuves avec plus d'avantage encore: n'etant que simple Capitaine dans l'Inde, il se trouva à la tête d'une petite armée, tous les officiers superieurs etant absens pour de bonnes ou mauvaises raisons, et il eut le bonheur, apres une marche bien combinée, de gagner sur les Anglois la bataille de [*blank in* MS.] Vous jugez bien que ces deux hommes là demanderoient à etre faits Officiers generaux.[4]

A l'egard des Ingenieurs, il y en a une quantite de surnumeraires en france, j'en ai arrêté deux de ceux là sous la simple assurance de leur passage franc, et de vous les bien recommander: l'un est M. Potier de Baldivia, tout jeune, mais bien instruit, et fils d'un Chevalier de st. Louis, Ingenieur attaché a M. Le Duc d'Orleans, et autrefois aide de camp du Marechal de Saxe; l'autre est M. Gillet de Lomont, jeune homme d'un merite peu commun, à qui il ne manque que d'avoir eté employé en guerre, comme il l'a eté dans des camps de paix.[5] Mais les Ingenieurs qui ont fait la guerre avec quelque distinction sont tous placés et contens de leur sort.

Vous savez que l'artillerie et le genie ont la plus grande affinité ensemble. Peutetre ignorez vous que ces deux corps ont eté plusieurs fois reunis et separés alternativement icy par nos Ministres divers; ainsi les uns peuvent tres bien suppléer aux autres, et tous les Militaires s'accordent à penser que dans la situation presente des Colonies, elles ont plus specialement besoin d'officiers d'artillerie que d'ingenieurs. C'est particulierement l'avis de l'homme de l'Europe le plus capable d'en juger, M. Le Comte de St. Germain.

Je suis assuré de la bonne volonté de quelques Officiers d'artillerie, habiles, experimentés et aguerris: mais j'ai un autre embarras. M. de Gribauval, Lieutenant general des armées du Roi, et Directeur general de l'artillerie de france, consequemment à la tête de ce corps, et jouissant de la plus grande consideration

---

4. We have found no evidence that Fareli and the two Geoghegans ever went to America, and it is unlikely that Davin did either; see Lasseray, *Les Français*, I, 179–81, 214, 231–2. René-Étienne-Henry de Vic Gaiault (or Gayault) de Boisbertrand (born 1746) was a former lieutenant of infantry, who held his brevet rank as an officer of mounted police (*ibid.*, II, 481–5); he carried the original of this letter to America, as explained below, and soon after his arrival was captured by the British.

5. Virtually nothing is known of Potier de Baldivia; for François-Pierre-Nicolas Gillet de Lomont see Thomas Balch, *The French in America during the War of Independence* . . . (Thomas W. Balch *et al.*, trans.; 2 vols., Philadelphia, 1891–95), II, 169.

publique,[6] avec qui j'ai eu plusieurs conferences à ce sujet, est d'avis que l'on vous fasse passer trois officiers d'artillerie à la fois, l'un pour etre en chef, et donner le branle à tout, les deux autres pour diriger toutes les operations, l'un dans les provinces du nord, et l'autre dans celles du midi. Pour la direction generale, il a jetté les yeux, de concert avec le Ministre, sur un Officier encore dans la fleur de l'age, que l'on juge egalement capable de l'ensemble et de tous les details, et dont on a deja eprouvé les grands talens en Corse, où on l'avoit chargé de tout, en le faisant passer sur le corps de 180 de ses anciens. Je vous envoye cyjoint un projet dressé par M. DuCoudray, l'Officier d'artillerie en question, et qui m'a paru fort bien; mais je dois vous informer en même tems que beaucoup de gens sont moins prevenus en sa faveur, tant dans le corps de l'artillerie, où il est fort jalousé, que hors de ce corps où il est engagé dans des controverses assez animées avec des militaires, avec des chymistes, avec M. de Buffon.[7]

   Entre les autres Officiers d'artillerie que l'on pourroit determiner à passer en Amerique, je distingue particulierement deux freres, MM. d'hangest, l'un Lieutenant colonel d'artillerie et chevalier de st. Louis, l'autre Capitaine d'artillerie, et ayant fait la

---

   6. He deserved it. Jean-Baptiste Vaquette de Gribeauval (1715–89) had been an artilleryman for forty years. After serving with distinction under Maria Theresa in the Seven Years' War he returned to France, where he completely overhauled the royal artillery by introducing lighter and more mobile guns and giving officers a more rigorous training. He was the chief architect of the system that Napoleon inherited.

   7. Dubourg's warning was well founded. Philippe-Charles-Jean-Baptiste Tronson Du Coudray (1738–77) was one of the leading young supporters of Gribeauval's ideas. He had already published works on artillery, metallurgy, and saltpetre; his career had shown enough brilliance to nourish his vanity and give scope to the singular gift for controversy on which Dubourg comments. See Pierre Chalmin, "La querelle des Bleus et des Rouges dans l'artillerie française à la fin du XVIIIe siècle," *Revue d'histoire économique et sociale*, XLVI (1968), 495. Deane, although unauthorized to do so commissioned Du Coudray a major general in the American army and permitted him to take a group of junior officers with him; he was thus the first high-ranking French recruit. He did some useful work, but also made a nuisance of himself. He had had the idea that he was to be commander of the artillery, a position to which Henry Knox had already been appointed; the ensuing complications, which promised to be endless, were terminated when the Frenchman drowned in the Schuylkill. Lasseray, *op. cit.*, II, 444–7; Freeman, *Washington*, IV, 422–4, 454–7, 538–9.

guerre aussi, et egalement chevalier de st. Louis.[8] Ces Messieurs d'hangest sont beaufreres de M. d'Antic, l'homme de france peut-etre qu'il importe le plus aux Colonies d'aquerir, tout le monde s'accordant à le regarder comme unique pour reunir ensemble la theorie et la pratique de tous les arts relatifs a la Chymie, et notamment de la verrerie et de la metallurgie. Ce savant artiste a eté friponné par de plus habiles financiers. M. Turgot se proposoit de lui donner la direction de toutes les manufactures de france, s'il etoit resté en place. M. d'Antic se retrouve dans l'embarras, chargé d'une femme et de quatre enfans, avec un patrimoine chargé de dettes criardes. Des gens que je crois de votre connoissance lui ont fait des offres tres avantageuses, M. hutton, chef des freres Moraves, et M. Johnson pour l'attirer en Angleterre, M. de Valtravers pour l'attacher à l'Electeur Palatin; d'autres font des projets pour le fixer icy, d'autres enfin voudroient le faire partir en Espagne. Mais je l'ai absolument decidé à vous donner la preference, si vous pouvez lui faire un sort convenable. Il ne peut s'engager à passer au nouveau Monde, à moins qu'on ne lui compte avant que de partir, vingt mille ecus de france, faisant deux mille cinq cent livres sterling, pour liquider ses biens, et assurer l'etat de sa famille. S'il obtient cela, il partira immediatement; une horde d'ouvriers de tous les genres s'empressera de le suivre, et on peut en quelque sorte assurer que cette seule transmigration avanceroit tous les arts d'un siecle en votre patrie.[9] Je vous envoye cyjoint un petit memoire dressé de concert avec lui.

Un autre homme qui ne vous seroit gueres moins utile, est plus qu'a moitié determiné à passer en Amerique, pour y etablir une manufacture d'armes telle qu'il n'y en a point en Europe, si vous pouvez lui faciliter les moyens d'y passer avec sûreté. Il est riche, il est extremement au fait de cette fabrication, il est mecontent de la cour: c'est M. de Montieu, cydevant entrepreneur de la manu-

8. For Louis-Augustin and Bernard-Remy Lamy d'Hangest see Lasseray, II, 514 ns.

9. Paul Bosc d'Antic (1726–84), formerly physician to Louis XV, was a student of natural history and physics but specialized in manufacturing glass and pottery: Larousse, *Dictionnaire universel*. Why he should have been in such demand, and how his expertise would have aided the American cause, we have no idea. For Hutton and Valltravers, old acquaintances of BF, see above, respectively, XVII, 223 n; XIV, 24 n.

facture royale des armes de st. Etienne en forez, qui a eté impliqué dans le fameux procès de M. de Bellegarde Inspecteur general d'artillerie son beaufrere. Cet honnete homme a tout prêts deux petits navires à lui, vingt deux petites pieces de canon de campagne de bronze, tout fondu, et les matieres toutes preparées pour une centaine de plus.[1] Il embarqueroit avec lui tous les outils et les materiaux necessaires; et tous ceux qui ont travaillé sous lui le suivroient en foule. Vous n'avez qu'a parler, et m'indiquer comment vous assureriez son passage, où il devroit se porter, et quelles facilités on lui procureroit pour tous ses etablissemens.

D'apres les conversations que nous avons eues ensemble, il a fait une autre speculation pour forcer le passage au travers de toutes les croisières de la marine Angloise, si les Colonies pouvoient fournir à une avance de deux, ou trois millions, argent de france, pour une expedition aussi decisive. Je vous envoye cyjoint le memoire qu'il m'a adressé à ce sujet.

D'autre part j'ai reflechi aux moyens de subvenir à tant de dépenses dans lesquelles votre Republique naissante se trouve engagée.

Le paquet que M. Penet m'a annoncé, il y a deja six semaines (ce 19 juin 1776) contenant des cartes de vos colonies, des plans, des brochures, une lettre de vous et une de M. Rush, ne m'est point encore parvenu; mais j'ai reçu, lu et relu le contrat en parchemin passé entre le Comité secret du Congrés d'une part, et Messieurs Pliarne, Penet et Comp. de l'autre, avec les instructions du même Comité aux memes commissionaires. Sur ces pieces authentiques, M. Penet m'a donné tous les eclaircissemens que je

---

1. The Bellegarde affair began in 1773, as part of an effort to discredit the fallen duc de Choiseul through one of his followers. Bellegarde and his brother-in-law, Jean-Joseph Carié de Montieu, were accused of furnishing to the royal arsenal as new weapons a vast quantity of old and defective muskets; the resultant legal procedures dragged on for years. [Honoré-Gabriel de Riquetti, comte de Mirabeau,] *Mémoires du ministère du duc d'Aiguillon* . . . (3rd ed., Paris, 1792), pp. 86–95. We are convinced that these were the 15,000 weapons for which Dubourg contracted, as he says earlier in the letter; the source was the same, and Montieu was involved. Dubourg checked the dealer's honesty by instructing Boisbertrand to inspect the firearms when he reached Nantes. The young man reported that they were extremely bad, and that the deal was an attempted swindle: Boisbertrand to the American commissioners, Sept. 5, 1778, Stevens, *Facsimiles*, XXIII, no. 1948. The commissioners, nevertheless, later bought the arms themselves.

pouvois desirer, et m'a detaillé ses divers projets d'operations, qui m'ont paru judicieux et bien combinés. Je l'avois fait revenir de Nantes pour le presenter secretement à M. le Cte. de V. Ministre des affaires etrangeres, qui vouloit le questioner sur l'etat de vos Colonies. Il est reparti quelques jours après, mais dans cet intervalle nous avions de nouveau concerté nos demarches ulterieures.

En consequence, j'ai pris des arrangemens avec la compagnie des fermiers generaux pour leur fournir directement par commission des Colonies unies, la provision de tabac necessaire à la consommation annuelle de ce royaume qu'ils tiroient cydevant par la voye de l'Angleterre, en œconomisant de part et d'autre ce que les douanes et les marchands de la grande Bretagne gagnoient tant sur les vendeurs Americains que sur les acheteurs françois. J'ai eté extremement satisfait de la franchise avec laquelle les fermiers generaux chargés de cette partie ont traité avec moi, en m'ouvrant tous leurs livres, et me montrant leurs factures en original.[2]

J'ai proposé à M. de S. Ministre de la Marine de lui fournir des farines et biscuits de mer, des bois de construction pour les navires (et par la suite du merrain pour le tonnelage) du chanvre, du goudron &c. Il m'a assuré qu'il ne s'informeroit point d'où je les tirerois, pourvu que je lui en procure à des prix raisonables: et que je pouvois prendre mes arrangemens en consequence.

Mais je ne vous dissimulerai point que j'ai trouvé ce Ministre prevenu de quelques idées mercantiles qu'il m'a fallu combattre, et dont j'aurai de la peine à le faire revenir, parcequ'elles lui ont eté suggerées par les gens qui sont reputés les plus au fait du commerce, et qui ont, ou croyent avoir interêt à entretenir les anciens prejugés à cet egard. Je l'ai cependant un peu ebranlé. Il m'a chargé de developer dans un petit memoire par ecrit mes idées particulieres sur les articles en quoi nous differons le plus; il donnera ce memoire à discuter à quelques habiles negocians, ou aux Deputés du commerce; apres quoi il pesera definitivement les raisons de part et d'autre. Je joindrai icy une copie de ce memoire, lorsque je l'aurai fait voir. J'ai pris des instructions de divers commerçans pour la traite des grains, des pelleteries, des indigos, des

2. Silas Deane, on his arrival, promptly set aside this agreement. He, Dubourg, and others then entered into protracted negotiations for a new contract, which were still incomplete when the American commissioners arrived. See Price, *France and the Chesapeake*, II, 702, 704–6.

fanons et blancs de baleine, et generalement de toutes les denrées et productions de votre sol; et nous pouvons nous flatter de vous en faire tirer un meilleur parti que vous n'avez jamais fait. Je suis encore plus assuré de pouvoir vous procurer en retour, toutes les marchandises Europeennes que vous souhaiterez, comme vins, huiles, draps, toiles, drogues, mercerie, quincaillerie &c., à meilleur compte que vous ne les tiriez d'Angleterre, parceque la france produit davantage, et que la main d'oeuvre y est moins chere.

J'ai actuellement un homme intelligent et plein d'ardeur qui parcourt toutes les manufactures d'aiguilles et d'epingles de Normandie &c., pour se mettre en etat d'en etablir bientôt une en Pensylvanie, où, moyennant les encouragemens que je lui ai fait esperer, il compte se rendre tres utile aux Americains, et se fonder lui même une tres bonne maison. Il paroit par vos instructions que l'objet dont vous avez le besoin le plus urgent, après les munitions de guerre, ce sont les aiguilles et les epingles.

M. Penet paroit un homme fidele, actif, intelligent, et tres connoisseur en armes de toutes especes; mais j'ai cru entrevoir que votre Comité ne le connoissant pas assez pour lui confier de gros fonds pecuniaires, n'avoit voulu s'engager qu'à lui rembourser amplement ses avances, et qu'il n'est pas en etat d'en faire de bien considerables, quelque bonne volonté qu'il ait. Voilà ce qui ralentit toutes les operations, que l'on auroit pu accelerer beaucoup si vous aviez eu quelquun icy duement autorisé à faire des marchés, et à prendre pour leur execution des engagemens au nom des 13 Colonies pour les payemens aux termes dont on pourroit convenir à l'amiable.

J'ai appris par nos Ministres que vous aviez donné des ordres à Liege pour y faire fondre du canon de campagne. Si nous avoins eu commission pour cela icy, nous aurions pu vous en faire fondre de meilleurs que les Liegeois et aurions eu plus de facilités pour vous les faire passer.

D'ailleurs j'ai eu sous les yeux tout recemment l'etat du canon de tous les arsenaux de france, où l'on m'a fait voir qu'il y en a par surabondance de differens calibres; et notamment que sur 1200 pieces de 4 livres, il n'y en a gueres que 500 pieces d'employées, et environ 700 pieces sans destination precise; moyennant quoi il ne nous seroit peutetre pas fort difficile d'en emprunter tacitement 2 ou 300, à charge de remplacement, et ces pieces de 4 livres sont justement celles dont on tire le meilleur service en campagne, où elles marchent à la tête des regimens. Si vous goûtez cette idée, ayez la bonté de nous envoyer des pouvoirs en bonne forme et d'y joindre, pour assurance des remplacemens, soit de l'argent, soit des marchandises, soit des lettres de change, soit des papiers-monnoye du Congrès.

Si je pouvois seulement repondre affirmativement de quelquune de ces choses pour une epoque fixe, on ne vous laisseroit manquer de rien. Denués de tout à cet egard, nous sommes obligés de nous reduire à vous faire passer peu à peu, par les vaisseaux qui viendront successivement de votre part pour en faire les chargemens, des fusils, de la poudre, du plomb, des pierres à fusil, du salpetre, et quelques Officiers subalternes d'artillerie, ou chefs-d'ouvriers, fondeurs, armuriers, &c.

Ce 29e juin

M. d'hangest l'ainé etoit venu exprès de la fère en cette ville pour conferer avec moi sur les moyens et les conditions de son passage en Amerique; mais apres avoir consulté un Ami commun, tous les deux ensemble et chacun separement, nous avons reconnu qu'il y avoit mieux à faire pour lui et pour nous; moyennant quoi il est retourné à son poste.

Reste à deliberer entre deux hommes tels que je doute qu'on puisse leur trouver un troisieme en Europe dans ce genre. L'un est ce M. DuCoudray dont je vous ai deja parlé cydessus, et pour qui mon estime n'a fait que s'accroitre. L'autre est le fameux Chevalier de Tot, arrivé avanthier de Constantinople, où, suivant le rapport de toutes les gazettes, il a dirigé l'artillerie des Turcs beaucoup mieux qu'on ne pouvoit l'esperer, etabli des fonderies de canons, dressé des batteries, construit des fortifications, et specialement au detroit des Dardanelles qu'il a mis à l'abri de l'invasion des Russes, tout puissans alors dans la Mediterranée.[3] Les gens de l'art n'en pensent pas tout a fait si avantageusement, et le regardent comme excellent peutetre en Turquie, et mediocre ailleurs; cependant je ne croirois point vous faire un mauvais present en vous

3. François, baron de Tott (1733–93), the son of a Hungarian exile, had been secretary to Vergennes at the embassy in Constantinople. During the recent Russo-Turkish war Tott had fortified the Dardanelles and reorganized the Ottoman army and navy: Larousse, *Dictionnaire universel*.

l'envoyant: au reste je menagerai vos interets autant qu'il me sera possible, mais vous concevez bien que tant l'un que l'autre de ces deux hommes là voudront se faire acheter le plus cher qu'ils pourront. M. Le chevalier de Tot se vantera d'avoir fait ses preuves avec le plus grand eclat. M duCoudray, par son credit aupres du Ministre de la guerre, etant en etat de vous rendre de plus grands services que persone, ne manque pas de faire valoir beaucoup cette consideration. Je le vois souvent depuis quelque tems, pour concerter ensemble les moyens d'obtenir un emprunt de quelques centaines de bouches à feu, et nous ne sommes pas sans esperances d'y reussir.

J'avois cherché à m'etayer pour cet effet de la protection du Comte d'Aranda, cy devant Ministre d'Espagne, et actuellement Ambassadeur icy.[4] Il m'a marqué beaucoup de bienveillance; mais des considerations importantes ne lui permettent pas de se compromettre vis avis du Ministere françois. Quoique M. Penet m'ait autorisé positivement, de vive voix et par ecrit à exercer pour lui, et comme lui même, les pouvoirs qu'il a reçus de votre Comité secret, je n'aurai point l'esprit entierement tranquille qu'il ne m'ait fait parvenir la lettre que vous m'avez fait l'honneur de m'ecrire de votre main. Dans cette perplexité, j'ai conçu l'idée de lier au moins une correspondance avec M. Arthur Lee, votre Deputé à Londres dont je pourrai avoir tres souvent des nouvelles. N'etant point connu de lui, j'ai eu recours a M. Le Comte de Lauraguais avec qui il est en liaison, pour lui faire passer ma premiere lettre.[5]

Je viens d'en recevoir une de M. Penet. Il s'agit de procurer à la colonie de Virginie douze pieces de canon de six. Ce calibre n'est pas commun icy; cependant nous tâcherons d'en trouver.

Il n'est pas tems encore de vous parler d'un fusil d'une nouvelle construction, beaucoup plus simple, et qu'on espere qui n'en sera

4. Pedro Pablo Abarca de Bolea, conde de Aranda (1718–98), had been the Spanish King's most influential minister until 1773, when he had fallen from power and been sent into ambassadorial exile.

5. For the comte de Lauraguais see above, XIX, 86 n. The well known playwright, amateur scientist, and eccentric was periodically in exile because of witticisms directed against the powerful; he was an outspoken friend of America, and had met Lee through John Wilkes. Larousse, *op. cit.* under Brancas; Burton J. Hendrick, *The Lees of Virginia* . . . (Boston, 1935), pp. 220, 235–6.

468

que plus solide; il y aura en même tems de l'epargne sur le prix. L'inventeur, nommé Reynard, m'en faisoit attendre le modele de jour en jour depuis plus d'un mois; il m'annonce enfin qu'il est terminé et l'epreuve en sera faite la semaine prochaine avec l'exactitude la plus scrupuleuse sous les yeux de M. de Gribauval qui veut bien s'y preter, et qui en cas de reussite, sera enchanté que le premier employ en soit consacré a la cause de la liberté, de la justice et de l'humanité, et que l'on ne commence a en faire pour le service des armées françoises que quand les votres en seront abondamment pourvues.

Je n'ai point encore reçu le paquet tant desiré de Roterdam, et il faut clore aujourd'huy cette lettre que je vais remettre a M. de Boisbertrand qui partira demain en poste pour aller s'embarquer à Nantes. Dieu veuille qu'il puisse vous la remettre bientôt. Soyez persuadé que je ne la lui ai confiée qu'apres m'etre assuré par de bons garants de sa fidelité, de son courage et de sa sagesse. Il m'a donné sa parole d'honneur qu'au moins ne tombera t'elle pas entre les mains de vos ennemis, telle chose qui puisse lui arriver à lui même.[6] Il m'en auroit fait serment si je faisois cas des sermens, mais je ne les ai jamais regardés que comme la derniere ressource des menteurs. Sans cela je jurerois icy entre vos mains un hommage lige et une fidelité inviolable à l'auguste Congrès de la plus respectable republique qui ait jamais existé. Mais mon attachement pour vous repond assez de mon devouement pour elle. Puisse t'elle conserver longtems un Sujet tel que vous, et en reproduire de semblables de generation en generation, et puissent mes services lui etre agreables en sousordre des votres. Je mourrois content si je pouvois voir ma patrie et la votre intimement unies, et

6. Dubourg revealed the contents of the letter and enclosures to his messenger, to enable him to make an oral report if they were lost. Boisbertrand was delayed at Nantes for more than two months, and did not sail until Sept. 10; with him were two low-ranking French officers whom he had recruited, and also a partner of Penet by the name of Couleaux. An American privateer intercepted their ship. Boisbertrand was landed alone at New Bedford as a prisoner, but was promptly released and went to Boston; his way was paid from there to Philadelphia. En route he stopped in New Jersey and took service with Gen. Lee, with whom he was captured three days later, Dec. 16, 1776. Meanwhile Couleaux had rejoined him and received his dispatches, which he delivered to Congress along with a covering letter from Boisbertrand that warned of Dubourg's naïveté. Force, 5 *Amer. Arch.*, III, 1162–3; Penet to BF below, Aug. 3; Stevens, *Facsimiles*, XXIII, no. 1948.

si j'avois pu y contribuer je serois au comble de mes voeux. Je suis avec la plus parfaite estime et la plus tendre affection Monsieur et cher Ami Votre tres humble et tres obeissant serviteur

BARBEU DUBOURG

Comme il est fort douteux que ces depeches puissent parvenir jusqu'a vous, tandis que la mer est herissée de vaisseaux Anglois, j'en fais faire deux autres copies que je ferai partir chacune par un navire different, afin qu'il puisse vous en arriver au moins une des trois.

Enfin je joins icy un modele d'alphabet en chiffres pour nous servir par la suite de part et d'autre, si vous le jugez à propos. Chaque lettre principale y est representée par plusieurs chiffres differens, dont on employera tantôt l'un et tantôt l'autre pour mettre les curieux en defaut. Les mots seront distingues par l'interposition d'un caractere Grec sans consequence; deux de ces caracteres auront la valeur d'une virgule, et trois vaudront un point. Il faudra effacer tous ces caracteres Grecs pour lire la lettre sans peine ni confusion. Faisons en immediatement l'essay.

3,2,β, 19, 5, 23, 16, 12, γc, 44, 53, δ, 10, 51, 4, 61, θ, 36, 17, 6, 24, 71, 1, λ, 42, 28, 37, 33, μ, 82, 54, 11, 9, 8, 47, 59, 88, 13, 69, ξι, 31, 92, ω, 72, 34, 56, 73, σ, 6, 94, 4, 20, ϕ, 40, 100, 68, 48, ψω

Pour dechiffrer cela, effacez les caracteres grecs,

3,	2,	β,	19,	5,	23,	16,	12,	γc,	44,	53,	δ,	10,	51,	4,	61, θ, 36,
m,	a,		f,	e,	m,	m,	e,		e,	t,		d,	e,	u,	x, f,
17,	6,	24,	71,	1,	λ,	42,	28,	37,	33,	μ,	82,	54,	11,	9,	8, 47, 59,
i,	l,	l,		e,	s,		v,	o,	u,		s,				
88,	13,	69,	ξι,	31,	92,	ω,	72,	34,	56,	73,	σ,	6,	94,	4,	20, ϕ, 40,
100,	68,	48,	ψω												

Cherchez maintenant les lettres correspondantes à chacun de ces chiffres dans l'alphabet cyjoint.

2e. juillet

M. de Boisbertrand emmene avec lui à ses propres depens, deux bas officiers d'une bravoure à toute epreuve, et d'une conduite irreprochable, dont on peut faire de tres bons Officiers, si l'on en a occasion, comme il est à presumer. Quant à Lui, je lui ai fait esperer le grade de Colonel, dans la persuasion où je suis qu'il peut bien le remplir a la satisfaction de vos Generaux. Je me suis cependant bien gardé de lui en donner de parole positive; mais je dois vous faire observer que c'est un usage constant d'avancer au moins d'un grade tout Officier que l'on fait passer d'icy dans les Indes.

Pour ce qui concerne tant M. DuCoudray que M. le Chevalier de Tot, comme il auroit fallu prendre beaucoup trop sur moi pour faire partir l'un ou l'autre immediatement je me crois obligé d'attendre vos ordres à cet égard.

P.S. Je rouvre ma lettre pour vous dire que depuis une heure, j'ai appris des choses qui me feroient un peu rabattre de l'idée que j'ai pu vous donner de M. de Montieux.[7] Adieu, portez vous bien, prosperez, vous et les votres et soyez sur que persone au monde ne vous est plus devoué.

Endorsed: Letter from Mr. Du Bourg Paris June 10th 1776 to July 2. to Doctor Franklin

From Lois Killcup[8]

ALS: American Philosophical Society

June 10 1776

Docr. you will be surprisd to see this from an old frind bute the grate love wee had for you and your brother[9] that when wee heard from time to time of honering conferd on you gave us such pleasure as I Doubte not you wolud [would] feel by puting out a litel finger to a frind passing by. Doctr. our frinds and relasons are gone from us.

Mr. Killcup has lost his mery thou [memory though] not his reson cante write his name. Docr. I hope you will see mr. bante a gentlman that is gone to mr. hancock which I should have wrote by but hard [heard] you was out a toune. Hee is a gentleman worth your notes you will admire him. He mared [married] mr.

---

7. Dubourg had undoubtedly received Boisbertrand's report from Nantes, discussed in an earlier note.

8. Mrs. Killcup or Kilcup (1702–90) was a native of Lynn who had married in sequence two Bostonians; the second, Dudson Killcup, was a merchant who died at the age of seventy-five in March, 1779. *New England Hist. and Geneal. Register,* V (1851), 327; Ogden Codman, *Index of Obituaries in Boston Newspapers, 1704–1800* (3 vols., Boston, 1968), I, 182.

9. Undoubtedly John Franklin, whose will Dudson Killcup had witnessed. Van Doren, *Franklin—Mecom*, p. 51.

Leewis Dauter.[1] Doct. I should not have seente you such a naked Leter had thar noot been such a frind as mr. bant for you to see and tell you all. I am Sir with the hiest regard and grateis respet your frind   LOIS KILLCUP

Addressed in another hand: To / The Honbl: / Benjamin Franklin Esqr / Philadelphia

From William Prichard[2]   ALS: American Philosophical Society

Honoured Sir,   Philada. June 10th 1776.

After being so far indebted to your clemency, nothing could give me more uneasiness than to be obliged to desire your assistance a second time, did not your former kindness encourage me to hope for a continuance of your favours. I have applied to several printers since my arrival in town, but have not been able to get employ, the want of paper having rendered work very scarce. Your honor has a quantity of old types[3] and a press, which if you would be pleased to let me have for a short time, I doubt not I could get my living by them, as I have met with a friend or two who have

1. William Bant (*c.* 1739–80) was a lawyer, merchant, and business associate of Hancock, and during the latter's absence in Philadelphia was managing his affairs in Boston. In 1765 Bant had married Mary Anna Lewis, who was related to the Killcups. Bant's trip to Philadelphia was to escort Katherine Quincy, Hancock's sister-in-law, who wanted to be with Mrs. Hancock at her lying in. *Sibley's Harvard Graduates,* IX, 550–1; Mass. Hist. Soc., *Proc.,* LIV (1922), 219; Samuel A. Green, *Groton Hist. Series* (4 vols., Groton, Mass., 1887–99), I, no. 13, p. 60; Herbert S. Allan, *John Hancock* . . . (New York, 1948), pp. 210, 224, 241; William T. Baxter, *The House of Hancock* . . . (Cambridge, Mass., 1945), pp. 241–2, 282, 287–8.

2. We know nothing more than this letter tells about the writer's background and difficulties. He seems to have been a recent arrival in Philadelphia, and he stayed in the city. The earliest book that he is known to have published was in 1782; four years later he owned a bookstore and circulating library and held book auctions until 1792. In 1798 a bookseller of the same name appeared in Richmond, Va. Charles Evans, *American Bibliography* (13 vols., Chicago and Worcester, Mass., 1903–55), VI, 167; XII, 419; George L. McKay, *American Book Auction Catalogues* (New York, 1937), p. 3.

3. Doubtless what BF had sent from London in 1774: above, XXI, 102, 210, 245.

offered me the printing of several small things if I could do them speedily. I shall take great care to weigh the types at taking them away, and return them safe whenever required, and thankfully pay your honour for the use of them; and if your honour would please to let me have those pamphlets and books in the Store to sell on commission, I should take a great care in rendering a proper account of all received, and pay for them regularly as I may chance to dispose of them. If your honour should have so good an opinion of my services and intentions, as to grant my request, it shall forever be remembered with gratitude, by Honoured Sir, Your faithful and affectionate Servant WM. PRICHARD.

Addressed: To / The Hone. B. Franklin Esqr.

From William Lee[4]

AL (letterbook draft): Robert E. Lee Memorial Foundation, Stratford Hall, Va.

Dear Sir   London 11 June 1776
    The Bill of Mess. W. & M. dated 12 Decr. 1775 on Mess. P. & J. Berthon value £300. which you remitted to my Brother,[5] is this day accepted payable at 60 daies by Agreement, this I doubt not you will think prudent to accept. I wish you long life, health, Success and happyness, and with a tender of any service, in my power, remain most sincerely Your Affectionate Humble Servant.

Dr. Benja. Franklin.

Editorial Note on the Plan of Treaties

The subjects of independence, foreign alliances, and confederation were closely interrelated, and Congress dealt with them together. They came

4. The alderman, brother of Arthur and Richard Henry: above xx, 308 n.
5. The committee of secret correspondence had remitted £200 with its letter above, Dec. 12; the "3" has been written over what was originally "£200." "W. and M." were undoubtedly Willing & Morris; Peter and John Berthon were a mercantile firm located in Lawrence-Pountney Lane: *Kent's Directory* . . . (London, 1776); *ibid* (1778).

before it formally in Richard Henry Lee's resolutions of June 7. On the 11th Franklin was put on a committee to draft a declaration of independence, and the next day on one to draft a plan of treaties.[6] Responsibility for the actual drafting fell in one case to Jefferson and in the other to John Adams; Franklin, though consulted, played a minor part.[7] He might have been expected to have a good deal to say about commercial treaties, because almost a year earlier he had proposed articles of confederation and the opening of American ports to foreign trade.[8] But, perhaps as a result of his bad health, he limited himself to providing precedents: he "had made some marks with a Pencil against some Articles in a printed Volume of Treaties, which he put into my hand," Adams wrote years later. "Some of these were judiciously selected, and I took them with others which I found necessary into the Draught. . . ."[9] The committee reported on July 18; the report was debated in August, resubmitted to an enlarged committee, and finally adopted on September 17.

We do not print the plan, despite its importance for the commissioners to France and for subsequent generations of policymakers, because Franklin had so little to do with it. It is printed in its various forms, furthermore, and the principles behind it are discussed with thoroughness and skill in a recent volume of the *Papers of John Adams*.[1]

From [Anthony Wayne[2]]

AL (draft): Historical Society of Pennsylvania

The writer, later known as "mad Anthony," needs no introduction. Deborah Franklin had dealt with him briefly a decade earlier about her husband's land speculations, but we have no evidence that Franklin knew him before they served together on the Pennsylvania committee of

6. *JCC*, V, 425–6, 431, 433.

7. His contributions to Jefferson's draft are discussed in the headnote on the latter's note to him below, under June 21.

8. See the articles and the resolution on trade above, under July 21, 1775.

9. Butterfield, *John Adams Diary*, III, 338. The volume was Henry Edmunds and William Harris, eds., *A Compleat Collection of All the Articles and Clauses Which Relate to the Marine, in the Several Treaties Now Subsisting between Great Britain, and Other Kingdoms and States* . . . (London, 1760). BF's copy, with treaty articles marked, is now in the Harvard University Library.

1. Taylor, *Adams Papers*, IV, 260–302.

2. Identified by the handwriting.

safety.[3] They may or may not have met in Canada; Franklin was en route from Montreal to New York while Wayne and his regiment, one of the six under General Sullivan, were on their way from New York to the St. Lawrence.

After the rout of the small American army and its retreat to Sorel, at the mouth of the Richelieu, the Canadian campaign was about to collapse. General Thomas was dying of smallpox at Chambly. He had turned over the command to General Wooster, who promptly departed for home and, at St. Johns, met Sullivan on his way north.[4] The new commander now had an army worth the name, he had brought with him enough provisions to supply it at least temporarily,[5] and he hoped to open a new offensive down the St. Lawrence toward Quebec.

The Canadians' hostility made intelligence hard to gather, and the Americans apparently had no idea that the enemy were moving toward them in force. The fleet from Britain had brought Carleton a large contingent of troops under General Burgoyne, and they were already on their way to Trois Rivières, roughly equidistant from Montreal and Quebec. This was also Sullivan's objective, but the British arrived first: six thousand regulars, it is estimated, were encamped around the village by the time the Americans, less than a quarter of that number, made their attack. Surprise was their only hope, and it was dissipated when local guides misled them in the night.[6] The result was the disaster recorded here, which ended the Canadian campaign.

Dear Sir   Camp at Sorell 13th. June 1776
After a long March by land and water Variated with Delightful as well as Gloomy prospects we Arrived here the night of the 4th. [?] Instant and on the 7th.[7] it was Agreed in a Council of War to Attack the Enemy at Three Rivers about 47 Miles lower down,

3. For the earlier contact see above, XIII, 32. During BF's service on the committee of safety from July to January, 1775–6, Wayne was one of the more faithful attenders: *Pa. Col. Recs.*, X, 285–452 *passim*.

4. Force, 4 *Amer. Arch.*, VI, 589; Otis G. Hammond, ed., *Letters and Papers of Major-General John Sullivan . . .* (3 vols., Concord, N.H., 1930–9), I, 212.

5. The stores were delayed beyond Albany by a shortage of boats and wagons, but at the end of May Schuyler reported to the commissioners that he had forwarded enough to supply the army for 20 to 25 days. *Ibid.*, pp. 202–3, 205–7, 211. For a return of what he had sent see Force, *op. cit.*, cols. 639–40.

6. Christopher Ward, *The War of the Revolution* (John R. Alden, ed.; 2 vols., New York, 1952), I, 198–9.

7. The first date was overwritten and is illegible. The second is incorrect; the expedition left late on the 6th: Force, *op. cit.*, col. 826.

whose Strength was Estimated at 3 or 4 Hundred. Genl. Thompson was appointed for this Command, the Disposition was as follows, 4 Attack's to be made at the same time viz. Col. Maxwell to Conduct the first, myself the Second Col. St. Clair the third and Col. Irvine the 4th. Liet. Col. Hartly the Reserves.[8]

On the same evening We Embarked and Arrivd at Col. St. Clairs Encampment about Midnight. It was Intended that the Attack shou'd be made at the dawn of day. This we found to be Impraketecable, therefore Remained where we were until the 7th. [?] when we took boats to the Number of 1450 Men all Pennslvanis except Maxwells Battalion.[9]

About 2 in the Morning we landed Nine Miles above the town, and after an Hours March day began to Appear, our Guides had mistook the road, the Enemy Discoverd and Cannonaded us from their ships. A Surprise was out of the Question. We therefore put our best face on and Continued our line of March thro' a thick deep Swamp three Miles wide and after four Hours Arrived at a more Open piece of Ground, amidst the thickest firing of the Shipping when all of a Sudden a large Body of Regulars Marched down in good Order Immediately in front of me to prevent our forming, in Consequence of which I Ordered my Light Infantry together with Capt. Hay's Company of Rifle men[1] to Advance and amuse them whilst I was forming, they began and Continued the Attack with great Spirit until I advanced to Support when I Orderd them to wheel to the Right and left and flank the Enemy at the same time we poured in a well Aimed and heavy fire in front as this:

8. For the three colonels, William Maxwell, William Irvine, and Arthur St. Clair, see the *DAB*. They commanded respectively the 2nd N.J. and the 6th and 2nd Pa. For Thomas Hartley, Irvine's second in command, see the minutemen officers' letter above, Aug. 31.

9. Again the date was overwritten and is illegible; the embarcation was at dusk on the 7th. St. Clair, who had been sent to observe the enemy and attack if he thought feasible, was encamped about ten miles from Trois Rivières and on the other side of the river. Force, *op. cit.*, cols. 684, 826.

1. Samuel Hay and riflemen of the 6th Pa.: Heitman, *Register of Officers*, p. 214.

They Attempted to Retreat in good Order at first but in a few Minutes broke and run in the Utmost Confusion. About this time the Other Divisions began to Immerge from the Swamp except Maxwell who with his was Advanced in a thicket a Considerable Distance to the left, our Rear now becoming our front. At this Instant we Recd. a heavy fire in flank from Muskettry field pieces Howitzers &ca. &ca. which threw us into some Confusion, but was Instantly Remedied. We Advanced in Colums up to their breast Work's which till then we had not Discovered. At this time Genl. Thompson with Cols. St. Clair Ervine and Hartly were Marching in full view to our Support, Col. Maxwell now began to Engage on the left of me, the fire was so hot he cou'd not mantain his post. The Other troops had Also fired off to the left. My Small Battalion Composed of my own and two Companis of Jersey men under Major Ray[2] amounting in the Whole to About 200 were left exposed to the Whole fire of the Shipping in flank and full three thousand men in front with all their Artilry under the Command of Genl. Burgoine. Our people taking example by others gave way. Indeed it was Imposible for them to stand it longer. Whilst Col. Allen[3] and myself were Employed in Ralling the troops Let. Col. Hartly had advanced with the Reserve and bravely Attacked the Enemy from a thiket in a Swamp to the left, this hardiness of his was of the Utmost Consequence to us, we having Rallied about 500 men from the Different Regiments. We now sent to find the Genl. and Other field Officers. At the same time the Rifle men of mine and Irvins kept up a Garding fire on the Enemy. The Swamp was so deep and thick with timber and Un-

2. Maj. David Rhea of the 2nd N.J.: *ibid.*, p. 344.

3. St. Clair had already become separated from his men, it seems, and his lieutenant colonel had taken charge. For William Allen see the commissioners to Schuyler above, May 10.

derwood that a man 10 Yards in front or Rear cou'd not see the
men Drawn up. This was the cause of the Genl. Col. St. Clair
Maxwell and Irvine missing us, or perhaps had taken for Granted
that we were all cut off. Col. Hartly who lay near retreated by
without a Discovery on either side, until he Crossed our line near
the left, which caused our people to follow him. Allen and myself
were now left on the field with only twenty men and five Officers,
the Enemy still Continuing their whole fire from Great and
[small?] guns upon us, but afraid to venture from their lines; we
thought it prudent to keept them in play by keeping up a small
fire in Order to gain time for our people to make good their
Retreat, in Consequence of which we Continued about an Hour
longer in the field, and then Retired back into the woods which
brought us to a Road on the far side of the Swamp. We followed
this Road about two Miles where we went from our Small party to
the place where our people had interd the Swamp by which means
we even Collected 6 or 700 men with whom we Retreated in good
Order but without Noureshmint of any kind, the Enemy who
were Strong in Number had Detatched in two or three bodies
about 1500 men to cut off our Retreat. They way laid and Engaged us again about 9 miles from the field of Battle, they did us
little damage[4] we Continued our March, and the third day Almost
worn out with fatague Hunger and Dificulties scarcely to be par-
ralleld we arrived here with 1100 men, but Genl. Thompson Col.
Irvine Doct. McCalla[5] and Several Officers are prisoners at three
Rivers. Col. St. Clair Arrived alone last night their Seperation
from the Army (which Appeared Indeed to be lost) was the cause
of their Misfortune. I believe it will be Universally Allowed that
Col. Allen and myself have saved the Army in Canada.[6] Capt.
Robinson has proved himself the Soldier and the Gentleman,[7] his

4. These were troops landed from the ships to block the retreat: Ward, *op.
cit.*, p. 199.
5. Daniel McCalla, D.D. (1748–1809), whom Congress had appointed
chaplain of the Pa. troops, was subsequently released on parole. William B.
Sprague, *Annals of the American Pulpit* . . . (9 vols., New York, 1859–73), III,
320–2.
6. Credit should also go to Carleton. His food supply was so low that he was
unable to feed prisoners; he consequently withdrew a force that could have
blocked the retreat: Ward, *op. cit.*, p. 200.
7. We have found no other reference to the part played by Thomas Robinson,
a captain in Wayne's 4th Pa. (Heitman, p. 349). "Colonel Wayne behaved

Conduct has Outgone the most Sanguine hopes of his friends, out of 150 of my own I have lost more than the One Quarter part, together with Slight touch in my Right leg, which is partly well already, we shall have more buisness soon, our people are in high Spirits and long for the Other bought [bout?] as well as your Humble Servant

Notation: Letter to Docr. Franklin John Martin, Delany &ca.[8] 13th. June 1776 Encl Giving an account of the Battle of Three rivers

The Pennsylvania Assembly: Instructions to Its Delegates in Congress

Printed in *Votes and Proceedings of the House of Representatives of . . . Pennsylvania . . .* (Philadelphia, 1776), VI, 740.

Since the previous autumn, when the Pennsylvania delegates had been instructed not to vote for independence,[9] the Assembly had come under mounting attack. One ground of attack was apportionment: Philadelphia, the center of radicalism, and the western counties were underrepresented. In March the house yielded to pressure and increased the number of their seats; the resulting by-election, on May 1, left the moderates in control but by a small margin.[1] The details of what followed remain obscure; only the outlines are clear. On May 10 Congress urged the colonies, if they had not already done so, to create governments adequate to the emergency, and five days later it adopted a preamble that spoke of substituting popular for royal authority.[2] A series of public meetings in Philadelphia culminated in one on May 20, which demanded that the Assembly cease to function, condemned its instructions against independence, and called for a provincial conference as prelude to the election of

exceedingly well," a participant reported, "and showed himself the man of courage and the soldier. Colonel Allen exerted himself several times, and is a fine fellow." Force, *op. cit.*, col. 828.

8. We cannot identify Martin. Sharpe Delany was a close friend in Pennsylvania with whom Wayne corresponded during the campaign: Harry E. Wildes, *Anthony Wayne* (New York, [1941]), p. 470.

9. Above, Nov. 9.

1. See David Hawke, *In the Midst of a Revolution* (Philadelphia, [1961]), pp. 13–31; Ryerson, *Revolution is Now Begun*, pp. 149–75.

2. *JCC*, IV, 342, 357–8.

a constituent convention "for carrying the said Resolve of Congress into execution."[3]

So began the revolution in Pennsylvania, while Franklin was on his way home from Montreal. By the time he reached Philadelphia on May 30 the Assembly was battling for survival, a battle in which he seems to have played little part.[4] On the day of the town meeting, May 20, the house reconvened after a recess, and almost immediately started to retreat on the issue of independence. On June 5 a committee was appointed to draw up new instructions. They were approved on the 8th, and entered on the record six days later, when the legislators adjourned until August.[5] By the time they met again independence was a fact, the convention was sitting, and the Assembly was a constitutional ghost.

Gentlemen,   [June 14, 1776]

When, by our Instructions of last November, we strictly enjoined you, in Behalf of this Colony, to dissent from and utterly reject any Propositions, should such be made, that might cause or lead to a Separation from Great-Britain, or a Change of the Form of this Government, our Restrictions did not arise from any Diffidence of your Ability, Prudence or Integrity, but from an earnest Desire to serve the good People of Pennsylvania with Fidelity, in Times so full of alarming Dangers and perplexing Difficulties.

The Situation of public Affairs is since so greatly altered, that we now think ourselves justifiable in removing the Restrictions laid upon you by those Instructions.

The Contempt with which the last Petition of the Honourable Congress has been treated: The late Act of Parliament, declaring the just Resistance of the Colonists, against Violences actually offered, to be Rebellion, excluding them from the Protection of

---

3. *Pa. Gaz.*, May 22, 1776; 8 *Pa. Arch.*, VIII, 7514–16. The conference and convention are discussed in the editorial note on the latter below, July 15. For descriptions and interpretations of the complex forces working against the Assembly see, in addition to Hawke's and Ryerson's works just cited, Charles H. Lincoln, *The Revolutionary Movement in Pennsylvania, 1760–1776* (Philadelphia, 1901), pp. 233–65; John Paul Selsam, *The Pennsylvania Constitution of 1776: a Study in Revolutionary Democracy* (Philadelphia and London, 1936), pp. 94–135; Theodore Thayer, *Pennsylvania Politics and the Growth of Democracy, 1740–1776* (Harrisburg, Pa., 1953), pp. 175–85; and Elisha P. Douglass, *Rebels and Democrats: the Struggle for Equal Political Rights and Majority Rule during the American Revolution* (Chicago, 1955), pp. 240–62.

4. See the editorial note just cited.

5. 8 *Pa. Arch.*, VIII, 7535, 7539, 7542–3.

the Crown, and even compelling some of them to bear Arms against their Countrymen: The Treaties of the King of Great-Britain, with other Princes, for engaging foreign Mercenaries to aid the Forces of that Kingdom, in their hostile Enterprizes, against America; and his Answer to the Petition of the Lord Mayor, Aldermen and Commons of the City of London, manifests such a determined and implacable Resolution to effect the utter Destruction of these Colonies, that all Hopes of a Reconciliation, on reasonable Terms, are extinguished.[6] Nevertheless, it is our ardent Desire, that a civil War, with all its attending Miseries, could be ended by a secure and honourable Peace.

We therefore hereby authorize you to concur with the other Delegates in Congress, in forming such further Compacts between the United Colonies, concluding such Treaties with foreign Kingdoms and States, and in adopting such other Measures as, upon a View of all Circumstances, shall be judged necessary for promoting the Liberty, Safety and Interests of America; reserving to the People of this Colony the sole and exclusive Right of regulating the internal Government and Police of the same.

The Happiness of these Colonies has, during the whole Course of this fatal Controversy, been our first Wish. Their Reconciliation with Great-Britain our next. Ardently have we prayed for the Accomplishment of both. But, if we must renounce the one or the other, we humbly trust in the Mercies of the Supreme Governor of the Universe, that we shall not stand condemned before his Throne, if our Choice is determined by that over-ruling Law of Self-preservation, which his divine Wisdom has thought fit to implant in the Hearts of his Creatures. Signed by Order of the House,   JOHN MORTON,[7] Speaker.

---

6. The rejection of the Olive Branch petition is discussed in the headnote on the previous instructions above, Nov. 9, the Prohibitory Act in the note on Hartley to BF, Nov. 23, the treaties for mercenaries in the note on BF to Carroll and Chase, May 27, 1776. The London petition and the King's reply in March, 1776, had appeared in the *Pa. Gaz.* of June 5; for the texts see Force, 4 *Amer. Arch.*, V, 462–3.

7. See the note on BF's letter to him above, Feb. 26.

Lambert Wickes[8] to the Committee of Secret Correspondence

ALS: National Archives

Gentlemen,　　　　　On Board the Reprisal 16th June 1776.

I received your orders and Instructions by Mr. Bingham, the 14th Inst. but the Shallop with the provisions did not Arrive till this day. We have now got all the provision on board both from the Wasp[9] and Shallop.

You may depend on my best endeavours in your Service to prosecute this Voyage with the Most expedition and Advantage in my power. My People, all to two are in good health, and the Officers are well Satisfied with this Cruize, hopeing thereby to render their Country an assential Service, as well as themselves. There is now One two Decker, two Frigates, one Twenty Gun Ship and a Sloop of War Lying in Old Kiln Road and we are waiting an Oppertunity to get out by them with impatience so that you may depend on our Embracing the first favorable oppertunity of getting out and proceeding on our intended Cruize. From Gentlemen Your most obliged humble Servant

LAMBT. WICKES

Addressed: To / The Honble: Committee of Secret / Correspondance / Philadelphia

Endorsed: Onbd. the Reprisal. 16 June 1776 Capt Wickes / Letter Captain Wickes onboard the Reprisal 16. June 1776

8. Wickes (1742?–77) showed himself in his short career to be one of the most promising American naval officers. He began as a Maryland captain and merchant, and became acquainted with Robert Morris. In March, 1776, the marine committee of Congress purchased a small ship, which was converted into an 18-gun sloop of war and christened the *Reprisal*, and in April Wickes was put in command of her. His first mission was to take Bingham to Martinique, along with a flotilla of merchant vessels; see Bingham's instructions above, June 3, 1776. The convoy, sheltered under Cape May, was blockaded for weeks by the British in Delaware Bay. Not until July 3 did Wickes and his charges elude the enemy and escape for the moment, but in the next two days four merchantmen were captured. Clark, *Wickes*, pp. 10–15, 42–6, 52–3.

9. A continental schooner which the committee had assigned, with the shallop, to carry the stores. *Ibid.*, p. 44.

From Lord Howe

Franklin's fellow negotiator in London, David Barclay, had written him in March to say that Lord Howe was coming as a commissioner and was as well disposed as ever.[1] After instructions to the Admiral and his brother were signed on May 6, Howe promptly left for America. He touched at Halifax in late June, learned that the General had sailed for New York, and followed him there. On the way he prepared a circular letter to the colonial governors, in which he enclosed a declaration to the American people. The circular informed the governors of his arrival and asked them to publicize the declaration, which announced that the commissioners were empowered to pardon those who promptly returned to their allegiance and to declare any colony or part of it to be at peace, and promised to reward all who helped to restore order.[2]

At the same time the Admiral wrote this letter to Franklin and two others to Congressional delegates. Bad weather delayed him, as he says, and he did not arrive at Sandy Hook until July 12. He promptly sent the documents ashore under a flag of truce. They were in Washington's hands on the 15th and before Congress on the 18th. Franklin was absent when they were delivered, and was sent for. When he entered the room he was given several letters sealed;[3] he opened and looked at them, then handed them to the President and asked that they be read to Congress. On the 19th the circular letter and declaration were ordered published, and the next day Franklin was authorized, if he thought best, to reply to Lord Howe.[4]

Eagle. June 20 [-July 12]. 1776.

I cannot my Worthy Friend, permit the Letters and Parcels which I have sent in the State I receiv'd them, to be landed without adding a word upon the subject of the injurious Extremities in which our unhappy Disputes have engaged us.

You will learn the Nature of my Mission from the Official Dispatches which I have recommended to be forwarded by the same Conveyance. Retaining all the Earnestness I ever express'd to see our Differences accomodated, I shall conceive, if I meet with the same Disposition in the Colonies which I was once taught to

1. Above, March 31, 1776.

2. For the text of the circular and declaration see Force, 5 *Amer. Arch.*, I, 605–6.

3. What the other letters were is not clear. One might have been Barclay's; the other, which has disappeared, could conceivably have been from Fothergill.

4. Smith, *Letters*, IV, 497–8; *JCC*, V, 592–3, 597; see also Gruber, *Howe Brothers*, pp. 89–99.

expect, the most flattering Hopes of proving serviceable in the Objects of the King's paternal Sollicitude, by promoting the re-establishment of lasting Peace and Union with the Colonies. But if the deep rooted Prejudices of America and the necessity of preventing her Trade from passing into foreign Channells, must keep us still a divided People, I shall from every private as well as public motive, most heartily lament, that this is not the moment wherein those great Objects of my Ambition are to be attain'd; and that I am to be longer deprived of an Opportunity to assure you personally of the Regard with which I am your sincere and faithfull humble servant HOWE.

P.S. I was disappointed of the Opportunity I expected for sending this Letter at the Time it was dated, and have been ever since prevented by Calms and contrary winds, from getting Here to inform Genl. Howe of the Commission with which I have the Satisfaction to be charged, and of his being join'd in it.

Sandy Hook. 12th. July.

Subscrib'd to Benjmn. Franklin Esq. Philadelphia. HOWE

Copy

To George Washington   AL (draft): New York Public Library

Dear Sir   Philadelphia, June 21. 76

I am much obliged by your kind Care of my unfortunate Letter, which at last came safe to hand. I see in it a Detail of the mighty Force we are threatned with;[5] which however I think it is not certain will ever arrive; and I see more certainly the Ruin of Britain if she persists in such expensive distant Expeditions, which will probably prove more disastrous to her than anciently her Wars in the Holy Land.

I return Gen. Sulivan's Letter enclos'd: Am glad to find him in such Spirits, and that the Canadians are returning to their Regard for us.[6] I am just recovering from a severe Fit of the Gout, which

5. The letter of Feb. 13 from Arthur Lee, with its enclosure, which Washington had forwarded with his own letter above, May 20; the packet had presumably gone to Canada while BF was on his way home.

6. This was Sulivan's letter to Washington of June 5–6, which the General had forwarded to Congress on the 16th. Otis G. Hammond, ed., *Letters and*

has kept me from Congress and Company almost ever since you left us,[7] so that I know little of what has pass'd there, except that a Declaration of Independence is preparing.[8] With the greatest Esteem and Respect, I am Dear Sir, Your most obedient and most humble Servant   B F

G Washington

From Thomas Jefferson   AL: American Philosophical Society

This note has probably far more importance than appears on the surface, because the likelihood is that Jefferson enclosed with it his draft of the Declaration of Independence. The evolution of that document has undergone repeated and microscopic analysis.[9] A number of minor questions remain unanswered, but the general outline is clear. On June 7 the issue of independence was raised, and four days later a committee, of which Franklin was a member, was appointed to draft a declaration, which was submitted to Congress on the 28th. The principal author was Jefferson, but he consulted with John Adams and Franklin, both of whom made small changes in phrasing.[1] A few of these alterations Jefferson identified

---

Papers of Major-General John Sullivan . . . (3 vols., Concord, N.H., 1930–39), I, 217–21; Fitzpatrick, *Writings of Washington*, V, 142. Sullivan, who had just arrived at Sorel with his reinforcements and taken the command, had been full of the optimism that ended a few days later in the disaster at Trois Rivières; see the headnote on Wayne to BF above, June 13, 1776.

7. Washington had left Philadelphia on June 4: Fitzpatrick, *op. cit.*, pp. 97–8.

8. See the following document.

9. John H. Hazelton, *The Declaration of Independence: Its History* (New York, 1906); Carl Becker, *The Declaration of Independence. A Study in the History of Political Ideas* (New York, [1922]); Julian P. Boyd, *The Declaration of Independence: the Evolution of the Text* (Princeton, N.J., 1945); Boyd, *Jefferson Papers*, I, 413–33; James Munves, *Thomas Jefferson and the Declaration of Independence: the Writing and Editing of the Document That Marked the Birth of the United States of America* (New York, 1978); Taylor, *Adams Papers*, IV, 341–51.

1. Congress treated the draft less tenderly, and in the ensuing debate made further changes and some significant deletions. To comfort Jefferson for the latter, BF told him the anecdote of a signboard: as originally composed it read "John Thompson, Hatter, makes and sells hats for ready money," followed by the picture of a hat; friends worked it over on logical grounds and reduced it to "John Thompson" and the picture. Paul Leicester Ford, ed., *The Works of Thomas Jefferson* (12 vols., New York, 1940–5), XII, 110 n. The famous remark attributed to BF at the signing of the Declaration, that "we must all hang together,

by name; the source of others remains conjectural.[2] Some of them may have been made in committee, but in that case Franklin was almost unquestionably absent. A fit of the gout had kept him from Congress and from meeting people since early in the month, he wrote on June 21, and on the 26th he was recuperating outside Philadelphia.[3] His few contributions to the document were presumably made on the draft that Jefferson sent him.

This note, if it accompanied the draft, must have been written between the appointment of the committee on June 11 and its report on the 28th, a Friday. Jefferson could scarcely have prepared his manuscript, submitted it to the committee, and had it returned to him in time to send it to Franklin on Friday the 14th. Hence the most likely date is the 21st.[4]

Friday morn. [June 21?, 1776]

The inclosed paper has been read and with some small alterations approved of by the committee. Will Doctr. Franklyn be so good as to peruse it and suggest such alterations as his more enlarged view of the subject will dictate? The paper having been returned to me to change a particular sentiment or two, I propose laying it again before the committee tomorrow morning, if Doctr. Franklyn can think of it before that time.

Th: J. to Doctr. Franklyn.

Addressed: To / Doctor Franklyn.

---

or most assuredly we shall all hang separately," was in all likelihood not his; see Carl Van Doren, *Benjamin Franklin's Autobiographical Writings* (New York, 1945), pp. 418–19.

2. Authorities differ on the question; see Boyd, *Declaration*, pp. 29–31; Munves, *op. cit.*, pp. 69–75.

3. Above, to Washington, June 21; below, to Rush, June 26.

4. Julian Boyd and his fellow editors deal at length with the questions, which are two sides of the same coin, of what Jefferson enclosed and when he did so, and after discarding a number of possibilities as unlikely they conclude that the most probable answers are the draft Declaration and June 21. *Jefferson Papers,* I, 404–6 n. Their analysis is persuasive, and to the best of our knowledge no evidence has since transpired that casts doubt on their conclusion.

Silas Deane to Robert Morris and the Committee of Secret Correspondence

ALS: (duplicate): Library of Congress

This letter, in form to Morris but in fact to the committee, is the only one from Deane that Franklin surely saw before his departure for France; it was therefore part of his small stock of information about what would face him in Europe.[5] The letter deals only with the preliminaries of

5. He may or may not have seen also Deane's three letters to Jay, dated June 11, which came by the same conveyance. They largely duplicated the contents of this one, and are discussed in L. Bendikson, "The Restoration of Obliterated Passages and of Secret Writing in Diplomatic Missives," *Franco-American Rev.*, I (1936–37), 248–54. Deane, just before leaving Bordeaux, gave the letters to Jay and Morris to a Capt. Leavey (he also appears as Lever or Leviz), who arrived in New Bedford on Sept. 5. The letters were forwarded to Washington, and by him to Philadelphia, together with one from the General that was read in Congress on Sept. 13. *Deane Papers*, I, 401; *Pa. Packet*, Sept. 24, and *Pa. Gaz.*, Sept. 25, 1776; Fitzpatrick, *Writings of Washington*, VI, 46; *JCC*, V, 755. Deane's communications, therefore, must have been in Philadelphia by Sept. 12.

Our rubric, to print communications to a group to which BF belonged, obviously does not apply when he ceased to be a member on leaving for France. We have therefore had to weigh probabilities. Letters from abroad that we are confident he read include the present one and the following: above, two from Dumas to the committee, one of April 30 to May 9, the other of May 14 to June 6, and one from Dubourg to BF, of June 10 to July 2; below, Dubourg to BF, July 5, Penet to BF, Aug. 3, and Story's report in the committee memorandum of Oct. 1. Four others to the committee, the dates of which suggest that they should have arrived in time, we omit because we do not believe that they did. They are:

(1) From Arthur Lee, June 3, 1776, Wharton, *Diplomatic Correspondence*, II, 95–6. This letter went by William Carmichael, a young Marylander who was later a member of Congress and who will be prominent in future volumes; he stayed so long in Paris that the dispatch was not delivered until December, 1778: *ibid.*, 95 n, 184–5; Smith, *Letters*, II, 410–11 n.

(2) From Dumas, June 30–August 10, 1776 (National Archives). Portions of this letter are printed in translation with an incorrect date in Wharton, *Diplomatic Correspondence*, II, 108–110. Because the letter went by St. Eustatius, according to Dumas, we do not believe it could have arrived before BF sailed.

(3) From Deane, July 20 to August 18, 1776, *Deane Papers*, I, 195–218. William McCreery, who like Carmichael was a young Marylander and future Congressman and, like him, will appear often in later volumes, carried this letter: Deane to the committee, Sept. 17, 1776 (transcript, Harvard University Library). McCreery's ship was chased and captured, and he threw the letter overboard: Lovell to BF, after May 26, 1777, APS.

(4) From Beaumarchais, Aug. 18, 1776, Wharton, *op. cit.*, II, 129–31. This letter also went by McCreery: *ibid.*, p. 201.

487

Deane's mission, because he reached France long after he had hoped to.
He sailed in early March, but his ship was forced to turn back. He left a
second time on April 3, bound for Bermuda; there he chartered a sloop
to take him to Bordeaux, where he arrived just over three months after
his first departure from Philadelphia.[6] He spent June in Bordeaux, and
did not reach Paris until July 6. There he expanded the range of his
activities, and they shaped in large degree those of his fellow commissioners when they joined him at the end of the year.[7]

Dear sir   Bordeaux June 23d. 1776
    I wrote you a Long Letter from 6th. to this Day which DD
[delivered?] Capt. Palmer of Portsmouth[8] and fearing Accidents
recapitulate the Heads in this (Via NYork). I arriv'd the 6th., sent
forward your Letters and the Bills for Acceptance. Messrs. Ds.[9]
have done everything in their power to assist me and have added
the utmost personal Kindness and hospitality. I could wish No
American Vessels were sent to any other address in this port as
theirs is a Capital House and may be relied on for secrecy and
Dispatch. Have critically attended to such Occurrences as might
point out the Disposition of this Kingdom and am of Opinion it
is much in Our Favor. Large Fleets are fitting out at Brest and
Toulon. Ammunition and other Stores are buying up by Order of
Court, and Spain is arming Ostensibly against Portugal.[1] The
Crop of Grain will be short in this Kingdom of Wheat one third,
of Rye one half the usual supply. This may be relied on.[2] Salt
Provisions are scarce and Dear. Beef 56. Sterling per Barrel see

    Subsequent communications from Deane, Dumas, and Beaumarchais we are
confident BF never saw. He sailed on Oct. 27, and six to seven weeks seems to
have been the minimal time for a direct crossing from France.
    6. Smith, *Letters*, II, 315 n; *Deane Papers*, I, 126–7, 134–5, 178; III, 146; V,
385, 394–6.
    7. For Deane's undertakings in the interval between this letter and BF's ar-
rival see the headnote on BF's letter to him below, Dec. 4, 1776.
    8. Capt. Thomas Palmer sailed from Bordeaux on Aug. 15 and reached
Portsmouth on Oct. 6; en route he was chased by a British man-of-war and
threw overboard all his dispatches, Deane's among them. *Naval Docs.*, VI, 1144.
    9. The two Delaps, for whom see the committee of secret correspondence to
Bingham above, June 3, 1776.
    1. The arming was more than ostensibly against Portugal. A dispute over
boundaries in South America was bringing the two countries close to war.
    2. Not so; the harvest was abundant. F. Braudel and E. Labrousse, eds.,
Histoire économique et sociale de la France (4 vols., Paris, 1970–80), II, 386–7,
392.

prices Current enclosed. Have wrote into Spain, Portugal, and England to find if they are in the same situation, and as I wrote immediately on my Arrival expect an Answer in a few Days. Messrs. Ds. have wrote on the same subject. I set out for Paris Tomorrow having obtaind Letters to Persons of Note there, particularly To *Monsr: Clugny Comptroller of Finances*,[3] Mons. Vergennes *Ministre des Affaires Etrangeres* and some others, also To The Farmers General on the subject of Tobacco from their Agent here, and a Memorial from some Merchants in this City on the subject of American Commerce, which indeed is in part already granted, it having been sent forward a few Days after my Arrival. My Letters are from persons of Influence and Note here. My immediate address will be To Messr. *Germany Gerardot & Co.* Bankers in Paris on whom have Letters of Credit from hence.[4] I have had all the success I could have wish'd for in this City, and have formed a Connection, (which may greatly promote my further Views,) by shewing them how deeply they were Interested in obtaining the Cheif Share of the American Commerce. The Ministry were Changed the Week I arrived. *Count Maurepas* is at the Head. *Mons. Clugny* late intendant of this City and province is *Comptroller of Finances*, a Circumstance which has greatly helped my obtaining Letters of Introduction. The Gentlemen who have Assisted me are of Note and stand well with the Ministry, but I may not mention them in my Letters. I leave the Sloop I came in here for the present for I expect to meet *Docr. Bancroft* at Paris and may send my first Dispatches from thence in her. None of the Articles of the Contract[5] are to be purchased in this part of France on any reasonable Terms and but few at any Rate. I have wrote To all the Ports where remittances were expected, for tho' I might obtain a Credit, the last Necessity only will induce me to Use it whilst remitting is so hazardous. But I am hourly in hopes of receiving something from you. I can add Nothing Material in this save My Respectful Compliments to the Gentlemen of the Congress, To your Worthy

3. Turgot's successor, Jean-Étienne-Bernard de Clugny, baron de Nuits-sur-Armançon, died after five months in office: *Dictionnaire de biographie française.*
4. For Deane's activities in Bordeaux see Crout, "Diplomacy of Trade," 120–3; Price, *France and the Chesapeake*, II, 704. Germany, Girardot & Co. was the successor of the bank established by Jacques Necker.
5. For presents to the Indians. The contract, and Deane's expectation of meeting Bancroft, are explained in his instructions above, March 2, 1776.

President and Gentlemen of the Committee with which I am more immediately connected in particular. I am with respects To Mrs. Morriss Dear sir Your Sincere Freind and Very Humble servant

S DEANE

P.S.: As my Letters will often refer To Matters concerning the Indian Contract in particular, as Well as to Those of a General Nature, it will be at Times much easier for Me, to direct my Letters and write them addressed individually to You, as in the present Case, than to write in the plural Stile of Address.[6]

(Duplicate)

To Robert Morriss Esqr, To be Communicated To The Honorable Committee for Secret Correspondence

From Horatio Gates

ALS: National Archives

Dear Sir   New York 23d: June 1776:
    This will be presented you by The Chevallier de Kermovant, who left Old France the Sixth of April, and arrived about Fourteen days ago at Stonington by the Way of Cape François; he desires me acquaint you that his Views are truly patriotic, and that he neither Seeks reward, or Honour, but as he shall Merit; he has Letters for you, and Doctor Rush, they probably will speak more for him, than I can presume to do.[7] He professes being an Engineer, and to have served all the last War with The Turks in that Line. I set out tomorrow afternoon, or Tuesday morning, for Albany, but have not yet received either Instructions, or the Resolves from Congress.[8] I am Dear Sir Your Affectionate Humble Servant

HORATIO GATES

6. A large blank in the MS at this point was apparently a communication in invisible ink, which is no longer decipherable; see Smith, *Letters*, V, 225 n.

7. Kermorvan carried two letters from Dubourg, one to BF and the other to Rush. An extract of the first is printed above, March 24, 1776, where the headnote quotes from the second. The Chevalier delivered both on June 26; see below, BF to Rush of that date and Kermorvan to BF the next day.

8. The resolutions creating a separate command in Canada and appointing Gates to it: *JCC*, V, 448. The General arrived in Albany at the end of the month to discover, now that the army was no longer in Canada, that Schuyler claimed command of it: Force, 4 *Amer. Arch.*, VI, 1199–1200.

Doctor Franklin,

Addressed: The Honble: / Doctor Benjamin Franklin, / Member of The Continental Congress / at / Philadelphia.

Notation: (Not ent'd.) 23 June 1776 Let Genl Gates to Dr. Franklin relating to Monsr. Kermovan read 27th [?] June 1776 before Board War

To Benjamin Rush

ALS: National Archives

Manor of Moreland, at Mr. Duffield's,[9] June 26. 76

Dear Doctor,

I have just received the enclos'd Letters by the Chevalier Kermorvan. By the Conversation I have had with him he appears to me skilful in his Profession. I hope in a few days to be strong enough to come to town and attend my Duty in Congress. In the mean time, I could wish you to introduce the Gentleman where it may be proper, and that you would translate the Passage relating to him that I have mark'd in M. Dubourg's Letter,[1] and show it with what you have receiv'd to the same purpose from the same Friend. As I think Philada. should be better fortify'd than it yet is, I hope some Use will be made of this Gentleman's Talents as an Engineer for that End.[2] With great Esteem, I am, Dear Doctor Your affectionate Friend and most obedient Servant B FRANKLIN

Respects to Mrs Rush

Doctor Rush

(not recorded)

Addressed: To / Dr Rush / Philadelphia

Endorsed: June 26th. 1776 Lre from Dr Franklin to Dr Rush relative to Mr Kermovan read 28h. June before Bd War

9. BF was staying at Moreland, northeast of Philadelphia, in the family house of his old friend Edward Duffield, the clock-maker. Above, VII, 211 n; Edward D. Neill, "Rev. Jacob Duché," *PMHB*, II (1878), 61–2 n.

1. The translated extract is above, March 24, 1776, and a note there identifies Kermorvan's letters.

2. In early June the Pa. committee of safety had appealed to Washington for an engineer to fortify the Delaware below Philadelphia. Rush saw to it that Kermorvan met members of Congress; that body recommended him to the

From the Chevalier de Kermorvan

ALS: American Philosophical Society

Monsieur   [June 27,³ 1776]

Vous trouverez les trois volumes de depravation, restauration, stabilité de l'ordre légal que m: du bourg m'a fait le plaisir de vous envoyer par moy.

Vous voudrez bien me faire la grace d'accepter les autres ouvrages que j'ai recueilli a paris d'après la notte que je demendai a m: du bourg, des livres qui pourroient vous faire plaisir.

J'ai remis hier au soir Votre lettre a M: Rush nous dévons aujourdhuy voir plusieurs membres du congrès.

J'ai l'honeur de vous prévenir que je ne communiquerai ce que je vous dis hier qu'aux membres du congrès. J'ai des raisons pour me comporter ainsi et si le congrès a le désir de réussir il est necessaire que tout ce qui est affaire de politique exterieure soit ignoré dans le public a cause des oppositions que les autres puissances ne manquent pas d'elever.

La hollande dans son commerce des indes, la Suisse dans ses contrats et renouvellemens d'alliance, en agissent ainsi. Le secret quand on a des ennemis est le plus nécessaire.

J'attends, Monsieur, avec impatience la nouvelle de votre parfaite convalescence, et le plaisir de vous voir ici accelerer le grand oeuvre. Je suis avec attachement et réconnoissance de vos politesses, Monsieur, Votre trés humble et trés obeissant serviteur

LE CHEVALIER DE KERMORVAN

Addressed: to / doctor fran [*torn*] / at the Countri

---

committee as the man for the job, and he was promptly engaged. Lyman H. Butterfield, "Franklin, Rush, and the Chevalier Kermorvan: an Episode of '76," APS *Library Bulletin*, 1946 (Philadelphia, 1947), pp. 36–7.

3. Kermorvan mentions having talked with BF "yesterday" and delivered his note to Rush (the preceding document) the same evening. The Chevalier therefore went in to Philadelphia from Moreland on the 26th, and was writing the next day.

In this and subsequent letters he capitalizes, consistently and meaninglessly, words within a sentence that begin with "l" or "s". To avoid confusion we have reduced them to lowercase.

From Charles Biddle

ALS: American Philosophical Society

Biddle (1745–1812), the brother of the more famous naval officer, Nicholas Biddle,[4] was a Philadelphia merchant captain. He had returned the previous January from a complicated but successful voyage to France for gunpowder,[5] and on the way back had injured himself badly in a fall. For a time in August he joined the army in New Jersey, and in September he left, bound for the Caribbean;[6] his lameness, in other words, did not prevent his resuming his "line of business" at sea. What office he held when he wrote we do not know. The office for which he was applying was that of an agent for the marine committee; these agents, who came to be known as the navy board, were first authorized in October,[7] but the need for them may well have been discussed much earlier. The wording of the second paragraph suggests the bracket of dates that we have supplied: gout kept Franklin out of circulation after his return to Philadelphia on May 30, and his presiding over the Pennsylvania convention when it assembled on July 15 publicized his recovery.

Sir   [June or early July?, 1776]

After the many strong instances of your freindship which I have received it is with great reluctance I trouble you once more on my Account. My lameness I fear will prevent my pursuing with Vigour the line of business in which I have been bred, and the Continuance of my present Office being uncertain, my freinds have advised me to apply for an establishment in the Navy board, which it is expected will be formed by Congress. If Sir you can consistent with your Judgment recommend me by a line to the President General[8] I make no doubt it will have the greatest weight and shall esteem it as the highest favor.

I am extremely sorry for your late Indisposition but hope for a speedy return of your health. I am just able to walk with the help

4. Above, XVIII, 84 n.
5. See Crout, "Diplomacy of Trade," pp. 85–7.
6. James S. Biddle, ed., *Autobiography of Charles Biddle . . . 1745–1812* (Philadelphia, 1883), pp. 80, 87, 90.
7. *JCC*, VI, 906; see also pp. 929, 933.
8. Hancock was a major general of Mass. militia.

of a Crutch and shall soon do myself the honor of waiting on you. With the Greatest respect I am Sir Your most Obedient Servant

CHAS. BIDDLE

Dr. Franklin

Addressed: Dr. Franklin

Endorsed: Cha Biddle

Thomas Hartley to the Pennsylvania Delegates in Congress

ALS: American Philosophical Society

⟨Crown Point, July 3, 1776: In the engagements near Three Rivers on June 8 the sixth Pennsylvania battalion, of which I have the honor to be lieutenant colonel, lost Colonel Irvine, Lieutenant Edie, and almost eighty privates, most of whom are prisoners.[9] On June 21 Captains McLean, Adams, and Rippie, Lieutenants McKerran, McCallister, and Hogg, Ensigns Lusk and Culbertson, and four privates crossed from Isle aux Noix to the west shore to fish in sight of the camp; they carried no arms. When they went to a house on the shore they were surrounded by Indians. Adams, Culbertson, and two privates were killed and scalped; McLean, McKerran, McCallister, Hogg, and two privates were captured; Rippie and Lusk escaped when a party of our men arrived.[10]

The battalion has suffered much from these accidents. The officers captured are the best we have, and we need their immediate release. The ones most recently seized were undoubtedly "carried directly to the Regulars at Montreal," and I beg you to make some arrangement for their prompt exchange.

P.S. It is the army's wish that General Thompson should be restored to us at once.⟩

9. For William Irvine see Wayne to BF above, June 13, 1776, and for Edie the letter from the York committee above, Jan. 29.

10. For McLean see the letter from the York committee above, Dec. 23. Brief notices of Robert Adams, William Rippey, Samuel McFerran, Abdiel McAllister, John Hoge, William Lusk, and Joseph Culbertson may be found in Heitman, *Register of Officers*, pp. 58, 141, 223, 271, 273, 277, 347, and in John B. Linn and William H. Egle, *Pennsylvania in the War of the Revolution* . . . (2 vols., Harrisburg, 1880), I, 167, 179, 182, 186, 188, 403, 602.

From Catharine Greene

ALS: American Philosophical Society

My Dearly beloved Friend   Warwick July the 3d 1776

I Gladly once more Welcom you To your own home though I Lament the occation hope by this you have Recoverd your Health and the Pheteiuge [Fatigue] of So Disagreeable a Tuor and have Resumd the Chearfull agreeable BENJAMIN FRANKLIN. Pray God to Preserve you long a Blessing to your family Friends and Injurd Country.

We have Disagreeable accounts from N. York and Quebeck[1] But Still hope there Is Virtue and Stability enough in our friends to Send our Enemies a Shamd to there own homes, and be Simple Bread and Water the Portion of theire Cheifs and that in a Dungeon. But I Reflect is not Such guilty Conciencions Punishment enought? Ile leave them to a Higer Power. And to our agreeable Corrispond which has been So long Bar'd I think your last favor is Jany. 27th a long while indeed But you have been Sick and in a Strange Land. Do give Sister Some little account of it and She will give it me for She is a Dear good Woman[2] and I know you have not time. In yours you wrote you had Put Ray to Lattin School which we was much Pleasd with as we Proposd giving him learning if his Capacity was good enough of which being Parents we did not think our Selves Judges. Mr. Greene was Just in Since my writeing and Designd to have wrote him Self to you but tis a Severe Drougth with us and has a Number of People makeing Hay So that is obligd to be with them But Desires his Kind Regards to you and Many thanks for your Care of his Boy and Says he hopes you will Call upon him for Money when ever you think fit for he does not love large Sums against him and would be Glad to know what Sum would Carry him throw Colledg. And if you think tis Best for him to Come home this Vacancy whether he would be Willing to go again or not I Could Deny my Self any Pleasure for My Childrens advantage. Those at home with Jenny and the family are all well and Joyn in Respects to you. I dont know but think Jenny is like to get one of our best Matches you are So good

---

1. The news from New York was that Gen. Howe and his army from Halifax had landed on Staten Island on June 25; the news from Quebec was that the siege had collapsed.

2. She doubtless meant to write "your Sister." She had a daughter's feeling for Jane Mecom; see Jane's letter to her above, Nov. 24.

a friend to Matrimony that you will be Glad to hear of it.[3] I Could Run much farther but fear the Post will be gone So I bid you Day Day God Bless. Your friend that loves you Dearly

CATY GREENE

Brother Hubbart[4] Desires his love to all.

Addressed: To / Doctr Franklin / Philadelphia / Free

From Frederick William de Woedtke

ALS: American Philosophical Society

Woedtke died shortly after writing this letter.[5] It is part of a series that he addressed to Franklin; the earlier ones have been lost, and another on July 4 is in large part illegible. His French bears out Father Carroll's comment that the Baron had picked up just enough polish to accentuate his awkwardness.[6] The handwriting is on a par with the spelling, which we have preserved at the cost of obscuring what he means; he writes "er" and "re" interchangeably, so that "notre" may appear as "noter," "maître" as "maiter," and "moindre" as "moinder." This letter and Wayne's above of June 13, 1776, as far as we know, are the only firsthand reports of the military debacle that Franklin received after leaving Canada.

Monsieur   Camp at Crown point, July 3d. 1776[7]

J'esper que vous aurai reçu mes deux dernieres Letters de sorel et de lile de noix. J'aurai eû lhonneur de vous ecrire plus souvent si je pouvois vous donner seulement une perspective d'une bonne nouvelle. Vous savez Monsieur que après que nos trouppes ont courrit [?] sans se tourner sans avoir eû ni mort ni blessé, sous les ordres de feu General Thoma; onts campé quelque tems à de-

3. In his missing letter of Jan. 27 BF must have mentioned entering Ray in school. The boy did come home for the vacation; see his letter below, Aug. 4. Jane Flagg, Jane Mecom's granddaughter, married Elihu Greene on Dec. 5, 1776: James M. Arnold, ed., *Vital Record of Rhode Island* . . . (21 vols., Providence, R.I., 1891–1912), I, 56 (1st pagination). The bridegroom was William Greene's cousin and the brother of Nathanael Greene: above, I, lxi, where the marriage is misdated by a year. Caty's calling BF "a friend to Matrimony" refers to his letter to her above, VI, 225.

4. Thomas Hubbart, the husband of Caty's sister: above, I, lviii.

5. He went into hospital in mid-July, and apparently died on the 29th or 30th. Force, 5 *Amer. Arch.*, I, 649, 698, 796.

6. See the note on the commissioners to Alexander above, March 27, 1776.

7. In another hand.

Chambo et de là sont arrivés à sorel, joinder le reste de nos
troupes, nous y avont campé de deux cotês de la riviere et out
[où] a force de fatuiger nos troupes nous avons fait des excellents
retranchements et par ce poste nous êtions encor toujours en grand
partiée maiter du pays mais aû lieu de penser a l'importance de ce
post, le G. Arnold propose lexpediton honteuse pour le céder
ayant sous lui le Colonel de Haas *!e plus grand Thorie de larmée.*[8]
Dans le meme interval le bon general Thomson, un homme respectable, enterprend l'expedition pour les Trois rivieres; expedition
mal conduit.[9] Les deux detachements celui du ceder et celui de
Trois rivieres etant rentré au camp de sorel il fuit [fut] presque
unaniment resoluit de quitter tout de suite le camp de sorel, et le
canada malgrez touttes les opositions et remontrances que jai fait
aû conseille, nous avons laissé noter camp sans ruiner la moinder
chose a nos batteries. Come le G. Sulivan avoit pris le dévant une
fausse alarmée vient. M. le Colonel de *Haas opina* tout de suite
pour precipiter noter marche de jetter deux canon dans l'eau ce
que j'ai heureusement empeché. Au camp de chambli on tient
conseille de guerre, on opina daller le plus tôt que possible à St.
Jean. Je fuit [fus] du sentiment *opposé* puisque nous ne savions pas
si l'enemi avoit pris possesion du post de sorel et non plûs sa force.
A St. Jean on tient conseille de guerre de nouvaux il fuit resoluit
de passer le lac champlain malgrez tout mes representations sans
savoir si l'enemie avoit pris poste à chambli. Avant de partir nous
avons brullé quelques maisons aû lieu de nous attacher a démolir
les fortifications de St. Jean. Avant de passer les Lacks nous nous
sommes arreté a lile de noix ou a la fin nous avons apris qu'il i
avoit quelques centaines dhommes a St. Jean. Nous avons laissé
une chaine de fer a lisle de noix laquelle êtant tiré pouvoit faire
bien de l'empechement aux battiments anglois pour venier de St.
Jean a nous. Les anglois onts jusqu'a present très peu des bauti-

8. A post had been established at the Cedars ("le céder"), up river from
Montreal, to impede communication between British sympathizers and the
western Indians. When the American garrison and a small relieving force were
captured, Gen. Arnold and John Philip de Haas (1735–86), lieut. col. of the
1st Pa., brought reinforcements from Sorel but succeeded only in securing
release of the prisoners. Justin H. Smith, *Our Struggle for the Fourteenth Colony:
Canada, and the American Revolution* (2 vols. New York, 1907), II, 365–80. De
Haas clearly had no Tory sympathies; see the *DAB.* Woedtke leveled the charge,
as the rest of the letter makes clear, against any one whom he disliked.

9. See Wayne's letter cited in the headnote.

ments, mais malheureusement nous leur laissont *le tems* de construire a St. Jean des batiments, nous voila arrivé a la Kronpointe,
campé et arrangué comme une horde de Tartares, lesquelles ont
cépendant une preference sur nous quils placent des guardes et
envoyent a reconoiter. Il i a Monsieur une desinuion total enter les
nouvaux anglois et les auters.[10] J'en crains avec certitude la suite.
Nous avons beaucoup d'officiers Thoris quil fauderoit renvoyer. Il
i a ici un colonel Antel du Reg. de Hesen regiment qui n'existe
presque plus, des Canadiens jeun homme sans conessance et experience qui fait malheureusement le service d'aide de Camp General qui se melle par désous du genie.[1] Nous faissons inocculé la
picote[2] a nos gens et la nouriture quils sonts eûs et [est] du cho-
chon [cochon] salé etc. etc. Nos Lazarets, nos hopitaux sonts ne-
gliges au dernier point. Breve nous sommes par *nous* mêmes bien
malheureux. Moimême j'ai un nomber d'enemie mais mes enemies sonts nos Thoris. Je commence et je finis toujours que le
respectable congres leurs fera confiscera leur bien et les fera abater
la tête a philadelphie. Je ne puis rien plus dire Monsieur que je
desireoit de faire honneur a voter recomendation faire honneur a
mon service mais je ne le puis nayant du puvooir a cet égard. Jai
nos soldats tout pour moi, mais a quoi cèla aboutit? Je crains je
crains que nous ne conservons ce poste. Si ma letter vous intresse
Monsieur et que vous ne pouvez la lire Mr. paul faiks Interpret
vous la lira tout de suite.[3] Je vous prie Monsieur de presenter mes

10. Friction between northerners and southerners, according to Gen. Sullivan, for a time threatened the army's existence. But he stressed the harmony
among officers, without mentioning Woedtke's opposition to the majority in
the councils of war. Otis G. Hammond, ed., *Letters and Papers of Major-General
John Sullivan* . . . (3 vols., Concord, N.H., 1930–39), I, 266–7.

1. Lieut. Col. Edward Antill was a lawyer like his brother John (above, XXI,
103–4 n), and emigrated from New Jersey to Quebec, where he joined the
American forces as an engineer. He was in the Canadian regiment commanded
by Moses Hazen ("Hesen"), and had been ordered to determine the number of
troops around Chambly and then to fortify St. Johns. *Ibid.*, pp. 234–5, 237;
Lasseray, *Les Français*, I, 120; Heitman, *Register of Officers*, p. 64; 3 N.J. Hist.
Soc. *Proc.*, II (1897), 43–6. The charge that the Colonel meddled in engineer-
ing, on top of everything else, ignores these orders.

2. Smallpox.

3. Paul Fooks (d. 1781) was a Philadelphian of French Huguenot extraction;
Woedtke had seen him just before leaving for Canada. Fooks was imprisoned in
his home during the British occupation, and in June, 1778, became interpreter

JULY 4, 1776

trés humbles civilités a Monsieur le president Hencko {Hancock]
et a Mr. Adam. Jai lhonneur de vous ecrire et de vous communiquer tout ce qui est passé en particulièr désirant cèpendant davoir
lhonneur et le plaisier d'avoir de vos nouvelles. 1500 homes de la
pensilvanie directement sous mes ordres avec le *brevet* d'eter leur
Chef me feroit du plaisir et peut êter que le respectable congre en
seroit content de leurs services[?]. Je finis puisque Mr. le Colonel
Alen[4] va partire a linstant et jai lhonneur de me dire avec la
consideration la plus distuingée Monsieur Votre trés humble et
tres obeissant serviteur   WOEDTKE

Franklin and James Wilson to Jasper Yeates

LS: Historical Society of Pennsylvania

⟨Philadelphia, July 4, 1776: The Congress has appointed you a
commissioner of Indian affairs in the middle department, and
asked us so to inform you. A conference will be held at Pittsburgh
on July 20, which Congress hopes you will attend. Although this
may be inconvenient, we know that your regard for the public
will outweigh any consideration of your private affairs. You will
shortly hear further from us. Signed by Franklin and Wilson.[5]⟩

---

for Congress. William Duane, ed., *Extracts from the Diary of Christopher Marshall* . . . (Albany, N.Y., 1877), pp. 63, 161, 272; *PMHB*, LXIII (1939), 331;
JCC, XI, 562.

4. For Lieut. Col. William Allen see Wayne's letter cited above.

5. For Yeates see the letter from the Pa. committee of safety above, Nov. 17.
His answer is below, July 6. This was the second treaty with the Indians at
Pittsburgh; for its predecessor see the note on BF to Mecom above, Aug. 2,
1775. On July 4 Congress appointed two commissioners, and instructed BF and
Wilson to write them to attend the conference mentioned here and to provide
the necessary gifts; the other letter is noted below, July 5. On the 20th the
Congress voted $3,000 for the gifts, and on Aug. 19 authorized the commis-
sioners to wait as long as necessary to complete their mission. The negotiations
at Pittsburgh were protracted until November and, like those in 1775, helped
to postpone an Indian war. *JCC*, V, 517, 595, 668; Force, 5 *Amer. Arch.*, II,
511–18; III, 599–600; *PMHB*, XXIX (1905), 359–61; Walter Mohr, *Federal
Indian Relations 1774–1788* (Philadelphia, 1933) pp. 49–50.

499

From Frederick William de Woedtke

ALS: American Philosophical Society

Monsieur, Kronpoint ce 4 Julei 1776

J'espere que le s. Colonel Allen vous aura remise ma letter[6] par laquelle vous ne savez que trop noter[7] situation, laquelle est la plus épineuse de nos trouppes, comme [*illegible*[8]] que avoire [*illegible*], par [*illegible*] juge [*illegible*] nous [*illegible*] experimenté et que les Generaux [*illegible*] Sulivan [*illegible*] gouverneur [*illegible*] de nos trouppes, cependant nous avons ici un nouveau Général qui dirige tout le monde—le s. Colonel Antheil il est Aide Camp General, il i a deux ans quil etoit [*illegible*] sans theorie sans pratique protegé du brave General [*illegible*] qui est l'ami intime de la femme d'Antheil. Le Capitaine Marquesi qui est le porteur de cette letter vous dira bien des choses. On a fait acroire au General Sulivan qu'il ne savoit son metier quoique j'ai vû de son travaille ce qui la si fort dégouté quil est parti pour philadelphie.[9] Il a eû le malheur de perder sans sa faute tout son [*illegible*] j'ai eû malheur de perder ses chevaux [*illegible*] voyage de philadelphis jusqu'a sorel je suis trè [*illegible*] Je ne puis [*illegible*] dans le nouveau [*illegible*] de plus vingt lieues autant que je [*illegible*] pour le bien être de nos trouppes tout ce quil i a [*illegible*] nous portent tout le mal imaginable au camp de chambli j'ai apris par plusieurs canadiens attaché aux Congres que les anglois avoit mis 500 Guines pour m'avoir prisonnier, je ne puis nier que cela ma flatté de beaucoup. Je desir fort, Monsieur, d'avoir un mot de reponse sur mes lettres, et recomende comme un citoyen comme un Géneral

6. The one above, written the previous day.

7. "Notre"; see the headnote on *ibid*.

8. The ink on the rest of the page has run, leaving only one coherent phrase decipherable, the attack on Col. Anthill continued from his previous letter. Much of the second page is also illegible; the third begins at "apris par plusieurs canadiens."

9. Capt. Bernard Mousac (Moussac, Maussac, or Moissac) de la Marquisie remains a shadowy figure. The commissioners to Canada, BF told Congress in August, 1776, had commissioned him a captain and engineer in one of the new companies to be raised there, but he had lost the document; a letter from Schuyler attested to the loss, and a new commission was issued him. *JCC*, V, 715; Force, 5 *Amer. Arch.*, I, 338. He apparently did know his business, for he is said to have served with distinction under Washington, St. Clair, and Wayne: Lasseray, *Les Français*, II, 630.

et comme un homme d'honneur de faire donner la place d'aide Camp Général a un homme experimenté. Si j'avois a proposer quelqu'n cela seroit le Colonel Scienkler [St. Clair].[1] La disharmonie enter nos trouppes continue.[2] Les 4 Vaisseau de Guerre que nous avons sur le lac sont en un très mauvaise état meme ils nónt point des balles quoique nous avons du plomb. Je vous écris tout sans déguisement, et j'ai l'honneur de me dire avec la plus grande considération Monsieur votre tres humble et très obeissant serviteur   WOEDTKE

Franklin and James Wilson to John Montgomery[3]

LS: Chicago Historical Society

⟨The letter, dated Philadelphia, July 5, 1776 is identical in wording with that to Jasper Yeates above, July 4, 1776.⟩

From Jacques Barbeu-Dubourg   ALS: National Archives

The news in this brief note, that France was arming and, Dubourg believed, about to go to war against Britain, was more arresting than any in his letter above of June 10 to July 2, 1776. The intelligence, false as it was, must have had considerable impact in Philadelphia. The question of when it arrived, however, seems to be unanswerable. Dubourg may have sent the note either with the original of the letter just mentioned, in which case Boisbertrand delivered both in mid-December, or with a duplicate of that letter which arrived, we conjecture, on September 13 and occasioned excitement in Congress.[4]

1. Arthur St. Clair (1736–1818), col. of the 2nd Pa., was promoted to brigadier general the following August; for his role in the Battle of Trois Rivières see Wayne to BF above, June 13, 1776.
2. See his previous letter.
3. A signer of the letter from the Carlisle committee above, Jan. 26.
4. See our annotation above, p. 455. Boisbertrand, although Dubourg expected him to leave with the letter on July 2 (p. 469), may have been delayed long enough to carry this note as well. The letter was translated and sent to Washington; the note may also have been, for a translation is with the original in the papers of Congress, although not now in the General's papers.

JULY 5, 1776

Monsieur   A Paris ce 5e. juillet 1776
On m'a averti sous main que l'on travaille extraordinairement
au Controlle general à faire des fonds pour un grand armement
tant par mer que par terre qui doit avoir lieu le plustôt possible.
Je n'ai reçu que d'hier au soir cet avis dans le plus grand secret. Je
me hate de vous en faire part, et vous pouvez bien compter que je
ne le negligerai pas de mon côté.
Je serai bien content quand ma chere patrie aura cause commune
avec la votre. Recommandez moi d'avance aux bonnes graces de
nos futurs alliés. Je suis de tout mon coeur, Monsieur et bon Ami,
Votre tres fidele et tres devoué serviteur   BARBEU DUBOURG

Endorsed: Paris July 5. 1776. Letter from Barbeu Dubourg.

Jasper Yeates to Franklin and James Wilson[5]

ALS: American Philosophical Society; copy: Historical Society of Pennsylvania

⟨Lancaster, July 6, 1776: I received your favor this afternoon, and
think it my duty cheerfully to accept the appointment by the
Congress. My company is under marching orders to Trenton, and
I am uneasy about leaving it; but I shall be happy to render my
country any service in the position assigned to me. Please express
to the Congress my grateful acknowledgement of the honor done
me. I shall expect to hear from you again when convenient.⟩

The Committee of Secret Correspondence to [Silas Deane]

Reprinted from *The North American and United States Gazette* (Philadelphia),
October 12, 1855.

Sir   Philadelphia, July 8th, 1776.
With this you will receive the Declaration of the Congress for a
final separation from Great Britain. It was the universal demand

5. See their letter to him above, July 4.

of the people, justly exasperated by the obstinate perseverance of the Crown in its tyrannical and destructive measures, and the Congress were very unanimous in complying with that demand. You will immediately communicate the piece to the Court of France, and send copies of it to the other Courts of Europe.[6] It may be well also to procure a good translation of it into French, and get it published in the gazettes.

It is probable that, in a few days, instructions will be formed in Congress directing you to sound the Court of France on the subject of mutual commerce between her and these States.[7]

It is expected you will send the vessel back as soon as possible, with the fullest intelligence of the state of affairs, and of everything that may affect the interest of the United States. And we desire that she may be armed and prepared for defence in her return, as far as the produce of her cargo will go for that purpose.

The Committee have sent Mr. William Bingham to Martinico, where he is to reside in character of a merchant, and occasionally correspond with you.[8] As we shall endeavor, by small armed vessels, to keep up a constant communication with that Island, we desire you would, from time to time, convey to and through him such information as you shall judge proper. He is a discreet young gentleman and worthy of confidence.

You will see in the newspapers that we have been obliged to quit Canada for the present. It was too bold a thing to block up Quebec a whole winter with an army much inferior in numbers to the garrison, and our troops sent too late to support them, not having had the small pox, have been much disabled by that distemper. But neither this disaster, nor the landing of an army in our neighborhood, have in the least dispirited the Congress, as

---

6. This letter and its enclosure, along with others to Deane, were thrown overboard when the *Dispatch*, the brigantine that was carrying them, was about to be captured: *Naval Docs.*, V, 1183; VI, 793. A copy of the letter went with the committee's next one: below, Aug. 7. Deane learned of the Declaration through English newspapers but did not receive another copy until November, when he communicated it to the French government. *Deane Papers*, I, 219–20, 358–9, 371–2.

7. See the editorial note on the plan of treaties above, under June 12, 1776.

8. See Bingham's instructions above, June 3, 1776.

you may perceive by our declaration being subsequent to both. With great esteem, we are, sir, Your very obedient servants,

> B. FRANKLIN
> ROBERT MORRIS.

[Copy.]

Notation: Letter to Mr. Deane, from Secret Committee, July 8, 1776, and Aug. 7, 1777(6)

The Committee of Secret Correspondence to Samuel and J. H. Delap[9]

Letterbook copy: National Archives

Gentlemen   Philada. July 10th. 1776

You will receive this by the Brigantine Dispatch Capt. Peter Parker and with it some letters for Silas Deane Esqr. which being of Considerable Consequence We beg you will cause them to be sent or delivered to him with the utmost Expedition and we make no doubt he has left his address with you shou'd he have left Bourdeaux.

You will find herein an Invoice and bill of Loading for some Goods we have shipped onboard this Brigt. Consigned to you for Sale. These Goods youl please to receive and make the most advantageous Sale of them that your market will admit.

Capt. Parker has orders to Arm and fit out the Dispatch in a Warlike manner and we hope You will advise and assist him in doing it, you'l please procure him the assistance of the most skillfull Persons Tradesmen &c. for doing that bussiness and supply him with Money to purchase Cannon, Swivels, Howitzers, Musquets, Powder, Ball &c. He must fit her in a very compleat manner and must have plenty of these kind of Stores. He is also to procure as many Seamen as he possibly can to come with him in this Brigt. in which we also pray for your assistance and that you will furnish with money to pay advance wages for Provisions and a New Suit of Sails all which we hope he will soon get Compleated with your assistance.[10] When you have paid all charges and Ex-

9. For the firm see the final note on Bingham's instructions above, June 3, 1776.
10. See the following letter.

pences relative to this vessell, whatever ballance remains from the Sale of her Cargo, you'l please to Invest in the purchase of some Brass Field Pieces Six and four pounder and if you can procure them, good Soldiers Muskets, Gun Locks, Powder or Salt Petre, or if you cannot ship such Articles, you may then Invest the said Ballance in Blankets and other Woollen Goods suitable for wear in a Cold Climate and whatever you buy, Ship onboard the said Brigt. Dispatch for address of the Committee of Secret Correspondance on Account and Risque of the United States of America and enclose to them an Invoice and bill of Loading for the same. It is necessary that Capt. Parker make dispatch in fitting the Brigt. and getting her ready for Sea and that you also compleat your bussiness for her soon as you can but she is not to sail untill Mr. Deane sends his dispatches for those are the most immediate object of the present Voyage. Therefore if Mr. Deane is not at Bourdeaux you will please to keep him well informed when the Brigt. will be ready to return and the Moment his dispatches come to your hands deliver them to Capt. Parker with an injunction to sail immediately for this Coast agreable to his orders. Shou'd Mr. Deane be in Bourdeaux Capt. Parker must be directed by him entirely in all his proceedings and if Mr. Deane desires any Goods to be shipped onboard the dispatch they must be received onboard inshort the Captain is ordered to receive onboard all Goods You recommend therefore you'l please to Ship any you may have or that Mr. Deane may order and inform Mr. John Danl. Schweighauser of Nantes that he may ship any he has for Account of this Continent.[1] We hope you will assist in making it known that great Wages and encouragement are given to Seamen in America and the Seamen of every Country will be alike Welcome. We shall have frequent opportunitys of addressing you and remain Gentlemen Your obedient Servants.

Messrs. Saml. & J.H. Delap

1. For Schweighauser see the note on Bonvouloir to de Guines above, Dec. 28.

The Committee of Secret Correspondence to Peter Parker[2]

Letterbook copy: National Archives

Sir   Philada. July 10th. 1776

The Brigt. Dispatch of which you are hereby appointed Commander in the Service of the United States of america, being now ready for Sea, You are to proceed immediately onboard said Brigantine for [the] Port of Bourdeaux in France and on your arrival there deliver the dispatches given [?] you herewith to Messrs. Saml. & J.H. Delap Merchts. at that place. You are to consider these letter's directed to those Gentlemen as very important and must deliver them yourself soon as possible. You must have them hung at Sea with a heavy weight ready to throw overboard and sink them in case you shou'd be unfortunately taken by the Enemy,[3] but to avoid that danger you must make it a standing rule to run from every Vessell you see at Sea. The Dispatch is well found with plenty of sails, rigging, stores and materials. You will therefore make good use of them and endeavour to make a short passage by a dilligent attention to Winds and Weather carrying at all times as much sail as is proper.

The Goods we have caused to be shipped onboard this Brigt. are Consignd to Messrs. Delap to whom you are to deliver the same and when this is done you must immediately set about arming the Brigt. with Eight or Ten four pounder Cannon, as many Swivels Blunderbusses, Cohorns, Howitzers and Muskets as you think proper, but take care that the Cannon &c. are of the best and handsomest, fit for ships use. You may if you think proper fit her with Close quarters and mount some Guns in the Cabin Steerage and Fore Castle, or you may Mount the whole on Deck and if she will bear more than Ten Cannon you may buy them. You must procure a suitable quantity of Powder and Ball for the Cannon, arms &c. with Cartridges, Cartridge Paper and all necessary apparatus thereto. You will Compleat this bussiness

2. A ship captain who, to judge by references to him in the *Pa. Gaz.*, had been plying for the past two years between Philadelphia and the West Indies. For further but meager information about him see [Augustus G. Parker,] *Parker in America, 1630–1910* (Buffalo, N.Y., 1911), pp. 421–4.

3. Parker did so; see the note on the committee to Deane above, July 8, 1776.

506

with Expedition and procure the best advice and assistance in doing it. Messrs. Delap will recommend you to proper People for this purpose and they will supply you with Money to pay the Cost. You must Ship as many Seamen as you can possibly get, especially American Seamen or those that have been much connected in this Country but you are not to confine yourself to these alone. We are in Want of Seamen and you may bring People of all Countrys or Nations that are willing to enter into the American Service. You must make it known in the best manner you can that great wages and encouragement is now given to Seamen in every part of America both for the Publick and for Merchant Service. You are therefore to bring over not only sufficient for your own Complement which as an Armed Vessell might be Thirty or forty, but as many as you can Conveniently give ship room to and you may Contract with them for such reasonable Wages as may be satisfactory to them. If any Masters or Mates Want passages home you are to Accommodate them free of any Charge to them.[4] You must lay in sufficient of Provisions and allow each man plenty but suffer no Waste. You are to receive from Messrs. Delap any Goods they may desire to Ship or from any other persons Goods that Messrs. Delap approve of being Shipped onboard and when you are ready for departure you are to wait [on?] those Gentln. for their dispatches and when you receive the same, with their approbation for your departure you are then to make the best of your way back for this Coast. You know how it is lined with British Men of Warr at present and it is not possible for us to say what Port may be safest by the time you return, but as we expect you will be well Armed and Manned you need not fear small Vessells, and by keeping Constantly a hand at each Mast head to look out we think you may avoid all large ones especially as we expect the Dispatch will be a Flyer and in France you may get another Compleat suit of Sails for her. You must therefore putt into the first safe Port you can any where in the United States of America and by the time you Return you may expect to Meet with some of our own Frigates, Galleys and Cruizers. Little Egg Harbour or Cape May will probably be as secure as any other places.

4. Seamen were in short supply, and Congress had recently offered a bounty for importing them: *JCC*, IV, 289–90; see also *Naval Docs.*, V, 398–9.

JULY 10, 1776

We deliver you herewith a Commission a list of agents for Prizes, and the Resolves of Congress respecting Captures[5] by which you will learn how to Conduct yourself in this respect. Your business however is not to Cruize but to make quick passage but if you meet any small prizes on your return so much the better provided you do not loose time in seeking them and in case of Capture you must send them in to some of the agents, who will do the needfull for all concerned. We expect you will be carefull of the Brigt. her stores and Materials, diligent in making dispatch both at Sea and in port, faithfull in the discharge of your Duty and the Moment you reach any port in America come or send the dispatches Express to the Committee of Secret Correspondance. We are Sir Your humble servants.

PS. Shoud you meet Silas Deane Esqr. who lately went from this place for Bourdeaux, you may Consult with and be advised and directed by him in all things relative to your business with the Brigt. Dispatch.

Capt. Peter Parker

Notation: Congr &c June 1776 to Wm Bingham &c Coppied.

Lambert Wickes to the Committee of Secret Correspondence

ALS: National Archives

Gentlemen   On board the Ship Reprisal July 11th. 1776

This will inform you of my proceedings since I left Cape May the 3d Instant. We left that place in Company with 13 Merchant Men, who I think all got Safe off, as we did not loose Sight of them till they got a good distance from the Land.[6] We Saw no Ships of War at all on the Coast.

We this Day fell in with Captain Mackay, in the Ship Friendship from Granada bound to London, loaded with Rum, Sugar, Cocoa and Coffee, which Ship I have taken, and sent John Parks in her prize Master and have given him orders to get into Philadelphia if Possible and if this should not be practicable, he is to Run her

---

5. For this material see *JCC*, IV, 229–32, 247–8, 253–4, 301.
6. In fact three were captured; Clark, *Wickes*, pp. 52–3.

508

into the first port in his power and Send an Express to Inform you Imeadiately.[7] Mr. Bingham is Well and desires his Complyments to you. From Gentlemen Your most Oblig'd humble Servant

LAMBT. WICKS

P. S: Our people are all well to 3 or 4. We are in Longitude 57 D, West and Lattd. 31 North   L: W:

Addressed: To / The Committee of Secret Correspondance / Philadelphia

Endorsed: July 11. 1776 Capt Lambert Wicks

From Noble Wimberly Jones

ALS: University of Pennsylvania Library

Dear Sir   Savannah 11. July 1776. 1. A:M

I received your kind favour of 12th Jany. but being out of Town just then, had not the pleasure of seeing and sending by Mr. Goddard,[8] and one or other accident hath prevented my answering it before. It gives me real concern that I could not attend that respectable Body the Continental Congress but can assure you, tho my person is not, my heart is most sincerely with them. Added to my own Ill state of health for above a twelve Month, my Dear and kind Father was sometime very Ill, and Died last November, which increased the difficulty of my being absent from hence[9] and deprived me also of the real pleasure of your Company, which tis now little probable I shall Ever Enjoy. It gave me great satisfaction to hear you were so well prepared for defence, tis I fear far from being our case. Indeed Am apprehensive without some timely Continental Assistance, we are in great danger. What most alarms, we hear within these few days, that the Cherokees have taken and killd some of our back settlers, Influenced and headed

7. The crew of the *Friendship*, to a man, joined the American service. The value of her cargo was estimated at £35,000, and Parks did succeed in bringing her in to Philadelphia. *Ibid.*, pp. 54–5, 66; *Naval Docs.*, VI, 64.

8. The Surveyor General had made a southern trip the year before; see BF to Hazard above, Sept. 25. We have found no other record of this trip.

9. The difficulty was compounded by the fact that the father was a Loyalist; out of respect for him Jones declined to attend Congress. *DAB*.

by Ministerial Emissaries and Troops, and we dayly expect to hear the same from the Creeks Chactaws &c. also tis said there are Troops and Indians on our southern frontiers from Augustine;[1] what Effect the severe rebuff the Troops or rather Ships against South Carolina Met with may have God knows, but as they are not gone from thence, cant say how matters may end there as yet;[2] we are however in both Provinces in as great Spirits as tis possible to conceive, considering our weak Situation, the Numerous Tribes of Indians and their Methods of War; It clearly appears a plan of the Vile Ministry, to carry on that at the same time the Fleet &c. is on our Sea coast. As there may be some matters in it that may not be disagreeable to [you[3]] I enclose a Letter that went to London for you but as the Gentleman found you were in America he sent it back lest it might miscarry.[4] The confused times prevents my being able to answer properly with respect to what the Province is justly in debt to you, shall keep it in Mind and trust it will not be ungrateful.[5]

Doubtless our President[6] has wrote fully our Situation and the Necessaty there is to the common cause our being supported without which little less than Miracles can save us, Spirits however I trust we don't want had we but Men. I beg leave to conclude with my best Respects to that [Respectable?] Assembly whereof you

1. These risings, known as the Cherokee War, were suppressed the following September; the British encouraged and in some cases armed the Indians. See James H. O'Donnell, *Southern Indians in the American Revolution* ([Knoxville, Tenn., 1973]), pp. 34–53.

2. British troops originally went from Boston to North Carolina, only to find that the local Loyalists had already been defeated. The expedition, after a juncture with reinforcements and a squadron from Britain, moved against South Carolina. On June 28 the warships attacked a fort on Sullivan's Island that guarded Charleston harbor, and were repulsed with heavy losses.

3. The word has been deleted in the MS.

4. Doubtless the letter above of May 16, 1775.

5. BF must have raised the question of the province's debt to him in his missing letter of Jan. 12, 1776, and after this vague reply he returned to the question just before he sailed for Europe: to Jones below, Oct. 25.

6. The Ga. provincial congress, after the Governor's departure and the collapse of the judicial system, established a temporary government on April 15, 1776, and named Archibald Bulloch (above, XV, 95–6 n) as president and commander in chief of the colony. Allen D. Candler, ed., *The Revolutionary Records of the State of Georgia* (3 vols., Atlanta, Ga., 1908), I, 274–77.

are a Worthy Member Sir Your Most Obedient and Very Humble
Servant   N W JONES

Addressed: To / Doctor Benjamin Franklin / Post Master General
of / North America / Philadelphia

Lambert Wickes to the Committee of Secret
Correspondence
ALS: National Archives

Gentlemen   On board the Reprisal July 13th: 1776
   This will inform of a Small Addition to our good fortune in the
Prize Way. We this day took Capt. Muckelno in the Schooner
Peter of Liverpool from St. Vincent bound to Liverpool in Brit-
tain, Loaded with: Rum: Sugar Coffee Cocoa and Cotton.[7] We
also took Capt. Mackey in the Ship Friendship from Granada,
bound to London, which I have wrote you of before,[8] and Now
Send a Coppy of that Letter. This Schooner, is ordered into one or
Either of the Egg Harbours, if She Can get in there, If not into
any other Port on the Coast. I have given orders to Mr. Jeremiah
Holden to Send this letter and the Schooners papers and letters to
you by Express on his Arrival in America.[9] We had very little
Wind this two or three days past and are but little further on our
Way, than when I Wrote you last, from Gentlemen your Most
Oblig'd humble Servant   LAMBT. WICKES

Addressed: To / The Committee of Secret Correspondence /
Philadelphia

Endorsed: July 13. 1776 Capt. Lambert Wickes

   7. See Clark, *Wickes*, p. 55.
   8. Above, July 11, 1776.
   9. Holden was prizemaster of the *Peter*. He sent the express as soon as he
anchored near the Egg Harbors, Little and Great, in southern N. J.: Clark,
Wickes, p. 66.

Editorial Note on the Pennsylvania Constitutional Convention

Franklin's deepest involvement in the affairs of Pennsylvania, aside from his work on the Assembly's committee of safety in 1775,[1] was as president of the convention that sat in Philadelphia from July 15 to September 28, 1776, and during those weeks governed the province. The convention and its administrative arm, a council of safety that replaced the committee, directed the war effort, provided for internal security, appointed new officers, chose and instructed Pennsylvania's delegation in Congress, approved American independence, and hammered out a new constitution for the new state.[2]

The first phase of this internal revolution was a provincial conference of committees held in Philadelphia on June 18 to 25. The city's committee of inspection and observation chose Franklin as a delegate to the conference, but he did not attend; he was suffering from gout and other ailments, and said that he knew little of what was going on in the city at the time.[3] The conference resolved that the existing government was inadequate, and called for a convention to form a new one "on the authority of the People only." All associators as well as those previously qualified were to vote for members, the city of Philadelphia and each county were allotted eight representatives apiece, and the election was set for July 8.[4] Franklin was returned for the city.

The day after the convention met it unanimously chose him as president, and four days later named him a delegate to Congress.[5] Both bodies, conveniently for him, were quartered in the State House. How he divided his time between them is impossible to tell, but he is known to have chaired the convention at a substantial proportion of its meetings.[6] Out of them came numerous executive and legislative documents,

1. See the note above, June 30, 1775.
2. The *Minutes of the Proceedings of the Convention of the State of Pennsylvania, Held at Philadelphia, the Fifteenth Day of July, 1776* (Philadelphia, 1776) is reprinted in Force, 5 *Amer. Arch.*, II, 1–62.
3. For the background of the conference see the headnote on the Assembly's instructions above, June 14. BF's ill health is discussed in a note on Mecom to Greene above, June 1, 1776.
4. Force, 4 *Amer. Arch.*, VI, 951–67; the quotation is col. 953.
5. 5 *Ibid.*, II, 1–2, 6.
6. On the assumption that he was absent when some one else either signed documents for the convention or resumed the chair after it had met as a committee of the whole (the only indications in the minutes of who the chairman was on a given day), and attended when the president is mentioned, he missed nine meetings, four of them while on his journey to Lord Howe, and presided at nineteen, a total of twenty-eight. The convention met sixty-three times in

such as commissions and ordinances, some of which he signed but none of which we print, because there is no indication that his concern with them went beyond the signature.[7]

The convention's chief impact on the future was through what proved to be the most controversial of the early state constitutions. It was in two parts, a declaration or bill of rights and a frame of government. The latter had remarkable features: a plural executive in the form of a council, elaborate provisions for rotation in office, a group of censors elected every seven years to review the operation of government and suggest constitutional changes, and a unicameral legislature.[8] These features, some of which are reminiscent of the articles of confederation that Franklin had proposed the previous summer,[9] aroused strong opposition. It began at once and continued for fourteen years, until it triumphed in the constitution of 1790. Both factions in this bitter struggle, the Constitutionalists and the Republicans, claimed Franklin for ally, and in doing so muddied such evidence as there is of his attitude toward the original document.[1]

---

all, and there is no way of knowing how many of the other thirty-five sessions he attended.

7. We have found five commissions that he signed in 1776 as president: to John Ewing as capt. of foot, York Co., Aug. 26 (Mrs. Henry M. Sage, Albany, N.Y.); to Garrat Dorland as 2nd lieut. of foot, York Co., Aug. 27 (Miss Helen Newman, Washington D.C.); to Jeremiah Cloud as 2nd lieut. of foot, Sept. 6 (Hist. Soc. of Pa.); to John Clark, Jr., as maj., 2nd battalion, York Co., Sept. 14 (N.-Y. Hist. Soc.); and to William Lowder as ensign of foot, York Co., Sept. 14 (APS). He also signed four ordinances, which illustrate the range of the convention's business. One of July 20, in response to a request from Congress, orders the transfer of ordinary prisoners of state; an attested copy is in the National Archives. A second of Sept. 3 appoints justices of the peace, BF among them; a broadside text is in the Hist. Soc. of Pa. A third of Sept. 5 requires allegiance to Pennsylvania, defines treason against it, and establishes penalties: *Pa. Evening Post*, Sept. 7, 1776. The final ordinance, of Sept. 14, provides support for the associators by a tax on all inhabitants over fifty, and by a fine and a tax on nonassociators: *ibid.*, Sept. 17–19, 1776. For the background proceedings and texts of these ordinances see Force, 5 *Amer. Arch.*, II, 7–8, 10, 13, 16–17, 19, 21, 24–8, 31–5, 42–5.

8. The printed text, *The Constitution of the Common-Wealth of Pennsylvania, as Established by the General Convention . . .* (Philadelphia, 1776), is reprinted in *ibid.*, cols. 51–9.

9. Above, under July 21.

1. The Republican Benjamin Rush, for example, subsequently did his best to dissociate BF from the constitution; see Lyman H. Butterfield, ed., *Letters of Benjamin Rush* (2 vols., Princeton, 1951), I, 336; "Excerpts from the Papers of Dr. Benjamin Rush," *PMHB*, XXIX (1905), 29. John Adams supported the Republicans and, as noted below, made the same attempt. When BF returned

We do not print the document itself, which he signed as president, because he played only a minor role in drafting it. He revised the wording, and to some extent the substance, of the bill of rights.[2] He was responsible for two small changes in the frame of government.[3] When the draft was complete, he was appointed to a three-man committee to make stylistic revisions and have copies printed for public consideration. There the record ends. The convention thanked him when it adjourned, for chairing the major debates on the constitution and for "his able and disinterested advice thereon."[4] But nowhere was that advice spelled out.

The belief soon took root, especially in Europe, that Franklin's role had been far more than advisory; and he did nothing to discourage the idea. "The Doctor," John Adams explained years later, "when he went to France in 1776, carried with him the printed copy of that Constitution, and it was immediately propagated through France that this was the plan of government of Mr. Franklin. . . . Mr. Turgot, the Duke de la Rochefoucauld, Mr. Condorcet, and many others, became enamored with the Constitution of Mr. Franklin."[5] The provision that was most often specifically attributed to him was that for a unicameral assembly. When this provision was adopted in August, 1776, Adams expressed surprise that "the American philosopher should . . . be a zealous advocate for it." Two and a half years later Timothy Matlack, who had helped to draft the constitution, declared in print that Franklin had been asked his opinion near the end of the debate, and had come out squarely in

to Pennsylvania in 1785, the Constitutional Society of Philadelphia hailed him as the father of the constitution, and the Assembly, dominated by Constitutionalists, asserted that he had been greatly instrumental in framing it. *Pa. Packet*, Sept. 19, 1785; *Minutes of the . . . Ninth General Assembly of the Commonwealth of Pennsylvania . . .* (Philadelphia, [1784–85]), pp. 376–7.

2. See his revisions below, under July 29.

3. He introduced a section drafted by Provost William Smith, which we assume became the second part of Article 45, to safeguard the chartered rights of religious, learned, and charitable institutions: Bird Wilson, *Memoir of the Life of the Right Reverend William White . . .* (Philadelphia, 1839), pp. 69–70. He opposed unsuccessfully the Assemblymen's profession of faith required in Article 10, but secured a proviso that it should never be made more exacting: Smyth, *Writings*, IX, 266–7.

4. Force, 5 *Amer. Arch.*, II, 62.

5. Charles F. Adams, ed., *The Works of John Adams* (10 vols., Boston, 1850–56), IX, 622–3. Adams did his best while abroad to disabuse Frenchmen of this idea; see Butterfield, *John Adams Diary*, II, 391. But he had little success; see J. Paul Selsam and Joseph G. Rayback, "French Comment on the Pennsylvania Constitution of 1776," *PMHB*, LXXVI (1952), 311–25.

favor of a single house. "La voix de M. Franklin," said Condorcet in 1790, "décida seule cette derniere disposition."[6]

Three Americans who had not been in the convention wrote long afterward that Franklin had given the delegates his opinion on how the legislature should be constituted, and had backed it with the analogy of a wagon pulled in two directions at once. They thoroughly disagreed, however, on what the analogy meant. To John Adams it was a wagon descending a steep grade, and the animals pulling it uphill prevented its crushing those pulling it down; Adams was arguing for checks and balances and persuaded himself—contrary to his statement in 1776—that Franklin had favored two houses. To Tom Paine, who favored a single house, the wagon was on the level, and the horses pulling in both directions either kept it from moving or tore it apart. To Alexander Graydon the analogy was an "équivoque," and its meaning an enigma not worth solving; Franklin calmed men as well as waves with oil, and his behavior to both factions was "oily and accommodating."[7]

But accommodation had its limits. The evidence strongly suggests that the President did, when called upon, express approval of the unicameral provision. At the end of his life, furthermore, when the old constitution was clearly doomed and many of his friends were leading the move to revise it, he wrote a defense of its salient points.[8] He was clearly not its author, as his French friends thought he was; the author was the convention itself, in which a number of younger men played the leading part.[9] Franklin, almost beyond question, approved in the main their handiwork and never ceased to approve. How much support he gave them in debate is conjectural. But at one point, if it is true that his opinion of a unicameral house was asked for and given, he put his mark on an essential part of the new government. Although he did not father the constitution, as he let it be thought, he had some reason to consider himself its godfather.

6. C. F. Adams, *op. cit.*, IX, 429; Matlack in the *Pa. Gaz.*, March 31, 1779; Condorcet, *Éloge de M. Franklin, lu à la séance publique de l'Académie des sciences, le 13 Nov. 1790* (Paris, 1791), p. 25.

7. Adams, *op. cit.*, IV, 389–91; Philip S. Foner, ed., *The Complete Writings of Thomas Paine* (2 vols., New York, [1945]), II, 1106; [Alexander Graydon,] *Memoirs of a Life, Chiefly Passed in Pennsylvania, within the Last Sixty Years . . .* (Harrisburg, Pa., 1811), pp. 266–7. The anecdote was also reported earlier; for an example see Smith, *Letters*, VI, 430.

8. Smyth, *Writings*, X, 54–60.

9. See Ryerson, *Revolution Is Now Begun*, p. 241 and the references cited there.

The Pennsylvania Convention to James Burd: a Circular Letter

Reprinted from [Thomas Balch, ed.,] *Letters and Papers Relating Chiefly to the Provincial History of Pennsylvania* . . . (Philadelphia, 1885), pp. 250–1.

During Washington's visit to Congress in late May and early June, the decision had been reached to establish a flying camp, or mobile reserve, to assist in defending New York. Congress set its size at 10,000 men, 6,000 of them Pennsylvanians. In late June the Pennsylvania provincial conference, in the absence of any other governmental authority, urged local committees to provide the troops; but the response was so slow that in early July all militiamen who were in readiness were ordered into New Jersey to provide support until the flying camp came into being. On July 19 the Pennsylvania convention received word from Congress that the associators' march, retarded by false reports, should be expedited. The result was circular letters of the same day from the convention to local committees and to the commanding officers of militia, urging them to have the troops on the road without delay.[1] The letter we publish was addressed to the commander of the fourth Lancaster County battalion.[2]

Sir: Philadelphia, July 19th, 1776.

The Congress of the United States of America, having recommended to this Convention to hasten, with all possible expedition, the march of the associators of this province into New Jersey, agreeable to a former request of Congress, we do earnestly recommend and require you to send forward into New Jersey your battalion, or as many companies as can possibly be armed, with all possible expedition, yielding a most exact obedience to the orders

1. Freeman, *Washington*, IV, 103; *JCC*, IV, 412–13; V, 519–20, 591; Force, 4 *Amer. Arch.*, VI, 961, 965–6; 5 *ibid.*, II, 5–6. The associators reinforced the N.J. militia, whose commander was glad to see the last of them. "The worst men . . . would be still pejorated," Brig. Gen. Livingston commented at the end of August, "by having been fellow-soldiers with that discipline-hating good-living-loving eternal-fame'd damn'd coxcomatical crew we lately had here from Philadelphia." Carl E. Prince *et al.*, eds., *The Papers of William Livingston* . . . (2 vols. to date, Trenton, N.J., 1979—), I, 128–9.

2. Burd was a Scottish immigrant and veteran of the French and Indian War, who had married into the Shippen family. He was a large landholder and prominent in the affairs of Lancaster Co., and had held his commission since the previous September. Lily L. Nixon, *James Burd, Frontier Defender, 1726–1793* (Philadelphia, 1941), especially pp. 167–8; see also Irma A. Watts, "Colonel James Burd—Defender of the Frontier," *PMHB*, L (1926), 29–37.

you may receive from this Convention, or from your superior officer, wholly disregarding all reports concerning the countermanding of orders received by you for marching the militia of this province, as such may be propagated by our enemies for wicked and destructive purposes. If you send forward only two companies, the second major is to march with them; if only three, the lieutenant-colonel, or first major; if only four, the lieutenant-colonel and second major; if only five, the colonel and both majors; if six, or the whole battalion, then all the field-officers.

Signed by Order of the Convention. BENJ. FRANKLIN

To James Burd, Esq., Colonel of his Battalion of the County of Lancaster.

From John Lawrence and William Smith[3]

ALS: American Philosophical Society

Sir   Burlington July 19th. 1776

At the Request of Mrs. Mecum (who has been an Inhabitant of this City for some time past and behav'd with Prudence and Industry) We take the Liberty to Inform you that her husband's Conduct is such, as to render her Scituation Disagreeable, and at times very Dangerous he being often Depriv'd of his Reason, and likely to become very Troublesome to the Inhabitants.[4] If a place

3. We have failed to identify Smith, who may have been a Burlington official. John Brown Lawrence (1729–96) was the mayor and a prominent local lawyer and member of the N.J. Council. He was suspected of being a Loyalist, and is said to have been imprisoned. He remained in Burlington until 1795 and died in Canada in 1796. Larry L. Gerlach, *Prologue to Independence: New Jersey in the Coming of the American Revolution* (New Brunswick, N.J., [1976]), pp. [361], 366; Sabine, *Loyalists*, II, 3; George M. Hills, *History of the Church in Burlington . . .* (Trenton, N. J., 1876), *passim*.

4. The request came from Elizabeth Ross Mecom, Benjamin's wife (above, I, lxi). Her husband apparently stayed in Burlington until the British invaded New Jersey at the end of the year. "He never could be kept in the place you Expected," Jane wrote her brother in 1779, "but was wandering about till the Hessians took possession of Burlington, when he disappeared and has never been heard of since." Van Doren, *Franklin—Mecom*, p. 188; see also pp. 182–3. Elizabeth Mecom paid £17 5s. 0d. for his support from July until the end of 1776; in 1791 she made a sworn statement that BF had engaged to reimburse her but that no one had: Jan. 7, 1791, Hist. Soc. of Pa.

in the Hospital of Philada. can be Procur'd or any other way of Confineing which may be thought more Eligeable she begs your Assistance And that you wo'd be pleas'd to favor us with an Answer on the Subject of this Letter. From Sir Your most Obedient Humble Servants (in haste)   JNO. LAWRENCE
WILLIAM SMITH

Addressed: To / The Honble / Benjamin Franklin Esqr. / At / Philada[5]

To Lord Howe

Copy: Henry E. Huntington Library; other copies: British Museum;[6] Library of Congress

When Franklin received permission from Congress to answer Howe's letter of June 20,[7] he did so on the same day. The reply went to Washington, who on July 30 sent it to the *Eagle* under a flag of truce. One of his emissaries described Howe's reception of the letter. "I watched his countenance, and observed him often to express marks of surprise. When he had finished reading it, he said his old friend had expressed himself very warmly; that when he had the pleasure of seeing him last in England, he made him acquainted with his sentiments respecting the dispute between Great Britain and the colonies, and of his earnest desire that a reconciliation might take place equally honorable and advantageous to both.[8] Possessed with these sentiments, and the most ardent desire to be the means of effecting this union, he had accepted the honor the King had done him in appointing him one of the commissioners; that, very unfortunately, a long passage prevented his arriving here before the declaration of independence took place. . . . I told him he had now a fair opportunity to mention to his friend Dr. Franklin, in a private letter, his design in coming out, and what his expectations from America were. This he declined; saying the doctor had grown too warm, and if

5. The address sheet has an irrelevant notation in BF's hand: "Officers of the British Army / Soldiers."
6. This copy is dated July 30, the others July 20. The earlier date must be correct because, as noted below, the letter was delivered to Howe on the 30th.
7. See the headnote on Howe's letter above, June 20.
8. See above, XXI, 408 *et seq.*

he expressed his sentiments fully to him, he should only give him pain, which he would wish to avoid."[9]

My Lord,   Philada. July 20th. 1776.

I received safe the Letters your Lordship so kindly forwarded to me, and beg you to accept my Thanks.

The Official Dispatches to which you refer me, contain nothing more than what we had seen in the Act of Parliament, viz. Offers of Pardon upon Submission;[10] which I was sorry to find, as it must give your Lordship Pain to be sent so far on so hopeless a Business.

Directing Pardons to be offered the Colonies, who are the very Parties injured, expresses indeed that Opinion of our Ignorance, Baseness, and Insensibility which your uninform'd and proud Nation has long been pleased to entertain of us; but it can have no other Effect than that of increasing our Resentment. It is impossible we should think of Submission to a Government, that has with the most wanton Barbarity and Cruelty, burnt our defenceless Towns in the midst of Winter, excited the Savages to massacre our Farmers, and our Slaves to murder their Masters, and is even now bringing foreign Mercenaries to deluge our Settlements with Blood.[1] These atrocious Injuries have extinguished every remaining Spark of Affection for that Parent Country we once held so dear: But were it possible for *us* to forget and forgive them, it is not possible for *you* (I mean the British Nation) to forgive the People you have so heavily injured; you can never confide again in those as Fellow Subjects, and permit them to enjoy equal Freedom, to whom you know you have given such just Cause of lasting Enmity. And this must impel you, were we again under your Government, to endeavour the breaking our Sprit by the severest Tyranny, and obstructing by every means in your Power our growing Strength and Prosperity.

9. Col. William Palfrey to Hancock, July 31, 1776, in John G. Palfrey, "Life of William Palfrey," Jared Sparks, ed., *The Library of American Biography* (25 vols., Boston and London, 1834–38), 2nd ser., VIII, 415, 417. Howe's guarded answer to BF is below, Aug. 16.

10. The "dispatches" were Howe's circular letter and declaration; see the headnote cited above. The statute was the Prohibitory Act.

1. The mercenaries were a recent addition; see the note on the Pa. Assembly's instructions above, June 14, 1776. The other atrocities had long been BF's stock in trade; see for example his letter to Hartley above, Sept. 12, 1775.

But your Lordship mentions "the Kings paternal Solicitude for promoting the Establishment of lasting *Peace* and Union with the Colonies." If by *Peace* is here meant, a Peace to be entered into between Britain and America as distinct States now at War, and his Majesty has given your Lordship Powers to treat with us of such a Peace, I may venture to say, tho' without Authority, that I think a Treaty for that purpose not yet quite impracticable, before we enter into Foreign Alliances. But I am persuaded you have no such Powers. Your Nation, tho' by punishing those American Governors who have created and fomented the Discord, rebuilding our burnt Towns, and repairing as far as possible the Mischiefs done us, She might yet recover a great Share of our Regard and the greatest part of our growing Commerce, with all the Advantage of that additional Strength to be derived from a Friendship with us; I know too well her abounding Pride and deficient Wisdom, to believe she will ever take such Salutary Measures. Her Fondness for Conquest as a Warlike Nation, her Lust of Dominion as an Ambitious one, and her Thirst for a gainful Monopoly as a Commercial one, (none of them legitimate Causes of War) will all join to hide from her Eyes every View of her true Interests; and continually goad her on in these ruinous distant Expeditions, so destructive both of Lives and Treasure, that must prove as perrnicious to her in the End as the Croisades formerly were to most of the Nations of Europe.

I have not the Vanity, my Lord, to think of intimidating by thus predicting the Effects of this War; for I know it will in England have the Fate of all my former Predictions, not to be believed till the Event shall verify it.

Long did I endeavour with unfeigned and unwearied Zeal, to preserve from breaking, that fine and noble China Vase the British Empire: for I knew that being once broken, the separate Parts could not retain even their Share of the Strength or Value that existed in the Whole, and that a perfect Re-Union of those Parts could scarce even be hoped for. Your Lordship may possibly remember the Tears of Joy that wet my Cheek, when, at your good Sister's in London, you once gave me Expectations that a Reconciliation might soon take place.[2] I had the Misfortune to find those Expectations disappointed, and to be treated as the Cause of the

2. Presumably at their second interview, on Dec. 28, 1774: above, XXI, 571.

Mischief I was labouring to prevent. My Consolation under that groundless and malevolent Treatment was, that I retained the Friendship of many Wise and Good Men in that Country, and among the rest some Share in the Regard of Lord Howe.

The well founded Esteem, and permit me to say Affection, which I shall always have for your Lordship, makes it painful to me to see you engag'd in conducting a War, the great Ground of which, as expressed in your Letter, is, "the Necessity of preventing the American Trade from passing into foreign Channels." To me it seems that neither the obtaining or retaining of any Trade, how valuable soever, is an Object for which Men may justly Spill each others Blood; that the true and sure means of extending and securing Commerce is the goodness and cheapness of Commodities; and that the profits of no Trade can ever be equal to the Expence of compelling it, and of holding it, by Fleets and Armies. I consider this War against us therefore, as both unjust, and unwise; and I am persuaded cool dispassionate Posterity will condemn to Infamy those who advised it; and that even Success will not save from some degree of Dishonour, those who voluntarily engag'd to conduct it. I know your great Motive in coming hither was the Hope of being instrumental in a Reconciliation; and I believe when you find *that* impossible on any Terms given you to propose, you will relinquish so odious a Command, and return to a more honourable private Station. With the greatest and most sincere Respect I have the honour to be, My Lord your Lordships most obedient humble Servant   B FRANKLIN

honble. Lord Howe

Copy

From William Alexander[3]   ALS: American Philosophical Society

Dear Sir   Lon[don 20 Ju]ly 1776

I consider it as one of the great misfortunes of the times in which we live, that we are deprived of the pleasure of hearing

---

3. Since the previous summer the banker had been in prison for debt; see the note on Stevenson to BF above, Nov. 16. He was released under a general act of Parliament (16 Geo. III, c. 38), which became law in May, and then fled to Dijon: Price, *France and the Chesapeake*, II, 694, 699. This letter was presumably

from you. I need hardly say that you have the wishes of all Good Men for your welfare, and That you may be the happy Instrument of Restoring the public tranquility on a permanent basis for the General Good of Mankind, And for the Benefit of our Country. This Goes by Monsr. de Cauveroz a French Gentleman a Great Traveller who having visited many Countries in Europe, is desirous of seeing and knowing Men, and a Country that is now the Object of Attention in Europe and promises to furnish Matter for future History.

As Monsr. de Cauveroz is Entirely disengaged and a Batchelor He may perhaps wish to pass his remaining days in that state of tranquility which is only to be found in a free Country. I doubt not in this Case but you will give Him your best assistance in procuring a Proper setlement. His own merit will I doubt not Soon procure Him that Esteem and Confidence, which He enjoys with those who know Him. Your Nephew and all your Friends are well, as is my litle Family. I am ever with the most Sincere Esteem [Dear] Sir your most obedient humble Servant

WILLIAM ALEXANDER

Addressed: To / Benjamin Franklin Esqr / Philadelphia / favour of / Mon de Cauveroz / QDC

Endorsed: Mr Alexander

Notations: Lett. from W Alexander London July 20. 1776. / Alexander William. July 20. 1776

To George Washington

ALS: Kunstsammlungen der Veste Coburg

Sir   Philada. July 22. 1776
The Bearer, Mr. Joseph Belton some time since petitioned the Congress for Encouragement to destroy the Enemy's Ships of War

---

written between his release and his flight. Penciled at the top of the page is a notation in an unidentifiable hand, "July 20 76 Hotel St. Louis, à Dijon," the address that Alexander provided in his letter to BF below, Dec. 22, 1776. Our guess is that BF took the present letter with him to France and, after receiving the later one, had the address noted.

by some Contrivances of his Invention.[4] They came to no Resolution on his Petition; and, as they appear to have no great Opinion of such Proposals, it is not easy, in the Multiplicity of Business before them, to get them to bestow any part of their Attention on his Request. He is now desirous of trying his Hand on the Ships that are gone up the North River; and as he proposes to work intirely at his own Expence, and only desires your Countenance and Permission, I could not refuse his Request of a Line of Introduction to you, the Trouble of which I beg you to excuse. As he appears to be a very ingenious Man, I hope his Project may be attended with Success. With the sincerest Esteem and Respect, I have the Honour to be, Your Excellency's most obedient and most humble Servant   B FRANKLIN

Genl. Washington

The Lancaster County Committee to the Pennsylvania Convention
Copy: Library of Congress

⟨Lancaster, July 23, 1776: Your ordinance for disarming the non-associators and the circular letters to the commanders of the county battalions of associators arrived last night.[5] This morning we forwarded them to each commander, who will receive them by noon or one P.M. and will doubtless do everything possible to forward the march of the militia.

We are making every effort to carry out the recommendations of Congress, that the troops be provided with what is needed.[6] Captains whose companies are ready or nearly so have received money, camp kettles, and a few muskets and bayonets; our gunsmiths have been busy in the past days repairing weapons, but our stores are almost exhausted. We have scarcely enough muskets for the necessary guards, and our tinsmiths lack tin for kettles. We have collected most of the available cash from our men of substance, so that something may be advanced to soldiers who need

---

4. For Joseph Belton see the note on BF to Deane above, Aug. 27.

5. For the convention's ordinance, of July 19, see Force, 5 *Amer. Arch.*, II, 6; one of the circular letters to the commanding officers is above, July 19, 1776.

6. *JCC*, V, 520.

it; and we submit to you whether money should not be sent for the purpose. Most of the militia require some small necessity, and many wish to leave a few shillings with their families; they apply to us and "expect to be here equipped and assisted and it gives us pain to see their disappointment." Our tinsmiths report no tin to be had in Philadelphia; should there be any to spare from public stores we could continue making kettles and canteens. "We shall use our best endeavour to keep our Gunsmiths busy and do every thing in our power to execute the orders of the Convention and promote the general Interest." Addressed to Franklin as president of the convention and signed on order of the committee by W. Atlee,[7] Chairman.)

From Benjamin Rush

AL: American Philosophical Society

Wednesday 3 oClock [July 24 or 31 or August 7, 1776]
Dr: Rush begs leave to inform Dr. Franklin that the members of the Canadian Committee will wait upon him this afternoon at 6 oClock at his own house.[8]

Addressed: Dr Franklin

The Pennsylvania Convention: Instructions to Its Delegates in Congress[9]

DS: Library of Congress

Gentlemen   In Convention, Philadelphia July [26] 1776.
This Convention confiding in your Wisdom and Virtue, has, by the Authority of the People, chosen and appointed you to repre-

7. For William Augustus Atlee (1735–93), a Lancaster lawyer and later a judge, see Charles I. Landis, "The Juliana Library Company in Lancaster," *PMHB*, XLIII (1919), 246–7.

8. The committee was to hear Canadian petitions; its meetings determine the note's possible dates. See Smith, *Letters*, IV, 537 n.

9. As soon as the convention met it became the government and behaved accordingly. One of its first actions, on July 20, was to appoint a delegation of its own to replace the Assembly's, with changes in membership but again including BF, and a committee to draft new instructions. On July 26 the draft was presented and unanimously approved. Force, 5 *Amer. Arch.*, II, 6–7, 11–12.

sent the Free State of Pennsylvania in the Congress of the United
States of America, and authorized you, or a Majority of such of
you as shall at any time be present to Vote, for and in the Name of
this State, in all and every Question there to be decided; And this
Convention apprehend it to be a Duty which they owe the Public
to give you the following general directions for your conduct,
confident that you will at all times pay the utmost attention to the
Instructions of your Constituents.

The immense and irreparable injury which a free Country may
sustain by, and the very great Inconveniencies which always arise
from a delay of its Councils, induce us in the first place, strictly to
enjoin and require you to give not only a constant, but, a punctual
Attendance in Congress.

The present Necessity of a vigorous exertion of the united force
of the Free States of America, against our British Enemies, is the
most important object of your immediate regard, and points out
the Necessity of cultivating and strengthening, by every means in
your power, the present happy Union of these States, untill such
a just, equal[1] and perpetual Confederation can be agreed upon and
finally effected, as will be the most likely to secure to each the
perfect direction of its own internal police, in the forming of
which Confederation you are to give your utmost assistance.

We recommend to you to use your utmost power and influence
in Congress, to have a due Attention paid to the establishing and
maintaining a respectable Naval Force: As such a Force is absolutely necessary to every trading Nation, and is the least expensive
or dangerous to the Liberties of Mankind.

With respect to the forming of Treaties with foreign powers, it
is necessary only to say, That we strictly charge and enjoin you,
not to agree to, or enter into any treaty of Commerce or Alliance
with Great Britain, or any other foreign power, but (on the part
of America) as Free and independent States, and that whenever
Great Britain shall acknowledge these States free and independent, you are hereby authorized, in conjunction with the Dele-

---

1. BF was soon involved in the controversy over what this adjective meant;
for his views see below, the editorial note under July 30 and his draft protest
under Aug. 20.

gates of the other united States, to treat with her concerning peace, Amity and Commerce on just and equal terms.

Extract from the Minutes

JOHN MORRIS Jr[2] Secretary

Notation: Convention Instructions to Delegates in Congress.

From the Chevalier de Kermorvan[3]

ALS: American Philosophical Society

Monsieur   26 juillet 1776.

Je jouis ici de la faveur de votre recommandation dans toutes les honnestetés et le bon accueil que j'ai recû de tout le monde. Je travaille tous les jours a m'en rendre digne et a mériter qu'on me continuë de l'amitié. J'ai vû une partie du terrein, et je me suis occupé de sa défense; j'ai trouvé dans le general mercer les meilleures intentions,[4] tous les jours je vais luy demender ses ordres, et ce qu'il veut que je fasse faire, cela me donne occasion de luy faire quelques questions sur la position des troupes, sur la communication des patrouilles d'ici a voodbridge et de voodbridge a Elizabeth town, cette partie là m'a l'air d'estre trés foible. Cependant depuis que j'ai parlé de la necessité de garder et de veiller exactement sur tous les points de la côte, je crois que le general roberdeau est allé a voodbridge profiter, et mettre en oeuvre ce que j'avois dit.[5] Je fais passer a m: hancok un plan genéral pour la

2. The previous phrase and the signature, unlike the rest of the document, are in Morris' hand. He was a Philadelphia lawyer and quartermaster of Pa. troops; see Robert C. Moon, *The Morris Family of Philadelphia* . . . (3 vols., Philadelphia, 1898), II, 428–33.

3. For the chevalier's reception in America see the headnote on Dubourg to BF above, March 24, 1776. On July 16 he was commissioned lieut. col. of engineers and ordered to the flying camp in New Jersey. 5 Force, *Amer. Arch.*, I, 367; *JCC*, V, 565.

4. Hugh Mercer (1727–77), a medical graduate of Aberdeen and a surgeon's mate in the Jacobite army at Culloden, emigrated to Pennsylvania and practiced there. After serving with distinction in the French and Indian War he moved to Virginia. Congress commissioned him brigadier general in June, 1776, and Washington assigned him to command the flying camp for defense of New Jersey. *DAB*.

5. For Roberdeau see the note on his letter above, March 6, 1776.

défense des côtes de l'amerique, je l'ai formé sur l'idée que j'ai pris du terrein d'amboy et sur les forces que nous y avons. Je doute que vous puissiez en mettre autant dans toutes les parties, mais il est très nécessaire de l'executer pour couvrir et proteger les villes de l'interieur. Nous n'avons pas une place forte pour arrester l'ennemi s'il avoit le moindre avantage. Or si nous formons quelques camps rétranchés a un mille ou a un demi mille de la coste je défie a toutes les puissances de l'europe de penetrer dans les terres, surtout si on fortifie l'entrée des rivieres des deux côtés. Si vous aviez fait ces manoeuvres là en canada vous n'auriez pas reculé plus loin que vos camps rétranchés où on augmente les rétranchemens en cas qu'on y soit attaqué, et où les troupes trouvent un azile a leur courage quand le nombre les accable. Si le congrés sent la necessité d'executer ce plan d'opérations il voudra bien l'ordonner a ses generaux, et si on prend confiance en moy j'insinuerai aux generaux les dispositions et les manoeuvres a faire quand l'ennemi descend a terre.

Je suis persuadé qu'ils conviendront que ce que je leur dirai vaut mieux que ce que je les vois pratiquer, a l'occasion des petites allertes que nous avons eu hier et avant hier, pour le passage de quelques petits bateaux qui cotoyoient staten island. J'ai eté ravi de la bonne volonté de nos troupes et de leur bonne contenance. En verité ce seroit un meurtre que de braves gens comme eux fussent victimes de mauvaises manoeuvres, ou dispositions. Avant hier pendant un orage considérable les sentinelles apperçurent un batteau qui cotoyoit staten island a la faveur de la nuit. Les eclairs qui etoient la seule lumiere du ciel le découvrirent aux sentinelles qui luy tirerent un coup de fusil. Aussitost toute la troupe de son propre mouvement prend les armes et descend au rivage. Le bateau fit sa route et nous nous rétirames dans nos quartiers. Hier quatre ou cinq autres petits bateaux vraisemblablement chargés de bled, parurent a quatre heures après midi, ils s'eloignoient le plus qu'ils pouvoient de notre coste, nous fimes feu de notre mauvaise batterie, d'abord avec deux petites pieces de canon; l'ennemi pour proteger ces batteaux canona notre batterie avec trois ou quatre grosses pieces de dix huit livres de balle. Ce petit combat dura environ deux heures, nos canonniers tirerent avec leur petites pieces aussi bien que nos ennemis, ils avoient la meilleure contenance. Je demeurai pendant tout le combat sur la batterie avec le general mercer qui fit venir nos deux plus grosses pieces avec lesquelles on toucha les voiles d'un de ces batteaux a une distance immense. La portée etoit trop forte pour nos pieces.

Je ne désirerois que de la celerité dans les opérations. On perd le temps sans rien faire. Depuis que je suis ici avec la bonne volonté qu'ont nos soldats de travailler j'aurois deja fait beaucoup d'ouvrage qui mettroit a couvert l'entrée de la riviere de brunsvick, ou l'ennemi peut nous attirer pour faire sa descente a amboy; nous craignant pour l'interieur de jersei nous nous y porterions tout de suite alors il s'empareroit d'amboy. En grace je demande a genoux au congrés d'ordonner de la celerité et tout ira bien dans notre guerre. De la lenteur extrême dans les conseils, mais la plus grande celerité dans les opérations militaires. De cette campagne ci dépend la liberté de l'amerique.

J'oubliois de vous dire, Monsieur, que trois de nos gens ont eté blessés hier, non sur la batterie, mais un dans une maison et les autres sur la coste où ils etoient a régarder, un cheval a eté tué d'un boulet a quelques toises de la maison du genéral mercer.[6]

Si on fait les batteries ou le fort que j'ai proposé de faire ici, sur la riviere, il faudroit envoyer des canons de fer avec des affuts de rempart. Ceux que j'ai vû dans la cour de l'hotel de ville seroient bons.[7] Faites, je vous supplie, en sorte, Monsieur, qu'on se décide et que le congrés ordonne de la celerité dans les opérations affin que nous soyons prests a recevoir milord how s'il vient sur quelqu'ne de nos costes avec un renfort qu'on dit qu'il amene. Je vous souhaite, Monsieur, une bonne santé, et vous prie de m'accorder et me continuer votre amitié que je travaille a mériter comme l'ami des hommes et de la liberté. Je suis avec respect, Monsieur, votre très humble serviteur

LE CH[EVALIE]R DE KERMORVAN

6. For another account of this episode see 5 Force, *Amer. Arch.*, I, 600–1.

7. On July 30 Mercer wrote Congress, and Roberdeau the Pa. committee of safety, suggesting that armed galleys be placed in the Raritan to prevent the British from moving up the river and cutting off Perth Amboy by land; this suggestion was presumably an alternative to Kermorvan's fort. Both generals mentioned that cannons for the galleys were available in Philadelphia. *Ibid.*, pp. 673–4.

An *ESSAY* of a DECLARATION of RIGHTS,

Brought in by the Committee appointed for that Purpose, and now under
the Confideration of the CONVENTION of the State of *Pennfylvania*.

1. THAT all Men are born equally free and independant, and have certain natural, inherent and unalienable Rights, amongft which are the enjoying and defending Life
and Liberty, acquiring, poffeffing and protecting Property, and purfuing and obtaining Happinefs and Safety.

2. That all Men have a natural and unalienable Right to worfhip almighty GOD according to the Dictates of their own Confciences and Underftandings: And that no Man ought
or of Right can be compelled to attend any Place of Religious Worfhip, or fupport any
him any Worfhip Place or Miniftry, contrary to, or againft his own free Will and Confent.
Nor can any Man be juftly deprived or abridged of any Civil Right as a Citizen, on account
of his peculiar Mode of religious Worfhip. And that no Authority can or ought to be vefted
in, or affumed by, any Power whatever that fhall in any Cafe interfere with, or in any Manner controul, the Right of Confcience in the free Exercife of religious Worfhip.

3. That the People of this State have the fole exclufive and inherent Right of governing
and regulating the internal Police of the fame.

4. That all Power being originally inherent in, and confequently derived from, the People,
therefore all Officers of Government, whether Legiflative or Executive, are their Truftees
and Servants, and at all Times accountable to them.

5. That Government is or ought to be inftituted for the common Benefit, Protection and
Security of the People, Nation or Community; and that a Majority of the Community hath
an indubitable, unalienable and indefeafible Right to reform, alter or abolifh it in fuch a
Manner as fhall be by that Majority judged moft conducive to the Public Weal.

6. That thofe who are employed in the Legiflative and Executive Bufinefs of the State
may be reftrained from Oppreffion, by feeling and participating the common Burthens, the
People have a Right, at fuch Periods as they may think proper, to reduce their Public Officers to a private Station, return them into that Body from which they were originally taken,
and fupply the Vacancies by certain and regular Elections: But that the having fo rule in any
Office, ought not in all Cafes to difqualify the Perfons now being thereout difpleafed

7. That all Elections ought to be free, and that all Men having an evident, permanent
and common Intereft with, and Attachment to, the Community, have a Right to elect Officers, or be elected into Office.

8. That all private Property, being protected by the State, ought to pay its juft Proportion
towards the Expence of that Protection; but that no Part of a Man's Property can be taken
from him, or applied to Public Ufes, without his own Confent, or that of his legal Reprefentatives: Nor are the People bound by any Laws but fuch as they have, in like Manner, affented to, for their common Good.

9. That in all Criminal Profecutions, a Man hath a Right to be heard by Council, to demand the Caufe and Nature of his Accufation, to be confronted with the Accufers or Wit-
neffes, to call for Evidence in his Favour, and a fpeedy public Trial by an impartial Jury of
the Country, without whofe unanimous Confent he cannot be found guilty, nor can he be
compelled to give Evidence againft himfelf, nor can any Man be juftly deprived of his Liberty, except by the Laws of the Land, or the Judgment of his Peers.

10. That the People have a Right to hold themfelves, their Houfes, Papers and Poffeffions free
from Search or Seizure, and therefore
for This Warrants without Oaths or Affirmations firft made, affording a fufficient Foundation for them, and whereby any Officer or Meffenger may be commanded or required to
fearch fufpected Places, or to feize any Perfon or Perfons his or their Property not particularly defcribed, are contrary to that Right, and ought not to be granted.

11. That in Controverfies refpecting Property, and in Suits between Man and Man, the
Parties have a Right to Trial by Jury, which ought to be held facred.

12. That the People have a Right to Freedom of Speech, and writing and publifhing their
Sentiments, therefore the Freedom of the Prefs ought not to be reftrained.

13. That the People have a Right to bear Arms for the Defence of themfelves and the
State, and as ftanding Armies in the Time of Peace are dangerous to Liberty, they ought
not to be kept up: And that the Military fhould be kept under ftrict Subordination to, and
governed by, the Civil Power.

14. That a frequent Recurrence to fundamental Principles, and a firm Adherence to
Juftice, Moderation, Temperance and Frugality are abfolutely neceffary to preferve the Bleff-
ings of Liberty, and keep a Government free, the People have therefore a Right to exact a
due and conftant Regard to thefe Points from their Officers and Reprefentatives.

15. That all Men have a natural inherent Right to Emigration from one State to any
other that will receive them, or for the Forming a new State in vacant Country whenever they find that thereby they may promote their own Happinefs.

16. That an enormous Proportion of Property vefted in a few Individuals is dangerous to
the Rights, and deftructive of the Common Happinefs, of Mankind; and therefore every
free State hath a Right by its Laws to difcourage the Poffeffion of fuch Property.

Franklin's Revisions of the Pennsylvania Bill of Rights

Revisions of the Pennsylvania Declaration of Rights

MS emendations of a broadside text, *An Essay of a Declaration of Rights, Brought in by the Committee Appointed for That Purpose, and Now under the Consideration of the Convention of the State of Pennsylvania* (Philadelphia, 1776): Library Company of Philadelphia.

The Pennsylvania constitution had two parts, a bill or declaration of rights and what became known as the frame of government.[8] The first was revised and adopted in its final form while the latter was still under consideration, and Franklin played a considerable part in the revision. On July 18 the convention appointed a drafting committee, which reported a week later. On the 26th the draft was recommitted for changes, which were completed the following day; and on the 29th the convention ordered this draft printed for its members. They resumed discussion of it at three meetings in August, one on the 13th and two on the 15th, and Franklin was present at all of them. On the 16th the document was adopted without debate.[9] The committee, of which Franklin was a member, that was appointed later to review the wording of the constitution left the bill of rights unaltered. Hence the present revisions were made between the printing of the draft, ordered on July 29, and the final debate upon it on August 15.

We cannot be completely certain that the revisions were Franklin's handiwork, rather than his notes of suggestions offered from the floor and adopted in the committee of the whole at one or more of the three August meetings; but the latter possibility is remote. He could not have recorded the entire process of revision, for the final draft adopted on August 16 contained further changes that are noted in our annotation. Why should he have recorded any, when the convention had both a secretary and a clerk? But the principal reason for rejecting this explanation is the stylistic care that went into the emendations and gives them, in our opinion, his particular hallmark. We are convinced that he reviewed the printed text, tightening the prose and slightly altering the substance, and that the convention then accepted most of what he had done and went on to make a few alterations of its own.

[Between July 29 and August 15, 1776]
AN ESSAY of a DECLARATION of RIGHTS,
Brought in by the Committee appointed for that Purpose, and

8. See the editorial note on the convention above, July 15, 1776.
9. Force, 5 *Amer. Arch.*, II, 5, 10–12, 21–4. The final text (*ibid.*, cols. 52–3) follows in general the printed draft as amended by BF; the exceptions we have noted below.

now under the Consideration of the CONVENTION of the State of Pennsylvania.

1. That all Men are born equally free and independant, and have certain natural, inherent and unalienable Rights, amongst which are the enjoying and defending Life and Liberty, acquiring, possessing and protecting Property, and pursuing and obtaining Happiness and Safety.

2. That all Men have a natural and unalienable Right to worship almighty GOD according to the Dictates of their own Consciences and Understandings:[10] And that no Man ought or of

                                     any

Right can be compelled to attend ∧any Place of Religious Wor-

          erect or   any place of Worship or maintain any

ship, or ∧ support or maintain any Worship, Place or Ministry, contrary to, or against his own free will and Consent. Nor can

  who acknowledges the Being of a God

any Man ∧ be justly deprived or abridged of any Civil Right as

               Religious Sentiments or

a Citizen, on account of his ∧peculiar Mode of religious Worship. And that no Authority can or ought to be vested in, or assumed by, any Power whatever that shall in any Case interfere with, or in any Manner controul, the Right of Conscience in the free Exercise of religious Worship.

3. That the People of this State have the sole exclusive and inherent Right of governing and regulating the internal Police of the same.

4. That all Power being originally inherent in, and consequently derived from, the People, therefore all Officers of Government, whether Legislative or Executive, are their Trustees and Servants, and at all Times accountable to them.

5. That Government is or ought to be instituted for the common Benefit, Protection and Security of the People, Nation or [*in the margin*: *And not[1]]
Community,* ∧and that a Majority of the Community hath an

---

10. Final version: "understanding."

1. Perhaps BF wrote the rest of what he had in mind on a separate sheet that has since disappeared. In any case the final version reads: "and not for the particular emolument or advantage of any single man, family, or set of men who are a part only of that community."

indubitable, unalienable and indefeasible Right to reform, alter
Government   Community
or abolish ~~it~~ ∧in such a Manner as shall be by that ~~Majority~~ judged
most conducive to the Public Weal.

6. That those who are employed in the Legislative and Executive Business of the State may be restrained from Oppression, ~~by
feeling and participating the common Burthens,~~ the People have
a Right, at such Periods as they may think proper, to reduce their
Public Officers to a private Station, ~~return them into that Body
from which they were originally taken,~~ and supply the Vacancies
by certain and regular Elections: ~~But that the having served in any
Office, ought not in all Cases to disqualify the Person from being re-
elected.~~

free

7. That all Elections ought to be free, and that all ∧Men hav-
a sufficient   and
ing ~~an~~ evident, ~~permanent and~~ common Interest with, and Attachment to, the Community, have a Right to elect Officers, or be
elected into Office.

8. That all private Property, being protected by the State,
ought to pay its just Proportion towards the Expence of that
justly
Protection; but ~~that~~ no Part of a Man's Property can be ∧taken
from him, or applied to Public Uses, without his own Consent,
or that of his legal Representatives: Nor are the People bound by
any Laws but such as they have, in like Manner, assented to, for
their common Good.[2]

for Criminal Offenses

9. That in all ~~Criminal~~ Prosecutions ∧a Man hath a Right to
himself and his
be heard by ∧Council, to demand the Cause and Nature of his

2. This article was much expanded in the final version, which reads: "That
every member of society hath a right to be protected in the enjoyment of life,
liberty, and property, and therefore is bound to contribute his proportion towards the expense of that protection, and yield his personal service when necessary, or an equivalent thereto; but no part of a man's property can be justly
taken from him, or applied to publick uses, without his own consent, or that of
his legal representatives; nor can any man who is conscientiously scrupulous of
bearing arms, be justly compelled thereto, if he will pay such equivalent; nor
are the people bound by any laws, but such as they have in like manner assented
to for their common good."

Accusation, to be confronted with the ~~Accusers or~~ Witnesses, to call for Evidence in his Favour, and a speedy public Trial by an

the

impartial Jury of the Country, without ~~whose~~ unanimous Consent

of which jury

∧he cannot be found guilty, nor can he be compelled to give Evidence against himself, nor can any Man be justly deprived of his Liberty, except by the Laws of the Land, or the Judgment of his Peers.

10[3] That the People have a Right to hold themselves, their Houses, Papers and Possessions free from Search or Seizure, and therefore

~~10. That~~ Warrants without Oaths or Affirmations first made, affording a sufficient Foundation for them, and whereby any Officer or Messenger may be commanded or required to search suspected Places, or to seize any Person or Persons his or their Property not particularly described, are contrary to that Right, and ought not to be granted.

11. That in Controversies respecting Property, and in Suits between Man and Man, the Parties have a Right to Trial by Jury, which ought to be held sacred.

12. That the People have a Right to Freedom of Speech, and of

∧writing and publishing their Sentiments, therefore the Freedom of the Press ought not to be restrained.

13. That the People have a Right to bear Arms for the Defence of themselves and the State, and as standing Armies in the Time of Peace are dangerous to Liberty, they ought not to be kept up: And that the Military should be kept under strict Subordination to, and governed by, the Civil Power.

14. That a frequent Recurrence to fundamental Principles, and

Industry

a firm Adherence to Justice, Moderation, Temperance ∧and Frugality are absolutely necessary to preserve the Blessings of Liberty, and keep a Government free, the People[4] have therefore a Right

3. The digits are in BF's hand.

4. At this point the final version begins a new sentence with a slight shift of emphasis: "The people ought therefore to pay particular attention to these points in the choice of officers and representatives, and have a right to exact a due and constant regard to them from their legislatures and magistrates in the

to exact a due and constant Regard to these Points from their Legislators or   in the making and Executing such Laws as ∧Officers ~~and Representatives~~ ∧are necessary for the good Govt. of the State.

                               to   e

15. That all Men have a natural inherent Right ~~of~~ Emigrat~~ion~~

                          to

from one State to any other[5] that will receive them, or ~~for the~~ vacant Countries, or in such Countries as they can purchase, Form~~ing~~ a new State in ~~vacant or purchased Countries~~, whenever they find that thereby they may promote their own Happiness.

16. That an enormous Proportion of Property vested in a few Individuals is dangerous to the Rights, and destructive of the Common Happiness, of Mankind; and therefore every free State hath a Right by its Laws to discourage the Possession of such Property.[6]

The Committee of Secret Correspondence to John Bradford[7]

Copy: National Archives; typescript of ALS: Yale University Library[8]

Sir   Philada. July 30th. 1776

We take the liberty to enclose herein some dispatches for Messrs. Saml. & J. H. Delap Merchts. in Bourdeaux which youl

---

making and executing such laws as are necessary for the good government of the State."

5. Final version: "another."

6. This article was deleted in the final version and a quite different one substituted: "That the people have a right to assemble together, to consult for their common good, to instruct their representatives, and to apply to the Legislature for redress of grievances, by address, petition, or remonstrance."

7. Bradford (1735–84) had been a member of the committee of correspondence. In April, 1776, Congress appointed him agent for prizes for Boston, the most important such position in the colonies, and also continental agent to assist the marine committee in purchasing and outfitting ships. Colonial Soc. of Mass., *Pubs.*, XL (1961), 404; Charles O. Paullin, *The Navy of the American Revolution* (Cleveland, Ohio, 1906), pp. 94–5; Smith, *Letters*, III, 642 n.

8. We print the copy, which ends before the signatures, and supply them, the postscript, and the endorsement from the typescript.

please to deliver into Capt. Clevelands own hands with a strict charge to take the utmost care of them and follow the orders also enclosed herein directed to him which you will be pleased to deliver and enjoin his punctual obedience on which will depend his future employment and advancement in the Public service. Mr. Morris informs us of the alacrity with which you have executed his Commissions in the purchase of the Brigantine Dispatch[9] and if any thing further of this kind offers this Committee will claim the liberty of troubling you again being respectfully Sir Your obedient Servants.

> BENJAMIN FRANKLIN
> BENJAMIN HARRISON
> ROBERT MORRIS

P.S. You will oblige me by putting up a Collection of the Public News Papers directed to Messers Samuel & J. H. Delap, Merchants in Bordeaux and send them by Captain Cleveland.

Jno Bradford Esqr

Endorsed: Mr. Morris, July 30th With Mr. Franklin's Letter. '76

The Committee of Secret Correspondence to Stephen Cleveland
LS: American Philosophical Society[1]

⟨Philadelphia, July 30, 1776: Bradford has informed us that he has outfitted the *Dispatch* and appointed you commander; "he gives you an extreme good Character." You will receive this from John Philip Merkle,[2] and you will be bound by the following

9. Stephen Cleveland, a veteran of the Royal Navy in the previous war, was commissioned captain of the brigantine *Dispatch* on Aug. 8, 1776; the ship had been the *Little Hannah* when taken as a prize the previous December, and Bradford had renamed her. *Naval Docs.*, V, 267, 1288 n; VI, 125. She is easily confused with another of the same name commanded by Capt. Peter Parker; see the committee's letters above to Deane, July 8, and to Parker, July 10, 1776. Cleveland's departure was delayed for almost two months, and when he left he carried with him, we believe, the committee's letter to Deane below of Aug. 7.

1. The complete text, printed from a copy, is in *Naval Docs.*, V, 1286–8.

2. For Bradford, Cleveland, and the *Dispatch* see the preceding letter. Merkle was a Dutch adventurer, who apparently turned up in New York in the spring of 1776. He was introduced to Congress as a man of wealth and integrity, and Carter Braxton and Robert Morris made a private contract with him to import £10,000 worth of goods. *Naval Docs.*, VI, 1039–40. As a purchasing agent for

instructions until they are superseded: You will give Bradford bills of lading for the cargo, which is consigned to Merkle, whom you will receive on board. You will make for France, put in at the first convenient port (Nantes or Bordeaux may be the safest), and there unload such of the cargo as Merkle wishes to sell. We enclose to Bradford a packet, which he will give you, addressed to Messrs. Samuel and J. H. Delap at Bordeaux. If you are captured, throw the packet overboard. If you land at Bordeaux deliver it to the Delaps; if you land at another port forward it by the best means available, tell them where Merkle is ordering you to call, and ask them how to address letters to Silas Deane so that they will surely reach him.[3] Merkle will, we expect, order you on to Amsterdam; you will deliver the remainder of the cargo at such ports as he directs and, when all is unloaded, will receive whatever goods, arms, and ammunition he wishes to ship. You are free to arm the brigantine as completely as you please, and to take on as many good seamen as you can accommodate.

Inform the Delaps and Deane how to reach you and when you intend to return. You will, we believe, receive from them letters and packets for us, which are to be seen by no one and thrown overboard if need be. When you are fitted and loaded, and have received your dispatches from Merkle, you are to make for the first safe harbor you find in the United States, and there enlist the help of local authorities in forwarding promptly to us whatever letters and packets you bring. Tell us the condition of your vessel, and we will give you further orders. We send you a commission, a book of regulations about captures, and a list of continental agents in case you take prizes.[4] But prizes are not your object; a fast and safe voyage is. "In time your utmost Ambition may be gratified provided Merit leads the Way to Promotion."

You may accommodate free of charge any American masters,

the committee in Europe Merkle turned out to be a disaster: Richard B. Morris *et al.*, eds., *John Jay, the Making of a Revolutionary: Unpublished Papers, 1745–1780* (New York, 1975), p. 270 n.

3. The committee explained these instructions in a separate letter to the Delaps of the same date (*Naval Docs.*, v, 1289–90); we do not summarize it because it adds no information, except that the firm would be expected to forward the committee's letters to Deane and he would pay the charges.

4. The committee sent the same material to Capt. Parker with its letter above, July 10, 1776.

mates, or seamen who want passage. Merkle will perhaps think it proper to make your ship French or Dutch, and to clear it for the West Indies. You are to co-operate with him, and do all you can to please him during the voyage.[5] Signed by Franklin, Benjamin Harrison, and Robert Morris.)

Editorial Note on Franklin's Part in the Congressional Debate of July 30 to August 1, 1776.

Richard Henry Lee's famous resolution of June 7, 1776, called for independence and confederation. Congress considered the resolution the next day, and on the 11th and 12th appointed a committee to draw up articles of confederation. The committee's report, commonly called the Dickinson draft after its chief architect, was presented on July 12. It was printed for the delegates, and intermittently discussed and amended from July 22 to August 20.[6] One of the crucial debates, on proportional versus equal representation of the states in Congress and on their financial contributions to the confederacy, was on July 30, 31, and August 1. Franklin spoke three times, contrary to his usual habit; neither the order of the speeches nor the days on which they were given is clear.[7] John Adams recorded them in his diary, in the first person and all, presumably, in shortened form. Jefferson described one of them; his version is in the third person and considerably longer than Adams', but even so is tantalizingly brief. The two reporters, nevertheless, provide the only record we have of Franklin's debating questions that went to the heart of the confederation.

5. Cleveland "must treat him with respect and all the attention he can," Morris wrote Bradford on the same day as this letter. "A hint from you to that effect will no doubt have its force." *Naval Docs.*, V, 1289.

6. *JCC*, V, 425–6, 431, 546–56. See also Burnett, *Continental Congress*, pp. 214–15; Merrill Jensen, *The Articles of Confederation: an Interpretation* . . . ([Madison, Wis.,] 1940), pp. 126–9; Herbert James Henderson, *Party Politics in the Continental Congress* ([New York, etc., 1974]), p. 136, 153 n; Jack N. Rakove, *The Beginnings of National Politics: an Interpretive History of the Continental Congress* (New York, 1979), pp. 151–62.

7. Jefferson opens his account of the debate with a proposal by Samuel Chase, to which first BF replies and then John Witherspoon, and implies that this succession of speeches was on July 30. Adams omits Chase's and assigns the other two to Aug. 1. We see no way to resolve this conflict of evidence, and in discussing BF's remarks have followed Adams' chronological order with no assurance that it is correct.

Article 17 of Dickinson's draft provided that each state should have a single vote in Congress. Franklin opened the debate, to judge by Adams' account, by stating bluntly the case for proportional representation. "Let the smaller Colonies give equal Money and Men, and then have an equal Vote. But if they have an equal Vote, without bearing equal Burthens, a Confederation upon such iniquitous Principles, will never last long."[8]

This was the nub of the question. Article 11, as formulated by Dickinson's committee, provided that all Congressional appropriations for defence and the general welfare be defrayed from a common treasury, into which each state would pay a quota determined by its population, Indians excluded. Were slaves also to be excluded? Here was another divisive issue, this time between northern and southern states. No union would be possible, protested Thomas Lynch of South Carolina, if slaves were considered people for the purposes of assessment, rather than property like land or sheep or horses. This reasoning, according to Adams, provoked Franklin to reply. "Slaves rather weaken than strengthen the State," he said, "and there is therefore some difference between them and Sheep. Sheep will never make any Insurrections."[9] Samuel Chase moved that the article be amended to include only white inhabitants, and after long discussion the amendment was defeated on August 1 by the seven northern states.[1]

The concomitant debate on Article 17 seems also to have reached its conclusion on August 1. Franklin moved an amendment, "that Votes should be in Proportion to Numbers."[2] This he considered to be equal representation, in the sense that population and votes were equated. The two accounts of what he said on that point, and the context in which he said it, differ markedly. He spoke, according to Adams, immediately after a member of the drafting committee had analyzed the position taken by the individual states. "I hear," Franklin said, "many ingenious Arguments to perswade Us that an unequal Representation is a very good Thing. If We had been born and bred under an unequal Representation We might bear it. But to sett out with an unequal Representation is unreasonable.

"It is said the great Colonies will swallow up the less. Scotland said the same Thing at the Union."[3]

This speech, according to Jefferson, had a quite different setting. It followed a compromise suggested by Samuel Chase, that when questions

8. Butterfield, *John Adams Diary*, II, 245. The editor argues (p. 246 n) that BF's speech was on July 31.

9. *Ibid.*, p. 246.

1. Boyd, *Jefferson Papers*, I, 320–1, 323.

2. Butterfield, p. 247.

3. *Ibid.*, p. 248.

of money came before Congress each state should have a voice proportioned to its population, and in all other questions an equal voice.

"Dr. Franklin [*deleted*: seconded the proposition] thought that the votes should be so proportioned in all cases. He took notice that the Delaware counties had bound up their Delegates to disagree to this article.[4] He thought it a very extraordinary language to be held by any state, that they would not confederate with us unless we would let them dispose of our money. Certainly if we vote equally we ought to pay equally: but the smaller states will hardly purchase the privilege at this price. That had he lived in a state where the representation, originally equal, had become unequal by time and accident he might have submitted rather than disturb government: but that we should be very wrong to set out in this practice when it is in our power to establish what is right. That at the time of the Union between England and Scotland the latter had made the objection which the smaller states now do. But experience had [*deleted*: shewn] proved that no unfairness had ever been shewn them. That their advocates had prognosticated that it would again happen as in times of old that the whale would swallow Jonas, but he thought the prediction reversed in event and that Jonas had swallowed the whale, for the Scotch had in fact got possession of the government and gave laws to the English. He reprobated the original agreement of Congress to vote by colonies, and therefore was for their voting in all cases according to the number of taxables [*deleted*: so far going beyond Mr. Chase's proposition]."[5]

The argument was unavailing; Article 17 was approved as the committee had reported it. Franklin considered entering a protest from the Pennsylvania convention, which was then sitting, and drafted one that put the case for the opposition in no uncertain terms; the draft is below under August 20. But he decided, as he explained there, to let the issue drop.

4. For the Delaware Assembly's instructions to its Congressional delegates see John A. Munroe, *Federalist Delaware, 1775–1815* (New Brunswick, N.J., 1954), pp. 81–2.
5. Boyd, p. 324. We have altered the punctuation and the handling of deletions to conform to our usage. Witherspoon, who according to Adams and Jefferson replied to BF, pointed out that the Scots had acquired a much larger share of representation than of taxation. *Ibid.*, p. 325.

From Anthony Wayne

LS: American Philosophical Society: AL (draft⁶): Historical Society of Pennsylvania

Dear Sir   Ticonderoga⁷ July 31st. 1776

We are so far remov'd from the Seat of Government of the free and independant States of America,⁸ and such an insurmountable Barrier (Alb . . . y) between Us, that scarcely One Letter or the least intelligence can reach here from your Quarter;⁹ through the medium of my Chaplain I hope this will find you, as he has promis'd to blow out the Brains of the Man who will attempt to take it from him.¹ We are inform'd by way of Boston that Lord Howe has joind the General before New-York with a large Fleet

---

6. The draft is dated July 29 and is docketed "Doct. Franklin Genl. Mifflin Abm. Robinson Esqr.," which we presume means that the same letter, as with Wayne's above of June 13, went to others as well as BF.

7. After the disaster at Trois Rivières the army retreated by way of Crown Point to Ticonderoga, where by mid-July some 2,500 men were assembled. Reinforcements over the next six weeks brought the force to over 10,000, of whom slightly more than half were fit for duty. Martin H. Bush, *Revolutionary Enigma: a Re-appraisal of General Philip Schuyler* . . . (Fort Washington, N.Y., 1969), pp. 64–7.

8. Three days earlier the Declaration of Independence had been read to the troops: Force, 5 *Amer. Arch.*, I, 630.

9. Two paragraphs added to the draft, but for some mysterious reason omitted in the LS, explain this statement: "Private, as well as publick letters (such as come to hand) we Receive Open, the Contents exposed to every Rascal whose Curiosity, or a worse and more Villainous motive induces to read; thro' this means the Enemy undoubtedly gain every Intelligence they can wish, and we have ground to believe that not more than one in ten of our letters ever come to us at all.

"The *State* of Massts. Bay has Established a post to this place and all letters carried free to the Army (as you'l see by the Inclosed note); can't you procure a Similar one to pass in our *State*, or are we less worthy than the Gentlemen from the Eastward? Be that as it may, an Inquiry into the cause of this shameful Conduct in some of the Different posts or Offices is a matter not to be neglected, as it may in the end be attended with bad and fatal Consequences."

Gates wrote much the same thing to Schuyler on July 22: Force, *op. cit.*, col. 512. For the Mass. postriders see *Resolves of the General Assembly of the Colony of Massachusetts Bay* . . . (Boston, 1776), p. 50.

1. The Rev. David Jones (died 1820), a chaplain of Pa. troops, was in action throughout the war and in many battles with Wayne; he later served in the War of 1812. Heitman, *Register of Officers*, p. 245; William B. Sprague, ed., *Annals of the American Pulpit* (9 vols., New York, 1859–69), VI, 85–9.

and Army, and that the Militia of York, Jersey, Connecticut &ca. have Assembled to the Amount of 60,000. Notwithstanding I own I have some apprehensions for the brave and generous Sons of America, who will be oblig'd to bear the brunt of the day; a raw undiciplin'd Militia (who have farms to mind and other concerns crowding in upon them) will in a few Weeks become impatient of Command; Fevers and other Camp disorders will be fatal to them at this time of Year. An artful Enemy will know how to wait and improve the favourable moment; General Howe is not un-aquainted with the wretched condition our people were in at Cambridge, he let slip the oppertunity; he will not be guilty of the like error again. I firmly believe that 20,000 men who wou'd engage to stay during the Campaign would be of less expence, and more Service then the whole.[2]

We are in high expectation of shortly seeing Burgoyne, who will attempt a junction with Howe, he'll not effect it without the loss of much blood.[3] Colo. St. Clair, Dehaase and myself are in possession of Mont Calms lines. We shall render them more formidable than ever in a few days, we are to be joind by Lieut. Col. Hartley and the 6th. Pennsa. Battallion we shall then Amount to about 1600 effective Men in these lines Officers included, under the Command of Colo. St. Clair. The Jersey and eastern Troops, are station'd on the opposite Side of Lake Champlain to Us, on a peninsula inaccessable, except at one Spot, which they are beginning to fortify; they are compos'd of three Brigades and Amount to about 1900 or 2,000 Men at most, so that our whole force of effective Men may be nearly 3,600.

Col. St. Clair and myself have commenced Engineers in chief, We amend, form and alter such part and parts of the old french Lines as We think proper a plan of which is here inclos'd.[4]

I rest assur'd that if Burgoyne makes an Attack upon Us, that

2. This sentence is omitted in the draft.

3. The British were planning to end the campaign with a two-pronged offensive, one army moving south from Canada and the other north from New York for a juncture at Albany; Burgoyne was Carleton's second in command: William B. Willcox, *Portrait of a General: Sir Henry Clinton in the War of Independence* (New York, 1964), pp. 95–8.

4. Cols. St. Clair, De Haas, and Hartley have appeared before in this volume. On the 18th the Pa. troops had encamped on the dilapidated French fortifications north and west of the fort; see *PMHB*, xxv (1901), 344. The enclosed plan is missing.

the British Troops will meet a worse fate than when under General Abercrombie in 1758.[5] They'll find an Enemy fertile in expedient, and altho' weak in Number yet brave by nature, who will push hard for Victory and long for revenge for the unforunate affair at *Three Rivers*. I am almost tempted to say with Macduff, "Gracious Heavens, cut short all intermission, and front to front set those Sons of War and Us; if they then escape may Heaven forgive them too."[6]

We are indefatigable in preparing to meet the Enemy by Water.[7] The superiority in a Naval force on this Lake is an object of the first moment. It has been hitherto shamefully neglected, but now in a fair way of becoming formidable as we have at present three Schooners and one Sloop well appointed and man'd with people drafted from the several Regiments; they carry from 8 to 16 Guns each which together with four Gondolaes[8] already built will be no contemptible fleet in the sea. 150 Carpenters from Philada. and Connecticut are arriv'd at Skeinsborough and are now at work in building more Arm'd Boats. The Enemy on the other hand are industriously employ'd in building Vessels of force, Batteaus &ca. at St. Johns they brought with them a considerable Number of Boats with a brass four Pounder in the bow of each. I saw and engag'd several of these boats near three Rivers they are between a Ships long boat and Batteau and carry about 50 or 60 Men.[9]

Our people have receiv'd three days fresh provisions, and have a prospect of being better supply'd, they begin to recover health

5. For James Abercromby's disastrous attack see Gipson, *British Empire*, VII, 208–36.

6. A considerable emendation of *Macbeth*, IV, iii, 231–4.

7. The draft adds at the beginning of the sentence that a force of 1,500 Conn. troops was expected shortly; in fact it stopped at Skenesborough: Force, *op. cit.*, cols. 660, 1071, 1199–1200.

8. Gondolas or gundelows, flush-decked and flat-bottomed river boats of shallow draft and with one square-rigged sail: William M. Fowler, Jr., *Rebels under Sail: the American Navy during the Revolution* (New York, [1976]), pp. 187–8. Gen. Arnold had just arrived to reinvigorate the shipbuilding program which made possible, at the end of the summer, his naval action that saved Ticonderoga: *ibid.*, chap. x.

9. This paragraph of the draft is differently organized and omits some sentences, but adds two statements: that on the water "I think we may ride Triumphant if we please," and that "in a few days we shall put the matter to the test." In fact, as already mentioned, the test did not come for more than a month.

and Spirits, but are still destitute of almost every necessary fit *for a Soldier*; Shoes stockings, Shirts and Soap are essential Articles in an Army and not easily done without, yet these cannot be had here on any terms.

I am sorry to have occasion to Write in this manner, but when objects of distress hourly strike the Eye—objects who look to me for relief—I can't but feel for their Situation tho unable to give them help. Cannot some means be fell on to send a speedy supply of these Articles? Interim I am with true regard Your most Obedient and very Humble Servant   ANTY. WAYNE

A Mr. Traverse, who was a Capt. in our Service, and has the Appearance of an Honest Intelligent man, has just Arrived from St. John's.[1] He Informs us that 8,000 Regulars are now there together with 4,000 Canadians, well Appointed Amounts in the whole to 12,000 men; that they have 150 Batteaus ready and three Armed vessels, and that we may expect them in a little time.

Addressed: Honbl. Doctr Benja. Franklin Esqr / Member Continental Congress / Philadelphia / favour'd per / Revd. Mr Jones

From Samuel J. Atlee[2]

ALS: Pennsylvania State Library, Harrisburg

⟨Perth Amboy, August 2, 1776: The service of the state required the battalion of musketeers that I command to march before it was ready.[3] The agent appointed to supply necessities was defi-

1. He had presumably not arrived on the 29th, for the draft omits this postscript. Capt. Joseph Traversé was a French Canadian who had been under Goforth's command at Trois Rivières and had had to flee the country; he had done so by a wide detour through Cohoes, near Albany. Force, *op. cit.*, cols. 548, 797. He reappeared in 1777 with news of a conspiracy among Canadian prisoners of war: Fitzpatrick, *Writings of Washington*, VI, 503.

2. For Atlee see Ross to BF above, Dec. 29. This letter was clearly intended for the Pa. committee of safety, from which BF had resigned in his letter to the Assembly above, Feb. 26. We have found no evidence that his resignation was formally accepted, and Atlee may have considered him as still at least titular president. The Colonel was captured soon afterward in the Battle of Long Island; see Anderson's letter below, Sept. 22.

3. Doubtless as a result of the circular letter from the convention above, July 19, 1776.

cient, and many of the men lack sheets, britches, and stockings, which are not to be had here. I should be obliged if the committee would order a quantity of them, for the soldiers in their present state cannot keep clean and therefore healthy. They justly complain, "and was it not for the Strictness of discipline kept up, I shou'd be difficulted to keep them to their duty. Were we situated any other where than in the Face of the Enemy I shou'd look upon it as a piece of cruelty to keep so strict a Hand over them in the Condition they are, but the least relaxation might be of infinite disservice." I earnestly beg for at least 500 sheets and pairs of stockings and 100 pairs of leather britches.

I recommend as adjutant Mr. Francis Mentges[4], who has much military knowledge and who should have, like the adjutants of other battalions, the rank and pay of a lieutenant.⟩

From Pierre Penet

Copy:[5] South Carolina Historical Society

Sir   At Nantes the 3 August 1776.

We have the Honour to write you by Capn. Crawford of Rhode Island that Mr. Brown of Providence consign'd to us at Nants, whoom we have dispatched with a Cargo of Powder Muschkets saltpeter &ca. who promiss'd to deliver you this.[6]

I had the honour to inform you in May last at my arrival in Europe of the success of my opperations, and of the advantageous dispositions I met with, now I will inform you have embarked in your ship the Hancock a Cargo of Muskets Saltpeter Powder tin Lead &ca. amounting to 60 or 70 thousand Livers, which sum

4. Mentges, whose name was variously spelled, was a French dancing master in Philadelphia; he subsequently became a lieut. col. in the Pa. line. W. A. N. Dorland, "The Second Troop Philadelphia City Cavalry," *PMHB*, XLV (1921), 385.

5. It could be a translation except that the slips in English are not the sort that a translator would be likely to make. Penet's later letters are in French, which at this early stage of their relationship he may not have known that BF understood. Although he is writing in the name of the company, he is clearly speaking for himself.

6. The firm of Nicholas Brown was Penet's principal American associate. Capt. Gideon Crawford left Nantes in early August in Brown's ship, the *Happy Return*, and by Oct. 1 her supplies were ashore in Providence. *Naval Docs.*, VI, 1078–9.

only M. Schweighauzer could pay us.[7] We are forced Sir to acquaint you that all the Houses you have in Spain and Portugal use you very Ill and make no remittances to Nantes, we have now in our stores Goods ready to send you to the amount of Forty thousand Guineas, but two of your Ships have arrived here from Cadiz in Ballast one is the Hancok and the other the Adams. The last brought no money. We askd Mr. Schweighauzer if he would answer for the Cargo which we were desirous to deliver to the Capn. on his paying us when he should have money of yours in his hands, he told us he could not take that on himself. Notwithstanding Sir as we have the greatest confidence in you and the Honourable Congress, we shall immediatly dispatch this Vessell with a Cargo of Ammunition provided however we can obtain from Manufactorers, the credit we require,[8] and we beg you will send us remittances by the first oppertunity, we request it less on our own Account than by the desire we have of serving so respectable a Nation as yours. You may depend on our willingness to do everything in our Power for your assistance.

I have seen Mr. Dean formerly a Member of your secret Committy as well as Mr. Morris's brother we have offer'd them our services at Paris,[9] we carry on our buisness seperately without communicating our Opperations to one another, if our house can be useful to them they may dispose of it.

7. "Only," we are convinced, modifies "sum"; see n. 10 below. For Schweighauser see Bonvouloir to de Guines above, Dec. 28.

8. The two ships mentioned earlier in the paragraph seem now to have become one, which in fact they were. "This vessel" was the *Hancock and Adams*, commanded by Capt. Samuel Smith, Jr., and under charter to the secret committee since February. She reached Nantes by way of Lisbon, and left in late August with arms and ammunition supposedly worth £35,000; so Penet must have obtained the needed credit. The ship carried Boisbertrand (*Naval Docs.*, VII, 576) and his three companions. An American privateer intercepted her, and she did not arrive until the beginning of November. On the 15th Congress ordered that the army should have all of her stores that it could use. *Ibid.*, VI, 7, 616; VII, 71, 72 n, 181; *JCC*, VI, 952–3; Smith, *Letters*, V, 491–3.

9. Thomas Morris (1750–78), Robert's illegitimate and much younger half-brother, was born after their father's death and raised as though Robert's son. The young man took to the bottle; his brother secured his appointment as Congress' commercial agent in Nantes, to separate him from his drinking companions, and recommended him to Deane's protection. Ellis P. Oberholtzer, *Robert Morris, Patriot and Financier* (New York, 1903), pp. 7, 44–5; *Deane Papers*, I, 173–4.

Several Vessells have been consign'd to us from Rhode Island and Virginia. They have been dispatched in few Days with good Cargos, and we can flatter Ourselves that all Vessells consign'd to us will meet with equal dispatch as we have taken our measures in consequence.

We have obtain'd a written Permission for twenty thousand Hogsheads of tobaco, but on recipt of this Congress may remit us what quantity they please and we will warrant their admition in our Ports.

If you have any yellow Wax Rice and Furs they are articles on which you might obtain great Profit.

We hope Sir that Congress will have sufficient Confidence in us to consign directly to us their Vessells loaded with your Produce, we can safely warrant and assure you that we can dispose annually of those four Articles to the Amount of Fifteen Millions this Currency, and send you in return immediatly, on the arrival of the ships any quantity and kind of Merchandize you may require.

We have now at our disposal and in our Manufactorys Cloth for your soldiers and Blankets of a good quality and Cheap. You may inquire of Mr. Brown of Providence to whoom we have remitted some.

If Mr. Dean applies to us for his opperations he shall be served immediatly if not he will find the difference, the name and Direction of our House at Nantes is Mr. Jques. Gruel Isle feydeau at Nantes, one of the best in the Place and in which you may place an entire confidence.[10] I recommend it to you as the fittest house for your Operations, and will serve you with all possible exactitude. I take the Liberty to recommend M. Pliarne to you and beg you will let him have what money he may want and Congress may take his Draughts on me for the amount.

Will you be pleased to assure the Members of the Honourable

10. The references to Schweighauser seem to imply that he was co-operating in a niggardly fashion: he paid only 60–70,000 livres, a paltry sum, for the military stores on the *Hancock and Adams*, and would not advance more for the rest of the cargo. If this interpretation is correct, it explains Penet's turning instead to one of his original backers, Jacques-Barthélémy Gruel. He was an opulent merchant and slave-trader in Nantes, who came from St. Domingue and was a landholder there. Price, *France and the Chesapeake*, II, 702; *Revue de l'histoire des colonies françaises*, XXIII (1930), 186. Penet was staying with him by the time he wrote, as he mentions below, and subsequently arranged for BF, when he reached Nantes, to be Gruel's guest.

the Congress Secret Committy and all those I have the honour to be acquainted with of my Zeal, and of the desire I have of procuring them all possible assistance. I dare flatter myself that I shall more and more merit their Confidence, [having] no other Interest than to oblige your Nation, support Liberty and sacrifice myself for your Country which I regard as my own, such are my Sentiments and those of my Freinds who are concernd with me.

My Presence in France is too necessary, beeing obliged to transact the secret affairs myself, to permit me to return to the Continent before the End of the Warr, unless you think proper I should go sooner. My residence is at Nants at the House of M. Jque. Gruel Mercht. It is the most advantageous Port in France for your ships, its River runs 150 Leagues into the heart of the Kingdom and facilitates the transport of all kind of Goods. Consequently there are large purchases made in this City of all kinds, which induced me to fix on it as the fittest for your affairs, here you may send all your ships. I will be answerable for the disposal of their Cargos. If you send to Bordeaux Direct to Messrs. Reculé de Basmarin & Raimbaux,[1] at Cadiz to Messrs. Delaville Brothers, with orders to advise Mr. Jques. Gruel at the arrival of each ship Consign'd to them, so that they may dispose of the Cargos and their produce to satisfie your demands.

Mistrust the Irish and scotch houses in Europe.[2] I have reasons to give you this Caution—send no more ships to Lisbon.

PLIARNE PENET & CO.

I have the Honour to write to General Washington, I ask him a favour. Would you be pleased to sollicit it for me, I shall think myself happy to merit it, that is that he would grant me the title and Commission without sallary, of his first Aid de Camp, that I may have the Honour to wear the uniform and the Ribbon they

1. One of the city's largest shipping firms; see Perry Viles, "The Shipping Interest of Bordeaux, 1774–1793" (doctoral dissertation, Harvard University, 1964), p. 220. Gruel, writing to BF below, Dec. 18, 1776, mentioned that he had a family connection with Basmarein's uncle.

2. He repeated the warning to Deane, and added that those houses "are our worst enemies." *Naval Docs.*, VI, 514–15. He doubtless feared competition from the Irish house of Delap, with which Deane had established close contact during his weeks in Bordeaux; see Deane to the committee above, June 23, 1776.

have when I shall have the pleasure to appear before,[3] I shall be greaty obliged to you if you can send me this Commission. Pardon my importunity, but I am too much attached to your Nation not to be honourd with a Rank which I hope I shall deserve, and may be given to me with all Confidence.

Make yourself easy Sir I can not say more by this. We are all your Freinds and will give you prooffs of it. Four Persons which I send will soon be with you, two of which are of Distinction and of great Merit, who will deliver you my Letters themselves.[4] I could not intrust them to anyone else as they are of great advantage and importance to you. I have the Honour to be with Respect Sir Your most humble and Obedient Servant   P. PENET & CO.

Doctr. Franklin Philadelphia

PS. I have the honour to observe, fear nothing as to Warlike Amunition. I will furnish all you may want, in as large quantitys as you can require as well as Cannon. I labour with your Freind Mr. Dubourg to whoom I have not yet deliverd your Letter having left it with my Effects in holland where I landed. I shall send it to him soon.[5]

I beg Mr. Franklin would inform Congress that we shall have besides the above mentioned Amunition a quantity of Cloths, Linnen Blanketts &ca. so as to dispatch the ships as soon as they arrive, that you may have them with you before the Winter.

PENET & CO.

Endorsed: Pliarne Penet & Co. Nantes 3d August 1776.

3. Before whom we do not conjecture. The application succeeded: Washington received Penet's letter on Oct. 6, in the middle of the retreat from Manhattan, and recommended that the request be granted and a brevet commission issued; Congress agreed. Fitzpatrick, *Writings of Washington,* VI, 174, 216.

4. One of the men of distinction and merit was Boisbertrand, and the second was Couleaux, Penet's partner, who eventually delivered the letters; the other two were French officers. See the penultimate note on Dubourg to BF above, June 10, 1776.

5. The delay in producing these credentials from BF had been worrying Dubourg for months; see his letter just cited.

From Charles-Guillaume-Frédéric Dumas

AL: (letterbook draft⁶): Algemeen Rijksarchief, the Hague

Dear Sir   4e. Août 1776 S.D. No. 1

A Gentleman belonging to Jam[aica] *a particular friend of Dr. B.F., and very well known to him* (je me sers de ces propres termes et il m'a assuré que vous le reconnoîtrez à ce signalement sans avoir besoin que je vous declare son nom) m'a chargé de bouche de lui écrire le plutôt possible pour . . . communes.⁷

Pour meilleure intelligence de ce que vous venez de lire M. je crois devoir vous dire que ce Gentilhomme m'a apporté une Lettre de celui avec qui vous savez que je corresponds par votre ordre en Europe, laquelle Lettre débute ainsi: *Dear Sir, this will be delivered to you by —— a friend of Dr. F., of Liberty; and of America. He is a Philosopher, very well instructed on the Subject of America; and I trust will be both an agreable and useful acquaintance, while he remains near you.*⁸

---

6. Dumas' letterbook is a chaos of drafts. If he turned this one into an ALS and sent it, as seems probable from his note at the end, it presumably went with his long communication of June 30 to Aug. 10 to the committee of secret correspondence, discussed in the note on Deane to Morris above, June 23, and arrived after BF's departure.

7. Dumas refers in abbreviated form to a passage that he repeated in full in his letter to the committee, just cited: The gentleman has instructed him to write BF "pour l'assurer de bonne part de l'estime singuliere qu'a pour lui et ses amis ce qu'il y a de plus sensé en Angleterre; qu'ils ne doivent pas croire, *and that he prays him to let them know it,* que la voix du Parliament actuel soit la voix du peuple Anglois; qu'il existe et se renforce *a great body,* qui, à la vérité, n'est pas le plus fort, mais qui regarde la cause des Americains comme la sienne propre, leur salut et leur liberté comme la sienne, qui prefereroit de les voir indépendants plutôt que subjugués, et qui fera à la future rentrée du Parlement les plus grands efforts en leur faveur; que la base de ce parti est déjà de 40 pairs, et de 160 membres des Communes."

8. Arthur Lee to Dumas, July 6, 1776, Jared Sparks, ed., *The Diplomatic Correspondence of the American Revolution* . . . (12 vols., Boston, 1829–30), IX, 276, where the blank space Dumas left was filled by "Mr. Ellis." This was presumably in Lee's ALS, which we have been unable to locate; Sparks (*loc. cit.*) silently interpolated the name in printing the extract as repeated by Dumas in his letter to the committee. We have found no Ellis who fits Lee's description. John Ellis, the British naturalist (above, XIX, 317 n), might have been called a philosopher and was an old acquaintance of BF, but as far as we know had no connection with America or friendship for the American cause. The only Jamaican Ellis we have found who might qualify was also John and also a natural-

Ce Gentilhomme m'a avoué qu'il . . . l'un de l'autre.[1]

Je vous ai écrit M. deux Lettres, la première que je nomme A en date du 30e. Avril, et l'autre B du 14e. May dernier, par la voie que vous m'avez indiquée dans votre Lettre du 12e. Xbre. passé, dans lesquelles je vous rends compte de la maniere dont j'ai exécuté les autres commissions que vous m'avez données. Ayez la bonté de m'en accuser la réception, comme aussi.d'une troisieme C, que je prépare pour vous l'envoyer par premier vaisseau qui fera voile pour le même Port que A et B, et enfin de la présente que je cote S.D. No. 1.

Recevez, M., les assurances de mon profond respect pour vous, pour Mr. D pour Mr. J—— et pour tous vos dignes et excellents amis. Après cela permettez que je fasse pour un moment abstraction de celui que m'imposent vos qualités représentatives, pour m'elever avec toute la vénération que je vous dois personnellement au précieux titre d'ami dont vous m'honorez. La souri de la fable le mérita de la part du lion. J'espere de le mériter par le zele, la fidelité, la joie avec laquelle j'obéirai constamment à vos ordres; et je m'estimerai moi-même à proportion de l'utilité dont je pourrai vous être.

Vous fixez sur vous, Messieurs, les yeux de l'humanité. Vous lui

---

ist, and was an important figure on the island: Noel B. Livingston, *Sketch Pedigrees of Some of the Early Settlers in Jamaica* . . . (Jamaica, 1909), p. 43; John Nichols, *Literary Anecdotes of the Eighteenth Century* . . . (9 vols., London, 1812–16), III, 196–7. But we have no evidence that this Ellis knew BF, or was in Europe at the time, or was familiar with the colonies.

1. Dumas again refers in abbreviated form to a passage that he intended to include, this time from a letter to the abbé Desnoyers of July 28–29 in the same letterbook. "Il m'a avoue," the passage reads, "qu'il étoit l'un des plus actifs dans ce parti, assistant à leurs conférences, les connoissant tous par noms et personnes, et que ce parti seroit bien aise qu'il y eût en Hollande un homme de confiance (un Agent) de la part du Congrès. Ce que me disoit Mr. Lee, dans sa lettre, de cet homme, achevant de me rassurer sur son caractère, je lui decouvris enfin qu'il voyoit devant lui cet homme, muni de créances et d'ordres suffisants du Congrès, pour laisser passer par mes mains tous les bons offices que voudroient lui rendre ses amis, mais que ni lui ni qui que ce soit autre ne devoit s'attendre que je rendisse compte en détail à personne de mes opérations; qu'il devoit suffire à chacun de savoir que je soignerai fidelement les commissions qui me seront adressées, et que je garderai à chacun en particulier le plus profond secret. Là dessus je lui montrai ma créance. Il en fut satisfait; me demanda mes adresses, donna les siennes, promit de ses nouvelles quand il en sera temps. Et nous nous sommes séparés satisfaits l'un de l'autre."

549

donnez un spectacle bien interessant, unique dans l'histoire: on s'attend à quelque chose de plus grand de votre part qu'à des batailles, des conquêtes, des Alexandres, des Césars et des Frederics, à une constitution et Législation qui par sa sagesse couronne tous vos nobles efforts.

Puisse-je vivre pour en être témoin, et dire en mourant: le république qui veulent le bonheur des peuples. En attendant *Concordia* etc.[2]

P.S. Dans ce moment, M., je recois la Lettre dont vous m'avez honnoré en date du 2e. Mars. Le porteur[3] me promet le plaisir de le voir au commencement du mois prochain. Je l'attends avec un coeur plein de votre recommandation. Entre ce Porteur et Mr. Storey vous faites mention d'une Lettre que Vous m'avez écrite Monsieur, *by another Conveyance*; elle ne m'est pas encore parvenue.

A Mr. B. F. à P. sous couvert de Mr. C. Marchand au Port St. Nicolas à St. D. voyez la Lettre précédente à Δ.[4]

From Ray Greene

ALS: American Philosophical Society

Honord Sir   Warwick August 4th, 1776

It would be Ungrateful in me not to Acknoqledge the many Obligations I am Under to you and my Good Granmah Mecom by so good an opportunity as this. Pappa and Mammah had thoughts of taking me with them.[5] My mamma wrote you of my getting home well or I should Certainly have done it as I know you thought of me. We had a very Pleasent journey I saw some of

2. He intended to repeat the quotation from Sallust in his letter above, April 30, 1776.

3. Silas Deane; see above, p. 375.

4. Dumas' sign for Desnoyers. In the letter to the abbé quoted above Dumas identified the merchant as a M. Caton, the Americans' chief agent in St. Domingue and supposedly loyal to their cause.

5. Jane Mecom was "Granmah" because she had become a quasi-mother to his mother; see her letter to Caty above, Nov. 24. In writing BF on July 3, 1776, Caty had asked his advice on whether to bring Ray, then eleven, home for vacation. The parents had done so, but had themselves left for Philadelphia so that William Greene might collect $120,000 due Rhode Island for troops taken into the continental service: William G. Roelker, *Benjamin Franklin and Catharine Ray Greene* . . . (Philadelphia, 1948), p. 77.

my relations in new york very intimate acquaintances that did not know me. They said I was so much altered and by their Smiles Concluded they thought it was for the better. Most all my friends wishes me to go back again shall I Conclude they love me? Indeed Sir I love you Dearly Gratitude says I must but had rather stay at home. Pray give my Duty to Mr. and Mrs. Bache and Sincere love to Mr. temple and all the family who I tenderly Regard. Permit to write a few lines to my Dear Granmah in your letter[6] I'm your Dutiful and Oblidged Servant   RAY GREENE

Addressed: To / Doctr. Franklin / Philadelphia

From Elizabeth Franklin   ALS: American Philosophical Society

Since the outbreak of hostilities William Franklin's position had become increasingly precarious. "At present we only live, as it were, upon Sufferance," he had written three days after Bunker Hill, "nor is it in our power to mend our Situation."[7] He managed to hold onto the remnants of his authority longer than most colonial governors, but by the beginning of 1776 the remnants were tatters. In early January he sent a confidential report to Lord George Germain, the new Secretary of State for the American Colonies; the report was intercepted and brought to the local commander of militia, Lord Stirling, who concluded that it traduced the American cause. The Governor's house was surrounded by soldiers, and invaded in the middle of the night; his wife was so frightened that he feared for her life. She had no relatives of her own to turn to, and had little support from the Baches and none from her father-in-law. William, distressed as he was for her, stood his ground and held onto office until June. Then, in response to a resolution of Congress urging the establishment of new governments in all the colonies,[8] the New Jersey provincial congress moved to secure his person. On June 19 he was removed from his house, and on the 21st examined before the congress, which recommended that the Continental Congress send him out of the province as soon as possible. On the 26th orders came from Philadelphia to transfer him to Connecticut; he arrived there on July 4, and on giving his parole was lodged in a private house in Wallingford.

6. The brief note to Jane (APS) explains that he has not written because he had "errands," and was "once Smart to work when the Post Past." He hopes that she is pleased with what he is told is to be Jenny Flagg's match (*i.e.*, to Elihu Greene), and that it will be "Pretty Soon if you like it. He comes Pretty often."
7. To Gage, June 20, 1775, Gage Papers, Clements Library.
8. See the headnote above, June 14, 1776.

His besetting worry was for his wife. She suffered from asthma,[1] and she had broken down at his forced departure from their home. Sally Bache invited her to Philadelphia, but she refused to leave her house for fear of pillagers. She was, as she says here, weighed down with troubles. By early August, however, her situation improved somewhat: Temple came to stay with her, bringing a note and some badly needed money from his grandfather. This letter was her acknowledgment, and her plea to have her husband back. The plea fell on deaf ears. The elder Franklin, as far as we know, did nothing more for her or for his son.[2]

Honored Sir   Amboy Augst: 6: 1776.

Your Favor by my Son I received Safe, and should have done myself the Honor of answering it by the first Post after, but I have been of late much Indisposed. I am infinitely obliged to you for the 60: Dollars, and as soon as Mr: Pettit Settles his Account with me[3] I will punctually repay you.

My Troubles do Indeed lie heavy on my Mind, and tho' many People may Suffer Still more than I do, yet that does not lessen the Weight of mine, which are really more than so weak a Frame is able to Support. I will not Disstress you by enumerating all my Afflictions, but allow me Dear Sir, to mention, that it is greatly in your Power to Relieve them. Suppose that Mr. Franklin would Sign a Parole not dishonorable to himself, and Satisfactory to Governor Trumbull, why may he not be permitted to return into this Province and to his Family? Many of the Officers that have been taken during the War has had that Indulgence shewn them, and why should it be denied to him? His private Affairs are unsettled, his Family Disstressd and he is living very uncomfortably, and at a great expence, which he can very illy afford at present. Consider my Dear and Honored Sir, that I am now pleading the Cause of your Son, and my Beloved Husband. If I have Said, or

1. Or so we assume because she had recently ordered a bottle of "Asthmatic Elixir": to WTF, July 29, 1776, APS. She died a year later.
2. Claude-Anne Lopez and Eugenia W. Herbert, *The Private Franklin: the Man and His Family* (New York, [1975]), pp. 206–12; William H. Mariboe, "The Life of William Franklin . . . " (doctoral dissertation, University of Pa., 1962), pp. 447–52, 459–71.
3. For Lieut. Col. Charles Pettit (1736–1806), who had been WF's aide since 1771 and was now transferring his allegiance to the new state government, see the *DAB*.

done anything wrong I beg to be forgiven. I am with great Respect Honored Sir Your Dutifull and affectionate Daughter

ELIZA. FRANKLIN

Addressed: To / Doctor Franklin / Philadelphia[4]

The Committee of Secret Correspondence to Silas Deane

LS: Maine Historical Society; letterbook copy: National Archives

Dear Sir   Philadelphia August 7th 1776

The above is a Copy of our last, which went by the Dispatch Captain Parker.[5]

The Congress have since taken into consideration the heads of a Treaty to be proposed to France, but as they are not yet concluded upon, we cannot say more of them per this conveyance.[6]

You will see by the Newspapers which accompany this, that the expedition against South Carolina is foiled by the gallant resistance made there. The Enemy, much diminished by Sickness, it is thought will attempt nothing farther in those parts. The people of North Carolina, who at first had taken up their Bridges, and broken the Roads, to prevent the Enemys penetrating their Country; have since, being ready to receive him, repaired the Roads and Bridges, and wish him to attempt making use of them.[7]

---

4. On the verso beside the address is a jotting by BF: "Taxing not all / Constitutions altered." We do not venture to guess why, as late as this, he was still concerned with those two old bones of contention.

5. The committee's letter above of July 8, 1776, which was thrown overboard before the *Dispatch* was captured. The present letter went, we believe, by the other *Dispatch*, Capt. Cleveland, for whom see the note on the committee to Bradford above, July 30, 1776. Cleveland left Beverly, Mass., on or about Sept. 22: *Naval Docs.*, VI, 953. Deane received the letter, with its enclosed copy of the Declaration of Independence, on Nov. 17, and complained that the ship carrying it had crossed in only thirty-eight days from Salem (adjacent to Beverly): *Deane Papers*, I, 371–2. We take this to mean that she arrived by early November, as Cleveland's ship might well have done, and that the letter was delayed in France.

6. See the editorial note on the plan of treaties above, under June 12, 1776.

7. For the attack on Charleston see the note on Jones to BF above, July 11, 1776. The British expedition, as mentioned there, went originally to North Carolina to aid the Loyalists; they planned a rendezvous on the coast, and the

Gen: Howe is posted now on Staten Island near New York, with the Troops he carried to Halifax when he was driven out of Boston. Lord Howe is also arrived there with some reinforcements, and more are expected, as the great push seems intended to be made in that Province. Gen. Washington's Army is in possession of the Town, about which many entrenchments are thrown up, so as to give an opportunity of disputing the possession with G: Howe; if he should attempt it, and of making it cost him something; but it is not so regularly fortified as to Stand a Siege. We have also a flying Camp in the Jerseys, to harrass the Enemy if he should attempt to penetrate thro' that Province to Philada.

In the different Colonies we have now near 80,000 men in the pay of the Congress. The Declaration of Independence meets with universal approbation, and the people every where seem more animated by it in defence of their Country. Most of our Frigates are Launched in the different Provinces, and are fitting for Sea with all the expedition in our power. They are fine ships, and will be capable of good service. Our small Privateers and Continental arm'd Vessells have already had great success as the papers will shew you; and by abstaining from Trade ourselves while we distress that of our enemys, we expect to make their men of war weary of their unprofitable and hopeless Cruisses, and their Merchants Sick of a Contest in which so much is risk'd and nothing gained. The forming a Navy is a very capital object with us, and the Marine Committee is ordered to bring in a plan for increasing it very considerably.[8] The Armed Boats for the defence of our

---

bridges were destroyed to impede their march rather than keep the British from moving inland. Hugh F. Rankin, *The North Carolina Continentals* (Chapel Hill, N.C., [1971]), pp. 40–3.

8. Congress, the previous December, had ordered thirteen frigates built. They were launched between May and November, 1776, but outfitting and arming them involved great delay; none of them was in service before 1777, and some never were. *JCC*, III, 425–6; Nathan Miller, *Sea of Glory: the Continental Navy Fights for Independence, 1775–1783* (New York, [1974]), pp. 203–10; William M. Fowler, Jr., *Rebels under Sail: the American Navy during the Revolution* (New York, [1976]), pp. 216–46. The instruction to the marine committee was not actually issued until Aug. 23, and its report was submitted in November; it called for the construction of three ships of the line, three more frigates, and two smaller craft. *JCC*, V, 700; VI, 970.

Rivers and Bays grow more and more in repute. They venture to attack large men of war, and are very troublesome to them. The papers will give you Several instances of their success.

We hope that by this time you are at Paris, and that Mr. Morris has joined you, whom we recommend to you warmly, and desire you may mutually co-operate in the public service.[9] With great esteem we are Dear sir Your very humble Servants

B FRANKLIN
BENJA HARRISON
ROBT MORRIS

Notation: Letter from Secret Committe August 7th. 1776.

John Dickinson to the Pennsylvania Convention[1]

ALS: National Archives

Sir,   Elizabeth Town Augt. 7th, 1776

I have this Moment recd. Information, that Adam Shetsline and Stophel Young two Privates of Capt. Goodwin's Company, have left the Camp without Leave, and are gone Homeward. One of them lives on Mr. Willing's Place, the other on Mr. York's, both in Moyamensing.[2] If some Measures are not immediately taken to discourage such Behaviour, it will be impossible to keep

9. For Thomas Morris see the note on Penet to BF above, Aug. 3, 1776. The young man, as subsequent volumes will make clear, was no boon to the public service.

1. Dickinson's brigade of Pennsylvania associators, attached to Gen. Mercer, was in New Jersey until the flying camp was formed; see the headnote on the convention's circular letter above, July 19, 1776. We have been unable to trace the two young men who were the subject of his letter, but desertion was a major problem when the flying camp was delayed. Dickinson had written the convention on Aug. 6 about unrest among his troops, and wrote again soon afterward about desertions. On the 23rd the associators were relieved from duty and returned home, and a month later Dickinson resigned. Force, 5 *Amer. Arch.*, II, 18, 20; Joseph M. Waterman, *With Sword and Lancet: the Life of General Hugh Mercer* . . . (Richmond, Va., [1941]), pp. 116–17, 120–1; Charles J. Stillé, *The Life and Times of John Dickinson* . . . (Philadelphia, 1891), p. 209.

2. Part of Philadelphia County.

the Troops here. I am, with great Esteem, sir, your very humble servant JOHN DICKINSON

Addressed: On public Service / To / Benjamin Franklin Esquire / President of the Convention / in / Philadelphia.

Endorsed: Augt. 7th. 1776 Letter from Col. Dickinson 2 Deserters.

Notation: Augt. 12th. 1776 read & referred to the Council of Safety.

From William Dunlap[3]   ALS: American Philosophical Society

Honord Sir   King and Queen: Aug: 10th: 1776.

Having lately labour'd under a most dangerous and severe Fit of Sickness, and being now but just able to hold my Pen, it will apologize for my Brevety and Imperfection of Expression. I have just received a Letter from my poor Son Ben, couch'd in Terms the most distressing to me: He tells me the worthy Dr. Witherspoon has apprized him, That the Exigencies of the Times, had intirely put it out of the Power of the truly benevolent Gentleman in England, to whom he owd his Education, from contributing any Thing further on that Head, and he must now shift for himself.[4] To your Humanity I can only appeal on this Occasion; whether you can find in your Heart to carry on the good Work begun by taking my poor Boy under your Patronage: He may yet live to be an Ornament by your means to his Country and a Blessing to his Friends. Or must, Oh Sir must his ardent Thirst for Knowledge be entirely quash'd, and must the worthy Youth have Recourse to the Plough or the Spade for a wretched Subsistance!

The Papers will inform you, I am married to a Woman of For-

3. The rector of Stratton Major, Va., who had married DF's niece: above, XV, 24 n.

4. Benjamin as a young man had been organist at his father's church (above, XIX, 38) and had attended the grammar school at Princeton; shortly thereafter he matriculated in the College of New Jersey, supported by the anonymous—and to us unknown—English benefactor, whose financial support came through President Witherspoon. When the College closed in the autumn of 1776, Benjamin is said to have enlisted and died in the service. We are indebted for this information to the editors of the forthcoming volume of *Princetonians . . . a Biographical Dictionary.*

tune.⁵ The Truth is, the Lady in Question is possess'd of upwards of £2000 in Land, Negroes, Stock, &c. but not a Farthing Cash: she never had a Child. Knowing I was in Debt, she secur'd every Farthing of the Income of her Estate for the Maintenance of herself and the Family. At her Death, *one Half* of the Estate is to go to my Children as I may Will: the other Half is at her own Disposal. Thus tho' my poor Ben: will one Day be entitled to Something, at present I cannot command a single Farthing to help him with. My unhappy Son Frank, engag'd some Months ago in the Marines, in which Service he died, having behav'd very well.⁶ I have now three Daughters besides my Ben. who are all well, and I hope will be a Blessing. Leaving the Event of this Application to you and a merciful God, I remain, Honor'd Sir, your most Obedient Humble Servant   W. DUNLAP

P.S. While Ben: was under the Patronage of his Unknown Benifactor, he was oblig'd to bend his Profession to Divinity; but I know Physick woud be most agreeable to him and me.

Endorsed: Letters of small Import.

The Pennsylvania Convention: Order to Pay George Ross and Others⁷   ALS: Rosenbach Foundation

⟨August 12, 1776: A note to the council of safety to pay George Ross, Timothy Matlack, and Henry Slagle £10,000 in the public service of the state of Pennsylvania, signed by Franklin as president of the convention, attested by John Morris, Jr., as secretary, and addressed to Jno. M. Nesbitt.⁸ Below Franklin's signature is

5. A few weeks before he wrote, Dunlap had married a widow, Mrs. Johanna Reeve: *ibid.* We know no more about her; neither have we any inkling, except what may be implied in BF's endorsement, about his response to Dunlap's request.

6. Francis Franklin Dunlap had been born in 1755: *ibid.* We have found no record of his service.

7. Pursuant to an order of the convention, of the same day, for setting up the flying camp in New Jersey; Ross, Matlack, and Slagle had been appointed commissioners for that purpose. Force, 5 *Amer. Arch.*, II, 20.

8. For Timothy Matlack and John Nesbitt, treasurer of the council of safety, see the *DAB*, and for Henry Slagle, a col. of associators, William H. Egle, "The Constitutional Convention of 1776," *PMHB*, IV (1880), 361–2.

an order to pay, dated August 13 and signed by Thomas Wharton, Jr., president of the council of safety. On the verso is a receipt, signed by Slagle, that he has received the full sum from Nesbitt.)

From the Chevalier de Kermorvan

ALS: American Philosophical Society

Monsieur [August 12?,[9] 1776.]

J'ai reçû l'honneur de votre Lettre. J'ai lû avec le plus grand plaisir votre judicieuse dissertation sur mon plan de défense.[1] J'ai parfaitement senti les raisons qui feront qu'on ne l'executera que quand l'ennemi seroit descendu. Vos peuples ne veulent pas travailler et ne voyent de danger que quand l'ennemi est sur eux. Le travail d'un camp rétranché n'est rien c'est l'affaire d'un jour pour la troupe qui est dans ce camp c'est seulement une elevation de terre plus ou moins haute plus ou moins epaisse selon le terrein; d'ailleurs je n'ai jamais entendu rétrancher 1500 milles d'etenduë de coste. Ce travail seroit aussi inutile ici que la grande muraille de la chine qui n'a pas préservé cet empire d'estre conquis par les tartares. Toutes les fois qu'on veut garder un pays, une province il n'y a de moyens que d'y mettre dans les endroits plats vuides de bois et d'autres défenses, un camp rétranché, et d'occuper les hauteurs par de bonne artillerie, et les bois par de l'infanterie, amboy est un point tout dècouvert de bois, qui a deux mille de circonference. S'il est vrai que dans toute l'amerique le pays soit couvert de bois, vous avez beaucoup moins a craindre. Mais dans la circonstance présente si l'on ne venoit pas a bout d'empescher l'ennemi de descendre au centre des colonies nous perdrions toute notre réputation dans l'europe qui a les yeux ouverts sur nous; ainsi le point interessant est de rapprocher les camps de la coste parcequ'ils sont trop eloignés; alors si par malheur l'ennemi descendoit vos peuples le voyant se rétrancher en arrivant ne se feront plus prier pour travailler, et quand ils auront de la bonne volonté vous conviendrez, Monsieur, que cela est possible.

9. We accept the date tentatively assigned by Lyman Butterfield in "Franklin, Rush, and Kermorvan," APS *Library Bulletin*, 1946, p. 40.
1. Kermorvan's plan was in his letter above, July 26, 1776; BF's reply has disappeared.

Pour ce qui est des forts aux embouchures des rivieres, comme vous n'avez point de gros canons de 24, 36, et 48, il est presque inutile de construire autre chose que de simples batteries pour empescher les descentes des troupes et le passage des batteaux, et la meilleure défense des rivieres dont l'embouchure est large sera d'y avoir des galleres armées de gros canons ou des batteaux armés; car des boulets de 4, six, huit, comme nous avons ici ne font pas d'effet sur un vaisseau et ne l'empescheront pas un moment de passer. Il est egalement nècessaire de couler bas au milieu des passages quelque môles enchainés, a fleur d'eau mais cela demendera a estre fait cet hyver car il est trop tard aujourdhuy. Je n'aurois jamais imaginé que, s'il est vrai que vous fondez du canon comme tout le monde le dit, vous n'en fondiez pas les deux tiers de gros calibre. On ne fait pas la guerre avec avantage sans le gros canon. Ainsi sur une riviere ou l'on veut empescher des citadelles flottantes comme des vaisseaux de passer il faut avoir dans les endroits etroits seulement, comme a billings-port des batteries de gros canon, alors il n'y a point de vaisseau de ligne qui ose passer sous un feu aussi prochain et qui le préviendra [*interlined*: battera] un mille avant qu'il soit sous le canon du fort. Nous eprouvons en europe que les vaisseaux n'osent passer sous le feu de St. malo et de brest. Mais ces avantages sont trop chers pour une république naissante, de simples batteries pour empescher les descentes des batteaux; des galleres ou batteaus armés, des masses coulées bas dans les passes des rivieres voilà tout ce qu'il vous faut comme vous l'avez pensé très judicieusement.

Il n'est pas aussi aisé dans une république d'executer des grandes choses tout de suite parceque le consentement de tout le monde n'est pas aisé a réunir et tous les hommes ne pensent pas egalement bien en faveur de la bonne cause; je vois qu'ils voudroient presque tous avoir la liberté sans l'acquerir. J'etois plus content de leur conduite a philadelphie qu'ici, vos bourgeois donnent un exemple de mauvaise volonté trés nuisible a notre cause. En verité je crois que les hommes sont nés pour estre esclaves, pour la plupart, encore ne meritent ils pas qu'on se donne la peine de veiller sur leurs interrests et de les commander. J'ai fait une batterie qui est trés bien placée, les canons batteront et défenderont bien la riviere, les feux sont bien dirigés, mais vos gens l'ont si mal faite contre ma volontè que je suis mortifié de l'avoir entreprise. Dès le premier jour ils se sont revoltés et m'ont fait dire que ma façon de leur faire placer le gazon et les fascines n'etoit pas de leur goust, et qu'ils ne vouloient faire que comme ils avoient toujours fait, qu'ils ne vouloient pas d'ailleurs travailler inutilement, que l'ennemi ne viendroit pas dans la riviere et qu'enfin ils n'etoient pas payés pour travailler. Tous ces propos et leur mécontentement m'anéantit. Je leur fis dire de faire comme ils voudroient; j'ai eté malgré cela deux fois par jour les voir travailler et les diriger dans la forme de l'ouvrage, ils ont mis le gazon qui a une apparence trés malpropre et qui ne peut pas se soutenir dans un temps aussi sec que l'été. Jugez, Monsieur, de ma position, faire un ouvrage mal executé, avoir la fievre continuelle, faire quatre mille a pieds tous les jours dans un etat de foiblesse, coucher sur la paille, avoir très peu de considération dans un pays où le genie est inutile et son métier est celuy d'un masson ou regardé comme tel, ne pouvoir rien dire pour le bien du service et pour epargner le sang des américains, parce que je crains de déplaire. J'ai pris le parti de faire dire le plus pressé d'executer par m. du bois qui parle volontiers.[2] Convenez, Monsieur, qu'il faut estre nè pour la cause generale de l'humanité, et n'avoir d'autre désir que de voir cette cause une fois triompher, pour souffrir patiemment tous ces désagrémens. Mais aussi je mourrois content, si votre independance etablie sous de bonnes loix, etoit en sureté et faisoit un exemple pour le reste du monde.

J'ai appris que m: de woëdké etoit mort au canada et n'avoit laissé que peu de regrets, j'en suis fâché sincerement. J'avois une lettre de recommandation pour luy, de m: du bourg qui nous invitoit a estre amis et nous lier pour la cause commune, voilà tous nos liens rompus. Si vous vouliez, Monsieur, me faire hériter de son grade le droit que j'aurois de participer aux conseils de guerre me donneroit plus d'influence et plus de droit a conseiller de

2. Col. Lewis Du Bois or Dubois, it has been suggested, was a descendant of the Huguenot immigrants who had long been settled at New Paltz, N.Y.: Lasseray, *Les Français*, pp. 188–9. He had served in Canada as a major and been recommended for promotion, after BF left Montreal, by the other commissioners. Congress named him to command a new regiment being raised in New York, the officers of which were to be veterans of the Canadian campaign; the N.Y. convention protested the arrangement, and much bickering ensued. Where Dubois and Kermorvan were together is not clear; in early August the Colonel was at Poughkeepsie. Force, 5 *Amer. Arch.*, I, 201, 393, 772; *JCC*, V, 440, 471–2, 479.

meilleures dispositions, sans avoir plus de commandement que je ne désire point, mais plus d'aisance qui m'est nécessaire. Je commence a parler tant soit peu l'anglois, a me faire entendre, je le lis parfaitement. Je vous suis, Monsieur, parfaitement et sincerement rèconnoissant de vos avis judicieux et de l'interrest que vous me marquez prendre a ma réputation. Je ne connoissois pas aussi bien l'esprit du peuple américain que je le connois ici. Ce peuple est le mesme partout inconstant et volage, de plus on devroit avoir des hommes d'esprit en qui ce peuple auroit quelque confiance qui leur parlât de tems en temps de leur devoir pour leur patrie et de la cause commune. Leurs generaux qu'ils ont elûs devroient aller les voir dans leurs tentes les exciter; les blessés devroient estre visités et soignés presque par les premiers officiers de l'armée, voilà comme se soutient l'ardeur patriotique qu'il est nècessaire d'infuser aux ames basses et populaires.

Dans un pays où il y a autant d'aisance il vous sera toujours difficile d'avoir des armées soudoyées que vous puissiez commander, il vaut mieux pour vous, pour un etat libre avoir une milice agricole.

Vous sçavez mieux que moy, Monsieur, qu'il est dangereux d'avoir des troupes dans son sein mesme a sa solde, que c'est l'origine de la corruption des états et des meurs du peuple, qu'un etat libre ne doit avoir qu'une bonne milice agricole, que tout le monde travaille la terre et fasse l'exercice, et qu'il n'y ait d'exempts que ceux qui ont des enfans qui les remplacent dans leur vieillesse.

Je partage bien sincerement le plaisir de la nouvelle que vous avez reçuë de france si elle est vraie je n'en suis pas surpris.[3] Mais a moins que vous n'ayez eû cette nouvelle de quelqu'un qui tienne cette permission secrettement du ministre, comme elle peut avoir ete donnée dans les ports de france secrettement de la part du ministre, car cette campagne n'est pas encore assez avancée, et nous n'avons pas encore eu assez d'avantages décisifs sur l'ennemi pour que la france se montre ouvertement opposée a la cour de Londres. La france ne pourroit pas mieux faire. Il y a long temps que m: de choiseul le conseille mais nous n'avons dans le ministere que de vieux procureurs qui ne sçavent faire la guerre qu'aux sujets

---

3. This was undoubtedly the report, which BF mentioned in his letters to Gates and Wayne below, Aug. 28, that the French government would turn a blind eye on the export of arms and ammunition.

de l'etat avec du papier timbré qui leur demende leur fortune, mais j'augure bien de l'interrest qu'offre votre commerce. Je suis avec le plus parfait respect, Monsieur Votre trés humble et trés obeissant serviteur LE CHEVALIER DE KERMORVAN

Je vous prie d'engager le congrés [à] ordonner au genéral de m'envoyer dans les lieux où l'on croit que l'ennemi attaquera. Je vais demender a m: mercer {d'aller?} a new york. Je ne sçais s'il le voudra.

From Mehetable Newland[4]

ALS: American Philosophical Society

Sir   Stafford Monmouth County Augst the 12th 76
   As Mr. Newland has the honour of being known to you, I have taken the liberty of asking the favour, whether you have heard, any thing of him, sence he Embark from New York for Quebec. From the deferent reports of the Success of our Troops, at that place, I am under the greatest uneasiness for his Welfare. Sir from the thousand Amiable qualities of your Character I flatter my self youl Pardon this Intrusion. I am Sir with the greatest Esteem Your Most Humble Servant   MEHETABLE NEWLAND

Addressed: To / The Honourable / Doct. Benjamin Franklen / at / Philadelphia

Proposal for the Great Seal of the United States

AD: Library of Congress

On July 4, 1776, Franklin, John Adams, and Jefferson were named as a committee to suggest a seal. Each man proposed designs, and one of Jefferson's closely resembled Franklin's. In addition the painter Pierre Du Simitière, who had been called in as a consultant, produced a version of his own. A letter from John Adams of August 14 described the various

4. All we know about her is in this note. For her missing husband see the annotation of his letter above, Feb. 5, 1776.

Robert Erskine's Chevaux-de-Frise

proposals;[5] hence Franklin's had been submitted by that time. On the 20th the committee brought in its report; one side of the seal, with the motto *E Pluribus Unum*,[6] was substantially what Du Simitière had suggested, and the other what Franklin and Jefferson had agreed upon. Congress tabled the report, and not until 1782 was the present seal adopted.[7] All that it retained of the first committee's handiwork was the Latin motto.

[Before August 14, 1776]
Moses standing on the Shore, and extending his Hand over the Sea, thereby causing the same to overwhelm Pharoah who is sitting in an open Chariot, a Crown on his Head and a Sword in his hand. Rays from a Pillar of Fire in the Clouds reaching to Moses, to express that he acts by Command of the Deity.
Motto, *Rebellion to Tyrants Is Obedience to God.*[8]

From Robert Erskine[9]

ALS: American Philosophical Society; AL (draft[1]), Ringwood Manor Museum, Ringwood State Park, Ringwood, N.J.

Dear sir   Newark August 16th. 1776.
I beg leave to enclose you a drawing of a new Contrivance for stopping Channels and Rivers, which I call Marine Chevaux de Frise; a model of which was exhibited at Headquarters in New York, the 20th of last month.

5. Butterfield, *Adams Correspondence*, II, 96–7. For Du Simitière see Richard S. Patterson and Richardson Dougall, *The Eagle and the Shield: a History of the Great Seal of the United States* (Washington, D.C. 1976), pp. 10–13.
6. The motto was taken from the *Gent. Mag.*: *ibid.*, pp. 22–4.
7. Boyd, *Jefferson Papers*, I, 494–7.
8. See Bradshaw's Epitaph above, under Dec. 14.
9. Erskine (1735–80) was a Scot who moved to London as an engineer and inventor. In 1771 he was elected to the Royal Society with BF's recommendation (above, VIII, 359), and the same year emigrated to Bergen Co., N.J., where he was an ironmaster; in 1775 he organized a militia company from his employees and became its captain. In 1777 he was surveyor general and cartographer of the continental army and produced a series of maps for Washington. *DAB*. BF's answer to this letter is below, Oct. 16.
1. Dated Aug. 15.

After the ships passed the Batteries with such facility, I considered with regret, that the Channel was not obstructed; and since the exegence required something both speedily executed and effectual, the Enclosed Construction occurred, which I have reason to beleive is now putting in practice.[2]

In addition to what is set forth on the Drawing, I beg leave to observe, that it may be described as a Tetrahedron with four horned Corners; having three Horns to each Corner; that the Consequence of a Ships running against it, must either be that she will stake upon it, or overset it, in which case the other horns will rise and take her in the bottom, and either overset her, go through her; or else she must break it with her weight; but here it is to be Considered, what force it will require to break a Beam 12 or 15 Inches square, standing only ⅓d from the perpendicular; which seems too great for any ship to apply, without injuring her so effectually, as to render her unfit for further service. Such Chevaux dropt here and there in Anchoring grounds and Harbours, would render them very unsafe. Supposing the Channel to be obstructed Seven fathoms deep, if it is made of Beams 32 feet long, its perpendicular height would be near 28 feet; the Horns would be within 14 feet of the surface, Consequently obstruct any vessel which drew more than that depth of water. Two Chevaux of these dimensions would stop 10 Fathoms, as the Horns of the one would be within 20 feet of those of the other. 20 would stop an hundred Fathoms, and require only 120 pieces of Timber. As the Current has full liberty to flow under, they Cannot injure Channels or sensibly obstruct the tide: indeed they need not be put in till an alarm, for if they are ready prepared, a number of them may be rigged up and thrown into a Channel in a few hours—but I need not enlarge or add a number of Circumstances which will naturally occur to any one Conversant in Mechanics.

I shall think my self happy if any endeavours of mine tend to serve the Cause of Freedom, Humanity and the States of America

2. In early July Washington had ordered the channel obstructed, but nothing effective had been achieved by the 12th, when H.M.S. *Phoenix* and *Rose* and three tenders sailed up the Hudson and anchored in the Tappan Zee, without receiving any damage worth mention from the shore batteries. Fitzpatrick, *Writings of Washington*, V, 129; *Naval Docs.*, V, 511, 1040.

and am Dear Sir with the Greatest respect Your most Obedient
humble servant   ROBT ERSKINE

Honble. Dr. Benjamin Franklin

Addressed: To / The Honble. / Dr. Benjamin Franklin / Philadelphia

From Lord Howe   Copy: Library of Congress

Eagle off Staten Island Augt. the 16: 1776.
I am sorry my worthy friend, that it is only on the assurances you
give me of my having still preserved a place in your esteem, that
I can now found a pretension to trouble you with a reply to your
favour of the 21st. past.[3]

I can have no difficulty to acknowledge that the powers I am
invested with, were never calculated to negociate a reunion with
America, under any other description than as subject to the crown
of Great Britain. But I do esteem those powers competent, not
only to confer and negotiate with any gentlemen of influence in
the Colonies upon the terms, but also to effect a lasting peace and
reunion between the two countries; were the temper of the Colonies such as professed in the last petition of the Congress to the
King.[4] America would have judged in the discussion how far the
means were adequate to the end; both for engaging her confidence
and proving our integrity. Nor did I think it necessary to say more
in my public declaration; not conceiving it could be understood
to refer to peace, on any other conditions but those of mutual
interest to both countries, which could alone render it permanent.

But as I perceive from the tenor of your letter, how little I am
to reckon upon the advantage of your assistance for restoring that
permanent union which has long been the object of my endeavours, and which I flattered myself when I left England would be
in the compass of my power; I will only add, that as the dishonour
to which you deem me exposed by my military situation in this

3. The letter above of July 20, 1776. This reply was sent ashore on the 17th
under a flag of truce and forwarded by Washington with his note to BF below,
Aug. 18.
4. The Olive Branch Petition; see the editorial note above, July 8, 1775.

country, has effected no change in your sentiments of personal regard towards me; so shall no difference in political points alter my desire of proving how much I am your sincere and obedient humble Servant HOWE

To Dr. Franklin

From William Temple Franklin

ALS: American Philosophical Society

Honored Sir Philada[5] Augst. 17th. 1776

It being rather late when I got to Mr. Duffields and the Road from there to Mr. Galloways being very bad; by the kind invitation of Mr. and Mrs. Duffield I staid that Night and waited on Mr. Galloway in the Morning, and proceeded on my way to this place where I arrived yesterday afternoon with out any accident. Let Mrs. Bache know that her Son William has been very well, except now and then the *Musick in his Ear*, but by Mrs. Duffields good nurseing is now much better.[6]

If it is not too much Trouble let Aunt Mecome know, that according to her desire I waited on Mrs. Van Voredice, who being indisposed I had not the pleasure of seeing, but I saw her Son, who told me that last they heard of Mrs. Turner and her husband, was, that they were both in London and that he was to have a Commission in the Guards.[7]

5. A slip of the pen: he was writing from Perth Amboy, where BF addressed his answer below, Aug. 27. WTF had visited Elizabeth Franklin little more than a fortnight earlier (see her letter to BF of Aug. 6 above), and then for some reason returned to Philadelphia. This second visit was presumably much longer, for BF was still writing him at Perth Amboy as late as Sept. 19.

6. BF had stayed with the Duffields in June to recuperate; see his letter to Rush above, June 26, 1776. They were old family friends, and we assume were again helping in an emergency, by taking William while his baby sister, Sarah, was desperately ill; she died on the day this letter was written.

7. Mrs. "Voredice" was Maria or Mary Ouke Van Vorhies, the sister of Catherine Ouke Mecom, and lived in New Brunswick: *N.J. Arch.*, XXII, 417; XXIX, 410. After John Mecom's death his widow had married Thomas Turner, a British officer who had been wounded at Lexington and Bunker Hill; above, I, lxii; XXI, 348 n; Jane Mecom to BF, July 14, 1775.

Mrs. Franklin desires her duty to you and aunt Mecome and Love to the Family, with that of Honored Sir your ever dutiful Grandson   W T FRANKLIN

Addressed: To / Dr. / Franklin / Philada / per Post

From John Kearsley Read[8]   ALS: American Philosophical Society

Honored Uncle   Wms. Burgh 18: Augt 76
    A series of years hath pass'd since you were troubled with a letter from me. My neglect of writing to you has been from a supposition that (hitherto) your engagements could not have allowed you time to attend to the less important concerns of a branch of the family so farr remote from you, as I have ever been. I hope however, should you find leisure, you will still remember a relation, who hath ever retained an affection for you and your family, and who would esteem it one of the greatest satisfactions of his life to *sometimes* hear from you.
    There is a Gentleman of Distinguished family and fortune, who commands the first Regiment now on its march from Virginia to New York (Colo. Read) he will I imagine make some stay in Phila. he will be accompanied by Dr. Skinner a gentleman of considerable Eminence in his profession.[9] I need only say, I should be exceedingly happy would take notice of those Gentlemen. Your attachment to this country, they are well apprized off, and a first acquaintance will convince you they merit your notice. I hope my Dear Uncle I do not intrude in the freedom I now take, and nothing but the confidence I have in your good nature, and your regard for those Gentlemen whose abilities intitle them to respect promps me to this freedom. I wish you great deal of happiness in

---

8. The son of DF's brother John: above, X, 69 n.
9. Isaac Read (1740–77) had been made colonel of the regiment a few days before, when it left Williamsburg to join Washington's army at New York. E. M. Sanchez-Saavedra, *A Guide to Virginia Military Organizations in the American Revolution* . . . ([Richmond, Va.,]1978), pp. 29–30; *Va. Hist. Mag.*, XX (1912), 280. Dr. Alexander Skinner (died 1788) was the regimental surgeon: *ibid.*, XIII (1906), 426; Heitman, *Register of Officers*, p. 368.

---

this world and I am with great truth Honored Uncle Your dutifull and affectionate Nephew   J. K. READ

Should you write please direct my letter to be left in the P. Office in Wm. Burgh to be left till calld for.

Addressed: Doctr. Benjn. Franklin / Philada.

From George Ross[1]   ALS: American Philosophical Society

Dear Sir   New York 18th. Augt: 1776

   The Phenix and Rose have Just now passed our Batterys and I fear without much damage. I was in one of the Batterys during the whole time they were within gun shot. The visit they had two nights agoe from our fire ships made them sick of their Station and they have now Joind the fleet at the Narrows.[2] Every countenance here is chearfull and if our Enemies dare attack they will undoubtedly procure themselves a severe drubbing. My complyments to friends. I am Sir Your very Humble Servant GEO: ROSS

Addressed: For / The Honble Docr: Benjn: Franklin / Philada:

From George Washington   ALS: American Philosophical Society

Sir,   New York Augt. 18th. 1776.

   I have been honourd with your favour of the 16th., and the several Inclosures contained therein, which are now return'd with my thanks for the oppertunity of perusing them. I also Inclose you a Letter from Lord Howe, sent out (with others) by a Flag in the Afternoon of yesterday. With it comes a Letter for Lieutt. Barrington, who if not among those who broke their Parole, and

---

1. On Aug. 10 the Pa. convention had ordered the colonels of associators, Ross among them, to join the N.J. flying camp with their men. Force, 5 *Amer. Arch.*, II, 19. Ross was also one of the commissioners for setting up the camp; see the convention's order to him above, Aug. 12.

2. The two ships were detached on the 15th to reconnoitre up the river, and fireships attacked them unsuccessfully on the night of the 16th. On the 18th they returned under heavy fire but were virtually undamaged. *Naval Docs.*, VI, 206–8, 225–7.

went of for Canada, is in York, Pensylvania.[3] With very great esteem and respect, I have the honour to be Sir Your Most Obedient Humble Servant   Go. WASHINGTON

The Honble. Benja. Franklin Esqr.

From James Bowdoin   ALS (draft): American Philosophical Society

Dear Sir   Boston Augst. 19th. 1776

I recd. per Mr. Gerry a Packet from you containing a Russian Book on Comets, and Vattel's Droit des Gens.

The former agreable to your desire I have sent to Mr. Oliver at Salem together with your Billet. The latter when I have looked over it I shall send to the President of Harvard College as a Present to the Library from you.[4] Dr. Cooper shewed me your letter to Lord Howe and his Lordships to you which occasioned it. It gave me great pleasure, as it has all that have seen it. His Lordship's sensibility must be touched with some parts of it, unless Court-Manners and Court-Politics have benumbed it. Some persons think they see a Treaty of Commerce growing out of this Correspondence with Lord Howe, and that he will take hold of the opportunity you give him of treating with Congress on that head. But from the Act of Parliament authorizing the King to appoint

3. Howe's letter to BF is above, Aug. 16, 1776. Lieut. William Barrington, of the 7th foot, had not gone to Canada, and was not at York but at Lancaster. When a group of his fellow officers had taken off northward the previous June from Lebanon, Pa., Barrington had stayed behind. He was now asking, after his release from the Lancaster jail, to have his baggage back and to be allowed parole, which on Aug. 24 the Pa. council of safety gave him. Force, 5 *Amer. Arch.*, I, 411–12, 761, 1325; see also Worthington C. Ford, *British Officers Serving in the American Revolution* . . . (Brooklyn, 1897), p. 24.

4. For Elbridge Gerry, who had taken his seat in February as a Mass. delegate to Congress, see the *DAB*. The "Russian" book on comets was, we assume, that by a Swedish scientist, Anders Johann Lexell, *Recherches et calculs sur la vraie orbite elliptique de la comète de l'an. 1769 et son tems périodique, executées sous la direction de Mr. Leonhard Euler* . . . (St. Petersburg, 1770). BF sent it with his "billet," a covering note that has disappeared, to Andrew Oliver, Jr. (1731–99), the son of the late Lieut. Gov., who had published in 1772 the earliest American work on comets: *DAB*; *Sibley's Harvard Graduates*, XII, 455–61. Vattel's work was the edition by Dumas that he had sent to BF and discussed in his letters above, May 17, June 30, 1775; see also BF's acknowledgement, Dec. 9.

Commissioners and from Lord Howe's circular Letter and Declaration grounded upon it, it seems very unlikely:[5] especially as Ministry appear very confident of Success in their military manoeuvres, and have declared by the King's Speech at the Late prorogation of Parliament that the Force in America with the blessing of Providence will be sufficient to quell the Rebels.[6] Can you my dear friend! with all your philosophical gravity refrain a Smile when you hear such men talk of a dependence on Providence?

As the Enemy have by this time collected all the Force designed against New York, it is probable we shall soon hear of a general attack. By what we learn here of the number and State of our Troops, we have reason to hope it will be an unsuccessful one. But it is proper to provide against the worst that may happen. If nothing decisive should take place before the first of Decr. I am under great concern lest the Continental Troops (whose inlistments expire at that time) or a great proportion of them will then quit the Service. The Re-inlistment last year you know was attended with great difficulty, and I am afraid it will be with much greater the present. But as this is a matter of capital importance, there's no doubt Congress will early take effectual care about it. As the giving great Bounties to inlist men for a short time cannot be supported long, we must fall upon some other method of raising them. For this purpose, would it do to form the militia in each Town into four or five divisions, as equal as may be as to number and circumstances, and require the personal service yearly of one of these divisions, they casting lots to determine the order or Succession of their Service? If any individuals in the division called to duty, could not attend, they should be obliged to procure able bodied men (voluntiers) in their stead, which the other divisions could supply. Such voluntiers having recd. an equivalent for this extra-Service not to be excused on that account from duty when called upon with the division they belong to. Or would it do to give a handsome bounty once for all of money or land, on condition of enlisting for as long a time as the war shall continue? This last method is liable to an objection from Desertions, Deaths

5. Howe's letter and BF's reply are above, June 20, July 20, 1776; the headnote on the former identifies the Admiral's circular letter and declaration; the statute was the Prohibitory Act.

6. Cobbett, *Parliamentary History*, XVIII (1774–77), 1366.

and other casualties: In which cases every campaign would make Recruits and further bounties necessary. I hope some effectual way will be found to procure men to engage in the Service during the war.

I am glad to find that notwithstanding your Countrymen have had so many good slices of you for those forty years past: there's enough remaining of you to afford them good Picking Still. Notwithstanding the past Regales[7] they still expect to feast upon you, and to feast as usual most deliciously. Like Beggars once indulged they ask for more. I am my dear Friend, with the sincerest Regard your affectionate humble servant   J B.

Copied

Dr. Benja. Franklin

Protest against the First Draft of the Articles of Confederation

AD (draft): American Philosophical Society; copy: Library of Congress

This document, as Franklin explains in his note at the end, is not what it appears to be. It was a protest from him and not, despite its opening sentence, from the convention. If he ever submitted it to that body, the meager minutes say nothing about it; and it was certainly not submitted to Congress. He wrote it at some period between late June and late August, 1776; the precise date cannot be determined, and our chronological placement is faute de mieux.

The background of the decision that Franklin is attacking, to accord the colonies equal representation in Congress, is explained in our note above, July 30, 1776, on his part in the debate on that issue. The protest is directed against Article 17, as numbered in the report of Dickinson's committee. The articles were discussed and amended until August 20, when a revised version was ordered printed for the delegates alone,[8] and in the process were renumbered, we do not know when. Hence Franklin was writing after the committee's draft neared completion (and probably after it was presented to Congress on July 12) and before the revision

7. Sumptuous repasts. "There's enough remaining of you," Bowdoin originally wrote, "to regale them further and to afford good Picking still and as 'tis said the sweetest meat grows upon old bones, and yours continue well fleshed, they still expect to feast," etc.

8. JCC, v, 628, 635–6, 639–40, 674–89.

went to press. His saying here that the small states have already voted in favor of Article 17 might suggest a date after August 1, if he did not also say that Congress has submitted the plan of confederation to the states, an action which in fact it delayed until late in 1777. The second statement, then, is prediction, and the first may equally well be. The most likely date of composition appears to be late July or early August.

The position that Franklin takes here is one that he had long held and continued to hold. The idea of proportioning a colony's representation according to its financial contribution to the confederacy or to its population—the two were closely related—was in his sketch of the Albany Plan and in the plan itself, and in his proposed articles in 1775; and he supported the same idea in the federal convention of 1787.[9] The tone in which he couches the present argument is harsh and uncompromising, like that of his memorandum to Dartmouth on a different subject just before leaving England; but in both cases he refrained from pushing to extremes. Dartmouth never saw the memorandum.[1] If the Pennsylvania convention saw this protest, Congress did not; and in 1787 Franklin helped engineer the "great compromise" between equal and proportional representation. Although anger might at times make him harsh, in the end he almost invariably gave way, as here, to "prudential Considerations" of the larger issues involved.

[Before August 20, 1776]

We the Representatives of the State of Pennsylvania in full Convention met, having duly considered the Plan of Confederation formed in Congress, and submitted to the several States for their Assent or Dissent, do hereby declare the Dissent of this State to the same, for the following Reasons, viz.

1. Because the Foundations of every Confederation intended to be lasting, ought to be laid in Justice and Equity, no unfair Advantage being given to, or taken by, any of the Contracting Parties.

2. Because it is in the Nature of things just and equal that the respective States of the Confederacy should be represented in Congress and have Votes there in proportion to their Importance, arising from their Numbers of People, and the degree [*interlined:* Share] of Strength they afford to the united Body. And therefore

9. For his proposals in 1754 and 1775 see above, V, 337, 387–8, and July 21, 1775, and for the proposal in 1787 Max Farrand, ed., *The Records of the Federal Convention of 1787* (revised ed.; 4 vols., New Haven and London, 1911), I, 197–200.

1. Above, XXI, 526–8.

the XVIIth Article, which gives one Vote to the smallest State, and no more to the largest when the Difference between them may be as 10 to 1, or greater, is unjust, and injurious to the larger States,[2] since all of them are by other Articles obliged to contribute in proportion to their respective Abilities.

3. Because the Practice hitherto in Congress, of allowing only one Vote to each Colony, was originally taken up under a Conviction of its Impropriety and Injustice, was intended to be in some future time corrected, and was then and since submitted to only as a temporary Expedient, to be used in ordinary Business until the Means of rectifying the same could be obtained. This clearly appears by the Resolve of Congress dated Sept. 6. 1774. being the Day of its Meeting, which Resolve is in these Words, "That in determining Questions in this Congress, each Colony or Province shall have one Vote; the Congress not being possessed of, or at present able to procure proper Materials for ascertaining the Importance of each Colony."[3] That Importance has since been suppos'd to be best found in the Numbers of People, for the Congress not only by their Resolution when the issuing Bills was agreed to,[4] but by this present Confederation have judged that the Contribution towards sinking those Bills and to the common Expence should be in proportion to such Numbers when they could be taken, which has not yet been done. And tho the larger Colonies submitted to this Temporary Inequality of Representation expecting it would much sooner have been rectified, it never was understood that by the Resolution above cited, a Power was given to the smaller States[5] to fix that Inequality upon them forever, as those small States have now attempted to do by combining to vote for this 17th Article, and thereby to deprive the larger States of their just Right acknowledged in the same Resolution. And the smaller States having given us in Advance this striking Instance of the Injustice they are capable of, and of the possible Effects of their Combination, is of itself a sufficient Reason for our determining not to put ourselves in their Power by agreeing to this

2. BF started to write "Colonies"; the "S" is superimposed on a "C." In the final paragraph he reverted to "Colonies," which was the term used for the individual states throughout the Dickinson draft.
3. *JCC*, I, 25.
4. *Ibid.*, II, 221–2; III, 458.
5. BF originally wrote, then deleted, "Colonies."

Article, as it stands connected with those concerning the Quota's of each State, since being a Majority of the States in Congress they may by the same Means at any time deprive the larger States of any Share in the Disposition of our Strength and Wealth and the Management of our common Interests.

But as the smaller Colonies may object, that if the larger are allowed a Number of Votes in proportion to their Importance, the smaller will then be equally in danger of being overpower'd and govern'd by them; We not having the least Desire of any Influence or Power that is unjust or unequal, or disproportion'd to the Burthens we are to bear, do hereby offer our Consent to the said 17th Article as it now stands, provided the Quotas to be contributed by the larger Provinces shall be reduced to an Equality with that of the smallest, in which Case, all by contributing equally will have a just right to equal Votes. Not that we mean thereby to avoid granting additional Aids when the Exigence of our common Interests shall appear to us to make them proper and necessary; but leaving to the Congress with regard to such additional Aids the Right of making Requisitions as enjoy'd by our late Kings we would reserve to ourselves the Right of judging of the Propriety of those Requisitions, and of Refusing or Complying with them in part or in the whole as to us shall seem best, and of modifying our Grants with such Conditions as we shall judge necessary, in like manner as our Assemblies might formerly do with regard to Requisitions from the Crown.[6] For it appears to us just and reasonable that we should retain the Disposition of what Strength we have above the equal Proportion contributed as aforesaid by our State to the common Service; with every Power necessary to apply the same, as Occasions may arise, for our own particular Security; this we mean to do from this time forward unless we are allow'd Votes in Congress proportion'd to the Importance of our State, as was originally intended.   Signed by Order of the Convention

Rough of Protest against the Inequality of Voting in Congress

[*Franklin's note:*] This Paper was drawn up by B Franklin in 1776, he being then President of the Convention of Pennsylvania; but he was dissuaded from endeavouring to carry it through, from

6. For the background of requisitions by the king see above, XXI, 136–7 n.

some prudential Considerations respecting the necessary Union at that time of all the States in Confederation.

To [Lord Howe]   AL (draft)[7]: American Philosophical Society

My Lord   Philada Aug 20. 76

The Temper of the Colonies as professed in their several Petitions to the Crown was sincere. The Terms they proposed should then have been closed with, and all might have been Peace. I dare say your Lordship as well as my self, laments they were not accepted. I remember I told you that better would never be offered, and I have not forgotten your just Comparison of the Sybyl's Leaves.[8] But the Contempt with which those Petitions were treated, none of them being vouchsaf'd an Answer; and the cruel Measures since taken, have chang'd that Temper. It could not be otherwise. To propose now to the Colonies a Submission to the Crown of Great Britain, would be fruitless. The Time is past. One might as well propose it to France, on the Footing of a former title.

From Emmanuel de Pliarne[9]

ALS: American Philosophical Society

Monsieur   Elisabeth town 22. aoust 1776

J'ay quitté Philadelphie pour passer quelque temps à La Campagne où La chaleur Est un peu plus supportable. Je ne comptais y Rester qu'une ou Deux semaines; Mais étant Voisin De L'endroit où se Doivent passer Les Grands Evenements de votre Continent,

7. The draft is apparently incomplete, and the letter was not sent. BF gave a clue to the reason in his answer of Sept. 8 to Howe's letter of Aug. 16: some delegates disliked the correspondence. BF presumably did not feel free to continue it until Congress appointed a committee to meet with the Admiral.

8. BF mentioned the petition from the first Continental Congress at his initial meeting with Howe in London, but did not record in his journal this part of the conversation: above, XXI, 568.

9. The merchant who was Pierre Penet's companion, and who stayed behind as the firm's representative when his partner returned to Europe; see above, the headnote of Dec. 28, 1775, and Penet to BF, Aug. 3, 1776.

J'ay Crû Devoir payer une Visite à tous Les ouvrages qu'on a elevé pour La Défense De La liberté.

J'ay été à Amboy. J'y ai Vû, Monsieur, vos Milices dans le plus grand désordre et cependant elles ont à leur tête de trés bons chefs; Mais En général c'est La même chose Dans le monde Entier avec de pareilles troupes.

J'étais hier à Newyork chez Le Général Washinton, et je Vis tous les ouvrages. Je ne suis pas ingenieur; mais J'ay vû nos fortifications En france, et Je trouve celles De Newyork bien Entendües pour sa défense; Mais il n'y a pas De troupes En proportion De L'etendüe des ouvrages. Je fus Dans L'isle du Gouverneur. Cette Défense Est belle elle Exige Deux Mille hommes et elle n'en a que 4 à 500.

Quoiqu'il En soit, Monsieur, L'ardeur des troupes suppléera au Nombre et personne ne Doute que La Réception Des Enemis sera chaude.

Hier au soir on attendait une attaque Dans Differentes parties. Le Général Levinston avait Envoyé La Nuit de 20 au 21 un Espion qui Revint hier matin et Raporta que tout était Disposé pour attaquer Ce Matin Newyork, Long Island, Amboy Elisabeth town et Blein star tout à La fois;[1] J'ignore si foy Doit être ajoutée à cé Raport; Mais on Doit s'attendre à quelque chose En peu et il Est essentiel que l'attaque se fasse bientot, parcequ'il Est à craindre que vos troupes ne se Découragent. Hier au moment où L'on se préparoit pour Le Combat, J'entendis Les Milices dans Le Camp Dire qu'on parloit chaque Jour D'une attaque pour Les Retenir Campées; Mais qu'elles ne seraient pas Dupes plus Long temps et à ce moment où Je vous Ecris, Monsieur, un Colonel m'assure que son Régiment Est Dans Cette Disposition.

D'apres cela il Est interessant Dêtre attaqué Dans ce moment où Les Esprits sont pleins De feu et où vos troupes sont trés Nombreuses.

J'imagine que L'orage De La Nuit derniere a Empêché

---

1. "Levinston" was William Livingston (1723–90), commanding the N.J. militia; on Aug. 31, he resigned to take WF's place as N.J. governor: Carl E. Prince *et al.*, eds., *The Papers of William Livingston* . . . (2 vols. to date, Trenton, N.J.—), I, 55–6. "Blein star" was Bergen Point (now in Bayonne), N.J.; see the spy's report in Force, 5 *Amer. Arch.*, I, 1110–11. The British preparations were in fact for the move to Long Island, which began on the 22nd.

L'attaque, et ce sera peut-être pour Demain Matin.[2] Je le Désire sincerement, et si Je suis a portée de Donner quelque secours, Je le ferai avec Coeur pour une Cause qui Est Devenüe La Mienne propre. Je vous instruirai De ce qui se passera avec attention, heureux si Je puis vous persuader que personne n'est avec plus de Reconnoissance et de Respect que Moi Monsieur Votre trés humble et tres obeissant serviteur PLIARNE

Mille Respects à Votre famille.

Si quelques lettres vous parvenaient de france à Mon adresse, Je vous prie de Les Mettre sous Le Couvert Du Général Mercer ou Général Roberdeau,[3] et elles Me seront Rendües.

From Cornelius Stevenson[4] ALS: Library of Congress

Sir   St. Eustatius Augt: 22 1776

I received some days past a pacquet from Amsterdam to my address for you which I forwarded by Mr: Russell Via Virginia whose Confidence and care I could safily rely on.

Yesterday I received a Second Marked B which will be handed you by Mr. Forbes bound for Phila.[5] I have his assurance of his particular attention and hope it will be received in safety. I shall at all times be ready to render you any services of this or any other

2. Tremendous thunderstorms continued during the day, and the Americans thought the enemy could not move in such weather; the initial landing on Long Island was therefore unopposed. William B. Willcox, *Portrait of a General: Sir Henry Clinton in the War of Independence* (New York, 1964), p. 104.

3. For Hugh Mercer, commanding the flying camp, and Daniel Roberdeau, brig. gen. of Pa. associators, see Kermorvan to BF above, July 26, 1776.

4. BF, writing Dumas above on Dec. 9, had suggested Robert and Cornelius Stevenson as forwarding agents. The firm was actively trading with America, as explained there, but we do not know even the partners' nationality. The only clue is the handwriting of this letter, which strongly suggests that Stevenson was Dutch.

5. The two packets were Dumas' letters above, under April 30 and May 14, 1776; he explained in the second one that they were marked A and B. Both had reached Philadelphia by Oct. 1; see BF to Dumas of that date. Capt. Thomas Russell, of Baltimore, had gone to St. Eustatius earlier in the year for gunpowder, and had left again for the island in mid-June. James Forbes, who was his second lieutenant on the latter voyage, subsequently rose to command a succession of ships. *Naval Docs.*, v, 606, 715–16; Charles H. Lincoln, *Naval Records*

kind without reserve and am with Every respectful attention Sir
Your most obedient humble Servant   CORNS: STEVENSON

Benjamin Frankland Esqr F.R.S.

To Thomas McKean[6]   ALS: Historical Society of Pennsylvania

Dear Sir,   Philada. Augt. 24. 1776

   I heard your Letter read in Congress relating to the Disposition
of the German Troops; and understanding from Col. Ross, that
they are canton'd on the Island opposite to the Jersey Shore, I send
you herewith some of the Resolutions of the Congress translated
into their Language, as possibly you may find some Opportunity
of conveying them over the Water, to those People.[7] Some of the
Papers have Tobacco Marks on the Back, it being suppos'd by the
Committee, that if a little Tobacco were put up in each as the
Tobacconists use to do, and a Quantity made to fall into the Hands
of that Soldiery, by being put into a Drift Canoe among some
other little Things, it would be divided among them as Plunder
before the Officers could know the Contents of the Paper and

---

of the American Revolution . . . (Washington, D.C., 1906), pp. 226, 274, 333,
404.

   6. McKean (1734–1817) was a lawyer and politician prominent in the affairs
of both Delaware and Pennsylvania. He was a Congressional delegate from the
former, a leader of the movement in Philadelphia toward independence, and at
the moment a col. of Pa. associators commanding a regiment at Perth Amboy.
DAB.

   7. McKean's letter to Congress is not mentioned in the *JCC* and seems to
have vanished. At Perth Amboy he was well placed to gather intelligence about
the newly arrived German mercenaries on Staten Island: a brigade of them had
taken position on the shore, separated by only a narrow channel from the
American post. Max von Eelking, *The German Allied Troops in the North American
War of Independence, 1776–1783* (trans. and abridged by J. S. Rosengarten;
Albany, N.Y., 1893), p. 27. On Aug. 14 Congress had passed a resolution
offering each German soldier who deserted a 50-acre bounty in land. *JCC*, v,
653–5. For a second offer along the same lines see BF to Gates below, Aug. 28,
and for a discussion of the whole episode Lyman H. Butterfield, "Psychological
Warfare in 1776: the Jefferson-Franklin Plan to Cause Hessian Desertions," APS
Proc., XCIV (1950), 234–41.

prevent it. With great Esteem, I am, Sir, Your most obedient humble Servant B FRANKLIN[8]

Col. McKean

Addressed: Free / To / The honble. Colonel McKean / of the Pennsylvania Forces / East Jersey / B Free Franklin

Endorsed: Letter. August 24th: 1776 Doctor Benjamin Franklin Member of Congress.

From John Fraser[9]   ALS: National Archives

Sir   Reading 24th August 1776

I took the liberty of addressing Some lines to you about two months ago, as I never was favour'd with an answer, perhaps they did not reach,[1] even if they did, I am not Surprised that matters of importance shoud prevent any attention to them; however as it was about business of the utmost consequence to myself and the peace of my Family, I hope you will excuse me if I intrude once more: when I'll have tried every possible chance, I'll have no neglect to reproach myself with, from such considerations I have wrote sundry letters to Mr. Clinton whom I personally knew at Esopus, I even wrote about four weeks ago to Messrs. McKean and Samuel Adams, but without so much as an answer. I write this however with confidence yet woud be extremely Sorry to be deemed trouble some. I'll certainly not be so after this, even if unsuccessfull now, but quietly trust to fate.

The cause of my writing the first time was from my receiving a letter from Montreal dated the 6th of may, wherein I was informed that you was so good as to agree to my return to Canada, the letter

8. "Inclos'd is the English Copy," BF added in the margin, "which is requested to be return'd, it belonging to the Congress." He then deleted this postscript and wrote under it "mislaid."

9. Fraser's troubles had long been before Congress, which had ordered the commissioners to Canada to look into the matter; see their instructions above, March 20. Gen. Wooster had ordered Fraser confined in Albany. How he got to Reading we do not know, but clearly by way of Esopus (Kingston), N.Y., where he was incarcerated, we assume, at the time when the commissioners requested his presence in Montreal in their letter to Schuyler above, May 4.

1. If they did the letter was subsequently lost.

however had scearcely come to hand when I learned that you was come back from Montreal and was on your way to Philadelphia. I therefore begg'd you would let me Know whither I had been misinformed or not: if I was not, I willingly hoped there was no impropriety in my getting even then my passport. In my first letter I said very little about my case, I will Say as little now, because I must Suppose you acquainted with the merits thereof: I'll only observe that I was treated with Such rigour in Canada that it was with pleasure I learned the order for Albany; altho' at the very worst and most inclement time of the winter Season: I looked on the cause of my apprehension So trivial and insufficient, that I never entertained the least doubt of procuring liberty to return to Canada as soon as I woud be hear'd here.

To demand papers that chanced to be in my custody in a publick and judicial capacity and which papers related to transactions prior to any footing in Canada, I thought there was no right to ask, therefore the greatest impropriety to grant and I have had the Satisfaction of never meeting with any whatever his politicks, that has differ'd with me in opinion. As to the papers in themselves they are not of the smallest consequence, they relate to private persons and were these papers in ashes there woud be just the same hold of the persons concerned had they remained in Canada: these papers however are the Cause of my being now eight long months torn from my Family—Sufferings to be sure of a private nature and nothing in the scales of publick matters, but for that very reason I woud fain expect not to be made to Suffer any longer for a Supposed private injury but be redressed and let go by the Gentlemen who are at the head of publick affairs:[2] I am really Sensible this is perhaps the worst time for an individual to expect any attention, but, sir, I have allready given my reasons and I hope you will easily forgive my being So full of my own personal affair, the obligation woud be greater then I Can express, woud you procure relief, was it even only to go to Canada on my Parole to return when required or at least to get leave to go to Philadelphia.[3]

2. Fraser described the affair of the papers, which caused Gen. Wooster to arrest and deport him, in his memorandum cited in the note on the commissioners' instructions of March 20.

3. BF did get him leave to return to Canada; see Fraser's letter below, Oct. 15.

I beg pardon for being so troublesome. I have the honor to be Sir your most humble and Obedient Servant   JOHN FRASER

Addressed: Benjamin Franklin Esqr.

Notation: Letter of John Frazier prisoner to Doctr B. Franklin

To John Bull[4]   ALS: American Philosophical Society

Sir,   Philada. Aug. 26. 76

I have the Pleasure to acquaint you, that upon the Reading of your Letter which I laid before Convention, the Leave which you desired was granted. I am, Sir, Your most obedient humble Servant   B FRANKLIN

Col Bull.

To William Temple Franklin   ALS: Haverford College Library

Dear Grandson   Philada Augt. 27. 1776

Your Letter acquainting us with your safe Arrival was very agreable to us all.[5] But as you are near the Scene of Action, we wish to hear from you by every Post, and to have all the News. It will cost you but little Trouble to write, and will give us much Satisfaction.

This Family has been in great Grief, from the Loss of our dear little Girl. She suffer'd much: but is now at Rest. Will is to come home to-morrow; he will help to comfort us.[6]

4. Bull (*c.* 1730–1824) had recruited and commanded a Pa. battalion until the previous January, when he resigned because many of his officers would no longer serve under him. He was named to the convention in July, and excused from it to visit his old battalion at Perth Amboy; his request for extension of his leave had just been granted. He tried to return to active command in 1777, but failed again because of officers' refusing to serve under him. John B. B. Trussell, Jr., *The Pennsylvania Line: Regimental Organization and Operations, 1776–1783* (Harrisburg, Pa., 1977), pp. 39, 169, 183; *PMHB*, III (1879), 197; Force, 5 *Amer. Arch.*, II, 24, 27–8.

5. The letter above of Aug. 17, 1776, announcing his arrival at Perth Amboy.

6. For the death of the baby, Sarah, and her brother's stay with the Duffields see the note on the letter just cited.

Give my Love to your Mother, and let me know what you hear from your Father. I am, Your affectionate Grand Father

B FRANKLIN

Say how you spend your time; I hope in some Improvement.

Addressed: Mr W. T. Franklin / at Mrs Franklin's / P. Amboy

To John Adams

ALS: National Archives

Sir,   Augt. 28.[7] 1776

The Bearer Mr. Measam was a Merchant of good Reputation at Montreal; but having engag'd warmly in the American Cause, has been oblig'd to abandon that Country, to the great Detriment of his Affairs. He was appointed by Gen. Wooster a Commissary of Stores there; and apprehending such an Officer to be at this time necessary in our Northern Army, he has apply'd to Congress for a Continuance in that Office.[8] I understand that his Memorial is referred to the Board of War. As I have had occasion to know Mr. Measam as a good Accomptant, a Man of Method, and very correct in Business, I cannot but think that if such an Officer is wanting, he is extremely well qualify'd for the Employ, and as such beg leave to recommend him to the Favour of the Board. With great Respect, I have the Honour to be Sir, Your most obedient humble Servant   B FRANKLIN

Honble. Jno Adams Esqr

Addressed: Honourable John Adams, Esqr

Notation: Dr Franklins Letter concerning Mr Measom

7. The "8" is differently formed from BF's usual digit, but can be no other.

8. His petition of Aug. 2, 1776, gives more information about him than was appropriate for the note on Hazard to BF above, May 3, 1776. Measam had been active in the Indian trade around Montreal, and had had land and other property, all of which he lost. After the American capture of Montreal he had been appointed by Gen. Montgomery, and commissioned by BF, postmaster of the province (a position that was doubtless the background for the present recommendation); he had also acted without rank or salary as commissary of all but artillery stores. He petitioned to have the latter appointment confirmed, with rank and salary, for the northern army or elsewhere. Force, 5 *Amer. Arch.*, I,

To Horatio Gates

Dear Sir,   Philadelphia August 28th. 1776.

The Congress being advised, that there was a probability that the Hessians might be induced to quit the British service by offers of land, &c., came to two resolves for this purpose, which, being translated into German and printed, are sent to Staten Island to be distributed, if practicable, among those people. Some of them have tobacco marks on the back, that so tobacco being put up in them in small quantities, as the tobacconists use, and suffered to fall into the hands of these people, they might divide the papers as plunder, before their officers could come to the knowledge of the contents, and prevent their being read by the men. That was the first resolve. A second has since been made for the officers themselves. I am desired to send some of both sorts to you, that, if you find it practicable, you may convey them among the Germans that shall come against you.[9]

The Congress continue firmly united, and we begin to distress the enemy's trade very much, many valuable prizes being continually brought in. Arms and ammunition are also continually arriving, the French having resolved to permit the exportation to us, as they heartily wish us success;[1] so that in another year we shall be well provided.

As you may not have seen Dr. Price's excellent pamphlet, for

725–6. The petition, and another from him of Aug. 25, were referred to the board of war, of which Adams was a member; it reported favorably on the 29th, and on Oct. 16 Measam was appointed commissary of clothing for the northern army. Taylor, *Adams Papers*, IV, 499–500 n.

9. The first Congressional resolve is discussed in BF to McKean above, Aug. 24, 1776. BF was promptly added to the committee that had drafted it, presumably to help in disseminating its offer. On the 26th he, Jefferson, and John Adams were appointed a second committee, and its report the next day, apparently by Jefferson, became the basis for another resolution that offered deserting German officers land bounties scaled according to their rank. *JCC*, V, 654–5, 705, 707–8; see also Boyd, *Jefferson Papers*, I, 509–10, and the article by Butterfield cited in BF to McKean. Gates, at Ticonderoga, forwarded the present letter to Arnold and promised to send on the tobacco that he assumed would follow it: Force, 5 *Amer. Arch.*, II, 302.

1. This conclusion was apparently based on rumors emanating from the West Indies; see Crout, "Diplomacy of Trade," pp. 37–60, *passim*.

writing which the City of London presented him a Freedom in a gold box of fifty pounds value, I send you one of them.[2]

My last advices from England say, that the Ministry have done their utmost in fitting out this armament, and that, if it fails, they cannot find means next year to go on with the war. While I am writing comes an account that the armies were engaged on Long Island, the event unknown, which throws us into anxious suspense. God grant success. I am &c.   B. FRANKLIN

From Dr. Franklin to Genl. Horatio Gates.

To Anthony Wayne   ALS: Historical Society of Pennsylvania

Dear Sir,   Philada Augt. 28. 1776

I have received two of your Favours, which were immediately communicated to the Board of War, who are a Committee of Congress appointed to take Care of every thing in that Department, and who will I make no doubt take the necessary Measures for supplying your Wants.[3] But as America is new in the Business of Providing for Armies, there must be for a time Deficiencies that are very inconvenient to the Troops, and which Experience only can bring us into the Mode of Preventing. I am pleas'd to find your People bear them with a Soldierly Spirit, and I hope they will soon be remedied.

A general Action is every day expected at New York. If the Enemy is beaten, it will probably be decisive as to them; for they can hardly produce such another Armament for another Campaign: But our growing Country can bear considerable Losses, and recover them, so that a Defeat on our part will not by any means occasion our giving up the Cause. Much depends on the Bravery of you who are posted at Ticonderoga. If you prevent the Junction of the two Armies, their Project for this Year will be broken, and the Credit of the British Arms thro'out Europe and of the Ministry in England will be demolish'd, and the Nation grow sick of the Contest.

I am much oblig'd by your Draft of the Situation of our Troops,

2. For Price's *Observations on the Nature of Civil Liberty* see Priestley to BF above, Feb. 13. The author received the freedom of the city in March: *Public Advertiser*, March 15, 1776.

3. Wayne's letters are above, June 13 and July 31, 1776.

and of the Defences. I pray heartily for your Success, not doubting you will deserve it.

The greatest Unanimity continues in the Congress. The Convention of this Province is sitting, engag'd in framing a new Government. The greatest Part of our Militia are in New Jersey. Arms and Ammunition are daily arriving, the French Government having resolv'd to wink at the Supplying of us:[4] So that in another Year our People throughout the Continent will be both better arm'd and better disciplin'd, as most of them will have some Experience of a Camp Life and actual Service. Present my best Respects to General Gates, and believe me, with sincere Esteem, Dear Sir Your most obedient humble Servant

B FRANKLIN

Col. Wayne

Endorsed: 28th Augt 1776. B Franklin Esqr Exd[?] Holding out encouragement to the Army &c.

From Anthony Wayne

ALS (draft): Historical Society of Pennsylvania

Dear Sir   Tyconderoga 1st. Septr. 1776

It was with the greatest Concern I recd. the Acct. of Liet. Col. Allen's Resignation. He undoubtedly at that time had his reasons for such a step. Circumstanced as he then was, and some unmerited Injuries recently Offered (as he thought) to his nearest Connections might percipitate him into a measure that strict prudence wou'd not justify. I yet hope it is not too late to Correct the *error.* Genl. St. Clairs promotion has opened the Door for his Admission to the Command of a Battalion who I know wishes for Nothing more than to see him at their head.[5] He was a young fellow who

4. BF had written much the same thing to Gates in the preceding document.

5. For William Allen see the note on the commissioners to Schuyler above, May 10, 1776. "My Brother Billy returning from Ticonderoga, soon after the Declaration of Independence," James Allen wrote in his diary, "immediately resigned his commission of Lieut. Col., as he always determined to do in case of such declaration. It gave great offense and it was insinuated to him, that if he would not resign his advancement, should be equal to his wishes." *PMHB*, IX (1885), 191. Allen subsequently raised a corps of Pa. loyalists, which he commanded for the rest of the war. *Ibid.*, pp. 193, 425, 440; Sabine, *Loyalists,*

gave up ease and Affluance for the fatagus and Dangers of a Camp. These he Indured with the fortitude becoming a true and Good Officer.

The share he had in Conducting the Retreat of our Shatter'd Army after the Defeat at three Rivers when left by every other field Officer but him and one more[6] Merits some Attention. I believe his Spirit wou'd not Admit him to ask for any such thing but I am well assured that he wou'd Accept of it and pledge myself for his being a Gentleman and a Soldier who will do honor to his Appointment.

I have nothing new to write you except that we have lately Recd. a Re enforcement of upwards of 4000 men from the East-ward,[7] that St. Clair and myself have Renderd the old french lines much Stronger than ever, that our men have Recoverd health and Spirits, and that we wish for nothing more than an Oppertunity of meeting that thundering son of Mars Burgoyne with all his Mercenaris face to face, when you may rest Assured we shall Pro-duce a Conviction to the World that the sons of America deserve to be free. Interim believe me Dear Sir Your Assured friend and most Obedient Humble Servant   ANTY WAYNE

Notation: 1 Septr. 1776 Doctr. Franklin

From Margaret Stevenson[8]   ALS: American Philosophical Society

My dearst Frind   Northumbland Court Sept. 3: 1776

I recived your kind faover March 29. By the same conveaes, as your sencer friend Sr.—told me he thought,[9] we offtin meet in Kensington Gardings inde [indeed] he shows me grate kindnss, for your sake but my dear sir you complan of my not writing I

I, 157–8. Col. Arthur St. Clair had been promoted to brigadier general on Aug. 9.

6. Wayne himself: see his letter above, June 13, 1776.

7. For its composition see Force, 5 *Amer. Arch.*, I, 293, 826, 1199–1200.

8. This was probably one of the letters that BF did not receive until years later; see his endorsement of the following document.

9. The sincere friend was William Strahan, who presumably thought that the conveyance was the same one that had brought a letter to him, now missing. BF wrote a number of his English friends at the same time, and enclosed the letters with his to Todd above, March 29, 1776.

have noe oppirtuny. Some few i have had, but suposs you not to receive them, the inclousd was brought me agane too Month after, Mr. Temple was gone,[1] so it is wee ar parted.

But I trust i am not forgottin, in some of your Lersure momments and sorey i am to thinke you have so few, but the disparce [dispenser] of all thinge, has given you head and heart to be a usfull mimber. I pray God you may be successfull in preseving your Country I wish for Peice a good one if you cane, or any Peice but that is silfich, hoping I may see Americae.

Now I know you Laugh and as [ask] poor old woman how can she expect; true, but I plese my self some times with talking about seeing you all your famliy, and Dear Timple, he I feear has forget me. I have pad mr. Elphiniston £12:14s: 0d. and news papers. Mr. E. has left of school.

I have your sword aand all other things which shall be Carfully preserved. I have not time metion them now Mr. Willoms left woord with Mr. Lichmer that Mr. Fergson[2] had a safe conveaes but he must have my Letter in a few hours and Mr. Lichmer will take my Lettere to Mr. Ferguson. I am to dine with Mr. L—. He sends Beast Complamens and I know he is afriend and well wisher to you and youer Country. As news i moste refer you to Jonthas Lette. Moly and all hers ar well[3] i fear she dos not [make use?] of this opertuty i am mostly with her but have bin Latly opun a Litle party of Pleasuer with Mr. Viny in his Long Carige to Cambig. Mrs. V and Mr. and Mrs. Willmot his Sister and Miss Mr. L— and my self wee was nine in Company and all in good humour, Thomas Viny is Prentices to his Uncle[4] his father Lamants the not seeing you thay Love and Honer you. I cant say more but wish you

1. The enclosure must have been her letter above, Nov. 16, which she had expected William Temple to carry.
2. For Charles Lechmere and Henry Hugh Fergusson see respectively the letter just cited and BF to JW above, Sept. 12.
3. "Jonthas Lette" is the following document; "Moly" can only be Polly Hewson, although we have never before encountered this nickname.
4. The others on the trip to Cambridge were Mr. and Miss Lechmere, Mr. and Mrs. Thomas Viny, their son (John Viny's apprentice must have been along to bring the total to nine), their daughter Mary and her husband, Edward Wilmott, and Edward's sister Ann. For the Wilmotts see William Berry, *County Genealogies. Pedigrees of the Families in the County of Kent* . . . (London, 1830), p. 280.

to say to your self everething in behalf of Dear sir your fathful and Seceir friend and Moste obligde Servant   MARGT STEVENSON

My Love to Mr. Mrs. Bach and kiss the Dear Children for me.

From [Jonathan Williams, Jr.]

AL: American Philosophical Society

Dear and honored Sir   London Sept. 3. 1776.

I have just heard of an Opportunity by which a Letter may possibly reach you, therefore sit down to acknowledge the Receipt of yours of the 29th March.

We are constantly wishing to hear from you again, all your Friends are extreemly anxious to know where you are and how you do: they are all well. You ask me if I am married, I am sorry to say I am not, nor am I likely to be, there are some Requisites which I can't at present command that I fear will prove an insurmountable Bar. Mr. A. says when I am master of £2000 and in Business, he will give me £ 3000 more, but it will be a long Time before I shall be in that Situation, and in the mean Time some other man may be more successfull. How can you suppose that I am turn'd Tory? If I thought you were serious in this indeed Sir it would hurt me, for I had rather part with my Life than my principles. If I dared say all I think, or could do all I wish, I should not be thought to deserve that name. I have often regretted that I was not in the Way when you sail'd.⁵ I did not follow because I never expected Things would have come to this pass, and because you advised such a plan as I have since adopted.

I am to be settled in a few Weeks and in a few years I hope to be in a tolerable Situation. If we were once more at peace and I had frequent Opport[unity] of being with you, I should not wish for a better.

I sometimes hear from France, by the last Letter I had, your

5. JW had been in France at the time of BF's departure. For the other matters in this paragraph see the letter that he is answering. "Mr. A." was William Alexander.

Friends there were well. I find New Jersey have appointed an agent, but I am afraid he will have little Business to do.[6]

I have inform'd Mrs. S. of this Opportunity but I don't know if she will have Time to write she and our Friend at Kensington with the little ones are all well. I am with the greatest Respect and Esteem Yours most dutifully and affectionately[7]

Addressed: Doctor Franklin / Market Street / Philadelphia

Endorsed: Old Letters not receiv'd till April 1786 Stevenson Hewson Williams[8]

From Mary Hewson[9]   ALS: American Philosophical Society

My dear Sir   London Septr. 5. 1776

Having a chance of sending a letter to you I would not neglect it. The Atlantic is now the *great gulph*, indeed; for there seems no possibility of passing over it to each other. However I hope you spoke in the spirit of prophecy when you said your public affairs might be settled by the time my private ones were finished. Both those events are yet only in expectation, but I fancy I shall conclude with Mr. Mure before next year, as he has agreed to let me have bonds for the payment of the money which he acknowledges my due in five, six, and seven years bearing 5 per cent interest. The sum they make out rather short, I think they allow about £7000. Mr. Henckell and Mr. Williams stood out for some hundreds more which they thought my right, but it was deter-

6. JW had acted as unofficial agent for a time in 1775, until the N.J. Assembly appointed Dennis DeBerdt, Jr., as BF's successor; see the note on JW to BF above, July 19, 1775.

7. "Williams" has been added in another hand. "Mrs. S." was of course Mrs. Stevenson and "our Friend" Polly Hewson.

8. See the note on Polly Hewson to BF above, Dec. 12. That letter and this one were unquestionably in the packet sent to RB, which he kept for more than a decade. So in all likelihood were Polly's two letters below, Sept. 5 and 8, her mother's above of Nov. 16 and Sept. 3 (which she sent together), and JW's below of Sept. 19.

9. Another of the letters that BF did not receive until 1786; see the preceding note.

mined against me by arbitration.[1] I shall be very well satisfied with my fortune, tho' I confess I am a little mortified at not having all that I ought to have, but it is all clear gain to me, for I never built much expectation upon it. If I could be in America I think I could do very well for my dear Children, who are very promising. William goes to a day school at Kensington where he has learnt to read very well; that is the only part of education he has received at present, for as I intended to take him with his brother and sister into the North to visit their grandmother as soon as I should be free to move, I delayed entering him at any superior school, and I proposed to take that journey before I determined where to fix my place of abode.[2] Tom continues a sprightly little fellow; and Elizabeth is a fine stout girl, and improves in beauty which I will do all I can to preserve. They have had the whooping cough, which prevented my having the girl inocculated last spring, but as our expectation of hot weather is over for this year I propose to have the operation performed very soon. God grant me success!

We came all the family this morning to visit Grandmama whom we had not seen for three weeks. She has been jaunting about since she left us, first at Richmond with James and Sally Pearce, and since with Mr. and Mrs. Viny to Cambridge in their long carriage.[3] I think my mother never was better than she is now. We talk of going to live together somewhere in the country, but when or where we cannot yet determine, our hankering after America makes us hope that this horrid war may be ended before our plan is fixed.

I wrote you a long letter many months ago which was to have

1. This was the end of the negotiations discussed in Polly's letter above, Dec. 12.

2. Polly's mother-in-law, Mary Heron Hewson, was a native of Hexham, Northumberland. Thomas J. Pettigrew, *Memoirs of the Life and Writings of the Late John Coakley Lettsom* . . . (3 vols., London, 1817), I, 137 (2d pagination).

3. For Mrs. Stevenson's trip to Cambridge see her letter above, Sept. 3, 1776. Sally Franklin (A.5.2.3.1.1.1) had married James Pearce in 1773 and settled at Ewell: above, XIX, 395 n; XX 382 n. They must have moved recently to Richmond, where their first child was born in April, 1775: John C. C. Smith, *The Parish Registers of Richmond, Surrey* . . . (2 vols., London, 1903–05), II, 107.

been conveyed by Mr. Temple but it came back to me, and I have had no opportunity of writing since.[4]

We drank your health to day, the person who first proposed the toast was my Son William who took up his glass of wine and water (for he is still very sober) and said "my Doctor papa's health." He came up to me this moment, whispering, "Give my love to Dr. papa." His nature is shy and he does not much exercise himself in ceremonies, therefore you may consider these two instances of his civility as somewhat extraordinary. I was determined to write and I had no other subjects but these to entertain you with. In the midst of your great avocations I know you will be pleased to hear of these domestic occurrences of her whom you have honoured with the name of Friend and who is most sincerely and affectionately yours   MARY HEWSON

I hope Mr. and Mrs. Bache with their two sons are well: And my old friend Temple. I rejoiced to hear he has the addition of Franklin, which I always knew he had some right to,[5] and I hope he will prove worthy the honourable Appellation.

To [Lord Howe]   AL (draft): American Philosophical Society

Whitehall had entrusted the peace mission to Lord Howe and his brother, but the Admiral played the leading part. He had carried on the lengthy maneuvering in London about the commission, he wrote the declaration that was disseminated on his arrival, and although he consulted with his brother he took charge of negotiating in America. His first problem was finding people with whom to negotiate. He approached Washington and Franklin and got nowhere.[6] He was not empowered to treat with Congress as representing the colonies, let alone as representing the independent United States; yet unless he found a way

4. That of Dec. 12, which she enclosed with hers below of Sept. 8, just as her mother enclosed hers of Nov. 16 with her letter of Sept. 3, 1776.

5. She later explained why she and her mother kept the knowledge to themselves; see the note on BF to Mecom above, June 17, 1775. In writing to Barbara Hewson, William's sister, in 1774 Polly referred to WTF as "Mr. Temple, a young gentleman who is at school here and is under the care of Dr. Franklin." Oct. 4, 1774, APS.

6. For his brother's role see Stevens, *Facsimiles*, XII, no. 1201, and for the approaches to Washington, Gruber, *Howe Brothers*, pp. 94–5, 108–9.

to sound out the delegates, and met some response from them, he could not treat at all. At the end of August the opportunity came, and he seized it. On the 27th the British won an overwhelming victory in the Battle of Long Island; three days later the remnant of the American forces retreated to Manhattan, where Washington's whole army was threatened with disaster. Now if ever Congress might be expected to listen to an overture for peace.

Howe paroled John Sullivan, captured in the battle, and sent him to Philadelphia with a message. The Admiral could not treat with Congress as such, Sullivan told that body on September 3, but wished to confer unofficially with some of its members, for the present as private individuals. The brothers had full power to settle the quarrel on terms advantageous to both sides, "the obtaining of which Delayed him near Two months in England, and prevented his arrival at this place before the Declaration of Independency took place."[7] Now was the time to reach agreement, before a decisive blow compelled one side or the other—a delicate euphemism—to sue for peace. In the event of such an agreement, the message added mysteriously, many things for which the Americans had not yet asked "might and ought to be granted Them"; and the authority of Congress would have to be acknowledged, for "otherwise The Compact would not be Compleat."[8]

This message put the delegates in a difficult position. If they agreed to an unofficial meeting, they might be accused of clutching at any straw to find a settlement; if they refused a meeting, they might be accused of brushing aside a genuine and promising overture.[9] After long debate they reached their decision on September 5: Congress would not send members to a private conference with Howe, but "will send a committee of their body to know whether he has any authority to treat with persons authorized by Congress for that purpose, in behalf of America, and what that authority is, and to hear such propositions as he shall think fit to make respecting the same."[1] The next day Franklin, John Adams, and Edward Rutledge were designated as the members of the committee.[2] It represented Congress, with which Howe had declined official dealing; and for that reason some expected him not to receive the three emissar-

7. For Howe's long and intricate negotiations with Whitehall see *ibid.*, pp. 72–8.

8. *JCC*, v, 730–1.

9. See Smith, *Letters*, v, 89–135.

1. *JCC*, v, 737.

2. *Ibid.*, p. 738. Rutledge and Richard Henry Lee were tied in the vote, but Lee opposed the mission and declined to serve. Although Adams considered doing the same, he was persuaded to accept. Smith, *op. cit.*, pp. 113–15.

ies.[3] He did so, nevertheless, and the account of the interview is below, September 11.

My Lord   Philada. Sept. 8. 1776
  I received your Favour of the 16th past. I did not immediately answer it, because I found that my Corresponding with your Lordship was dislik'd by some Members of Congress. I hope now soon to have an Opportunity of discussing with you, vivâ voce, the Matters mention'd in it; as I am with Mr. Adams and Mr. Rutledge appointed to wait on your Lordship in consequence of a Desire you exprest in some Conversation with Gen. Sullivan, and of a Resolution of Congress made thereupon which that Gentleman has probably before this time communicated to you. We purpose to set out on our Journey to-morrow Morning, and to be at Amboy on Wednesday about 9 aClock, where we should be glad to meet a Line from your Lordship, appointing the Time and Place of Meeting. If it would be agreable to your Lordship, we apprehend that either at the House on Staten Island, opposite to Amboy, or at the Governor's House in Amboy, we might be accommodated with a Room for the purpose. With the greatest Esteem and Respect, I have the Honour to be My Lord, &c.

To George Washington   ALS: Yale University Library

Sir   Philada. Sept. 8. 1776
  The Congress having appointed Mr. Adams, Mr. Rutledge and my self, to meet Lord Howe, and hear what Propositions he may have to make, we purpose setting out to-morrow, and to be at Perth Amboy on Wednesday morning, as you will see by the enclos'd, which you are requested immediately to forward to his Lordship;[4] and if an Answer comes to your hands, that you would send it to meet us at Amboy. What we have heard of the Badness of the Roads between that Place and New York, makes us wish to

3. *Ibid.*, pp. 115–17, 122–3.
4. The finished form of the preceding document. Washington sent it to Howe the next day and promised to forward a reply by express. Fitzpatrick, *Writings of Washington*, VI, 38.

be spar'd that part of the Journey.[5] With great Respect and Esteem, I have the honour to be, Sir, Your Excellency's most obedient and most humble Servant   B FRANKLIN

His Excy. Gen. Washington

Notation: Phila. Septr. 8. 1776 From Dr. Franklin

From Mary Hewson   ALS: American Philosophical Society

My dear Sir   Kensington Sepr. 8. 1776

As I was yesterday informed that my letter of thursday was not then gone[6] I sit down now to make a little addition, fancying that I have not said all I have to say, for I wrote in haste. I think I gave you my family history pretty fully, as to public concerns, I know nothing, nor should I write of them to you if I knew anything, so I will give you some account of some friends of whom you may not hear by other means; tho' as my mother has written you a long letter she probably has given you all the intelligence that I shall.[7]

Dolly is now upon a tour in Wales with Mrs. Scott, who (if I may say it) is a warm friend of the Americans; she declares were she a man she would go to America, to serve the country and exalt her character. I hope this jaunt will be of service to Dolly by amusing her mind which was much depressed by her long and close attendance upon her dying sister; and the unexpected distribution of her fortune almost overset her, for Mrs. C. B. left all to her except £100 to each of her brothers and £300 to one of her nieces who was her god-daughter. Mrs. Hawkesworth and I with some difficulty prevailed on Dolly not to give up the fortune her sister bequeathed her; she really was hardly in her senses for some time after her sister's death.[8]

---

5. The journey, that is, to Washington's headquarters if Howe did not choose to meet there. If he did elect New York, the committee arranged to bypass Perth Amboy by having the Admiral's answer brought to it on the road from New Brunswick; see BF to WTF below, Sept. 10.

6. The letter of Sept. 5 above, which, like this one, did not reach BF until 1786.

7. Mrs. Stevenson had not; see her letter above, Sept. 3, 1776.

8. Mrs. Scott was undoubtedly the same woman with whom Dolly Blunt had visited Bath the year before, and whom we conjecturally identified as the novelist and historian; see the note on Blunt to BF above, April 19, 1775. For

The W[ilkses] are in the same situation in which you left them, if one can call that the same which must have been every day growing worse; however they are still in the House in Yorkbuildings—upon recollection, I believe you were gone before they came to it. Poor woman! She supports her spirits amazingly, and he is not more gloomy than he used to be. Some of her friends have proposed her keeping a boarding house in London; others have proposed her setting up a school at Durham where they say a good one is wanted. He is inclined to the London scheme; she would like the other better, and in my opinion it is most eligible, but no step is yet taken for either. Fanny is much improved, and may be called a fine young woman.[9]

When I mentioned Dolly's accession of fortune I forgot to tell you one instance of kindness it has enabled her to perform. She lent £50 to James Pearce with which he has furnished his house so as to let it in lodgings which will make him stand rent free at least. Do you not think Mrs. C B's fortune is in good hands, and better disposed than if it had been parcelled out in shares to her brothers? The Pearces have a little girl, they are very industrious, and I believe succeed very well at Richmond.[1]

I sold my aunt's goods and moved out of Church Lane last spring, and have now a house in the Square at 30 guineas a year, the other was forty, so I save something, and have nearly the same accommodation. I have taken the house but for one year, and I hope before that term expires my affairs will be so settled that I may fix upon some other spot to sit down in with my little folks where I can bring them up in the manner I like and give them an education that shall be of future advantage to them. Mr. Elphinston has given up his school, but he continues his house, which he means to let out in apartments, and has just published *A finishing plan of education*, which is a proposal for taking pupils at 100 guineas a year. Mr. Williams perhaps you may have heard has

---

Catherine Blunt's illness see Polly's letter above, Dec. 12. Mrs. Hawkesworth, Dr. John's widow, had long been part of Dolly's circle.

9. The name at the beginning of the paragraph has been crossed out as indicated, but BF supplied it in commenting on this letter in 1786 (above, p. 299 n). Fanny was presumably a daughter of Israel and Elizabeth Wilkes, who were old London friends of Polly and BF; see for example above, XV, 238; XVII, 222.

1. For Dolly's legacy and the Pearces see Polly's letter of Sept. 5.

opened a chapple in Margarette Street Cavendish Square. I have not yet been there, but I intend to satisfy my curiosity some day.[2]

My letters are a kind of private newspaper, I give the articles just as they happen to occur without regard to order or connection. I fancy this kind will be most pleasing to you, as it will not require an answer, and will make you feel somewhat like having your English friends about you.

If the Congress and the Ministry will agree you shall have some of those friends really with you; but we must wait on this side the water till those mighty powers determine our lot.

As I do not chuse my labour should be lost I send you with this the letter I wrote you last year,[3] it may divert you to read it when you have nothing else to do.

My mother came hither last night, she is just now gone to bed and desired me to give her love to you, wishing you a good night. I hope you will be able to recollect how you slept on the 8th of Sepr. Tho' I fancy there is no night on which her good wishes do not rise for you. In those good wishes she is most heartily joined by your faithful and affectionate   MARY HEWSON

To William Temple Franklin

ALS: Bruce Gimelson, Chalfont, Pa. (1978)

Dear Grandson,   Brunswick, Sept. 10. 1776

It is possible that a Line from Lord Howe may be left for me at your good Mother's, as I have appointed to be there to morrow Morning, in order to meet a Notice from his Lordship relating to the Time and Place of a proposed Interview. If it should come there to night, or very early in the Morning I could wish you would set out with it on horseback so as to meet us on the Road not far from hence, that if NYork should be the Place, we may not go so far out of our way as Amboy would be. Besides I should be

2. We have not located a copy of Elphinston's pamphlet, which he had printed by Dodsley and circulated to friends: *Gent. Mag.*, XLVI (1776), 374; James Elphinston, *Forty Years' Correspondence* . . . (8 vols., London, 1791–94), II, 200–4. For the Rev. David Williams, the dissenting clergyman, see his letter above, Aug. 16, 1775.

3. The December letter mentioned in Polly's of Sept. 5.

glad to see you. My Love to your Mother. Mr. Adams and Mr. Rutledge are with me. If Amboy or the House opposite to it on Staten Island is to be the Place of Meeting, we shall want private Lodgings there. I am as ever, Your affectionate Grandfather

B FRANKLIN

If no Letter is come to your House enquire at Headquarters if any for me is come there:[4] but do not mention from whom, or the Occasion.

Master W. Franklin

From Lord Howe

Copy: Library of Congress

Eagle off Bedlows Island[5] Sepr. 10: 1776.

Lord Howe presents his compliments to Dr. Franklin, and according to the tenor of his favour of the 8th.[6] will attend to have the pleasure of meeting him and Messrs. Adams and Rutledge tomorrow morning at the house on Staten Island opposite to Amboy, as early as the few conveniencies for travelling by land on Staten Island will admit. Lord Howe upon his arrival at the place appointed, will send a boat (if he can procure it in time) with a flag of truce over to Amboy. And requests the Dr. and the other gentlemen will postpone their intended favour of passing over to meet him untill they are informed as above of his arrival to attend them there.

In case the weather should prove unfavourable for Lord Howe to pass in his boat to Staten Island tomorrow as from the present appearance there is some reason to suspect, he will take the next earliest opportunity that offers for that purpose. In this intention he may be farther retarded, having been an invalid lately; but will certainly give the most timely notice of that inability. He however

4. The headquarters in Perth Amboy, we assume, of Gen. Mercer, who was commanding in New Jersey.

5. Near the New Jersey shore and several miles north of the northeastern point of Staten Island. At this anchorage the *Eagle*, three days before, had been attacked by David Bushnell's submarine: Frederick Wagner, *Submarine Fighter of the American Revolution* . . . (New York, [1963]), pp. 59–64; see also Gale to BF above, Aug. 7, 1775.

6. This is the first letter in Howe's correspondence with BF that is in the third person.

flatters himself he shall not have occasion to make farther excuses on that account.

Lord Howe's Conference with the Committee of Congress

AD: New York Public Library

The committee appointed by Congress left Philadelphia on September 9, Franklin and Rutledge in carriages and Adams on horseback.[7] They spent the night of the 10th in New Brunswick, where the taverns were full. Adams and Franklin had to share a bed in a room with one small window, which the younger man wanted shut for fear of catching cold; Franklin, delighted at the chance to make a convert, lectured him on colds until he talked them both to sleep. The next morning the three continued to Perth Amboy, where Lord Howe had a barge waiting for them, and one of his officers to be left ashore as a hostage. The precaution struck Adams as childish, and the others agreed; the officer returned with them to Staten Island.[8]

The interview that followed was the only meeting, before the final peace negotiations, between officially constituted representatives of the two sides; and it aroused a great deal of attention. Three authoritative and more or less full accounts of it survive.[9] One is the terse report printed below, September 17, that the committee delivered to Congress. The second is John Adams' long narrative in his autobiography, written a quarter-century later but embellished with extracts from his correspondence at the time.[1] The third and least known is in effect the minutes of the meeting. They were kept by the secretary of the commission, Henry Strachey,[2] and they are no more sprightly than minutes usually are; but

7. For the background of their journey see the headnote on BF to Howe above, Sept. 8.

8. Butterfield, *John Adams Diary*, III, 417–19. Gen. Howe, according to his brother, was absent because he had to be with the army: Stevens, *Facsimiles*, XII, no. 1201.

9. Two others are equally authoritative but not full. One is the printed extract, couched in generalities, of Howe's letter to Germain of Sept. 20: Smith, *Letters*, V, 142–3 n. The other, brief and uninformative, is in Rutledge to Washington of Sept. 11: *ibid.*, p. 137. A number of second-hand references to the meeting are in *ibid.*, pp. 154–89 *passim*.

1. Butterfield, III, 419–20, 422–31. Adams included (pp. 426–9) his long letter to Sam Adams of Sept. 14, which may also be found in Smith, *Letters*, V, 159–62.

2. Strachey (1737–1810) had been secretary to Lord Clive in India, and through his influence entered Parliament in 1768; he was secretary to the

they have the compensating advantage of a contemporary eyewitness account, which is as reliable as the committee's report to Congress and much more detailed. We print Strachey's version, and note what we consider substantial variations from Adams', but not minor differences in who said what and when.

11th. Septr. 1776.

Lord Howe received the Gentlemen on the Beach. Dr. Franklin introduced Mr. Adams and Mr. Rutledge. Lord Howe very politely expressed the Sense he entertained of the Confidence they had placed in him, by thus putting themselves in his hands.[3]

A general and immaterial Conversation from the Beach to the House. The Hessian Guard saluted, as they passed.

A cold dinner was on the Table. Dined, the Hessian Colonel present. Immediately after dinner he retired.[4]

Lord Howe informed them it was long since he had entertained an opinion that the Differences between the two Countries might be accommodated to the Satisfaction of both, that he was known to be a Well Wisher to America, particularly to the Province of Massachusets' Bay, which had endeared itself to him by the very high Honors it had bestowed upon the Memory of his eldest Brother.[5] That his going out as Commissioner from the King had

---

commission until it was terminated in 1778: Namier and Brooke, *House of Commons*, III, 488.

3. In other words by bringing the hostage with them. "Gentlemen, you make me a very high Compliment," were Howe's words as Adams reported them (Butterfield, p. 419), "and you may depend upon it, I will consider it as the most sacred of Things."

4. "We walked up to the House between Lines of Guards of Grenadiers, looking as fierce as ten furies," Adams remembered (pp. 419–20), "and making all the Grimaces and Gestures and motions of their Musquets with Bayonets fixed, which I suppose military Ettiquette requires but which We neither understood nor regarded.

"The House had been the Habitation of military Guards, and was as dirty as a stable: but his Lordship had prepared a large handsome Room, by spreading a Carpet of Moss and green Spriggs from Bushes and Shrubbs in the Neighbourhood, till he had made it not only wholesome but romantically elegant, and he entertained Us with good Claret, good Bread, cold Ham, Tongues and Mutton." The meal and the conference together lasted about three hours: Smith, *Letters*, V, 154.

5. Howe had made this point on first meeting BF: above, XXI, 565–6. The Admiral went on to say, according to Adams (p. 422), that he felt for America as a brother, and would lament her fall as a brother would. "Dr. Franklin, with

been early mentioned, but that afterwards for some time he had heard no more of it. That an Idea had then arisen of sending several Commissioners, to which he had objected. That his Wish was to go out singly and with a Civil Commission only, in which case, his Plan was to have gone immediately to Philadelphia. That he had even objected to his Brother's being in the Commission, from the Delicacy of the Situation and his desire to take upon himself all the Reproach that might be the Consequence of it. That it was however thought necessary that the General should be joined in the Commission (for reasons which he explained [*in the margin:* having their hands upon the Two Services]) and that he Lord Howe should also have the naval Command, in which he had acquiesced. That he had hoped to reach America before the Army had moved, and did not doubt but if their Disposition had been the same as expressed in their Petition to the King, he should have been able to have brought about an Accommodation to the Satisfaction of both Countries. That he thought the Petition was a sufficient Basis to confer upon, that it contained Matter, which, with Candour and Discussion might be wrought into a Plan of Permanency. That the Address to the People, which accompanied the Petition to His Majesty, tended to destroy the good Effects that might otherwise have been hoped for from the Petition.[6] That he had however still flattered himself that upon the Grounds of the Petition, he should be able to do some good. That they themselves had changed the ground since he left England by their Declaration of Independency, which, if it could not be got over, precluded him from all Treaty, as they must know, and he had explicitly said so in his Letter to Dr. Franklin.[7] That he had not, nor did he expect ever to have, Powers to consider the Colonies in the light of Independent States. That they must also be sensible, he could not confer with them as a Congress. That he could not

an easy Air and a collected Countenance, a Bow, a Smile and all the Naivetee which sometimes appeared in his Conversation and is often observed in his Writings, replied 'My Lord, We will do our Utmost Endeavours, to save your Lordship that mortification.' His Lordship appeared to feel this, with more Sensibility, than I could expect: but he only returned 'I suppose you will endeavour to give Us employment in Europe.'"

6. For the petition see the editorial note above, July 8, 1775, and for the accompanying address to the British people *JCC*, II, 163–71.

7. Above, Aug. 16, 1776.

acknowledge that Body which was not acknowledged by the King, whose Delegate he was, neither, for the same reason, could he confer with these Gentlemen as a Committee of the Congress. That if they would not lay aside that Distinction, it would be improper for him to proceed. That he thought it an unessential Form, which might for the present lie dormant. That they must give him leave to consider them merely as Gentlemen of great Ability, and Influence in the Country, and that they were now met to converse together, and to try if any Outline could be drawn to put a stop to the Calamities of War, and to bring forward some Plan that might be satisfactory both to America and to England. He desired them to consider the Delicacy of his Situation, the Reproach he was liable to, if he should be understood by any step of his, to acknowledge, or to treat with, the Congress, that he hoped they would not by any Implication commit him upon that Point, that he was rather going beyond his Powers in the present Meeting. [Dr. Franklin said You may depend upon our taking care of that, my Lord.[8]] That he thought the Idea of a Congress might easily be thrown out of the Question at present, for that if Matters could be so settled that the King's Government should be reestablished, the Congress would of course cease to exist, and that if they meant such Accommodation, they must see how unnecessary and useless it was to stand upon that Form which they knew they were to give up upon the Restoration of legal Government.

Dr. Franklin said that His Lordship might consider the Gentlemen present in any view he thought proper, that they were also at liberty to consider themselves in their real Character, that there was no necessity on this occasion to distinguish between the Congress and Individuals, and that the Conversation might be held as amongst friends.

The Two other Gentlemen assented, in very few Words, to what the Doctor had said.

Lord Howe then proceeded, that on his Arrival in this Country he had thought it expedient to issue a Declaration, which they

8. The brackets, here and in the similar interpolations by BF that follow, are in the original. His comment seems to make no sense in this context; we are inclined to believe that it is misplaced, and is a garbled version of the remark, quoted above, that Adams attributed to BF earlier in the interview.

had done him the honor to comment upon,[9] that he had endeavored to couch it in such Terms as would be the least exceptionable, that he concluded they must have judged he had not expressed in it all he had to say, though enough, he thought, to bring on Discussion which might lead the way to Accommodation.[1] That their Declaration of Independency had since rendered him the more cautious of opening himself, that it was absolutely impossible for him to treat, or confer, upon that Ground, or to admit the Idea in the smallest degree, that he flattered himself if That were given up, their was still room for him to effect the King's Purposes. That His Majesty's most earnest desire was to make his American Subjects happy, to cause a Reform in whatever affected the Freedom of their Legislation, and to concur with his Parliament in the Redress of any real Grievances.[2] That his Powers were, generally, to restore Peace and grant Pardons, to attend to Complaints and Representations, and to confer upon Means of establishing a Re Union upon Terms honorable and advantageous to the Colonies as well as to Great Britain. That they knew We expected Aid from America, that the Dispute seemed to be only concerning the Mode of obtaining it.

[Doctor Franklin here said, *That* we never refused, upon *Requisition*.[3]]

Lord Howe continued, that their Money was the smallest Consideration, that America could produce more solid Advantages to Great Britain, that it was her Commerce, her Strength, her Men, that we chiefly wanted.

[Here, Dr. Franklin, said with rather a sneering Laugh, Ay, my Lord, we have a pretty considerable Manufactory of *Men*, alluding as it should seem to their numerous Army.[4]]

Lord Howe continued, it is desireable to put a stop to these

9. For Howe's declaration see the headnote on his letter above, June 20, 1776. "They" who commented on it were Congress: *JCC*, v, 592–3.

1. A phrase and the beginning of another have here been deleted in the MS: "that He would so far communicate his Powers as to say generally that they were: to confer with any Persons upon the Subject of Peace and Re-Union; that the King was disposed".

2. Howe is alluding to the second stage of pacification; see the headnote above, March 31, 1776.

3. An old point; see above, XXI, 136–7.

4. Here a badly faded note is penciled in the margin: "No—To their increasing population." The hand cannot be surely identified, but looks like Howe's.

ruinous Extremities, as well for the sake of our Country, as Yours. When an American falls, England feels it. Is there no way of treading back this Step of Independency, and opening the door to a full discussion?

Lord Howe concluded with saying that having thus opened to them the general Purport of the Commission, and the King's Disposition to a permanent Peace, he must stop to hear what they might chuse to observe.

Dr. Franklin said he supposed His Lordship had seen the Resolution of the Congress which had sent them hither, that the Resolution contained the whole of their Commission, that if this Conversation was productive of no immediate good Effect, it might be of Service at a future time. That America had considered the Prohibitory Act as the Answer to her Petition to the King; Forces had been sent out, and Towns destroyed. That they could not expect Happiness now under the *Domination* of Great Britain, that all former Attachment was *obliterated*, that America could not return again to the Domination of Great Britain, and therefore imagined that Great Britain meant to rest it upon Force. The other Gentlemen will deliver their Sentiments.

Mr. Adams said that he had no objection to Lord Howe's considering him, on the present Occasion, merely as a private Gentleman, or in any Character except that of a British Subject. That the Resolution of the Congress to declare the Independency was not taken up upon their own Authority, that they had been instructed so to do, by *all* the Colonies, and that it was not in their power to treat otherwise than as independent States. He mentioned warmly his own Determination not to depart from the Idea of Independency, and spoke in the common way of the Power of the Crown, which was comprehended in the Ideal Power of Lords and Commons.

Mr. Rutledge began by saying he had been one of the oldest Members of the Congress, that he had been one from the beginning.[5] [*In the margin:* Mr. Rutledge mentioned (by way of Answer to Lord Howe's Remark upon that point) that their Petition to the King contained all which they thought was proper to be addressed

5. And only in that sense one of the oldest: he was not yet twenty-seven. In the first Congress John Adams had called him puerile, among other things; in the second Rutledge led the S.C. delegation. *DAB*.

to His Majesty, that the other Matters which could not come under the head of a Petition and therefore could not with Propriety be inserted, were put into the Address to the People, which was only calculated to shew them the Importance of America to Great Britain, and that the Petition to King was by all of them meant to be respectful.] That he thought it was worth the Consideration of Great Britain whether she would not receive greater Advantages by an Alliance with the Colonies as independent States, than she had ever hitherto done, that she might still enjoy a *great Share* of the Commerce, that she would have their raw Materials for her Manufactures, that they could protect the West India Islands much more effectually and more easily than she can, that they could assist her in the Newfoundland Trade. That he was glad this Conversation had happened, as it would be the occasion of opening to Great Britain the Consideration of the Advantages she might derive from America by an Alliance with her as an independent State, before any thing is settled with other foreign Powers. That it was impossible the People should consent to come again under the English Government. He could answer for South Carolina, that Government had been very oppressive, that the Crown Officers had claimed Privilege and confined People upon pretence of a breach of Privilege,[6] that they had at last taken the Government into their own hands, that the People were now settled and happy under that Government, and would not (even if they, the Congress, could desire it) return to the King's Government.

Lord Howe said, that if such were their Sentiments, he could only lament it was not in his Power to bring about the Accommodation he wished. That he had not Authority, nor did he expect he ever should have, to treat with the Colonies as States independent of the Crown of Great Britain, and that he was sorry the Gentlemen had had the trouble of coming so far, to so little purpose. That if the Colonies would not give up the System of Inde-

6. Rutledge was referring to the case that had brought him to fame three years before. The S.C. Council imprisoned the printer of a protest against its actions. Rutledge, suing for his release, attacked the Council's authority as derived from the crown and not the electorate, and won the verdict; the constitutional issue thus precipitated was carried to London. Edward McCrady, *The History of South Carolina under the Royal Government, 1719–1776* (New York and London, 1899), 716–23.

pendency, it was impossible for him to enter into any Negociation.

Dr. Franklin observed that it would take as much time for them to refer to, and get an Answer from their Constituents, as it would the Commissioners to get fresh Instructions from home, which he supposed might be done in about 3 Months.

Lord Howe replied it was in vain to think of his receiving Instructions to treat upon that ground.

After a little Pause, Dr. Franklin suddenly said, well my Lord, as America is to expect nothing but upon unconditional Submission, [*In the margin:* Lord Howe interrupted the Doctor at the Word Submission, said that Great Britain did not require unconditional Submission, that he thought what he had already said to them, proved the contrary, and desired the Gentlemen would not go away with such an Idea.

Memorandum. Perhaps Dr. Franklin meant Submission to the Crown, in opposition to their Principle of Independency.] and Your Lordship has no Proposition to make us, give me leave to ask whether, if *we* should make Propositions to Great Britain (not that I know, or am authorised to say we shall) You would receive and transmit them?

Lord Howe said he did not know that he could avoid receiving any Papers that might be put into his hands. Seemed rather doubtful about the Propriety of transmitting home, but did not say that he would decline it.

Notation: Important Document Containing an Account of the Interview between Lord Howe and Dr Franklin, J. Adams and others Sep. 1776. Written by Ld Howe's Secretary

The Secret Committee to the Maryland Council of Safety[7]

LS: Maryland Historical Society

⟨Philadelphia, Sept. 13, 1776: We have been asked for powder for the continental frigate built at Baltimore.[8] The powder should

7. This letter was ordered written in a committee meeting on Sept. 5, at which BF was not present: Smith, *Letters*, V, 108. He does not appear to have attended after June, 1776, as mentioned in our editorial note on the committee above, Sept. 18, 1775; why he signed the letter we have no idea.

8. The *Virginia*; see the complete text of the letter in *Naval Docs.*, VI, 807.

SEPTEMBER 13, 1776

have been ordered there, and we understand you have a considerable supply; please furnish four and a half tons for the purpose to Messrs. William Lux, Samuel Purviance, and David Stewart.[9] We will repay you in kind or supply more if necessary. Signed by Franklin, Josiah Bartlett, Richard Henry Lee, and Robert Morris.⟩

The Committee of Conference: Report to Congress

DS: New York Public Library; DS: American Philosophical Society;[1] copy: Library of Congress

The committee returned to Philadelphia on the morning of September 13.[2] On the same day it gave an oral report to Congress, and was asked for a written one as soon as possible. The latter was presented on the 17th, and the same committee was ordered to publish it with other documents relating to the negotiations.[3] The report needs no annotation of its substance; the background of the meeting is discussed in earlier headnotes,[4] and the most complete account of what took place is above, September 11, 1776.

Sept 17. [1776]

In Obedience to the order of Congress we have had a meeting with Lord Howe. It was on Wednesday last upon Staten island opposite to Amboy where his lordship received and entertained us with the utmost politeness.

His Lordship opened the Conversation by acquainting us that though he could not treat with us as a committee of Congress yet as his powers enabled him to confer and consult with any private gentlemen of influence in the colonies on the means of restoring peace between the two countries he was glad of this opportunity of conferring with us on that subject, if we thought ourselves at liberty to enter into a conference with him in that character.

9. For these three Baltimore merchants see Robert Purviance, *A Narrative of Events Which Occurred in Baltimore Town during the Revolutionary War* . . . (Baltimore, 1849), pp. 31–2, 105.
1. The first DS, which we print, is in Thomson's hand; the second is in an unidentified hand with his and Hancock's signatures.
2. Smith, *Letters*, V, 158.
3. *JCC*, V, 755, 765–7.
4. March 31, June 20, July 20, and Sept. 8, 1776.

We observed to his lordship that as our business was to hear he might consider us in what light he pleased and communicate to us any propositions he might be authorised to make for the purpose mentioned; but that we could consider ourselves in no other character than that in which we were placed by the order of Congress.

His lordship then entered into a discourse of considerable length which contained no explicit proposition of peace except one viz. That the colonies should return to their allegiance and obedience to the government of great Britain. The rest consisted principally of assurances that there was an exceeding good disposition in the King and his ministers to make that government easy to us, with intimations that in case of our submission, they would cause the offensive acts of parliament to be revised and the instructions to Governors to be reconsidered, that so if any just causes of complaint were found in the acts or any errors in government were perceived to have crept into the instructions they might be amended or withdrawn.

We gave it as our opinion to his lordship that a return to the domination of great Britain was not now to be expected. We mentioned the repeated humble petitions of the colonies to the King and parliament, which had been treated with contempt and answered only by additional injuries, the unexampled patience we had shewn under their tyrannical government and that it was not till the last act of parliament, which denounced war against us and put us out of the King's protection that we declared our independance. That this declaration had been called for by the people of the colonies in general; that every colony had approved of it when made and all now considered themselves as independant states and were settling or had settled their governments accordingly, so that it was not in the power of Congress to agree for them that they should return to their former dependant state. That there was no doubt of their inclination to peace and their willingness to enter into a treaty with Britain, that might be advantageous to both countries. That though his lordship had at present no power to treat with them as independant states, he might, if there was the same good disposition in Britain, much sooner obtain fresh powers from thence for that purpose than powers could be obtained by Congress from the several colonies to consent to a submission. His lordship then saying that he was sorry to find that no accommodation was like to take place put an end to the conference.

Upon the whole it did not appear to your committee, that his lordship's commission contained any other authority of importance than what is expressed in the act of parliament, viz. that of granting pardons with such exceptions as the commissioners shall think proper to make and of declaring America or any part of it to be in the King's peace upon submission. For as to the power of enquiring into the state of America, which his lordship mentioned to us and of conferring and consulting with any persons the commissioners might think proper and representing the result of such conversations to the Ministry, who, provided the colonies would subject themselves, might after all, or might not, at their pleasure, make any alterations in the former instructions to governors or propose in parliament any amendments of the acts complained of, we apprehended any expectation from the effect of such a power would have been too uncertain and precarious to be relyed on by America, had she still continued in her state of dependance.

Ordered that the above be published.

Extract from the minutes.   CHAS THOMSON secy.

By order of Congress   JOHN HANCOCK Presidt.[5]

From Samuel Cooper   ALS: American Philosophical Society

My dear Sir   Boston N.E 17 Septr 1776.

I cannot forbear expressing to you the Pleasure I receivd from hearing you were appointed by Congress with others to confer with Lord and Genl. Howe. The Subject of this Conference we do not as yet certainly know, but suppose it was desird on their Part for something more than settling an Exchange of Prisoners. I am not sorry our Enemies appear so eager for Negotiating. It looks as if they were not quite certain of their first grand Object, the Subduing us by Arms; and must give us Spirits. I suspect their Accounts from Europe are not the most favorable, and that France has made some Motion that alarms Britain. I doubt not however, we shall be cautious of their Designs, and that you will shew the World we have Negotiators as well as Soldiers. I can most chear-

5. This line is in Hancock's hand.

fully trust the important Affairs of America at this critical Season in such Hands. We have Nothing new here except Captures from the British Trade, which are likely to increase. Our own Navigation is almost wholly turn'd into Privateering, so that their Cruizers can take little or Nothing from us but empty Hulls, while their Ships come fast to us richly laden'd. It is regretted among us that the American Fleet is not in greater Forwardness. We have two fine Frigates built at Newbury and Portsmouth, but after so long a Time, not yet ready to put to Sea: Many are the more uneasy at this, as two Frigates of the Enemy have had the undisturb'd Range of our Bay for five or six Weeks past, retaken some valuable Prizes; and greatly prevented the Coasters from coming in with Supplies to this Town.[6] Whether there be any Fault in this or where it lies, I am unable to determine. I expect Mr. Austin, a worthy Gentleman, and Select Man of this Town will call for this Letter, and deliver it to you.[7] I am Sir, With very great Esteem and Affection, Your obedient humble Servant   SAM COOPER

[*In the margin:*] I wrote an Answer to your's enclosing your Correspondence with L. Howe immediately after receiving it.[8]

Dr. Franklin.

Addressed: To / The Honorable / Benjn. Franklin Esqr. L.L.D. F.R.S. / Member of the American Congress / Philadelphia

6. For the difficulties in getting into commission the new frigates that Congress had ordered see the note on the committee of secret correspondence to Deane above, Aug. 7, 1776. The *Raleigh* at Portsmouth had been launched in May, and the *Boston* and *Hancock* at Newburyport in June and July; but all were delayed for want of cannon. Nathan Miller, *Sea of Glory: the Continental Navy Fights for Independence* . . . (New York, [1974]), pp. 204, 209; William M. Fowler, Jr., *Rebels Under Sail* . . . (New York, [1976]), pp. 217–18, 222–3, 238–44. The British frigates were the *Liverpool* and *Milford: Naval Docs.*, VI, 892; their captures are listed in the index of that volume.

7. For Austin and his errand in Philadelphia see the following document.

8. Cooper had shown Bowdoin BF's letter to Howe of July 20: Bowdoin to BF above, Aug. 19, 1776. BF's letter to Cooper and the latter's reply are missing.

From Elizabeth Hubbart Partridge[9]

ALS: American Philosophical Society

Dear and Ever Honoured Uncle   Boston Septr: 17 1776

Would my Vanity permitt me to think, my long Silence Requier'd an Apology, I might justly Plead ill Health, and want of Spirets, (not want of affection) has deprived me of the Honor and Pleasure, of writing to you before this Time, but I now take up my Pen, to beg the Favour of your kind assistance to the two Gentlemen Messrs: Austen, and Barrett, they are Our Friends, and come with this, on Bussiness to the Congress in which We are Interested; Viz. when Genl: How left this Town, he took a large Quantity of Goods, from Us and others; which was taken from him, on their Passage to Hallifax, by some of the Arm'd Vessels belonging to the United States; an Carri'd into Portsmouth where they ware Libeled, Tryed, and Acquited, but the Capturs have Appealed to Congress.[1] The Gentlemen will Acquant you with the perticulars, and if you can Render them any Servis in this affair, it will be Greatfully Acknowledged by Us.

Pleas to present Our affectionate Regards to Aunt Mecome, to Mr. and Mrs. Beach, and their Little ones, to Our good Friends Mr. and Mrs. Green if they are still with you, and Our Sincere Congratulations if they have got well through the Small Pox.[2]

Mr. Partridge and Our Daughter joyn in Duty to you. May Heaven Smile on your Endeavours to Save your Country from

9. BF's stepniece had returned to Boston after her sojourn with the Greenes at Warwick, for which see Mecom to BF above, May 14, 1775.

1. The British, on leaving Boston, had confiscated goods of three local merchants, Samuel Austin, Samuel Barrett, and Samuel Partridge, Elizabeth's husband, to keep them out of the hands of the American forces. A British ship carrying the goods to Halifax was captured by an American privateer. The Portsmouth prize court awarded the goods to the owners, and Congress eventually modified the decision by stipulating that the captors should receive a portion of the value. William B. Clark, *George Washington's Navy* . . . (Baton Rouge, La., [1960]), pp. 130–2, 136–8, 140, 151, 166–7, 179, 185–7; *Naval Docs.*, IV-VI, *passim*.

2. One of William Greene's reasons for going to Philadelphia was to have himself inoculated: William G. Roelker, ed., *Benjamin Franklin and Catharine Ray Greene: Their Correspondence, 1755–1790* (Philadelphia, 1949), p. 79. His wife apparently had the same intention.

Ruin, and that Every Blessing here and hear after may be your Reward is the Ardent Prayer of Your affectionate Neice

ELIZA PARTRIDGE

From N[icholas] Barker   ALS: American Philosophical Society

Sir   Rotterdam the 18th. of Septr. 1776

I take the liberty to recommend the bearer of this letter Mr. Chas. Fred. Bedaulx a Swiss gentleman who was Lieutenant of Grenadiers in the service of this country, to your notice as an officer of merit.[3] He could have found employment in the Royal Army, but this being inconsistent with his principles, he rather chose to hazard a voyage at his own expence to the Continent of America, in hopes an Opportunity may be given him to use his sword in the cause of Liberty. Born in a country where this Blessing is religiously maintained, he knows how to value it and seems determined not to serve in any Army of Oppressors. I, tho' an Englishman, cannot but applaud his ardour and wish him success.

I hope, Sir, you will pardon the liberty I take. You will not, I believe, recollect my Name, but I beg leave to put you in mind that I had the honour to dine with you and Sir John Pringle, some years ago at the house of Mr. Davidson, whose partner I am.[4]

My little, tho' best endeavours have been used to inspire my country-men with a better sense of Justice and their own Interest. Unknown to any gentleman in America, my pen has been employed, so far as my other occupations would permit, in the cause of Civil Liberty and against the violent measures of our ministry, while I thought it was not yet too late for reconciliation. It was all

3. Bedaulx, also known as Lebrun de Bedeaux, was born in Switzerland in 1752; see Lasseray, *Les Français*, I, 128–9. He embarked for America, but the British captured his ship. He escaped to France with this letter, showed it to Silas Deane, and then forwarded it to BF with the covering letter below, Dec. 16, 1776. Barker was, we assume, the Nicholas Barker of Rotterdam who was in France in 1779, when an acquaintance tried to reintroduce him to BF: Joshua Johnson to Bancroft, July 13, 1779, APS.

4. William Davidson (died 1794) was a Scot who became one of the leading merchants of Rotterdam: *Gent. Mag.*, LXIV (1794), 1055. BF and Sir John presumably dined with him and his partner during their European tour in 1766.

SEPTEMBER 18, 1776

I could do at this distance. Others have reasoned on this Subject in a very Masterly manner, but all in vain. The same measures were still pursued. A Separation, the natural result, has taken place, and the curse denounced, is fallen on our own guilty heads! I have the honour to be, with great veneration, Sir Your most humble and Most obedient Servant   N: BARKER

The Honble. Benjamin Franklin Esqr.

Notations: W. Barker 18. Sept. 1776. M. Bedaulx

To William Temple Franklin

ALS: American Philosophical Society

Dear Billy   Philada Sept. 19. 1776
I received yours of the 16th, in which you propose going to your Father, if I have no Objection. I have consider'd the matter, and cannot approve of your taking such a Journey at this time, especially alone, for many reasons which I have not time to write. I am persuaded, that if your Mother should write a sealed Letter to her Husband, and enclose it under Cover to Govr. Trumbull of Connecticut, acquainting him that it contains nothing but what relates to her private Family Concerns, and requesting him to forward or deliver it, (opening it first if he should think fit) he would cause it to be deliver'd safe without opening. I hope you do not feel any Reluctance in returning to your Studies. This is the Time of Life in which you are to lay the Foundations of your future Improvement, and of your Importance among Men. If this Season is neglected, it will be like cutting off the Spring from the Year.

Your Aunt had the Carelessness to send the Bundle containing your Wastecoat, undirected, by Prichard. He forgot where he was to leave it, and with his usual Stupidity carried it to your House and brought it away again without asking a Question about it till he came home. He has also brought away the Razor Case you lent to Mr. Adams. We shall send both when there is *another* Opportunity; for one has since been miss'd, that of Mr. Bache, who intended calling to see Mrs. Franklin. There seems to be a kind of Fatality attending the Conveyance of your Things between Amboy and Philadelphia. Benny had written as I told you, but his Letter it seems was not sent. It was thought to be too full of

Pothooks and Hangers, and so unintelligible by the dividing Words in the Middle, and joining Ends of some to Beginnings of others, that if it had fallen into the Hands of some Committee it might have given them too much Trouble to decypher it, on a Suspicion of its containing Treason, especially as directed to a Tory House. He is now diligent in learning to write better, that he may arrive at the Honour of Corresponding with his Aunt after you leave her. Mr. and Mrs. Green went from hence on Monday, on their Return. I wish they may be in time to cross the North River safely at some of the upper Ferries.[5] My Love to your good Mama, and Respects to her Friends in the Family. Your Aunts join in best Wishes, with Your affectionate Grandfather   B FRANKLIN

They desire I would express more particularly their Love to Mrs Franklin.

Addressed: To / Mr William Temple Franklin, / at Mrs Franklin's / Perth Amboy / B Free Franklin

Notation: B. Franklin Esqr to his Grandson Philada. Sepr. 19th. 1776

From [Jonathan Williams, Jr.]

AL: American Philosophical Society

Dear and honored Sir   Sept. 19. 1776.

I am happy to convey to you two Letters which I think must give you pleasure because they come from your old Friends.[6] I wish I could convey to you as many more as (if it was thought they would arrive safe) your other Friends wish to write. I know of no material alteration among them, all I have lately seen are well. The good Bishop with his amiable Family are gone into Wales.

5. The Greenes had started on the 16th, the day after the British had over-run New York and forced the Americans back to high ground on northern Manhattan.
6. Mrs. Stevenson's of Sept. 3 and her daughter's double letter of Sept. 5 and 8, 1776. Each woman enclosed an earlier letter to BF that had been returned to her. JW had been uncertain about the conveyance he had heard of for his letter above of Sept. 3, and clearly did not use it. Instead he sent the whole batch to RB with the present letter, and the packet did not reach BF until 1786; see the note on Hewson to BF above, Dec. 12.

Mr. A. with his lovely Daughters are in France, I believe I have before told you he was liberated tho' the affairs are not yet brought to a Conclusion, but he seems very confident that they will at last happily terminate. Mrs. DB is journeying about the Country for her amusement with a party consisting wholly of Ladies, they set off upon an unconfined plan or rather no plan at all, for they go to one place without determining how long to stay or where to go next 'till they arrive there, and then they follow their Inclinations and Convenience according as Circumstances happen.[7]

I am in the same Situation but am just upon the Eve of entering into a considerable Scene of Business, which as yet seems to promise well.

I have had several Letters from your French Translator,[8] he seems in good Spirits and speaks of you with great affection.

The Son of your philosophic Friend whose House we were at in Wanstead,[9] is about publishing an Edition of your political Works, it is under the Inspection of two Gentlemen of your intimate acquaintance who will take Care that nothing shall appear that you can object to. I have added your albany plan with Reasons and Motives to the Collection, which I found among the provincial papers, and consulted the Bishop and several other of your Friends upon the Occasion, who unanimously were of Opinion that you would not be displeased with me for it.[1] Your Reputation is the only Object with any of us, so we hope that it will meet with your approbation.

I beg Sir that you will take the earliest Opportunity of informing my Friends about me, and if it be possible favour me with a

---

7. The Bishop was of course Shipley. William Alexander had fled to France with his family after his release from debtors' prison; see the note on his letter above, July 20, 1776. Dolly Blunt was traveling in Wales with Mrs. Scott and others; see Hewson to BF above, Sept. 8.

8. Dubourg, who had met and entertained JW in Paris: above, XXI, 535 n.

9. Benjamin and Samuel Vaughan respectively.

1. This is the first reference to the edition that appeared three years later; see Edwin Wolf, II, "Benjamin Franklin's *Political, Miscellaneous and Philosophical Pieces,* 1779," *Library Chronicle,* XVI (1950), 50–63. The document that JW contributed, the reasons and motives for the Albany Plan, is reprinted from Vaughan above, V, 397–416.

Letter and some account of them. I am as ever with the greatest Respect most affectionately Yours &c.

This and the other Letters comes under Cover to Mr Bache.

Addressed: Doctor Franklin / Philadelphia

The Committee of Secret Correspondence to William Bingham

LS: Yale University Library

Sir   Philadelphia September 21st [-October 1] 1776

Your several letters of the 4th. 15th. and 26th August to this Committee have been duely received with the several enclosures and the whole have been laid before the Congress. We can therefore communicate that satisfaction which we dare say it must afford you to know that you have so far obtained the approbation of that August Body. It is not necessary that we should enter into minute replys to the Contents of your letters, therefore we shall only notice such parts as seem to require it.[2]

Captain Wickes behaviour meets the approbation of his country and fortune seems to have had an Eye to his merit when she conducted his three prizes safely in.[3] You made a very proper use of his engagement, by your question to the General and it is extreamly satisfactory, that our prizes may be carried into and protected in the French ports,[4] but hitherto the Congress have not thought proper to intrust blank Commissions beyond Seas. Neither can their Resolve for bringing prizes into some of these States for Condemnation be dispensed with; these matters are now under

2. The letters have all disappeared, and their contents can only be inferred from this reply. For Bingham's mission see the committee's instructions and letter to him above, June 3, 1776.

3. The *Friendship*, *Peter*, and *Neptune* were all dispatched to American ports. Clark, *Wickes*, pp. 54–5.

4. Off the harbor of St. Pierre, Martinique, the *Reprisal* had engaged a British sloop of war, which left when fired upon by a shore battery: *ibid.*, pp. 57–60. After what was hailed as an American victory Bingham apparently asked Gen. d'Argout, the French commandant, what his attitude was toward American operations off the island. The General answered that he had been ordered to protect American shipping, and would permit prizes to be brought into port and disposed of there: Crout, "Diplomacy of Trade," p. 50.

consideration of a Committee and should any alteration take place you shall be informed of it.[5] We are bound to return thanks to his Excellency the General for the information he authorized you to give us as mentioned in your letter of the 4th and particularly for his disposition to Favour our Commerce in Port and protect it at sea and likewise for that concern he expressed at not having it in his power to assist us with the Arms and Powder we requested. You will therefore signify to His Excellency that this Committee entertain the warmest sentiments of esteem and respect for his person and character, and of gratitude for His Favourable attention to the concerns of our much injured Country, that we request the continuance of his Friendship and hope during your residence at Martinico there will be many opportunities of benefiting by His Favourable disposition, particularly in countenancing you in the purchase and exportation of Arms, ammunition and Clothing.

We are not surprized that Admiral Young's letter shou'd alter the Generals sentiments respecting Convoys, but we esteem much his spirited answer to the Admiral which may probably be productive of some alteration.[6] We like well your proposal for a Constant intercourse by Packets, and the Sloop Independance Capt. Young is now sent on that service in which we hope she will be successfull and continue.[7] More of the like kind shall follow and probably this may be found the best method of supporting our intercourse with Europe, and as these Vessels are properly Commissioned we cannot see any impropriety in fitting out Tenders with Coppies of their Commissions provided the Commanding officer of those Tenders are really officers belonging to the Vessel whose Commissions they bear, but the prizes must be sent to America for condemnation (unless the Cargoes are perishable) and

5. A committee had been appointed on Aug. 21 to consider whether prizes might be sent to ports outside the United States: *JCC*, v, 694.

6. After the action mentioned above Vice Adm. James Young, commanding the British West Indian squadron, demanded that the *Reprisal* be delivered to him, or he would inform Whitehall that a breach of the peace had occurred. D'Argout threatened in turn to inform Versailles, but he also retracted his earlier offer to convoy American shipping. Robert C. Alberts, *The Golden Voyage. The Life and Times of William Bingham* (Boston, 1939), p. 31.

7. The committee had instructed Capt. John Young to take dispatches to Bingham and return with arms and ammunition: *Naval Docs.*, VI, 912. For Young's career see William B. Clark, *The First Saratoga: Being the Saga of John Young and His Sloop-of-War* (Baton Rouge, La., 1953).

in such case if properly certifyed it might be best to make sale of them.

We thank you for Mr. Prices Pamphlet[8] and wish you woud write to Mr. Deane and Mr. Morris to contrive you a Constant and ample Supply of the English, Irish, and French Newspapers Political publications &c. We send you by this opportunity the Journals of Congress as far as published and the News Papers to this time. We received the Arms and Powder by the Reprisal they came seasonably, and we wish there had been more of them. The Secret Committee will supply you with Funds for the payments for these and more.

Since the arrival of Ld: Howe and Gen: Howe in the Neighbourhood of New York with their Forces, they have been rather too Strong for our people to cope with, and consequently have succeeded in their interprizes, which however have not been of that importance that they will probably [seem?] to the World. They have been ten or twelve weeks with a powerfull Fleet and a [i.e., are] well provided and appointed with every thing necessary and what have they done? They have got possession of three small Islands on the Coast of America, these were hardly disputed with them and yet if every Acre of American teritory is to cost them in the same proportion the Conquest woud ruin all Europe. Our Army are now collected to a point and are strongly entrenched on New York Island and at Kingsbridge, so that in fact Mr. Howe is hemmed in as he was at Boston, except that he has more Elbow Room and a powerfull Fleet commanding an extensive Inland Navigation.[9] Our Northern Army are Strongly posted at Tyconderago and expect they will be able to keep Mr. Burgoyne from crossing the Lakes this Campaigne.

We are worse off for Woolen Cloathing for our Army than any other matter, and you must exert your utmost industry to buy and send us every thing of that kind you can meet with in Martinico or any of the Neighbouring Islands. We have gone into this detail of our present situation that you may have a just Idea of it and be

8. Presumably *Observations on the Nature of Civil Liberty* . . . , discussed in a note on Priestley to BF above, Feb. 13.

9. The disastrous outcome of the campaign is well disguised. The British, in control of Staten Island, western Long Island, and all but the northern end of Manhattan, were slowly preparing the final move that drove Washington across the Hudson and out of New Jersey.

able to make proper representations to the General and inhabitants of Martinico.

We recommended the French officers that came with Captain Wickes to Congress, and the board of War have provided for them to their Satisfaction, on this subject your remarks have been very proper. Officers unacquainted with our Language cannot be Usefull, therefore we do not wish to encourage such to come amongst us, at the same time Men of Merit and abilities will always meet with suitable encouragement. You must therefore pursue the line you set out in, give general discouragement to those that apply and recommend none but such as the General will pledge his word for, and you May even intimate to him that if too many come over the Congress will not know what to do with them.[1]

We are now at the 1st of October and have heard from Mr. Deane after his arrival at Bourdeaux, his last letter is dated the 23d June when he was just setting out for Paris. We have later than his.[2] In consequence of which we desire you to enquire of the General and Governor whither they have received any Arms or ammunition from Monsr. Hortalez with directions to deliver the same to any person properly authorized by Congress to receive them. If they have we hereby authorize you to receive the same giving you receipts on behalf of the United States of America. If none such are arrived, enquire if they have any advice of such and request they will make known to you when they do arrive.

We desire you to make the like application to the Governor of st. Eustatia, but proceed cautiously in this bussiness. We think you should go there yourself in a French Vessel or if that might be unsafe or make a noise, get Mr. Richard Harrison or some person in whose prudence you can confide. Let the first question be, whether His Excellency has received any advices from Monsr. Hortalez. If the answer be in the negative, tell him he will receive letters from such a person and that those advices have reference to you therefore request the Favour of being immediately made ac-

1. Gen. d'Argout at Martinique had recommended four French officers who had no English and no money. Bingham, perhaps for political reasons that he explained in a missing letter, persuaded Wickes to take them with him on his return voyage; and the board of war reluctantly took care of them. Clark, *Wickes*, pp. 64, 68.

2. Deane's letter is above. The later word was Thomas Story's verbal report from Arthur Lee; see the committee's memorandum below, Oct. 1.

quainted when they come to hand when you will wait on him or send a proper person in your stead. If the answer be in the affirmative then enquire if His Excellency has received any thing beside advice from Monsr. Hortalez and if he has, inform him you are empowered to receive the same from him agreeable to the directions sent with the Goods. We belive you had best proceed in the same cautious manner at Martinico and open no more of this bussiness than circumstances shall make absolutely necessary. We also enjoin you to the stricktest secrecy and herewith enclose you two seperate letters as your proper authority for receiving any goods or money Mr. Hortalez our Agent in Europe may Remit.[3] It was intended that Capt. Young should deliver you this letter but as we have some important dispatches to send to Mr. Deane, we have concluded to send Mr. Wm. Hodge junr. the bearer hereof with the same in order that he may deliver them with his own hands. You'l please to shew Mr. Hodge proper attention and assist him to the utmost of your power in procuring him a passage immediately from Martinico to France in a good ship. If any Men of War or packet should be going, make application to the General to recommend Mr. Hodge to the Commander, also to the Governor or commander of the port where he goes to in France, to give him support and assistance from thence to Paris with the best dispatch. If Mr. Hodge should want money for his expences supply him and transmit us his Receipts for the same. You will serve your Country by forwarding Mr. Hodge without delay, but you need not mention to the General how urgent we are on this point unless you find it will promote his dispatch.[4]

We learn from many quarters that a Fleet of twenty sail of the line are fitting out at Brest and Toulon.[5] Shou'd they come out to

3. One of the letters of Oct. 1, signed by BF and Morris, is below; the other, of the same date and mentioned in our note on the memorandum just cited, was Hancock's authorization of the two to act for the committee.

4. William Hodge (born 1750) was a Philadelphia merchant who had been commissioned to go to Europe and there purchase, outfit, and man a privateer to cruise in the Channel and, if the French permitted, bring prizes into their ports. He carried with him copies of the proposed commercial treaty and of BF's credentials as commissioner to France, along with a blank commission for Deane to sign for the commander of the privateer. Hugh L. Hodge, *Memoranda of Family History* (Philadelphia, 1903), pp. 11–12; *Naval Docs.*, VI, 1120–1.

5. The ships were being made ready, but none was yet in active service: Dull, *French Navy*, pp. 52–3, 60–1.

the West Indies and be destined to commit Hostilities against the British Trade or Territorys, they have a fair opportunity to strike a Capital Stroke at New york where they have upwards of 400 Sail of Ships Guarded only by two Sixty four Gun Ships, two fiftys and Six Fortys the rest are all Frigates &c: Twenty Sail of the line wou'd take their whole Fleet with ease, and then we cou'd as easily manage their Army.

We had Ommitted above to desire that you should send back in the Sloop Independance Captain Young a proportion of the Arms, ammunition Money or other Stores you May receive either at Martinico or st. Eustatia from Monsr. Hortalez, taking bills of loading for the same, deliverable to us or our order and if the quantity you receive should be considerable you may send by Captain Young about the value of Three or four Thousand pounds Sterling observing that we want muskets and woolen Cloathing most immediately. We shall send more armed vessels after Capt. Young to bring away the Remainder of what you may receive or buy, and are, Sir Your Obedient humble Servants   B Franklin
Robt Morris

William Bingham Esqr.

Notations: Committee of Secret Correspondence September 21 1776 No 4 / Committee of S C Septr 21st 1776

From William Temple Franklin

ALS: American Philosophical Society

Honoured Sir,   Perth-Amboy Septr: 21st: 1776

I am very sorry to find, that my intended visit to my Father, does not meet with your approbation;[6] and it likewise makes my Mother very uneasy; as she will not now be able to communicate the situation of her Family concerns, nor get that advice she is desirous of having, and without which she knows not how to act.

The method you mention of encloseing her Letters seal'd to Govr. Trumbull, she has tried with Col. Hamlen in her two last Letters, but has had no account of their being receiv'd, either open'd or unopened, tho' there has been sufficient time for that

---

6. See BF's letter of two days before.

purpose: she likewise knows not how to take the Liberty of encloseing a Letter to a Gentleman, with whom she is totally unacquainted, and who has not shewn any favour to her husband during his Imprisonment, but on the contrary, has rather been severe.[7]

In my going, you might perhaps imagine, I should give such intelligence to my Father, as would not be thought proper for him to know, but I can assure you sir, that I am entirely ignorant of every thing relating to Publick Affairs, except the petty News, which is talk'd of by every body, and is in all the Publick Prints.

In my Fathers last Letter to my mother he leaves it to her, concerning my return to Philadelphia, while she continues in the same situation, that she is in now, and I believe she will keep me, unless she can hear from my Father, concerning her removal, as she will not be able to effect it without the assistance of Thomas;[8] and as I mention'd before the Winter is approaching so fast, and the present troubles not likely to end, that there is no time to be lost.

Mr. Bache did not favour us with a call as he went along, but I suppose he will on his return.

My mother joins me in Duty to you and Aunt Mecome, and in desireing to be affectionately remember'd to Mrs. Bache and the Children. I am Honoured Sir, Your ever dutiful Grandson

W. T. FRANKLIN

Addressed: To / Dr: Franklin / Philadelphia / per Post

7. Col. "Hamlen," we conjecture, was Jabez Hamlin (1709–91), a prominent resident of Middletown and a member of the state council of safety, for whom see H. Franklin Andrews, *The Hamlin Family, a Genealogy of Capt. Giles Hamlin* . . . (Exira, Ia., 1900), pp. 44–61. We have found no other Conn. colonel of that name.

8. Thomas Park or Parke, the Franklins' steward, attended WF in confinement and was still with him when Elizabeth died the following summer. E. Alfred Jones, *The Loyalists of New Jersey* . . . (N.J. Hist. Soc. *Coll.*, x; Newark, N.J., [1927]), p. 169; William H. Mariboe, "The Life of William Franklin . . . " (doctoral dissertation, University of Pa., 1962), p. 480.

To William Temple Franklin

ALS: American Philosophical Society

Dear Grandson,   Philada. Sept. 22. 1776

You are mistaken in imagining that I am apprehensive of your carrying dangerous Intelligence to your Father;[9] for while he remains where he is, he could make no use of it were you to know and acquaint him with all that passes. You would have been more in the right if you could have suspected me of a little tender Concern for your Welfare, on Account of the Length of the Journey, your Youth and Inexperience, the Number of Sick returning on that Road with the Infectious Camp Distemper, which makes the Beds unsafe, together with the Loss of Time in your Studies, of which I fear you begin to grow tired. To send you on such a Journey merely to avoid the being oblig'd to Govr. Trumbull for so small a Favour as the forwarding a Letter, seems to me inconsistent with your Mothers usual Prudence. I rather think the Project takes its rise from your own Inclination to a Ramble, and Disinclination for Returning to College, join'd with a Desire I do not blame of seeing a Father you have so much Reason to love. They send to me from the Office for my Letter, so I cannot add more than to acquaint you, I shall by next post if desired send several Frank'd Covers directed to Govr. Trumbull, for Mrs. F. to use as she has occasion. I write to him in the first now sent, to introduce her Request. She may desire her Husband to send his Letters to her under Cover to me: It will make but 2 Days odds. The Family is well and join in Love to her and you. Your affectionate Grandfather   B FRANKLIN

Addressed: Free / To / Mr William Temple Franklin / at Mrs Franklin's / Perth Amboy / B Free Franklin

Notation: B. Franklin Esqr to his Grand child. Philada Sepr. 22d 1776

---

9. See the preceding document.

Patrick Anderson to the Pennsylvania Convention

ALS: National Archives[1]

⟨Camp above Kingsbridge, September 22, 1776: My zeal for the cause, my difficulties, "our present shattered condition," and the lack of orders from the convention or council of safety compel me to trouble you with the following account.

After our defeat on Long Island the command of the musketry battalion devolved on me. About 200 men remained fit for duty, but had lost most of their baggage and some of their arms and accoutrements. No field officers were left, and I applied for advice to Lieut. Col. Brodhead, who soon afterward told me that he had been ordered to annex my battalion to the rifle regiment, and had so informed you; I complied while awaiting your further instructions. "Want of Necessarys Sowered the men's minds." Shortage of rations and unpunctual pay have increased their discontent, and so many have deserted that scarcely eighty-three remain. They believe that, if captured, they will not be exchanged while any continental prisoners are still in enemy hands.

I have, with Col. Brodhead's permission, sent Lieut. Lang after the deserters. I have confidence in him, and he can inform you fully of our situation. Capt. Dehuff will tell you more when he arrives.[2] I will await your further orders and cheerfully obey them. If the battalion is to be recruited I will recommend several for promotion, of whose good behavior and courage on Long Island and elsewhere I have proof. Addressed to Franklin as president of the convention.⟩

1. The complete text is in 1 *Pa. Arch.*, V, 27–8.
2. Capt. Anderson, of Chester Co., was a company commander before the action on Long Island, in which his battalion was heavily engaged and its colonel, Samuel Atlee (whose letter is above, Aug. 2, 1776), was captured. Lieut. James Lang was promoted to captain the following December; he and Capt. Abraham Dehuff were respectively from York and Lancaster Co. John B. B. Trussell, *The Pennsylvania Line: Regimental Organization and Operations, 1776–1783* (Harrisburg, Pa., 1977), pp. 122–3, 167–8, 176–81. For Daniel Brodhead (1736–1809) see *ibid.*, p. 165, and the *DAB*.

James Ewing and Michael Swoope[3] to the Pennsylvania
Convention LS: Morristown National Historical Park

Dated Septr. 23d. 1776. Fort Constitution[4]
We the Subscribers do beg Leave to recommend the Bearer Mr.
James Lang Lieutenant in The Pennsylvania Battalion of Mus-
quetry, for the Commission of Captain (there being at present a
Vacancy in said Battalion). We further beg Leave to represent him
as a very proper and fit Person for said Post.[5]

JAMES EWING Br. Gl.
MICH. SWOOPE Colol.

To the Honorable Benjn Franklin Esqr President of the Convention

The Continental Congress: Instructions to Franklin, Silas Deane, and Arthur Lee as Commissioners to France

Attested copy: Harvard University Library

This document was long in the making. On August 27 Congress expanded the committee that was drafting the proposed treaty of commerce with France, and ordered it to draft also instructions to the commissioners who were to carry the treaty. The committee reported the
instructions on September 10.[6] On the 24th, a week after Congress
approved the treaty, it amended and adopted the instructions after a
lively debate. The principal question at issue was what assurances the
commissioners might offer if, as a result of signing the treaty, France
were drawn into war, and the final decision was to offer nothing more
than American neutrality.[7] On the 26th Franklin, Deane, and Jefferson
were elected commissioners. John Adams apparently refused nomination, and Jefferson, after thinking over the offer for days, declined it on

3. For Gen. James Ewing (1736–1806) see the *DAB*, and for Col. Swoope
the letter from York above, Aug. 31, 1775.
4. Better known as Fort Lee, on the west side of the Hudson facing Fort
Washington in upper Manhattan.
5. For Lang see the preceding document.
6. Butterfield, *John Adams Diary*, III, 413; *JCC*, V, 710, 817 n. For the draft
treaty of commerce see the editorial note above under June 12, 1776.
7. The issue appears in the draft of the instructions as printed in the *JCC*, V,
813–7, where the editor has indicated the amendments rejected and adopted in
debate.

October 11.[8] Franklin had no hesitation. "I have only a few years to live," he told Benjamin Rush, "and I am resolved to devote them to the work that my fellow citizens deem proper for me; or speaking as old-clothes dealers do of a remnant of goods, 'You shall have me for what you please.'"[9] On September 28 Congress made provision for the commissioners' maintenance in France. On October 16 it gave them additional instructions on foreign alliances, and learned of Jefferson's refusal to serve. On the 22nd Arthur Lee was elected as his replacement, and Congress appended a final directive to procure from the French court eight ships of the line.

The instructions of September 24 and October 16 have survived in a number of forms;[1] only one copy, that which we print, contains the additions made on September 28 and October 22. Franklin took this document with him to France, and the signatures of the three commissioners attest its accuracy. It is, however, inaccurate in two minor respects: the instructions of September 24 and October 16 include Lee's name, though he had not yet been elected; and most of the references to articles in the proposed treaty are misnumbered.

[September 24 – October 22, 1776]

Instructions to, Benjamin Franklin, Silas Deane and Arthur Lee, Commissioners appointed by the Congress of the United States of America.

There is herewith delivered to you a Plan of a Treaty with his most Christian Majesty of France, approved of in Congress on the part of the United States of America.

It is the wish of Congress that the Treaty should be concluded

8. Butterfield, *op. cit.*, IV, 70; Charles Francis Adams, ed., *The Works of John Adams* . . . (10 vols., Boston, 1856), I, 248; Boyd, *Jefferson Papers*, I, 524.

9. Lyman H. Butterfield, ed., *Letters of Benjamin Rush* (2 vols., Princeton, N.J., 1951), I, 118. For Rush's later and slightly different versions of the quotation see the *PMHB*, XXIX (1905), 29, and George W. Corner, ed., *The Autobiography of Benjamin Rush* . . . (Princeton, N.J., 1948), p. 149. BF was elected by unanimous vote: Smith, *Letters*, V, 380.

1. The original draft of the Sept. 24 instructions, printed in the *JCC* and addressed to no one, is in the National Archives. Three copies signed by Hancock are extant. Two are in the Harvard University Library, one with BF's, Deane's, and Jefferson's names filled in and the other with BF's, Deane's, and Lee's; in the third, in the APS, Lee's name is interlined above Jefferson's. Two copies of the Oct. 16 instructions, again signed by Hancock, are respectively in the New York Public Library and the APS. In the first the name of the third commissioner is blank; in the second Lee's has been added in another ink, and BF has appended a notation: "Additional Instructions to Treat with foreign Ambassadors Oct. 16, 1776." An extract in his hand is also in the APS.

and you are hereby instructed to use every means in your Power for concluding it conformable to the plan you have received.

If you shall find that to be impracticable, you are hereby authorised to relax the demands of the United States, and to enlarge their Offers agreable to the following Directions.

If his most Christian Majesty shall not consent that the subjects, people and Inhabitants of the United States, shall have the Priviledges proposed in the second Article, then the United States ought not to give the Subjects of his most Christian Majesty the Privileges proposed in the first Article;[2] but that the United States shall give to the Subjects of his most Christian Majesty the same Privileges, Liberties and Immunities at least and the like favour in all things which any Foreign Nation the most favoured shall have; provided his most Christian Majesty shall give to the Subjects People and Inhabitants of the United States, the same benefits Privileges and immunities which any the most favoured Foreign Nation now has, uses or enjoys. And in case neither of these Propositions of equal Advantages are agreed to, then the whole of the said Articles are to be rejected rather than obstruct the farther Progress of the Treaty.

The third Article must be insisted on.[3]

The sixth Article ought to be obtained if possible; but should be waved rather than the Treaty should be interrupted by insisting upon it; his most Christian Majesty agreeing nevertheless, to use his Interest and Influence to procure Passes from the States mentioned in this Article for the Vessels of the Subjects and Inhabitants of the United States upon the Mediterranean.[4]

The seventh Article will probably be attended with some Diffuculty. If you find his most Christian Majesty determined not to

2. The first two articles of the treaty provided that in commercial affairs each nation should treat the citizens of the other as if they were its own. This radical break with tradition is discussed in Felix Gilbert, *To the Farewell Address: Ideas of Early American Foreign Policy* (Princeton, 1961), p. 51; James H. Hutson, "Intellectual Foundations of Early American Diplomacy," *Diplomatic History*, I (1977), 5; and Vernon G. Setser, "Did Americans Create the Conditional Most-Favored-Nation Clause?," *Journal of Modern History*, V (1933–4), 319–23.

3. Here the numbering begins to be erroneous: each article referred to is in fact the following one. Article 4 provided that France should protect, and convoy when requested, American ships in its territorial waters.

4. Article 7 committed France to protecting American trade from attack by corsairs on the Barbary coast.

agree to it, you are impower'd to add to it as follows.[5] That the United States will never be subject or acknowledge allegiance or obedience to the King or Crown or Parliament of Great Britain, nor grant to that Nation any exclusive Trade or any advantages or Priviledges in Trade more than to his most Christian Majesty; neither shall any Treaty for terminating the present War between the King of Great Britain and the United States or any War which may be declared by the King of Great Britain against his most Christian Majesty in consequence of this Treaty take Effect untill the expiration of six Calender Months after the Negotiation for that purpose shall have been duly notified, in the former instance, by the United States to his most Christian Majesty, and in the other instance by his most Christian Majesty to the United States, to the end that both these Parties may be included in the Peace, if they think proper.

The eleventh and twelth Articles are to be waved if you find that the Treaty will be interrupted by insisting on them.[6]

You will press the thirteenth Article but let not the fate of the Treaty depend upon obtaining it.[7]

If his most Christian Majesty should be unwilling to agree to the fifteenth and twenty fifth Articles you are directed to consent that the Goods and effects of Enemies on board the Ships and Vessels of ether Party shall be liable to seizure and confiscation.[8]

The twenty fourth Article is not to be insisted on.[9]

You will solicit the Court of France for an immediate supply of twenty or thirty thousand Muskets and bayonets, and a large

5. Article 8 bristled with difficulties for the commissioners because it promised only that the United States, in the event of an Anglo-French war, would not render Britain any assistance. What follows was an amendment by George Wythe to the instructions: *JCC*, v, 815.

6. Articles 12 and 13 had to do with duties on imports from the French West Indies to the United States.

7. Article 14 exempted from confiscation the estates of American merchants who died while resident in France.

8. Article 16 restricted the condemnation in wartime of goods captured en route to an enemy port; Article 26 guaranteed that subjects of both nations, except soldiers in the service of an enemy, might sail and trade where they pleased, and that all goods they carried, contraband excepted, should be free from seizure.

9. Article 25 stipulated that privateers commissioned by any state at war with either of the contracting parties might receive no protection in French or American ports.

supply of Ammunition, and Brass Field Pieces to be sent under convoy by France. The United States engage for the Payment of the Arms, Artillery and Ammunition and to indemnify France for the Expence of the Convoy.

Engage a few good Engineers in the Service of the United states.

It is highly probable that France means not to let the United States sink in the present Contest; but as the Difficulty of obtaining true accounts of our Condition may cause an Opinion to be entertain'd, that we are able to support the War on our own Strength and resources, longer than in fact we can do, it will be proper for you to press for the immediate and explicit declaration of France in our Favour, upon a sugestion that a reunion with Great Britain may be the consequence of a Delay.

Should Spain be disinclined to our Cause from an Apprehension of Danger to her Dominions in South America, you are impowered to give the Strongest Assurances, that that Crown will receive no molestation from the United states in the Possession of those Territories.

You will transmit to us the most speedy and full intelligence of your Progress in this Business and of any other European Transactions that it may import us to know.

You are desired to get the best and earliest information that you possibly can of any negotiations that the Court of London may be carrying on for obtaining Foreign Mercenaries to be sent against these states, the next Campaign; and if any such design is in agitation you will endeavour to prevail with the Court of France to exert its influence in the most effectual manner to prevent the execution of such Designs.[1]

You are desired to obtain as early as possible a publick acknowledgement of the Independancy of these States on the Crown and Parliament of Great Britain by the Court of France.

In conducting this important Business the Congress have the greatest Confidence in your address, Abilities, Vigilance and Attachment to the interests of the United States and wish you every success.

By order of Congress   JOHN HANCOCK Presidt. . . .[2]

1. This and the following paragraph were Richard Henry Lee's amendments to the instructions: *JCC*, V, 816–17; Smith, *Letters*, V, 131–2.

2. This entry is followed in the MS by one of Sept. 26, which we omit; it records that Congress elected BF, Deane, and Lee as commissioners.

Septr. 28.

Resolved that the Commissioners should live in such stile and manner at the Court of France as they may find suitable and necessary to support the Dignity of their Publick Character, keeping an account of their Expences, which shall be reimbursed by the Congress of the United States of America.

That besides the actual Expences of the Commissioners, a Handsome allowance be made to each of them as a compensation for their Time, trouble, risque and Services.

That the secretary of the Embassy be allowed a salary of one thousand pounds sterling per annum, with the expences of his Passage out and Home.

That the secret Committee be directed to export Produce or remit Bills untill they make an effectual lodgement in France of 10,000 Pounds Sterling subject to the Order of the said Commissioners for their present support, and report to Congress when it is effected, in order that Congress may then consider what further Remittances to order for this purpose.

Extract from the Minutes   CHAS THOMSON secy.

In Congress October 16. 1776.

Additional Instructions to Benjamin Franklin, Silas Deane, and Arthur Lee, Commissioners from the United states of America to the King of France.[3]

Whilst you are negotiating the Affairs you are charged with at the Court of France, you will have opportunities of conversing frequently with the Ministers and agents of other European Princes and States residing there.

You shall endeavour when you find Occasion fit and convenient to obtain from them a recognition of our Independancy and Sovereignty, and to conclude Treaties of peace Amity and Commerce between their Princes or States and us; provided that the same be not inconsistent with the Treaty you shall make with his most Christian Majesty; that they do not oblige us to become a party in any War, which may happen in consequence thereof, and that the immunities, exemptions, privileges, protection, defence and ad-

---

3. These instructions foreshadow the Congressional decision at the end of the year to send emissaries to various European courts, for which see the committee of secret correspondence to the commissioners below, Dec. 30, 1776.

629

vantages Or the contrary, thereby stipulated, be equal and reciprocal.

If that cannot be effected, you shall to the Utmost of your
power, prevent their taking part with Great Britain in the War
which his Britannic Majesty prosecutes against us, or entering
into offensive Alliances with that King, and protest and present
remonstrances against the same, desiring the interposition, mediation and good offices, on our behalf of his most Christian Majesty the King of France and of any other Princes or States whose
dispositions are not hostile towards us.

In case overtures be made to you by the Ministers or agents of
any European Princes or States for Commercial Treaties between
them and us, you may conclude such treaties accordingly.

By order of Congress   JOHN HANCOCK Presidt.

In Congress October 22. 1776.

Resolved, That the Commissioners going to the Court of France
be directed to procure from that Court at the Expence of these
United States either by purchase or Loan, eight Line of battle ships
of 74 and 64 Guns, well manned, and fitted in every respect for
Service; That as these Ships may be useful in proportion to the
quickness with which they reach North-America, the Commissioners, be directed to expedite this Negotiation with all possible
diligence.   JOHN HANCOCK Presidt.

Paris, Feb. 5. 1777.

The within is a true Copy of the original Instructions examined
by us,   B FRANKLIN
SILAS DEANE
ARTHUR LEE

Endorsed: Instructions

Sketch of Propositions for a Peace   Copy: Library of Congress

This document, in an unidentified hand, was among the papers that
Franklin left to his grandson and editor. When William Temple Franklin
eventually published it, he gave two possible explanations of it. The first
was that his grandfather thought it advisable to carry with him propositions for peace with Great Britain, and therefore drew up these and

submitted them to the "secret committee," presumably the committee of secret correspondence; Congress may or may not have acted upon them. The second was that the committee provided Franklin with these or similar proposals in case he were captured at sea.[4] The first explanation, that he wrote them himself, is by far the more plausible. The idea of securing the United States by expanding its borders was consonant with his thinking,[5] the offer of an annual subsidy to Great Britain for the next century was one that he had already suggested in another context,[6] and the economic arguments advanced here are ones that might be expected of him; "He thinks," furthermore, that his visiting England would be useful. These signs all suggest that the proposals were his, but if so he seems to have discarded them. No evidence has come to light that they were discussed in Congress, or that he took them with him on his voyage.

[After September 26 and before October 25, 1776.[7]]
Sketch of Propositions for a peace 1776.

There shall be a perpetual peace between Great Britain and the United States of America on the following conditions.

Great Britain shall renounce and disclaim all pretence of right or authority to govern in any of the United States of America.

To prevent those occasions of misunderstanding which are apt to arise where the territories of different powers border on each other through the bad conduct of frontier inhabitants on both sides, Britain shall cede to the United states the provinces or Colonies of Quebec, St. John's, Nova Scotia, Bermuda, East and West Florida, and the Bahama islands, with all their adjoining and intermediate territories now claimed by her.

In return for this Cession, the United States shall pay to Great Britain the sum of [*blank in* MS] Sterling in annual payments that is to say [*blank*] per annum for and during the term of [*blank*] years.

And shall moreover grant a free trade to all British subjects throughout the United States and the ceded Colonies And shall guarantee to Great Britain the Possession of her islands in the West Indies.

4. WTF, *Memoirs*, I, 307, 308–9.
5. See Gerald Stourzh, *Benjamin Franklin and American Foreign Policy* (2nd ed.; Chicago, 1969), pp. 65–82, 198–213.
6. "Intended Vindication and Offer of Congress to Parliament" above, under July 21, 1775.
7. *I.e.*, after his election as commissioner and before his departure.

Motives for proposing a peace at this time.

1. The having such propositions in charge, will by the Law of nations be some protection to the Commissioners or Ambassadors if they should be taken.

2. As the news of our declared independence will tend to unite in Britain all parties against us; so our offering peace with commerce and payments of money, will tend to divide them again. For peace is as necessary to them as to us: our commerce is wanted by their merchants and manufacturers, who will therefore incline to the accommodation, even though the monopoly is not continued, since it can be easily made appear their *share* of our growing trade, will soon be greater than the *whole* has been heretofore. Then for the landed interest, who wish an alleviation of taxes, it is demonstrable by figures that if we should agree to pay suppose ten millions in one hundred years, viz. £100,000 per annum for that term, it would being faithfully employed [as] a sinking fund more than pay off all their present national debt. It is besides a prevailing opinion in England, that they must in the nature of things sooner or later lose the Colonies, and may think they had better be without the government of them, so that the Proposition will on that account have more supporters and fewer opposers.

3. As the having such propositions to make; or any powers to treat of peace, will furnish a pretence for BF's going to England, where he has many friends and acquaintance, particularly among the best writers and ablest speakers in both Houses of Parliament, he thinks he shall be able when there if the terms are not accepted, to work up such a division of sentiments in the nation as greatly to weaken its exertions against the United States and lessen its credit in foreign countries.

4. The knowledge of there being powers given to the Commissioners to treat with England, may have some effect in facilitating and expediting the proposed treaty with France.[8]

5. It is worth our while to offer such a sum for the countries to be ceded, since the vacant lands will in time sell for a great part of what we shall give, if not more; and if we are to obtain them by conquest, after perhaps a long war, they will probably cost us

8. This attempt at persuasion by threat, if it is BF's, modifies what he said later was his consistent view "that a Virgin State should preserve the Virgin Character, and not go about suitering for Alliances, but wait with decent Dignity for the Applications of others." To Arthur Lee below, March 21, 1777.

more than that sum. It is absolutely necessary for us to have them for our own security, and though the sum may seem large to the present generation, in less than half the term, it will be to the whole United States, a mere trifle.

The Secret Committee to John Ross[9]

LS:[1] New York Public Library

⟨Philadelphia, September 27, 1776: Several vessels bringing clothing have been captured. Please purchase on the best possible terms 10,000 striped blankets, 30,000 yards of blue and brown broadcloth at 3*s.* to 6*s.* the yard, 3,000 yards of different colors for facings at about 4*s.*, and 1,000 pieces of Duffields[2] or the equivalent at about 90*s.* Use either funds on hand or credit; we are buying rice, indigo, tobacco, etc., for immediate export, and the season will give us a fair opportunity of getting them to market, whereas enemy cruisers have hampered us this summer. Get the cloth wherever it can be most quickly procured, except in Great Britain or Ireland; if need be charter a foreign ship to carry it, and we will promptly return her loaded. If you cannot send directly to America, consign the goods to William Bingham at Martinique, Cornelius Stevenson at St. Eustatius, Isaac Gouverneur at Curaçao, or Stephen Ceronio at Cap François,[3] with orders to forward them at once. Signed by Franklin, Robert Morris, Richard Henry Lee, Francis Lewis, and Philip Livingston.⟩

9. Ross (1729–1800) was a Scot who settled in Philadelphia and was active in the East Indian trade. He had recently gone to Europe, under contract with the committee, to oversee purchases. *PMHB*, XXIII (1899), 78; *Naval Docs.*, IV, 580. His resultant financial troubles will appear in later volumes.

1. The complete text in *Naval Docs.*, VI, 1024–5, omits a notation on the MS that the letter was received on Feb. 12, 1777.

2. A coarse woolen cloth now known as duffel.

3. For Bingham and Stevenson see above, the letter to the first of June 3 and from the second of Aug. 22, 1776. Isaac Gouverneur, scion of a prominent N.Y. mercantile family, was in business on both Curaçao and St. Eustatius; see John A. Stevens, Jr., *Colonial New York, Sketches Biographical and Historical* . . . (New York, 1867), pp. 136–7; *Political Mag. and Parliamentary, Naval, Military and Literary Jour.*, II (1781), 564–5. A letter to Ceronio is below, Oct. 23.

To William Temple Franklin

ALS: American Philosophical Society

Dear Tempe   Philada. Sept. 28. 1776

I hope you will return hither immediately, and that your Mother will make no Objection to it, something offering here that will be much to your Advantage if you are not out of the Way.[4] I am so hurried that I can only add Ever your affectionate Grandfather   B FRANKLIN

My Love to her.

Addressed: To / Mr William Temple Franklin / at Mrs Franklins / Perth Amboy / B Free Franklin

Notation: B. Franklin Esqr to his Grand child. Phila Sepr. 28th. 1776

The Continental Congress: Letter of Credence to Franklin, Silas Deane, and Thomas Jefferson as Commissioners to France

DS: Harvard University Library; incomplete copy (?):[5] American Philosophical Society

[September 30, 1776]

The Delegates of the united States of New-hampshire, Massachusetts bay, Rhode-island, Connecticut, New-york, New-jersey, Pensylvania, Delaware, Maryland, Virginia, North-carolina, South-carolina and Georgia to all who shall see these presents greeting.

Whereas a trade upon equal terms between the subjects of his most Christian Majesty the king of France and the people of these states will be beneficial to both nations, Know ye therefore that we confiding in the prudence and integrity of Benjamin Franklin one of the delegates in Congress from the state of Pensylvania and

4. BF had been elected two days before as one of the commissioners to France, and he took WTF with him.

5. Or a DS if it originally bore Hancock's signature; the conclusion is missing. Later copies, which replace Jefferson's name with Lee's, are in the APS, Harvard University Library, and the Conn. Hist. Soc.; the last is for some reason dated Oct. 23. For the committee that drafted the letter see the *JCC*, V, 827.

president of the Convention of the said state &c. Silas Deane late a delegate from the state of Connecticut, now in France, and Thomas Jefferson a delegate from the state of Virginia have appointed and deputed and by these presents do appoint and depute them the said Benjamin Franklin, Silas Deane and Thomas Jefferson our Commissioners, giving and granting to them the said Benjamin Franklin, Silas Deane and Thomas Jefferson or to any two of them and in case of the death, absence or disability of any two, to any one of them full power to communicate, treat, agree and conclude with his most Christian Majesty the king of France, or with such person or persons as shall by him be for that purpose authorised, of and upon a true and sincere friendship and a firm, inviolable and universal peace for the defence protection and safety of the navigation and mutual commerce of the subjects of his most Christian Majesty and the people of the united states, and to do all other things which may conduce to those desirable ends, and promising in good faith to ratify whatsoever our said commissioners shall transact in the premisses. Done in Congress at Philadelphia the thirtieth day of September in the year of our Lord one thousand, seven hundred and seventy six. In testimony whereof the president by order of the said Congress hath hereunto subscribed his name and affixed his seal. JOHN HANCOCK Presid't

Attest Cha Thomson secy

Vote of Thanks from Harvard College

Text in William C. Lane, "Harvard College and Franklin," *Publications of the Colonial Society of Massachusetts*, x (1907), 238–9.

⟨Sept. 30, [1776]: The President and Fellows vote their thanks to Franklin for the gift, transmitted by James Bowdoin, of Vattel's *Droit des gens*,[6] and ask Bowdoin to present him with a copy of their vote.⟩

6. See above, Dumas to BF, May 17, 1775, and Bowdoin to BF, Aug. 19, 1776.

Report of Thomas Story[7] to the Committee of Secret Correspondence and the Committee's Memorandum upon It[8]

DS and copy:[9] National Archives

[October 1, 1776]

"On my leaving London Arthur Lee Esqr. requested me to inform the Committee of Correspondence, that he had several conferences with the French Embassador who had communicated the same to the French Court, that in consequence thereof the Duke De Vergennes had sent a gentleman to Mr. Lee, [who informed] him that the French Court could not think of entering into a War with England, but that they would assist America by sending from Holland this Fall £200,000 Sterling worth of Arms and Ammunition to St. Eustatius, Martinico or Cape Francois, that application was to be made to the Governors or Commandants of those Places, by enquiring for Monsr. Hortalez and that on applying Persons properly authorised, the above articles would be delivered to them."[1]

---

7. For the little we know about Arthur Lee's emissary see BF to Dumas above, Dec. 9. Story's report brought the first definite news of the French decision to send aid, and of the means agreed upon. The news could not have come at a more welcome moment, for the future looked dark: Long Island had been lost, New York had been lost, and Washington's army was waiting for the enemy to dislodge it from the hills of northern Manhattan. Hence the possibility of further misfortune mentioned in the last paragraph of the memorandum.

8. The memorandum is in a different hand.

9. The copy gives in an introductory statement the date of the report, which was used in a hearing in 1808 on the claim of Beaumarchais' daughter to be reimbursed for what her father had spent for the United States, and adds that the committee, on Dec. 13, 1775, had sent Story on a mission to France, Holland, and England. Two words illegible in the DS are supplied from the copy.

1. Story probably left London on his return in late May or early June, by which time Beaumarchais had assumed the pseudonym of Hortalez although the company had not yet been organized; see Lee to Dumas, May 20 to June 11, *Deane Papers*, I, 136. Lee said later that the grant was 200,000 louis d'or, which is close to £200,000 but vastly in excess of the actual sum, a million livres or less than £50,000; he said at the same time that the funds were a gift. Stevens, *Facsimiles*, III, no. 271. Story's report may be so interpreted, but the committee speaks of a loan.

Philada. October 1st. 1776. The above intelligence was Communicated to the Subscribers being the only two Members of the Committee of Secret Correspondence now in this City,[2] and on considering the Nature and importance of it, We agree in opinion that it is our indispensable duty to keep it Secret, even from Congress for the following reasons.

First. Shou'd it get to the ears of our Enemies at New York they wou'd undoubtedly take measures to intercept the Supplies and thereby deprive us not only of these succours but of others expected by the same route.

Second. As the Court of France have taken Measures to Negotiate this loan and succour in the most cautious and Secret Manner, shou'd we divulge it immediately, we may not only loose the present benefit, but also render that Court Cautious of any further Connection with such unguarded People and prevent their granting other Loans and assistance that we stand in need of, and have directed Mr. Deane to ask of them, for it appears from all our Intelligence they are not disposed to Enter into an immediate War with Britain altho disposed to support us in our Contest with them, we therefore think it our duty to Cultivate their favourable disposition toward us, draw from them all the support we can and in the end their private Aid must assist us to establish Peace or inevitably draw them in as Parties to the War.

Third. We find by Fatal Experience the Congress Consists of too many Members to keep Secrets, as none cou'd be more strongly enjoined than the present Embassy to France, notwithstanding which Mr. Morris was this day asked by Mr. Reese Meredith[3] whether Doctor Franklin and others were really going Ambassadors to France, which plainly proves, that this Committee ought to keep this Secret if Secrecy is required.

Fourthly We are also of opinion that it is *unnecessary* to inform Congress of this Intelligence at present because Mr. Morris belongs to all the Committees that can properly be employed in

2. Johnson and Jay had left to attend their respective state conventions, and Dickinson had withdrawn from Congress: Burnett, *Letters*, I, xlvi, liv, lix. On Oct. 1 Hancock had certified that BF and Morris were authorized to act for the full committee: *ibid.*, II, 111–12.

3. An elderly Quaker merchant in Philadelphia, frequently mentioned in passing in earlier volumes.

receiving and Importing the expected supplys from Martinico, St. Eustatia or Cape Francois and will immediately influence the necessary measures for that purpose. Indeed we have already authorized Wm. Bingham Esqr. to apply at Martinico and St. Eustatia for what comes there and remit part by the Armed Sloop Independance Capt. Young promising to send others for the rest.[4] Mr. Morris will apply to the Marine Committee to send other armed Vessells after her and also to Cape Francois (without Communicating this advice) in Consequence private Intelligence lately recd that Arms, Ammunition and Cloathing can now be procured at those places.

But shou'd any unexpected misfortune befall the States of America so as to depress the spirits of the Congress, it is our opinion that on any event of that kind, Mr. Morris (if Doctr. Franklin shou'd be absent) shou'd communicate this Important matter to Congress. Otherwise keep it untill part of or the whole supplys arrive, unless other events happen to render the Communication of it more proper than it appears to be at this time.

B FRANKLIN
ROBT MORRIS

Endorsements: Communicated to me the 11th October 1776 and I concur heartily in the measure.   RICHARD HENRY LEE

Communicated to me the 10th of October 1776 and I do also sincerely approve of the Measure.   WM HOOPER[5]

4. The committee to Bingham above, Sept. 21 to Oct. 1, 1776.

5. These were two of the three members elected to the committee on Oct. 11; the third was John Witherspoon: *JCC*, VI, 867. For all three see the *DAB*.

The Committee of Secret Correspondence to William Bingham[6]

LS: American Philosophical Society; LS:[7] New York Public Library; LS:[8] Harvard University Library

Sir   Philada. October 1st 1776

Having received advice that our Agent Monsr. Hortalez is dispatching Sundry Articles wanted for the Service of the United States of America to Martinico recommended to the care of his Excellency the General or the Governor and Intendant there, to be by them delivered to whoever Shall be properly authorized by Congress to receive the Same, We hereby request that you will make application for all Arms, ammunition Money cloathing or other Articles, that may arrive in Martinico with the above directions, and you are hereby empowered to receive and Grant Receipts for the Same on behalf of the United States of America, or to Sign Certificates or any other writing that may be required purporting the delivery thereof to you as Agent for the Congress. We are sir Your most humble Servants   B FRANKLIN

ROBT MORRIS

Notation: C of Secret Correspondence October 1 177[6]

The Committee of Secret Correspondence to Silas Deane

LS: Harvard University Library; letterbook copy: National Archives[9]

Dear Sir,   Philadelphia October 1st 1776

Mr. Morris has communicated to us the substance of your letters to him down to the 23rd June when you was near setting out for Paris.[1] We hope your reception there has been equal to your ex-

---

6. This letter is essentially a repetition in more formal terms of the instructions, also written on Oct. 1, in the second part of the committee's letter to Bingham above, Sept. 21. Those instructions were the outcome of the committee's interview with Story, for which see the document preceding this one.

7. Where by a clerk's error Martinique, when it first appears, becomes St. Eustatia.

8. Signed by BF alone.

9. From the copy we have silently corrected a few slips of the pen and deciphered some illegible words in the LS.

1. See Deane's letter of that date above.

pectation and our wishes, indeed we have no reason to doubt it considering the countenance we have met with amongst the French Islands, and their sea ports in Europe. It woud be very agreeable and usefull to hear from you just now in order to form more certain of the designs of the French Court respecting us and our contest, especially as we learn by various ways they are fitting out a considerable squadron at Brest and Toulon. What a noble Stroke they might now Strike at Newyork. Twenty Sail of the line wou'd take the whole Fleet there consisting of between 4 and 500 Sail of Men War, Transports, Stores Ships and Prizes; was that piece of business once effected by a French Fleet we wou'd engage to give them a very good Account of Genl. Howes Army in A Short time,[2] but alas we fear the Court of France will let Slip the Glorious opportunity and go to war by halves as we have done. We say go to war because we are of opinion they must take part in the war, sooner or later and the longer they are about it, the worse terms will they come in upon. We doubt not you will obtain from England a regular account of the proceedings of Ld. Howe and his Brother and we suppose the Generals Military opperations will be ushered into the World with an eclat beyond their true merits or at least, the conduct of our people and their present Situation will be misrepresented as ten times worse than the reality. We shall therefore State these things to you as they really are. The Fleet under Ld: Howe you know is vastly superiour to any thing we have in the Navy way; consequently where ever Ships can move they must command, therefore it was long foreseen that we cou'd not hold either Long Island or Newyork. Nevertheless as our fortifications were chiefly built with Axes and Spades the time and trouble in raising them was not mispent, for it must have been oweing to those works that they remained several Weeks at Staten Island without making any attempt. The first they did make was on Long Island when they landed 20,000 men or upwards at this time we had our Army consisting of not more than 20,000 Effective men stationed at Kings bridge, New York and on Long Island. 6 to 7000 was the whole of our Force on the latter and about 3000, of them commanded by Genl. Sullivan and Ld. Sterling turned out of the Lines took possession of some heights and in-

2. The later part of the committee's letter to Bingham above, Sept. 21, was written on the same day as this one and said much the same thing.

tended to annoy the Enemy in their approaches. They however out General'd us, and got a body of 5000 Men between our people and the Lines, so that we were surrounded and of course came off second best, but they purchased the victory dear and many such wou'd be their ruin. Sullivan, Ld. Stirling and many other officers fell into their hands, these with privates amounted to from 800 to 1000 Men in killed, wounded and taken Prisoners. They lost a greater number in killed and wounded[3] but we took but few prisoners as you may suppose. Genl. Howe then laid a Trap in which he fully expected to have caught every man we had on that Island, but Genl. Washington saw and frustrated his design by an unexpected and well conducted retreat across the Sound. This retreat is Spoke of on both Sides as a master Stroke.

The Enemy immediately marched up a large Body of Men opposite to Hell Gate. Our people threw up entrenchments on York Island to oppose their landing, but Shame to say it, on the day of Tryal two Brigades behaved infamously and cou'd not be Stopped by the intreatys or Threats of the General who came up in the midst of their flight.[4]

It had been previously determined to abandon New York and most of our Cannon and military stores were removed from thence in time. The Enemy took possession of the city and incamped on the plains of Harlem. Our side occupy the Heights of Harlem, Kings bridge and Mount Washington where they have made Lines as Strong as can be. In this situation they had a Skirmish between about 1000 to 1200 men on each Side in which we gained greatly the advantage, beat them off the Feild and took three Feild pieces from them, having killed and wounded Considerable Numbers of their men. Since then the City of New York has been on Fire and its said one fifth or one sixth of it is reduced to Ashes. The Enemy charged some stragglers of our people that happened to be in New York with having set the City on Fire designedly and took that occasion as we were told to exercise some inhuman Crueltys on those poor Wretches that were in their power.[5] They will no doubt

3. More than 10,000 American troops were on Long Island, according to the best estimates, and some 1,400 were casualties; the British reported losing less than 400: Freeman, *Washington*, IV, 157 n, 167 n.

4. *Ibid.*, pp. 193–4.

5. Was one of the cruelties the execution of Nathan Hale on Sept. 22, the day after the fire?

endeavour to throw the odium of such a measure on us, but in this they will fail, for Genl. Washington previous to the evacuation of that City whilst it was in his power to do as he pleased with it, desired to know the sense of Congress, respecting the destruction of the City as many officers had given it as their opinion it would be an adviseable measure, but Congress Resolved that it should be evacuated and left unhurt as they had no doubt of being able to take it back at a future day.[6] This will convince all the World we had no desire to burn Towns or destroy Citys but that we left such Meritorious works to grace the History of our Enemies. Upon the whole our Army near New York are not sufficiently strong to Cope with Genl. Howe in the open Feild they have therefore entrenched themselves and act on the defensive. They want better Arms, better Tents, and more Cloathing than they now have, or is in our power at this time to supply them with, consequently we cannot recruit or encrease that Army under these discouragements. Men cannot chearfully enter a service where they have the prospect of facing a powerfull Enemy and encountering the inclemencys of a hard, Cold Winter, without covering at the same time. These are discouraging circumstances but we must encounter them with double dilligence and we still have hopes to procure Cloathing partly by Importation, partly by Capture and chiefly by purchasing all that can be found on the Continent. If France means to befreind us or wishes us well they shoud send us succours in good Muskets, Blankets Cloaths Coatings and proper Stuff for Tents, and also in ammunition, but not like the Venetians wait untill we are beat and then send assistance. We are willing to pay for them, and shall be able soon as we can safely export our Tobacco and other valuable produce.

Our Northern Army is strong, well entrenched in an advantegeous Post at Tyconderago which can only be taken from them by storm as it cannot be approached in a regular manner on account of the situation. We are also formidable in the Lakes in Galleys, Boats and Gondolas under command of your freind Arnold, and that Army is better provided than the other so that we do not seem to apprehend any danger in that quarter at present. The Southern States are for the present in peace and quietness except some interruptions from the Indians who were instigated thereto

6. *JCC*, v, 733.

by Mr. Stewart the Superintendant and other Agents from our Enemies, however they have not any cause to rejoice in those machinations as yet for the Carolineans and Virginians have attacked and beat them several times, destroyed several of thier Towns and Corn Feilds and made them repent sorely what they have done, so that we have little to apprehend on account of Indians.[7]

The Only Sourse of uneasiness amongst us arises from the Number of Tories we find in every State. They are More Numerous than formerly and Speak more openly but Tories are now of various kinds and various principles, some are so from real attachment to Britain, some from interested views, many very many from fear of the British Force, some because they are dissatisfied with the General Measures of Congress, more because they disapprove of the Men in power and the measures in their respective States, but these different passions veiws and expectations are so combined in their Consequences that the parties affected by them, either withhold their assistance or oppose our operations and if America falls it will be oweing to such divisions more than the force of our Enemies. However there is much to be done before America can be lost and if France will but join us in time there is no danger but America will soon be established an Independant Empire and France drawing from her the principal part of those sources of Wealth and power that formerly flowed into Great Britain will immediately become the greatest power in Europe. We have given you as just a Picture of our present Situation as we can draw in the compass of a Letter, in Order that you may be well informed, but you will only impart such circumstances as you may think prudent.

Our Frigates are fine Vessels but we meet with dificulty in procuring Guns and Anchors. Our people are but young in casting the former, and we want Coals to make the latter; however these

7. For details of the naval dispositions on the lakes see Wayne to BF below, Oct. 3. Arnold's fleet was destroyed on Oct. 11, but the lateness of the season induced Carleton to retire from Ticonderoga. The Indian incursions on the frontier of Virginia and North Carolina had been contrary to the wishes of Stuart, the Indian superintendant for the British in the southern department, whose agents had sought to restrain the attacks: Philip M. Hamer, "John Stuart's Indian Policy during the Early Months of the American Revolution," *Miss. Valley Hist. Rev.*, XVII (1930–31), 351–66.

dificulties we shall surmount and are bent on building some Line of Battle Ships immediately.[8] The success in privateering and encouragement given by the Merchants will inevitably bring Seamen amongst us, this with the measures that will be adopted to encourage the breeding of seamen amongst ourselves, will in a few Years make us respectable on the Ocean. Surely France cannot be so blind to her own Interest as to neglect this Glorious opportunity of destroying the power and humbling the pride of her natural and our declared enemy.

We make no doubt you have been made acquainted with the Negotiations of Monsr. Hortalez and in consequence thereof we conclude that you will be at no loss to obtain the supplies of Goods wanted for a particular department, notwithstanding we know that the greatest part of those Remittances that were intended you have been intercepted by one means or other. It is unfortunate and much to be regretted that those remittances have had such Ill fate, but we hope you have obtained the Goods on Credit, and you may depend that Remittances will be continued until all your engagements are discharged.

Cloathing and Tents are so much wanted for our Army, that we intreat you to apply immediately to the Court of France for a Loan of money sufficient to dispatch immediately very considerable quantities of stuff fit for Tents and of Coarse Cloths, Coatings, Stockings and such other comfortable necessarys for any Army as you can readily judge will be proper.

You will get these goods sent out direct in French Vessels or to their Islands where we can send for them but if you cou'd prevail on the Court of France to send out men of war with them it wou'd be most acceptable.

Whatever engagements you make for payment of the cost of such Cloathing and Necessarys the Congress will order sufficient Remittances to fullfill the same but in our circumstances it requires time to accomplish them.

You'l Observe the Secret Committee have given orders to Mr. Thomas Morris to procure sundry articles and dispatch them immediately, and if you succeed in the negotiation of a loan from the Court for this purpose you may employ him or act in Conjunction with him, to procure and dispatch those articles ordered by them

8. See the note on the committee's letter to Deane above, Aug. 7, 1776.

and such others as you shall judge necessary and the Remittances to be made him will serve to refund the Loan. Should the Court decline this matter perhaps the Farmers General may be induced to advance the money or stake their Credit, for the sake of securing the Tobacco the Secret Committee will Remit to Europe.[9] These things we throw out as hints and shall only further observe that you cannot render your injured Country more essential service at this time than by procuring these supplies immediately.

We are told our vigilant enemies have demanded of the Courts of France, Spain, and Portugal to deliver up the American Ships in their Ports, and to forbid their having any further intercourse with them, that the Court of Portugal has complied so far as to order our Ships away on ten days notice.[10] That France and Spain gave evasive answers. This is private uncertain intelligence, but we think you will do well, to intimate to the Ministers of those Nations, that first impressions are lasting, that the time has been when they stood much in need of American Supplies, that such time may come again, that altho we are Stiled Rebels by Britain, yet our Freindship may hereafter be of the utmost importance to those powers particularly that possess American Colonies, and that injuries now done us will not be easilly effaced. These hints and arguments you'l offer as the suggestions of your own mind and endeavour to influence them by Interest or fear from taking any part against us. On the contrary as it is evidently their Interest to encourage our Commerce, so we hope you'l be able to influence them by One Means or other to protect and Licence it in the utmost extent. We shall not take up more of your time at present but remain Sir Your very humble Servants   B FRANKLIN
ROBT MORRIS

To Silas Deane Esqr

9. For Thomas Morris see the note on Penet to BF above, Aug. 3, 1776. Deane had already begun to negotiate with the farmers general, both as agent and for himself; see Price, *France and the Chesapeake*, II, 704–5.

10. An edict of July 4, published on the 16th, gave American shipping eight days' notice to leave Portuguese waters: Armando Marques Guedes, *A Aliança Inglêsa (Notas de História Diplomática)* (Lisbon, 1938), p. 241.

To Charles-Guillame-Frédéric Dumas

ALS: Yale University Library; copy: Archives du Ministère des affaires étrangères

Sir,   Philada. Oct. 1. 1776

I have just time to acknowledge the Receipt of your two Packets, A and B. with the Pamphlets enclos'd, the Contents of which are very satisfactory.[1] You will hear from me more fully in a little time.[2] With great Esteem I am, Sir, Your most obedient humble Servant   B FRANKLIN

We have a great Force brought against us here, but continue firm.

Mr Dumas.

From Catharine Greene   ALS: American Philosophical Society

My Dear Friend   Warwick Octr the 1st 1776

You will be Glad to hear of our geting home Safe which we did Friday night being 9½ Days on our Journey 10 on the Rhode layd by one throw a Careless trick of Catharines[3] but as Dont Choose to Leson her in your esteem Shall not tell the Particuliars. I wrote you from New Rochell after we had Past the troubled Waters[4] which hope you have Receivd. After that had nothing Remarkable except at the Publick houses. Wonderful accounts from N. york Such as was Never there Supposd. We Come from Newhaven to Harford and then to Windham and then to Providence where we Deliverd our treasure Meeting with no other trouble with it then the Bulk and heft.[5] We there heard of Celias haveing the Small Pox finely at Medfield and was expeckted to be

1. See Cornelius Stevenson to BF above, Aug. 22, 1776.
2. He apparently did so, but the letter miscarried; see BF to Dumas below, Jan. 28, 1777.
3. They left Philadelphia on Sept. 16; see BF to WTF above, Sept. 19. If they reached Warwick on Friday the 27th, Caty's "trick" must have immobilized them for more than a day.
4. Of the Hudson. Her letter has not survived, but see the final note below.
5. Doubtless the money that William Greene had gone to Philadelphia to collect from Congress; payment had been authorized on Sept. 2. See the note on Ray's letter above, Aug. 4, 1776, and *JCC*, V, 728.

out in a day or two.[6] Calld upon a few friends and Came home where we was So Joyfully Receivd as was worth takeing the Journey for had we had no other Pleasure. They had all been Very Clever and Sayd there had been but one or two Disagreeable things had happend which Desird not to hear of. Comeing from your house first I hardly knew whether to be Glad or Sorry you was not at home as the Parting from those we love is Sorrow, but when I Pleasd my Self with the Wish you had to Run away from hurry and Come to New England I was Sorry as I Wanted you to Strengthen the hope but not without you Could Pass the North River with great Safety and you Could be made Very Comfortable on the Rhode and then I Could wish you to take your Dear Sister with you whoes Heart is So Divided between So good a Brother and a Distrest Daugter[7] that though She appears Chearfull is Very un happy and for fear of makeing her friends So keeps all to her Self. She is a Dear good Woman and in whatever would Contribute to her happines, Should do it Willingly. Our Best Regard to Mr. and Mrs. Beach Beney and Dear little Willy. All of you I long to feast with us on fine Peaches and Pares and Bakt Sweet apples all which we have in great Plenty. Uncle Philip is here the Person you Visited with me and adds his love as does Jenny Phebe and Ray who is a good Boy as is Samey and other Children.[8] I am with Due Respect and as much love as you wish, your friend

CATY GREENE

Be kind enough to give our love to Mr. Elery[9] and mention our geting home well. Mr. Greene would have wrote but has Company.

6. Celia, the Greenes' second daughter, was then fourteen; for the children see above, x, 191 n. Medfield had just established a hospital for inoculation against smallpox: William S. Tilden, *History of the Town of Medfield, Massachusetts* . . . (Boston, 1887), p. 167.

7. Jane Collas was constantly worried about her seafaring husband, and with reason: during the war he was captured at least four times. "She looks on herself alredy," her mother had written in the spring of 1776, "as a Disconsolat widdow." Van Doren, *Franklin—Mecom*, p. 167; see also p. 189.

8. For Philip Greene (1727–91), Caty's maternal uncle, see Louise B. Greene, *The Greenes of Rhode Island* . . . (New York, 1903), pp. 104–5. Jenny Flagg was about to marry Elihu Greene, William's cousin; the others were Caty's children.

9. For Ellery see the note on Williams to BF above, March 1.

We feasted upon you a great deal Since we left your house for all there is but Such a Morsal of you left. Poor Doctr. Babcock with Mr. Collins the Gentleman that was to Come to us was at New york at the time the City was given up the Doctr. Run and Lost his horse for a time. Mr. Collins got over the Jersey Side and left both his horses but the Doctr. got his again one of our officers had Rhode it off.[1]

I askt Genll. Greene if there was any Prospect of our Prisoners being Release from Quebeck he Sayd it lay with the Congress.[2] Do my Dear Friend if there is any exchangeing them let it be done for they have Past throw Such ameseing hardships [*torn* a]s makes it Nessary for there Country to [*torn* th]em Selves in there Cause.

When I Say or write too free Pray tel me.

Addressed: To / Doctr Franklin / Philadelphia

The Committee of Secret Correspondence to Silas Deane

ALS: Haverford College Library; letterbook copy: National Archives

Sir   Philada. October 2d. 1776

We have this day received from the Honorable Congress of Delegates of the United States of America the important papers that accompany this letter being,

> first, a Treaty of Commerce and Alliance between the Court of France and these States.

> second, Instructions to their Commissioners relative to the said Treaty.

> lastly, A Commission, whereby you will see that Doctr. Franklin, The Honorable Thos. Jefferson Esqr. and your-

---

1. The Rhode Island Assembly had appointed John Collins of Newport, BF's old friend Joshua Babcock (above, XXI, 96 n), and another to confer with Washington on defense of the state: John R. Bartlett, ed., *Record of the Colony of Rhode Island . . .* (10 vols., Providence, R.I., 1856–65), VII, 609, 619–20.

2. This conversation indicates where the Greenes crossed the Hudson. On Sept. 17 Nathanael Greene was put in command in New Jersey, and established his headquarters at Fort Lee (Constitution): George W. Greene, *The Life of Nathanael Greene . . .* (3 vols., New York, 1867–71), I, 217–19. The fort was across the river from the American position in northern Manhattan.

self are appointed Commissioners for Negotiating said Treaty at the Court of France.[3]

These papers speak for themselves and need no Strictures or remarks from us, neither is it our business to make any. You will observe, that in case of the absence or disability of any one or two of the Commissioners the other has full Power to Act.

We therefore think it proper to inform you that Doctr. Franklin and Mr. Jefferson will take Passage with all Speed but it is necessary that their appointment on this business remain a profound Secret and we do not choose even to trust this paper with their rout. Suffice it therefore, that you expect them soon after this reaches your hands, but by different conveyances. And If you do not see some evident advantage will arise by Communicating this Commission to the French Ministry immediately, We give it as our opinion You had best suspend it, untill the arrival of one or both these Gentlemen, because You will then benefit of each others advice and abilities, and we apprehend their arrival will give additional Importance to the Embassy.

But should you be of opinion that delay will be in the least degree injurious to our Country or its Cause you must by all means use your own discretion in this matter, wherein we are not authorised to instruct or advise; we only offer our own thoughts on the Subject. Shou'd you think proper to disclose this Commission to the Ministers of France, enjoin the Stricktest Secrecy respecting the Names, or rather insist that it be not made known to any persons, but those whose office and employments entitle them to the communication that any others are joined with you in it because if that Circumstance reaches England before their arrival it will evidently endanger their Persons. The Congress have ordered the Secret Committee to lodge Ten thousand Pounds Sterling in France subject to the drafts or orders of the Commissioners for their support, and you may depend that remittances will be made for that purpose with all possible dilligence.[4] We can also inform you, that you may expect instructions for forming Treaties with

3. The commission or letter of credence is above, Sept. 30, 1776. The instructions were in fact incomplete, for others were added on Oct. 16 and 22; all are printed together above, under Sept. 24.

4. The *Reprisal*, on which BF sailed, carried £3,000 worth of indigo as a first instalment: BF to Deane below, Dec. 4, 1776.

other Nations. Consequently you will Cultivate a good understanding with all the Foreign Ministers.

We have Committed these Important dispatches to the care of
Mr. Wm. Hodge junr. who we hope will in due time have the
pleasure to deliver them in person, he knows nothing more of
their Contents, than that they are Important and in case of Capture his orders are to sink them in the Sea. This Young Gentle-
mans Character, Family, and alertness in the Publick Service, all
entitle him to your Notice. He is also charged with some business
from the Secret Committee wherein your Countenance and assistance may be usefull.[5] You will no doubt extend it to him and also
engage Mr. Morris's exertions therein.

You will please to advance Mr. Hodge the Value of One hundred
and fifty pounds Sterling for his Expences and transmit us his
receipt for the same. We most fervently pray for a successfull
negotiation and are with the utmost attention and regard Dear Sir
Your affectionate Friends and Obedient humble Servants

B FRANKLIN

ROBT MORRIS

PS Mr. Hodge has some instructions from the Secret Committee
which he will lay before you and if the Negotiation of Monsr.
Hortalez respecting Arms and Ammunition has been Conducted
with success it will be needless for Mr. Hodge to make Contracts
for those Articles. You will know how that matter is and direct
Mr. Hodge accordingly, and if you shoud think it of more Consequence to send him immediately back here with dispatches than
to employ him in the business that Committee have proposed he
will obey your orders and Mr. Morris may do the other.

To The Honorable Silas Deane Esqr.

5. See the note on the committee to Bingham above, Sept. 21, 1776.
Hodge's instructions, dated Oct. 3, are in *Naval Docs.*, VI, 1120–1.

The Committee of Secret Correspondence to William Hodge, Jr.[6]

Copy: National Archives

Sir,   Philada, October 3d 1776

We Commit to your care sundry dispatches delivered you herewith, and you are immediately to repair onboard the Sloop Independance John Young Commander now waighting for you between this and Rheedy Island. This Sloop will carry you and Said dispatches with the utmost Expedition to the Island of Martinico, where you must apply to Wm. Bingham Esqr. delivering to him all the letters and Packages directed for him. This Gentn. will assist in procuring you an immediate Passage from thence to some port in France onbd. a French Vessel. Choose a good one if you have a Choice and a Man of War or Packet in preferance to a Merchantman. The General of Martinico will give you a letter to the Commander of the Port you Sail for, requesting him to grant you a Passport, and to expedite you immediately to Paris, on your arrival there you must find out Silas Deane Esqr. and Mr. Thos. Morris and deliver to each the letters and Packages directed for them. If you arrive at Nantes apply to Mr. John Danl. Schweighauser. At Bourdeaux to Messrs. Saml. & Jno. Hans Delap. At Havre de Grace to Mr. Andw. Limozin. At Dunkirk to Messrs. P. Stival & Son, in the name of Willing Morris & Co. to furnish you with the Address of Mr. Deane and Mr. Morris at Parris, as it will be well known to them all, and they will also render you any other Services you may Stand in need of.[7] Should you go to Paris without previously finding out the Address of these Gentn. Apply to Messrs. [blank in MS] Bankers in Paris, who can direct you to Mr. Deane.

The Letters and Packet directed for him and Thos. Morris you are to consider as dispatches of the utmost Importance, you must never Suffer them to be out of your possession one Moment untill you deliver them safe with untouched Seals to those two Gentle-

6. See the note on the committee to Bingham above, Sept. 21, 1776.

7. The committee furnished Hodge with a letter of the same date introducing him to these four firms: Force, 5 *Amer. Arch.*, II, 852–3. Schweighauser and the Delaps have often appeared before; for meager information about Limozin and Pierre Stival & fils see respectively Pierre Dardel, *Navires et marchandises dans les ports de Rouen et du Havre au XVIIIe siècle* (Paris, 1963), p. 408, and *Almanach général des marchands* . . . for 1779, p. 193.

men, unless you should unfortunately be taken, and in that case you must throw them overboard, always keeping them ready Slung with a Weight to Sink them if that Measure Should be necessary, and for your faithful discharge of this trust, you are answerable to your God, Your Country and to us that have reposed this Confidence in you. We have desired Mr. Bingham to supply you with what Money you want at Martinico, and to transmit us your receipts for the Amount. Mr. Deane will supply you with any sum not Exceeding One Hundred and fifty Pounds Sterlg in France. You will keep an account of your Expences, which will be paid by the Congress, who will also Compensate you Generously hereafter for your time trouble and Risque in this Voyage. Should Mr. Deane think proper to send you immediately back with dispatches for us, you will no doubt take charge of them, and proceed according to his Instructions. You must Cautiously avoid letting any person whatever know what is your Business or that you have the least Connection with Publick business. We wish you a Safe and Successfull Voyage and are Sir Your Obedient humble Servants

Mr. Wm. Hodge Junr.

From Anthony Wayne

ALS: University of Pennsylvania Library; two drafts:[8] Historical Society of Pennsylvania

Dear sir   Tyconderoga, 3rd Octr: 1776

I shou'd have acknowledged the Rect. of your favour of the 28th of Augt. sooner but for want of time; I am glad to find that unanimity prevails in Congress. Whilst that Continues I am under no Apprehension but that we shall rise Superior to every Dificulty. The Settling the boundaries of the Respective States is an event that has given the highest Satisfaction to every thinking Gentn. in this Army and is truly worthy of Congress.[9]

8. The shorter draft is a reworking of the first two paragraphs of the longer one; the latter breaks off after the passage quoted below about Wayne's troops.

9. Congress had debated the Articles of Confederation at length, but had postponed a decision; see BF's protest above under Aug. 20, 1776. A rumor may have reached the army that jurisdiction over boundaries had actually been assumed by Congress, as the Articles proposed.

I am also pleased to hear that the Convention is engaged in framing a new Government, a Government which I hope will be permanent; but as I am not well acquainted with the present *Current* of Politicks, I shall wave the Subject, and like unkle *Toby*, ride my own hobby.[10]

We are not a little Surprized at the Avacuation of Long Island, the Surrender of that was Opening the door to the Island of New York. Our people can't possibly hold that place, when the North and East Rivers are free for the Enemies fleet, as by that means they can at anytime land troops on the back of our Posts, a Circumstance which I fear has not been sufficiently guarded against.[11] In Order to Gain time for that purpose, the Sacrafice of four, five, or even ten thousand men (in my humble Opinion) ought to have been Risqued, rather than give up Ground, that will not only Supply the Enemy with every Necessary, but reduce us to the hard Necessity of making a Winter Campaign in the open field, to watch their motion, whilst they have a good Cover in the City of New York.

In this Quarter we have had greatly the Advantage of the Enemy in point of time and Materials for the purpose of building a fleet, which we have so well Improved that at this juncture we have on lake Champlain three Schooners, a Sloop Eight Gondolas and three fine Row Galley's the last of which sail'd yesterday so that Unless Burgoyne can prevail over that force, he can't come here this Season. However they have not been Idle on their part as our Accounts generally agree that they have two Schooners Mounting each twelve Gun's and a Vessel odly riged mounting

10. Each of the drafts contains a passage of some interest that the ALS omits. In the longer draft the addition is: "I Observe we have an extraordinary House of Convention and as an extraordinary a Bench of the *peace*. But the old Addage holds, that a Desprate Disorder requires a Desprate cure. Our Constitution was Convulsed; these may be the most proper state Physicians to restore it to its native Vigor. I hope they will effect it." The addition in the shorter draft is: "The Provision made for the Wounded Soldier, has had the Greatest good effect." For the ordinance about justices of the peace see the note on the convention above, July 15, 1776, and for Congress' action on wounded soldiers *JCC*, V, 702–5.

11. Wayne had in mind the obvious British move, a landing on northern Manhattan to bottle up the American army; Howe's second in command vainly urged this course upon him: William B. Willcox, *Portrait of a General* . . . (New York, 1964), pp. 108–10.

twenty eighteen Pounders together with a number of Gondola's. The Number of Cannon we have on the lake I believe is nearly about Ninety, which is no Contemptible force and I believe, will not be redely Subdued; but shou'd they prevail by Water, on the land side our lines are so Strengthen'd by Redouts, that they can not be Carri'd by storm, and the Season is too far Advanced for a Regular Approach. The former I hope will be their Choice, when I rest Assured that their Impetuosity and eagerness to form a Junction at New York will prove fatal to them. Our people are in high Spirits at the Idea of the Enemies Advancing, and their minds are prepared for the Worst event.[1]

The Situation of our Brigade woud not be very pleasing to some; to us its become familiar, and I trust we shall meet *Death or Glory* with a fortitude becoming Americans.

A Strong Garrisson must at all events be Statened here during the Winter, Composed of Troops engaged during the War. The sooner they are sent the Better, as the time of these now on the Ground, will all expire in January. The first Pennsa. and two New Jersey Regiments are only Engaged for three Weeks after this date, all the New England Militia until the last of next Month; you therefore see that no time is to be lost.

I also think it would Conduce greatly to the Publick service, if those Regiments raised in Pennsa. last Jany. were call'd home (as soon as the safety of this post will Admit) In Order to Recruit, under the present Encouragement given by Congress; were they brought home paid Off and a little refreshed from their hard Fatague, I verily believe that every man would Inlist again. They have gone thro' every Dificulty with chearfulness, and without

1. The longer draft expands upon this observation: "Our people are in high Spirits, tho' poorly and thinly clad; yet they will sell their Lives, or Liberty dear. The fatague they have Undergone in this place is Inexpressible, yet they go thro' all without a murmour; and if I can gather anything from some casual Allarms that happen, they wish for nothing more than to meet the Enemy *Communis Armis*.

"It was not unpleasing the Other evening on hearing a Number of Gun's fired from some of our own Indians to see the Convelations [? Convalescents?] and all the Sick in the Doctr. Report turning out as one man, in the Pennsa. lines, and Refusing to return whilst there was the least appearance of an Enemy Approaching.

"You'l excuse me for mentioning this triffling Circumstance, but it shews the Martial Spirit which yet Animates, our worthy poor fatagued fellows."

Murmour, add to this that they are Second to none in point of Decipline and real Bravery, Seasoned and Inured to hardship and a Soldiers life, Consequently far Superior to any New Recruits.

Present my best Compliments to Genl. Hancock and tell Col. Wilson that he has my sincere friendship.[2] Interim I am with the highest Esteem Dear sir Your Most Obedient Humble Servant

ANTY. WAYNE

Doct. Franklin

From Alexandre Pochard[3]   ALS: American Philosophical Society

Monsieur,   Montreal Le 11 8bre. 1776.

Cette Lettre ne vous parviendra que lorsque des tems plus calmes et plus heureux auront ramené la paix en Canada, et ouvert une communication libre de cette province aux vôtres. J'espere et je souhaitte encore plus que cette communication soit le fruit de vos genereux efforts pour le maintien de la liberté; actuellement on ne prononce ici ce nom qu'avec horreur. Tout le monde les prêtres, et quelques gentillâtres à la tête se prosterne lâchement devant l'Idole de la tyrannie. Le peu d'honnêtes-gens qui soupirent pour le retour de vos troupes sont persecutés. L'Imprimeur M. Mesplet, ses ouvriers et moi avons ressenti les coups de la vengeance des Suppôts du Roi. On nous a trainé en prison comme des coupables, on nous y a retenu 26 jours sans nous interroger, pendant ce tems L'Imprimerie et nos effets ont été a la Disposition d'une soldatesque qui ne cherche qu'à piller, et a la discretion de la justice de Sa Majesté, qui ne differe de l'injustice que par le nom.[4]

M. Mesplet S'est consolé des ses malheurs dans la vue que le

2. John Hancock was a major general of the Massachusetts militia and James Wilson a colonel of the Pennsylvania associators.

3. He had arrived in Philadelphia the previous autumn with an introduction from Dumas and no knowledge of English; see BF to Dumas above, Dec. 9.

4. Fleury Mesplet went to Montreal in March, 1776, as printer for the Americans; see the note on the commissioners' instructions above, March 20. Pochard accompanied him, and they arrived just as the retreat began. They elected to stay, with the results mentioned here. See R. W. McLachlan, "Fleury Mesplet, the First Printer at Montreal," 2 Royal Soc. of Canada, *Proc. and Trans.*, XII (1906), 2d section, pp. 203–5.

Corps respectable qui l'a engagé dans ces embarras saura quelque jour le dédommager des pertes quil a faittes. Je ne demande pour la reparation des torts que jai endurés en mon particulier que la Continuation de vos bontés pour mon ami.[5] Si vous croyez Monsieur que ma bonne volonté et mes malheurs soient quelque chose qui meritent l'attention du Congrès, que cette attention se tourne sur cet ami; on fera mon bonheur en concourant au sien.

Les troubles m'obligent de quitter L'amerique, je vais hyverner à Londres ou j'ai quelque raison d'Interêt à dêmeler. Je laisse entre les mains de M. Mesplet une traduction du Sens commun, et une lettre sur les affaires du tems de ma façon. Ces productions ressemblent à ces enfans des hébreux que leurs parens cachoient avec soin pour les soustraire aux fureurs du tyran de l'Egipte.[6] J'ai dépensé de l'encre pour votre parti, j'aurais versé mon sang si je l'avois cru necessaire au succès des enfans de la vertu et de la Liberté.

Puisse-je à mon retour vous retrouver paisibles et triomphans. Puisse-je travailler de concert avec M. Mesplet à persuader au Canadiens que leurs vainqueurs sont leurs plus grands amis. Jouissez M., d'une sante egale à vos vertus la posterité placera votre nom a côte [de] ceux des Pompée des Brutus et des Catons. Je suis avec respect Monsieur Votre tres humble tres obéissant serviteur

POCHARD

Addressed: To / Dr. frankelin, / Philadelphia

5. The M. Vaillant who had come with him to America; see BF to Dumas above, Dec. 9. We know nothing about him except that his family was connected with Pochard's, and that he remained in America. On Feb. 17, 1781, an abbé Pochard wrote BF enclosing a letter that he asked to have forwarded to Vaillant, who was then in Philadelphia. APS.

6. Mesplet hid them so successfully that, as far as we know, they were never published. The "tyran de l'Egipte" appears to be an amalgam of Pharaoh and Herod: Exodus 2: 1–3; Math. 2: 16.

Discharge of the Mortgage of Mary Pitts[7]

DS: American Philosophical Society

⟨October 14, 1776: Appeared before me, William Parr, recorder of deeds,[8] Benjamin Franklin, the mortgagee, who has received from the representative of Mary Pitts, the mortgagor, the money and interest due for the discharge of the mortgage. Signed by Franklin and attested by Parr.⟩

Testimony in a Prize Case

D: National Archives

Seth Jenkins, to whose character Franklin was testifying, was a Nantucket relative and sea captain who had visited him in London in 1773.[9] Jenkins was again in town in March, 1775, when he appeared before the House of Lords. In October of the same year he and some fellow Nantucketers arrived once more in London, and began the adventure that eventually brought them before a Philadelphia prize court. They purchased a ship, the brig *Richmond*, in which to get home; unnamed "friends of America" gave them letters to Franklin, Hancock, and others explaining British designs against the colonies, and the *Richmond* also carried, for reasons unknown, some £20,000. She sailed under false registry for the West Indies, cleared there for Halifax (but actually bound for Nantucket), and was captured by an American privateer, John Craig. He considered her a legitimate prize because of her clearance, and sent her to Philadelphia and her owners to the Bahamas; they eventually found their way home and contested the seizure. Litigation followed in the Philadelphia admiralty court, punctuated by appeals to Congress. The owners, although they won their case, apparently failed to recover their property.[1]

7. BF had first tried to attach this mortgage in 1753, and the affair had dragged on for years. The mortgagor died in 1772; now BF, presumably as part of winding up his affairs before leaving for France, recovered from her representative £502 16s.: above, XIV, 191 n; XIX, 192, 395.

8. Also a lawyer and judge and member of the Philadelphia common council; see E. James Ferguson *et al.*, eds., *The Papers of Robert Morris . . .* (5 vols. to date, [Pittsburgh, 1973—]), II, 346 n.

9. Above, XX, 74 n, 290.

1. The litigation is recorded in Craig v. Brig *Richmond*, from which our excerpt is taken; the case is the seventh in Revolutionary War Prize Cases: Records of the Court of Admiralty in Cases of Captures, National Archives. See also Alexander Starbuck, *The History of Nantucket*, (Rutland, Vt., 1969), pp. 198–200; *Naval Docs.*, VI, 104–5, 1446–7; VII, 98; *JCC*, VII, 13, 188–9.

[October 14, 1776²]
Doctor Benjamin Franklin being examined declared that he remembered hearing Seth Jenkins examined in the House of Lords
on the Prohibitory Bill . . . that the Testimony he gave in the
Course of his Examination was in Favour of the Merchants' Petition and such as shewed the said Jenkins to be a Friend to
America.³

[*In the margin:*] Evid. of Doct. Franklyn.

From John Fraser

ALS: American Philosophical Society

Sir   Reading 15th 8br 1776
I received your favor of the 28. Ulto.⁴ and I am exceedingly
obliged to you for the trouble you have been at on my account, I
am only unelucky in having got my Second leave for Canada when
I can not make use of it. I have been very much indisposed these
three weeks and I am yet too weak to undertake the journey, as
soon as my health will permit, I'll go to Philada. to take the
benefit of the indulgence of the Congress⁵ and then will take the
opportunity of thanking you for your good Offices. I Remain
sincerely Sir your most Obedient and humble servant
                                              JOHN FRASER

Benjamin Franklin Esqre

Endorsed: From J Fraiser

2. The record states that after BF's testimony the court was adjourned to the
next day, and reconvened on Oct. 15.
3. Jenkins was actually examined on the first, or New England, Restraining
Bill; the examination is printed in Cobbett, *Parliamentary History*, XVIII
(1774–77), 423–5. The *London Chron.* summarized it and the debate in its issue
of March 16, 1775, and printed the merchants' petition on the 18th.
4. He is acknowledging BF's reply, now lost, to his letter above of Aug. 24,
1776.
5. The *JCC* make no mention of him. He was presumably back in Montreal
by the following June, when a petition was circulated to have him restored to
his judgeship: Hilda M. Neatby, *The Administration of Justice under the Quebec Act*
(Minneapolis, Minn., 1937), p. 57.

To Robert Erskine

ALS (draft):⁶ American Philosophical Society

Sir   Philada. Oct. 16. 76

I should sooner have acknowledged your Favour of Aug. 16. containing the Drawing of your Chevaux de Frise: but that I have been so extreamly occupy'd as to be oblig'd to postpone writing to many of my Correspondents.

Please to accept my Thanks for the Communication of your Contrivance, which I am persuaded will answer the Purpose where ever the Bottom is so hard as to prevent the Points being press'd into the Ground by the passing Ship before the Resistance shall become great enough to force the upper Points thro' her Bottom. The Ground being soft in our Channel, we were oblig'd to fix our pointer Beams to a Floor, in the Chevaux we plac'd there during the Summer of the preceding Year.⁷ That Floor gives them so firm a Stand, that all the Vessels which thro' Inadvertence have run upon them, have had such Breaches made in their Bottoms as immediately sunk them. One was a large Ship. I am, Sir, with great Esteem, Your most obedient humble Servant B FRANKLIN

Notation: A Letter to Dr. B. Franklin and a letter of B Franklin.⁸

6. On the back of Erskine's letter above, Aug. 16, 1776; hence the notation below.

7. For a discussion of these Pa. chevaux-de-frise and BF as their purported designer see John W. Jackson, *The Pennsylvania Navy, 1775–1783* . . . (New Brunswick, N. J., 1974), pp. 353–76, and the editorial note on the committee of safety above, June 30, 1775. BF must have considered the new design of some importance, because before embarking for France he left what we assume was Erskine's drawing, along with other papers, in the hands of David Rittenhouse: Memorandum Book (above, VII, 167–8), entry of Oct. 21, 1776.

8. On the verso, in a different hand from that of the notation, is "Bernard Maussac de Lamarquisie," for whom see Woedtke to BF above, July 4, 1776. We assume, knowing nothing about his movements, that he carried either Erskine's letter or this one in final form, or both.

The Attempt to Settle Franklin's Post Office Account

(I) DS;[9] (II) three ADS:[1] American Philosophical Society

In the period between Franklin's dismissal as deputy postmaster general in January, 1774, and his departure from England in March, 1775, he tried to settle his indebtedness to the General Post Office. The account that he submitted in December, 1774, showed a balance due from him of £973 0s. 5d.; he offered to pay, as he says here, and was told to settle in America.[2] His final effort to do so is described in these documents. Again he failed, and the whole matter was open when he sailed for France. On his return in 1785 it was still open. At some point thereafter he achieved a settlement, for his own private satisfaction, by composing an account against the King for losses (including house rent) resulting from the British occupation of Philadelphia.[3]

I.

Philada. Oct. 18. 1776

We the Subscriber's Deputy Postmaster General and Secretary of the Post Office in America, appointed by the Postmaster General of Great Britain, do hereby certify, that Benjamin Franklin, late in the same Office, did this Day exhibit to us his Accounts, which we have examined and compared with the Comptrollers Books, and with Receipts of the Receiver-General produc'd to us, and do find the same to agree, some small additional Charges excepted for Horns and Stamps;[4] and that there is remaining in his Hands due to the said Office the Sum of Nine Hundred and seventy three Pounds and Fivepence Sterling, which Ballance he tendred to us in Currency; but we having no Authority or Orders to settle the said Account and receive the Ballance, did refuse the same. Witness our Hands.

JOHN FOXCROFT
FR. DASHWOOD.[5]

9. A certificate in BF's hand attached to the last page of his Ledger, and signed by the others.

1. BF's marginal notes in *ibid.*, p. 11.

2. Above, XXI, 226–7, 376, 530–1.

3. This account, which includes some interesting details, is on the penultimate page of the Ledger; our successors will presumably publish it in a later volume.

4. The stamps, no doubt for postmarking, were apparently disallowed; the post horns had already been: above, XVI, 42; XVII, 130; XXI, 227.

5. For Dashwood see Foxcroft's letter above, Sept. 15, 1775.

II.

[October 18–21, 1776.]

Memorandum, Philada Oct. 18. 1776. that I this Day got Messrs. Foxcroft and Dashwood to compare this Acct. with the Comptroller's Books and the Receiver-General's Receipts with other Vouchers, and obtain'd from them a Certificate that they found the Accounts to agree, and the above Ballance to be right, with an Acknowledgement that I tendred them the said Ballance in Currency which they could not receive for want of Orders.

B FRANKLIN

See the Certificate fix'd with Wafers at the End of this Book. Note, the said Ballance, and more, as appears by the opposite Page, was received by me in Currency, and the Exchange generally estimated at 166 ⅔, at which Rate I would have repaid it. While in England I offer'd the Ballance in Sterling at the Office, but was referr'd here for a Settlement with Mr. Foxcroft, for which I have never till now had an Opportunity. BF. At the Exchange of 166 ⅔ the Sum of £973 0s. 3¼d. comes to £1621 13s. 9¼d. which I offered to pay.

Memorandum Oct. 21, 1776 This day obtained from Mr. Amos Strettell an Acct. of Cash paid by Mrs. Franklin in my Absence in Discharge of Interest due on Mortgages of some Post Office Land, amounting to £36 Pensilva Currency,[6] which must be deducted from the above Ballance, being Sterling £21 12s.   BF.

The Committee of Secret Correspondence to William Bingham   LS: American Philosophical Society; copy: National Archives

Sir   Philadelphia October 21st 1776

We send you herewith a copy of what we wrote you the 1st Inst. per the Sloop Independance Capt. Young and hope some of the articles that were to be forwarded to your Island or St. Eustatia by

---

6. See above, XI, 419 n, 469 n.

Monsr. Hortalez have arrived. In that case you will apply for, receive and Ship them by these opportunities of our Continental Cruizers, which are sent for that purpose, and also to bring back such woolen Goods as can be procured agreeable to the Orders of the Secret Committee.

You'l observe this goes by the Sachem Captain Robinson to Martinico, a Copy of it we send by the Armed Brigantine Andrea Doria[7] Capt. Isaiah Robinson to St. Eustatia where he values on Mr. Samuel Curson[8] Mercht., and if you have made application to the Governor there in consequence of our former letter, you must renew it now and give orders for some of the articles to be Remitted by the Andrea Doria, or the vessel that is to Sail under her Convoy, and we think you had best send us by every good conveyance both from St. Eustatia and Martinico a part of these Supplies. We are Sir Your obedient Servants   B FRANKLIN
ROBT MORRIS

Wm Bingham Esqr.

Addressed: William Bingham Esquire / Martinico [*In Morris' hand:*] To be forwarded or / carried by Capt Robison / R. Morris

Endorsed: Committee of S Correspondence, October 21st 1776

From Amos Strettell: Statement of Account[9]

AD: American Philosophical Society

⟨Monday, October 21, 1776: George McCleave gave mortgages, dated respectively May 13 and December 18, 1762, to the execu-

---

7. See the note on the committee's second letter to Bingham, below, Oct. 23.

8. The copy appears to read "where the value's on," and presumably means that the agent will value the cargo. Curson was representing his father, a prominent Baltimore banker and shipowner, and was also in partnership with Isaac Gouverneur on St. Eustatius. See Jacob H. Pleasants, *The Curzon Family of New York and Baltimore* . . . (Baltimore, 1919), pp. 35–8, 41–5; *Public Papers of George Clinton* . . . (10 vols., Albany, 1899–1914), V, 270.

9. For the background of the account, which was due from the Post Office, see above, XI, 469 n. We cannot explain the disparity, amounting to one year's

tors of Robert Strettell's estate. On the first mortgage McCleave paid one year's interest, £3 12s., and on the second none. Between November 27, 1765, and May 17, 1768, Mrs. Franklin paid £36 for interest on both mortgages, and in 1772 John Foxcroft paid £33 19s. The balance due for the four years thereafter is £28 16s.

Amos Strettell hopes that this "Scetch" will answer Franklin's purposes, and inquires of him whether he, or the late partnership of Franklin & Hall, has a claim on the estate of Robert Strettell, or on the late partnership of Robert and Amos Strettell, or on the latter alone.⟩

The Committee of Secret Correspondence to William Bingham

LS: Historical Society of Pennsylvania; copy: National Archives

Sir   Philada. October 23d. 1776

We have wrote you already by this Conveyance of the Brigantine Andrew Doria to St. Eustatia which we deem safer than the Sachem as she sails faster and is of more Force.[1] Therefore we now enclose you some very Important dispatches for Mr. Dean[2] and request you will forward them by the very first good Conveyance advising us hereafter the Vessell and Masters name by which they

---

interest on the two mortgages, between the sum of £21 12s. noted there as owed to the Strettell estate and the £28 16s. that is mentioned here. Neither have we any idea of what claim BF, or he and his erstwhile partner, might have had on the Strettells.

1. This is ambiguous, but the letter went by both ships; see the next note. The *Sachem* was a ten-gun sloop and the *Andrew Doria* a fourteen-gun brig: Nathan Miller, *Sea of Glory* . . . (New York, [1974]), p. 528.

2. These were two letters, dated Oct. 23, for Bingham to forward. One went directly to Martinique by the *Sachem*, as mentioned in the committee's letter to Bingham of Oct. 21, and the other by the *Andrew Doria* via St. Eustatius. The first, signed by Morris alone, merely enclosed the commissioners' additional instructions of Oct. 16. A summary of the second is below. Morris added a note to Bingham, of the same date, urging him to take particular care of these dispatches: Force, 5 *Amer. Arch.*, II, 1198.

go and also of their arrival when you hear it. We are Sir Your
Obedient Servants   B FRANKLIN
                                               ROBT MORRIS
                                               RICHARD HENRY LEE
                                               WM HOOPER
                                               JNO WITHERSPOON

Wm Bingham Esqr.

Addressed: To / Wm Bingham Esqr. / Martinico

Endorsed: C of Secret Correspondence October 23d 1776

The Committee of Secret Correspondence to Stephen Ceronio[3]
Letterbook copy: National Archives

In Committee of Secret Correspondence Philada.
Sir   October 23 1776
The Inclosed letter[4] was wrote and signed before we had an
opportunity to transmit it and having now so good a conveyance
as the Brigantine Lexington we transmit the Same to you as an
official Letter from the Committee of Secret Correspondence
which you'l observe is distinct from the Secret Committee with
whom you also Correspond, by this letter you'l find we expect
Some Arms, ammunition Money or Cloathing may be sent out by
Our Agent Monsr. Hortalez to the Governor at Cape François,
with orders for the delivery of them to whoever may be properly
empowered by Congress to recieve the same,[5] that power is

3. A young Genoese who had lived for a time in America before being sent
to St. Domingue as an American agent; see *Naval Docs.*, VI, 244.

4. Now lost. It is identified by a note in another hand at this point in the MS
as "a letter similar to that written to Mr. Bingham Oct. 1st. only substituting
Cape Francois for Martinique and St. Eustatius."

5. The *Lexington*, a 16-gun Continental ship, was commanded by Capt. William Hallock: *Naval Docs.*, VI, 1201, 1355. For the Governor, Victor-Thérèse
d'Ennery, see Crout, "Diplomacy of Trade," pp. 55–9. With this letter went a
number of enclosures. One was a packet of dispatches for Ceronio to send to
Deane via the Delaps in Bordeaux; for the contents see the *Deane Papers*, I,
335–6. Morris wrote a covering note to Deane, and also sent one to Ceronio
and another to the Delaps to expedite the forwarding: Force, 5 *Amer. Arch.*, II,
1198.

granted to you, and you'l please to apply to the Governor with our respectfull Compliments, desire to know if he has received Such supply, if he has produce the letter to him if he has not, then request he will inform you when such Supplies do Arrive or any advice respecting them. When you receive the Goods in consequence of this appointment, Ship a quantity of them by the Lexington if they are ready, if not you may Charter suitable French Vessels to bring them here dividing them into many Bottoms and Sending an Assortment consisting of part of every Article you recieve. In short you must transmit the Whole to us in the Safest and most expeditious manner you can Contrive, Consigning to this Committee for the Use and on Acct. of the United States of America. We are sir your Obedient servants   B F.

                                          R M

Mr. Stephen Ceronio

The Committee of Secret Correspondence to Silas Deane

Copy:[6] Haverford College Library; copy: National Archives

⟨Philadelphia, October 23, 1776: We have written you twice today by different ships.[7] This letter goes by the *Andrew Doria* to St. Eustatius, to be forwarded to William Bingham and by him to you in a French vessel. We enclose two resolutions of Congress.[8] The first replaces Thomas Jefferson as commissioner with Arthur Lee, whom you will immediately ask to join you; then give him the resolution and the enclosed letter. The other resolution instructs you to hire or buy eight ships of the line; if you are successful, we hope that France and Spain will send a large fleet to convoy these ships, and order its commander to make for the first safe port, preferably Philadelphia, and put himself totally under the direction of Congress. Signed by Franklin, Robert Morris, Richard Henry Lee, William Hooper, and John Witherspoon.⟩

6. In Robert Morris' hand; for the full text see Smith, *Letters*, V, 367–8.
7. These letters are discussed in *ibid.*, p. 368 n.
8. *JCC*, VI, 895–7.

The Committee of Secret Correspondence to Arthur Lee

LS: Yale University Library; two copies and extract: National Archives

Sir   Philadelphia October 23rd 1776

By this conveyance we transmit to Silas Deane Esq. a Resolve of the Honble. the continental congress of Delegates from the Thirteen United States of America, whereby you are appointed one of their Commissioners for negotiationg a treaty of alliance, Amity and Commerce with the Court of France, and also for negotiating Treaties with other Nations agreeable to certain plans and instructions of Congress, which we have transmitted by various conveyances to Mr. Deane another of the Commissioners. We have requested him to give you immediate notice to join him, and on your Meeting to deliver this letter and lay before you all the Papers and instructions, also to deliver you the Resolve whereby you are appointed.[9] We flatter ourselves from the assurances of your Freinds here, that you will chearfully undertake this important bussiness and that our Country will greatly benefit of those abilities and that attachment you have already manifested in sundry important services, which at a proper period, shall be made known to those you woud wish.

This Committee will think it proper to address all their dispatches unto Mr. Deane untill they have certain advice that his Colleagues have joined him, but the communication of them will be the same as if addressed to the whole. We remain with much Esteem and regard Sir Your most Obedient humble Servants

ROB MORRIS
B FRANKLIN

Arthur Lee Esqr.

Notation: 1776. Letter from Morriss & Co. Philada. 23. Octor. No. 1.

---

9. These conveyances, including BF on the *Reprisal*, are described in the committee's letter to Deane of Oct. 24, which we are not publishing because BF did not sign it. The committee instructed Deane to use the greatest caution in notifying Lee, in order not to endanger him, and suggested having the letter sent to London in the diplomatic pouch of the French Ambassador and delivered in secret: Smith, *Letters*, V, 378–9. Deane reported merely that he had notified Lee by express: *Deane Papers*, I, 417–18.

The Committee of Secret Correspondence to the American Commissioners to France

LS: American Philosophical Society; letterbook copies: Library of Congress; National Archives

Gentlemen   Philada. October 24th 1776

The Congress having Committed to our Charge and Management their Ship of War called the Reprisal, Commanded by Lambert Wickes Esqr. carrying sixteen Six pounders and about one hundred and twenty Men, We have allotted her to carry Doctor Franklin to France and directed Capt. Wickes to proceed for the Port of Nantes where the Doctor will land and from thence proceed to Paris, and he will either carry with him or send forward this letter by express as to him may then appear best. The Reprisal is a fast sailing Ship and Capt. Wickes has already done honor in Action to the American Flagg.[10] We have therefore ordered him to land at Nantes some Indico he has onboard[11] take in any Refreshments, Stores, Provisions or other necessarys he may want and immediately to proceed on a Cruize against our Enemies, and we think he will not be long before he meets with a sufficient Number of Prizes. We have directed him to send them into such of the French Ports as are most Convenient addressing them at Dunkirk to Messrs. P. Stival & Son, at Havre de Grace to Mr. Andw Limozin, at Bourdeaux to Messrs. Saml & J H Delap at Nantes to Messrs. Pliarne, Penet & Company and at any other Ports in France to such persons as you may appoint to receive them, when he finishes his Cruize he will call in at Nantes, Bourdeaux or Brest for your orders and advices which we beg you will have ready for him lodged at those places. In Consequence of this plan for the Reprisals Cruize we desire you to make immediate application to the Court of France to Grant the Protection of their Ports to American Men of War and their Prizes, shew them that British Men of War under Sanction of an act of Parliament are daily Capturing American Ships and Cargoes. Shew them the Resolves of Congress for making Reprisals on British and West India property[1] and that our Continental Men of War and Numer-

10. See Clark, *Wickes*, pp. 52–65.

11. See the note on the committee to Deane above, Oct. 2, 1776.

1. Presumably the resolutions of March 23, 1776, although they made no mention of West Indian property: *JCC*, IV, 230–2.

ous private Ships of War are most successfully employed in executing those Resolutions of the Congress. Shew them the Justice
and equity of this proceeding and surely they cannot, they will
not refuse the protection of their Ports to American Ships of War,
Privateers and their Prizes. If your application on this head is
crowned with success, try another which it is their interest to
grant. That is to obtain leave to make Sale of those Prizes and
their Cargoes or any part thereof that may be suitable for that
Country.[2] If you succeed in this also, you must appoint some
person to Act as judge of the Admiralty who shoud give the Bond
prescribed for those Judges to determine in all Cases agreable to
the Rules and Regulations of Congress and for this purpose we
will Report to Congress some Resolves Vesting you with Authority to make such appointment and Authorizing such judge to
Condemn without a jury as required here. If these Resolves are
agreed to by Congress they shall be immediately transmitted to
you. If they are not that plan must drop and the Prizes must all
proceed for America for Condemnation. You can in the mean time
consult the Ministers whether they will permit such Courts in
France and in the French West India Islands. If protection is
granted to our Cruizers and their Prizes you will immediately
procure proper orders to be sent to the Officers of all their Ports
on this subject, and write yourselves to those House's we have
named at the several Ports that the Prizes are to remain for Capt.
Wickes's further orders, also lodge such orders with proper persons at the other Ports in France. On the Contrary if The Prizes
are not to be protected in their Ports then give immediate Notice
to all those Houses and proper persons at the other Ports to furnish
the Prizes that Capt. Wickes of the Reprisal may send into their
port with any Necessarys the Prize master may judge they stand
in need of and to order him immediately to make the best of his
way with the Prize to the first safe Port he can make in the United
States of America lodge advice also for Cap. Wickes at Bourdeaux
Brest and Nantes whether his Prizes are to be protected in Port or
not and whether or not any sales will be permitted. If they are
protected he can take his own time to Collect and bring them

2. France could not give such permission without violating a treaty obligation to Britain, as BF pointed out in his letter to Hancock below, Dec. 8, 1776;
the committee obviously hoped that the French court was much nearer than it
was to abandoning official neutrality.

Home under his own Convoy, if any sale is permitted he can sell perishable Commodities and Vessels unfit for so long a Voyage as to this Coast. If no protection for Prizes they will be come away by your orders and need not stay for his, and If they deny Protection to our Cruizers themselves, he will only remain in Port for your advices and to obtain such supplys as may be necessary. We have recommended Cap. Wickes[3] to take onboard his own Ship as many Valuable Commodities as he can if he is successfull but shou'd he be unsuccessfull in Cruizing then Messrs. Pliarne & Co. may put some Goods onboard when he is coming away. You will readily see the Tendancy these measures have, and as their consequences may be very important so we hope your attention to them will be immediate and Constant whilst necessary. Capt. Wickes is a Worthy Man as such we recommend him and shou'd he have the misfortune to be taken or meet with any other misfortune we hope you will adopt measures for his relief. He will treat Prisoners with Humanity and we are Convinced his Conduct will do honor to his appointment. We have the honor to be Gentlemen Your most obedient and Most humble Servants   ROBT MORRIS
RICHARD HENRY LEE
JNO WITHERSPOON
WILL HOOPER

To The Commissioners of the United States of America at the Court of France

Notation: 1776 Letter from Morriss Lee & Co Philadelphia 24 Octor. To Commissioners

3. In their letter to him of the same date, which repeated the instructions here in greater detail and survives only in a copy without signatures: *Naval Docs.*, VI, 1400–3. We have no evidence that BF signed any of the committee's letters on the 24th, two days before he sailed. One, to Dumas, we know he did not: Smith, *Letters*, V, 380. Another to Deane is also, like that to Wickes, an unsigned copy: *ibid.*, pp. 378–9.

To [Samuel Cooper[4]]   Extract: Massachusetts Archives

[October 25, 1776]

Being once more order'd to Europe, and to embark this day, I write this Line &c.

As to our publick Affairs, I hope our People will keep up their Courage. I have no Doubt of their finally succeeding by the Blessing of God, nor have I any Doubt, that so good a Cause will fail of that Blessing. It is computed here that we have already taken a Million Sterling from the Enemy. They must soon be sick of their piratical Project. No Time should be lost in fortifying three or four Ports on our extended Coast as strong as Art and Expence can make them: Nothing will give us greater Weight and Importance in the Eyes of the Commercial States, than a Conviction that we can annoy, on Occasion, their Trade, and carry our Prizes into safe Harbors; and whatever Expence we are at in such fortifying will be soon repaid by the Encouragement and Success of Privateering.

Extract of a Letter from Dr. Franklin to D. C.[5] dated Philada. Octr 25. 1776.

Notation: In Council Novr. 20. 1776 Read and Sent down[6] John Avery Dpty Secy

To [Noble Wimberly Jones]

ALS: Massachusetts Historical Society

Sir   Philada. Oct. 25. 1776

Being just about to embark for Europe, I take the Liberty of troubling you with my Acct.[7] and requesting you would be so good as to procure an Adjustment of it from your Government, and remit the Sum you receive to my Son-in-law Richard Bache,

4. Cooper referred to this letter by date in his reply below, Feb. 27, 1777, and added that he had "read your affectionate Leave to all our Friends."

5. Dr. Cooper.

6. To the House of Representatives.

7. Presumably the same account that he had compiled in London in May, 1774: above, XXI, 205–6. A copy dated Philadelphia, Oct. 7, 1776, which may have been what he enclosed, was published in the *Hist. Mag.*, I (1857), 311, and has since disappeared.

Secretary of the General Post Office Residing in this Place, whose Rect. shall be a Discharge.

I congratulate you on the Success against the Cherokees; I hope it will tend to the Security of your Frontiers. I hope your Health is re-establish'd.[8] If on the other side the Water I can in anything render you either Service or Pleasure, be so good as to command freely, Dear Sir, Your obliged Friend and most obedient Servant

B FRANKLIN

Notes for Books Borrowed from the Library Company of Philadelphia
AD: American Philosophical Society

These two notes for borrowers from the Library Company demarcated the sheep from the goats. The sheep, who were the members, promised to pay for books not returned on time and in good condition; the goats put down a refundable deposit. The requirement of a promissory note from a member went back at least to 1732, and a note to accompany a nonmember's deposit was in use by 1763;[9] but the printed forms themselves have not survived. The earliest promissory note extant in the Company is dated 1780; another, undated and signed by Franklin, is among his papers in the American Philosophical Society. The two differ slightly in wording, and both refer to the Company instead of leaving a blank, as in these texts, for the Librarian's name. The forms that Franklin here seems to be copying, doubtless in answer to some query, were dated for use in the 1770's; and he would have been unlikely to have had them with him, or to have received an inquiry about them, during his years in England or later in France. Hence our guess is that he copied them during his months in Philadelphia.

Forms of Notes, used in the publick Library at Philadelphia

I promise to pay to [*blank in MS*] the Sum of [*blank*] within [*blank*] Weeks from the Date hereof, being for Value receiv'd. Nevertheless if at or before the Expiration of the said Term, I return undefac'd to the said [*blank*] a Book entitled [*blank*] which I have this Day borrowed of him, this Note is to be void, otherwise of full

---

8. See the note on the letter above of July 11, 1776, to which BF is replying.
9. Above, I, 251; X, 387.

1775–1776?

force and effect. Witness my hand, the [*blank*] Day of [*blank*] 177[.].

[*In the margin:*] Note given by a Member

I acknowledge to have this Day borrowed of [*blank*] a Book entitled[*blank*] belonging to the Library Compy. of Philadelphia, and have deposited in his Hands the Sum of [*blank*] as a Security for returning the said Book undefac'd within [*blank*] Weeks from the Date hereof; which if I fail to do, I hereby agree that the said Sum be forfeited to the Use of the Library. Witness my Hand this [*blank*] Day of [*blank*] 177[.].

[*In the margin:*] Note [given] by a [Nonmem?]ber

Notation: Hand writing of B. Franklin

From Giambatista Beccaria

Incomplete draft: American Philosophical Society

Illustrissimo Signor Signor Padrone mio Colendissimo.

A quest'ora avrete ricevuto risposta alle vostre direttavi per mezzo [*blank in* MS] riceverete anche questa per l'istesso canale, e potrete rispondermi per il medesimo; che così La spesa sarà tutta addosso a me, e riceverò le lettere sicuramente; perciocchè le due penultime vostre hanno tardato, e le ho ricevute dalla posta come procedenti da questo nostro stato. Circa il fosforo repplico, che pe' cristalli colorati non passano i raggi dell'istesso colore unicamente; ma passa la Luce composta con solamente alcun predominio del raggio del colore del cristallo; chè è (in confidenza) un' asinagine il supporre altrimenti, e pretendere che il virefieri, rubescere, flavescere importi verde, rosso, giallo deciso; che per provare, che il fosforo rende la luce quale la bee appunto si dee provare, nel nostro caso, che rende la luce composta con quel predominio, ossia la luce ordinaria tinta più o meno del colore del cristallo secondochè il colore del cristallo traguardato contro un oggetto bianco è più intenso, e secondo chè la vivezza dell'altra luce traggittante ha meno eficacia a spegnere la tinta procedente dal colore del cristallo. Spero, che a quest'ora il Sig. Wilson sarà persuaso almanco dalla considerazione del fatto suo medesimo. E perchè il

672

Sig. Wilson in questa occasione non [*ha voluto*] Onorarmi di alcuna sua, come io altra volta a lui mi dicessi. Ciò avrebbe risparmiato pena a me più lunga, e a lui una svista. Per altro rallegratevi con lui sinceramente delle belle osservazioni sue. Avrete veduto, che io ingenuamente ho esposta la mia congettura sulla osservazione del fosforo rosso immerso ne' raggi primigenii. Io ho vero piacere, se posso contribuire alla perfezione delle cose altrui; e altri pare, che non abbia maggior gusto, che di trovare in altri errore. E ciò fa, chè talora si pecchi de chi vuole trovare il peccato. Bramo sapere, se il Signr. Cavaliere Pringle ha ricevuto copia del mio nuovo libro, dell'elettricità del cièl sereno, nel quale sono dirette a lui due lettere; e se abbia egli preso ciò in buon grado. Quando scrissi primamente dell'elettricismo artificiale mi dressi al Sig. Beccari presidente allora della academia di bologna; il quale essendo ora mancato (esso era osservatore diligente dell'atmosfera) m'è paruto bene dirigermi al Presidente di cotesta reale società, ove e le altre, e questa parte massimamente della Fisica particolarmente si coltiva etc. Mi sono diretto al Sig. Nawse, perchè ho dubitato, che voi seguitaste ad oscillare trall'inghilterra e la francia. Ora mi riraccomando per la distribuzione delle copie etc. etc. comè anche per la correzione della traduzione circa i seguenti punti massimamente.

Alla pag. 354 alla linea 22 si dee leggere. *I. Due corpi similmente elettrizzati si discostano amendue direttamente giusta La somma delle elettricità loro simili, e ciascuno giusta La massa sua inversamente. II. Due corpi contrariamente elettrizzati si accostano amendue direttamente giusta la somma delle elettricità loro contrarie, e ciascuno giusta la massa sua inversamente.*

Alla pag. 355 al principio della linea seconda del num. 839 in vece di viluppo A si dee leggere viluppo B.

Alla pag. 394 si vogliono cambiare i due num. 915, 916 come segue.

915. In quarto Luogo se N abbia La dose naturale di fuoco (Tav. VIII), ed E (fig. 1.) sia elettrizzato per eccesso; ovvero D (fig. 2.) per difetto; allora il fuoco naturale di N nelle diverse parti della superficie sua senza dipartirsi da esso corpo N seconderà nelle diverse parti della superficie sua la tensione, o il rilassamento, cui L'eccesso di E, o il difetto di D inducono nel fuoco naturale dell'aria ambiente senza scagliarnelo via da ess' aria; sicchè il fuoco

naturale di N si bilicherà col fuoco rilassato, o teso dell'aria ambiente similmente che si bilicherebbe il fuoco di altr'aria, che fosse nel luogo di N; Epperò, siccome quest'aria, che fosse in Luogo di N per tale tensione o rilassamento non moverebbe, così non moverà il corpo N.

915. E di nuovo, siccome non moverebbe il corpo E, nè il corpo D, se dall'aria fossero unicamente attorniati, per la tensione, o rilassamento, che spanderebbero uniformemente in giro nel fuoco naturale di Lei, così non moveranno neppur' essendovi il corpo N; perciocchè nel fuoco naturale di N si propagherà da E, o da D l'istessa azione, che si propagherebbe nel fuoco naturale dell'aria, che occupasse il luogo di N, e ne risulterà l'istessa reazione, che ne risulterebbe dal fuoco naturale di ess'aria.

La nota apposta al num. 915, la quale principia—*Universalmente* etc. si vuole lasciare.

Alla pag. 408 al principio della Linea 34 in vece di due avanti, si vuole leggere che avanti.

Alla pag. 412 lin. 20 elettricità che nel disgiungimento, si legga delle elettricità nel disgiungimento.

Alla pag. 418 al principio della lin. 35 si legga in MN.

Alla pag. 419 lin. 10 maggiore in Mn si legga maggiore in MN.

Queste correzioni sono oltre quelle che si trovano al fine del libro nell'errata corrige.

TRANSLATION[1]

My most illustrious and revered Master,　　[1775–1776[2]]
You will have by now received the answer to your letter, sent you through [*blank in MS*]. You will receive this, too, and be able to answer through the same channel; the cost will then be entirely mine, and I shall be sure of receiving the letters. Your two pre-

1. For our caveat about translating these drafts see above, xx, 356.
2. Beccaria asks whether Pringle had received a pamphlet of his, described below, which could not have been printed, sent from Italy, and in Pringle's hands before the autumn of 1775. Beccaria also mentions that he has not heard from Wilson, who in fact wrote him on March 19, 1776, and received a reply: *A Letter from F. Beccaria to Mr. Wilson, Concerning the Light Exhibited in the Dark by Bologna Phosphorous* . . . ([London,] 1776), p. [1]. Hence the Italian must have been writing between the autumn of 1775 and the arrival of Wilson's communication in, say, the late spring of 1776.

vious ones before the last were delayed, as a matter of fact, and I received them in the mail as if coming from our own state.

My answer about phosphorus is that rays of the same color as a crystal are not the only ones that pass through it, but that they pass through more brilliantly when they and it are the same color. It is stupid, between you and me, to suppose anything else, or that becoming greenish, reddish, yellowish means being actually green, red, yellow. In order to prove that phosphorus creates light, as it is absorbed by it, we have to prove in this case that it creates light by combining with that color which ordinary light receives from the crystal, depending on how strongly the crystal is colored when seen against a white background, and on the degree to which light passing through it can extinguish that color.

I hope that Mr. Wilson will by now be convinced, by studying his own facts if nothing else. For Mr. Wilson has not [seen fit?] on this occasion to honor me with any [communication], as [he did when] I addressed him before;[3] it would have spared me a further effort and him an oversight. Congratulate him sincerely, nevertheless, on his sound observations.[4] You will see that I have naively exposed my guess about the observations of red phosphorus immersed in the original rays. I am truly pleased if I can contribute to perfecting the ideas of others; some people, it seems, find their keenest pleasure in catching others at fault, and this sometimes leads the fault-finder into being at fault himself.

I should like to know whether Sir Pringle has received my new book on electricity in the serene sky, containing two letters addressed to him, and whether he took that in good part.[5] When I first wrote about artificial electricity I addressed myself to Mr. Beccari, then president of the Bologna Academy;[6] as he has now

3. Doubtless in 1766, when Beccaria sent him observations on the electricity of glasses: above, XIII, 452.

4. Beccaria must have received a copy of Wilson's *A Series of Experiments Relating to Phosphori and the Prismatic Colors They Are Found to Exhibit in the Dark* (London, 1775). BF could not have sent the pamphlet, for it was published months after his departure: *Gent. Mag.*, XLV (1775), 442.

5. Beccaria's pamphlet, *Della elettricità terrestre atmosferica a cielo sereno . . .* [Turin, 1775], was cast in the form of three letters; two of them were to Pringle, the later one on August, 1775. The pamphlet was included in the translation referred to at the end of the paragraph.

6. A reference to his *Dell'elettricismo, lettere . . . dirette al chiarissimo Sig. Giacomo Bartolomeo Beccari* (Bologna, 1758). Beccari (1682–1766) was a Bolo-

died (he was a diligent observer of the atmosphere) I thought it proper to address the president of the Royal Society in which physics is studied in all its branches, and particularly in this one. I addressed myself to Mr. Nourse because I did not know whether you were still shuttling between England and France. Now I again recommend distributing copies, etc., as well as correcting the translation,[7] particularly on the following points:

On p. 354, line 22, it must read "*I. Two bodies similarly electrified both move apart, directly according to the sum of their similar electricities and inversely according to their masses. II. Two bodies oppositely electrified move together, directly according to the sum of their opposite electricities and inversely according to their masses.*"

On p. 355, at the beginning of the second line of paragraph 839, instead of "tassel[8] A" it must be read "tassel B."

On page 394 the two paragraphs 915, 916,[9] ought to be changed as follows:

915. "In the fourth place, if N (Plate VIII) is not electrified and E (fig. 1) is positively electrified or D (fig. 2) negatively electrified, then the natural fire of N will correspond in the different parts of its surface to the tension or relaxation which the excess of E or the deficiency of D bring about in the natural fire of the surrounding air, without drawing it out of that air. Thus the natural fire of N will balance the tense or relaxed fire of the surrounding air, just as the fire of air in the place of N would balance. Because such air that replaced N would not move in consequence of that tension or relaxation, so the body N will not move."

915. "Again, just as the body E and the body D, if surrounded only by air, would not move because of the tension or relaxation that they uniformly release, so they will not move in the presence

gnese scientist who experimented with luminescence and published a series of papers on the subject; see E. Newton Harvey, *A History of Luminescence* . . . (Philadelphia, 1957), pp. 156–8.

7. The translation that BF had initiated in 1773 and that John Nourse was supervising; it was finally published as *A Treatise upon Artificial Electricity* . . . (London, 1776): above, XX, 355; XXI, 149–50; *Public Advertiser*, Oct. 23, 1776. The translator made all these suggested changes except the long revision of pp. 394–5 of *Elettricismo artificiale, e naturale* . . . [Turin, 1772].

8. "Viluppo" in the original and "leaf" in the translation.

9. Beccaria mistook his own numbers. They should have been 925 and 926, and in fact the alterations were all in 925.

of the body N. For the same action that would spread from E or D into the natural fire of air in the place of N will spread into the natural fire of N, and with the same effect as would result from the natural fire of that air."

The note to paragraph 915, which begins "Universally," etc., should be deleted.

On p. 408 at the beginning of line 34, instead of "two before" it ought to read "that before."

On p. 412 line 20, "electricity that in the disconnection" must read "the electricity in the disconnection."

On p. 418 at the beginning of line 35 make it read "MN."

On p. 419 line 10, "greater in Mn," make it read "greater in MN."

These corrections are in addition to those found in the errata at the end of the book.

Index

Compiled by William B. Willcox
(Semicolons separate subentries; colons separate divisions within subentries.)

Army, American (*continued*) and Ammunition; Articles of War; Artillery; Enlistments; Firearms; Gunpowder.

Arnold, Benedict: early exploits of, 94 n; Gates's encomium on, 285; on Canadian expedition, 350, 378 n, 414 n, 420, 426, 430, 497; receives commissioners at Montreal, 413; BF's loan to, for northern army, 418 n; quarrel with Hazen, 420 n, 431 n; on American debts in Canada, 425; and defense of Lake Champlain, 541 n, 642; to assist Hessian desertions, 583 n

Ars Amatoria (Ovid), quoted, 222

Articles of Confederation: BF proposes, xlv, 103, 120–5, 474, 513, 572; adoption of (1781), 120–1; Dickinson draft of, debated in Congress, 536–8: BF's protest against, 571–5; and interstate boundary disputes, 652

Articles of war: in Pa., 147–8, 188; Congress adopts, 147; Cambridge conference, Congress revises, 224, 230–3

Artillery: importation, manufacture of, 104, 290, 372, 627–8; from N.Y., Crown Point for siege of Boston, 238; Newland on use of, against ships, 336–9; ordered from Liége, 466; availability of, in France, 466–7; Va. seeks, in France, 468; from Philadelphia for defense of N.J., 528; Americans lack heavy, 559

Arundel, Louis O'hickey d', Gen. Lee introduces to BF, 342; biog. note, 342–3 n

Asia, H.M.S., open to attack at N.Y., 335

Assemblies, colonial: proposed acknowledgment by, of Parliamentary commercial regulation, 119; in BF's proposed Articles of Confederation, 122–3, 125; and new post offices, 133; militia officers appointed by, 135–6; in recommendations of Cambridge conference, 228–9, 231; in Hartley's plan of reconciliation, 254, 256–8, 266; Washington appeals to, for weapons, 331 n; in instructions to British peace commissioners, 395–6; and royal requisitions, 574

Assembly, Conn.: requests explanation of Lexington and Concord, 39 n; establishes postriders, 157 n

Assembly, Del., instructs delegates on state representation in Congress, 538

Assembly, Ga., and BF's agency, 45, 510, 670–1

Assembly, Jamaica, Congress addresses, 364

Assembly, Mass. *See* House of Representatives, Mass.

Assembly, N.J.: London agents of, 8–9 n, 110–11, 197–8, 280, 589; petition to King from, 9 n, 110–11, 197–8; WF addresses, 32 n, 191; on North's conciliatory resolution, 131; questions WF's letter to Dartmouth, 191. *See also* Committee of correspondence, N.J. Assembly.

Assembly, N.Y.: refuses to approve proceedings of first Congress or elect delegates to second, 11–12, 31 n; petitions King and Parliament, 49; Schuyler's role in, 159 n

Assembly, Pa.: elects BF as delegate to Congress, xli, 32, 35–6, 42, 44, 51, 86, 94, 251; appoints committee of safety, xliii, 72–3, 94, 140, 186 n; abolition of, xliii, 251, 480; BF does not attend, resigns from, 35, 367–8; instructs Congressional delegates, 35–6, 251–2, 293–4, 296, 479–81; elections for, 35, 251, 479; on North's conciliatory resolution, 131; and associators, 135, 141, 147, 158, 188–9, 208, 210–11; and port of Philadelphia, 140 n; BF to recommend musket contract for, 184; recommends raising minutemen, 188; and naval commodore, 213; earlier petitions from, forwarded to BF, 215; BF's responsibility for unicameral form of, 514–15; profession of faith required for members of, 514 n; hails BF's role in framing Pa. constitution (1785), 514 n

Assembly, R.I.: and postal system, 168, 172; displaces Gov. Wanton, 171 n; appoints committee to confer on defense, 648 n

Assembly, Va. *See* House of Burgesses, Va.

Associators, Pa.: genesis and formation of, 34 n, 72–3, 135–6, 178, 180, 188–9, 201–2; Bradford's capts. in, 42–3 n; officers of, 73, 189, 295–6, 318–19, 332; discontent in, 141–2, 147–8, 209–10, 212–13; local supplies of arms for, 158, 265, 277, 296, 523–4; articles for, 178, 180; as voters to elect convention, 512; convention requires tax support for, 513 n; ordered into N.J., 516–17, 523–4, 542, 568 n; W. Livingston's opinion of, 516 n. *See also* Deserters; Militia; Nonassociators.

Atkinson, Richard: Mary Hewson negotiates with, 300–1; army contract of, 301 n

Atlantic: BF on different speed of crossing, east and west, 16; "great gulph" between BF and Mary Hewson, 589

Bordeaux (*continued*)
Cleveland sent to, 504–8, 533–6; message for Wickes at, 668
Bosc d'Antic. *See* Antic, Paul Bosc d'.
Boston: British troops in, xli, 11–12, 38, 44, 96, 177: Chatham's motion to withdraw (1775), 401 n; activities of Loyalists in, 3–4; British gifts to relieve inhabitants of, 13, 100–1 n; postriders to, from N.Y., 15 n; Howe, Clinton, Burgoyne sail for, 24; hardships of inhabitants of, 37–8, 92, 96, 105, 175, 200, 241, 387–8, 610; Jonathan Williams, Sr., loses goods in, 68–9; town meeting, selectmen of, agree with Gage on refugees, 68–9 n; BF's proposed reparation to, 96, 125, 139; incidents in siege of, 100, 107, 110, 295; contemplated American assault upon, 207 n, 225, 240; arrival of British troops at (1768), 261; British evacuate, 387–8, 394, 400, 434–5, 610; BF urges fortification of, 400. *See also* Army, American; Boston Massacre; Boston Neck; Boston Port Act.
Boston (continental frigate), launched, 609 n
Boston Massacre: Warren's, Lovell's orations on anniversaries of, 14 n, 393 n; trials resulting from, 28 n
Boston Neck, British fortifications on, 44 n
Boston Port Act: hardships caused by, 11; Ga. resolutions against, 46 n; BF proposes reparation for, 125; Hartley proposes, abandons suspension of, 257, 268 n; North moves repeal of, 267–8, 270
Boulton, Matthew, BF's debt to, for tea urn, 100
Bounties in land, for deserting Hessian officers, 583 n
Bourbon, Don Gabriel Antonio of. *See* Gabriel Antonio.
Bouts-rimés, JW probably sends BF, 50 n
Bowdoin, Elizabeth (Mrs. James): BF and others houseguests of, 387 n; BF's love to, 390
Bowdoin, James: at Cambridge conference, 226, 387 n; BF and others houseguests of, 387; transmits books sent by BF, 389–90, 569, 635; president of Mass. Executive Council, 389 n; BF too busy to write to, 401; letter from, 569–71; letter to, 389–90
Bows and arrows, BF on advantages of, 343–4
Boyne, H.M.S., carries Burgoyne to England, 283

Braddock, Edward, defeat of (1755), 277 n
Bradford, John, Boston agent for prizes, letter to, 533–4
Bradford, Thomas, in Philadelphia associators, 42–3 n
Bradford, William, capt. of associators: BF on bad terms with, 43 n; arrests British soldiers, 175, 176 n; letter to(?), 42–3
Bradshaw, John, epitaph on, 303–4
Bradstreet, John, expedition of, against Fort Frontenac (1758), 340 n
Brandywine, Battle of the (1777), James Ross in, 308 n
Braxton, Carter: Congress refers BF letter to, *et al.*, 400; business association with J. P. Merkle, 534 n
Brest: French naval preparations reported at, 488, 619, 640; message for Wickes at, 668
Bristol, England, *Dickinson* diverted to, 333, 408
Briton, William, master of *Fanny*, 447–8
Brodeau, Ann (Anna): BF, Morris recommend, on opening of her boarding school, 282–3; biog. note, 282–3 n
Brodeau, Anna Maria, marries William Thornton, 283 n
Brodhead, Daniel, Lieut. Col., commands Pa. regiment, 623
Bromfield, Henry, brother of Thomas, 161 n
Bromfield, Henry, nephew of Thomas, 161 n
Bromfield, Thomas, American merchant in London: biog. note, 161 n; letter from, 161–2
Brooks, James, imprisoned with Kearsley, 265
Brown, John, Providence merchant, contracts of, with secret committee, 326–7, 341, 354–5
Brown, Nicholas, Providence merchant: contracts of, with secret committee, 327, 341, 354–5; Penet sends cargo in ship of, 543
Brown, Nicholas, & Co., association with Pliarne, Penet & Cie., 326 n, 543, 545
Browns & Collinson: receives gift from Bostonians, 52; BF closes account with, 71–2; draft on, for Mrs. Stevenson, 108; letter to, 71
Brunswick, Germany, British treaty for mercenaries with ruler of, 440 n
Brunswick, N.J. *See* New Brunswick.
Bryson, James, witnesses power of attorney, bond, 21, 146
Bucks Co., Pa.: manufacture of firearms

Continental Congress, second (*continued*) suggested proportioning of requisitions by, 266–7; and supply of gunpowder, 278, 375, 378–9; dissension in, over independence, 286, 401; members of, esteem Dumas' Vattel, 287–8; proceedings of, sent to Dumas, 288, 411: Spanish Infante, 298: Bingham, 617; and Deane's mission, 310–11, 370–3; Pliarne, Penet appear before, 311, 333; BF's proposed preambles to resolutions of, 322–3, 388–9; authorizes privateering, 322, 388; and prisoners of war, 328; and O'hickey d'Arundel, 342: Woedtke, 362 n, 379 n, 499; imposes secrecy on its members, 345 n: to little effect, 637; addresses Jamaica Assembly, 364; Hartley on failure of, to propose terms, 366; to memorialize Montgomery, 376; and Hudson forts, 397 n; BF on obstacles in, to independence, 401; Washington visits, 439, 516; excitement in, over news from France, 455, 501; fears Franco-British rapprochement, 456; and Howes' peace commission, 483, 569, 575 n, 591–3, 600–1, 603, 606–8; and Declaration of Independence, 485–6; Kermorvan recommended by, 491–2: sends advice to, 526–8; suggested punishment of Loyalists by, 498; undiscouraged by setbacks, 503–4; offers bounty for imported seamen, 507 n: for deserting Hessians, 578 n, 583; establishes N.J. flying camp, 516; unexcited by Belton's submersible cannon, 522–3; debate in, on Articles of Confederation, 536–8, 571–2; and great seal, 563; unanimity in, 583, 585, 652; appeal to, from prize court, 610 n; and commissioners to France, 624–30, 634–5, 648–9: to other courts, 629 n; committee of secret correspondence withholds news of French assistance from, 636–8; decides not to destroy N.Y., 642; dissatisfaction with, 643. *See also* Assembly, N.Y.; Assembly, Pa.; Petitions to Congress; Petitions to crown.

Convention, Conventions, provincial. *See* Provincial convention; Provincial conventions.

Convention, U.S. constitutional (1787), BF's role in, 572

Cooke, John, debt of, to Howard, 162–3

Cooke, Nicholas: and postal arrangements in R.I., 171–2, 183; succeeds to governorship, 171 n; BF addresses as Providence postmaster, 183; at Cambridge conference, 225, 235, 246; and Penet

and Pliarne, 311; letter from, 171–2; letter to, 183

Cooper, Samuel: sends news, 11–12, 387–8; on British evacuation of Boston, 387; house guest, with BF, at Bowdoins, 387; BF too busy to write to, 401; shows Bowdoin BF's correspondence with Lord Howe, 569, 609; BF says farewell to, 670; conveys BF's farewell to friends, 670 n; letters from, 11–12, 387–8, 608–9; letter to, 670

Corn. *See* Grain.

Cornelia (brigantine), charter party for, 333–4

Coudray. *See* Du Coudray.

Couleaux, Mons., Penet's partner: delivers Boisbertrand's dispatches to Congress, 469 n; letters to BF, 547 n

Council, Executive, in BF's Articles of Confederation, 124

Council, Mass.: appointed members of, resign, 10; reimbursement of BF by, 60 n, 244; Winthrop serves on, 93 n; committee of, attends Cambridge conference, 225–6, 235, 246; extract of BF letter read to, 243–4 n

Council, N.H., William Temple member of, 394 n

Council, N.J., WF meets with, 32 n

Council, S.C., legal challenge to power of (1773), 604 n

Council of safety, Md., letter to, from secret committee, 605–6

Council of safety, Pa.: creation of, 512; payment by, for flying camp, 557–8; and Lieut. Barrington, 569 n; Anderson requests orders from, 623

Council of war, American: on Benjamin Church, 234 n; on proposal to attack Boston, 240: Trois Rivières, 475; commissioners to Canada empowered to vote in, 384, 414; in retreat from Canada, 422–3, 426, 497; Kermorvan wants to participate in, 560–1

Court martial: in Pa. militia, 147, 178; in articles of war, 230–3; on deserters from Arnold, 285 n; on Hazen, 420 n

Crafton, Robert: supports Hartley's plan of reconciliation, 262–3; suggests Congress authorize requisitions, 266–7; letters from, 262–3, 266–7

Craig, John, American privateer, captures *Richmond*, 657

Craven Street, Mrs. Stevenson moves from, 263 n

"Cravenstreet Gazette" (1770), Hutton in, 26 n

Crawford, Gideon, brings supplies from Nantes, 543

INDEX

Credence, Letter of. *See* Letter of credence.
Credit, American: low in Canada for want of specie, 413–14, 417–18, 424–5; bills of, *see* Bills of credit
Creditors, British, supposedly defrauded by American customers, 115, 119, 138, 193
Creeks, threaten Ga., 510
Croghan, George, WF's loan to, 170
Croker, Francis, marriage of, 279
Croker, John, father of Catherine Meed, 279, 304
Croker, Joseph, conjecturally identified, 279
Crown Point: Skene lieut. gov. of, 84; Americans capture, 94 n; lead, arms, artillery from, 161 n, 179, 184 n, 238; Mass. committee visits, 226 n; Woedtke at, 362 n; Americans abandon, 539 n
Culbertson, Joseph, American ensign, killed, 494
Cumberland Co., Pa.: officers in, recommended, 318–19; manufacture of arms and accoutrements in, 342; letters from committee of correspondence of, 318–19, 331; letter from commissioners of, 342
Curaçao, European supplies to be transshipped at, 633
Currency, American: BF's concern with paper, 54 n: design of, 126 n, 357–8; Pa.'s issue of paper, 140, 141 n; Canadians' attitude toward, in paper and specie, 353, 385, 413–14, 417–18, 425–6, 438–9; Dubourg asks for, in paper or specie, 467. *See also* Bills of credit.
Curson, Samuel, American agent on St. Eustatius, 662
Curwin, George, commands *Hope*, 176 n
Cushing, Caleb, on Mass. Council, 244
Customs houses, British, BF's proposal to close, 127

Dagge, Henry: brother of John, 21 n; legal opinion of, on Indian land titles, 25 n, 102–3
Dagge, John, witnesses signature on power of attorney, 21
Dalrymple, Alexander: recommends writing engraver, 22; career in India, 22 n; letter from, 22
Dalrymple, Sir John, ministerial pamphlet by, 81–2
Dana, Francis, on mission to England, 8 n, 10, 12, 14
Dartmouth, William Legge, Earl of: and N.J. petition, 9 n, 110–11; circular letter to govs. from, 11, 191 n; receives

news of Lexington and Concord, 29 n; Strahan's letters intercepted for, 60 n; Strahan on purported concessions by, 86; transmits conciliatory resolution, 131; letter from WF to, 191; and plot to deliver Philadelphia, 241 n; BF's memorandum to (1775), 572
Dartmouth, Mass. *See* New Bedford.
Dashwood, Francis, John Foxcroft's secretary: arrives in America, 203; signs certificate about BF's postal account, 660–1
Davenport, Josiah, WF's secretary, 171
Davidson, William, Scots merchant in Rotterdam, BF and Pringle dine with (1766), 611
Davin, Mons., Dubourg offers American service to, 460, 461 n
Davis, Mrs. (Hugh?), affair of, 50
Dawson, Richard, leaves Club of Thirteen to be lieut. gov. of Isle of Man, 173
Daymon, Francis: introduces Bonvouloir to committee of secret correspondence, 312–13, 315; biog. note, 313 n
Deane, Silas: as agent in France for committee of secret correspondence, xlv, 310–11, 355, 443, 652: certificate for, instructions to, 369–75: to make contact with Bancroft, Dumas, 373–4, 550: go-betweens for correspondence of, 445–6, 503–5, 535, 619: commissions Du Coudray, 462 n: negotiates for tobacco, 465 n, 489: voyage to France, 487–8: in Bordeaux, 488–9, 508, 618: Declaration of Independence sent to, 502–3: association with Penet, Delaps, 544–5, 546 n: to send newspapers home, 617; election of, instructions to, as commissioner to France, xlvi, 624–30, 648–50, 666; on BF's vindication and offer, 112–13; interest of, in New England confederation, 120 n; Saltonstall's son-in-law, 157 n; business connection with Bromfield, 161 n; BF confirms postal arrangements of, 183–4; biog. note, 183 n; on secret committee, 204 n, 277–8, 324, 354; secret committee contract with, *et al.*, 354–6; Bancroft's former teacher, 373 n; sees recommendation of Bedaulx, 611 n; letter from, 488–90; letters to, 183–5, 502–4, 553–5, 639–45, 648–50, 665
DeBerdt, Dennis, Jr., agent for N.J., 111 n, 589 n
Declaration of Causes and Necessity for Taking up Arms: Washington reads to army, 69 n; BF's involvement with, 88–9, 92 n; sent to Grand Duke Leopold, 309

691

INDEX

Declaration of Independence: preparation of, xlv, 474, 485–6; Col. Allen resigns because of, 428 n, 585; sent to Deane, 502, 503 n, 553 n; popularity of, in America, 502–3, 554, 603, 607; dissemination of, 503, 539 n; timing of, as sign of Congress' mood, 503–4; effect of, on Lord Howe's mission, 518, 592, 600, 602, 607

Declaration of Rights, Pa., BF's revisions of, 514, 529–33

Declaration to American people (Lord Howe), 483, 519, 601–2

Declaratory Act: for colonies (1766), Shipley on, 79–80; for Ireland (1719), 259 n

Deer Island, Mass., raided, 110

De Haas, Philip, Lieut. Col.: on expedition to Cedars and subsequent retreat, 497; at Ticonderoga, 540

De Huff, Abraham, Capt., sent from army to Pa. convention, 623

De Lancey family, Whitehall relies on loyalty of, 24

Delap, J. H. and Samuel, Bordeaux mercantile firm: as agent for transmitting correspondence, 445, 504–7, 533, 535, 664 n; assists, praised by Deane, 488; will furnish Deane's address, 651; inquires about prices, 489; as Penet's competitor for American business, 546 n; to receive Wickes's prizes, 667; letter to, 504–5

Delaville Bros., Cadiz merchants, recommended by Penet, 546

Delaware. See Assembly, Del.

Delaware River: defense, fortification of, 73, 135, 241 n, 491–2 n; coal deposits near, 320

Della elettricità terrestre atmosferica a cielo sereno . . . (Beccaria), sent to Pringle, 675 n

Dell' elettricismo . . . (Beccaria), addressed to Beccari, 675 n

Denmark: Moravians tolerated in, 57 n; Queen of, *see* Caroline Matilda

Deodands, captures from British as, 249

Derby, John, carries news of Lexington and Concord to England, 29 n, 30

Derby, Richard, provides schooner for John Derby, 29 n

Deschambault, Que., in American retreat from Quebec, 423, 427, 430, 496–7

Deserters: among Pa. associators, 555–6, 623; means of encouraging, among Hessians, 578–9, 583

Desnoyers, Abbé, French chargé d'affaires at the Hague, Dumas' dealings with, 406–7, 412, 433–4, 436, 549 n, 550 n

"Dialogue between Britain, France, Spain, Holland, Saxony and America" (BF), paraphrased in "Intended Vindication and Offer," 119–20

Dickinson, John: asked to confirm opinion on Indian land titles, 25; helps draft declaration, petition, 88–9, 99; on secret committee, 204 n; role of, in Pa. Assembly, 251, 286; on committee of secret correspondence, 280, 291: signs Deane's certificate, instructions, 369, 374: Bingham's instructions, 447; Dumas' admiration for, regards to, 410 n, 411–12, 436, 549; drafts Articles of Confederation, 536–7, 571–2; desertions in brigade of, 555–6; resigns from army, 555 n; leaves Congress, 637 n; letters from, *et al.*, 84, 131, 296–7, 447–8, 449, 450; letter from, 555–6; letter to, *et al.*, 188–9

Dickinson (*Dickenson*; snow): sails for Nantes and puts in at Bristol, 332–3, 408; BF's memorandum about, 332–3

Dill, James, Capt. of York Co. associators, discontented with his colonel, 202

Dill, Matthew, Col. of York Co. associators, discontent with, 202, 220

Dilly, Charles and Edward, publish William Smith's sermon, 190 n

Directions to the Deputy Post-Masters, for Keeping Their Accounts . . . , 134 n

Discourse on the Different Kinds of Air . . . (Priestley), 10 n

Discours . . . *sur les droits des souverains* . . . (Noodt), Dumas sends BF, 75

Dispatch (brigantine, Capt. Cleveland), voyage to France, 534–5, 553 n

Dispatch (brigantine, Capt. Parker): planned armament of, 503, 506–7; to carry dispatches, 503 n, 504, 506, 534 n, 553; captured, 503 n, 553 n

Dodd, William, Rev., putative father of Anna Maria Brodeau, 282 n

Doolittle, Isaac, works on *Turtle*, 156

Dorchester, Mass., Heights of, and evacuation of Boston, 387

Dorland, Garret, 2nd Lieut. of York Co. foot, 513 n

Downes, Anna Hill, invited to take refuge with Greenes, 38

Draper, Richard, newspaper of, 4

Draper, Sir William, on means of coercing colonists, 96–7

Dresden, damaged by Prussians (1756), 120

Droit de Dieu, de la nature et des gens . . . (Abbadie), Dumas sends BF, 75

Droit des gens, ou Principes de la loi naturelle . . . (Vattel): Dumas sends BF, 48, 74–

1. We include under this heading only (1) items that cannot readily be found under BF's correspondents, organizations with which he was connected, etc.; (2) cross references to writings by or attributed to him that appear for the first time in this volume.

Gage, Thomas (*continued*)
Hill, 144 n; responsible for beginning war, 37–8, 39 n, 44, 59, 91; detains Bostonians' goods, 39, 68–9 n, 92, 96, 105 n, 175, 176 n, 200; calls General Court, 41–2, 44; strengthens Boston fortifications, 44; authorized to grant pardons, 86 n; letter of, falsified when laid before Parliament, 137 n; returns home, 248; BF satirizes, 276
Gaiault (Gayault) de Boisbertrand. *See* Boisbertrand.
Gale, Benjamin: describes Bushnell's submarine, 155–7; BF calls on, 155 n; recommends postal appointments, 157; letter from, 154–8
Galleys: in Pa. navy, 135 n, 416; suggested for coastal defense, 528 n, 559; and defense of Ticonderoga, 642, 653
Galloway, Joseph: BF's breach with, xliii–xliv, 32–3; on BF's expecting independence, xlv, 33; British reactions to plan of union of, 23–4; to be asked to confirm legal opinion on Indian land titles, 25; retires from public life, 32, 36 n; program of, for Pa. fails, 36; and reorganization of Indiana Co., 325–6; WTF visits, 566; letter to, 33–4
Gardiners Island, attempted British raid on, 167
Gardner, Henry, treasurer of Mass., 244
Garnier, Charles-Jean: as suggested contact for Deane, 374; biog. note, 374 n
Garth, Charles, and Olive Branch Petition, 281 n
Garver, George, manufactures saltpetre, 207
Gaspee, H.M.S., captured on St. Lawrence, 328 n
Gates, Elizabeth (Mrs. Horatio), joins husband in regards to BF and family, 362
Gates, Horatio: at Cambridge council of officers, 227 n; sends BF news, Gen. Lee's letters to Thanet, Burgoyne, 249–50, 283–4, 293; biog. note, 249 n; on dissension in Congress over independence, 286; opinion of Newland, 343; introduces Woedtke, 362; introduces Kermorvan, 390, 490; and Canadian command, 490; on interception of mail to northern army, 539 n; asked to help procure Hessian desertions, 583; BF sends Price pamphlet to, 584; letters from, 249–50, 283–6, 362–3, 490–1; letter to, 583–4
"G.B." (Hartley's alias), 31, 130, 138, 260, 262, 268, 366

General Court, Mass.: called by Gage, 41–2, 44; Cambridge conference refers matters to, 234–5: recommends that Congress authorize establishment of prize court by, 241
General Post Office, British: functions in colonies despite disturbances, 14–15; BF's advice on packet service of, to America (1768), 55; discontinues packets, 60 n, 348 n; BF dismissed from, 132, 660; collapses, 132–3; BF attempts to settle accounts with, 660–1; mortgages on land held by, 661, 662 n
Genn, Thomas, master of *Cornelia*, 334
Geoghegans, Messrs., Dubourg recommends for American service, 460–1
George III: declares colonies in rebellion, xlv, 251, 281; receives petition from first Congress, 11 n; hope for dismissal of ministry by, 45–6; Germain's influence with, 89; and petitions from City of London, 90 n, 130 n, 203 n, 481: from N.J., 110–11; from second Congress (Olive Branch), 251, 280; Canadians urged to appeal to, 136; speech to Parliament, 255, 570; BF satirizes, 275–6; and Burgoyne's return on leave, 284 n; as author of American grievances, 322–3, 481; suggested removal of name of, from Prayer Book, 360; letter of, to Maria Theresa, 434; supposedly wants peace, 484, 520, 602, 607; does not acknowledge Congress, 601; BF's account against (1785?), 660
George, Lake: in French and Indian War, 277 n; open for boats, 353; closed by ice, 402 n, 413. *See also* Lakes.
Georgia: opinion in, at outbreak of war, 45; BF's agency for, 45, 510, 670–1; settlement of, at British expense, 114 n, 116; slow to send delegates to Congress, 114 n, 116 n; post office established in, 183; precarious situation of, 509–10. *See also* Provincial congress, Ga.
Germain, Lord George: increasingly influences King and ministry, 89; rescinds Thomas Carleton's appointment, 347 n; Priestley on policy of, 348; WF's report to, 551
Germantown, Pa., powder mill at, 324 n
Germany, Girardot & Cie., Deane's bankers, 489
Germany township, Pa., associators in, 202
Gerrish, Joseph, on Mass. Council, 244
Gerry, Elbridge, delivers books to Bowdoin from BF, 569
Gibbs, W. P., witnesses deed, 302

Morris, Robert (*continued*)
322 n; warden of port of Philadelphia, 140; Tucker's negotiations with, over Bermuda, 166; BF informs, of decision to return gunpowder, 186–7; biog. note, 186 n; on secret committee, 204 n: signs committee license, contracts, charter parties, 323–4, 327, 334, 353 n; Gates's regards to, 286; recommends Mrs. Brodeau, 302–3; contract of *et al.*, with secret committee, 335–6; influence of, through committees, 637–8; letters from BF and, 502–4, 615–20, 639–45, 648–50, 661–2; letters from, *et al.*, 447–50, 533–6, 553–5, 605–6, 633, 663–4; letters to, 186–7, 322; letters to, *et al.*, 304–5, 332, 488–90
Morris, Thomas: as American agent in France, 544, 555, 644–5, 650–1; biog. note, 544 n; to provide Bingham with newspapers, 617
Mortar. *See* "Congress."
Morton, John: speaker of Pa. Assembly, 36, 481; letter to, 367–8
Morton, Perez, deputy secretary of Mass. Council, 244
Mousac (Moussac, Maussac, Moissac) de la Marquisie. *See* Marquisie.
Moyamensing, Pa., deserters from, 555
Muckelno, John, master of captured British merchantman, 511
Mumford, Benjamin: postrider captured and detained by British, 167, 171, 197 n; establishes Newport post office, 171 n; in Philadelphia(?), 273
Mumford, Peter, establishes Newport post office, 171 n; in Philadelphia(?), 273
Mumford, Thomas, Conn. merchant: contract of, with secret committee, 277–8; biog. note, 277 n
Mure, Hutchinson: Mary Hewson negotiates with, about inheritance, 63, 300–1, 589–90; army contract of, helps to feed fish, 301; biog. note, 301 n
Mure, Son, & Atkinson, army contractors, and Mary Hewson's legacy, 301
Murray, Lord John, commands Highland regiment sent to America, 89

Nantes: consignment to Schweighauser at, 314; as center for shipping American supplies, 314 n, 332, 334, 408, 535, 543–6; dispatches sent via, 455 n, 501 n; Penet, Boisbertrand at, 456, 459, 464 n, 465, 469 n; Thomas Morris agent at, 544; fitness of, for American

trade, 546; BF bound for, 667; message for Wickes to be left at, 668
Nantucket: Jane Mecom invited to, 106; Congress limits imports by, 106 n; oil for export bought at, 327; Seth Jenkins's odyssey in returning to, 657
Narragansett Road, R.I., as postal route, 168, 172
Narrows of Hudson River, in campaign of 1776, 338, 568
Navigation Acts: BF's proposal to abolish, xlv, 126; in peace negotiations (1774–75), 114 n; alleged American aim to abolish, 115, 119; proposed re-enactment of, by colonies, 119
Navy, American: BF, others lament lack of, 184–5, 312, 401, 609: hope for, 289, 644; Pa. delegates to press for creation of, 525. *See also* Frigates; Ships of the line.
Navy, British: harassment of coast by, 167–8, 171–2, 196, 199–200, 609; controls American waters, 640, 653. *See also* Howe, Richard.
Navy, French: preparing for war, 454, 488, 502; appearance of, at N.Y. hoped for, 620, 640
Navy, Pa.: officers commissioned in, 135; choice of commodore for, 213, 252
Navy board, American, established, 493
Negroes, excluded from American army, 237
Neptune (British brigantine), captured, 615 n
Nesbitt, John M., treasurer of Pa. council of safety, 557–8
Netherlands: American agents in, xliii; and exportation of arms and ammunition, 96–7 n, 165; Story sent to, 290 n, 636 n; Deane's suggested visit to, 373; Penet in, 455, 547. *See also* Dumas.
Neversink, N.J., gunpowder landed at, 186, 187 n
Neveu-Sevestre, Lieut. Col., imprisoned by Wooster, 384
Newark, N.J.: committee of, to forward gunpowder, 172, 187; commissioners to Canada at, 391
New Bedford (Dartmouth), Mass.: ships arrive at, 39; post office in, 389; Boisbertrand lands at, 469 n
New Bern, N.C., post office and committee of safety of, 163 n
New Brunswick, N.J.: consignment of gunpowder at, 186–7, 344–5; commissioners to Canada, Woedtke at, 392 n; committee of conference at, en route to

INDEX

Song (BF's): "The King's Own Regulars,"
274–7, 401
Sorel, Que.: in American retreat from
Canada, 421 n, 427 n, 428, 475, 485,
497
Sorel River. *See* Richelieu River.
South Carolina: newspapers from, for BF,
50; gunpowder arrives from, 159 n,
178; Gen. Lee proposes exempting,
from military obligation, 292–3; British attack on, 510, 553; hostility in, to
British rule, 604; constitutional dispute
in (1773), 604 n
Southwick, Samuel, Newport postmaster,
168, 172
Spain: provides money for colonies, xlvi,
454; and Pope Alexander's demarcation
line, 150; BF foresees close American relations with, 298; committee of secret
correspondence on sea power of, 314; in
dispute with Portugal, 488; commercial
houses in, 544; commissioners to reas-
sure, about South American possessions,
628; asked to ban American shipping,
645; asked to provide fleet, 665
Spangenburg, Augustus Gottlief: Seidel's
predecessor, 55 n; BF's acquaintance
with (1755–56), 58
Speculation on speed of ships (BF), 16
Spencer, Joseph, Brig. Gen., at Cambridge council of officers, 227 n
Spinning and knitting, BF on, as means of
paying for war, 242
Spooner, Walter, at Cambridge conference, 226
Staten Island: in campaign of 1776, xli,
495 n, 527, 554, 617 n, 640; committee confers with Lord Howe on, xlii,
xlv, 593, 597–608; Hessians on, 578,
599
Steele, Joshua, sends book to BF, 264
Stevenson, Cornelius, American agent on
St. Eustatius: forwards letters, 291,
577–8; goods consigned to, 633; letter
from, 577–8
Stevenson, Margaret: low spirits of, in BF's
absence, 26, 28, 63; sends news, letters,
newspapers, 27–8; wants granddaughter weaned, 63 n; letter of, to BF as journal of a month, 65; and WTF's identity,
68 n; BF hopes to dance with, at Hew-
son-Bache wedding, 100; BF abandons
American investment for, 108, 269;
health of, 263, 299, 589, 590; letters
from, decade in reaching BF, 263 n,
589, 613 n; William Temple returns
letters to, 347 n, 587; Priestley reports
on, 350; longs to emigrate to America,

590; visits Pearces, Vinys, Mary Hew-
son, 590, 596; letters from, 27–8, 263–
5, 586–8; letter to, 108–9
Stevenson, Robert, American agent on St.
Eustatius, 291
Stevenson, Robert, maj. of Pa. troops, 220
Stewart, David, Baltimore merchant,
gunpowder to be delivered to, 606
Stiles, Ezra: friends of, 52 n, 168 n; meets
Goddard, 248 n
Stirling, Lord. *See* Alexander, William.
Stival, Pierre & Fils, Dunkirk firm: will
give Deane's address, 651; receive
Wickes's prizes, 667
Stockbridge (Indian tribe), offers services
through chief, 239
Stock market: unaffected by start of war,
82; BF expects decline in, 108
Stockton, Samuel: BF introduces to JW,
198; biog. note, 198 n; visits Mrs. Ste-
venson, 264
Stonington, Conn.: British fire on, 196 n,
200 n; Kermorvan arrives at, 490
Story, Thomas: carries dispatches to, from
BF, committee of secret correspondence,
290, 291 n, 297, 374, 403, 407, 435–
6, 550; biog. note, 290 n; verbal report
by, 290 n, 618 n, 636, 639 n; visits
London, 403, 407
Strachey, Henry: account of Staten Island
conference by, 598–605; biog. note,
598–9 n
Strahan, William: at Bath to recover
health, 27–8; strained relationship with
BF, 60, 85; BF vents anger on, 85; letters of, intercepted, 60 n; writes as
promised by each packet, 60 n, 143–4;
hopes Congress will send BF to England,
61, 88, 145–6; on nature and consequences of civil war, 86–7, 144–5,
192, 222; prophesies American dicta-
torship, 86, 196, 222; queries of, to BF
(1769), 193 n, 221; visits Mrs. Stevenson, 264, 586; letters from, 61, 85–8,
143–6, 192–6, 220–3; letters to, 85,
218–19
Stratton Major, Va., William Dunlap rector of, 556 n
Strettel, Amos, accounts to BF for interest
on mortgages, 661, 662–3
Strettell, Robert, claims on estate of, 663
Stringer, Samuel, army surgeon: implied
neglect of duty, 420–1; biog. note,
421 n
Stuart (Stewart), John, and Indian incursions in south, 642–3
Stuckey, A., Rotterdam merchant, to
transmit letters, 297, 412, 436

720

INDEX

Woedtke, Frederick William, Baron de (*continued*)
   Dubourg hopes for Kermorvan's collaboration with, 560; letters from, 496–9, 500–1
Wolves, proverb about, 51
Woodbridge, N.J., in campaign of 1776, 526
Woodhull ("Woshon"), Ebenezer, minuteman officer at Fort Constitution, 398
Woolford, Mrs.: WTF asked to write to, 27; biog. note, 27 n
Wooster, David, Brig. Gen.: in Canadian campaign, 352; commands at Montreal, 384 n, 385 n; at Quebec, 403 n, 422, 579 n, 580 n, 582; assumes Canadian command, returns home, 475
Worcester, Mass.: refugees from Boston in, 38–9, 51 n, 69–70, 106, 197; Jane Mecom, Catharine Greene in, 169
Wright, Sir James, as gov. of Ga., 45 n
Wrixon, Elias: Bancroft, Samuel Wharton introduce to BF, 305–6, 307; biog. note, 306 n
Wynkoop, Cornelius, in charge of captured British officers, 417 n
Wythe, George, amendment to commissioners' instructions by, 627 n

Yates, Abraham, Jr., chairs Albany committee, 179; letter from, 179
Yates, Richard, Samuel Vaughan's dealings with, 70–1
Yeates, Jasper: chairs Lancaster Co. committee, 266; commissioner of Indian affairs, 499, 501–2; letter from, 502; letter to, 499
York, Mr., recommended as postrider, 149
York Co., Pa.: committee of, on conscientious objectors, 141–2; officers' report on minutemen in, 188–9; saltpetre manufactured in, 207; supply of powder and lead in, 219–20; army officers in, 304–5, 332; letters from committee of, 141–2, 201–2, 207, 219–20, 304–5, 332
Young, James, Vice Adm., R.N., threatens commander of Martinique, 616
Young, John, American naval capt., carries dispatches to Bingham, 616, 619, 651, 661: to return with arms, 620, 638
Young, Stophel, Pa. deserter, 555

Zara (Hill), play performed in Boston, 285 n

726